SELECTED WRITINGS OF

FRANCIS BACON

Library of Congress Catalog Card Number: 55-6393

The text of this edition follows that of the definitive edition of Bacon's *Works*, edited by James Spedding, R. L. Ellis, and D. D. Heath, London, 1857–74. Most of the bracketed translations of foreign phrases within the text are from the Spedding edition, except that those preceded by asterisks have been added by Professor Dick.

Random House IS THE PUBLISHER of *The Modern Library*

BENNETT A. CERF — DONALD S. KLOPFER — ROBERT K. HAAS

Manufactured in the United States of America

By H. Wolff

SELECTED WRITINGS OF

FRANCIS BACON

WITH AN INTRODUCTION AND NOTES BY

HUGH G. DICK

Professor of English, University of California at Los Angeles

THE MODERN LIBRARY · NEW YORK

CONTENTS

INTRODUCTION

"The monuments of wit survive the monuments of power"

Bacon, *Gesta Grayorum.*

THE DEBT the modern world owes to science is so pervasive and so profound that no man can measure it. But before science and its resultant technologies could be freed for their development in the modern world, a revolution in human attitudes had to be achieved, and that revolution was not accomplished solely by the continuous impact of scientific discovery. Men's minds had to be prepared, older habits of thought challenged, and the areas of faith enlarged. The idea and the ideals of science had to be brought home to the human heart and mind. The idea and the ideals found their architect and their spokesman in Francis Bacon, whom the late Alfred North Whitehead called "one of the great builders who constructed the mind of the modern world."

What Bacon contributed was less a philosophical system than an irresistible conviction and a poet's vision. In a sense, Bacon is incomparably the greatest poet of science. The core of his thought is the dignity of man and the greatness of man's future. His avowed purpose was "to try whether I cannot in very fact lay more firmly the foundations and extend more widely the limits of the power and greatness of man." His conception is at once humble and magnificently arrogant—an expression of faith from one of the universal men of the High Renaissance. To understand it is to face a basic problem for the modern mind. Those who believe that we live in an appalling age in which man's ability to know and command nature has far outstripped his ability to know and command himself may be repelled by much (though certainly not all) of what Bacon has to offer. Those who believe that the limits of learning are not yet in sight or have hardly begun to emerge may take added faith from him. His ultimate vision reaches far beyond our own times to embrace the conception of a unified science spanning the whole realm of the knowable, by which man's command of himself and of nature may be joined.

Bacon spoke of himself as "a bell-ringer which is first up to call others to church." In a more militant mood he described himself as a trumpeter who "summons and excites men not to cut each other to pieces with mutual contradictions, or to quarrel and fight with one another; but rather to make peace between themselves, and turning with united forces against the Nature of Things, to storm and occupy her castles and strongholds, and extend the bounds of human empire, as far as God Almighty in his goodness may permit." As herald of the scientific movement, Bacon uttered three challenges to his time. He called for a total reform of human knowledge, a true advancement of learning, and a revolution in the conditions of life.

His challenge for what he called "a total reconstruction of sciences, arts, and all human knowledge" sprang from disappointment with his own university training, which he felt to be out of touch with the needs of life. At Cambridge, according to his chaplain and first biographer William Rawley, "he first fell into the dislike of Aristotle, not for the worthlessness of the author, to whom he would ever ascribe all high attributes, but for the unfruitfulness of the way: being a philosophy (as his lordship used to say) only strong for disputation and contentions, but barren of production of works for the benefit of the life of man; in which mind he continued to his dying day." The starting point, then, was Bacon's reaction against the decadent Aristotelianism of the schools; but this was only the starting point.

When he looked about him, he came to realize (as others had done) that three recent discoveries—printing, gunpowder, and the compass—had done more to transform the world in which he lived than had any political theory or any school of philosophy. "For these three have changed the whole face and state of things throughout the world; the

first in literature, the second in warfare, the third in navigation; whence have followed innumerable changes; insomuch
that no empire, no sect, no star seems to have exerted
greater power and influence in human affairs than these
mechanical discoveries." Awakened by these realizations,
Bacon felt impelled to review the whole intellectual history
of the western world to see why philosophy had been so
productive of words but so barren of fruit for the "benefit
and use of life."

He emerged with a religious and historical generalization
of imposing scope. In the beginning God gave mankind
command over the realm of nature, a dominion impaired
but not annulled by man's fall. In the time following, the
primeval age of antiquity, mankind survived and civiliza-
tions grew insofar as nameless men learned to command
nature by obeying her. The growth of science continued
intermittently through the pre-Platonic philosophers and
(with reservations) through Plato and Aristotle as culminat-
ing figures. But with them the process of investigating nature received a decisive check, although it was renewed for
a time in the culture of Rome until the barbarians overran
the Roman Empire. It slowed down because Plato and,
above all, Aristotle (and with them intellectuals in general)
grew more interested in speculative questions—in metaphysics, in theories of knowledge, in logic itself—than in
man's divinely ordained rule of nature.

Bacon saw the medieval synthesis, which moved even
further in the same direction, as the work of profoundly
cloistered men cut off from the roots of life. "This kind of
degenerate learning did chiefly reign amongst the schoolmen; who having sharp and strong wits, and abundance of
leisure, and small variety of reading; but their wits being
shut up in the cells of monasteries and colleges; and knowing little history, either of nature or time; did out of no
great quantity of matter, and infinite agitation of wit, spin
out unto us those laborious webs of learning which are extant in their books." Bacon's comment here is directed not
to the history of philosophy alone but to the whole history

of western society. Because its intellectual leaders were immersed in speculation rather than in observation and experiment, all too little was being done to "subdue and overcome the necessities and miseries of humanity." The basis for the badly needed reform of knowledge lay not in metaphysics on the one hand nor (as is sometimes said) in simple empiricism on the other but in "a true and lawful marriage between the empirical and the rational faculty, the unkind and ill-starred divorce and separation of which has thrown into confusion all the affairs of the human family."

What that reform was, how it was to be accomplished, and the spirit in which it was to be conducted do not require statement here. These things have been unforgettably set down by Bacon himself in the "Proemium," "Preface," and "Plan" of *The Great Instauration*. In less than two dozen pages his overarching scheme is set forth, and one could do worse than begin reading Bacon with these pages.

Bacon's second challenge to his time rang in his trumpet call for the *advancement* of knowledge, the phrase itself suggesting the idea of progress, which J. B. Bury termed "the animating and controlling idea" of the modern western mind. Since the doctrine of progress comes to us most immediately from Bacon and Descartes, we need to examine the background against which it arose, a complex of ideas which Bacon felt to be long-standing counsels of despair and which are nowadays grouped as theories of the decay of nature. The origin of these counsels lay in Greek thought. One of the most powerful of Greek myths was that of the Golden Age, which gave rise to two distinct approaches to the history of nature and of man. The simpler approach was that of an almost unqualified pessimism: man had once lived in perfect harmony with nature and himself, his subsequent story being that of a prolonged decline from the Golden Age to the Silver and thence through various stages of human disharmony and natural degeneration into the ages of Lead and Clay. This view of universal history was readily adaptable to the purposes of some early Fathers of the Church, who seized the analogy between the Golden

Age and the Garden of Eden with the subsequent Fall of Man and the Biblical prophecies of a Doomsday to come. Their teachings became so fixed in the Christian tradition that there was a widespread tendency for men to regard themselves as living in the twilight sickness of a dying world. As one of Bacon's contemporaries put it, the created universe "is not only in the staggering and declining age, but, which exceedeth dotage, at the very upshot, and like a sick man which lyeth at death's door, ready to breathe out the last gasp"—or again, "Man himself whom all these things do serve, is of lower stature, less strength, shorter life than at the first he was, so that there is a general decay of nature, and in every leaf of that book [the Bible] it is written, that the frame of the heavenly arch erected over our heads must very shortly loose and dissolve itself."

The second and more sophisticated approach to universal history arising out of the myth of the Golden Age was a concept of cycles or vast rhythms affecting the totality of things. On the surface this concept offered a more hopeful view, but only on the surface. Plato taught that the physical universe and everything in it is organic and mortal, moving from birth through growth to death in huge cycles of time which may be endlessly repeated, and that within these cycles of time human institutions are also organic, moving through growth to their decay and end. Aristotle's view did not greatly differ from Plato's except in stressing that these rhythms of change are certainly eternal, a view that Christian thought could not accommodate. But if the sole prospect is that of renewal and decay, some necessary emphasis falls on human resignation to a fixed pattern of things: the only prospect for a high civilization, for example, is simply to defer as long as possible the irresistible decline to which it is doomed. This is something less than a counsel of hope.

Such views, whether accepted directly or transmitted through Christian thinkers, were powerfully reinforced in some Renaissance quarters by a despairing sense of cultural inferiority. The moderns bowed before the ancients: the Homeric heroes and the golden ages of Periclean Greece and Augustan Rome seemed to some thinkers like human splendors that the modern world could never match. Even the Reformation added some sense of splendors not to be regained or equaled when the cohesion and purity of the primitive Church were contrasted with the spectacle of Christendom fragmented and at bitterest war with itself.

Against these manifold counsels of despair Bacon advanced his arguments of hope. Like others of his time, but perhaps less whole-heartedly than they, he too felt that he was living in the old age of the universe. But because he believed that knowledge is cumulative, he saw no reason to despair. His imagination was haunted by the discovery of the New World, which moved him as a symbol of how men might add productively to knowledge and discover new realms undreamed of in the youthful times of the so-called ancients. The two persistent images of his prose are of planting and discovery. Again, Bacon shared to a degree the organic cyclical concept of history, but he utterly refused to accept the prevalent implication of this view. For Bacon asserted that man can control his destiny: he is not the slave of implacable decay *unless he chooses to be* because knowledge, being incremental, need not be subject to the unalterable laws of change that create and destroy empires. What Bacon feared and fought was any spirit of resignation or of complacency toward human knowledge. He had faith in its dynamic capacities.

Bacon sounded his third challenge by his call for a revolution in the conditions of life. The tenor of his call is profoundly humanitarian, and perhaps his noblest achievement was to awaken the consciences of men. The twin labels of "materialist" and "utilitarian" have been applied to him by some whom he would have thought guilty of counsels of despair. No man of his time saw more clearly the importance of technological discovery, none set a higher value on it, and none more exultantly predicted the changes that organized research and applied science would bring about in human life. For him a main (though not the chief) value of science was the hope of "a line and race of inventions that may in some degree subdue and overcome the necessities and miseries of humanity." He unweariedly proclaimed the worth of knowledge sought for "the benefit and use of life," and in supporting his appeal for the development of science he declared that "the matter in hand is no mere felicity of speculation but the real business and fortunes of the human race."

At the same time he had a clear-sighted sense of values. He had no disposition to exalt applied science, which he valued greatly, over pure science, which he valued more. He vigorously condemned those who seek only "experiments of Fruit, not experiments of Light" and those who drop out of the race for theoretical knowledge to pick up the golden ball of some immediately practical discovery. In his eyes all scientific activity should be conducted with twin goals in mind, "the glory of the Creator and the relief of man's estate," his ultimate dream being that of "an apocalypse or true vision of the footsteps of the Creator imprinted on his creatures." Again, when he urged men to seek discoveries and to extend their command over nature, he was not thinking of physical science alone. He was no less concerned with all other disciplines in which men may approach truth by bowing their minds to facts. Indeed his breadth of view is such that a distinguished modern thinker has called for a return to Bacon on the grounds that science itself during the past three and a half centuries has been too much under the spell of the triumphs in the physical sciences with a concomitant narrowing of intellectual horizons. Man's knowledge of himself and of his own institutions is central to Bacon's concept of nature. His dream of a science beyond the sciences and his prayer for the apocalyptic vision furnish the just context in which he must be read.

2

The works by which Bacon helped shape the course of western civilization are four: successively the *Essays*, *The Advancement of Learning*, *The Great Instauration* (which includes *The New Organon*), and the *New Atlantis*. These are the four monuments of Bacon's mind, and no list of the world's great books would be complete without at least one of them. In the pages that follow, all of them are printed entire except for the omission of Book II of *The New Organon*, which contains Bacon's premature and unfinished attempt to construct a scientific logic. In addition to these major works, Bacon produced a large body of occasional writing: legal, political, historical, devotional, and literary, including even poetic and dramatic. Part of these materials appeared during his lifetime, but far more was left in manuscript at his death. Some of these shorter pieces have unusual autobiographical interest. Through them we can see how thoroughly Bacon was committed to the ideas he gave the world and how he felt about the Faustian drama of his own life. These short pieces include Bacon's most famous letter, his nearest approach to an autobiography, selections from his search for meaning in classic myth, and the moving prayer written immediately after his fall from high estate. These writings, some of them highly personal, set in their proper order, are here used to introduce and link the four master works. The result, it is hoped, is a coherent autobiography of a mind often at war with itself yet sustained by massive, even momentous convictions.

Bacon's *Essays*, his first published work, appeared in 1597. Of all his writings these have been the most popular because, as he was fond of remarking, these most of all "come home to men's business and bosoms." (In a sense their popularity has been unfortunate, since one cannot know Bacon from the *Essays* alone any more than one can know Shakespeare simply from his *Sonnets*.) The first edition carried only ten essays proper; and these sometimes seem almost like a bare scaffolding for the essays in their final form. What Bacon aimed at and achieved was the utmost terseness of expression, a taut, curt, aphoristic style. To achieve it he stripped away transitions, adjectives, adverbs, and even concrete illustrations. When he later revised and expanded these essays into their ultimate form, he tempered his original austerity somewhat but never so much as to impair their striking compactness.

All this was a conscious piece of prose artistry. Since the general Elizabethan tradition was toward a copious style, Bacon's break with the dominant tradition helped produce what one contemporary called "schisms of eloquence." Bacon, to be sure, was not the first English prose stylist to aim at an Attic simplicity. Others had known the brevity of Tacitus and the superb directness of the English Bible stemming from William Tyndale. Every Elizabethan schoolboy had been taught to keep a commonplace book of "sayings" drawn from his reading, every Elizabethan writer knew the telling power of *sententiae* or proverbial-like utterances, and a good many Elizabethans besides Bacon had been trained at the Inns of Court, where the chant of *pauca verba, pauca verba* (few words, few words) was the price of prolixity in a speaker. But none before Bacon had braved the outermost limits of terseness. Even from the first, however, Bacon did not deny himself the advantages of balance, cadence, and metaphor which were to give his prose its quotability, its popularity, and its power.

That Bacon first conceived the *Essays* as a series of aphorisms is characteristic, and his original intentions are made clear in *The Advancement of Learning*, in which he distinguishes between two kinds of prose, the one "magistral," the other "probative." The magistral writer, he explains, operates from a ground of certitude and delivers knowledge "in such form as may best be believed, and not as may best be examined." The probative writer, on the other hand, is an explorer, not a preacher. By reducing his statements to bare aphorisms he deliberately strips off his defenses and cuts away everything that may hide "whether he be superficial or solid." More important still, the stark aphorism challenges readers to pit their observations against the writer's and thus add to the ultimate attainment of truth. The provisional, "scientific" attitude here implied is borne out by the fact that Bacon called these sketches merely *Essays*— i.e., tentative explorations. Not until more than a quarter of a century later, when he gave the essays their final form and modified their original austerity into something more nearly magistral, did he add—*or Counsels, Civil and Moral*.

One thing may be said with assurance of them: they never leave readers indifferent. They delighted Bacon's contemporaries and successors, including the Puritans, who transplanted them to this country. But later Puritans of a different stamp have often taken a strong moral line. William Blake penciled an outraged protest on the title page of his copy, "Good advice for Satan's kingdom"; and subsequent critics have at times labeled them "counsels of expediency" or studies in the ignoble art of getting ahead. The charge cannot be altogether dismissed. As a courtier Bacon was fascinated by what he called "the architecture of fortune," a phrase that had Machiavellian as well as classical connotations—hence his tough-minded and at times insensitive concern with the ways of getting and holding power. But we do well to remember that he was as much concerned to explore and to challenge as to counsel. "We are much beholden," he writes, "to Machiavel and others, that write what men do and not what they ought to do," and the *Essays* owe no small part of their impact to the writer's unsparing insight into the gullibilities, self-delusions, and pretenses of men. Bacon's desire "to join serpentine wisdom with columbine innocency" was part of his whole-hearted acceptance of life and a phase of his Renaissance gusto. One always has the sense of a shrewd and insatiable intelligence exploring the ways of men with extraordinary penetration and with the art of coalescing a world of experience in a phrase. But the unique triumph of the *Essays* comes in the great themes greatly handled, the discourses of truth, beauty, studies, death, and the vicissitude of things.

Of the Proficience and Advancement of Learning appeared in 1605, but seems to have been in gestation from at least 1592 when Bacon, writing to Lord Burghley, announced: "I have taken all knowledge to be my province." His famous remark has sometimes been misconstrued. He did not mean that he intended to *master* all fields of human knowledge but rather to *survey* them, and *The Advancement* is the result of that survey. Even in an age when verifiable knowledge was far less extensive than now—and far less multi-branched—it was remarkable that any man should have attempted what Bacon did. What is even more astonishing is that such a survey should retain its impressiveness. The feat could have been accomplished only by a writer of commanding power and breadth of vision.

Book I, which was written under conditions of relative leisure, is much the more finished of the two Books. Bacon cast it in the form of a great oration to be delivered before a discerning, dispassionate judge. Since the work was conceived under Elizabeth, whose learning was an unfailing source of national pride, and completed under James I, who had just come to the throne with an enviable reputation for scholarship, Bacon wrote with a royal judge in mind. The occasion, so to speak, was one of high dignity, and Bacon brought to it all the lucidity, conciseness, and magnificence of his prose. He here displays consummate literary tact and fully bears out Ben Jonson's well-known description of him as a speaker in Parliament: "No man ever spoke more neatly, more pressly, more weightily, nor suffered less emptiness, less idleness in what he uttered. No member of his speech but consisted of his own graces. His hearers could not cough, or look aside from him, without loss. He commanded where he spoke." Book I of *The Advancement of Learning* is Bacon's greatest English exercise in the magistral style.

The essential theme of Book I being the dignity of learning, Bacon proceeds from a defense of secular learning against those inclined to attack or, at best, to undervalue it on to a statement of its positive values. What Bacon has to say in defense and in praise of learning was not a work of supererogation because the Renaissance was not exempt from anti-intellectual currents of considerable violence. In fact, Sir Philip Sidney was obliged to defend the values of the imagination and the function of literature at the very time when Spenser had emerged and when Marlowe, Shakespeare, and a host of major writers were shortly to create a literature in English that would take rank with any in the world. So Bacon, standing at the threshold of the seven-

teenth century—the first great age of science in the modern
world—had similarly to defend enterprises of the inquiring
mind. But Bacon's defense and laudation were the work not
of a blind partisan of learning but of a far-seeing critic as
well. Hence he manages to heighten the effectiveness of his
defense by the discernment of his criticism and at the same
time to establish by contrast with prevailing attitudes the
values of the empirical position which he felt to be necessary for the development of science.

Book II, after a preliminary discussion of needed university reforms, embarks on Bacon's circumnavigation of what
he calls "the small Globe of the Intellectual World," an
image designedly evoking the exploits of Magellan and
Drake. Bacon's purpose was to determine "what parts
thereof lie fresh and waste, and not improved by the industry of man." His main interest, therefore, was in the unsur-
veyed realm of secular learning rather than in what was for
his readers the familiar old world of Divinity, in which he
pauses only briefly at the end of the Book. His explorations
in the realm of the secular are conducted according to a
careful plan, which in its broadest outlines is a psychological scheme that takes him through the continents of History
(corresponding to memory), Poetry or imaginative literature (corresponding to imagination), and Philosophy (corresponding to reason). He sets foot briefly on the continent
of History, which he finds reasonably well peopled; he
merely skirts the shore of imaginative literature, which did
not greatly interest him; and he hurries on to the dark continent of Philosophy, which embraced all learning other
than history and literature. Bacon had to the full the trav-
eler's gifts of a fresh eye and a questing mind, so that what
he has to say is invariably illuminating—and he touches
everything under the sun from astrology and athletics (including cosmetics) to logic and the art of government, all
according to a scheme unfolded as he goes along. The
seventeenth century was an age of curious and compendious
minds; it was also about the last age in which anyone would
undertake such a voyage of discovery; and what Bacon

embarked on was a larger enterprise of the kind than any-one before or since has dared attempt. Two discoveries emerge from his voyage, one important for an understanding of his age, the other important for an understanding of Bacon. He vigorously called attention to the lack of verified and verifiable knowledge about the whole realm of nature, and he made it unmistakably clear that the realm of nature included man and man's institutions.

Bacon published *The Great Instauration*, his chief philo-sophical work, in 1620, when he was at the height of his public career. He had drafted it at least twelve years earlier and had revised it yearly. He wrote in Latin in order to address an international audience. He opens the work with a stately "Proemium" couched in the third person, but for all that an intensely personal statement of his hopes for his own philosophy. There follows a dedication to the King, who Bacon hoped would support the development of a vast program for scientific research. The dedication gives way to the noble "Preface," which has, among the most powerful and impressive pages that Bacon ever wrote, a great prae-ludium which reaches its climax in prayer. Then comes "The Plan," or the outline for a sixfold scheme for the de-velopment of science which Bacon trusted that future ages would realize. Like the best of human predictions, time has proved his scheme wrong in details but right in spirit. Its central thesis embodies the spirit of science as we know it: "Those . . . who aspire not to guess and divine but to dis-cover and know; who propose not to devise mimic and fabu-lous worlds of their own, but to examine and dissect the nature of this very world itself; must go to facts themselves for everything."

The rest of the volume is occupied by *The New Organon*, which Bacon intended as merely the second part in his six-fold scheme for the great renewal of learning—i.e., a system of inductive logic appropriate to the investigation of nature. The full realization of his purpose proved to be beyond him, and Book II of *The New Organon*, though not without its interest to logicians, must be written off as an heroic failure.

Book I, on the other hand, is the cardinal statement of Bacon's philosophy and contains in a series of memorable aphorisms his demand for the reform of knowledge, the advancement of learning, and a revolution in the conditions of life. By general consent Bacon reaches his deepest psychological and philosophical insight in his recognition of the four Idols of the Mind (Aphorisms XXXIX to LXVIII), the four basic impediments of the human mind in any search for absolute truth. They can be summarized, but no summary does them justice. Like all great preceptions, they sound simple once they are made; but in truth their recognition marks a forward step in the human mind's critical awareness of itself, and Bacon's discussion of them is timeless.

The last of Bacon's major works, the *New Atlantis*, appeared posthumously in the year of his death, 1626. Like much of his writing, it is incomplete, a fragment of a larger dream. On the surface it is the sunniest and most immediately engaging of all his works. It has an enchanted sense of voyaging, wonder, and of fable come true, of rich costumes and gentle customs. It is the imaginative realization of a wise and tolerant people, of a harmonious society, and of an island world in which the great instauration moves toward reality. It is, Bacon's chaplain tells us, a story devised "to the end that he might exhibit therein a model or description of a college instituted for the interpreting of nature and the producing of great and marvellous works for the benefit of man." It is all that, and something more. It stands to the total of Bacon's work very much as *The Tempest* stands to Shakespeare's. But whereas *The Tempest* is a supreme expression of serenity, the *New Atlantis* is an expression of hope, which is another way of saying an expression of some discontent and lack of present fulfillment. Discussing the uses of imaginative literature in *The Advancement of Learning*, Bacon explains: "The use of this Feigned History hath been to give some shadow of satisfaction to the mind of man in those points wherein the nature of things doth deny it; the world being in proportion inferior to the soul; by reason whereof there is agreeable to the spirit of man a more ample greatness, a more exact goodness, and a more absolute variety, than can be found in the nature of things." The phrase "some *shadow* of satisfaction" is revealing. Couple it with the appearance of the Father of Salomon's House, who "had an aspect as if he pitied men," and you reach a sense of the Faustian discontent behind the *New Atlantis* and in truth behind Bacon's whole life and thought.

3

The same Faustian elements emerge in the tragedy of Bacon's public career. He was born January 22, 1561, in the golden reign of Elizabeth I. He was, superficially, most fortunate in his birth. His mother was notable among the learned women of her time. His father, Sir Nicholas Bacon, was an outstanding statesman of the day. His uncle, William Cecil, later Lord Burleigh, was Elizabeth's greatest minister, and even the Queen herself was charmed by the precocious child. The boy was plainly destined for a career in public life, to which, as he grew older, he was drawn partly by a fierce desire for the kind of place and power his father had won, partly by a deep sense of duty. The Bacons, like the Cecils, were not of the Old Nobility: they were among the New Men who had just emerged in the breakup of the feudal world. Lawyers, Humanists, and Protestants, they were men dedicated to the service of the Crown. For them the noblest way to serve God was to serve the state. Thus the ideal of the active life was part of Bacon's birthright, and the tragic polarity of his life was fixed for him by his birth and training.

The other polarity of the contemplative life he soon found for himself. He was educated privately, then sent in 1573 at the age of twelve to Trinity College, Cambridge, but with no intention on his or his parents' part that he should take a degree. He remained at Cambridge three years, long enough, however, to start him on his lifelong quest. His feelings toward Cambridge were ambivalent. He was repelled by its traditionalism yet was deeply drawn to the kind of life he found there.

By the time he was fifteen his father had definitely settled on the decision "to mould and frame him for the arts of state," so that he was withdrawn from the university to start reading law at Gray's Inn. But he had barely entered his legal studies when an opportunity opened for foreign experience and some acquaintance with diplomacy in the service of Sir Amias Paulet, newly-made English Ambassador to France. In 1579 his stay abroad was cut short by his father's death, an event that threw a far deeper shadow over Bacon's brilliant prospects than even he could have realized at the time. His father, who had settled generous estates on his other sons, had by sheer mischance failed to make provision for his youngest son, and Bacon was left without an income adequate to a courtier's career and without the influence that would have assured his way. It is easy enough for us to see that Bacon at eighteen might have been wise to renounce all political ambitions and dreams of place and power, no matter how deeply they were ingrained or how much they were expected of him. As time went on, he was again and again tempted to do so and at the last bitterly to regret his lack of decision.

He returned to Gray's Inn to qualify himself for the bar, to which he was admitted in 1586. In 1584, however, he was elected to the House of Commons and began his distinguished Parliamentary career. In 1593 he led a vigorous fight for the rights of the Commons and the people against what he regarded as dangerous proposals urged by the House of Lords, the chief ministers of the Queen, and the Queen herself. His independence cost him dearly. The great Queen had a long memory for those who opposed her wishes, and when during the 1590's Bacon became a candidate first for the Attorney-Generalship and later for the Solicitorship, she allowed him to dangle interminably in hopes and then appointed others. Through Cecil's influence he was promised a lucrative post and through his own abilities he won unofficial status on Elizabeth's legal staff, but the inescapable fact was that he held no appointed office during the reign of Elizabeth, whom he loved and revered.

A second source of sorrow and distress came from his association with the rising young Earl of Essex, beginning in the 1590's. Essex, a brilliant, virile, volatile youth of extraordinary promise, was the last of Elizabeth's favorites. He was drawn to Bacon by respect for the latter's conspicuous abilities, which he fought valiantly, though unsuccessfully, to have the Queen reward. When she failed to bestow offices which Essex and Bacon had thought were half-promised, Essex with characteristic generosity gave Bacon a rich gift of land. But as the decade wore on, Essex increasingly discovered that being an Elizabethan favorite was not always a happy lot; and although Bacon, who was one of his chief mentors, tried to moderate his courses and counsel temperance, the inevitable break occurred between the aging Queen and the ambitious favorite. Bacon did everything in his power to effect a reconciliation, urging obedience on Essex and understanding on the Queen; but when it became all too evident that pride and self-will in Essex were going to triumph over his loyalty, Bacon refused to be party to any courses headed toward treason, and the two men drew apart. Essex and his followers raised an armed rebellion to seize the Queen. They failed, were arraigned on charges of treason, and the leaders were executed. In the course of the trial Bacon was obliged to appear among the Queen's Counsel so that it seemed to some as though he were heartlessly prosecuting a friend and ardent benefactor. But we know today that, however distasteful the role was to Bacon, he behaved with entire probity. He had foreseen the Essex rebellion and had struggled manfully to prevent it. When the act of treason occurred, he could only accept it for what it was. When the trial came on, he could have withdrawn in a romantic, futile gesture that could in no way have helped Essex and that would have embarrassed the Crown's handling of its problem. He was in a cruel position, but in putting the security of the state ahead of personal considerations when treason was the issue, he had done, as he said, his "duty to the Queen and State; in which I would not show myself false-hearted nor faint-hearted for any man's sake living."

Upon the death of Elizabeth and the accession of James I in 1603, the pattern of Bacon's public life began to change, slowly at first and then with increasing rapidity. He was knighted in 1603, sworn as King's Counsel in 1604, made Solicitor-General in 1607 and Attorney-General in 1613, placed on the Privy Council in 1616, created Lord Keeper of the Great Seal in 1617 and Lord Chancellor in 1618. These last were the highest appointive offices of the realm and made the holder technically the principal officer of state after the King. In 1618 he was raised to the peerage as Baron Verulam, and in January, 1621, he was further advanced as Viscount St. Alban. But the days of his glory were appallingly brief. Four months later he was indicted by the House of Lords, of which he was a member, on charges of corruption, specifically for accepting gifts from parties who had suits before him. Bacon made no effort to defend himself but pled guilty and threw himself on the mercy of the Peers. He was sentenced to a fine of £40,000, to imprisonment in the Tower at the King's pleasure, to banishment from London and the court, and to permanent disbarment from public office and from Parliament. If the Lords were not disposed to be merciful, the King was. The fine was remitted, his imprisonment lasted only a few days, and the banishment was subsequently removed. What was left was the disbarment from Parliament and public office.

That the long years of Bacon's distinguished public life ended in ignominy has caused much speculation. Why did he not defend himself? There have been hints, on the one hand, that he was betrayed by the rapacity of his servants, who unquestionably were all too free in accepting gifts in his name from litigants; and there have been hints, on the other hand, that Bacon threw himself down as a willing sacrifice to enemies of the King and of the Duke of Buckingham, Bacon's principal supporter. Perhaps so, but this is to multiply mystery needlessly. Up to a point Bacon was guilty as charged—which is not to say that he was guilty of corruption in the layman's sense of the term. None of the gifts had affected his decisions, and in fact none of his several thousand decisions was ever reversed. He could say with a clear heart what he said to the King: "I had no bribe or reward in my eye or thought, when I pronounced any sentence or order." Yet he was guilty of indulging in a practice of the time common enough, but wholly indefensible in a judge. He might have blurred the issue by a defense. He might have taken refuge in the legal subtlety that there was no law forbidding the Lord Chancellor to receive gifts and nothing either in his oath of office. He might have answered the allegations in detail, pointing out that some of the gifts were made well after the suits in question had been settled, that other gifts were made by persons whom he subsequently ruled against (no bribery here), and that not a single perversion of justice had occurred. But he did none of these things: he sought no refuge and he blurred no issues. Nowhere in his life did Bacon so well display the largeness of his soul as in his unsparing and unequivocal confession of fault, in his unwillingness to defend himself, and in his assertion after his sentence had been passed: "I was the justest judge that was in England these fifty years. But it was the justest censure in Parliament that was these two hundred years."

In the first days of his disgrace Bacon felt that he could not outlive his humiliation and made a hurried draft of his will, which in its final form contained the famous provision: "For my name and memory, I leave it to men's charitable speeches, and to foreign nations, and the next ages." He was saved from utter despair by his religious faith, by the consciousness that he had never knowingly perverted justice, and by an unquenchable force of spirit that drew from Prince Charles the admiring comment: "This man scorns to go out like snuff."

Then the contemplative polarity exerted its magic force. It had been with him always through the years of his disappointments under Elizabeth until he was in his forties. It had given him the strength in the midst of an amazingly full career to produce the Essays, The Advancement of

Learning, and *The Great Instauration*, among countless other writings. Besides, he had always had the unfulfilled impulse "with God's assistance to retire myself to Cambridge, and there spend my life in studies and contemplations, without looking back." There had steadily been moments of self-awareness—"knowing myself by inward calling to be fitter to hold a book than to play a part, I have led my life in civil causes; for which I was not very fit by nature, and more unfit by the preoccupation of my mind"—but even as he wrote, he had already decided "that in this theatre of man's life it is reserved only for God and Angels to be lookers-on." Now, having tasted the glory and the dust, he felt shame that he had misspent so much of his life "in things for which I was least fit; so as I may truly say, my soul hath been a stranger in the course of my pilgrimage." Yet he took comfort from the fact that time remained to him, and his mind turned eagerly to projects he had long wanted to attempt: a history of England under the Tudors, an analytical digest of English law, the final shaping of his major works, and the first samples of the natural history which he hoped future ages would perfect. His five remaining years were too short for all he hoped to do, yet his output was impressive for a man of his years and troubles, including, among other works, his able *History of the Reign of King Henry VII*, the expansion and Latin translation of *The Advancement of Learning* (called *De Dignitate et Augmentis Scientiarum*), the final form of the *Essays*, and the *New Atlantis*.

Bacon died April 9, 1626, an enigmatic yet mighty figure, whose monuments of wit have survived his monuments of power. A contemporary who knew him intimately has perhaps characterized him best: "A man most sweet in his conversation and ways, grave in his judgments, invariable in his fortunes, splendid in his expenses; a friend unalterable to his friends; an enemy to no man; above all, a most hearty and indefatigable servant of the King and a most earnest lover of the Public, having all the thoughts of his large heart set on adorning the age in which he lives and benefiting as far as possible the whole human race."

A SELECTED BIBLIOGRAPHY

EDITIONS

Works, ed. James Spedding, R. L. Ellis, D. D. Heath. 14 vols. London, 1857-74. The definitive edition and the definitive biography used for all texts and translations in the present volume. Vols. 1-7 contain the works in original and in translation; vols. 8-14 contain James Spedding's *The Letters and the Life of Francis Bacon.*

Philosophical Works, ed. J. M. Robertson. London, Routledge, 1905. A one-volume reprint of all Bacon's chief writings based on the Spedding, Ellis, Heath edition with the latter editors' introductions and notes. Contains also the earliest biography of Bacon by his chaplain William Rawley.

BIBLIOGRAPHY

Gibson, R. W. *Francis Bacon. A Bibliography of His Works and Baconiana to the Year 1750.* Oxford, Scrivener Press, 1950.

BIOGRAPHY AND CRITICISM IN ENGLISH

Since virtually all histories of science, philosophy, English literature, and English law contain more or less extensive discussions of Bacon, such works are not included below. Also excluded are any selections from the vast body of Continental literature about Bacon.

Anderson, F. H. *The Philosophy of Francis Bacon.* University of Chicago Press, 1948. A carefully organized, objective account.

Broad, C. D. *The Philosophy of Francis Bacon.* Cambridge University Press, 1926. A lucid, witty explication, which minimizes Bacon's influence on the development of science but ranks him high as the first philosopher to grapple with the as yet unsolved problems of inductive logic.

Church, R. W. *Bacon*. (English Men of Letters). London, 1884. A readable bigraphy, hostile to Bacon as a personality.

Craig, Hardin. *The Enchanted Glass. The Elizabethan Mind in Literature.* 2nd edn. Oxford, Blackwell, 1950. Useful for general intellectual background.

Ducasse, C. J. "Francis Bacon's Philosophy of Science," in *Structure, Method and Meaning,* ed. Paul Henle. New York, Liberal Arts Press, 1951.

Farrington, Benjamin. *Francis Bacon.* New York, Schuman, 1949. The best short book on Bacon.

Farrington, Benjamin. "On Misunderstanding the Philosophy of Francis Bacon," in *Science, Medicine, and History,* ed. E. A. Underwood. 2 vols. Oxford University Press, 1954.

Fowler, Thomas. *Bacon.* London, 1881. A sane, well-balanced study.

Gordon, George. *The Lives of Authors.* London, Chatto & Windus, 1950. Contains an essay, "Francis Bacon and the Revival of English Humanism."

James, D. G. *The Dream of Learning.* Oxford, Clarendon Press, 1951. Compares and contrasts the essential perceptions of Bacon and Shakespeare.

Jones, Richard Foster. *Ancients and Moderns.* (Washington University Studies: Language and Literature). St. Louis, 1936. Authoritative study furnishing an account of Bacon's influence on the development of English attitudes toward science in the seventeenth century.

Jones, Richard Foster, and others. *The Seventeenth Century. Studies in the History of English Thought and Literature from Bacon to Pope.* Stanford University Press, 1951.

Knights, L. C. *Explorations.* London, Chatto & Windus, 1946. Bacon as seen by a New Critic in the chapter entitled "Bacon and the Seventeenth-Century Dissociation of Sensibility."

Krapp, G. P. *The Rise of English Literary Prose.* New York, Oxford University Press, 1915. Devotes a chapter to the importance of Bacon.

Lemmi, Charles W. *The Classic Deities in Bacon.* Baltimore, The Johns Hopkins University Press, 1933. A scholarly study of *The Wisdom of the Ancients.*

Macaulay, T. B. "Francis Bacon," *Edinburgh Review,* LXV (1837), 277ff. The classic essay. A violent diatribe against Bacon's character and an excessive laudation of him as a philosopher, "the British Plato."

MacDonald, W. L. *Beginnings of the English Essay*. University of Toronto Press, 1914.

Merton, Robert K. "Science, Technology and Society in Seventeenth Century England," *Osiris*, IV (1938), 360-632. A sociological study.

Napier, Macvey. "Remarks, Illustrative of the Scope and Influence of the Philosophical Writings of Lord Bacon," *Transactions of the Royal Society of Edinburgh*, VIII (1818), 373-425. Still useful for its account of Bacon's Continental reputation and influence.

Robertson, J. M. *Pioneer Humanists*. London, Watts, 1907. Offers a critical review of various conflicting Bacon biographies and holds that Bacon's greatness was as a writer, not as a philosopher.

Schelling Anniversary Papers. New York, Century, 1923. Contains two significant studies: Morris Croll, "Attic Prose: Lipsius, Montaigne, and Bacon"; and Ronald S. Crane, "The Relation of Bacon's Essays to His Program for the Advancement of Learning."

Seventeenth-Century Studies Presented to Sir Herbert Grierson. Oxford, Clarendon Press, 1938. Contains two important essays: Geoffrey Bullough, "Bacon and the Defence of Learning"; and Rudolph Metz, "Bacon's Part in the Intellectual Movement of His Time."

Spedding, James. *Evenings with a Reviewer*. 2 vols. London, 1881. A patient demolition of Macaulay's account of Bacon's life.

Sturt, Mary. *Francis Bacon*. London, Kegan Paul, 1932. A laudatory biography.

Taylor, A. E. *Francis Bacon*. (British Academy Master-Mind Lecture). Oxford University Press, 1927. A stimulating appraisal.

Tillotson, Geoffrey. "Words for Princes: Francis Bacon in His Essays," [London] *Times Literary Supplement* (Feb. 6, 1937), p. 8.

Tuveson, Ernest. *Millennium and Utopia*. Berkeley and Los Angeles, University of California Press, 1949. A study of the religious backgrounds of the idea of progress.

Wallace, Karl R. *Francis Bacon on Communication and Rhetoric*. Chapel Hill, University of North Carolina Press, 1948. Helpful scholarly study of the principles behind Bacon's art as a writer and speaker.

Whitehead, Alfred North. *Science and the Modern World.* New York, Macmillan, 1925. Brilliant account of the changing concepts of science and their impact on Western culture.

Willey, Basil. *The Seventeenth Century Background.* London, Chatto & Windus, 1934. Outstanding study in the history of ideas with a chapter on "Bacon and the Rehabilitation of Nature."

Williams, Charles. *Bacon.* London, Barker, 1933. A sympathetic biography.

Wilson, F. P. *Elizabethan and Jacobean.* Oxford, Clarendon Press, 1945. Contains an excellent analysis of Bacon's prose.

Wolf, Abraham. *A History of Science, Technology and Philosophy in the XVIth and XVIIth Centuries.* 2nd edn. London, Allen & Unwin, 1950. The standard history copiously illustrated.

Zeitlin, J. "The Development of Bacon's Essays," *Journal of English and Germanic Philology,* XXVII (1928), 496-519.

SELECTED WRITINGS OF

FRANCIS BACON

My Lord,

With as much confidence as mine own honest and faithful
devotion unto your service and your honourable correspondence unto me and my poor estate can breed in a man, do I
commend myself unto your Lordship. I wax now somewhat
ancient; one and thirty years is a great deal of sand in the
hour-glass. My health, I thank God, I find confirmed; and
I do not fear that action shall impair it, because I account
my ordinary course of study and meditation to be more
painful than most parts of action are. I ever bare a mind (in
some middle place that I could discharge) to serve her
Majesty; not as a man born under Sol, that loveth honour;
nor under Jupiter, that loveth business (for the contemplative planet carrieth me away wholly); but as a man born
under an excellent Sovereign, that deserveth the dedication
of all men's abilities. Besides, I do not find in myself so
much self-love, but that the greater parts of my thoughts are
to deserve well (if I were able) of my friends, and namely
of your Lordship; who being the Atlas of this commonwealth, the honour of my house, and the second founder of
my poor estate, I am tied by all duties, both of a good
patriot, and of an unworthy kinsman, and of an obliged
servant, to employ whatsoever I am to do you service.
Again, the meanness of my estate doth somewhat move me:
for though I cannot accuse myself that I am either prodigal
or slothful, yet my health is not to spend, nor my course to
get. Lastly, I confess that I have as vast contemplative ends,
as I have moderate civil ends: for I have taken all knowledge to be my province; and if I could purge it of two sorts
of rovers, whereof the one with frivolous disputations, confutations, and verbosities, the other with blind experiments
and auricular traditions and impostures, hath committed so
many spoils, I hope I should bring in industrious observa-

tions, grounded conclusions, and profitable inventions and discoveries; the best state of that province. This, whether it be curiosity, or vain glory, or nature, or (if one take it favourably) *philanthropia*, is so fixed in my mind as it cannot be removed. And I do easily see, that place of any reasonable countenance doth bring commandment of more wits than of a man's own; which is the thing I greatly affect. And for your Lordship, perhaps you shall not find more strength and less encounter in any other. And if your Lordship shall find now, or at any time, that I do seek or affect any place whereunto any that is nearer unto your Lordship shall be concurrent, say then that I am a most dishonest man. And if your Lordship will not carry me on, I will not do as Anaxagoras did, who reduced himself with contemplation unto voluntary poverty: but this I will do; I will sell the inheritance that I have, and purchase some lease of quick revenue, or some office of gain that shall be executed by deputy, and so give over all care of service, and become some sorry bookmaker, or a true pioner in that mine of truth, which (he said) lay so deep. This which I have writ unto your Lordship is rather thoughts than words, being set down without all art, disguising, or reservation. Wherein I have done honour both to your Lordship's wisdom, in judging that that will be best believed of your Lordship which is truest, and to your Lordship's good nature, in retaining nothing from you. And even so I wish your Lordship all happiness, and to myself means and occasion to be added to my faithful desire to do you service. From my lodging at Gray's Inn.

THE

ESSAYES OR COUNSELS

CIVILL AND MORALL

OF

FRANCIS LO. VERULAM,

VISCOUNT ST. ALBAN

NEWLY ENLARGED

[Unpublished dedication to Prince Henry — 1612]

TO THE MOST HIGH AND EXCELLENT PRINCE, HENRY, PRINCE OF WALES, DUKE OF CORNWALL, AND EARL OF CHESTER.

It may please your Highness,

Having divided my life into the contemplative and active part, I am desirous to give his Majesty and your Highness of the fruits of both, simple though they be.

To write just treatises requireth leisure in the writer, and leisure in the reader, and therefore are not so fit, neither in regard of your Highness' princely affairs, nor in regard of my continual services; which is the cause that hath made me choose to write certain brief notes, set down rather significantly than curiously, which I have called *Essays*. The word is late, but the thing is ancient. For Seneca's epistles to Lucilius, if one mark them well, are but *Essays*, that is, dispersed meditations, though conveyed in the form of epistles. These labours of mine I know cannot be worthy of your Highness, for what can be worthy of you? But my hope is, they may be as grains of salt, that will rather give you an appetite than offend you with satiety. And although they handle those things wherein both men's lives and their pens are most conversant, yet (what I have attained I know not) but I have endeavoured to make them not vulgar, but of a nature whereof a man shall find much in experience, and little in books; so as they are neither repetitions nor fancies. But howsoever, I shall most humbly desire your Highness to accept them in gracious part, and to conceive, that if I cannot rest, but must shew my dutiful and devoted affection to your Highness in these things which proceed from myself, I shall be much more ready to do it in performance of any your princely commandments. And so wishing your Highness all princely felicity I rest,

Your Highness's most humble servant.

ESSAYS OR COUNSELS

CIVIL AND MORAL

[1625]

1
OF TRUTH

What is Truth? said jesting Pilate; and would not stay for
an answer. Certainly there be that delight in giddiness, and
count it a bondage to fix a belief; affecting[1] free-will in
thinking, as well as in acting. And though the sects of philosophers[2] of that kind be gone, yet there remain certain discoursing wits[3] which are of the same veins, though there be
not so much blood in them as was in those of the ancients.
But it is not only the difficulty and labour which men take
in finding out of truth; nor again that when it is found it
imposeth upon men's thoughts; that doth bring lies in favour;
but a natural though corrupt love of the lie itself. One of the
later school of the Grecians[4] examineth the matter, and is at
a stand to think what should be in it, that men should love
lies, where neither they make for pleasure, as with poets,
nor for advantage, as with the merchant; but for the lie's
sake. But I cannot tell: this same truth is a naked and open
day-light, that doth not shew the masks and mummeries and
triumphs of the world, half so stately and daintily as candle-

lights. Truth may perhaps come to the price of a pearl, that sheweth best by day; but it will not rise to the price of a diamond or carbuncle, that sheweth best in varied lights. A mixture of a lie doth ever add pleasure. Doth any man doubt, that if there were taken out of men's minds vain opinions, flattering hopes, false valuations, imaginations as one would, and the like, but it would leave the minds of a number of men poor shrunken things, full of melancholy and indisposition, and unpleasing to themselves? One of the Fathers,[5] in great severity, called poesy *vinum dæmonum* [devil's-wine], because it filleth the imagination; and yet it is but with the shadow of a lie. But it is not the lie that passeth through the mind, but the lie that sinketh in and settleth in it, that doth the hurt; such as we spake of before. But howsoever these things are thus in men's depraved judgments and affections, yet truth, which only doth judge itself, teacheth that the inquiry of truth, which is the love-making or wooing of it, the knowledge of truth, which is the presence of it, and the belief of truth, which is the enjoying of it, is the sovereign good of human nature. The first creature of God, in the works of the days, was the light of the sense; the last was the light of reason; and his sabbath work ever since, is the illumination of his Spirit. First he breathed light upon the face of the matter or chaos; then he breathed light into the face of man; and still he breatheth and inspireth light into the face of his chosen. The poet[6] that beautified the sect that was otherwise inferior to the rest, saith yet excellently well: *It is a pleasure to stand upon the shore, and to see ships tossed upon the sea; a pleasure to stand in the window of a castle, and to see a battle and the adventures thereof below: but no pleasure is comparable to the standing upon the vantage ground of Truth,* (a hill not to be commanded, and where the air is always clear and serene,) *and to see the errors, and wanderings, and mists, and tempests, in the vale below;* so always that this prospect be with pity, and not with swelling or pride. Certainly, it is heaven upon earth, to have a man's mind move in charity, rest in providence, and turn upon the poles of truth.

To pass from theological and philosophical truth, to the truth of civil business; it will be acknowledged even by those that practise it not, that clear and round dealing is the honour of man's nature; and that mixture of falsehood is like allay in coin of gold and silver, which may make the metal work the better, but it embaseth it. For these winding and crooked courses are the goings of the serpent; which goeth basely upon the belly, and not upon the feet. There is no vice that doth so cover a man with shame as to be found false and perfidious. And therefore Montaigne saith prettily, when he inquired the reason, why the word of the lie should be such a disgrace and such an odious charge? Saith he, *If it be well weighed, to say that a man lieth, is as much to say, as that he is brave towards God and a coward towards men.* For a lie faces God, and shrinks from man. Surely the wickedness of falsehood and breach of faith cannot possibly be so highly expressed, as in that it shall be the last peal to call the judgments of God upon the generations of men; it being foretold, that when Christ cometh, *he shall not find faith upon the earth.*

2

OF DEATH

MEN fear Death, as children fear to go in the dark; and as that natural fear in children is increased with tales, so is the other. Certainly, the contemplation of death, as the wages of sin and passage to another world, is holy and religious; but the fear of it, as a tribute due unto nature, is weak. Yet in religious meditations there is sometimes mixture of vanity and of superstition. You shall read in some of the friars' books of mortification, that a man should think with himself what the pain is if he have but his finger's end pressed or tortured, and thereby imagine what the pains of death are, when the whole body is corrupted and dissolved; when many times death passeth with less pain than the torture of a limb: for the most vital parts are not the quickest of sense. And by him that spake only as a philosopher[1] and natural man, it was well said, *Pompa mortis magis terret, quam mors ipsa:* [it is the accompaniments of death that are frightful rather than death itself.] Groans and convulsions, and a discoloured face, and friends weeping, and blacks, and obsequies, and the like, shew death terrible. It is worthy the observing, that there is no passion in the mind of man so weak, but it mates and masters the fear of death; and therefore death is no such terrible enemy when a man hath so many attendants about him that can win the combat of him. Revenge triumphs over death; Love slights it; Honour aspireth to it; Grief flieth to it; Fear pre-occupateth it; nay we read, after Otho the emperor had slain himself, Pity (which is the tenderest of affections) provoked many to die, out of mere compassion to their sovereign, and as the truest sort of followers. Nay Seneca adds niceness and satiety: *Cogita quamdiu eadem feceris; mori velle, non tantum fortis, aut miser, sed etiam fastidiosus potest.* A man would die, though he were neither valiant nor miserable, only upon a weariness to do the same thing so oft over and over. It is no less worthy to observe, how little alteration in good spirits the approaches of death make; for they appear to be the same men till the last instant. Augustus Cæsar died in a compliment; *Livia, conjugii nostri memor, vive et vale:* [farewell, Livia; and forget not the days of our marriage.] Tiberius in dissimulation; as Tacitus saith of him, *Jam Tiberium vires et corpus, non dissimulatio, deserebant*: [his powers of body were gone, but his power of dissimulation still remained.] Vespasian in a jest; sitting upon the stool, *Ut puto Deus fio:* [I think I am becoming a god.] Galba with a sentence; *Feri, si ex re sit populi Romani:* [strike, if it be for the good of Rome;] holding forth his neck. Septimius Severus in despatch; *Adeste si quid mihi restat agendum:* [make haste, if there is anything more for me to do.] And the like. Certainly the Stoics bestowed too much cost upon death, and by their great preparations made it appear more fearful. Better saith he,[2] *qui finem vitæ extremum inter munera ponat naturæ:* [who accounts the close of life as one of the benefits of nature.] It is as natural to die as to be born;

and to a little infant, perhaps, the one is as painful as the other. He that dies in an earnest pursuit, is like one that is wounded in hot blood; who, for the time, scarce feels the hurt; and therefore a mind fixed and bent upon somewhat that is good doth avert the dolours of death. But above all, believe it, the sweetest canticle is, *Nunc dimittis;*[3] when a man hath obtained worthy ends and expectations. Death hath this also; that it openeth the gate to good fame, and extinguisheth envy. *Extinctus amabitur idem:* [the same man that was envied while he lived, shall be loved when he is gone].

3

OF UNITY IN RELIGION

RELIGION being the chief band of human society, it is a happy thing when itself is well contained within the true band of Unity. The quarrels and divisions about religion were evils unknown to the heathen. The reason was, because the religion of the heathen consisted rather in rites and ceremonies, than in any constant belief. For you may imagine what kind of faith theirs was, when the chief doctors and fathers of their church were the poets. But the true God hath this attribute, that he is a *jealous God;* and therefore his worship and religion will endure no mixture nor partner. We shall therefore speak a few words concerning the Unity of the Church; what are the Fruits thereof; what the Bounds; and what the Means.

The Fruits of Unity (next unto the well pleasing of God, which is all in all) are two; the one towards those that are without the church, the other towards those that are within. For the former; it is certain that heresies and schisms are of all others the greatest scandals; yea, more than corruption of manners. For as in the natural body a wound or solution of continuity is worse than a corrupt humour; so in the spiritual. So that nothing doth so much keep men out of the church, and drive men out of the church, as breach of unity. And therefore, whensoever it cometh to that pass,

that one saith *Ecce in deserto* [*Behold! in the desert], another saith *Ecce in penetralibus* [*Behold! in the sanctuary];
that is, when some men seek Christ in the conventicles of
heretics, and others in an outward face of a church, that
voice had need continually to sound in men's ears, *Nolite
exire,—Go not out.* The Doctor of the Gentiles[1] (the propriety of whose vocation drew him to have a special care of
those without) saith, *If an heathen come in, and hear you
speak with several tongues, will he not say that you are
mad?* And certainly it is little better, when atheists and profane persons do hear of so many discordant and contrary
opinions in religion; it doth avert them from the church, and
maketh them *to sit down in the chair of the scorners.* It is
but a light thing to be vouched in so serious a matter, but
yet it expresseth well the deformity. There is a master of
scoffing,[2] that in his catalogue of books of a feigned library
sets down this title of a book, *The morris-dance of Heretics.*
For indeed every sect of them hath a diverse posture or
cringe by themselves, which cannot but move derision in
worldlings and depraved politics, who are apt to contemn
holy things.

As for the fruit towards those that are within; it is peace;
which containeth infinite blessings. It establisheth faith. It
kindleth charity. The outward peace of the church distilleth
into peace of conscience. And it turneth the labours of
writing and reading of controversies into treatises of mortification and devotion.

Concerning the Bounds of Unity; the true placing of them
importeth exceedingly. There appear to be two extremes.
For to certain zelants all speech of pacification is odious. *Is
it peace, Jehu? What hast thou to do with peace? turn thee
behind me.* Peace is not the matter, but following and party.
Contrariwise, certain Laodiceans and lukewarm persons
think they may accommodate points of religion by middle
ways, and taking part of both, and witty reconcilements; as
if they would make an arbitrement between God and man.
Both these extremes are to be avoided; which will be done,
if the league of Christians penned by our Saviour himself

were in the two cross[3] clauses thereof soundly and plainly expounded: *He that is not with us is against us;* and again, *He that is not against us is with us;* that is, if the points fundamental and of substance in religion were truly discerned and distinguished from points not merely of faith, but of opinion, order, or good intention. This is a thing may seem to many a matter trivial, and done already. But if it were done less partially, it would be embraced more generally.

Of this I may give only this advice, according to my small model. Men ought to take heed of rending God's church by two kinds of controversies. The one is, when the matter of the point controverted is too small and light, not worth the heat and strife about it, kindled only by contradiction. For as it is noted by one of the fathers,[4] *Christ's coat indeed had no seam, but the church's vesture was of divers colours;* whereupon he saith, *In veste varietas sit, scissura non sit,* [let there be variety in the garment, but let there be no division:] they be two things, Unity and Uniformity. The other is, when the matter of the point controverted is great, but it is driven to an over-great subtilty and obscurity; so that it becometh a thing rather ingenious than substantial. A man that is of judgment and understanding shall sometimes hear ignorant men differ, and know well within himself that those which so differ mean one thing, and yet they themselves would never agree. And if it come so to pass in that distance of judgment which is between man and man, shall we not think that God above, that knows the heart, doth not discern that frail men in some of their contradictions intend the same thing; and accepteth of both? The nature of such controversies is excellently expressed by St. Paul in the warning and precept that he giveth concerning the same, *Devita profanas vocum novitates, et oppositiones falsi nominis scientiæ:* [Avoid profane novelties of terms, and oppositions of science falsely so called.] Men create oppositions which are not; and put them into new terms so fixed, as whereas the meaning ought to govern the term, the term in effect governeth the meaning. There be also two false peaces or unities: the one, when the peace is grounded but upon an implicit ignorance; for all colours will agree in the dark: the other, when it is pieced up upon a direct admission of contraries in fundamental points. For truth and falsehood, in such things, are like the iron and clay in the toes of Nabuchadnezzar's image; they may cleave, but they will not incorporate.

Concerning the Means of procuring Unity; men must beware, that in the procuring or muniting of religious unity they do not dissolve and deface the laws of charity and of human society. There be two swords amongst Christians, the spiritual and temporal; and both have their due office and place in the maintenance of religion. But we may not take up the third sword, which is Mahomet's sword, or like unto it; that is, to propagate religion by wars or by sanguinary persecutions to force consciences; except it be in cases of overt scandal, blasphemy, or intermixture of practice against the state; much less to nourish seditions; to authorise conspiracies and rebellions; to put the sword into the people's hands; and the like; tending to the subversion of all government, which is the ordinance of God. For this is but to dash the first table against the second; and so to consider men as Christians, as we forget that they are men. Lucretius the poet, when he beheld the act of Agamemnon, that could endure the sacrificing of his own daughter, exclaimed:

Tantum Relligio potuit suadere malorum:

[to such ill actions Religion could persuade a man.] What would he have said, if he had known of the massacre in France, or the powder treason[5] of England? He would have been seven times more Epicure and atheist than he was. For as the temporal sword is to be drawn with great circumspection in cases of religion; so it is a thing monstrous to put it into the hands of the common people. Let that be left unto the Anabaptists, and other furies. It was great blasphemy when the devil said, *I will ascend and be like the Highest;* but it is greater blasphemy to personate God, and bring him in saying, *I will descend, and be like the prince of darkness:* and what is it better, to make the cause of religion to descend to the cruel and execrable actions of murthering princes, butchery of people, and subversion of states and governments? Surely this is to bring down the Holy Ghost, instead of the likeness of a dove, in the shape of a vulture or raven; and set out of the bark of a Christian church a flag of a bark of pirates and Assassins. Therefore it is most necessary that the church by doctrine and decree, princes by their sword, and all learnings, both Christian and moral, as by their Mercury rod,[6] do damn and send to hell for ever those facts and opinions tending to the support of the same; as hath been already in good part done. Surely in counsels concerning religion, that counsel of the apostle[7] would be prefixed, *Ira hominis non implet justitiam Dei:* [The wrath of man worketh not the righteousness of God.] And it was a notable observation of a wise father,[8] and no less ingenuously confessed; *that those which held and persuaded pressure of consciences, were commonly interested therein themselves for their own ends.*

4

Of Revenge

REVENGE is a kind of wild justice; which the more man's nature runs to, the more ought law to weed it out. For as for the first wrong, it doth but offend the law; but the revenge of that wrong putteth the law out of office. Certainly, in taking revenge, a man is but even with his enemy; but in passing it over, he is superior; for it is a prince's part to pardon. And Salomon, I am sure, saith, *It is the glory of a man to pass by an offence.* That which is past is gone, and irrevocable; and wise men have enough to do with things present and to come; therefore they do but trifle with themselves, that labour in past matters. There is no man doth a wrong for the wrong's sake; but thereby to purchase himself profit, or pleasure, or honour, or the like. Therefore why should I be angry with a man for loving himself better than me? And if any man should do wrong merely out of ill-nature, why, yet it is but like the thorn or briar, which prick and scratch, because they can do no other. The most tolerable sort of revenge is for those wrongs which there is no law to remedy; but then let a man take heed the revenge be such as there is no law to punish; else a man's enemy is still before hand, and it is two for one. Some, when they take revenge, are desirous the party should know whence it cometh. This the more generous. For the delight seemeth to be not so much in doing the hurt as in making the party repent. But base and crafty cowards are like the arrow that flieth in the dark. Cosmus, duke of Florence, had a desperate saying against perfidious or neglecting friends, as if those wrongs were un-pardonable; *You shall read* (saith he) *that we are com-manded to forgive our enemies; but you never read that we are commanded to forgive our friends.* But yet the spirit of Job was in a better tune: *Shall we* (saith he) *take good at God's hands, and not be content to take evil also?* And so of friends in a proportion. This is certain, that a man that studieth revenge keeps his own wounds green, which other-wise would heal and do well. Public revenges are for the most part fortunate; as that for the death of Cæsar; for the death of Pertinax; for the death of Henry the Third of France; and many more. But in private revenges it is not so. Nay rather, vindictive persons live the life of witches; who, as they are mischievous, so end they infortunate.

5

OF ADVERSITY

IT was a high speech of Seneca (after the manner of the Stoics), *that the good things which belong to prosperity are to be wished; but the good things that belong to adversity are to be admired. Bona rerum secundarum optabilia; ad-versarum mirabilia.* Certainly if miracles be the command over nature, they appear most in adversity. It is yet a higher speech of his than the other (much too high for a heathen), *It is true greatness to have in one the frailty of a man, and the security of a God. Vere magnum habere fragilitatem hominis, securitatem Dei.* This would have done better in poesy, where transcendences are more allowed. And the poets indeed have been busy with it; for it is in effect the thing which is figured in that strange fiction of the ancient poets, which seemeth not to be without mystery; nay, and to have some approach to the state of a Christian; that *Hercules, when he went to unbind Prometheus* (by whom human nature is represented), *sailed the length of the great ocean in an earthen pot or pitcher;* lively describing Christian resolution, that saileth in the frail bark of the flesh thorough the waves of the world. But to speak in a mean. The virtue of Prosperity is temperance, the virtue of Adversity is fortitude; which in morals is the more heroical virtue. Prosperity is the blessing of the Old Testament; Adversity is the blessing of the New; which carrieth the greater benediction, and the clearer revelation of God's favour. Yet even in the Old Testament, if you listen to David's harp, you shall hear as many hearse-like airs as carols; and the pencil of the Holy Ghost hath laboured more in describing the afflictions of Job than the felicities of Salomon. Prosperity is not without many fears and distastes; and Adversity is not without comforts and hopes. We see in needle-works and embroideries, it is more pleasing to have a lively work upon a sad and solemn ground, than to have a dark and melancholy work upon a lightsome ground: judge therefore of the pleasure of the heart by the pleasure of the eye. Certainly virtue is like precious odours, most fragrant when they are incensed or crushed: for Prosperity doth best discover vice, but Adversity doth best discover virtue.

6

Of Simulation and Dissimulation

Dissimulation is but a faint kind of policy or wisdom; for it asketh a strong wit and a strong heart to know when to tell truth, and to do it. Therefore it is the weaker sort of politics that are the great dissemblers.

Tacitus saith, *Livia sorted well with the arts of her husband and dissimulation of her son;* attributing arts or policy to Augustus, and dissimulation to Tiberius. And again, when Mucianus encourageth Vespasian to take arms against Vitellius, he saith, *We rise not against the piercing judgment of Augustus, nor the extreme caution or closeness of Tiberius.* These properties, of arts or policy and dissimulation or closeness, are indeed habits and faculties several, and to be distinguished. For if a man have that penetration of judgment as he can discern what things are to be laid open, and what to be secreted, and what to be shewed at half lights, and to whom and when, (which indeed are arts of state and arts of life, as Tacitus well calleth them,) to him a habit of dissimulation is a hinderance and a poorness. But if a man cannot obtain to that judgment, then it is left to him generally to be close, and a dissembler. For where a man cannot choose or vary in particulars, there it is good to take the safest and wariest way in general; like the going softly, by one that cannot well see. Certainly the ablest men that ever were have had all an openness and frankness of dealing; and a name of certainty and veracity; but then they were like horses well managed; for they could tell passing well when to stop or turn; and at such times when they thought the case indeed required dissimulation, if then they used it, it came to pass that the former opinion spread abroad of their good faith and clearness of dealing made them almost invisible.

There be three degrees of this hiding and veiling of a man's self. The first, Closeness, Reservation, and Secrecy; when a man leaveth himself without observation, or without hold to be taken, what he is. The second, Dissimulation, in the negative; when a man lets fall signs and arguments, that he is not that he is. And the third, Simulation, in the affirmative; when a man industriously and expressly feigns and pretends to be that he is not.

For the first of these, Secrecy; it is indeed the virtue of a confessor. And assuredly the secret man heareth many confessions. For who will open himself to a blab or babbler? But if a man be thought secret, it inviteth discovery; as the more close air sucketh in the more open; and as in confession the revealing is not for worldly use, but for the ease of a man's heart, so secret men come to the knowledge of many things in that kind; while men rather discharge their minds than impart their minds. In few words, mysteries are due to secrecy. Besides (to say truth) nakedness is uncomely, as well in mind as body; and it addeth no small reverence to men's manners and actions, if they be not altogether open. As for talkers and futile persons, they are commonly vain and credulous withal. For he that talketh what he knoweth, will also talk what he knoweth not. Therefore set it down, *that an habit of secrecy is both politic and moral.* And in this part, it is good that a man's face give his tongue leave to speak. For the discovery of a man's self by the tracts of his countenance is a great weakness and betraying; by how much it is many times more marked and believed than a man's words.

For the second, which is Dissimulation; it followeth many times upon secrecy by a necessity; so that he that will be secret must be a dissembler in some degree. For men are too cunning to suffer a man to keep an indifferent carriage between both, and to be secret, without swaying the balance on either side. They will so beset a man with questions, and draw him on, and pick it out of him, that, without an absurd silence, he must shew an inclination one way; or if he do not, they will gather as much by his silence as by his speech. As for equivocations, or oraculous speeches, they cannot hold out long. So that no man can be secret, except he give himself a little scope of dissimulation; which is, as it were, but the skirts or train of secrecy.

But for the third degree, which is Simulation and false profession; that I hold more culpable, and less politic; except it be in great and rare matters. And therefore a general custom of simulation (which is this last degree) is a vice, rising either of a natural falseness or fearfulness, or of a mind that hath some main faults, which because a man must needs disguise, it maketh him practise simulation in other things, lest his hand should be out of ure.

The great advantages of simulation and dissimulation are

three. First, to lay asleep opposition, and to surprise. For where a man's intentions are published, it is an alarum to call up all that are against them. The second is, to reserve to a man's self a fair retreat. For if a man engage himself by a manifest declaration, he must go through or take a fall. The third is, the better to discover the mind of another. For to him that opens himself men will hardly shew themselves adverse; but will (fair) let him go on, and turn their freedom of speech to freedom of thought. And therefore it is a good shrewd proverb of the Spaniard, *Tell a lie and find a troth*. As if there were no way of discovery but by simulation. There be also three disadvantages, to set it even. The first, that simulation and dissimulation commonly carry with them a shew of fearfulness, which in any business doth spoil the feathers of round flying up to the mark. The second, that it puzzleth and perplexeth the conceits of many, that perhaps would otherwise co-operate with him; and makes a man walk almost alone to his own ends. The third and greatest, is, that it depriveth a man of one of the most principal instruments for action; which is trust and belief. The best composition and temperature is to have openness in fame and opinion; secrecy in habit; dissimulation in seasonable use; and a power to feign, if there be no remedy.

7

Of Parents and Children

The joys of parents are secret; and so are their griefs and fears. They cannot utter the one; nor they will not utter the other. Children sweeten labours; but they make misfortunes more bitter. They increase the cares of life; but they mitigate the remembrance of death. The perpetuity by generation is common to beasts; but memory, merit, and noble works, are proper to men. And surely a man shall see the noblest works and foundations have proceeded from childless men; which have sought to express the images of their minds, where those of their bodies have failed. So the care of posterity is most in them that have no posterity. They that are the first raisers of their houses are most indulgent towards their children; beholding them as the continuance not only of their kind but of their work; and so both children and creatures.

The difference in affection of parents towards their several children is many times unequal; and sometimes unworthy; especially in the mother; as Salomon saith, *A wise son rejoiceth the father, but an ungracious son shames the mother.* A man shall see, where there is a house full of children, one or two of the eldest respected, and the youngest made wantons; but in the midst some that are as it were forgotten, who many times nevertheless prove the best. The illiberality of parents in allowance towards their children is an harmful error; makes them base; acquaints them with shifts; makes them sort with mean company; and makes them surfeit more when they come to plenty. And therefore the proof is best, when men keep their authority towards their children, but not their purse. Men have a foolish manner (both parents and schoolmasters and servants) in creating and breeding an emulation between brothers during childhood, which many times sorteth to discord when they are men, and disturbeth families. The Italians make little difference between children and nephews or near kinsfolks; but so they be of the lump, they care not though they pass not through their own body. And, to say truth, in nature it is much a like matter; insomuch that we see a nephew sometimes resembleth an uncle or a kinsman more than his own parent; as the blood happens. Let parents choose betimes the vocations and courses they mean their children should take; for then they are most flexible; and let them not too much apply themselves to the disposition of their children, as thinking they will take best to that which they have most mind to. It is true, that if the affection or aptness of the children be extraordinary, then it is good not to cross it; but generally the precept is good, *optimum elige, suave et facile illud faciet consuetudo:* [choose the best—custom will make it pleasant and easy.] Younger brothers are commonly fortunate, but seldom or never where the elder are disinherited.

8

OF MARRIAGE AND SINGLE LIFE

HE that hath wife and children hath given hostages to fortune; for they are impediments to great enterprises, either of virtue or mischief. Certainly the best works, and of greatest merit for the public, have proceeded from the unmarried or childless men; which both in affection and means have married and endowed the public. Yet it were great reason that those that have children should have greatest care of future times; unto which they know they must transmit their dearest pledges. Some there are, who though they lead a single life, yet their thoughts do end with themselves, and account future times impertinences. Nay, there are some other that account wife and children but as bills of charges. Nay more, there are some foolish rich covetous men, that take a pride in having no children, because they may be thought so much the richer. For perhaps they have heard some talk, *Such an one is a great rich man,* and another except to it, *Yea, but he hath a great charge of children;* as if it were an abatement to his riches. But the most ordinary cause of a single life is liberty, especially in certain self-pleasing and humorous minds, which are so sensible of every restraint, as they will go near to think their girdles and garters to be bonds and shackles. Unmarried men are best friends, best masters, best servants; but not always best subjects; for they are light to run away; and almost all fugitives are of that condition. A single life doth well with churchmen; for charity will hardly water the ground where it must first fill a pool. It is indifferent for judges and magistrates; for if they be facile and corrupt, you shall have a servant five times worse than a wife. For soldiers, I find the generals commonly in their hortatives put men in mind of their wives and children; and I think the despising of marriage amongst the Turks maketh the vulgar soldier more base. Certainly wife and children are a kind of discipline of humanity; and single men, though they may be many times more charitable, because their means are less exhaust, yet, on the other side, they are more cruel and hardhearted (good to make severe inquisitors,) because their tenderness is not so oft called upon. Grave natures, led by custom, and therefore constant, are commonly loving husbands; as was said of Ulysses, *vetulam suam prætulit immortalitati:* [he preferred his old wife to immortality.] Chaste women are often proud and froward, as presuming upon the merit of their chastity. It is one of the best bonds both of chastity and obedience in the wife, if she think her husband wise; which she will never do if she find him jealous. Wives are young men's mistresses; companions for middle age; and old men's nurses. So as a man may have a quarrel to marry when he will. But yet he was reputed[1] one of the wise men, that made answer to the question, when a man should marry?—*A young man not yet, an elder man not at all.* It is often seen that bad husbands have very good wives; whether it be that it raiseth the price of their husband's kindness when it comes; or that the wives take a pride in their patience. But this never fails, if the bad husbands were of their own choosing, against their friends' consent; for then they will be sure to make good their own folly.

9

Of Envy

THERE be none of the affections which have been noted to fascinate or bewitch, but love and envy. They both have vehement wishes; they frame themselves readily into imaginations and suggestions; and they come easily into the eye, especially upon the presence of the objects; which are the points that conduce to fascination, if any such thing there be. We see likewise the scripture calleth envy an *evil eye;* and the astrologers call the evil influences of the stars *evil aspects;* so that still there seemeth to be acknowledged, in the act of envy, an ejaculation or irradiation of the eye. Nay some have been so curious as to note, that the times when the stroke or percussion of an envious eye doth most hurt, are when the party envied is beheld in glory or triumph; **for** that sets an edge upon envy: and besides, at such times the spirits of the person envied do come forth most into the outward parts, and so meet the blow.

But leaving these curiosities, (though not unworthy to be thought on in fit place,) we will handle, what persons are apt to envy others; what persons are most subject to be envied themselves; and what is the difference between public and private envy.

A man that hath no virtue in himself, ever envieth virtue in others. For men's minds will either feed upon their own good or upon others' evil; and who wanteth the one will prey upon the other; and whoso is out of hope to attain to another's virtue, will seek to come at even hand by depressing another's fortune.

A man that is busy and inquisitive is commonly envious. For to know much of other men's matters cannot be because all that ado may concern his own estate; therefore it must needs be that he taketh a kind of play-pleasure in looking upon the fortunes of others. Neither can he that mindeth but his own business find much matter for envy. For envy is a gadding passion, and walketh the streets, and doth not keep home: *Non est curiosus, quin idem sit malevolus:* [There is no curious man but has some malevolence to quicken his curiosity.]

Men of noble birth are noted to be envious towards new men when they rise. For the distance is altered; and it is like a deceit of the eye, that when others come on they think themselves go back.

Deformed persons, and eunuchs, and old men, and bastards, are envious. For he that cannot possibly mend his own case will do what he can to impair another's; except these defects light upon a very brave and heroical nature, which thinketh to make his natural wants part of his honour; in that it should be said, that an eunuch, or a lame man, did such great matters; affecting the honour of a miracle; as it was in Narses the eunuch, and Agesilaus and Tamberlanes, that were lame men.

The same is the case of men that rise after calamities and misfortunes. For they are as men fallen out with the times;

and think other men's harms a redemption of their own sufferings.

They that desire to excel in too many matters, out of levity and vain glory, are ever envious. For they cannot want work; it being impossible but many in some one of those things should surpass them. Which was the character of Adrian the Emperor; that mortally envied poets and painters and artificers, in works wherein he had a vein to excel.

Lastly, near kinsfolks, and fellows in office, and those that have been bred together, are more apt to envy their equals when they are raised. For it doth upbraid unto them their own fortunes, and pointeth at them, and cometh oftener into their remembrance, and incurreth likewise more into the note of others; and envy ever redoubleth from speech and fame. Cain's envy was the more vile and malignant towards his brother Abel, because when his sacrifice was better accepted there was no body to look on. Thus much for those that are apt to envy.

Concerning those that are more or less subject to envy: First, persons of eminent virtue, when they are advanced, are less envied. For their fortune seemeth but due unto them; and no man envieth the payment of a debt, but rewards and liberality rather. Again, envy is ever joined with the comparing of a man's self; and where there is no comparison, no envy; and therefore kings are not envied but by kings. Nevertheless it is to be noted that unworthy persons are most envied at their first coming in, and afterwards overcome it better; whereas contrariwise, persons of worth and merit are most envied when their fortune continueth long. For by that time, though their virtue be the same, yet it hath not the same lustre; for fresh men grow up that darken it.

Persons of noble blood are less envied in their rising. For it seemeth but right done to their birth. Besides, there seemeth not much added to their fortune; and envy is as the sunbeams, that beat hotter upon a bank or steep rising ground, than upon a flat. And for the same reason those that are advanced by degrees are less envied than those that are advanced suddenly and *per saltum* [*by a leap].

Those that have joined with their honour great travels,

cares, or perils, are less subject to envy. For men think that they earn their honours hardly, and pity them sometimes; and pity ever healeth envy. Wherefore you shall observe that the more deep and sober sort of politic persons, in their greatness, are ever bemoaning themselves, what a life they lead; chanting a *quanta patimur* [*how we suffer!]. Not that they feel it so, but only to abate the edge of envy. But this is to be understood of business that is laid upon men, and not such as they call unto themselves. For nothing increaseth envy more than an unnecessary and ambitious engrossing of business. And nothing doth extinguish envy more than for a great person to preserve all other inferior officers in their full rights and pre-eminences of their places. For by that means there be so many screens between him and envy.

Above all, those are most subject to envy, which carry the greatness of their fortunes in an insolent and proud manner; being never well but while they are shewing how great they are, either by outward pomp, or by triumphing over all opposition or competition; whereas wise men will rather do sacrifice to envy, in suffering themselves sometimes of purpose to be crossed and overborne in things that do not much concern them. Notwithstanding so much is true, that the carriage of greatness in a plain and open manner (so it be without arrogancy and vain glory) doth draw less envy than if it be in a more crafty and cunning fashion. For in that course a man doth but disavow fortune; and seemeth to be conscious of his own want in worth; and doth but teach others to envy him.

Lastly, to conclude this part; as we said in the beginning that the act of envy had somewhat in it of witchcraft, so there is no other cure of envy but the cure of witchcraft; and that is, to remove the *lot*[1] (as they call it) and to lay it upon another. For which purpose, the wiser sort of great persons bring in ever upon the stage somebody upon whom to derive the envy that would come upon themselves; sometimes upon ministers and servants; sometimes upon colleagues and associates; and the like; and for that turn there are never wanting some persons of violent and undertaking natures, who, so they may have power and business, will take it at any cost.

Now, to speak of public envy. There is yet some good in public envy, whereas in private there is none. For public envy is as an ostracism, that eclipseth men when they grow too great. And therefore it is a bridle also to great ones, to keep them within bounds.

This envy, being in the Latin word *invidia,* goeth in the modern languages by the name of *discontentment;* of which we shall speak in handling Sedition. It is a disease in a state like to infection. For as infection spreadeth upon that which is sound, and tainteth it; so when envy is gotten once into a state, it traduceth even the best actions thereof, and turneth them into an ill odour. And therefore there is little won by intermingling of plausible actions. For that doth argue but a weakness and fear of envy, which hurteth so much the more; as it is likewise usual in infections; which if you fear them, you call them upon you.

This public envy seemeth to beat chiefly upon principal officers or ministers, rather than upon kings and estates themselves. But this is a sure rule, that if the envy upon the minister be great, when the cause of it in him is small; or if the envy be general in a manner upon all the ministers of an estate; then the envy (though hidden) is truly upon the state itself. And so much of public envy or discontentment, and the difference thereof from private envy, which was handled in the first place.

We will add this in general, touching the affection of envy; that of all other affections it is the most importune and continual. For of other affections there is occasion given but now and then; and therefore it was well said, *Invidia festos dies non agit:* [Envy keeps no holidays:] for it is ever working upon some or other. And it is also noted that love and envy do make a man pine, which other affections do not, because they are not so continual. It is also the vilest affection, and the most depraved; for which cause it is the proper attribute of the devil, who is called *The envious man, that soweth tares amongst the wheat by night;* as it always cometh to pass, that envy worketh subtilly, and in the dark; and to the prejudice of good things, such as is the wheat.

10

OF LOVE

THE stage is more beholding to Love, than the life of man. For as to the stage, love is ever matter of comedies, and now and then of tragedies; but in life it doth much mischief; sometimes like a syren, sometimes like a fury. You may observe, that amongst all the great and worthy persons (whereof the memory remaineth, either ancient or recent,) there is not one that hath been transported to the mad degree of love: which shews that great spirits and great business do keep out this weak passion. You must except nevertheless Marcus Antonius, the half partner of the empire of Rome, and Appius Claudius, the decemvir and lawgiver; whereof the former was indeed a voluptuous man, and inordinate; but the latter was an austere and wise man: and therefore it seems (though rarely) that love can find entrance not only into an open heart, but also into a heart well fortified, if watch be not well kept. It is a poor saying of Epicurus, *Satis magnum alter alteri theatrum sumus:* [Each is to other a theatre large enough]; as if man, made for the contemplation of heaven and all noble objects, should do nothing but kneel before a little idol, and make himself a subject, though not of the mouth (as beasts are), yet of the eye; which was given him for higher purposes. It is a strange thing to note the excess of this passion, and how it braves the nature and value of things, by this; that the speaking in a perpetual hyperbole is comely in nothing but in love. Neither is it merely in the phrase; for whereas it hath been well said that the archflatterer, with whom all the petty flatterers have intelligence, is a man's self; certainly the lover is more. For there was never proud man thought so absurdly well of himself as the lover doth of the person loved; and therefore it was well said, *That it is impossible to love and to be wise.* Neither doth this weakness appear to others only, and not to the party loved; but to the loved most of all, except the love be reciproque. For it is a true rule, that love is ever rewarded either with the reciproque or with an inward and secret contempt. By how much the more men ought to beware of this passion, which loseth not only other things, but itself. As for the other losses, the poet's relation doth well figure them; That he that preferred Helena,[1] quitted the gifts of Juno and Pallas. For whosoever esteemeth too much of amorous affection quitteth both riches and wisdom. This passion hath his floods in the very times of weakness; which are great prosperity and great adversity; though this latter hath been less observed: both which times kindle love, and make it more fervent, and therefore shew it to be the child of folly. They do best, who if they cannot but admit love, yet make it keep quarter; and sever it wholly from their serious affairs and actions of life; for if it check once with business, it troubleth men's fortunes, and maketh men that they can no ways be true to their own ends. I know not how, but martial men are given to love: I think it is but as they are given to wine; for perils commonly ask to be paid in pleasures. There is in man's nature a secret inclination and motion towards love of others, which if it be not spent upon some one or a few, doth naturally spread itself towards many, and maketh men become humane and charitable; as it is seen sometime in friars. Nuptial love maketh mankind; friendly love perfecteth it; but wanton love corrupteth and embaseth it.

11

OF GREAT PLACE

MEN in great place are thrice servants: servants of the sovereign or state; servants of fame; and servants of business. So as they have no freedom; neither in their persons, nor in their actions, nor in their times. It is a strange desire, to seek power and to lose liberty: or to seek power over others and to lose power over a man's self. The rising unto place is laborious; and by pains men come to greater pains; and it is sometimes base; and by indignities men come to dignities.

The standing is slippery, and the regress is either a down-fall, or at least an eclipse, which is a melancholy thing. *Cum non sis qui fueris, non esse cur velis vivere:* [When a man feels that he is no longer what he was, he loses all his interest in life.] Nay, retire men cannot when they would, neither will they when it were reason; but are impatient of private-ness, even in age and sickness, which require the shadow; like old townsmen, that will be still sitting at their street door, though thereby they offer age to scorn. Certainly great persons had need to borrow other men's opinions, to think themselves happy; for if they judge by their own feeling, they cannot find it: but if they think with themselves what other men think of them, and that other men would fain be as they are, then they are happy as it were by report; when perhaps they find the contrary within. For they are the first that find their own griefs, though they be the last that find their own faults. Certainly men in great fortunes are stran-gers to themselves, and while they are in the puzzle of busi-ness they have no time to tend their health either of body or mind. *Illi mors gravis incubat, qui notus nimis omnibus, ig-notus moritur sibi:* [It is a sad fate for a man to die too well known to every-body else, and still unknown to himself.] In place there is licence to do good and evil; whereof the latter is a curse: for in evil the best condition is not to will; the second not to can. But power to do good is the true and law-ful end of aspiring. For good thoughts (though God accept them) yet towards men are little better than good dreams, except they be put in act; and that cannot be without power and place, as the vantage and commanding ground. Merit and good works is the end of man's motion; and conscience of the same is the accomplishment of man's rest. For if a man can be partaker of God's theatre, he shall likewise be partaker of God's rest. *Et conversus Deus, ut aspiceret opera quæ fecerunt manus suæ, vidit quod omnia essent bona nimis;* [And God turned to look upon the works which his hands had made, and saw that all were very good;] and then the sabbath. In the discharge of thy place set before thee the best examples; for imitation is a globe of precepts. And after a time set before thee thine own example; and examine thyself strictly whether thou didst not best at first. Neglect not also the examples of those that have carried themselves ill in the same place; not to set off thyself by taxing their memory, but to direct thyself what to avoid. Reform therefore, without bravery or scandal of former times and persons; but yet set it down to thyself as well to create good precedents as to follow them. Reduce things to the first institution, and observe wherein and how they have degenerate; but yet ask counsel of both times; of the ancient time, what is best; and of the latter time, what is fittest. Seek to make thy course regular, that men may know beforehand what they may expect; but be not too positive and peremptory; and express thyself well when thou digressest from thy rule. Preserve the right of thy place; but stir not questions of jurisdiction: and rather assume thy right in silence and *de facto* [*as an accepted fact], than voice it with claims and challenges. Preserve likewise the rights of inferior places; and think it more honour to direct in chief than to be busy in all. Embrace and invite helps and advices touching the execution of thy place; and do not drive away such as bring thee information, as meddlers; but accept of them in good part. The vices of authority are chiefly four; delays, corruption, roughness, and facility. For delays; give easy access; keep times appointed; go through with that which is in hand, and interlace not business but of necessity. For corruption; do not only bind thine own hands or thy servants' hands from taking, but bind the hands of suitors also from offering. For integrity used doth the one; but integrity professed, and with a manifest detestation of bribery, doth the other. And avoid not only the fault, but the suspicion. Whosoever is found variable, and changeth manifestly without manifest cause, giveth suspicion of corruption. Therefore always when thou changest thine opinion or course, profess it plainly, and declare it, together with the reasons that move thee to change; and do not think to steal it. A servant or a favourite, if he be inward, and no other apparent cause of esteem, is commonly thought but a by-way to close corruption. For roughness; it is a needless cause of discontent: severity breedeth fear, but roughness breedeth hate. Even reproofs from authority ought to be grave, and not taunting. As for facility; it is worse than bribery. For bribes come but now and then; but if importunity or idle respects lead a man, he shall never be without. As Salomon saith, *To respect persons is not good; for such a man will transgress for a piece of bread.* It is most true that was anciently spoken, *A place sheweth the man.* And it sheweth some to the better, and some to the worse. *Omnium consensu capax imperii, nisi imperasset,* [a man whom every body would have thought fit for empire if he had not been emperor,] saith Tacitus of Galba; but of Vespasian he saith, *Solus imperantium, Vespasianus mutatus in melius:* [He was the only emperor whom the possession of power changed for the better;] though the one was meant of sufficiency,[1] the other of manners and affection. It is an assured sign of a worthy and generous spirit, whom honour amends. For honour is, or should be, the place of virtue; and as in nature things move violently to their place and calmly in their place, so virtue in ambition is violent, in authority settled and calm. All rising to great place is by a winding stair; and if there be factions, it is good to side a man's self whilst he is in the rising, and to balance himself when he is placed. Use the memory of thy predecessor fairly and tenderly; for if thou dost not, it is a debt will sure be paid when thou art gone. If thou have colleagues, respect them, and rather call them when they look not for it, than exclude them when they have reason to look to be called. Be not too sensible or too remembering of thy place in conversation and private answers to suitors; but let it rather be said, *When he sits in place he is another man.*

12

Of Boldness

It is a trivial grammar-school text, but yet worthy a wise man's consideration. Question was asked of Demosthenes, *what was the chief part of an orator?* he answered, *action:*

what next? *action.* what next again? *action.* He said it that knew it best, and had by nature himself no advantage in that he commended. A strange thing, that that part of an orator which is but superficial, and rather the virtue of a player, should be placed so high, above those other noble parts of invention, elocution, and the rest; nay almost alone, as if it were all in all. But the reason is plain. There is in human nature generally more of the fool than of the wise; and therefore those faculties by which the foolish part of men's minds is taken are most potent. Wonderful like is the case of Boldness, in civil business; what first? Boldness: what second and third? Boldness. And yet boldness is a child of ignorance and baseness, far inferior to other parts. But nevertheless it doth fascinate and bind hand and foot those that are either shallow in judgment or weak in courage, which are the greatest part; yea and prevaileth with wise men at weak times. Therefore we see it hath done wonders in popular states;[1] but with senates and princes less; and more ever upon the first entrance of bold persons into action than soon after; for boldness is an ill keeper of promise. Surely as there are mountebanks for the natural body, so are there mountebanks for the politic body; men that undertake great cures, and perhaps have been lucky in two or three experiments, but want the grounds of science, and therefore cannot hold out. Nay you shall see a bold fellow many times do Mahomet's miracle. Mahomet made the people believe that he would call an hill to him, and from the top of it offer up his prayers for the observers of his law. The people assembled; Mahomet called the hill to come to him, again and again; and when the hill stood still, he was never a whit abashed, but said, *If the hill will not come to Mahomet, Mahomet will go to the hill.* So these men, when they have promised great matters and failed most shamefully, yet (if they have the perfection of boldness) they will but slight it over, and make a turn, and no more ado. Certainly to men of great judgment, bold persons are a sport to behold; nay and to the vulgar also, boldness has somewhat of the ridiculous. For if absurdity be the subject of laughter, doubt you not but great boldness is seldom without some absurdity. Especially it is a sport to see, when a bold fellow is out of countenance; for that puts his face into a most shrunken and wooden posture; as needs it must; for in bashfulness the spirits do a little go and come; but with bold men, upon like occasion, they stand at a stay; like a stale at chess, where it is no mate, but yet the game cannot stir. But this last were fitter for a satire than for a serious observation. This is well to be weighed; that boldness is ever blind; for it seeth not dangers and inconveniences. Therefore it is ill in counsel, good in execution; so that the right use of bold persons is, that they never command in chief, but be seconds, and under the direction of others. For in counsel it is good to see dangers; and in execution not to see them, except they be very great.

13

OF GOODNESS AND GOODNESS OF NATURE

I TAKE Goodness in this sense, the affecting of the weal of men, which is that the Grecians call *Philanthropia;* and the word *humanity* (as it is used) is a little too light to express it. Goodness I call the habit, and Goodness of Nature the inclination. This of all virtues and dignities of the mind is the greatest; being the character of the Deity: and without it man is a busy, mischievous, wretched thing; no better than a kind of vermin. Goodness answers to the theological virtue Charity, and admits no excess, but error. The desire of power in excess caused the angels to fall; the desire of knowledge in excess caused man to fall: but in charity there is no excess; neither can angel or man come in danger by it. The inclination to goodness is imprinted deeply in the nature of man; insomuch that if it issue not towards men, it will take unto other living creatures; as it is seen in the Turks, a cruel people, who nevertheless are kind to beasts, and give alms to dogs and birds; insomuch as Busbechius reporteth, a Christian boy in Constantinople had like to have been stoned for gagging in a waggishness a long-billed fowl. Errors indeed in this virtue of goodness or charity may be committed. The Italians have an ungracious proverb, *Tanto buon che val niente; So good, that he is good for nothing.* And one of the doctors of Italy, Nicholas Machiavel, had the confidence to put in writing, almost in plain terms, *That the Christian faith had given up good men in prey to those that are tyrannical and unjust.* Which he spake, because indeed there was never law, or sect, or opinion, did so much magnify goodness, as the Christian religion doth. Therefore, to avoid the scandal and the danger both, it is good to take knowledge of the errors of an habit so excellent. Seek the good of other men, but be not in bondage to their faces or fancies; for that is but facility or softness; which taketh an honest mind prisoner. Neither give thou Æsop's cock a gem, who would be better pleased and happier if he had a barley-corn. The example of God teacheth the lesson truly; *He sendeth his rain, and maketh his sun to shine, upon the just and unjust;* but he doth not rain wealth, nor shine honour and virtues, upon men equally. Common benefits are to be communicate with all; but peculiar benefits with choice. And beware how in making the portraiture thou breakest the pattern. For divinity maketh the love of ourselves the pattern; the love of our neighbours but the portraiture. *Sell all thou hast, and give it to the poor, and follow me:* but sell not all thou hast, except thou come and follow me; that is, except thou have a vocation wherein thou mayest do as much good with little means as with great; for otherwise in feeding the streams thou driest the fountain. Neither is there only a habit of goodness, directed by right reason; but there is in some men, even in nature, a disposition towards it; as on the other side there is a natural malignity. For there be that in their nature do not affect the good of others. The lighter sort of malignity turneth but to a crossness, or frowardness, or aptness to oppose, or difficilness, or the like; but the deeper sort to envy and mere mischief. Such men in other men's calamities are, as it were, in season, and are ever on the loading part: not so good as the dogs that licked Lazarus' sores; but like flies that are still buzzing upon any thing that is raw;

misanthropi, that make it their practice to bring men to the bough,[1] and yet have never a tree for the purpose in their gardens, as Timon had. Such dispositions are the very errours of human nature; and yet they are the fittest timber to make great politiques of; like to knee timber,[2] that is good for ships, that are ordained to be tossed; but not for building houses, that shall stand firm. The parts and signs of goodness are many. If a man be gracious and courteous to strangers, it shews he is a citizen of the world, and that his heart is no island cut off from other lands, but a continent that joins to them. If he be compassionate towards the afflictions of others, it shews that his heart is like the noble tree[3] that is wounded itself when it gives the balm. If he easily pardons and remits offences, it shews that his mind is planted above injuries; so that he cannot be shot. If he be thankful for small benefits, it shews that he weighs men's minds, and not their trash. But above all, if he have St. Paul's perfection, that he would wish to be an *anathema* from Christ for the salvation of his brethren, it shews much of a divine nature, and a kind of conformity with Christ himself.

14

Of Nobility

WE will speak of Nobility first as a portion of an estate; then as a condition of particular persons. A monarchy where there is no nobility at all, is ever a pure and absolute tyranny; as that of the Turks. For nobility attempers sovereignty, and draws the eyes of the people somewhat aside from the line royal. But for democracies, they need it not; and they are commonly more quiet and less subject to sedition, than where there are stirps[1] of nobles. For men's eyes are upon the business, and not upon the persons; or if upon the persons, it is for the business sake, as fittest, and not for flags and pedigree. We see the Switzers last well, notwithstanding their diversity of religion and of cantons. For utility is their bond, and not respects. The united provinces of the Low

Countries in their government excel; for where there is an equality, the consultations are more indifferent, and the payments and tributes more cheerful. A great and potent nobility addeth majesty to a monarch, but diminisheth power; and putteth life and spirit into the people, but presseth their fortune. It is well when nobles are not too great for sovereignty nor for justice; and yet maintained in that height, as the insolency of inferiors may be broken upon them before it come on too fast upon the majesty of kings. A numerous nobility causeth poverty and inconvenience in a state; for it is a surcharge of expense; and besides, it being of necessity that many of the nobility fall in time to be weak in fortune, it maketh a kind of disproportion between honour and means.

As for nobility in particular persons; it is a reverend thing to see an ancient castle or building not in decay; or to see a fair timber tree sound and perfect. How much more to behold an ancient noble family, which hath stood against the waves and weathers of time. For new nobility is but the act of power, but ancient nobility is the act of time. Those that are first raised to nobility are commonly more virtuous, but less innocent, than their descendants; for there is rarely any rising but by a commixture of good and evil arts. But it is reason the memory of their virtues remain to their posterity, and their faults die with themselves. Nobility of birth commonly abateth industry; and he that is not industrious, envieth him that is. Besides, noble persons cannot go much higher: and he that standeth at a stay when others rise, can hardly avoid motions of envy. On the other side, nobility extinguisheth the passive envy from others towards them; because they are in possession of honour. Certainly, kings that have able men of their nobility shall find ease in employing them, and a better slide into their business; for people naturally bend to them, as born in some sort to command.

15

OF SEDITIONS AND TROUBLES

SHEPHERDS of people had need know the calendars of tempests in state; which are commonly greatest when things grow to equality;[1] as natural tempests are greatest about the *Equinoctia*. And as there are certain hollow blasts of wind and secret swellings of seas before a tempest, so are there in states:

> ————Ille etiam cæcos instare tumultus
> Sæpe monet, fraudesque et operta tumescere bella.
> [Of troubles imminent and treasons dark
> Thence warning comes, and wars in secret gathering.]

Libels and licentious discourses against the state, when they are frequent and open; and in like sort, false news often running up and down to the disadvantage of the state, and hastily embraced; are amongst the signs of troubles. Virgil giving the pedigree of Fame, saith *she was sister to the Giants:*

> Illam Terra parens, irâ irritata Deorum,
> Extremam (ut perhibent) Cœo Enceladoque sororem
> Progenuit.

As if fames were the relics of seditions past; but they are no less indeed the preludes of seditions to come. Howsoever he noteth it right, that seditious tumults and seditious fames differ no more but as brother and sister, masculine and feminine; especially if it come to that, that the best actions of a state, and the most plausible, and which ought to give greatest contentment, are taken in ill sense, and traduced: for that shews the envy great, as Tacitus saith, *conflata magna invidia, seu bene seu male gesta premunt:* [when dislike prevails against the government, good actions and bad offend alike.] Neither doth it follow, that because these fames are a sign of troubles, that the suppressing of them with too much severity should be a remedy of troubles. For the despising of them many times checks them best; and the going about to stop them doth but make a wonder long-lived. Also that kind of obedience which Tacitus speaketh of, is to be held suspected: *Erant in officio, sed tamen qui mallent mandata imperantium interpretari quam exequi;* [ready to serve, and yet more disposed to construe commands than execute them;] disputing, excusing, cavilling upon mandates and directions, is a kind of shaking off the yoke, and assay of disobedience; especially if in those disputings they which are for the direction speak fearfully and tenderly, and those that are against it audaciously.

Also, as Machiavel noteth well, when princes, that ought to be common parents, make themselves as a party, and lean to a side, it is as a boat that is overthrown by uneven weight on the one side; as was well seen in the time of Henry the Third of France; for first himself entered league for the extirpation of the Protestants; and presently after the same league was turned upon himself. For when the authority of princes is made but an accessary to a cause, and that there be other bands that tie faster than the band of sovereignty, kings begin to be put almost out of possession.

Also, when discords, and quarrels, and factions, are carried openly and audaciously, it is a sign the reverence of government is lost. For the motions of the greatest persons in a government ought to be as the motions of the planets under *primum mobile;*[2] (according to the old opinion,) which is, that every of them is carried swiftly by the highest motion, and softly in their own motion. And therefore, when great ones in their own particular motion move violently, and, as Tacitus expresseth it well, *liberius quam ut imperantium meminissent,* [unrestrained by reverence for the government], it is a sign the orbs are out of frame.[3] For reverence is that wherewith princes are girt from God; who threateneth the dissolving thereof; *Solvam cingula regum:* [I will unbind the girdles of kings.]

So when any of the four pillars of government are mainly shaken or weakened (which are Religion, Justice, Counsel, and Treasure), men had need to pray for fair weather. But let us pass from this part of predictions (concerning which,

nevertheless, more light may be taken from that which followeth); and let us speak first of the Materials of seditions;
then of the Motives of them; and thirdly of the Remedies.

Concerning the Materials of seditions. It is a thing well to
be considered; for the surest way to prevent seditions (if the
times do bear it) is to take away the matter of them. For
if there be fuel prepared, it is hard to tell whence the spark
shall come that shall set it on fire. The matter of seditions is
of two kinds; much poverty and much discontentment. It is
certain, so many overthrown estates, so many votes for
troubles. Lucan noteth well the state of Rome before the
civil war,

> Hinc usura vorax, rapidumque in tempore fœnus,
> Hinc concussa fides, et multis utile bellum:

[estates eaten up by usurious rates of interest, credit shaken,
war a gain to many.]

This same *multis utile bellum* [*war a gain to many], is an
assured and infallible sign of a state disposed to seditions
and troubles. And if this poverty and broken estate in the
better sort be joined with a want and necessity in the mean
people, the danger is imminent and great. For the rebellions
of the belly are the worst. As for discontentments, they are
in the politic body like to humours in the natural, which are
apt to gather a preternatural heat and to inflame. And let no
prince measure the danger of them by this, whether they be
just or unjust: for that were to imagine people to be too reasonable; who do often spurn at their own good: nor yet by
this, whether the griefs whereupon they rise be in fact great
or small: for they are the most dangerous discontentments
where the fear is greater than the feeling: *Dolendi modus,
timendi non item:* [Suffering has its limit, but fears are endless.] Besides, in great oppressions, the same things that pro-
voke the patience, do withal mate the courage; but in fears
it is not so. Neither let any prince or state be secure concerning discontentments, because they have been often, or
have been long, and yet no peril hath ensued: for as it is
true that every vapour or fume doth not turn into a storm;

so it is nevertheless true that storms, though they blow over divers times, yet may fall at last; and, as the Spanish proverb noteth well, *The cord breaketh at the last by the weakest pull.*

The Causes and Motives of seditions are, innovation in religion; taxes; alteration of laws and customs; breaking of privileges; general oppression; advancement of unworthy persons; strangers; dearths; disbanded soldiers; factions grown desperate; and whatsoever, in offending people, joineth and knitteth them in a common cause.

For the Remedies; there may be some general preservatives, whereof we will speak: as for the just cure, it must answer to the particular disease; and so be left to counsel rather than rule.

The first remedy or prevention is to remove by all means possible that material cause of sedition whereof we spake; which is, want and poverty in the estate. To which purpose serveth, the opening and well-balancing of trade; the cherishing of manufactures; the banishing of idleness; the repressing of waste and excess by sumptuary laws; the improvement and husbanding of the soil; the regulating of prices of things vendible; the moderating of taxes and tributes, and the like. Generally, it is to be foreseen that the population of a kingdom (especially if it be not mown down by wars) do not exceed the stock of the kingdom which should maintain them. Neither is the population to be reckoned only by number; for a smaller number that spend more and earn less, do wear out an estate sooner than a greater number that live lower and gather more. Therefore the multiplying of nobility and other degrees of quality in an over proportion to the common people, doth speedily bring a state to necessity; and so doth likewise an overgrown clergy; for they bring nothing to the stock; and in like manner, when more are bred scholars than preferments can take off.

It is likewise to be remembered, that forasmuch as the increase of any estate must be upon the foreigner (for whatsoever is somewhere gotten is somewhere lost), there be but three things which one nation selleth unto another; the commodity as nature yieldeth it; the manufacture; and the vecture, or carriage. So that if these three wheels go, wealth will flow as in a spring tide. And it cometh many times to pass, that *materiam superabit opus;* that the work and carriage is more worth than the material, and enricheth a state more; as is notably seen in the Low-Countrymen, who have the best mines above ground[4] in the world.

Above all things, good policy is to be used that the treasure and monies in a state be not gathered into few hands. For otherwise a state may have a great stock, and yet starve. And money is like muck, not good except it be spread. This is done chiefly by suppressing, or at the least keeping a strait hand upon the devouring trades of usury, ingrossing, great pasturages, and the like.

For removing discontentments, or at least the danger of them; there is in every state (as we know) two portions of subjects; the nobless and the commonalty. When one of these is discontent, the danger is not great; for common people are of slow motion, if they be not excited by the greater sort; and the greater sort are of small strength, except the multitude be apt and ready to move of themselves. Then is the danger, when the greater sort do but wait for the troubling of the waters amongst the meaner, that then they may declare themselves. The poets feign, that the rest of the gods would have bound Jupiter; which he hearing of, by the counsel of Pallas, sent for Briareus, with his hundred hands, to come in to his aid. An emblem, no doubt, to show how safe it is for monarchs to make sure of the good will of common people.

To give moderate liberty for griefs and discontentments to evaporate (so it be without too great insolency or bravery), is a safe way. For he that turneth the humours back, and maketh the wound bleed inwards, endangereth malign ulcers and pernicious imposthumations.

The part of Epimetheus mought well become Prometheus, in the case of discontentments; for there is not a better provision against them. Epimetheus, when griefs and evils flew abroad, at last shut the lid, and kept hope in the bottom of the vessel. Certainly, the politic and artificial nourishing and entertaining of hopes, and carrying men from hopes to hopes, is one of the best antidotes against the poison of discontentments. And it is a certain sign of a wise government and proceeding, when it can hold men's hearts by hopes, when it cannot by satisfaction; and when it can handle things in such manner, as no evil shall appear so peremptory but that it hath some outlet of hope: which is the less hard to do, because both particular persons and factions are apt enough to flatter themselves, or at least to brave that they believe not.

Also the foresight and prevention, that there be no likely or fit head whereunto discontented persons may resort, and under whom they may join, is a known, but an excellent point of caution. I understand a fit head to be one that hath greatness and reputation; that hath confidence with the discontented party, and upon whom they turn their eyes; and that is thought discontented in his own particular: which kind of persons are either to be won and reconciled to the state, and that in a fast and true manner; or to be fronted with some other of the same party, that may oppose them, and so divide the reputation. Generally, the dividing and breaking of all factions and combinations that are adverse to the state, and setting them at distance, or at least distrust, amongst themselves, is not one of the worst remedies. For it is a desperate case, if those that hold with the proceeding of the state be full of discord and faction, and those that are against it be entire and united.

I have noted that some witty and sharp speeches which have fallen from princes have given fire to seditions. Cæsar did himself infinite hurt in that speech, *Sylla nescivit literas, non potuit dictare:* [Scylla was no scholar, he could not dictate:] for it did utterly cut off that hope which men had entertained, that he would at one time or other give over his dictatorship. Galba undid himself by that speech, *legi a se militem, non emi;* [that he did not buy his soldiers, but levied them:] for it put the soldiers out of hope of the donative. Probus likewise, by that speech, *si vixero, non opus erit amplius Romano imperio militibus;* [if I live, the Roman empire shall have no more need of soldiers:] a speech of great despair for the soldiers. And many the like. Surely princes had need, in tender matters and ticklish times, to beware what they say; especially in these short speeches, which fly abroad like darts, and are thought to be shot out of their secret intentions. For as for large discourses, they are flat things, and not so much noted.

Lastly, let princes, against all events, not be without some great person, one or rather more, of military valour, near unto them, for the repressing of seditions in their beginnings. For without that, there useth to be more trepidation in court upon the first breaking out of troubles than were fit. And the state runneth the danger of that which Tacitus saith; *Atque is habitus animorum fuit, ut pessimum facinus auderent pauci, plures vellent, omnes paterentur:* [A few were in a humour to attempt mischief, more to desire, all to allow it.] But let such military persons be assured, and well reputed of, rather than factious and popular; holding also good correspondence with the other great men in the state; or else the remedy is worse than the disease.

16

OF ATHEISM

I HAD rather believe all the fables in the Legend,[1] and the Talmud, and the Alcoran, than that this universal frame is without a mind. And therefore God never wrought miracle to convince atheism, because his ordinary works convince it. It is true, that a little philosophy inclineth man's mind to atheism; but depth in philosophy bringeth men's minds about to religion. For while the mind of man looketh upon second causes scattered, it may sometimes rest in them, and go no further; but when it beholdeth the chain of them, confederate and linked together, it must needs fly to Providence and Deity. Nay, even that school[2] which is most accused of atheism doth most demonstrate religion; that is, the school of Leucippus and Democritus and Epicurus. For it is a thousand times more credible, that four mutable elements, and one immutable fifth essence,[3] duly and eternally placed, need no God, than that an army of infinite small portions or seeds unplaced, should have produced this order and beauty without a divine marshal. The scripture saith, *The fool hath said in his heart, there is no God;* it is not said, *The fool hath thought in his heart;* so as he rather saith it by rote to himself, as that he would have, than that he can throughly believe it, or be persuaded of it. For none deny there is a God, but those for whom it maketh that there were no God. It appeareth in nothing more, that atheism is rather in the lip than in the heart of man, than by this; that atheists will ever be talking of that their opinion, as if they fainted in it within themselves, and would be glad to be strengthened by the consent of others. Nay more, you shall have atheists strive to get disciples, as it fareth with other sects. And, which is most of all, you shall have of them that will suffer for atheism, and not recant; whereas if they did truly think that there were no such thing as God, why should they trouble themselves? Epicurus is charged that he did but dissemble for his credit's sake, when he affirmed there were blessed natures, but such as enjoyed themselves without having respect to the government of the world. Wherein they say he did temporize; though in secret he thought there was no God. But certainly he is traduced; for his words are noble and divine: *Non Deos vulgi negare profanum; sed vulgi opiniones Diis applicare profanum:* [There is no profanity in refusing to believe in the Gods of the vulgar: the profanity is in believing of the Gods what the vulgar believe of them.] Plato could have said no more. And although he had the confidence to deny the administration, he had not the power to deny the nature. The Indians of the west have names for their particular gods, though they have no name for God: as if the heathens should have had the names Jupiter, Apollo, Mars, &c. but not the word *Deus;* which shews that even those barbarous people have the notion, though they have not the latitude and extent of it. So that against atheists the very savages take part with the very subtlest philosophers. The contemplative atheist is rare: a Diagoras, a Bion, a Lucian perhaps, and some others; and yet they seem to be more than they are; for that all that impugn a received religion or superstition are by the adverse part branded with the name of atheists. But the great atheists indeed are hypocrites; which are ever handling holy things, but without feeling; so as they must needs be cauterized in the end. The causes of atheism are; divisions in religion, if they be many; for any one main division addeth zeal to both sides; but many divisions introduce atheism. Another is, scandal of priests; when it is come to that which St. Bernard saith, *Non est jam dicere, ut populus sic sacerdos; quia nec sic populus ut sacerdos:* [One cannot now say, the priest is as the people, for the truth is that the people are not so bad as the priest.] A third is, custom of profane scoffing in holy matters; which doth by little and little deface the reverence of religion. And lastly, learned times, specially with peace and prosperity; for troubles and adversities do more bow men's minds to religion. They that deny a God destroy man's nobility; for certainly man is of kin to the beasts by his body; and, if he be not of kin to God by his spirit, he is a base and ignoble creature. It destroys likewise magnanimity, and the raising of human nature; for take an example of a dog, and mark what a generosity and courage he will put on when he finds himself maintained by a man; who to him is instead of a God, or *melior natura;* which courage is manifestly such as that creature, without that confidence of a better nature than his own, could never attain. So man, when he resteth and assureth himself upon divine protection and favour, gathereth a force and faith which human nature in itself could not obtain. Therefore, as atheism is in all respects hateful, so in this, that it depriveth human nature of the means to exalt itself above human frailty. As it is in particular persons, so it is in nations. Never was there such a state for magnanimity as Rome. Of this state hear what Cicero saith: *Quam volumus licet, patres conscripti, nos amemus, tamen nec numero Hispanos, nec robore Gallos, nec calliditate Pœnos, nec artibus Græcos,*

nec denique hoc ipso hujus gentis et terræ domestico nati-
voque sensu Italos ipsos et Latinos; sed pietate, ac religione,
atque hac una sapientia, quod Deorum immortalium nu-
mine omnia regi gubernarique perspeximus, omnes gentes
nationesque superavimus: [Pride ourselves as we may upon
our country, yet are we not in number superior to the Spaniards, nor in strength to the Gauls, nor in cunning to the
Carthaginians, nor to the Greeks in arts, nor to the Italians
and Latins themselves in the homely and native sense which
belongs to this nation and land; it is in piety only and religion, and the wisdom of regarding the providence of the Immortal Gods as that which rules and governs all things, that
we have surpassed all nations and peoples.]

17

OF SUPERSTITION

IT were better to have no opinion of God at all, than such
an opinion as is unworthy of him. For the one is unbelief,
and other is contumely: and certainly superstition is the re-
proach of the Deity. Plutarch saith well to that purpose:
Surely (saith he) *I had rather a great deal men should say*
there was no such man at all as Plutarch, than that they
should say that there was one Plutarch that would eat his
children as soon as they were born; as the poets speak of
Saturn. And as the contumely is greater towards God, so the
danger is greater towards men. Atheism leaves a man to
sense, to philosophy, to natural piety, to laws, to reputation;
all which may be guides to an outward moral virtue, though
religion were not; but superstition dismounts all these, and
erecteth an absolute monarchy in the minds of men. Therefore atheism did never perturb states; for it makes men
wary of themselves, as looking no further: and we see the
times inclined to atheism (as the time of Augustus Cæsar)
were civil times. But superstition hath been the confusion of
many states, and bringeth in a new *primum mobile,* that
ravisheth all the spheres of government. The master of
superstition is the people; and in all superstition wise men

follow fools; and arguments are fitted to practice, in a reversed order. It was gravely said by some of the prelates
in the council of Trent, where the doctrine of the schoolmen
bare great sway, *that the schoolmen were like astronomers,
which did feign eccentrics and epicycles, and such engines
of orbs, to save[1] the phænomena; though they knew there
were no such things;* and in like manner, that the schoolmen
had framed a number of subtle and intricate axioms and
theorems, to save the practice of the church. The causes of
superstition are, pleasing and sensual rites and ceremonies;
excess of outward and pharisaical holiness; over-great reverence of traditions, which cannot but load the church; the
stratagems of prelates for their own ambition and lucre; the
favouring too much of good intentions, which openeth
the gate to conceits and novelties; the taking an aim at
divine matters by human, which cannot but breed mixture
of imaginations: and, lastly, barbarous times, especially
joined with calamities and disasters. Superstition, without a
veil, is a deformed thing; for as it addeth deformity to an
ape to be so like a man, so the similitude of superstition to
religion makes it the more deformed. And as wholesome
meat corrupteth to little worms, so good forms and orders
corrupt into a number of petty observances. There is a
superstition in avoiding superstition, when men think to do
best if they go furthest from the superstition formerly received; therefore care would be had that (as it fareth in ill
purgings) the good be not taken away with the bad; which
commonly is done when the people is the reformer.

18

Of Travel

Travel, in the younger sort, is a part of education; in the
elder, a part of experience. He that travelleth into a country
before he hath some entrance into the language, goeth to
school, and not to travel. That young men travel under some
tutor, or grave servant, I allow well; so that he be such a
one that hath the language, and hath been in the country

before; whereby he may be able to tell them what things are worthy to be seen in the country where they go; what acquaintances they are to seek; what exercises or discipline the place yieldeth. For else young men shall go hooded, and look abroad little. It is a strange thing, that in sea voyages, where there is nothing to be seen but sky and sea, men should make diaries; but in land-travel, wherein so much is to be observed, for the most part they omit it; as if chance were fitter to be registered than observation. Let diaries therefore be brought in use. The things to be seen and observed are, the courts of princes, specially when they give audience to ambassadors; the courts of justice, while they sit and hear causes; and so of consistories ecclesiastic; the churches and monasteries, with the monuments which are therein extant; the walls and fortifications of cities and towns, and so the havens and harbours; antiquities and ruins; libraries; colleges, disputations, and lectures, where any are; shipping and navies; houses and gardens of state and pleasure, near great cities; armories; arsenals; magazines; exchanges; burses; warehouses; exercises of horsemanship, fencing, training of soldiers, and the like; comedies, such whereunto the better sort of persons do resort; treasuries of jewels and robes; cabinets and rarities; and, to conclude, whatsoever is memorable in the places where they go. After all which the tutors or servants ought to make diligent inquiry. As for triumphs, masks, feasts, weddings, funerals, capital executions, and such shows, men need not to be put in mind of them; yet are they not to be neglected. If you will have a young man to put his travel into a little room, and in short time to gather much, this you must do. First as was said, he must have some entrance into the language before he goeth. Then he must have such a servant or tutor as knoweth the country, as was likewise said. Let him carry with him also some card [1] or book describing the country where he travelleth; which will be a good key to his inquiry. Let him keep also a diary. Let him not stay long in one city or town; more or less as the place deserveth, but not long; nay, when he stayeth in one city or town, let him change his lodging from one end and part of the town to another; which is a great adamant of acquaintance. Let him sequester himself from the company of his countrymen, and diet in such places where there is good company of the nation where he travelleth. Let him upon his removes from one place to another, procure recommendation to some person of quality residing in the place whither he removeth; that he may use his favour in those things he desireth to see or know. Thus he may abridge his travel with much profit. As for the acquaintance which is to be sought in travel; that which is most of all profitable, is acquaintance with the secretaries and employed men of ambassadors: for so in travelling in one country he shall suck the experience of many. Let him also see and visit eminent persons in all kinds, which are of great name abroad; that he may be able to tell how the life agreeth with the fame. For quarrels, they are with care and discretion to be avoided. They are commonly for mistresses, healths, place, and words. And let a man beware how he keepeth company with choleric and quarrelsome persons; for they will engage him into their own quarrels. When a traveller returneth home, let him not leave the countries where he hath travelled altogether behind him; but maintain a correspondence by letters with those of his acquaintance which are of most worth. And let his travel appear rather in his discourse than in his apparel or gesture; and in his discourse let him be rather advised in his answers, than forward to tell stories; and let it appear that he doth not change his country manners for those of foreign parts; but only prick in² some flowers of that he hath learned abroad into the customs of his own country.

19

OF EMPIRE

IT is a miserable state of mind to have few things to desire, and many things to fear; and yet that commonly is the case of kings; who, being at the highest, want matter of desire, which makes their minds more languishing; and have many representations of perils and shadows, which makes their minds the less clear. And this is one reason also of that effect which the Scripture speaketh of, *That the king's heart is inscrutable.* For multitude of jealousies, and lack of some predominant desire that should marshal and put in order all the rest, maketh any man's heart hard to find or sound. Hence it comes likewise, that princes many times make themselves desires, and set their hearts upon toys; sometimes upon a building; sometimes upon erecting of an order; sometimes upon the advancing of a person; sometimes upon obtaining excellency in some art or feat of the hand; as Nero for playing on the harp, Domitian for certainty of the hand with the arrow, Commodus for playing at fence, Caracalla for driving chariots, and the like. This seemeth incredible unto those that know not the principle *that the mind of man is more cheered and refreshed by profiting in small things, than by standing at a stay in great.* We see also that kings that have been fortunate conquerors in their first years, it being not possible for them to go forward infinitely, but that they must have some check or arrest in their fortunes, turn in their latter years to be superstitious and melancholy; as did Alexander the Great;[1] Dioclesian; and in our memory, Charles the Fifth; and others: for he that is used to go forward, and findeth a stop, falleth out of his own favour, and is not the thing he was.

To speak now of the true temper of empire; it is a thing rare and hard to keep; for both temper and distemper consist of contraries. But it is one thing to mingle contraries, another to interchange them. The answer of Apollonius to Vespasian is full of excellent instruction. Vespasian asked him, *what was Nero's overthrow?* He answered, *Nero could touch and tune the harp well; but in government sometimes he used to wind the pins too high, sometimes to let them down too low.* And certain it is that nothing destroyeth authority so much as the unequal and untimely interchange of power pressed too far, and relaxed too much.

This is true, that the wisdom of all these latter times in princes' affairs is rather fine deliveries and shiftings of dangers and mischiefs when they are near, than solid and grounded courses to keep them aloof. But this is but to try masteries with fortune. And let men beware how they neglect and suffer matter of trouble to be prepared; for no man can forbid the spark, nor tell whence it may come. The difficulties in princes' business are many and great; but the greatest difficulty is often in their own mind. For it is common with princes (saith Tacitus) to will contradictories, *Sunt plerumque regum voluntates vehementes, et inter se contrariæ:* [Their desires are commonly vehement and incompatible one with another.] For it is the solecism of power, to think to command the end, and yet not to endure the mean.

Kings have to deal with their neighbours, their wives, their children, their prelates or clergy, their nobles, their second-nobles or gentlemen, their merchants, their commons, and their men of war; and from all these arise dangers, if care and circumspection be not used.

First for their neighbours; there can no general rule be given (the occasions are so variable,) save one, which ever holdeth; which is, that princes do keep due sentinel, that none of their neighbours do overgrow so (by increase of territory, by embracing of trade, by approaches, or the like), as they become more able to annoy them than they were. And this is generally the work of standing counsels to foresee and to hinder it. During that triumvirate of kings, King Henry the Eighth of England, Francis the First King of France, and Charles the Fifth Emperor, there was such a watch kept, that none of the three could win a palm of ground, but the other two would straightways balance it, either by confederation, or, if need were, by a war; and would not in any wise take up peace at interest. And the like was done by that league (which Guicciardine saith was the security of Italy) made between Ferdinando King of Naples, Lorenzius Medices, and Ludovicus Sforza, potentates, the one of Florence, the other of Milan. Neither is the opinion of some of the schoolmen to be received, *that a war cannot justly be made but upon a precedent injury or provo-*

cation. For there is no question but a just fear of an imminent danger, though there be no blow given, is a lawful cause of a war.

For their wives; there are cruel examples of them. Livia is infamed for the poisoning of her husband; Roxalana, Solyman's wife, was the destruction of that renowned prince Sultan Mustapha, and otherwise troubled his house and succession; Edward the Second of England his queen had the principal hand in the deposing and murther of her husband. This kind of danger is then to be feared chiefly, when the wives have plots for the raising of their own children; or else that they be advoutresses.

For their children; the tragedies likewise of dangers from them have been many. And generally, the entering of fathers into suspicion of their children hath been ever unfortunate. The destruction of Mustapha (that we named before) was so fatal to Solyman's line, as the succession of the Turks from Solyman until this day is suspected to be untrue, and of strange blood; for that Selymus the Second was thought to be suppositious. The destruction of Crispus, a young prince of rare towardness, by Constantinus the Great, his father, was in like manner fatal to his house; for both Constantinus and Constance, his sons, died violent deaths; and Constantius, his other son, did little better; who died indeed of sickness, but after that Julianus had taken arms against him. The destruction of Demetrius, son to Philip the Second of Macedon, turned upon the father, who died of repentance. And many like examples there are; but few or none where the fathers had good by such distrust; except it were where the sons were up in open arms against them; as was Selymus the First against Bajazet; and the three sons of Henry the Second, King of England.

For their prelates; when they are proud and great, there is also danger from them; as it was in the times of Anselmus and Thomas Becket, Archbishops of Canterbury; who with their crosiers did almost try it with the king's sword; and yet they had to deal with stout and haughty kings; William Rufus, Henry the First, and Henry the Second. The danger is not from that state, but where it hath a dependance of foreign authority; or where the churchmen come in and are elected, not by the collation of the king, or particular patrons, but by the people.

For their nobles; to keep them at a distance, it is not amiss; but to depress them, may make a king more absolute, but less safe; and less able to perform any thing that he desires. I have noted it in my History of King Henry the Seventh of England, who depressed his nobility; whereupon it came to pass that his times were full of difficulties and troubles; for the nobility, though they continued loyal unto him, yet did they not co-operate with him in his business. So that in effect he was fain to do all things himself.

For their second-nobles; there is not much danger from them, being a body dispersed. They may sometimes discourse high, but that doth little hurt; besides, they are a counterpoise to the higher nobility, that they grow not too potent; and, lastly, being the most immediate in authority with the common people, they do best temper popular commotions.

For their merchants; they are *vena porta;*[2] and if they flourish not, a kingdom may have good limbs, but will have empty veins, and nourish little. Taxes and imposts upon them do seldom good to the king's revenue; for that that he wins in the hundred he leeseth in the shire; the particular rates being increased, but the total bulk of trading rather decreased.

For their commons; there is little danger from them, except it be where they have great and potent heads; or where you meddle with the point of religion, or their customs, or means of life.

For their men of war; it is a dangerous state where they live and remain in a body, and are used to donatives; whereof we see examples in the janizaries, and pretorian bands of Rome; but trainings of men, and arming them in several places, and under several commanders, and without donatives, are things of defence, and no danger.

Princes are like to heavenly bodies, which cause good or

evil times; and which have much veneration, but no rest. All precepts concerning kings are in effect comprehended in those two remembrances; *memento quod es homo;* and *memento quod es Deus,* or *vice Dei;* [Remember that you are a man; and remember that you are a God, or God's lieutenant:] the one bridleth their power, and the other their will.

20
OF COUNSEL

THE greatest trust between man and man is the trust of giving counsel. For in other confidences men commit the parts of life; their lands, their goods, their child, their credit, some particular affair; but to such as they make their counsellors, they commit the whole: by how much the more they are obliged to all faith and integrity. The wisest princes need not think it any diminution to their greatness, or derogation to their sufficiency to rely upon counsel. God himself is not without, but hath made it one of the great names of his blessed Son; *The Counsellor.* Salomon hath pronounced that *in counsel is stability.* Things will have their first or second agitation: if they be not tossed upon the arguments of counsel, they will be tossed upon the waves of fortune; and be full of inconstancy, doing and undoing, like the reeling of a drunken man. Salomon's son¹ found the force of counsel, as his father saw the necessity of it. For the beloved kingdom of God was first rent and broken by ill counsel; upon which counsel there are set for our instruction the two marks whereby bad counsel is for ever best discerned; that it was young counsel, for the persons; and violent counsel, for the matter.

The ancient times do set forth in figure both the incorporation and inseparable conjunction of counsel with kings, and the wise and politic use of counsel by kings: the one, in that they say Jupiter did marry Metis, which signifieth counsel; whereby they intend that Sovereignty is married to Counsel: the other in that which followeth, which was thus:

They say, after Jupiter was married to Metis, she conceived by him and was with child, but Jupiter suffered her not to stay till she brought forth, but eat her up; whereby he became himself with child, and was delivered of Pallas armed, out of his head. Which monstrous fable containeth a secret of empire; how kings are to make use of their counsel of state. That first they ought to refer matters unto them, which is the first begetting or impregnation; but when they are elaborate, moulded, and shaped in the womb of their counsel, and grow ripe and ready to be brought forth, that then they suffer not their counsel to go through with the resolution and direction, as if it depended on them; but take the matter back into their own hands, and make it appear to the world that the decrees and final directions (which, because they come forth with prudence and power, are resembled to Pallas armed) proceeded from themselves; and not only from their authority, but (the more to add reputation to themselves) from their head and device.

Let us now speak of the inconveniences of counsel, and of the remedies. The inconveniences that have been noted in calling and using counsel, are three. First, the revealing of affairs, whereby they become less secret. Secondly, the weakening of the authority of princes, as if they were less of themselves. Thirdly, the danger of being unfaithfully counselled, and more for the good of them that counsel than of him that is counselled. For which inconveniences, the doctrine of Italy, and practice of France, in some kings' times, hath introduced *cabinet* counsels;[2] a remedy worse than the disease.

As to secrecy; princes are not bound to communicate all matters with all counsellors; but may extract and select. Neither is it necessary that he that consulteth what he should do, should declare what he will do. But let princes beware that the unsecreting of their affairs comes not from themselves. And as for cabinet counsels, it may be their motto, *plenus rimarum sum:* [they are full of leaks:] one futile person that maketh it his glory to tell, will do more hurt than many that know it their duty to conceal. It is true there be some affairs which require extreme secrecy, which will hardly go beyond one or two persons besides the king: neither are those counsels unprosperous; for, besides the secrecy, they commonly go on constantly in one spirit of direction, without distraction. But then it must be a prudent king, such as is able to grind with a hand-mill;[3] and those inward counsellors had need also be wise men, and especially true and trusty to the king's ends; as it was with King Henry the Seventh of England, who in his greatest business imparted himself to none, except it were to Morton and Fox.[4]

For weakening of authority; the fable[5] showeth the remedy. Nay, the majesty of kings is rather exalted than diminished when they are in the chair of counsel; neither was there ever prince bereaved of his dependances by his counsel; except where there hath been either an over-greatness in one counsellor or an over-strict combination in divers; which are things soon found and holpen.

For the last inconvenience, that men will counsel with an eye to themselves; certainly, *non inveniet fidem super terram* [he will not find faith on the earth,] is meant of the nature of times, and not of all particular persons. There be that are in nature faithful, and sincere, and plain, and direct; not crafty and involved; let princes, above all, draw to themselves such natures. Besides, counsellors are not commonly so united, but that one counsellor keepeth sentinel over another; so that if any do counsel out of faction or private ends, it commonly comes to the king's ear. But the best remedy is, if princes know their counsellors, as well as their counsellors know them:

Principis est virtus maxima nosse suos.

[*The chief virtue of a ruler is to know his own counsellors]

And on the other side, counsellors should not be too speculative into their sovereign's person. The true composition of a counsellor is rather to be skilful in their master's business, than in his nature; for then he is like to advise him, and not feed his humour. It is of singular use to princes if they take the opinions of their counsel both separately and together. For private opinion is more free; but opinion before others is more reverent. In private, men are more bold in their own humours; and in consort, men are more obnoxious to others' humours; therefore it is good to take both; and of the inferior sort rather in private, to preserve freedom; of the greater rather in consort, to preserve respect. It is in vain for princes to take counsel concerning matters, if they take no counsel likewise concerning persons; for all matters are as dead images; and the life of the execution of affairs resteth in the good choice of persons. Neither is it enough to consult concerning persons *secundum genera* [*according to types], as in an idea, or mathematical description, what the kind and character of the person should be; for the greatest errors are committed, and the most judgment is shown, in the choice of individuals. It was truly said, *optimi consiliarii mortui:* [the best counsellors are the dead:] books will speak plain when counsellors blanch. Therefore it is good to be conversant in them, specially the books of such as themselves have been actors upon the stage.

The counsels at this day in most places are but familiar meetings, where matters are rather talked on than debated. And they run too swift to the order or act of counsel. It were better that in causes of weight, the matter were propounded one day and not spoken to till the next day; *in nocte consilium:* [night is the season for counsel.] So was it done in the Commission of Union between England and Scotland; which was a grave and orderly assembly. I commend set days for petitions; for both it gives the suitors more certainty for their attendance, and it frees the meetings for matters of estate, that they may *hoc agere* [*stick to business]. In choice of committees for ripening business for the counsel, it is better to choose indifferent[6] persons, than to make an indifferency by putting in those that are strong on both sides. I commend also standing commissions; as for trade, for treasure, for war, for suits, for some provinces; for where there be divers particular counsels and but one counsel of estate (as it is in Spain), they are, in effect, no more than standing commissions: save that they have greater authority. Let such as are to inform counsels out of their particular professions, (as lawyers, seamen, mintmen, and the like,) be first heard before committees; and then, as occasion serves, before the counsel. And let them not come in multitudes, or in a tribunitious manner; for that is to clamour counsels, not to inform them. A long table and a square table, or seats about the walls, seem things of form, but are things of substance; for at a long table a few at the upper end, in effect, sway all the business; but in the other form there is more use of the counsellors' opinions that sit lower. A king, when he presides in counsel, let him beware how he opens his own inclination too much in that which he propoundeth; for else counsellors will but take the wind of him,[7] and instead of giving free counsel, sing him a song of *placebo*.[8]

21
Of Delays

FORTUNE is like the market; where many times, if you can stay a little, the price will fall. And again, it is sometimes like Sibylla's offer;[1] which at first offereth the commodity at full, then consumeth part and part, and still holdeth up the price. For occasion (as it is in the common verse) *turneth a bald noddle, after she hath presented her locks in front, and no hold taken;* or at least turneth the handle of the bottle first to be received, and after the belly, which is hard to clasp. There is surely no greater wisdom than well to time the beginnings and onsets of things. Dangers are no more light, if they once seem light; and more dangers have deceived men than forced them. Nay, it were better to meet some dangers half way, though they come nothing near, than to keep too long a watch upon their approaches; for if a man watch too long, it is odds he will fall asleep. On the other side, to be deceived with too long shadows (as some have been when the moon was low and shone on their enemies' back), and so to shoot off before the time; or to teach dangers to come on, by over early buckling towards them; is another extreme. The ripeness or unripeness of the occasion (as we said) must ever be well weighed; and generally it is good to commit the beginnings of all great actions to Argos with his hundred eyes, and the ends to Briareus with his hundred hands; first to watch, and then to speed. For the helmet of Pluto, which maketh the politic man go invisible, is secrecy in the counsel and celerity in the execution. For when things are once come to the execution, there is no secrecy comparable to celerity; like the motion of a bullet in the air, which flieth so swift as it outruns the eye.

22

OF CUNNING

WE take Cunning for a sinister or crooked wisdom. And certainly there is a great difference between a cunning man and a wise man; not only in point of honesty, but in point of ability. There be that can pack the cards, and yet cannot play well; so there are some that are good in canvasses and factions, that are otherwise weak men. Again, it is one thing to understand persons, and another thing to understand matters; for many are perfect in men's humours, that are not greatly capable of the real part of business; which is the constitution of one that hath studied men more than books. Such men are fitter for practice than for counsel; and they are good but in their own alley: turn them to new men, and they have lost their aim; so as the old rule to know a fool from a wise man, *Mitte ambos nudos ad ignotos, et videbis,* [Send them both naked to those they know not,] doth scarce hold for them. And because these cunning men are like haberdashers of small wares, it is not amiss to set forth their shop.

It is a point of cunning, to wait upon him with whom you speak, with your eye;[1] as the Jesuits give it in precept: for there be many wise men that have secret hearts and transparent countenances. Yet this would be done with a demure abasing of your eye sometimes, as the Jesuits also do use.

Another is, that when you have any thing to obtain of present despatch, you entertain and amuse the party with whom you deal with some other discourse; that he be not too much awake to make objections. I knew a counsellor and secretary, that never came to Queen Elizabeth of England with bills to sign, but he would always first put her into some discourse of estate, that she mought the less mind the bills.

The like surprise may be made by moving things when the party is in haste, and cannot stay to consider advisedly of that is moved.

If a man would cross a business that he doubts some other would handsomely and effectually move, let him pretend to wish it well, and move it himself in such sort as may foil it.

The breaking off in the midst of that one was about to say, as if he took himself up, breeds a greater appetite in him with whom you confer to know more.

And because it works better when any thing seemeth to be gotten from you by question, than if you offer it of yourself, you may lay a bait for a question, by showing another visage and countenance than you are wont; to the end to give occasion for the party to ask what the matter is of the change? As Nehemias did; *And I had not before that time been sad before the king.*

In things that are tender and unpleasing, it is good to break the ice by some whose words are of less weight, and to reserve the more weighty voice to come in as by chance, so that he may be asked the question upon the other's speech; as Narcissus did,[2] in relating to Claudius the marriage of Messalina and Silius.

In things that a man would not be seen in himself, it is a point of cunning to borrow the name of the world; as to say, *The world says,* or *There is a speech abroad.*

I knew one that, when he wrote a letter, he would put that which was most material in the postscript, as if it had been a bye-matter.

I knew another that, when he came to have speech, he would pass over that that he intended most; and go forth, and come back again, and speak of it as of a thing that he had almost forgot.

Some procure themselves to be surprised at such times as it is like the party that they work upon will suddenly come upon them; and to be found with a letter in their hand, or doing somewhat which they are not accustomed; to the end they may be apposed[3] of those things which of themselves they are desirous to utter.

It is a point of cunning, to let fall those words in a man's own name, which he would have another man learn and use, and thereupon take advantage. I knew two that were competitors for the secretary's place in Queen Elizabeth's time, and yet kept good quarter between themselves; and would confer one with another upon the business; and the one of them said, That to be a secretary *in the declination of a monarchy* was a ticklish thing, and that he did not affect it: the other straight caught up those words, and discoursed with divers of his friends, that he had no reason to desire to be secretary in the declination of a monarchy. The first man took hold of it, and found means it was told the Queen; who hearing of *a declination of a monarchy,* took it so ill, as she would never after hear of the other's suit.

There is a cunning, which we in England call *The turning of the cat in the pan;* which is, when that which a man says to another, he lays it as if another had said it to him. And to say truth, it is not easy, when such a matter passed between two, to make it appear from which of them it first moved and began.

It is a way that some men have, to glance and dart at others by justifying themselves by negatives; as to say *This I do not;* as Tigellinus did towards Burrhus, *Se non diversas spes, sed incolumitatem imperatoris simpliciter spectare:* [That he had not several hopes to rest on, but looked simply to the safety of the Emperor.]

Some have in readiness so many tales and stories, as there is nothing they would insinuate, but they can wrap it into a tale; which serveth both to keep themselves more in guard, and to make others carry it with more pleasure.

It is a good point of cunning, for a man to shape the answer he would have in his own words and propositions; for it makes the other party stick the less.

It is strange how long some men will lie in wait to speak somewhat they desire to say; and how far about they will fetch; and how many other matters they will beat over, to come near it. It is a thing of great patience, but yet of much use.

A sudden, bold, and unexpected question doth many times surprise a man, and lay him open. Like to him that, having changed his name and walking in Paul's, another suddenly came behind him and called him by his true name, whereat straightways he looked back.

But these small wares and petty points of cunning are infinite; and it were a good deed to make a list of them; for that nothing doth more hurt in a state than that cunning men pass for wise.

But certainly some there are that know the resorts and falls of business, that cannot sink into the main of it; like a house that hath convenient stairs and entries, but never a fair room. Therefore you shall see them find out pretty looses in the conclusion, but are no ways able to examine or debate matters. And yet commonly they take advantage of their inability, and would be thought wits of direction. Some build rather upon the abusing of others, and (as we now say) *putting tricks upon them*, than upon soundness of their own proceedings. But Salomon saith, *Prudens advertit ad gressus suos: stultus divertit ad dolos*: [The wise man taketh heed to his steps: the fool turneth aside to deceits.]

23

OF WISDOM FOR A MAN'S SELF

An ant is a wise creature for itself, but it is a shrewd thing in an orchard or garden. And certainly men that are great lovers of themselves waste the public. Divide with reason between self-love and society; and be so true to thyself, as thou be not false to others; specially to thy king and coun-

try. It is a poor centre of a man's actions, *himself*. It is right
earth. For that only stands fast upon his own centre; whereas
all things that have affinity with the heavens, move upon
the centre of another, which they benefit. The referring of
all to a man's self is more tolerable in a sovereign prince; because themselves are not only themselves, but their good
and evil is at the peril of the public fortune. But it is a desperate evil in a servant to a prince, or a citizen in a republic. For whatsoever affairs pass such a man's hands, he
crooketh them to his own ends; which must needs be often
eccentric to the ends of his master or state. Therefore let
princes, or states, choose such servants as have not this mark;
except they mean their service should be made but the accessary. That which maketh the effect more pernicious is
that all proportion is lost. It were disproportion enough for
the servant's good to be preferred before the master's; but
yet it is a greater extreme, when a little good of the servant
shall carry things against a great good of the master's. And
yet that is the case of bad officers, treasurers, ambassadors,
generals, and other false and corrupt servants; which set a
bias upon their bowl,[1] of their own petty ends and envies, to
the overthrow of their master's great and important affairs.
And for the most part, the good such servants receive is after the model of their own fortune; but the hurt they sell for
that good is after the model of their master's fortune. And
certainly it is the nature of extreme self-lovers, as they will
set an house on fire, and it were but to roast their eggs; and
yet these men many times hold credit with their masters, because their study is but to please them and profit themselves;
and for either respect they will abandon the good of their
affairs.

Wisdom for a man's self is, in many branches thereof, a
depraved thing. It is the wisdom of rats, that will be sure to
leave a house somewhat before it fall. It is the wisdom of
the fox, that thrusts out the badger, who digged and made
room for him. It is the wisdom of crocodiles, that shed tears
when they would devour. But that which is specially to be
noted is, that those which (as Cicero says of Pompey) are

sui amantes, sine rivali, [lovers of themselves without rival,] are many times unfortunate. And whereas they have all their times sacrificed to themselves, they become in the end themselves sacrifices to the inconstancy of fortune; whose wings they thought by their self-wisdom to have pinioned.

24

OF INNOVATIONS

As the births of living creatures at first are ill-shapen, so are all Innovations, which are the births of time. Yet notwithstanding, as those that first bring honour into their family are commonly more worthy than most that succeed, so the first precedent (if it be good) is seldom attained by imitation. For Ill, to man's nature as it stands perverted, hath a natural motion, strongest in continuance; but Good, as a forced motion, strongest at first. Surely every medicine is an innovation; and he that will not apply new remedies must expect new evils; for time is the greatest innovator; and if time of course[1] alter things to the worse, and wisdom and counsel shall not alter them to the better, what shall be the end? It is true, that what is settled by custom, though it be not good, yet at least it is fit; and those things which have long gone together, are as it were confederate within themselves; whereas new things piece not so well; but though they help by their utility, yet they trouble by their inconformity. Besides, they are like strangers; more admired and less favoured. All this is true, if time stood still; which contrariwise moveth so round, that a froward retention of custom is as turbulent a thing as an innovation; and they that reverence too much old times, are but a scorn to the new. It were good therefore that men in their innovations would follow the example of time itself; which indeed innovateth greatly, but quietly, and by degrees scarce to be perceived. For otherwise, whatsoever is new is unlooked for; and ever it mends some, and pairs[2] other; and he that is holpen takes it for a fortune, and thanks the time; and he that is hurt, for a wrong, and imputeth it to the author. It is good also not to try experiments in states, except the necessity be urgent, or the utility evident; and well to beware that it be the reformation that draweth on the change, and not the desire of change that pretendeth the reformation. And lastly, that the novelty, though it be not rejected, yet be held for a suspect; and, as the Scripture saith, *that we make a stand upon the ancient way, and then look about us, and discover what is the straight and right way, and so to walk in it.*

25

Of Dispatch

AFFECTED dispatch is one of the most dangerous things to business that can be. It is like that which the physicians call *predigestion,* or hasty digestion; which is sure to fill the body full of crudities and secret seeds of diseases. Therefore measure not dispatch by the times of sitting, but by the advancement of the business. And as in races it is not the large stride or high lift that makes the speed; so in business, the keeping close to the matter, and not taking of it too much at once, procureth dispatch. It is the care of some only to come off speedily for the time; or to contrive some false periods of business, because they may seem men of dispatch. But it is one thing to abbreviate by contracting, another by cutting off. And business so handled at several sittings or meetings goeth commonly backward and forward in an unsteady manner. I knew a wise man that had it for a by-word, when he saw men hasten to a conclusion, *Stay a little, that we may make an end the sooner.*

On the other side, true dispatch is a rich thing. For time is the measure of business, as money is of wares; and business is bought at a dear hand where there is small dispatch. The Spartans and Spaniards have been noted to be of small dispatch; *Mi venga la muerte de Spagna; Let my death come from Spain;* for then it will be sure to be long in coming.

Give good hearing to those that give the first information in business; and rather direct them in the beginning, than interrupt them in the continuance of their speeches; for he that is put out of his own order will go forward and backward, and be more tedious while he waits upon his memory, than he could have been if he had gone on in his own course. But sometimes it is seen that the moderator is more troublesome than the actor.

Iterations are commonly loss of time. But there is no such gain of time as to iterate often the state of the question; for it chaseth away many a frivolous speech as it is coming forth. Long and curious speeches are as fit for dispatch, as a robe or mantle with a long train is for race. Prefaces and passages,[1] and excusations, and other speeches of reference to the person,[2] are great wastes of time; and though they seem to proceed of modesty, they are bravery. Yet beware of being too material[3] when there is any impediment or obstruction in men's wills; for pre-occupation of mind ever requireth preface of speech; like a fomentation to make the unguent enter.

Above all things, order, and distribution, and singling out of parts, is the life of dispatch; so as the distribution be not too subtle: for he that doth not divide will never enter well into business; and he that divideth too much will never come out of it clearly. To choose time is to save time; and an unseasonable motion is but beating the air. There be three parts of business; the preparation, the debate or examination, and the perfection. Whereof, if you look for dispatch, let the middle only be the work of many, and the first and last the work of few. The proceeding upon somewhat conceived in writing doth for the most part facilitate dispatch: for though it should be wholly rejected, yet that negative is more pregnant of direction[4] than an indefinite; as ashes are more generative than dust.

26
OF SEEMING WISE

IT hath been an opinion, that the French are wiser than they seem, and the Spaniards seem wiser than they are. But howsoever it be between nations, certainly it is so between man and man. For as the Apostle[1] saith of godliness, *Having a shew of godliness, but denying the power thereof;* so certainly there are in point of wisdom and sufficiency, that do nothing or little very solemnly: *magno conatu nugas* [*trifles achieved by great effort]. It is a ridiculous thing and fit for a satire to persons of judgment, to see what shifts these formalists have, and what prospectives to make *superficies* to seem body that hath depth and bulk. Some are so close and reserved, as they will not shew their wares but by a dark light; and seem always to keep back somewhat; and when they know within themselves they speak of that they do not well know, would nevertheless seem to others to know of that which they may not well speak. Some help themselves with countenance and gesture, and are wise by signs; as Cicero saith of Piso, that when he answered him, he fetched one of his brows up to his forehead, and bent the other down to his chin; *Respondes, altera ad frontem sublato, altero ad mentum depresso supercilio, crudelitatem tibi non placere* [*You answer, with one brow raised to your forehead and the other dropped to your chin, that cruelty does not please you]. Some think to bear it[2] by speaking a great word, and being peremptory; and go on, and take by admittance that which they cannot make good. Some, whatsoever is beyond their reach, will seem to despise or make light of it as impertinent or curious; and so would have their ignorance seem judgment. Some are never without a difference, and commonly by amusing men with a subtilty, blanch[3] the matter; of whom A. Gellius saith, *Hominem delirum, qui verborum minutiis rerum frangit pondera:* [a trifler, that with verbal points and niceties breaks up the mass of matter]. Of which kind also, Plato in his Protagoras bringeth in Prodicus in scorn, and maketh him make a speech that consisteth of distinctions from the beginning to the end. Generally, such men in all deliberations find ease to be of the negative side, and affect a credit to object and foretell difficulties; for when propositions are denied, there is an end of them; but if they be allowed, it requireth a new work; which false point of wisdom is the bane of business. To conclude, there is no decaying merchant, or inward beggar,[4] hath so many tricks to uphold the credit of their wealth, as these empty persons have to maintain the credit of their sufficiency. Seeming wise men may make shift to get opinion; but let no man choose them for employment; for certainly you were better take for business a man somewhat absurd than over-formal.

27

OF FRIENDSHIP

IT had been hard for him that spake it[1] to have put more truth and untruth together in few words, than in that speech, *Whosoever is delighted in solitude is either a wild beast or a god.* For it is most true that a natural and secret hatred and aversation towards society in any man, hath somewhat of the savage beast; but it is most untrue that it should have any character at all of the divine nature; except it proceed, not out of a pleasure in solitude, but out of a love and desire to sequester a man's self for a higher conversation: such as is found to have been falsely and feignedly in some of the heathen; as Epimenides[2] the Candian, Numa the Roman, Empedocles the Sicilian, and Apollonius of Tyana; and truly and really in divers of the ancient hermits and holy fathers of the church. But little do men perceive what solitude is, and how far it extendeth. For a crowd is not company; and faces are but a gallery of pictures; and talk but a tinkling cymbal, where there is no love. The Latin adage meeteth with it a little: *Magna civitas, magna solitudo;* [a great town is a great solitude;] because in a great town friends are scattered; so that there is not that fellowship, for the most part, which is in less neighbourhoods. But we may go further, and affirm most truly that it is a mere and miserable solitude to want true friends; without which the world is but a wilderness; and even in this sense also of solitude, whosoever in the frame of his nature and affections is unfit for friendship, he taketh it of the beast, and not from humanity.

A principal fruit of friendship is the ease and discharge of the fulness and swellings of the heart, which passions of all kinds do cause and induce. We know diseases of stoppings and suffocations are the most dangerous in the body; and it is not much otherwise in the mind; you may take sarza to open the liver, steel to open the spleen, flower of sulphur for the lungs, castoreum for the brain; but no receipt openeth the heart, but a true friend; to whom you may impart griefs, joys, fears, hopes, suspicions, counsels, and whatsoever lieth upon the heart to oppress it, in a kind of civil shrift or confession.

It is a strange thing to observe how high a rate great kings and monarchs do set upon this fruit of friendship whereof we speak: so great, as they purchase it many times at the hazard of their own safety and greatness. For princes, in regard of the distance of their fortune from that of their subjects and servants, cannot gather this fruit, except (to make themselves capable thereof) they raise some persons to be as it were companions and almost equals to themselves, which many times sorteth to inconvenience. The modern languages give unto such persons the name of favourites, or privadoes; as if it were matter of grace, or conversation. But the Roman name attaineth the true use and cause thereof, naming them *participes curarum* [*sharers of cares]; for it is that which tieth the knot. And we see plainly that this hath been done, not by weak and passionate princes only, but by the wisest and most politic that ever reigned; who have oftentimes joined to themselves some of their servants; whom both themselves have called friends, and allowed others likewise to call them in the same manner; using the word which is received between private men.

L. Sylla, when he commanded Rome, raised Pompey (after surnamed the Great) to that height, that Pompey vaunted himself for Sylla's over-match. For when he had carried the consulship for a friend of his, against the pursuit of Sylla, and that Sylla did a little resent thereat, and began to speak great, Pompey turned upon him again, and in effect bade him be quiet; *for that more men adored the sun rising than the sun setting*. With Julius Cæsar, Decimus Brutus had obtained that interest, as he set him down in his testament for heir in remainder after his nephew. And this was the man that had power with him to draw him forth to his death. For when Cæsar would have discharged the senate, in regard of some ill presages, and specially a dream of Calpurnia; this man lifted him gently by the arm out of his chair, telling him he hoped he would not dismiss the senate till his wife had dreamt a better dream. And it seemeth his favour was so great, as Antonius, in a letter which is recited *verbatim* in one of Cicero's Philippics, calleth him *venefica, witch;* as if he had enchanted Cæsar. Augustus raised Agrippa (though of mean birth) to that height, as when he consulted with Mæcenas about the marriage of his daughter Julia, Mæcenas took the liberty to tell him, *that he must either marry his daughter to Agrippa, or take away his life: there was no third way, he had made him so great.* With Tiberius Cæsar, Sejanus had ascended to that height, as they two were termed and reckoned as a pair of friends. Tiberius in a letter to him saith, *hæc pro amicitiâ nostrâ non occultavi;* [these things, as our friendship required, I have not concealed from you;] and the whole senate dedicated an altar to Friendship, as to a goddess, in respect of the great dearness of friendship between them two. The like or more was between Septimius Severus and Plautianus. For he forced his eldest son to marry the daughter of Plautianus; and would often maintain Plautianus in doing affronts to his son; and did write also in a letter to the senate, by these words: *I love the man so well, as I wish he may over-live me.* Now if these princes had been as a Trajan or a Marcus Aurelius, a man might have thought that this had proceeded of an abundant goodness of nature; but being men so wise, of such strength and severity of mind, and so extreme lovers of themselves, as all these were, it proveth most plainly that they found their own felicity (though as great as ever happened to mortal men) but as an half piece, except they mought have a friend to make it entire; and yet, which is more, they were princes that had wives, sons, nephews; and yet all these could not supply the comfort of friendship.

It is not to be forgotten what Comineus observeth of his

first master, Duke Charles the Hardy; namely, that he would communicate his secrets with none; and least of all, those secrets which troubled him most. Whereupon he goeth on and saith that towards his latter time *that closeness did impair and a little perish his understanding.* Surely Comineus mought have made the same judgment also, if it had pleased him, of his second master Lewis the Eleventh, whose closeness was indeed his tormentor. The parable of Pythagoras is dark, but true; *Cor ne edito; Eat not the heart.* Certainly, if a man would give it a hard phrase, those that want friends to open themselves unto are cannibals of their own hearts. But one thing is most admirable (wherewith I will conclude this first fruit of friendship), which is, that this communicating of a man's self to his friend works two contrary effects; for it redoubleth joys, and cutteth griefs in halfs. For there is no man that imparteth his joys to his friend, but he joyeth the more: and no man that imparteth his griefs to his friend, but he grieveth the less. So that it is in truth of operation upon a man's mind, of like virtue as the alchymists use to attribute to their stone for man's body; that it worketh all contrary effects, but still to the good and benefit of nature. But yet without praying in aid of alchymists, there is a manifest image of this in the ordinary course of nature. For in bodies, union strengtheneth and cherisheth any natural action; and on the other side weakeneth and dulleth any violent impression: and even so it is of minds.

The second fruit of friendship is healthful and sovereign for the understanding, as the first is for the affections.[3] For friendship maketh indeed a fair day in the affections, from storm and tempests; but it maketh daylight in the understanding, out of darkness and confusion of thoughts. Neither is this to be understood only of faithful counsel, which a man receiveth from his friend; but before you come to that, certain it is that whosoever hath his mind fraught with many thoughts, his wits and understanding do clarify and break up, in the communicating and discoursing with another; he tosseth his thoughts more easily; he marshalleth them more orderly; he seeth how they look when they are turned into words: finally, he waxeth wiser than himself; and that more by an hour's discourse than by a day's meditation. It was well said by Themistocles to the king of Persia, *That speech was like cloth of Arras,*[4] *opened and put abroad; whereby the imagery doth appear in figure; whereas in thoughts they lie but as in packs.* Neither is this second fruit of friendship, in opening the understanding, restrained only to such friends as are able to give a man counsel; (they indeed are best;) but even without that, a man learneth of himself, and bringeth his own thoughts to light, and whetteth his wits as against a stone, which itself cuts not. In a word, a man were better relate himself to a statua or picture, than to suffer his thoughts to pass in smother.

Add now, to make this second fruit of friendship complete, that other point which lieth more open and falleth within vulgar observation; which is faithful counsel from a friend. Heraclitus saith well in one of his enigmas, *Dry light is ever the best.* And certain it is, that the light that a man receiveth by counsel from another, is drier and purer than that which cometh from his own understanding and judgment; which is ever infused and drenched in his affections and customs. So as there is as much difference between the counsel that a friend giveth, and that a man giveth himself, as there is between the counsel of a friend and of a flatterer. For there is no such flatterer as is a man's self; and there is no such remedy against flattery of a man's self, as the liberty of a friend. Counsel is of two sorts; the one concerning manners, the other concerning business. For the first, the best preservative to keep the mind in health is the faithful admonition of a friend. The calling of a man's self to a strict account is a medicine, sometime, too piercing and corrosive. Reading good books of morality is a little flat and dead. Observing our faults in others is sometimes improper for our case. But the best receipt (best, I say, to work, and best to take) is the admonition of a friend. It is a strange thing to behold what gross errors and extreme absurdities many (especially of the greater sort) do commit, for want of a friend to tell them of them; to the great damage both of their fame and fortune: for, as St. James saith, they are as men *that look sometimes into a glass, and presently forget their own shape and favour.* As for business, a man may think, if he will, that two eyes see no more than one; or that a gamester seeth always more than a looker-on; or that a man in anger is as wise as he that hath said over the four and twenty letters;[5] or that a musket may be shot off as well upon the arm as upon a rest; and such other fond and high imaginations, to think himself all in all. But when all is done, the help of good counsel is that which setteth business straight. And if any man think that he will take counsel, but it shall be by pieces; asking counsel in one business of one man, and in another business of another man; it is well, (that is to say, better perhaps than if he asked none at all;) but he runneth two dangers; one, that he shall not be faithfully counselled; for it is a rare thing, except it be from a perfect and entire friend, to have counsel given, but such as shall be bowed and crooked to some ends which he hath that giveth it. The other, that he shall have counsel given, hurtful and unsafe, (though with good meaning,) and mixed partly of mischief and partly of remedy; even as if you would call a physician that is thought good for the cure of the disease you complain of, but is unacquainted with your body; and therefore may put you in way for a present cure, but overthroweth your health in some other kind; and so cure the disease and kill the patient. But a friend that is wholly acquainted with a man's estate will beware, by furthering any present business, how he dasheth upon other inconvenience. And therefore rest not upon scattered counsels; they will rather distract and mislead, than settle and direct.

After these two noble fruits of friendship, (peace in the affections, and support of the judgment,) followeth the last fruit; which is like the pomegranate, full of many kernels; I mean aid and bearing a part in all actions and occasions. Here the best way to represent to life the manifold use of friendship, is to cast and see how many things there are which a man cannot do himself; and then it will appear that it was a sparing speech of the ancients, to say, *that a friend is another himself;* for that a friend is far more than himself. Men have their time, and die many times in desire of some things which they principally take to heart; the bestowing of a child, the finishing of a work, or the like. If a man have a true friend, he may rest almost secure that the care of those things will continue after him. So that a man hath, as it were, two lives in his desires. A man hath a body, and that body is confined to a place; but where friendship is, all offices of life are as it were granted to him and his deputy. For he may exercise them by his friend. How many things are there which a man cannot, with any face or comeliness, say or do himself? A man can scarce allege his own merits with modesty, much less extol them; a man cannot sometimes brook to supplicate or beg; and a number of the like. But all these things are graceful in a friend's mouth, which are blushing in a man's own. So again, a man's person hath many proper relations which he cannot put off. A man cannot speak to his son but as a father; to his wife but as a husband; to his enemy but upon terms: whereas a friend may speak as the case requires, and not as it sorteth with the person. But to enumerate these things were endless; I have given the rule, where a man cannot fitly play his own part; if he have not a friend, he may quit the stage.

28

OF EXPENSE

RICHES are for spending, and spending for honour and good actions. Therefore extraordinary expense must be limited by the worth of the occasion; for voluntary undoing may be as well for a man's country as for the kingdom of heaven. But ordinary expense ought to be limited by a man's estate; and governed with such regard, as it be within his compass; and not subject to deceit and abuse of servants; and ordered to the best shew, that the bills may be less than the estimation abroad. Certainly, if a man will keep but of even hand,[1] his ordinary expenses ought to be but to the half of his receipts; and if he think to wax rich, but to the third part. It is no baseness for the greatest to descend and look into their own estate. Some forbear it, not upon negligence alone, but doubting to bring themselves into melancholy, in respect they shall find it broken. But wounds cannot be cured without searching. He that cannot look into his own estate at all, had need both choose well those whom he employeth, and change them often; for new are more timorous and less subtle. He that can look into his estate but seldom, it behoveth him to turn all to certainties.[2] A man had need, if he be plentiful in some kind of expense, to be as saving again in some other. As if he be plentiful in diet, to be saving in apparel; if he be plentiful in the hall, to be saving in the stable; and the like. For he that is plentiful in expenses of all kinds will hardly be preserved from decay. In clearing of a man's estate, he may as well hurt himself in being too sudden, as in letting it run on too long. For hasty selling is commonly as disadvantageable as interest.[3] Besides, he that clears at once will relapse; for finding himself out of straits, he will revert to his customs: but he that cleareth by degrees induceth a habit of frugality, and gaineth as well upon his mind as upon his estate. Certainly, who hath a state to repair, may not despise small things; and commonly it is less dishonourable to abridge petty charges, than to stoop to petty gettings. A man ought warily to begin charges which once begun will continue: but in matters that return not he may be more magnificent.

29

Of the True Greatness of Kingdoms and Estates

The speech of Themistocles the Athenian, which was haughty and arrogant in taking so much to himself, had been a grave and wise observation and censure, applied at large to others. Desired at a feast to touch a lute, he said, *He could not fiddle, but yet he could make a small town a great city.* These words (holpen a little with a metaphor) may express two differing abilities in those that deal in business of estate. For if a true survey be taken of counsellors and statesmen, there may be found (though rarely) those which can make a small state great, and yet cannot fiddle: as on the other side, there will be found a great many that can fiddle very cunningly, but yet are so far from being able to make a small state great, as their gift lieth the other way; to bring a great and flourishing estate to ruin and decay. And, certainly those degenerate arts and shifts, whereby many counsellors and governors gain both favour with their masters and estimation with the vulgar, deserve no better name than fiddling; being things rather pleasing for the time, and graceful to themselves only, than tending to the weal and advancement of the state which they serve. There are also (no doubt) counsellors and governors which may be held sufficient (*negotiis pares*), able to manage affairs, and to keep them from precipices and manifest inconveniences; which nevertheless are far from the ability to raise and amplify an estate in power, means, and fortune. But be the workmen what they may be, let us speak of the work; that is, the true Greatness of Kingdoms and Estates, and the means thereof. An argument fit for great and mighty princes to have in their hand; to the end that neither by over-measuring their forces, they leese themselves in vain enterprises; nor on the other side, by undervaluing them, they descend to fearful and pusillanimous counsels.

The greatness of an estate in bulk and territory, doth fall under measure; and the greatness of finances and revenew doth fall under computation. The population may appear by musters; and the number and greatness of cities and towns by cards and maps. But yet there is not any thing amongst civil affairs more subject to error, than the right valuation and true judgment concerning the power and forces of an estate. The kingdom of heaven is compared, not to any great kernel or nut, but to a grain of mustard-seed; which is one of the least grains, but hath in it a property and spirit hastily to get up and spread. So are there states great in territory, and yet not apt to enlarge or command; and some that have but a small dimension of stem, and yet apt to be the foundations of great monarchies.

Walled towns, stored arsenals and armories, goodly races of horse, chariots of war, elephants, ordnance, artillery, and the like; all this is but a sheep in a lion's skin, except the breed and disposition of the people be stout and warlike. Nay, number (itself) in armies importeth not much, where the people is of weak courage; for (as Virgil saith) *It never troubles a wolf how many the sheep be.* The army of the Persians in the plains of Arbela was such a vast sea of people, as it did somewhat astonish the commanders in Alexander's army; who came to him therefore, and wished him to set upon them by night; but he answered, *He would not pilfer the victory.* And the defeat was easy. When Tigranes the Armenian, being encamped upon a hill with four hundred thousand men, discovered the army of the Romans, being not above fourteen thousand, marching towards him, he made himself merry with it, and said, *Yonder men are too many for an ambassage, and too few for a fight.* But, before the sun set, he found them enow to give him the chase with infinite slaughter. Many are the examples of the great odds between number and courage: so that a man may truly make a judgment, that the principal point of greatness in any state is to have a race of military men. Neither is money the sinews of war (as it is trivially said), where the sinews of men's arms, in base and effeminate people, are failing. For Solon said well to Crœsus (when in ostentation he shewed him his gold), *Sir, if any other come that hath better iron than you, he will be master of all this gold.* Therefore let any prince or state think soberly of his forces, except his militia of natives be of good and valiant soldiers. And let princes, on the other side, that have subjects of martial disposition, know their own strength; unless they be otherwise wanting unto themselves. As for mercenary forces (which is the help in this case), all examples show that whatsoever estate or prince doth rest upon them, *he may spread his feathers for a time, but he will mew them soon after.*

The blessing of Judah and Issachar will never meet; *that the same people or nation should be both the lion's whelp and the ass between burthens;* neither will it be, that a people overlaid with taxes should ever become valiant and martial. It is true that taxes levied by consent of the estate do abate men's courage less: as it hath been seen notably in the excises of the Low Countries; and, in some degree, in the subsidies of England. For you must note that we speak now of the heart and not of the purse. So that although the same tribute and tax, laid by consent or by imposing, be all one to the purse, yet it works diversly upon the courage. So that you may conclude, *that no people over-charged with tribute is fit for empire.*

Let states that aim at greatness, take heed how their nobility and gentlemen do multiply too fast. For that maketh the common subject grow to be a peasant and base swain, driven out of heart, and in effect but the gentleman's labourer. Even as you may see in coppice woods; if you leave your staddles[1] too thick, you shall never have clean underwood, but shrubs and bushes. So in countries, if the gentlemen be too many, the commons will be base; and you will bring it to that, that not the hundred poll will be fit for an helmet; especially as to the infantry, which is the nerve of an army; and so there will be great population and little strength. This which I speak of hath been no where better seen than by comparing of England and France; whereof England, though far less in territory and population, hath been (nevertheless) an over-match; in regard the middle people of England make good soldiers, which the peasants of France do not. And herein the device of king Henry the Seventh (whereof I have spoken largely in the history of his life) was profound and admirable; in making farms and houses of husbandry of a standard; that is, maintained with such a proportion of land unto them, as may breed a subject to live in convenient plenty and no servile condition; and to keep the plough in the hands of the owners, and not mere hirelings. And thus indeed you shall attain to Virgil's character which he gives to ancient Italy:

Terra potens armis atque ubere glebæ:

[A land powerful in arms and in productiveness of soil.] Neither is that state (which, for any thing I know, is almost peculiar to England, and hardly to be found any where else, except it be perhaps in Poland) to be passed over; I mean the state of free servants and attendants upon noblemen and gentlemen; which are no ways inferior unto the yeomanry for arms. And therefore out of all question, the splendour and magnificence and great retinues and hospitality of noblemen and gentlemen, received into custom, doth much conduce unto martial greatness. Whereas, contrariwise, the close and reserved living of noblemen and gentlemen causeth a penury of military forces.

By all means it is to be procured, that the trunk of Nebuchadnezzar's tree of monarchy[2] be great enough to bear the branches and the boughs; that is, that the natural subjects of the crown or state bear a sufficient proportion to the stranger subjects that they govern. Therefore all states that are liberal of naturalisation towards strangers are fit for empire. For to think that an handful of people can, with the greatest courage and policy in the world, embrace too large extent of dominion, it may hold for a time, but it will fail suddenly. The Spartans were a nice people in point of naturalisation; whereby, while they kept their compass, they stood firm; but when they did spread, and their boughs were becomen too great for their stem, they became a windfall upon the sudden. Never any state was in this point so open to receive strangers into their body as were the Romans. Therefore it sorted with them accordingly; for they grew to the greatest monarchy. Their manner was to grant naturalisation (which they called *jus civitatis*), and to grant it in the highest degree; that is, not only *jus commercii, jus connubii, jus hæreditatis;* but also *jus suffragii,* and *jus honorum.*[3] And this not to singular persons alone, but likewise to whole families; yea to cities, and sometimes to nations. Add to this their custom of plantation of colonies; whereby the Roman plant was removed into the soil of other nations. And putting both constitutions together, you will say that it was not the Romans that spread upon the world, but it was the world that spread upon the Romans; and that was the sure way of greatness. I have marvelled sometimes at Spain, how they clasp and contain so large dominions with so few natural Spaniards; but sure the whole compass of Spain is a very great body of a tree; far above Rome and Sparta at the first. And besides, though they have not had that usage to naturalise liberally, yet they have that which is next to it; that is, to employ almost indifferently all nations in their militia of ordinary soldiers; yea and sometimes in their highest commands. Nay it seemeth at this instant they are sensible of this want of natives; as by the Pragmatical Sanction,[4] now published, appeareth.

It is certain, that sedentary and within-door arts, and delicate manufactures (that require rather the finger than the arm), have in their nature a contrariety to a military disposition. And generally, all warlike people are a little idle, and love danger better than travail. Neither must they be too much broken of it, if they shall be preserved in vigour. Therefore it was great advantage in the ancient states of Sparta, Athens, Rome, and others, that they had the use of slaves, which commonly did rid those manufactures. But that is abolished, in greatest part, by the Christian law. That which cometh nearest to it, is to leave those arts chiefly to strangers (which for that purpose are the more easily to be received), and to contain the principal bulk of the vulgar natives within those three kinds,—tillers of the ground; free servants; and handicraftsmen of strong and manly arts, as smiths, masons, carpenters, &c: not reckoning professed soldiers.

But above all, for empire and greatness, it importeth most, that a nation do profess arms as their principal honour, study, and occupation. For the things which we formerly have spoken of are but habilitations toward arms; and what is habilitation without intention and act? Romulus, after his death (as they report or feign), sent a present to the Romans, that above all they should intend arms; and then they should prove the greatest empire of the world. The fabric of the state of Sparta was wholly (though not wisely) framed and composed to that scope and end. The Persians and Macedonians had it for a flash. The Gauls, Germans, Goths, Saxons, Normans, and others, had it for a time. The Turks have it at this day, though in great declination. Of Christian Europe, they that have it are, in effect, only the Spaniards. But it is so plain *that every man profiteth in that he most intendeth*, that it needeth not to be stood upon. It is enough to point at it; that no nation which doth not directly profess arms, may look to have greatness fall into their mouths. And on the other side, it is a most certain oracle of time, that those states that continue long in that profession (as the Romans and Turks principally have done) do wonders. And those that have professed arms but for an age, have notwithstanding commonly attained that greatness in that age which maintained them long after, when their profession and exercise of arms hath grown to decay.

Incident to this point is, for a state to have those laws or customs which may reach forth unto them just occasions (as may be pretended) of war. For there is that justice imprinted in the nature of men, that they enter not upon wars (whereof so many calamities do ensue) but upon some, at the least specious, grounds and quarrels. The Turk hath at hand, for cause of war, the propagation of his law or sect; a quarrel that he may always command. The Romans, though they esteemed the extending the limits of their empire to be great honour to their generals when it was done, yet they never rested upon that alone to begin a war. First therefore, let nations that pretend to greatness have this; that they be sensible of wrongs, either upon borderers, merchants, or politic ministers; and that they sit not too long upon a provocation. Secondly, let them be prest[5] and ready to give aids and succours to their confederates; as it ever was with the Romans; insomuch, as if the confederates had leagues defensive with divers other states, and, upon invasion offered, did implore their aids severally, yet the Romans would ever be the foremost, and leave it to none other to have the honour. As for the wars which were anciently made on the behalf of a kind of party, or tacit conformity of estate, I do not see how they may be well justified: as when the Romans made a war for the liberty of Græcia; or when the Lacedæmonians and Athenians made wars to set up or pull down democracies and oligarchies; or when wars were made by foreigners, under the pretence of justice or protection, to deliver the subjects of others from tyranny and oppression; and the like. Let it suffice, that no estate expect to be great, that is not awake upon any just occasion of arming.

No body can be healthful without exercise, neither natural body nor politic; and certainly to a kingdom or estate, a just and honourable war is the true exercise. A civil war indeed is like the heat of a fever; but a foreign war is like the heat of exercise, and serveth to keep the body in health; for in a slothful peace, both courages will effeminate and manners corrupt. But howsover it be for happiness, without all question, for greatness it maketh, to be still for the most part in arms; and the strength of a veteran army[6] (though it be a chargeable business) always on foot, is that which commonly giveth the law, or at least the reputation, amongst all neighbour states; as may well be seen in Spain, which hath had, in one part or other, a veteran army almost continually, now by the space of six score years.

To be master of the sea is an abridgment[7] of a monarchy. Cicero, writing to Atticus of Pompey his preparation against Cæsar, saith, *Consilium Pompeii plane Themistocleum est; putat enim, qui mari potitur, eum rerum potiri;* [Pompey is going upon the policy of Themistocles; thinking that he who commands the sea comands all.] And, without doubt, Pompey had tired out Cæsar, if upon vain confidence he had not left that way. We see the great effects of battles by sea. The battle of Actium decided the empire of the world. The battle of Lepanto arrested the greatness of the Turk. There be many examples where sea-fights have been final to the war; but this is when princes or states have set up their rest[8] upon the battles. But thus much is certain, that he that commands the sea is at great liberty, and may take as much and as little of the war as he will. Whereas those that be strongest by land are many times nevertheless in great straits. Surely, at this day, with us of Europe, the vantage of strength at sea (which is one of the principal dowries of this kingdom of Great Britain) is great; both because most of the kingdoms of Europe are not merely inland, but girt with the sea most part of their compass; and because the wealth of both Indies seems in great part but an accessary to the command of the seas.

The wars of latter ages seem to be made in the dark, in respect of the glory and honour which reflected upon men from the wars in ancient time. There be now, for martial encouragement, some degrees and orders of chivalry; which nevertheless are conferred promiscuously upon soldiers and no soldiers; and some remembrance perhaps upon the scutcheon; and some hospitals for maimed soldiers; and such like things. But in ancient times, the trophies erected upon the place of the victory; the funeral laudatives and monuments for those that died in the wars; the crowns and garlands personal; the style of Emperor, which the great kings of the world after borrowed; the triumphs of the generals upon their return; the great donatives and largesses upon the disbanding of the armies; were things able to inflame all men's courages. But above all, that of the Triumph, amongst the Romans, was not pageants or gaudery, but one of the wisest and noblest institutions that ever was. For it contained three things; honour to the general; riches to the treasury out of the spoils; and donatives to the army. But that honour perhaps were not fit for monarchies; except it be in the person of the monarch himself, or his sons; as it came to pass in the times of the Roman emperors, who did impropriate the actual triumphs to themselves and their sons, for such wars as they did achieve in person; and left only, for wars achieved by subjects, some triumphal garments and ensigns to the general.

To conclude: no man can *by care taking* (as the Scripture saith) *add a cubit to his stature,* in this little model of a man's body; but in the great frame of kingdoms and commonwealths, it is in the power of princes or estates to add amplitude and greatness to their kingdoms; for by introducing such ordinances, constitutions, and customs, as we have now touched, they may sow greatness to their posterity and succession. But these things are commonly not observed, but left to take their chance.

30

OF REGIMENT OF HEALTH

THERE is a wisdom in this beyond the rules of physic: a man's own observation, what he finds good of, and what he finds hurt of, is the best physic to preserve health. But it is a safer conclusion to say, *This agreeth not well with me, therefore I will not continue it;* than this, *I find no offence of this, therefore I may use it.* For strength of nature in youth passeth over many excesses, which are owing a man till his age. Discern of the coming on of years, and think not to do the same things still; for age will not be defied. Beware of sudden change in any great point of diet, and if necessity inforce it, fit the rest to it. For it is a secret both in nature and state, that it is safer to change many things than one. Examine thy customs of diet, sleep, exercise, apparel, and the like; and try, in any thing thou shalt judge hurtful, to discontinue it by little and little but so, as if thou dost find any inconvenience by the change, thou come back to it again: for it is hard to distinguish that which is generally held good and wholesome, from that which is good particularly, and fit for thine own body. To be free-minded and cheerfully disposed at hours of meat and of sleep and of exercise, is one of the best precepts of long lasting. As for the passions and studies of the mind; avoid envy; anxious fears; anger fretting inwards; subtle and knotty inquisitions; joys and exhilarations in excess; sadness not communicated. Entertain hopes; mirth rather than joy; variety of delights, rather than surfeit of them; wonder and admiration, and therefore novelties; studies that fill the mind with splendid and illustrious objects, as histories, fables, and contemplations of nature. If you fly physic in health altogether, it will be too strange for your body when you shall need it. If you make it too familiar, it will work no extraordinary effect when sickness cometh. I commend rather some diet for certain seasons, than frequent use of physic, except it be grown into a custom. For those diets alter the body more, and trouble it less. Despise no new accident in your body, but ask opinion of it. In sickness, respect health principally; and in health, action. For those that put their bodies to endure in health, may in most sicknesses, which are not very sharp, be cured only with diet and tendering. Celsus could never have spoken it as a physician, had he not been a wise man withal, when he giveth it for one of the great precepts of health and lasting, that a man do vary and interchange contraries, but with an inclination to the more benign extreme: use fasting and full eating, but rather full eating; watching and sleep, but rather sleep; sitting and exercise, but rather exercise; and the like. So shall nature be cherished, and yet taught masteries. Physicians are some of them so pleasing and conformable to the humour of the patient, as they press not the true cure of the disease; and some other are so regular in proceeding according to art for the disease, as they respect not sufficiently the condition of the patient. Take one of a middle temper; or if it may not be found in one man, combine two of either sort; and forget not to call as well the best acquainted with your body, as the best reputed of for his faculty.

31

OF SUSPICION

SUSPICIONS amongst thoughts are like bats amongst birds, they ever fly by twilight. Certainly they are to be repressed, or at the least well guarded: for they cloud the mind; they leese friends; and they check with business, whereby business cannot go on currently and constantly. They dispose kings to tyranny, husbands to jealousy, wise men to irresolution and melancholy. They are defects, not in the heart, but in the brain; for they take place in the stoutest natures; as in the example of Henry the Seventh of England. There was not a more suspicious man, nor a more stout. And in such a composition they do small hurt. For commonly they are not admitted, but with examination, whether they be likely or no? But in fearful natures they gain ground too fast. There is nothing makes a man suspect much, more than to know little; and therefore men should remedy suspicion by procuring to know more, and not to keep their suspicions in smother. What would men have? Do they think those they employ and deal with are saints? Do they not think they will have their own ends, and be truer to themselves than to them? Therefore there is no better way to moderate suspicions, than to account upon such suspicions as true[1] and yet to bridle them as false. For so far a man ought to make use of suspicions, as to provide, as if that should be true that he suspects, yet it may do him no hurt. Suspicions that the mind of itself gathers are but buzzes; but suspicions that are artificially nourished, and put into men's heads by the tales and whisperings of others, have stings. Certainly, the best mean to clear the way in this same wood of suspicions, is frankly to communicate them with the party that he suspects; for thereby he shall be sure to know more of the truth of them than he did before; and withal shall make that party more circumspect not to give further cause of suspicion. But this would not be done to men of base natures; for they, if they find themselves once suspected, will never be true. The Italian says, *Sospetto licentia fede;*[2] as if suspicion did give a passport to faith; but it ought rather to kindle it to discharge itself.

32

OF DISCOURSE

SOME in their discourse desire rather commendation of wit, in being able to hold all arguments, than of judgment, in discerning what is true; as if it were a praise to know what might be said, and not what should be thought. Some have certain common places and themes wherein they are good, and want variety; which kind of poverty is for the most part tedious, and when it is once perceived, ridiculous. The honourablest part of talk is to give the occasion; and again to moderate and pass to somewhat else; for then a man leads the dance. It is good, in discourse and speech of conversation, to vary and intermingle speech of the present occasion with arguments, tales with reasons, asking of questions with telling of opinions, and jest with earnest: for it is a dull thing to tire, and, as we say now, to jade, any thing too far. As for jest, there be certain things which ought to be privileged from it; namely, religion, matters of state, great persons, any man's present business of importance, and any case that deserveth pity. Yet there be some that think their wits have been asleep, except they dart out somewhat that is piquant, and to the quick. That is a vein which would be bridled;

Parce, puer, stimulis, et fortius utere loris.
[*Spare the whip, boy, and use the reins more strongly.]

And generally, men ought to find the difference between saltness and bitterness. Certainly, he that hath a satirical vein, as he maketh others afraid of his wit, so he had need be afraid of others' memory. He that questioneth much, shall learn much, and content much; but especially if he apply his questions to the skill of the persons whom he asketh; for he shall give them occasion to please themselves in speaking, and himself shall continually gather knowledge. But let his questions not be troublesome; for that is fit for a poser. And let him be sure to leave other men their turns to speak. Nay, if there be any that would reign and take up all the time, let him find means to take them off, and to bring others on; as musicians use to do with those that dance too long galliards. If you dissemble sometimes your knowledge of that you are thought to know, you shall be thought another time to know that you know not. Speech of a man's self ought to be seldom, and well chosen. I knew one was wont to say in scorn, *He must needs be a wise man, he speaks so much of himself:* and there is but one case wherein a man may commend himself with good grace; and that is in commending virtue in another; especially if it be such a virtue whereunto himself pretendeth. Speech of touch[1] towards others should be sparingly used; for discourse ought to be as a field, without coming home to any man. I knew two noblemen, of the west part of England, whereof the one was given to scoff, but kept ever royal cheer in his house; the other would ask of those that had been at the other's table, *Tell truly, was there never a flout or dry blow[2] given?* To which the guest would answer, *Such and such a thing passed.* The lord would say, *I thought he would mar a good dinner.* Discretion of speech is more than eloquence; and to speak agreeably to him with whom we deal, is more than to speak in good words or in good order. A good continued speech, without a good speech of interlocution,[3] shews slowness; and a good reply or second speech, without a good settled speech, sheweth shallowness and weakness. As we see in beasts, that those that are weakest in the course, are yet nimblest in the turn; as it is betwixt the greyhound and the hare. To use too many circumstances ere one come to the matter, is wearisome; to use none at all, is blunt.

33

Of Plantations

PLANTATIONS are amongst ancient, primitive, and heroical works. When the world was young it begat more children; but now it is old it begets fewer: for I may justly account new plantations to be the children of former kingdoms. I like a plantation in a pure soil; that is, where people are not displanted to the end to plant in others. For else it is rather an extirpation than a plantation. Planting of countries is like planting of woods; for you must make account to leese almost twenty years profit, and expect your recompense in the end. For the principal thing that hath been the destruction of most plantations, hath been the base and hasty drawing of profit in the first years. It is true, speedy profit is not to be neglected, as far as may stand with the good of the plantation, but no further. It is a shameful and unblessed thing to take the scum of people, and wicked condemned men, to be the people with whom you plant; and not only so, but it spoileth the plantation; for they will ever live like rogues, and not fall to work, but be lazy, and do mischief, and spend victuals, and be quickly weary, and then certify over to their country[1] to the discredit of the plantation. The people wherewith you plant ought to be gardeners, plough-men, labourers, smiths, carpenters, joiners, fishermen, fowl-ers, with some few apothecaries, surgeons, cooks and bakers. In a country of plantation, first look about what kind of victual the country yields of itself to hand; as chestnuts, wallnuts, pine-apples, olives, dates, plums, cher-ries, wild honey, and the like; and make use of them. Then consider what victual or esculent things there are, which grow speedily, and within the year; as parsnips, carrots, turnips, onions, radish, artichokes of Hierusalem,[2] maize, and the like. For wheat, barley, and oats, they ask too much labour; but with pease and beans you may begin, both because they ask less labour, and because they serve for meat as well as for bread. And of rice likewise cometh a great increase, and it is a kind of meat. Above all, there ought to be brought store of biscuit, oat-meal, flour, meal, and the like, in the beginning, till bread may be had. For beasts, or birds, take chiefly such as are least subject to diseases, and multiply fastest; as swine, goats, cocks, hens, turkeys, geese, house-doves, and the like. The victual in plantations ought to be expended almost as in a besieged town; that is, with certain allowance. And let the main part of the ground employed to gardens or corn, be to a common stock; and to be laid in, and stored up, and then delivered out in proportion; besides some spots of ground that any particular person will manure for his own private. Consider likewise what commodities the soil where the plantation is doth naturally yield, that they may some way help to defray the charge of the plantation, (so it be not, as was said, to the untimely prejudice of the main business,) as it hath fared with tobacco in Virginia.[3] Wood commonly aboundeth but too much; and therefore timber is fit to be one. If there be iron ore, and streams whereupon to set the mills, iron is a brave commodity where wood aboundeth. Making of bay-salt,[4] if the climate be proper for it, would be put in experience. Growing silk likewise, if any be, is a likely commodity. Pitch and tar, where store of firs and pines are, will not fail. So drugs and sweet woods, where they are, cannot but yield great profit. Soap-ashes[5] likewise, and other things that may be thought of. But moil not too much under ground; for the hope of mines is very uncertain, and useth to make the planters lazy in other things. For government, let it be in the hands of one, assisted with some counsel; and let them have commission to exercise martial laws, with some limitation. And above all, let men make that profit of being in the wilderness, as they have God always, and his service, before their eyes. Let not the government of the plantation depend upon too many counsellors and undertakers in the country that planteth, but upon a temperate number; and let those be rather noblemen and gentlemen, than merchants; for they look ever to the present gain. Let there be freedoms from custom, till the plantation be of strength; and not only freedom from custom, but freedom to carry their commodities where they may make their best of them, except there be some special cause of caution. Cram not in people, by sending too fast company after company; but rather harken how they waste, and send supplies proportionably; but so as the number may live well in the plantation, and not by surcharge be in penury. It hath been a great endangering to the health of some plantations, that they have built along the sea and rivers, in marish and unwholesome grounds. Therefore, though you begin there, to avoid carriage and other like discommodities, yet build still rather upwards from the streams, than along. It concerneth likewise the health of the plantation that they have good store of salt with them, that they may use it in their victuals when it shall be necessary. If

you plant where savages are, do not only entertain them
with trifles and gingles; but use them justly and graciously,
with sufficient guard nevertheless; and do not win their
favour by helping them to invade their enemies, but for
their defence it is not amiss; and send oft of them over to
the country that plants, that they may see a better condition
than their own, and commend it when they return. When
the plantation grows to strength, then it is time to plant
with women as well as with men; that the plantation may
spread into generations, and not be ever pieced from without. It is the sinfullest thing in the world to forsake or
destitute a plantation once in forwardness; for besides the
dishonour, it is the guiltiness of blood of many commiser-
able persons.

34

OF RICHES

I CANNOT call Riches better than the baggage of virtue. The
Roman word is better, *impedimenta.* For as the baggage
is to an army, so is riches to virtue. It cannot be spared nor
left behind, but it hindereth the march; yea and the care of
it sometimes loseth or disturbeth the victory. Of great riches
there is no real use, except it be in the distribution; the rest
is but conceit. So saith Salomon, *Where much is, there are
many to consume it; and what hath the owner but the sight
of it with his eyes?* The personal fruition in any man cannot
reach to feel great riches: there is a custody of them; or a
power of dole and donative of them; or a fame of them; but
no solid use to the owner. Do you not see what feigned
prices are set upon little stones and rarities? and what works
of ostentation are undertaken, because there might seem to
be some use of great riches? But then you will say, they may
be of use to buy men out of dangers or troubles. As Salomon
saith, *Riches are as a strong hold, in the imagination of the
rich man.* But this is excellently expressed, that it is in imagination, and not always in fact. For certainly great riches
have sold more men than they have bought out. Seek not

proud riches, but such as thou mayest get justly, use soberly, distribute cheerfully, and leave contentedly. Yet have
no abstract nor friarly contempt of them. But distinguish,
as Cicero saith well of Rabirius Posthumus, *In studio rei
amplificandæ apparebat, non avaritiæ prædam, sed instru-
mentum bonitati quæri;* [In seeking to increase his estate it
was apparent that he sought not a prey for avarice to feed
on, but an instrument for goodness to work with.] Hearken
also to Salomon, and beware of hasty gathering of riches;
Qui festinat ad divitias, non erit insons: [He that maketh
haste to be rich shall not be innocent.] The poets feign, that
when Plutus (which is Riches) is sent from Jupiter, he
limps and goes slowly; but when he is sent from Pluto, he
runs and is swift of foot. Meaning that riches gotten by
good means and just labour pace slowly; but when they
come by the death of others (as by the course of inheritance, testaments, and the like), they come tumbling upon
a man. But it mought be applied likewise to Pluto, taking
him for the devil. For when riches come from the devil (as
by fraud and oppression and unjust means), they come
upon speed. The ways to enrich are many, and most of
them foul. Parsimony is one of the best, and yet is not
innocent; for it withholdeth men from works of liberality
and charity. The improvement of the ground is the most
natural obtaining of riches; for it is our great mother's blessing, the earth's; but it is slow. And yet where men of great
wealth do stoop to husbandry, it multiplieth riches exceedingly. I knew a nobleman in England, that had the greatest
audits of any man in my time; a great grazier, a great sheep-
master, a great timber man, a great collier, a great corn-mas-
ter, a great lead-man, and so of iron, and a number of the like
points of husbandry. So as the earth seemed a sea to him,
in respect of the perpetual importation. It was truly observed by one, that himself came very hardly to a little
riches, and very easily to great riches. For when a man's
stock is come to that, that he can expect the prime of markets, and overcome those bargains which for their greatness
are few men's money, and be partner in the industries of

younger men, he cannot but increase mainly. The gains of ordinary trades and vocations are honest; and furthered by two things chiefly; by diligence, and by a good name for good and fair dealing. But the gains of bargains are of a more doubtful nature; when men shall wait upon others' necessity, broke by servants and instruments to draw them on, put off others cunningly that would be better chapmen, and the like practices, which are crafty and naught. As for the chopping of bargains, when a man buys not to hold but to sell over again, that commonly grindeth double, both upon the seller and upon the buyer. Sharings do greatly enrich, if the hands be well chosen that are trusted. Usury is the certainest means of gain, though one of the worst; as that whereby a man doth eat his bread *in sudore vultûs alieni;* [in the sweat of another man's face;] and besides, doth plough upon Sundays. But yet certain though it be, it hath flaws; for that the scriveners and brokers do value unsound men[1] to serve their own turn. The fortune in being the first in an invention or in a privilege, doth cause sometimes a wonderful overgrowth in riches; as it was with the first sugar man in the Canaries.[2] Therefore if a man can play the true logician, to have as well judgment as invention, he may do great matters; especially if the times be fit. He that resteth upon gains certain, shall hardly grow to great riches; and he that puts all upon adventures, doth oftentimes break and come to poverty: it is good therefore to guard adventures with certainties, that may uphold losses. Monopolies, and coemption of wares for re-sale, where they are not restrained, are great means to enrich; especially if the party have intelligence what things are like to come into request, and so store himself beforehand. Riches gotten by service, though it be of the best rise, yet when they are gotten by flattery, feeding humours, and other servile conditions, they may be placed amongst the worst. As for fishing for testaments and executorships (as Tacitus saith of Seneca, *testamenta et orbos tamquam indagine capi,* [*wills and childless couples are caught with a net]) it is yet worse; by how much men submit themselves to meaner persons than in service. Believe not much them that seem to despise riches; for they despise them that despair of them; and none worse when they come to them. Be not penny-wise; riches have wings, and sometimes they fly away of themselves, sometimes they must be set flying to bring in more. Men leave their riches either to their kindred, or to the public; and moderate portions prosper best in both. A great state left to an heir, is as a lure to all the birds of prey round about to seize on him, if he be not the better stablished in years and judgment. Likewise glorious[3] gifts and foundations are like *sacrifices without salt;* and but the painted sepulchres of alms, which soon will putrefy and corrupt inwardly. Therefore measure not thine advancements by quantity, but frame them by measure: and defer not charities till death; for, certainly, if a man weigh it rightly, he that doth so is rather liberal of another man's than of his own.

35

OF PROPHECIES

I MEAN not to speak of divine prophecies; nor of heathen oracles; nor of natural predictions; but only of prophecies that have been of certain memory, and from hidden causes. Saith the Pythonissa to Saul, *To-morrow thou and thy son shall be with me.* Homer hath these verses:

> At domus Æneæ cunctis dominabitur oris,
> Et nati natorum, et qui nascentur ab illis.

[The house of Æneas shall reign in all lands, and his children's children, and their generations.] A prophecy, as it seems, of the Roman empire. Seneca the tragedian hath these verses:

> ———— Venient annis
> Sæcula seris, quibus Oceanus
> Vincula rerum laxet, et ingens
> Pateat Tellus, Tiphysque novos
> Detegat orbes; nec sit terris
> Ultima Thule:

[There shall come a time when the bands of ocean shall be loosened, and the vast earth shall be laid open; another Tiphys shall disclose new worlds, and lands shall be seen beyond Thule:] a prophecy of the discovery of America. The daughter of Polycrates dreamed that Jupiter bathed her father, and Apollo anointed him; and it came to pass that he was crucified in an open place, where the sun made his body run with sweat, and the rain washed it. Philip of Macedon dreamed he sealed up his wife's belly; whereby he did expound it, that his wife should be barren; but Aristander the soothsayer told him his wife was with child, because men do not use to seal vessels that are empty. A phantasm that appeared to M. Brutus in his tent, said to him, *Philippis iterum me videbis:* [Thou shalt see me again at Philippi.] Tiberius said to Galba, *Tu quoque, Galba, degustabis imperium:* [Thou likewise shall taste of empire.] In Vespasian's time, there went a prophecy in the East, that those that should come forth of Judea should reign over the world: which though it may be was meant of our Saviour, yet Tacitus expounds it of Vespasian. Domitian dreamed, the night before he was slain, that a golden head was growing out of the nape of his neck: and indeed the succession that followed him, for many years, made golden times. Henry the Sixth of England said of Henry the Seventh, when he was a lad, and gave him water, *This is the lad that shall enjoy the crown for which we strive.* When I was in France, I heard from one Dr. Pena, that the Queen Mother, who was given to curious arts, caused the King her husband's nativity to be calculated, under a false name; and the astrologer gave a judgment, that he should be killed in a duel; at which the Queen laughed, thinking her husband to be above challenges and duels: but he was slain upon a course at tilt, the splinters of the staff of Montgomery going in at his beaver. The trivial prophecy, which I heard when I was a child, and queen Elizabeth was in the flower of her years, was,

> When hempe is sponne
> England's done:

whereby it was generally conceived, that after the princes had reigned which had the principial letters of that word *hempe* (which were Henry, Edward, Mary, Philip, and Elizabeth), England should come to utter confusion; which, thanks be to God, is verified only in the change of the name; for that the King's style[1] is now no more of England, but of Britain. There was also another prophecy, before the year of eighty-eight, which I do not well understand.

> There shall be seen upon a day,
> Between the Baugh and the May,
> The black fleet of Norway.
> When that that is come and gone,
> England build houses of lime and stone,
> For after wars shall you have none.

It was generally conceived to be meant of the Spanish fleet that came in eighty-eight: for that the king of Spain's surname, as they say, is Norway. The prediction of Regiomontanus,

> Octogesimus octavus mirabilis annus,[2]

was thought likewise accomplished in the sending of that great fleet, being the greatest in strength, though not in number, of all that ever swam upon the sea. As for Cleon's dream, I think it was a jest. It was, that he was devoured of a long dragon; and it was expounded of a maker of sausages, that troubled him exceedingly. There are numbers of the like kind; especially if you include dreams, and predictions of astrology. But I have set down these few only of certain credit, for example. My judgment is, that they ought all to be despised; and ought to serve but for winter talk by the fireside. Though when I say *despised*, I mean it as for belief; for otherwise, the spreading or publishing of them is in no sort to be despised. For they have done much mischief; and I see many severe laws made to suppress them. That that hath given them grace, and some credit, consisteth in three things. First, that men mark when they hit, and never mark when they miss; as they do generally also of dreams. The second is, that probable conjectures, or obscure traditions, many times turn themselves into prophecies; while the nature of man, which coveteth divination, thinks it no peril to foretell that which indeed they do but collect.[3] As that of Seneca's verse. For so much was then subject to demonstration, that the globe of the earth had great parts beyond the Atlantic, which mought be probably conceived not to be all sea: and adding thereto the tradition in Plato's Timæus, and his Atlanticus, it mought encourage one to turn it to a prediction. The third and last (which is the great one) is, that almost all of them, being infinite in number, have been impostures, and by idle and crafty brains merely contrived and feigned after the event past.

36
OF AMBITION

AMBITION is like choler;[1] which is an humour that maketh men active, earnest, full of alacrity, and stirring, if it be not stopped. But if it be stopped, and cannot have his way, it becometh adust,[2] and thereby malign and venomous. So ambitious men, if they find the way open for their rising, and still get forward, they are rather busy than dangerous; but if they be checked in their desires, they become secretly discontent, and look upon men and matters with an evil eye, and are best pleased when things go backward; which is the worst property in a servant of a prince or state. Therefore it is good for princes, if they use ambitious men, to handle it so as they be still progressive and not retrograde; which because it cannot be without inconvenience, it is good not to use such natures at all. For if they rise not with their service, they will take order to make their service fall with them. But since we have said it were good not to use men of ambitious natures, except it be upon necessity, it is fit we speak in what cases they are of necessity. Good commanders in the wars must be taken, be they never so ambitious; for the use of their service dispenseth with the rest; and to take a soldier without ambition is to pull off his spurs. There is also great use of ambitious men in being screens to princes in matters of danger and envy; for no man will take that part, except he be like a seeled[3] dove, that mounts and mounts because he cannot see about him. There is use also of ambitious men in pulling down the greatness of any subject that overtops; as Tiberius used Macro in the pulling down of Sejanus. Since therefore they must be used in such cases, there resteth to speak how they are to be bridled, that they may be less dangerous. There is less danger of them if they be of mean birth, than if they be noble; and if they be rather harsh of nature, than gracious and popular: and if they be rather new raised, than grown cunning and fortified in their greatness. It is counted by some a weakness in princes to have favourites; but it is of all others the best remedy against ambitious great-ones. For when the way of pleasuring and displeasuring lieth by the favourite, it is impossible any other should be over-great. Another means to curb them, is to balance them by others as proud as they. But then there must be some middle counsellors, to keep things steady; for without that ballast the ship will roll too much. At the least, a prince may animate and inure some meaner persons, to be as it were scourges to ambitious men. As for the having of them obnoxious[4] to ruin; if they be of fearful natures, it may do well; but if they be stout and daring, it may precipitate their designs, and prove dangerous. As for the pulling of them down, if the affairs require it, and that it may not be done with safety suddenly, the only way is, the interchange continually of favours and disgraces; whereby they may not know what to expect, and be as it were in a wood. Of ambitions, it is less harmful, the ambition to prevail in great things, than that other to appear in every thing; for that breeds confusion, and mars business. But yet it is less danger to have an ambitious man stirring in business, than great in dependances. He that seeketh to be eminent amongst able men hath a great task; but that is ever good for the public. But he that plots to be the only figure amongst ciphers is the decay of a whole age. Honour hath three things in it; the vantage ground to do good; the approach to kings and principal persons; and the raising of a man's own fortunes. He that hath the best of these intentions, when he aspireth, is an honest man; and that prince that can discern of these intentions in another that aspireth, is a wise prince. Generally, let princes and states choose such ministers as are more sensible of duty than of rising; and such as love business rather upon conscience than upon bravery;[5] and let them discern a busy nature from a willing mind.

37

OF MASQUES AND TRIUMPHS[1]

THESE things are but toys, to come amongst such serious observations. But yet, since princes will have such things, it is better they should be graced with elegancy than daubed with cost. Dancing to song, is a thing of great state and pleasure. I understand it, that the song be in quire, placed aloft, and accompanied with some broken music;[2] and the ditty fitted to the device. Acting in song, especially in dialogues, hath an extreme good grace; I say acting, not dancing (for that is a mean and vulgar thing); and the voices of the dialogue would be strong and manly, (a base and a tenor; no treble;) and the ditty high and tragical; not nice or dainty. Several quires, placed one over against another, and taking the voice by catches,[3] anthem-wise, give great pleasure. Turning dances into figure[4] is a childish curiosity. And generally let it be noted, that those things which I here set down are such as do naturally take the sense, and not respect petty wonderments. It is true, the alterations of scenes, so it be quietly and without noise, are things of great beauty and pleasure; for they feed and relieve the eye, before it be full of the same object. Let the scenes abound with light, specially coloured and varied; and let the masquers, or any other, that are to come down from the scene, have some motions upon the scene itself before their coming down; for it draws the eye strangely, and makes it with great pleasure to desire to see that it cannot perfectly discern. Let the songs be loud and cheerful, and not chirpings or pulings. Let the music likewise be sharp and loud, and well placed. The colours that shew best by candle-light, are white, carnation, and a kind of sea-water-green; and oes, or spangs,[5] as they are of no great cost, so they are of most glory. As for rich embroidery, it is lost and not discerned. Let the suits of the masquers be graceful, and such as become the person when the vizards are off; not after examples of known attires; Turks, soldiers, mariners, and the like. Let anti-masques[6] not be long; they have been commonly of fools, satyrs, baboons, wild-men, antics, beasts, sprites, witches, Ethiops, pigmies, turquets,[7] nymphs, rustics, Cupids, statua's moving, and the like. As for angels, it is not comical enough to put them in anti-masques; and any thing that is hideous, as devils, giants, is on the other side as unfit. But chiefly, let the music of them be recreative, and with some strange changes. Some sweet odours suddenly coming forth, without any drops falling, are, in such a company as there is steam and heat, things of great pleasure and refreshment. Double masques, one of men, another of ladies, addeth state and variety. But all is nothing except the room be kept clear and neat.

For justs, and tourneys, and barriers;[8] the glories of them are chiefly in the chariots, wherein the challengers make their entry; especially if they be drawn with strange beasts: as lions, bears, camels, and the like; or in the devices of their entrance; or in the bravery of their liveries; or in the goodly furniture of their horses and armour. But enough of these toys.

38

OF NATURE IN MEN

NATURE is often hidden; sometimes overcome; seldom extinguished. Force maketh nature more violent in the return; doctrine and discourse maketh nature less importune; but custom only doth alter and subdue nature. He that seeketh victory over his nature, let him not set himself too great nor too small tasks; for the first will make him dejected by often failings; and the second will make him a small proceeder, though by often prevailings. And at the first let him practise with helps, as swimmers do with bladders or rushes; but after a time let him practise with disadvantages, as dancers do with thick shoes. For it breeds great perfection, if the practice be harder than the use. Where nature is mighty, and therefore the victory hard, the degrees had need be, first to stay and arrest nature in time; like to him that would say over the four and twenty letters when he was angry; then to go less in quantity; as if one should, in forbearing wine, come from drinking healths to a draught at a meal; and lastly, to discontinue altogether. But if a man have the fortitude and resolution to enfranchise himself at once, that is the best:

> Optimus ille animi vindex lædentia pectus
> Vincula qui rupit, dedoluitque semel.

> [Wouldst thou be free? The chains that gall thy breast
> With one strong effort burst, and be at rest.]

Neither is the ancient rule amiss, to bend nature as a wand to a contrary extreme, whereby to set it right; understanding it, where the contrary extreme is no vice. Let not a man force a habit upon himself with a perpetual continuance, but with some intermission. For both the pause reinforceth the new onset; and if a man that is not perfect be ever in practice, he shall as well practise his errors as his abilities, and induce one habit of both; and there is no means to help this but by seasonable intermissions. But let not a man trust his victory over his nature too far; for nature will lay buried a great time, and yet revive upon the occasion or temptation. Like as it was with Æsop's damsel, turned from a cat to a woman, who sat very demurely at the board's end, till a mouse ran before her. Therefore let a man either avoid the occasion altogether; or put himself often to it, that he may be little moved with it. A man's nature is best perceived in privateness, for there is no affectation; in passion, for that putteth a man out of his precepts; and in a new case or experiment, for there custom leaveth him. They are happy men whose natures sort with their vocations; otherwise they may say, *multum incola fuit anima mea,* [my soul hath been a stranger and a sojourner;] when they converse in those things they do not affect.[1] In studies, whatsoever a man commandeth upon himself, let him set hours for it; but whatsoever is agreeable to his nature, let him take no care for any set times; for his thoughts will fly to it of themselves; so as the spaces of other business or studies will suffice. A man's nature runs either to herbs or weeds; therefore let him seasonably water the one, and destroy the other.

39

OF CUSTOM AND EDUCATION

MEN's thoughts are much according to their inclination; their discourse and speeches according to their learning and infused opinions; but their deeds are after as they have been accustomed. And therefore as Machiavel well noteth (though in an evil-favoured instance,) there is no trusting to the force of nature nor to the bravery of words, except it be corroborate by custom. His instance is, that for the achieving of a desperate conspiracy, a man should not rest upon the fierceness of any man's nature, or his resolute undertakings; but take such an one as hath had his hands formerly in blood. But Machiavel knew not of a friar Clement,[1] nor a Ravillac, nor a Jaureguy, nor a Baltazar Gerard; yet his rule holdeth still, that nature, nor the engagement of words, are not so forcible as custom. Only superstition is now so well advanced, that men of the first blood[2] are as firm as butchers by occupation; and votary resolution[3] is made equipollent to custom even in matter of blood. In other things the predominancy of custom is every where visible; insomuch as a man would wonder to hear men profess, protest, engage, give great words, and then do just as they have done before; as if they were dead images, and engines moved only by the wheels of custom. We see also the reign or tyranny of custom, what it is. The Indians (I mean the sect of their wise men[4]) lay themselves quietly upon a stack of wood, and so sacrifice themselves by fire. Nay the wives strive to be burned with the corpses of their husbands. The lads of Sparta, of ancient time, were wont to be scourged upon the altar of Diana, without so much as queching.[5] I remember, in the beginning of Queen Elizabeth's time of England, an Irish rebel condemned, put up a petition to the Deputy that he might be hanged in a with,[6] and not in an halter; because it had been so used with former rebels. There be monks in Russia, for penance, that will sit a whole night in a vessel of water, till they be engaged with hard ice. Many examples may be put of the force of custom, both upon mind and body. Therefore, since custom is the principal magistrate of man's life, let men by all means endeavour to obtain good customs. Certainly custom is most perfect when it beginneth in young years: this we call education; which is, in effect, but an early custom. So we see, in languages the tongue is more pliant to all expressions and sounds, the joints are more supple to all feats of activity and motions, in youth than afterwards. For it is true that late learners cannot so well take the ply; except it be in some minds that have not suffered themselves to fix, but have kept themselves open and prepared to receive continual amendment, which is exceeding rare. But if the force of custom simple and separate be great, the force of custom copulate and conjoined and collegiate is far greater. For there example teacheth, company comforteth, emulation quickeneth, glory raiseth: so as in such places the force of custom is in his exaltation. Certainly the great multiplication of virtues upon human nature resteth upon societies well ordained and disciplined. For commonwealths and good governments do nourish virtue grown, but do not much mend the seeds. But the misery is, that the most effectual means are now applied to the ends least to be desired.

40

Of Fortune

It cannot be denied, but outward accidents conduce much to fortune; favour, opportunity, death of others, occasion fitting virtue. But chiefly, the mould of a man's fortune is in his own hands. *Faber quisque fortunæ suæ* [*every man is the architect of his own fortune], saith the poet. And the most frequent of external causes is, that the folly of one man is the fortune of another. For no man prospers so suddenly as by others' errors. *Serpens nisi serpentem comederit non fit draco.* [A serpent must have eaten another serpent, before he can become a dragon.] Overt and apparent virtues bring forth praise; but there be secret and hidden virtues that bring forth fortune; certain deliveries of a man's self, which have no name. The Spanish name, *desemboltura*,[1] partly expresseth them; when there be not stonds[2] nor restiveness in a man's nature; but that the wheels of his mind keep way with the wheels of his fortune. For so Livy (after he had described Cato Major in these words, *In illo viro tantum robur corporis et animi fuit, ut quocunque loco natus esset, fortunam sibi facturus videretur*) [Such was his strength of body and mind, that wherever he had been born he could have made himself a fortune;] falleth upon that, that he had *versatile ingenium:* [a wit that could turn well.] Therefore if a man look sharply and attentively, he shall see Fortune: for though she be blind, yet she is not invisible. The way of fortune is like the milken way in the sky; which is a meeting or knot of a number of small stars; not seen asunder, but giving light together. So are there a number of little and scarce discerned virtues, or rather faculties and customs, that make men fortunate. The Italians note some of them, such as a man would little think. When they speak of one that cannot do amiss, they will throw in into his other conditions, that he hath *Poco di matto* [*a little of the fool]. And certainly there be not two more fortunate properties, than to have a little of the fool, and not too much of the honest. Therefore extreme lovers of their country or masters were never fortunate, neither can they be. For when a man placeth his thoughts without himself, he goeth not his own way. An hasty fortune maketh an enterpriser and remover; (the French hath it better, *enterprenant*, or *remuant;*) but the exercised fortune maketh the able man. Fortune is to be honoured and respected, and it be but for her daughters, Confidence and Reputation. For those two felicity breedeth; the first within a man's self, the latter in others towards him. All wise men, to decline the envy of their own virtues, use to ascribe them to Providence and Fortune; for so they may the better assume them: and, besides, it is greatness in a man to be the care of the higher powers. So Cæsar said to the pilot in the tempest, *Cæsarem portas, et fortunam ejus:* [You carry Cæsar and his fortune.] So Sylla chose the name of *Felix* [*Fortunate], and not of *Magnus* [*Great]. And it hath been noted, that those who ascribe openly too much to their own wisdom and policy, end infortunate. It is written that Timotheus the Athenian, after he had, in the account he gave to the state of his government, often interlaced this speech, *and in this Fortune had no part,* never prospered in any thing he undertook afterwards. Certainly there be, whose fortunes are like Homer's verses, that have a slide and easiness more than the verses of other poets; as Plutarch saith of Timoleon's fortune, in respect of[3] that of Agesilaus or Epaminondas. And that this should be, no doubt it is much in a man's self.

41

OF USURY[1]

MANY have made witty invectives against Usury. They say that it is a pity the devil should have God's part, which is the tithe.[2] That the usurer is the greatest sabbath-breaker, because his plough goeth every Sunday. That the usurer is the drone that Virgil speaketh of;

Ignavum fucos pecus a præsepibus arcent.
[*They drive the lazy swarm of drones from the hive.]

That the userer breaketh the first law that was made for mankind after the fall, which was, *in sudore vultûs tui comedes panem tuum;* not, *in sudore vultûs alieni;* [in the sweat of thy face shalt thou eat bread—not in the sweat of another's face.] That usurers should have orange-tawny bonnets,[3] because they do judaize. That it is against nature for money to beget money; and the like. I say this only, that usury is a *concessum propter duritiem cordis:* [a thing allowed by reason of the hardness of men's hearts:] for since there must be borrowing and lending, and men are so hard of heart as they will not lend freely, usury must be permitted. Some others[4] have made suspicious and cunning propositions of banks, discovery of men's estates, and other inventions. But few have spoken of usury usefully. It is good to set before us the incommodities and commodities of usury, that the good may be either weighed out or culled out; and warily to provide, that while we make forth to that which is better, we meet not with that which is worse.

The discommodities of usury are, First, that it makes fewer merchants. For were it not for this lazy trade of usury, money would not lie still, but would in great part be employed upon merchandizing; which is the *vena porta*[5] of wealth in a state. The second, that it makes poor merchants. For as a farmer cannot husband his ground so well if he sit at a great rent; so the merchant cannot drive his trade so well, if he sit at great usury. The third is incident to the other two; and that is the decay of customs of kings or states, which ebb or flow with merchandizing. The fourth, that it bringeth the treasure of a realm or state into a few hands. For the usurer being at certainties, and others at uncertainties, at the end of the game most of the money will be in the box; and ever a state flourisheth when wealth is more equally spread. The fifth, that it beats down the price of land; for the employment of money is chiefly either merchandizing or purchasing; and usury waylays both. The sixth, that it doth dull and damp all industries, improvements, and new inventions, wherein money would be stirring, if it were not for this slug. The last, that it is the canker and ruin of many men's estates; which in process of time breeds a public poverty.

On the other side, the commodities of usury are, first, that howsoever usury in some respect hindereth merchandizing, yet in some other it advanceth it; for it is certain that the greatest part of trade is driven by young merchants, upon borrowing at interest; so as if the usurer either call in or keep back his money, there will ensue presently a great stand of trade. The second is, that were it not for this easy borrowing upon interest, men's necessities would draw upon them a most sudden undoing; in that they would be forced to sell their means (be it lands or goods) far under foot; and so, whereas usury doth but gnaw upon them, bad markets would swallow them quite up. As for mortgaging or pawning, it will little mend the matter: for either men will not take pawns without use; or if they do, they will look precisely for the forfeiture. I remember a cruel monied man in the country, that would say, The devil take this usury, it keeps us from forfeitures of mortgages and bonds. The third and last is, that it is a vanity to conceive that there would be ordinary borrowing without profit; and it is impossible to conceive the number of inconveniences that will ensue, if borrowing be cramped. Therefore to speak of the abolishing of usury is idle. All states have ever had it, in one kind or rate, or other. So as that opinion must be sent to Utopia.

To speak now of the reformation and reiglement of usury; how the discommodities of it may be best avoided, and the commodities retained. It appears by the balance of commodities and discommodities of usury, two things are to be reconciled. The one, that the tooth of usury be grinded, that it bite not too much; the other, that there be left open a means to invite monied men to lend to the merchants, for the continuing and quickening of trade. This cannot be done, except you introduce two several sorts of usury, a less and a greater. For if you reduce usury to one low rate, it will ease the common borrower, but the merchant will be to seek for money. And it is to be noted, that the trade of merchandize, being the most lucrative, may bear usury at a good rate: other contracts not so.

To serve both intentions, the way would be briefly thus. That there be two rates of usury; the one free, and general for all; the other under licence only, to certain persons and in certain places of merchandizing. First therefore, let usury in general be reduced to five in the hundred;[6] and let that rate be proclaimed to be free and current; and let the state shut itself out to take any penalty for the same. This will preserve borrowing from any general stop or dryness. This will ease infinite borrowers in the country. This will, in good part, raise the price of land,[7] because land purchased at sixteen years' purchase will yield six in the hundred, and somewhat more; whereas this rate of interest yields but five. This by like reason will encourage and edge industrious and profitable improvements; because many will rather venture in that kind than take five in the hundred, especially having been used to greater profit. Secondly, let there be certain persons licensed to lend to known merchants upon usury at a higher rate; and let it be with the cautions following. Let the rate be, even with the merchant himself, somewhat more easy than that he used formerly to pay; for by that means all borrowers shall have some ease by this reformation, be he merchant, or whosoever. Let it be no bank or common stock, but every man be master of his own money. Not that I altogether mislike banks, but they will hardly be brooked, in regard of certain suspicions. Let the state be answered some small matter for the licence, and the rest left to the lender; for if the abatement be but small, it will no whit discourage the lender. For he, for example, that took before ten or nine in the hundred, will sooner descend to eight in the hundred, than give over his trade of usury, and go from certain gains to gains of hazard. Let these licensed lenders be in number indefinite, but restrained to certain principal cities and towns of merchandizing; for then they will be hardly able to colour other men's monies[8] in the country: so as the licence of nine will not suck away the current rate of five; for no man will lend his monies far off, nor put them into unknown hands.

If it be objected that this doth in a sort authorize usury, which before was in some places but permissive; the answer is, that it is better to mitigate usury by declaration, than to suffer it to rage by connivance.

42

Of Youth and Age

A MAN that is young in years may be old in hours, if he have lost no time. But that happeneth rarely. Generally, youth is like the first cogitations, not so wise as the second. For there is a youth in thoughts, as well as in ages. And yet the invention of young men is more lively than that of old; and imaginations stream into their minds better, and as it were more divinely. Natures that have much heat and great and violent desires and perturbations, are not ripe for action till they have passed the meridian of their years; as it was with Julius Cæsar, and Septimius Severus. Of the latter of whom it is said, *Juventutem egit erroribus, imo furoribus, plenam;* [He passed a youth full of errors, yea of madnesses.] And yet he was the ablest emperor, almost, of all the list. But reposed natures may do well in youth. As it is seen in Augustus Cæsar, Cosmus[1] Duke of Florence, Gaston de Fois, and others. On the other side, heat and vivacity in age is an excellent composition for business. Young men are fitter to invent than to judge; fitter for execution than for counsel; and fitter for new projects than for settled business. For the experience of age, in things that fall within the compass of it, directeth them; but in new things, abuseth them. The errors of young men are the ruin of business; but the errors of aged men amount but to this, that more might have been done, or sooner. Young men, in the conduct and manage of actions, embrace more than they can hold; stir more than they can quiet; fly to the end, without consideration of the means and degrees; pursue some few principles which they have chanced upon absurdly; care not to innovate,[2] which draws unknown inconveniences; use extreme remedies at first; and that which doubleth all errors, will not acknowledge or retract them; like an unready horse, that will neither stop not turn. Men of age object too much, consult too long, adventure too little, repent too soon, and seldom drive business home to the full period, but content themselves with a mediocrity of success. Certainly it is good to compound employments of both; for that will be good for the present, because the virtues of either age may correct the defects of both; and good for succession, that young men may be learners, while men in age are actors; and, lastly, good for extern accidents, because authority followeth old men, and favour and popularity youth. But for the moral part, perhaps youth will have the pre-eminence, as age hath for the politic. A certain rabbin, upon the text, *Your young men shall see visions, and your old men shall dream dreams,* inferreth that young men are admitted nearer to God than old, because vision is a clearer revelation than a dream. And certainly, the more a man drinketh of the world, the more it intoxicateth: and age doth profit rather in the powers of understanding, than in the virtues of the will and affections. There be some have an over-early ripeness in their years, which fadeth betimes. These are, first, such as have brittle wits, the edge whereof is soon turned; such as was Hermogenes[3] the rhetorician, whose books are exceeding subtle; who afterwards waxed stupid. A second sort is of those that have some natural dispositions which have better grace in youth than in age; such as is a fluent and luxuriant speech; which becomes youth well, but not age: so Tully saith of Hortensius, *Idem manebat, neque idem decebat:* [He continued the same, when the same was not becoming.] The third is of such as take too high a strain at the first, and are magnanimous more than tract of years can uphold. As was Scipio Africanus, of whom Livy saith in effect, *Ultima primis cedebant:* [His last actions were not equal to his first.]

43
Of Beauty

Virtue is like a rich stone, best plain set; and surely virtue is best in a body that is comely, though not of delicate features; and that hath rather dignity of presence, than beauty of aspect. Neither is it almost[1] seen, that very beautiful persons are otherwise of great virtue; as if nature were rather busy not to err, than in labour to produce excellency. And therefore they prove accomplished, but not of great spirit; and study rather behaviour than virtue. But this holds not always: for Augustus Cæsar, Titus Vespasianus, Philip le Bel of France, Edward the Fourth of England, Alcibiades of Athens, Ismael the Sophy of Persia, were all high and great spirits; and yet the most beautiful men of their times. In beauty, that of favour[2] is more than that of colour; and that of decent and gracious motion[3] more than that of favour. That is the best part of beauty, which a picture cannot express; no nor the first sight of life. There is no excellent beauty that hath not some strangeness in the proportion. A man cannot tell whether Apelles or Albert Durer were the more trifler; whereof the one would make a personage by geometrical proportions; the other, by taking the best parts out of divers faces, to make one excellent. Such personages, I think, would please nobody but the painter that made them. Not but I think a painter may make a better face than ever was; but he must do it by a kind of felicity, (as a musician that maketh an excellent air in music,) and not by rule. A man shall see faces, that if you examine them part by part, you shall find never a good; and yet altogether do well. If it be true that the principal part of beauty is in decent motion, certainly it is no marvel though persons in years seem many times more amiable; *pulchrorum autumnus pulcher;* [beautiful persons have a beautiful Autumn;] for no youth can be comely but by pardon,[4] and considering the youth as to make up the comeliness. Beauty is as summer fruits, which are easy to corrupt, and cannot last; and for the most part it makes a dissolute youth, and an age a little out of countenance; but yet certainly again, if it light well, it maketh virtue shine, and vices blush.

44

OF DEFORMITY

DEFORMED persons are commonly even with nature; for as nature hath done ill by them, so do they by nature; being for the most part (as the Scripture saith) *void of natural affection;* and so they have their revenge of nature. Certainly there is a consent between the body and the mind; and where nature erreth in the one, she ventureth in the other. *Ubi peccat in uno, periclitatur in altero.* But because there is in man an election touching the frame of his mind, and a necessity in the frame of his body, the stars of natural inclination are sometimes obscured by the sun of discipline and virtue. Therefore it is good to consider of deformity, not as a sign, which is more deceivable; but as a cause, which seldom faileth of the effect. Whosoever hath any thing fixed in his person that doth induce contempt, hath also a perpetual spur in himself to rescue and deliver himself from scorn. Therefore all deformed persons are extreme bold. First, as in their own defence, as being exposed to scorn; but in process of time by a general habit. Also it stirreth in them industry, and especially of this kind, to watch and observe the weakness of others, that they may have somewhat to repay. Again, in their superiors, it quencheth jealousy towards them, as persons that they think they may at pleasure despise: and it layeth their competitors and emulators asleep; as never believing they should be in possibility of advancement, till they see them in possession. So that upon the matter, in a great wit, deformity is an advantage to rising. Kings in ancient times (and at this present in some countries) were wont to put great trust in eunuchs; because they that are envious towards all are more obnoxious and officious[1] towards one. But yet their trust towards them hath rather

been as to good spials and good whisperers, than good
magistrates and officers. And much like is the reason of deformed persons. Still the ground is, they will, if they be of
spirit, seek to free themselves from scorn; which must be
either by virtue or malice; and therefore let it not be marvelled if sometimes they prove excellent persons; as was
Agesilaus,[2] Zanger the son of Solyman, Æsop, Gasca President of Peru; and Socrates may go likewise amongst them;
with others.

45

OF BUILDING

HOUSES are built to live in, and not to look on; therefore let
use be preferred before uniformity, except where both may
be had. Leave the goodly fabrics of houses, for beauty only,
to the enchanted palaces of the poets; who build them with
small cost. He that builds a fair house upon an ill seat,[1] com-
mitteth himself to prison. Neither do I reckon it an ill seat
only where the air is unwholesome; but likewise where the
air is unequal; as you shall see many fine seats set upon a
knap[2] of ground, environed with higher hills round about it;
whereby the heat of the sun is pent in, and the wind gathereth as in troughs; so as you shall have, and that suddenly,
as great diversity of heat and cold as if you dwelt in several
places. Neither is it ill air only that maketh an ill seat, but
ill ways, ill markets: and, if you will consult with Momus,[3]
ill neighbours. I speak not of many more; want of water;
want of wood, shade, and shelter; want of fruitfulness, and
mixture of grounds of several natures; want of prospect;
want of level grounds; want of places at some near distance
for sports of hunting, hawking, and races; too near the sea,
too remote; [not] having the commodity of navigable rivers,
or the discommodity of their overflowing; too far off from
great cities, which may hinder business, or too near them,
which lurcheth[4] all provisions, and maketh every thing dear;
where a man hath a great living laid together, and where he is
scanted: all which, as it is impossible perhaps to find to-

gether, so it is good to know them, and think of them, that a man may take as many as he can; and if he have several dwellings, that he sort them so, that what he wanteth in the one he may find in the other. Lucullus answered Pompey well; who, when he saw his stately galleries, and rooms so large and lightsome, in one of his houses, said, *Surely an excellent place for summer, but how do you in winter?* Lucullus answered, *Why, do you not think me as wise as some fowl are, that ever change their abode towards the winter?*

To pass from the seat to the house itself; we will do as Cicero doth in the orator's art; who writes books *De Oratore,* and a book he entitles *Orator;* whereof the former delivers the precepts of the art, and the latter the perfection. We will therefore describe a princely palace, making a brief model thereof. For it is strange to see, now in Europe, such huge buildings as the Vatican and Escurial and some others be, and yet scarce a very fair room in them.

First therefore, I say you cannot have a perfect palace, except you have two several sides; a side for the banquet, as is spoken of in the book of Hester, and a side for the household; the one for feasts and triumphs, and the other for dwelling. I understand both these sides to be not only returns,[5] but parts of the front; and to be uniform without, though severally partitioned within; and to be on both sides of a great and stately tower in the midst of the front, that, as it were, joineth them together on either hand. I would have on the side of the banquet, in front, one only goodly room above stairs, of some forty foot high; and under it a room for a dressing or preparing place at times of triumphs. On the other side, which is the household side, I wish it divided at the first into a hall and a chapel, (with a partition between;) both of good state and bigness; and those not to go all the length, but to have at the further end a winter and a summer parlour, both fair. And under these rooms, a fair and large cellar sunk under ground; and likewise some privy kitchens, with butteries and pantries, and the like. As for the tower, I would have it two stories, of eighteen foot high a piece, above the two wings; and a goodly leads upon the

top, railed with statua's interposed; and the same tower to
be divided into rooms, as shall be thought fit. The stairs
likewise to the upper rooms, let them be upon a fair open
newel,[6] and finely railed in with images of wood, cast into a
brass colour; and a very fair landing-place at the top. But
this to be, if you do not point any of the lower rooms for a
dining place of servants. For otherwise you shall have the
servants' dinner after your own: for the steam of it will
come up as in a tunnel. And so much for the front. Only I
understand the height of the first stairs to be sixteen foot,
which is the height of the lower room.

Beyond this front is there to be a fair court, but three
sides of it, of a far lower building than the front. And in all
the four corners of that court fair stair-cases, cast into turrets, on the outside, and not within the row of buildings
themselves. But those towers are not to be of the height of
the front, but rather proportionable to the lower building.
Let the court not be paved, for that striketh up a great heat
in summer, and much cold in winter. But only some side
alleys, with a cross, and the quarters to graze, being kept
shorn, but not too near shorn. The row of return on the banquet side, let it be all stately galleries: in which galleries let
there be three, or five, fine cupolas in the length of it, placed
at equal distance; and fine coloured windows of several
works. On the household side, chambers of presence[7] and
ordinary entertainments, with some bed-chambers; and let
all three sides be a double house, without thorough lights on
the sides, that you may have rooms from the sun, both for
forenoon and afternoon. Cast it also, that you may have
rooms both for summer and winter; shady for summer, and
warm for winter. You shall have sometimes fair houses so
full of glass, that one cannot tell where to become to be out
of the sun or cold. For inbowed[8] windows, I hold them of
good use; (in cities, indeed, upright do better, in respect of
the uniformity towards the street;) for they be pretty retiring
places for conference; and besides, they keep both the wind
and sun off; for that which would strike almost thorough the
room doth scarce pass the window. But let them be but few,
four in the court, on the sides only.

Beyond this court, let there be an inward court, of the same square and height; which is to be environed with the garden on all sides; and in the inside, cloistered on all sides, upon decent and beautiful arches, as high as the first story. On the under story, towards the garden, let it be turned to a grotta, or place of shade, or estivation. And only have opening and windows towards the garden; and be level upon the floor, no whit sunken under ground, to avoid all dampishness. And let there be a fountain, or some fair work of statua's in the midst of this court; and to be paved as the other court was. These buildings to be for privy lodgings on both sides; and the end for privy galleries. Whereof you must foresee that one of them be for an infirmary, if the prince or any special person should be sick, with chambers, bed-chamber, antecamera, and recamera,[9] joining to it. This upon the second story. Upon the ground story, a fair gallery, open, upon pillars; and upon the third story likewise, an open gallery, upon pillars, to take the prospect and freshness of the garden. At both corners of the further side, by way of return, let there be two delicate or rich cabinets, daintily paved, richly hanged, glazed with crystalline glass, and a rich cupola in the midst; and all other elegancy that may be thought upon. In the upper gallery too, I wish that there may be, if the place will yield it, some fountains running in divers places from the wall, with some fine avoidances.[10] And thus much for the model of the palace; save that you must have, before you come to the front, three courts. A green court plain, with a wall about it; a second court of the same, but more garnished, with little turrets, or rather embellishments, upon the wall; and a third court, to make a square with the front, but not to be built, nor yet enclosed with a naked wall, but enclosed with tarrasses,[11] leaded aloft, and fairly garnished, on the three sides; and cloistered on the inside, with pillars, and not with arches below. As for offices, let them stand at distance, with some low galleries, to pass from them to the palace itself.

46

OF GARDENS

GOD ALMIGHTY first planted a Garden. And indeed it is the purest of human pleasures. It is the greatest refreshment to the spirits of man; without which buildings and palaces are but gross handyworks: and a man shall ever see that when ages grow to civility and elegancy, men come to build stately sooner than to garden finely; as if gardening were the greater perfection. I do hold it, in the royal ordering of gardens, there ought to be gardens for all the months in the year; in which severally things of beauty may be then in season. For December, and January, and the latter part of November, you must take such things as are green all winter: holly; ivy; bays; juniper; cypress-trees; yew; pine-apple-trees;[1] fir-trees; rosemary; lavender; periwinkle, the white, the purple, and the blue; germander; flags;[2] orange-trees; lemon-trees; and myrtles, if they be stoved;[3] and sweet marjoram, warm set.[4] There followeth, for the latter part of January and February, the mezereon-tree,[5] which then blossoms; crocus vernus, both the yellow and the grey; primroses; anemones; the early tulippa; hyacinthus orientalis; chamaïris;[6] fritellaria. For March, there come violets, specially the single blue, which are the earliest; the yellow daffodil; the daisy; the almond-tree in blossom; the peach-tree in blossom; the cornelian-tree in blossom; sweet-briar. In April follow, the double white violet; the wall-flower; the stock-gilliflower; the cowslip; flower-de-lices, and lilies of all natures; rosemary-flowers; the tulippa; the double piony; the pale daffodil; the French honeysuckle; the cherry-tree in blossom; the dammasin and plum-trees in blossom; the white thorn in leaf; the lilac-tree. In May and June come pinks of all sorts, specially the blush-pink; roses of all kinds, except the musk, which comes later; honey-suckles; strawberries; bugloss; columbine; the French marigold; flos Africanus; cherry-tree in fruit; ribes;[7] figs in fruit; rasps;[8] vine-flowers; lavender in flowers; the sweet satyrian, with the white flower; herba muscaria; lilium convallium; the apple-tree in blossom. In July come gilliflowers of all varieties; musk-roses; the lime-tree in blossom; early pears and plums in fruit; genitings, quadlins.[9] In August come plums of all sorts in fruit; pears; apricocks; berberries; filberds; musk-melons; monks-hoods, of all colours. In September come grapes; apples; poppies of all colours; peaches; melocotones;[10] nectarines; cornelians; wardens;[11] quinces. In October and the beginning of November come services; medlars; bullaces;[12] roses cut or removed to come late; holly-oaks; and such like. These particulars are for the climate of London; but my meaning is perceived, that you may have *ver perpetuum* [*eternal spring], as the place affords.

And because the breath of flowers is far sweeter in the air (where it comes and goes like the warbling of music) than in the hand, therefore nothing is more fit for that delight, than to know what be the flowers and plants that do best perfume the air. Roses, damask and red, are fast flowers of their smells; so that you may walk by a whole row of them, and find nothing of their sweetness; yea though it be in a morning's dew. Bays likewise yield no smell as they grow. Rosemary little; nor sweet marjoram. That which above all others yields the sweetest smell in the air, is the violet, specially the white double violet, which comes twice a year; about the middle of April, and about Bartholomew-tide. Next to that is the musk-rose. Then the strawberry-leaves dying, with a most excellent cordial smell. Then the flower of the vines; it is a little dust, like the dust of a bent,[13] which grows upon the cluster in the first coming forth. Then sweet-briar. Then wallflowers, which are very delightful to be set under a parlour or lower chamber window. Then pinks and gilliflowers, specially the matted pink and clove gilliflower. Then the flowers of the lime-tree. Then the honeysuckles, so they be somewhat afar off. Of bean-flowers I speak not, because they are field flowers. But those which perfume the air most delightfully, not passed by as the rest, but being trodden upon and crushed, are three; that is, burnet, wild-thyme, and watermints. Therefore you are to set whole alleys of them, to have the pleasure when you walk or tread.

For gardens (speaking of those which are indeed prince-like, as we have done of buildings), the contents ought not well to be under thirty acres of ground; and to be divided into three parts; a green in the entrance; a heath or desert in the going forth; and the main garden in the midst; besides alleys on both sides. And I like well that four acres of ground be assigned to the green; six to the heath; four and four to either side; and twelve to the main garden. The green hath two pleasures: the one, because nothing is more pleasant to the eye than green grass kept finely shorn; the other, because it will give you a fair alley in the midst, by which you may go in front upon a stately hedge, which is to enclose the garden. But because the alley will be long, and, in great heat of the year or day, you ought not to buy the shade in the garden by going in the sun thorough the green, therefore you are, of either side the green, to plant a covert alley, upon carpenter's work, about twelve foot in height, by which you may go in shade into the garden. As for the making of knots or figures with divers coloured earths, that they may lie under the windows of the house on that side which the garden stands, they be but toys: you may see as good sights many times in tarts. The garden is best to be square, encompassed on all the four sides with a stately arched hedge. The arches to be upon pillars of carpenter's work, of some ten foot high, and six foot broad; and the spaces between of the same dimension with the breadth of the arch. Over the arches let there be an entire hedge of some four foot high, framed also upon carpenter's work; and upon the upper hedge, over every arch, a little turret, with a belly, enough to receive a cage of birds: and over every space between the arches some other little figure, with broad plates of round coloured glass gilt, for the sun to play upon. But this hedge I intend to be raised upon a bank, not steep, but gently slope, of some six foot,

set all with flowers. Also I understand, that this square of
the garden should not be the whole breadth of the ground,
but to leave on either side ground enough for diversity of
side alleys; unto which the two covert alleys of the green
may deliver you. But there must be no alleys with hedges
at either end of this great enclosure; not at the hither end,
for letting your prospect upon[14] this fair hedge from the
green; nor at the further end, for letting your prospect from
the hedge through the arches upon the heath.

For the ordering of the ground within the great hedge,
I leave it to variety of device; advising nevertheless that
whatsoever form you cast it into, first, it be not too busy, or
full of work. Wherein I, for my part, do not like images
cut out in juniper or other garden stuff; they be for children. Little low hedges, round, like welts, with some pretty
pyramides, I like well; and in some places, fair columns
upon frames of carpenter's work. I would also have the
alleys spacious and fair. You may have closer alleys upon
the side grounds, but none in the main garden. I wish also,
in the very middle, a fair mount, with three ascents, and
alleys, enough for four to walk abreast; which I would
have to be perfect circles, without any bulwarks or em-
bossments; and the whole mount to be thirty foot high;
and some fine banqueting-house, with some chimneys
neatly cast, and without too much glass.

For fountains, they are a great beauty and refreshment;
but pools mar all, and make the garden unwholesome, and
full of flies and frogs. Fountains I intend to be of two
natures: the one that sprinkleth or spouteth water; the
other a fair receipt of water, of some thirty or forty foot
square, but without fish, or slime, or mud. For the first, the
ornaments of images gilt, or of marble, which are in use,
do well: but the main matter is so to convey the water, as
it never stay, either in the bowls or in the cistern; that the
water be never by rest discoloured, green or red or the
like; or gather any mossiness or putrefaction. Besides that,
it is to be cleansed every day by the hand. Also some steps
up to it, and some fine pavement about it, doth well. As

for the other kind of fountain, which we may call a bathing pool, it may admit much curiosity and beauty; wherewith we will not trouble ourselves: as, that the bottom be finely paved, and with images; the sides likewise; and withal embellished with coloured glass, and such things of lustre; encompassed also with fine rails of low statua's. But the main point is the same which we mentioned in the former kind of fountain; which is, that the water be in perpetual motion, fed by a water higher than the pool, and delivered into it by fair spouts, and then discharged away under ground, by some equality of bores, that it stay little. And for fine devices, of arching water without spilling, and making it rise in several forms (of feathers, drinking glasses, canopies, and the like), they be pretty things to look on, but nothing to health and sweetness.

For the heath, which was the third part of our plot, I wish it to be framed, as much as may be, to a natural wildness. Trees I would have none in it, but some thickets made only of sweet-briar and honeysuckle, and some wild vine amongst; and the ground set with violets, strawberries, and primroses. For these are sweet, and prosper in the shade. And these to be in the heath, here and there, not in any order. I like also little heaps, in the nature of mole-hills (such as are in wild heaths), to be set, some with wild thyme; some with pinks; some with germander, that gives a good flower to the eye; some with periwinkle; some with violets; some with strawberries; some with cowslips; some with daisies; some with red roses; some with lilium convallium; some with sweet-williams red; some with bear's-foot: and the like low flowers, being withal sweet and sightly. Part of which heaps are to be with standards of little bushes pricked upon their top, and part without. The standards to be roses; juniper; holly; berberries; (but here and there, because of the smell of their blossom;) red currants; gooseberry; rosemary; bays; sweetbriar; and such like. But these standards to be kept with cutting, that they grow not out of course.

For the side grounds, you are to fill them with variety of

alleys, private, to give a full shade, some of them, wheresoever the sun be. You are to frame some of them likewise
for shelter, that when the wind blows sharp, you may walk
as in a gallery. And those alleys must be likewise hedged
at both ends, to keep out the wind; and these closer alleys
must be ever finely gravelled, and no grass, because of
going wet. In many of these alleys likewise, you are to set
fruit-trees of all sorts; as well upon the walls as in ranges.
And this would be generally observed, that the borders
wherein you plant your fruit-trees be fair and large, and
low, and not steep; and set with fine flowers, but thin and
sparingly, lest they deceive[15] the trees. At the end of both
the side grounds, I would have a mount of some pretty
height, leaving the wall of the enclosure breast high, to
look abroad into the fields.

For the main garden, I do not deny but there should be
some fair alleys ranged on both sides, with fruit trees; and
some pretty tufts of fruit trees, and arbours with seats, set
in some decent order; but these to be by no means set
too thick; but to leave the main garden so as it be not close,
but the air open and free. For as for shade, I would have
you rest upon the alleys of the side grounds, there to walk, if
you be disposed, in the heat of the year or day; but to make
account that the main garden is for the more temperate parts
of the year; and in the heat of summer, for the morning and
the evening, or overcast days.

For aviaries, I like them not, except they be of that
largeness as they may be turfed, and have living plants and
bushes set in them; that the birds may have more scope,
and natural nestling, and that no foulness appear in the
floor of the aviary. So I have made a platform of a princely
garden, partly by precept, partly by drawing, not a model,
but some general lines of it; and in this I have spared for
no cost. But it is nothing for great princes, that for the
most part taking advice with workmen, with no less cost
set their things together; and sometimes add statua's, and
such things, for state and magnificence, but nothing to the
true pleasure of a garden.

47

OF NEGOCIATING

IT is generally better to deal by speech than by letter; and
by the mediation of a third than by a man's self. Letters
are good, when a man would draw an answer by letter
back again; or when it may serve for a man's justification
afterwards to produce his own letter; or where it may be
danger to be interrupted, or heard by pieces. To deal in
person is good, when a man's face breedeth regard, as
commonly with inferiors; or in tender cases, where a man's
eye upon the countenance of him with whom he speaketh
may give him a direction how far to go; and generally,
where a man will reserve to himself liberty either to disavow or to expound. In choice of instruments, it is better
to choose men of a plainer sort, that are like to do that that
is committed to them, and to report back again faithfully
the success, than those that are cunning to contrive out of
other men's business somewhat to grace themselves, and
will help the matter in report for satisfaction sake. Use also
such persons as affect the business wherein they are employed; for that quickeneth much; and such as are fit for
the matter; as bold men for expostulation, fair-spoken men
for persuasion, crafty men for inquiry and observation,
froward and absurd men for business that doth not well
bear out itself. Use also such as have been lucky, and
prevailed before in things wherein you have employed
them; for that breeds confidence, and they will strive to
maintain their prescription. It is better to sound a person
with whom one deals afar off, than to fall upon the point
at first; except you mean to surprise him by some short
question. It is better dealing with men in appetite, than
with those that are where they would be. If a man deal
with another upon conditions, the start or first performance
is all; which a man cannot reasonably demand, except
either the nature of the thing be such, which must go
before; or else a man can persuade the other party that he

shall still need him in some other thing; or else that he be counted the honester man. All practice[1] is to discover, or to work. Men discover themselves in trust, in passion, at unawares, and of necessity, when they would have somewhat done and cannot find an apt pretext. If you would work any man, you must either know his nature and fashions, and so lead him; or his ends, and so persuade him; or his weakness and disadvantages, and so awe him; or those that have interest in him, and so govern him. In dealing with cunning persons, we must ever consider their ends, to interpret their speeches; and it is good to say little to them, and that which they least look for. In all negociations of difficulty, a man may not look to sow and reap at once; but must prepare business, and so ripen it by degrees.

48

OF FOLLOWERS AND FRIENDS

COSTLY followers are not to be liked; lest while a man maketh his train longer, he make his wings shorter. I reckon to be costly, not them alone which charge the purse, but which are wearisome and importune in suits. Ordinary followers ought to challenge no higher conditions than countenance, recommendation, and protection from wrongs. Factious followers are worse to be liked, which follow not upon affection to him with whom they range themselves, but upon discontentment conceived against some other; whereupon commonly ensueth that ill intelligence[1] that we many times see between great personages. Likewise glorious[2] followers, who make themselves as trumpets of the commendation of those they follow, are full of inconvenience; for they taint business through want of secrecy; and they export honour from a man, and make him a return in envy. There is a kind of followers likewise which are dangerous, being indeed espials; which inquire the secrets of the house, and bear tales of them to others. Yet such men, many times, are in great favour; for they are officious, and commonly exchange tales. The following by certain estates of men, answerable to that which a great person himself professeth, (as of soldiers to him that hath been employed in the wars, and the like,) hath ever been a thing civil, and well taken even in monarchies; so it be without too much pomp or popularity. But the most honourable kind of following is to be followed as one that apprehendeth to advance virtue and desert in all sorts of persons. And yet, where there is no eminent odds in sufficiency, it is better to take with the more passable, than with the more able. And besides, to speak truth, in base times active men are of more use than virtuous. It is true that in government it is good to use men of one rank equally: for to countenance some extraordinarily, is to make them insolent, and the rest discontent; because they may claim a due. But contrariwise, in favour, to use men with much difference and election is good; for it maketh the persons preferred more thankful, and the rest more officious: because all is of favour.³ It is good discretion not to make too much of any man at the first; because one cannot hold out that proportion. To be governed (as we call it) by one, is not safe; for it shews softness, and gives a freedom to scandal and disreputation; for those that would not censure or speak ill of a man immediately, will talk more boldly of those that are so great with them, and thereby wound their honour. Yet to be distracted with many is worse; for it makes men to be of the last impression,⁴ and full of change. To take advice of some few friends is ever honourable; *for lookers-on many times see more than gamesters; and the vale best discovereth the hill.* There is little friendship in the world, and least of all between equals, which was wont to be magnified. That that is, is between superior and inferior, whose fortunes may comprehend the one the other.

49

Of Suitors

MANY ill matters and projects are undertaken; and private suits do putrefy the public good. Many good matters are undertaken with bad minds; I mean not only corrupt minds, but crafty minds, that intend not performance. Some embrace suits, which never mean to deal effectually in them; but if they see there may be life in the matter by some other mean, they will be content to win a thank, or take a second reward, or at least to make use in the mean time of the suitor's hopes. Some take hold of suits only for an occasion to cross some other; or to make an information[1] whereof they could not otherwise have apt pretext; without care what become of the suit when that turn is served; or, generally, to make other men's business a kind of entertainment to bring in their own. Nay some undertake suits, with a full purpose to let them fall; to the end to gratify the adverse party or competitor. Surely there is in some sort a right in every suit; either a right in equity, if it be a suit of controversy; or a right of desert, if it be a suit of petition. If affection lead a man to favour the wrong side in justice, let him rather use his countenance to compound the matter than to carry it. If affection lead a man to favour the less worthy in desert, let him do it without depraving or disabling the better deserver. In suits which a man doth not well understand, it is good to refer them to some friend of trust and judgment, that may report whether he may deal in them with honour: but let him choose well his referendaries, for else he may be led by the nose. Suitors are so distasted with delays and abuses, that plain dealing in denying to deal in suits at first, and reporting the success barely, and in challenging no more thanks than one hath deserved, is grown not only honourable but also gracious. In suits of favour, the first coming ought to take little place: so far forth consideration may be had of his trust, that if intelligence of the matter could not otherwise have been had but by him, advantage be not taken of the note, but the party left to his other means; and in some sort recompensed for his discovery.[2] To be ignorant of the value of a suit is simplicity; as well as to be ignorant of the right thereof is want of conscience. Secrecy in suits is a great mean of obtaining; for voicing them to be in forwardness may discourage some kind of suitors, but doth quicken and awake others. But timing of the suit is the principal. Timing. I say, not only in respect of the person that should grant it, but in respect of those which are like to cross it. Let a man, in the choice of his mean, rather choose the fittest mean than the greatest mean; and rather them that deal in certain things, than those that are general. The reparation of a denial is sometimes equal to the first grant; if a man shew himself neither dejected nor discontented. *Iniquum petas ut æquum feras,* [Ask more than is reasonable, that you may get no less,] is a good rule, where a man hath strength of favour: but otherwise a man were better rise in his suit;[3] for he that would have ventured at first to have lost the suitor, will not in the conclusion lose both the suitor and his own former favour. Nothing is thought so easy a request to a great person, as his letter; and yet, if it be not in a good cause, it is so much out of his reputation. There are no worse instruments than these general contrivers of suits; for they are but a kind of poison and infection to public proceedings.

50

OF STUDIES

STUDIES serve for delight, for ornament, and for ability. Their chief use for delight, is in privateness and retiring; for ornament, is in discourse; and for ability, is in the judgment and disposition of business. For expert men can execute, and perhaps judge of particulars, one by one; but the general counsels, and the plots and marshalling of affairs, come best from those that are learned. To spend too much time in studies is sloth; to use them too much for ornament, is affectation; to make judgment wholly by their rules, is the humour of a scholar. They perfect nature, and are perfected by experience: for natural abilities are like natural plants, that need proyning[1] by study; and studies themselves do give forth directions too much at large, except they be bounded in by experience. Crafty men contemn studies, simple men admire them, and wise men use them; for they teach not their own use; but that is a wisdom without them, and above them, won by observation. Read not to contradict and confute; nor to believe and take for granted; nor to find talk and discourse; but to weigh and consider. Some books are to be tasted, others to be swallowed, and some few to be chewed and digested; that is, some books are to be read only in parts; others to be read, but not curiously; and some few to be read wholly, and with diligence and attention. Some books also may be read by deputy, and extracts made of them by others; but that would be only in the less important arguments, and the meaner sort of books; else distilled books are like common distilled waters, flashy[2] things. Reading maketh a full man; conference a ready man; and writing an exact man. And therefore, if a man write little, he had need have a great memory; if he confer little, he had need have a present wit: and if he read little, he had need have much cunning, to seem to know that he doth not. Histories make men wise; poets witty; the mathematics subtile; natural philosophy deep; moral grave; logic and rhetoric able to contend. *Abeunt studia in mores.* [The studies pass into the manners.] Nay there is no stond or impediment in the wit, but may be wrought out by fit studies: like as diseases of the body may have appropriate exercises. Bowling is good for the stone and reins;[3] shooting for the lungs and breast; gentle walking for the stomach; riding for the head; and the like. So if a man's wit be wandering, let him study the mathematics; for in demonstrations, if his wit be called away never so little, he must begin again. If his wit be not apt to distinguish or find differences, let him study the schoolmen; for they are *cymini sectores*, [splitters of hairs.] If he be not apt to beat over[4] matters, and to call up one thing to prove and illustrate another, let him study the lawyers' cases. So every defect of the mind may have a special receipt.

[°*So that readers can see how Bacon habitually developed and expanded his essays, we print the original curt version of "Of Studies" from the first edition of 1597.*]

STUDIES serue for pastimes, for ornaments and for abilities. Their chiefe vse for pastime is in priuatenes and retiring; for ornamente is in discourse, and for abilitie is in iudgement. For expert men can execute, but learned men are fittest to iudge or censure.

¶To spend too much time in them is slouth, to vse them too much for ornament is affectation: to make iudgement wholly by their rules, is the humour of a Scholler. ¶They perfect *Nature,* and are perfected by experience. ¶Craftie men continue them, simple men admire them, wise men vse them: For they teach not their owne vse, but that is a wisedome without them: and aboue them wonne by observation. ¶Reade not to contradict, nor to belieue, but to waigh and consider. ¶Some bookes are to bee tasted, others to bee swallowed, and some few to bee chewed and disgested: That is, some bookes are to be read only in partes; others to be read, but cursorily, and some few to be read wholly and with diligence and attention. ¶Reading maketh a full man, conference a readye man, and writing an exacte man. And therefore, if a man write little, he had neede haue a great memorie, if he conferre little, he had neede haue a present wit, and if he reade little, hee had neede haue much cunning, to seeme to know that he doth not. ¶Histories make men wise, Poets wittie: the Mathematickes subtle, naturall Phylosophie deepe: Morall graue, Logicke and Rhetoricke able to contend.

51

OF FACTION

MANY have an opinion not wise, that for a prince to govern his estate, or for a great person to govern his proceedings, according to the respect of factions, is a principal part of policy; whereas contrariwise, the chiefest wisdom is either in ordering those things which are general, and wherein men of several factions do nevertheless agree; or in dealing with correspondence to particular persons, one by one. But I say not that the consideration of factions is to be neglected. Mean men, in their rising, must adhere; but great men, that have strength in themselves, were better to maintain themselves indifferent[1] and neutral. Yet even in beginners, to adhere so moderately, as he be a man of the one faction which is most passable with the other, commonly giveth best way. The lower and weaker faction is the firmer in conjunction; and it is often seen that a few that are stiff do tire out a greater number that are more moderate. When one of the factions is extinguished, the remaining subdivideth; as the faction between Lucullus and the rest of the nobles of the senate (which they called *Optimates*) held out awhile against the faction of Pompey and Cæsar; but when the senate's authority was pulled down, Cæsar and Pompey soon after brake. The faction or party of Antonius and Octavianus Cæsar against Brutus and Cassius, held out likewise for a time; but when Brutus and Cassius were overthrown, then soon after Antonius and Octavianus brake and subdivided. These examples are of wars, but the same holdeth in private factions. And therefore those that are seconds in factions do many times, when the faction subdivideth, prove principals; but many times also they prove cyphers and cashiered; for many a man's strength is in opposition; and when that faileth he groweth out of use. It is commonly seen that men once placed take in with the contrary faction to that by which they enter: thinking belike that they have the first sure, and now are ready for a new purchase. The traitor in faction lightly goeth away with it;[2] for when matters have stuck long in balancing, the winning of some one man casteth them, and he getteth all the thanks. The even carriage between two factions proceedeth not always of moderation, but of a trueness to a man's self, with end to make use of both. Certainly in Italy they hold it a little suspect in popes, when they have often in their mouth *Padre commune* [*the Common Father]: and take it to be a sign of one that meaneth to refer all to the greatness of his own house. Kings had need beware how they side themselves, and make themselves as of a faction or party; for leagues within the state are ever pernicious to monarchies: for they raise an obligation paramount to obligation of sovereignty, and make the king *tanquam unus ex nobis* [like one of themselves]; as was to be seen in the League of France.[3] When factions are carried too high and too violently, it is a sign of weakness in princes; and much to the prejudice both of their authority and business. The motions of factions under kings ought to be like the motions (as the astronomers speak) of the inferior orbs, which may have their proper motions, but yet still are quietly carried by the higher motion of *primum mobile*.[4]

52

OF CEREMONIES AND RESPECTS

HE that is only real,[1] had need have exceeding great parts of virtue; as the stone had need to be rich that is set without foil. But if a man mark it well, it is in praise and commendation of men as it is in gettings and gains: for the proverb is true, *That light gains make heavy purses;* for light gains come thick, whereas great come but now and then. So it is true that small matters win great commendation, because they are continually in use and in note: whereas the occasion of any great virtue cometh but on festivals. Therefore it doth much add to a man's reputation, and is (as queen Isabella[2] said) *like perpetual letters commendatory,* to have good forms. To attain them it almost sufficeth not to despise them; for so shall a man observe them in others; and let him trust himself with the rest. For if he labour too much to express them, he shall lose their grace; which is to be natural and unaffected. Some men's behaviour is like a verse, wherein every syllable is measured; how can a man comprehend great matters, that breaketh his mind too much to small observations? Not to use ceremonies at all, is to teach others not to use them again; and so diminisheth respect to himself; especially they be not to be omitted to strangers and formal natures; but the dwelling upon them, and exalting them above the moon, is not only tedious, but doth diminish the faith and credit of him that speaks. And certainly there is a kind of conveying of effectual and imprinting passages amongst compliments, which is of singular use, if a man can hit upon it. Amongst a man's peers a man shall be sure of familiarity; and therefore it is good a little to keep state. Amongst a man's inferiors one shall be sure of reverence; and therefore it is good a little to be familiar. He that is too much in anything, so that he giveth another occasion of satiety, maketh himself cheap. To apply one's self to others is good; so it be with demonstration that a man doth it upon regard, and not upon facility. It is a good precept generally in seconding another, yet to add somewhat of one's own: as if you will grant his opinion, let it be with some distinction; if you will follow his motion, let it be with condition; if you allow his counsel, let it be with alleging further reason. Men had need beware how they be too perfect in compliments; for be they never so sufficient otherwise, their enviers will be sure to give them that attribute, to the disadvantage of their greater virtues. It is loss also in business to be too full of respects, or to be curious in observing times and opportunities. Salomon saith, *He that considereth the wind shall not sow, and he that looketh to the clouds shall not reap.* A wise man will make more opportunities than he finds. Men's behaviour should be like their apparel, not too strait or point device,[3] but free for exercise or motion.

53

OF PRAISE

PRAISE is the reflexion of virtue. But it is as the glass or body which giveth the reflexion. If it be from the common people, it is commonly false and naught; and rather followeth vain persons than virtuous. For the common people understand not many excellent virtues. The lowest virtues draw praise from them; the middle virtues work in them astonishment or admiration; but of the highest virtues they have no sense of perceiving at all. But shews, and *species virtutibus similes* [*appearances resembling virtues], serve best with them. Certainly fame is like a river, that beareth up things light and swoln, and drowns things weighty and solid. But if persons of quality and judgment concur, then it is (as the Scripture saith), *Nomen bonum instar unguenti fragrantis;* [a good name like unto a sweet ointment.] It filleth all round about, and will not easily away. For the odours of ointments are more durable than those of flowers. There be so many false points of praise, that a man may justly hold it a suspect. Some praises proceed merely of flattery; and if he be an ordinary flatterer, he will have certain common attributes, which may serve every man; if he be a cunning flatterer, he will follow the arch-flatterer, which is a man's self; and wherein a man thinketh best of himself, therein the flatterer will uphold him most: but if he be an impudent flatterer, look wherein a man is conscious to himself that he is most defective, and is most out of countenance in himself, that will the flatterer entitle him to perforce, *spretâ conscientiâ* [*in spite of his conscience]. Some praises come of good wishes and respects, which is a form due in civility to kings and great persons, *laudando præcipere* [*to teach by praising]; when by telling men what they are, they represent to them what they should be. Some men are praised maliciously to their hurt, thereby to stir envy and jealousy towards them; *pessimum genus inimicorum laudantium;* [the worst kind of enemies are they that praise;] insomuch as it was a proverb amongst the Grecians, that *he that was praised to his hurt, should have a push rise upon his nose;* as we say, *that a blister will rise upon one's tongue that tells a lie.* Certainly moderate praise, used with opportunity, and not vulgar, is that which doth the good. Salomon saith, *He that praiseth his friend aloud, rising early, it shall be to him no better than a curse.* Too much magnifying of man or matter doth irritate contradiction, and procure envy and scorn. To praise a man's self cannot be decent, except it be in rare cases; but to praise a man's office or profession, he may do it with good grace, and with a kind of magnanimity. The Cardinals of Rome, which are theologues, and friars, and schoolmen, have a phrase of notable contempt and scorn towards civil business: for they call all temporal business of wars, embassages, judicature, and other employments, *shirrerie*, which is *under-sheriffries;* as if they were but matters for under-sheriffs and catch-poles:[1] though many times those under-sheriffries do more good than their high speculations. St. Paul, when he boasts of himself, he doth oft interlace, *I speak like a fool;* but speaking of his calling, he saith, *magnificabo apostolatum meum:* [I will magnify my mission.]

54
OF VAIN-GLORY

IT was prettily devised of Æsop; *the fly sat upon the axletree of the chariot wheel, and said, What a dust do I raise!* So are there some vain persons, that whatsoever goeth alone or moveth upon greater means, if they have never so little hand in it, they think it is they that carry it. They that are glorious[1] must needs be factious; for all bravery[2] stands upon comparisons. They must needs be violent, to make good their own vaunts. Neither can they be secret, and therefore not effectual; but according to the French proverb, *Beaucoup de bruit, peu de fruit; Much bruit, little fruit.* Yet certainly there is use of this quality in civil affairs. Where there is an opinion and fame to be created either of virtue or greatness, these men are good trumpeters. Again, as Titus Livius noteth in the case of Antiochus and the Ætolians, *There are sometimes great effects of cross lies,*[3] as if a man that negociates between two princes, to draw them to join in a war against the third, doth extol the forces of either of them above measure, the one to the other: and sometimes he that deals between man and man, raiseth his own credit with both, by pretending greater interest than he hath in either. And in these and the like kinds, it often falls out that somewhat is produced of nothing; for lies are sufficient to breed opinion, and opinion brings on substance. In militar commanders and soldiers, vain-glory is an essential point; for as iron sharpens iron, so by glory one courage sharpeneth another. In cases of great enterprise upon charge and adventure, a composition of glorious natures doth put life into business; and those that are of solid and sober natures have more of the ballast than of the sail. In fame of learning, the flight will be slow without some feathers of ostentation. *Qui de contemnendâ gloriâ libros scribunt, nomen suum inscribunt.* [They that write books on the worthlessness of glory, take care to put their names on the title page.] Socrates, Aristotle, Galen, were men full of ostentation. Certainly vain-glory helpeth to perpetuate a man's memory; and virtue was never so beholding to human nature, as it received his due at the second hand.[4] Neither had the fame of Cicero, Seneca, Plinius Secundus, borne her age so well, if it had not been joined with some vanity in themselves; like unto varnish, that makes ceilings not only shine but last. But all this while, when I speak of vain-glory, I mean not of that property that Tacitus doth attribute to Mucianus; *Omnium, quæ dixerat feceratque, arte quâdam ostentator:* [A man that had a kind of art of setting forth to advantage all that he had said or done:] for that proceeds not of vanity, but of natural magnanimity and discretion; and in some persons is not only comely, but gracious. For excusations, cessions,[5] modesty itself well governed, are but arts of ostentation. And amongst those arts there is none better than that which Plinius Secundus speaketh of, which is to be liberal of praise and commendation to others, in that wherein a man's self hath any perfection. For saith Pliny very wittily, *In commending another you do yourself right; for he that you commend is either superior to you in that you commend, or inferior. If he be inferior, if he be to be commended, you much more; if he be superior, if he be not to be commended, you much less.* Glorious men are the scorn of wise men, the admiration of fools, the idols of parasites, and the slaves of their own vaunts.

55

OF HONOUR AND REPUTATION

THE winning of Honour is but the revealing of a man's virtue and worth without disadvantage. For some in their actions do woo and affect honour and reputation; which sort of men are commonly much talked of, but inwardly little admired. And some, contrariwise, darken their virtue in the shew of it; so as they be undervalued in opinion. If a man perform that which hath not been attempted before; or attempted and given over; or hath been achieved, but not with so good circumstance; he shall purchase more honour, than by effecting a matter of greater difficulty or virtue, wherein he is but a follower. If a man so temper his actions, as in some one of them he doth content every faction or combination of people, the music will be the fuller. A man is an ill husband of his honour, that entereth into any action, the failing wherein may disgrace him more than the carrying of it through can honour him. Honour that is gained and broken upon another[1] hath the quickest reflexion, like diamonds cut with fascets. And therefore let a man contend to excel any competitors of his in honour, in outshooting them, if he can, in their own bow. Discreet followers and servants help much to reputation. *Omnis fama a domesticis emanat* [*All fame comes from servants]. Envy, which is the canker of honour, is best extinguished by declaring a man's self in his ends rather to seek merit than fame; and by attributing a man's successes rather to divine Providence and felicity, than to his own virtue or policy. The true marshalling of the degrees of sovereign honour are these. In the first place are *conditores imperiorum,* founders of states and commonwealths; such as were Romulus, Cyrus, Cæsar, Ottoman, Ismael. In the second place are *legislatores,* lawgivers; which are also called *sec-*

ond founders, or *perpetui principes,* because they govern by their ordinances after they are gone; such were Lycurgus, Solon, Justinian, Eadgar, Alphonsus of Castile, the wise, that made the *Siete partidas.*[2] In the third place are *liberatores,* or *salvatores,* such as compound the long miseries of civil wars, or deliver their countries from servitude of strangers or tyrants; as Augustus Cæsar, Vespasianus, Aurelianus, Theodoricus, King Henry the Seventh of England, King Henry the Fourth of France. In the fourth place are *propagatores* or *propugnatores imperii* [*extenders or defenders of empire]; such as in honourable wars enlarge their territories, or make noble defence against invaders. And in the last place are *patres patriæ,* [fathers of their country;] which reign justly, and make the times good wherein they live. Both which last kinds need no examples, they are in such number. Degrees of honour in subjects are, first *participes curarum* [*sharers of cares], those upon whom princes do discharge the greatest weight of their affairs; their *right hands,* as we call them. The next are *duces belli,* great leaders; such as are princes' lieutenants, and do them notable services in the wars. The third are *gratiosi,* favourites; such as exceed not this scantling, to be solace to the sovereign, and harmless to the people. And the fourth, *negotiis pares* [*those equal to the business]; such as have great places under princes, and execute their places with sufficiency. There is an honour, likewise, which may be ranked amongst the greatest, which happeneth rarely; that is, of such as sacrifice themselves to death or danger for the good of their country; as was M. Regulus, and the two Decii.[3]

56

OF JUDICATURE

JUDGES ought to remember that their office is *jus dicere,* and not *jus dare;* to interpret law, and not to make law, or give law. Else will it be like the authority claimed by the church of Rome, which under pretext of exposition of Scripture doth not stick to add and alter; and to pronounce that which they do not find; and by shew of antiquity to introduce novelty. Judges ought to be more learned than witty, more reverend than plausible, and more advised than confident. Above all things, integrity is their portion and proper virtue. *Cursed* (saith the law) *is he that removeth the landmark.* The mislayer of a mere-stone is to blame. But it is the unjust judge that is the capital remover of landmarks, when he defineth amiss of lands and property. One foul sentence doth more hurt than many foul examples. For these do but corrupt the stream, the other corrupteth the fountain. So saith Salomon, *Fons turbatus, et vena corrupta, est justus cadens in causâ suâ coram adversario:* [A righteous man falling down before the wicked is as a troubled fountain or a corrupt spring.] The office of judges may have reference unto the parties that sue, unto the advocates that plead, unto the clerks and ministers of justice underneath them, and to the sovereign or state above them.

First, for the causes or parties that sue. *There be* (saith the Scripture) *that turn judgment into wormwood;* and surely there be also that turn it into vinegar; for injustice maketh it bitter, and delays make it sour. The principal duty of a judge is to suppress force and fraud; whereof force is the more pernicious when it is open, and fraud when it is close and disguised. Add thereto contentious suits, which ought to be spewed out, as the surfeit of courts. A judge ought to prepare his way to a just sentence, as God useth to prepare his way, by raising valleys and taking down hills: so when there appeareth on either side an high hand, violent prosecution, cunning advantages taken, combination, power, great counsel, then is the virtue of a judge seen, to make inequality equal; that he may plant his judgment as upon an even ground. *Qui fortiter emungit, elicit sanguinem;* [Violent blowing makes the nose bleed;] and where the wine-press is hard wrought, it yields a harsh wine, that tastes of the grape-stone. Judges must beware of hard constructions and strained inferences; for there is no worse torture than the torture of laws. Specially in case of laws penal, they ought to have care that that which was meant for terror be not turned into rigour; and that they bring not upon the people that shower whereof the Scripture speaketh, *Pluet super eos laqueos* [*He shall rain snares upon them]; for penal laws pressed are a *shower of snares* upon the people. Therefore let penal laws, if they have been sleepers of long, or if they be grown unfit for the present time, be by wise judges confined in the execution: *Judicis officium est, ut res, ita tempora rerum, &c.* [A judge must have regard to the time as well as to the matter.] In causes of life and death, judges ought (as far as the law permitteth) in justice to remember mercy; and to cast a severe eye upon the example, but a merciful eye upon the person.

Secondly, for the advocates and counsel that plead. Patience and gravity of hearing is an essential part of justice; and an overspeaking judge is no well-tuned cymbal. It is no grace to a judge first to find that which he might have heard in due time from the bar; or to show quickness of conceit in cutting off evidence or counsel too short; or to prevent information by questions, though pertinent. The parts of a judge in hearing are four: to direct the evidence; to moderate length, repetition, or impertinency of speech; to recapitulate, select, and collate the material points of that which hath been said; and to give the rule or sentence. Whatsover is above these is too much; and proceedeth either of glory and willingness to speak, or of impatience to hear, or of shortness of memory, or of want of a staid and equal attention. It is a strange thing to see that the boldness of advocates should prevail with judges; whereas they should imitate God, in whose seat they sit; who *represseth the presumptuous, and giveth grace to the modest.* But it is more strange, that judges should have noted favourites; which cannot but cause multiplication of fees, and suspicion of bye-ways. There is due from the judge to the advocate some commendation and gracing, where causes are well handled and fair pleaded; especially towards the side

which obtaineth not; for that upholds in the client the reputation of his counsel, and beats down in him the conceit of
his cause. There is likewise due to the public a civil reprehension of advocates, where there appeareth cunning counsel, gross neglect, slight information, indiscreet pressing, or
an over-bold defence. And let not the counsel at the bar
chop[1] with the judge, nor wind himself into the handling
of the cause anew after the judge hath declared his sentence; but on the other side, let not the judge meet the cause
half way, nor give occasion for the party to say his counsel
or proofs were not heard.

Thirdly, for that that concerns clerks and ministers. The
place of justice is an hallowed place; and therefore not only
the bench, but the foot-pace and precincts and purprise[2]
thereof, ought to be preserved without scandal and corruption. For certainly *Grapes* (as the Scripture saith) *will not
be gathered of thorns or thistles;* neither can justice yield
her fruit with sweetness amongst the briars and brambles
of catching and polling[3] clerks and ministers. The attendance of courts is subject to four bad instruments. First, certain persons that are sowers of suits; which make the court
swell, and the country pine. The second sort is of those that
engage courts in quarrels of jurisdiction, and are not truly
amici curiæ, [*friends of the court] but *parasiti curiæ*
[*parasites of the court], in puffing a court up beyond her
bounds, for their own scraps and advantage. The third sort
is of those that may be accounted the left hands of courts;
persons that are full of nimble and sinister tricks and shifts,
whereby they pervert the plain and direct courses of courts,
and bring justice into oblique lines and labyrinths. And the
fourth is the poller and exacter of fees; which justifies the
common resemblance of the courts of justice to the bush
whereunto while the sheep flies for defence in weather, he
is sure to lose part of his fleece. On the other side, an ancient clerk, skilful in precedents, wary in proceeding, and
understanding in the business of the court, is an excellent
finger of a court; and doth many times point the way to the
judge himself.

Fourthly, for that which may concern the sovereign and estate. Judges ought above all to remember the conclusion of the Roman Twelve Tables; *Salus populi suprema lex;* [The supreme law of all is the weal of the people;] and to know that laws, except they be in order to that end, are but things captious, and oracles not well inspired. Therefore it is an happy thing in a state when kings and states do often consult with judges; and again when judges do often consult with the king and state: the one, when there is matter of law intervenient in business of state; the other, when there is some consideration of state intervenient in matter of law. For many times the things deduced to judgment may be *meum* and *tuum,* when the reason and consequence thereof may trench to point of estate:[4] I call matter of estate, not only the parts of sovereignty, but whatsoever introduceth any great alteration or dangerous precedent; or concerneth manifestly any great portion of people. And let no man weakly conceive that just laws and true policy have any antipathy; for they are like the spirits and sinews, that one moves with the other. Let judges also remember, that Salomon's throne was supported by lions on both sides: let them be lions, but yet lions under the throne; being circumspect that they do not check or oppose any points of sovereignty. Let not judges also be so ignorant of their own right, as to think there is not left to them, as a principal part of their office, a wise use and application of laws. For they may remember what the apostle saith of a greater law than theirs; *Nos scimus quia lex bona est, modo quis eâ utatur legitime.* [We know that the law is good, if a man use it lawfully.]

57

OF ANGER

To seek to extinguish Anger utterly is but a bravery of the Stoics. We have better oracles: *Be angry, but sin not. Let not the sun go down upon your anger.* Anger must be limited and confined both in race and in time. We will first speak how the natural inclination and habit to be angry may be attempered and calmed. Secondly, how the particular motions of anger may be repressed, or at least refrained from doing mischief. Thirdly, how to raise anger or appease anger in another.

For the first; there is no other way but to meditate and ruminate well upon the effects of anger, how it troubles man's life. And the best time to do this, is to look back upon anger when the fit is throughly over. Seneca saith well, *That anger is like ruin, which breaks itself upon that it falls.*[1] The Scripture exhorteth us *To possess our souls in patience.* Whosoever is out of patience, is out of possession of his soul. Men must not turn bees;

. . . . . . animasque in vulnere ponunt:

[that put their lives in the sting.]

Anger is certainly a kind of baseness; as it appears well in the weakness of those subjects in whom it reigns; children, women, old folks, sick folks. Only men must beware that they carry their anger rather with scorn than with fear; so that they may seem rather to be above the injury than below it; which is a thing easily done, if a man will give law to himself in it.

For the second point; the causes and motives of anger are chiefly three. First, to be too sensible of hurt; for no man is angry that feels not himself hurt; and therefore tender and delicate persons must needs be oft angry; they have so many things to trouble them, which more robust natures have little sense of. The next is, the apprehension and construction of the injury offered to be, in the circumstances thereof, full of contempt: for contempt is that which putteth an edge upon anger, as much or more than the hurt itself. And therefore when men are ingenious in picking out circumstances of contempt, they do kindle their anger much. Lastly, opinion of the touch of a man's reputation doth multiply and sharpen anger. Wherein the remedy is, that a man should have, as Consalvo[2] was wont to say, *telam honoris crassiorem,* [an honour of a stouter web.] But in all refrainings of anger, it is the best remedy to win time; and to make a man's self believe, that the opportunity of his revenge is not yet come, but that he foresees a time for it; and so to still himself in the mean time, and reserve it.

To contain anger from mischief, though it take hold of a man, there be two things whereof you must have special caution. The one, of extreme bitterness of words, especially if they be aculeate and proper; for *communia maledicta*[3] are nothing so much; and again, that in anger a man reveal no secrets; for that makes him not fit for society. The other, that you do not peremptorily break off, in any business, in a fit of anger; but howsoever you shew bitterness, do not act anything that is not revocable.

For raising and appeasing anger in another; it is done chiefly by choosing of times, when men are frowardest and worst disposed, to incense them. Again, by gathering (as was touched before) all that you can find out to aggravate the contempt. And the two remedies are by the contraries. The former to take good times, when first to relate to a man an angry business; for the first impression is much; and the other is, to sever, as much as may be, the construction of the injury from the point of contempt; imputing it to misunderstanding, fear, passion, or what you will.

58

OF VICISSITUDE OF THINGS

SALOMON saith, *There is no new thing upon the earth.* So that as Plato had an imagination, *That all knowledge was but remembrance;* so Salomon giveth his sentence, *That all novelty is but oblivion.* Whereby you may see that the river of Lethe runneth as well above ground as below. There is an abstruse astrologer that saith, *if it were not for two things that are constant, (the one is, that the fixed stars ever stand at like distance one from another, and never come nearer together, nor go further asunder; the other, that the diurnal motion perpetually keepeth time,) no individual would last one moment.* Certain it is, that the matter is in a perpetual flux, and never at a stay. The great winding-sheets, that bury all things in oblivion, are two; deluges and earthquakes. As for conflagrations and great droughts, they do not merely dispeople and destroy. Phaëton's car went but a day. And the three years' drought in the time of Elias[1] was but particular, and left people alive. As for the great burnings by lightnings, which are often in the West Indies, they are but narrow. But in the other two destructions, by deluge and earthquake, it is further to be noted, that the remnant of people which hap to be reserved, are commonly ignorant and mountainous people, that can give no account of the time past; so that the oblivion is all one as if none had been left. If you consider well of the people of the West Indies, it is very probable that they are a newer or a younger people than the people of the old world. And it is much more likely that the destruction that hath heretofore been there, was not by earthquakes (as the Ægyptian priest told Solon concerning the island of Atlantis, *that it was swallowed by an earthquake),* but rather that it was desolated by a particular deluge. For earthquakes are seldom in those parts. But on the other side, they have such pouring rivers, as the rivers of Asia and Africk and Europe are but brooks to them. Their Andes likewise, or mountains, are far higher than those with us; whereby it seems that the remnants of generation of men were in such a particular deluge saved. As for the observation that Machiavel hath, that the jealousy of sects doth much extinguish the memory of things; traducing Gregory the Great, that he did what in him lay to extinguish all heathen antiquities; I do not find that those zeals do any great effects, nor last long; as it appeared in the succession of Sabinian,[2] who did revive the former antiquities.

The vicissitude or mutations in the Superior Globe are no fit matter for this present argument. It may be, Plato's great year,[3] if the world should last so long, would have some effect; not in renewing the state of like individuals, (for that is the fume of those that conceive the celestial bodies have more accurate influences upon these things below than indeed they have,) but in gross. Comets, out of question, have likewise power and effect over the gross and mass of things; but they are rather gazed upon, and waited upon in their journey, than wisely observed in their effects; specially in their respective effects; that is, what kind of comet, for magnitude, colour, version of the beams, placing in the region of heaven, or lasting, produceth what kind of effects.

There is a toy which I have heard, and I would not have it given over, but waited upon a little. They say it is observed in the Low Countries (I know not in what part) that every five and thirty years the same kind and suit of years and weathers comes about again; as great frosts, great wet, great droughts, warm winters, summers with little heat, and the like; and they call it the *Prime.* It is a thing I do the rather mention, because, computing backwards, I have found some concurrence.

But to leave these points of nature, and to come to men. The greatest vicissitude of things amongst men, is the vicissitude of sects and religions. For those orbs rule in men's minds most. The true religion is *built upon the rock;* the rest are tossed upon the waves of time. To speak therefore of the causes of new sects; and to give some counsel concerning them, as far as the weakness of human judgment can give stay to so great revolutions.

When the religion formerly received is rent by discords; and when the holiness of the professors of religion is decayed and full of scandal; and withal the times be stupid, ignorant, and barbarous; you may doubt the springing up of a new sect; if then also there should arise any extravagant and strange spirit to make himself author thereof. All which points held when Mahomet published his law. If a new sect have not two properties, fear it not; for it will not spread. The one is, the supplanting or the opposing of authority established; for nothing is more popular than that. The other is, the giving licence to pleasures and a voluptuous life. For as for speculative heresies, (such as were in ancient times the Arians, and now the Arminians,) though they work mightily upon men's wits, yet they do not produce any great alterations in states; except it be by the help of civil occasions. There be three manner of plantations of new sects.By the power of signs and miracles; by the eloquence and wisdom of speech and persuasion; and by the sword. For martyrdoms, I reckon them amongst miracles; because they seem to exceed the strength of human nature: and I may do the like of superlative and admirable holiness of life. Surely there is no better way to stop the rising of new sects and schisms, than to reform abuses; to compound the smaller differences; to proceed mildly, and not with sanguinary persecutions; and rather to take off the principal authors by winning and advancing them, than to enrage them by violence and bitterness.

The changes and vicissitude in wars are many; but chiefly in three things; in the seats or stages of the war; in the weapons; and in the manner of the conduct. Wars, in ancient time, seemed more to move from east to west; for the Persians, Assyrians, Arabians, Tartars, (which were the invaders,) were all eastern people. It is true, the Gauls were western; but we read but of two incursions of theirs: the one to Gallo-Græcia, the other to Rome. But East and West have no certain points of heaven; and no more have the wars, either from the east or west, any certainty of observation. But North and South are fixed; and it hath seldom or never been seen that the far southern people have invaded the northern, but contrariwise. Whereby it is manifest that the northern tract of the world is in nature the more martial region: be it in respect of the stars of that hemisphere; or of the great continents that are upon the north, whereas the south part, for aught that is known, is almost all sea; or (which is most apparent) of the cold of the northern parts, which is that which, without aid of discipline, doth make the bodies hardest, and the courages warmest.

Upon the breaking and shivering of a great state and empire, you may be sure to have wars. For great empires, while they stand, do enervate and destroy the forces of the natives which they have subdued, resting upon their own protecting forces; and then when they fail also, all goes to ruin, and they become a prey. So was it in the decay of the Roman empire; and likewise in the empire of Almaigne, after Charles the Great, every bird taking a feather; and were not unlike to befal to Spain, if it should break. The great accessions and unions of kingdoms do likewise stir up wars: for when a state grows to an over-power, it is like a great flood, that will be sure to overflow. As it hath been seen in the states of Rome, Turkey, Spain, and others. Look when the world hath fewest barbarous peoples, but such as commonly will not marry or generate, except they know means to live, (as it is almost every where at this day, except Tartary,) there is no danger of inundations of people: but when there be great shoals of people, which go on to populate, without foreseeing means of life and sustentation, it is of necessity that once in an age or two they discharge a portion of their people upon other nations; which the ancient northern people were wont to do by lot; casting lots what part should stay at home, and what should seek their fortunes. When a war-like state grows soft and effeminate, they may be sure of a war. For commonly such states are grown rich in the time of their degenerating; and so the prey inviteth, and their decay in valour encourageth a war.

As for the weapons, it hardly falleth under rule and ob-servation: yet we see even they have returns and vicissi-tudes. For certain it is, that ordnance was known in the city of the Oxidrakes in India; and was that which the Macedonians called thunder and lightning, and magic. And it is well known that the use of ordnance hath been in China above two thousand years. The conditions of weap-ons, and their improvement, are, First, the fetching afar off; for that outruns the danger; as it is seen in ordnance and muskets. Secondly, the strength of the percussion; wherein likewise ordnance do exceed all arietations[4] and ancient inventions. The third is, the commodious use of them; as that they may serve in all weathers; that the car-riage may be light and manageable; and the like.

For the conduct of the war: at the first, men rested extremely upon number: they did put the wars likewise upon main force and valour; pointing days for pitched fields, and so trying it out upon an even match: and they were more ignorant in ranging and arraying their battles. After they grew to rest upon number rather competent than vast; they grew to advantages of place, cunning diversions, and the like: and they grew more skilful in the ordering of their battles.

In the youth of a state, arms do flourish; in the middle age of a state, learning; and then both of them together for a time; in the declining age of a state, mechanical arts and merchandise. Learning hath his infancy, when it is but beginning and almost childish: then his youth, when it is luxuriant and juvenile: then his strength of years, when it is solid and reduced: and lastly, his old age, when it waxeth dry and exhaust. But it is not good to look too long upon these turning wheels of vicissitude, lest we become giddy. As for the philology[5] of them, that is but a circle of tales, and therefore not fit for this writing.

OF THE INTERPRETATION OF NATURE

[DE INTERPRETATIONE NATURAE]

[*ca* 1603]

PROEM

BELIEVING that I was born for the service of mankind, and regarding the care of the commonwealth as a kind of common property which like the air and the water belongs to everybody, I set myself to consider in what way mankind might be best served, and what service I was myself best fitted by nature to perform.

Now among all the benefits that could be conferred upon mankind, I found none so great as the discovery of new arts, endowments, and commodities for the bettering of man's life. For I saw that among the rude people in the primitive times the authors of rude inventions and discoveries were consecrated and numbered among the Gods. And it was plain that the good effects wrought by founders of cities, law-givers, fathers of the people, extirpers of tyrants, and heroes of that class, extend but over narrow spaces and last but for short times; whereas the work of the Inventor, though a thing of less pomp and shew, is felt everywhere and lasts for ever. But above all, if a man could succeed, not in striking out some particular invention, however useful, but in kindling a light in nature—a light which should in its very rising touch and illuminate all the border-regions that confine upon the circle of our present knowledge; and so spreading further and further should presently disclose and bring into sight all that is most hidden and secret in the world,—that man (I thought) would be the benefactor indeed of the human race,—the propagator of man's empire over the universe, the champion of liberty, the conqueror and subduer of necessities.

For myself, I found that I was fitted for nothing so well as for the study of Truth; as having a mind nimble and versatile enough to catch the resemblances of things (which is the chief point), and at the same time steady enough to fix and distinguish their subtler differences; as being gifted by nature with desire to seek, patience to doubt, fondness to meditate, slowness to assert, readiness to reconsider, carefulness to dispose and set in order; and as being a man that neither affects what is new nor admires what is old, and that hates every kind of imposture. So I thought my nature had a kind of familiarity and relationship with Truth.

Nevertheless, because my birth and education had seasoned me in business of state; and because opinions (so young as I was) would sometimes stagger me; and because I thought that a man's own country has some special claims upon him more than the rest of the world; and because I hoped that, if I rose to any place of honour in the state, I should have a larger command of industry and ability to help me in my work;—for these reasons I both applied myself to acquire the arts of civil life, and commended my service, so far as in modesty and honesty I might, to the favour of such friends as had any influence. In which also I had another motive: for I felt that those things I have spoken of—be they great or small—reach no further than the condition and culture of this mortal life; and I was not without hope (the condition of Religion being at that time not very prosperous) that if I came to hold office in the state, I might get something done too for the good of men's souls.

When I found however that my zeal was mistaken for ambition, and my life had already reached the turning-point, and my breaking health reminded me how ill I could afford to be so slow, and I reflected moreover that in leaving undone the good that I could do by myself alone, and applying myself to that which could not be done without the help and consent of others, I was by no means discharging the duty that lay upon me,—I put all those thoughts aside, and (in pursuance of my old determination) betook myself wholly to this work. Nor am I discouraged from it because I see signs in the times of the decline and overthrow of that knowledge and erudition which is now in use. Not that I apprehend any more barbarian invasions (unless possibly the Spanish empire should recover its strength, and having crushed other nations by arms should itself sink under its own weight): but the civil wars which may be expected, I think, (judging from certain fashions which have come in of late) to spread through many countries,—together with the malignity of sects, and those compendious artifices and devices which have crept into the place of solid erudition—seem to portend for literature and the sciences a tempest not less fatal, and one against which the Printing-office will be no effectual security. And no doubt but that fair-weather learning which is nursed by leisure, blossoms under reward and praise, which cannot withstand the shock of opinion, and is liable to be abused by tricks and quackery, will sink under such impediments as these. Far otherwise is it with that knowledge, whose dignity is maintained by works of utility and power. For the injuries therefore which should proceed from the times, I am not afraïd of them; and for the injuries which proceed from men I am not concerned. For if any one charge me with seeking to be wise overmuch, I answer simply that modesty and civil respect are fit for civil matters; in contemplations nothing is to be respected but Truth. If any one call on me for *works*, and that presently; I tell him frankly, without any imposture at all, that for me—a man not old, of weak health, my hands full of civil business, entering without guide or light upon an argument of all others the most obscure,—I hold it enough to have constructed the machine, though I may not succeed in setting

it on work. Nay with the same candour I profess and declare, that the Interpretation of Nature, rightly conducted,
ought in the first steps of the ascent, until a certain stage of
Generals[1] be reached, to be kept clear of all application
to Works. And this has in fact been the error of all those
who have heretofore ventured themselves at all upon the
waves of experience—that being either too weak of purpose or too eager for display, they have all at the outset
sought prematurely for works, as proofs and pledges of
their progress, and upon that rock have been wrecked and
cast away. If again any one ask me, not indeed for actual
works, yet for definite promises and forecasts of the works
that are to be, I would have him know that the knowledge
which we now possess will not teach a man even what to
wish. Lastly—though this is a matter of less moment—if any
of our politicians, who use to make their calculations and
conjectures according to persons and precedents, must
needs interpose his judgment in a thing of this nature,—I
would but remind him how (according to the ancient fable)
the lame man keeping the course won the race of the swift
man who left it: and that there is no thought to be taken
about precedents, for the thing is without precedent.

Now for my plan of publication—those parts of the work
which have it for their object to find out and bring into
correspondence such minds as are prepared and disposed
for the argument, and to purge the floors of men's understandings, I wish to be published to the world and circulate
from mouth to mouth: the rest I would have passed from
hand to hand, with selection and judgment. Not but I
know that it is an old trick of impostors to keep a few of
their follies back from the public which are indeed no
better than those they put forward: but in this case it is
no imposture at all, but a sober foresight, which tells me
that the formula itself of interpretation, and the discoveries
made by the same, will thrive better if committed to the
charge of some fit and selected minds, and kept private.
This however is other people's concern. For myself, my
heart is not set upon any of those things which depend

upon external accidents. I am not hunting for fame: I have no desire to found a sect, after the fashion of heresiarchs; and to look for any private gain from such an undertaking as this, I count both ridiculous and base. Enough for me the consciousness of well-deserving, and those real and effectual results with which Fortune itself cannot interfere.

THE
TWOO BOOKES OF FRANCIS BACON
OF THE
PROFICIENCE
AND
ADVANCEMENT OF LEARNING
DIVINE AND HUMANE

TO THE KING

[1605]

THE
FIRST BOOK OF FRANCIS BACON
OF THE
PROFICIENCE
AND
ADVANCEMENT OF LEARNING
DIVINE AND HUMAN

To the King

THERE were under the Law[1] (excellent King) both daily sacrifices and freewill offerings; the one proceeding upon ordinary observance, the other upon a devout cheerfulness. In like manner there belongeth to kings from their servants both tribute of duty and presents of affection. In the former of these I hope I shall not live to be wanting, according to my most humble duty, and the good pleasure of your Majesty's employments: for the later, I thought it more respective to make choice of some oblation which might rather refer to the propriety and excellency of your individual person, than to the business of your crown and state.

Wherefore representing your Majesty many times unto my mind, and beholding you not with the inquisitive eye of presumption to discover that which the Scripture telleth me is inscrutable, but with the observant eye of duty and admiration; leaving aside the other parts of your virtue and fortune, I have been touched, yea and possessed with an extreme wonder at those your virtues and faculties which the philosophers call intellectual; the largeness of your capacity, the faithfulness of your memory, the swiftness of your apprehension, the penetration of your judgment, and the facility and order of your elocution: and I have often thought that of all the persons living that I have known, your Majesty were the best instance to make a man of Plato's opinion, that all knowledge is but remembrance, and that the mind of man by nature knoweth all things, and hath but her own native and original notions (which by the strangeness and darkness of this tabernacle of the body are sequestered) again revived and restored: such a light of nature I have observed in your Majesty, and such a readiness to take flame and blaze from the least occasion presented, or the least spark of another's knowledge delivered. And as the Scripture saith of the wisest king,[2] *That his heart was as the sands of the sea;* which though it be one of the largest bodies yet it consisteth of the smallest and finest portions; so hath God given your Majesty a composition of understanding admirable, being able to compass and comprehend the greatest matters, and nevertheless to touch and apprehend the least; whereas it should seem an impossibility in nature for the same instrument to make itself fit for great and small works. And for your gift of speech, I call to mind what Cornelius Tacitus saith of Augustus Cæsar; *Augusto profluens, et quæ principem deceret, eloquentia fuit;* [that his style of speech was flowing and prince-like:] for if we note it well, speech that is uttered with labour and difficulty, or speech that savoureth of the affectation of art and precepts, or speech that is framed after the imitation of some pattern of eloquence, though never so excellent,—all this has somewhat servile, and holding of the subject. But your Majesty's manner of speech is indeed prince-like, flowing as from a fountain, and yet streaming and branching itself into nature's order, full of facility and felicity, imitating none, and inimitable by any. And as in your civil estate there appeareth to be an emulation and contention of your Majesty's virtue with your fortune; a virtuous disposition with a fortunate regiment; a virtuous expectation (when time was) of your greater fortune, with a prosperous possession thereof in the due time; a virtuous observation of the laws of marriage, with most blessed and happy fruit of marriage; a virtuous and most Christian desire of peace, with a fortunate inclination in your neighbour princes thereunto: so likewise in these intellectual matters, there seemeth to be no less contention between the excellency of your Majesty's gifts of nature and the universality and perfection of your learning. For I am well assured that this which I shall say is no amplification at all, but a positive and measured truth; which is, that there hath not been since Christ's time any king or temporal monarch which hath been so learned in all literature and erudition, divine and human. For let a man seriously and diligently revolve and peruse the succession of the emperors of Rome, of which Cæsar the dictator, who lived some years before Christ, and Marcus Antoninus were the best learned; and so descend to the emperors of Græcia, or of the West, and then to the lines of France, Spain, England, Scotland, and the rest; and he shall find this judgment is truly made. For it seemeth much in a king, if by the compendious extractions of other men's wits and labours he can take hold of any superficial ornaments and shews of learning, or if he countenance and prefer learning and learned men: but to drink indeed of the true fountains of learning, nay to have such a fountain of learning in himself, in a king, and in a king born, is almost a miracle. And the more, because there is met in your Majesty a rare conjunction as well of divine and sacred literature as of profane and human; so as your Majesty standeth invested of that triplicity which in great veneration was ascribed to the ancient Hermes; the power and fortune of a King, the knowledge and illumination of a Priest, and the learning and universality of a Philosopher. This propriety inherent and individual attribute in your Majesty deserveth to be expressed not only in the fame and admiration of the present time, nor in the history or tradition of the ages succeeding; but also in some solid work, fixed memorial, and immortal monument, bearing a character or signature both of the power of a king and the difference and perfection of such a king.

Therefore I did conclude with myself, that I could not make unto your Majesty a better oblation than of some treatise tending to that end; whereof the sum will consist of these two parts: the former concerning the excellency of learning and knowledge, and the excellency of the merit and true glory in the augmentation and propagation thereof; the later, what the particular acts and works are which have been embraced and undertaken for the advancement of learning, and again what defects and undervalues I find in such particular acts; to the end that though I cannot positively or affirmatively advise your Majesty, or propound unto you framed particulars, yet I may excite your princely cogitations to visit the excellent treasure of your own mind, and thence to extract particulars for this purpose agreeable to your magnanimity and wisdom.

IN the entrance to the former of these,—to clear the way, and as it were to make silence to have the true testimonies concerning the dignity of learning to be better heard without the interruption of tacit objections,—I think good to deliver it from the discredits and disgraces which it hath received; all from ignorance; but ignorance severally disguised; appearing sometimes in the zeal and jealousy of divines, sometimes in the severity and arrogancy of politiques, and sometimes in the errors and imperfections of learned men themselves.

I hear the former sort say, that knowledge is of those things which are to be accepted of with great limitation and caution; that the aspiring to over-much knowledge was the original temptation and sin, whereupon ensued the fall of man; that knowledge hath in it somewhat of the serpent, and therefore where it entereth into a man it makes him swell,—*Scientia inflat*, [knowledge puffeth up;] that Salomon gives a censure, *That there is no end of making books, and that much reading is weariness of the flesh;* and again in another place, *That in spacious knowledge there is much contristation, and that he that increaseth knowledge increaseth anxiety;* that St. Paul gives a caveat, *That we be not spoiled through vain philosophy;* that experience demonstrates how learned men have been arch-heretics, how learned times have been inclined to atheism, and how the contemplation of second causes doth derogate from our dependence upon God, who is the first cause.

To discover then the ignorance and error of this opinion and the misunderstanding in the grounds thereof, it may well appear these men do not observe or consider that it was not the pure knowledge of nature and universality, a knowledge by the light whereof man did give names unto other creatures in Paradise, as they were brought before him, according unto their proprieties, which gave the occasion to the fall; but it was the proud knowledge of good and evil, with an intent in man to give law unto himself and to depend no more upon God's commandments, which was the form of the temptation. Neither is it any quantity of knowledge how great soever that can make the mind of man to swell; for nothing can fill, much less extend, the soul of man, but God and the contemplation of God; and therefore Salomon speaking of the two principal senses of inquisition, the eye and the ear, affirmeth that the eye is never satisfied with seeing, nor the ear with hearing; and if there be no fulness, then is the continent greater than the content: so of knowledge itself and the mind of man, whereto the senses are but reporters, he defineth likewise in these words, placed after that calendar or ephemerides which he maketh of the diversities of times and seasons for all actions and purposes; and concludeth thus: *God hath made all things beautiful, or decent, in the true return of their seasons: Also he hath placed the world in man's heart, yet cannot man find out the work which God worketh from the beginning to the end:* declaring not obscurely that God hath framed the mind of man as a mirror or glass capable of the image of the universal world, and joyful to receive the impression thereof, as the eye joyeth to receive light; and not only delighted in beholding the variety of things and vicissitude of times, but raised also to find out and discern the ordinances and decrees which throughout all those changes are infallibly observed. And although he doth insinuate that the supreme or summary law of nature, which he calleth *the work which God worketh from the beginning to the end,* is not possible to be found out by man; yet that doth not derogate from the capacity of the mind, but may be referred to the impediments, as of shortness of life, ill conjunction of labours, ill tradition of knowledge over from hand to hand, and many other inconveniences whereunto the condition of man is subject. For that nothing parcel of the world is denied to man's inquiry and invention he doth in another place rule over, when he saith, *The spirit of man is as the lamp of God, wherewith he searcheth the inwardness of all secrets.* If then such be the capacity and receit of the mind of man, it is manifest that there is no danger at all in the proportion or quantity of knowledge, how large soever, lest it should make it swell or out-compass itself; no, but it is merely the quality of knowledge, which be it in quantity more or less, if it be taken without the true corrective thereof, hath in it some nature of venom or malignity, and some effects of that venom, which is ventosity or swelling. This corrective spice, the mixture whereof maketh knowledge so sovereign, is Charity, which the apostle[3] immediately addeth to the former clause; for so he saith, *knowledge bloweth up, but charity buildeth up;* not unlike unto that which he delivereth in another place: *If I spake* (saith he) *with the tongues of men and angels, and had not charity, it were but as a tinkling cymbal;* not but that it is an excellent thing to speak with the tongues of men and angels, but because if it be severed from charity, and not referred to the good of men and mankind, it hath rather a sounding and unworthy glory than a meriting and substantial virtue. And as for that censure of Salomon concerning the excess of writing and reading books and the anxiety of spirit which redoundeth from knowledge, and that admonition of St. Paul, *That we be not seduced by vain philosophy;* let those places be rightly understood, and they do indeed excellently set forth the true bounds and limitations whereby human knowledge is confined and circumscribed; and yet without any such contracting or coarctation,[4] but that it may comprehend all the universal nature of things. For these limitations are three. The first, *that we do not so place our felicity in knowledge, as we forget our mortality.* The second, *that we make application of our knowledge to give ourselves repose and contentment, and not distaste or repining.* The third, *that we do not presume by the contemplation of nature to attain to the mysteries of God.* For as touching the first of these, Salomon doth excellently expound himself in another place of the same book, where he saith; *I saw well that knowledge recedeth as far from ignorance as light doth from darkness, and that the wise man's eyes keep watch in his head, whereas the fool roundeth about in darkness: but withal I learned that the same mortality involveth them both.* And for the second, certain it is, there is no vexation or anxiety of mind which resulteth from knowledge otherwise than merely by accident; for all knowledge and wonder (which is the seed of knowledge) is an impression of pleasure in itself: but when men fall to framing conclusions out of their knowledge, applying it to their particular, and ministering to themselves thereby weak fears or vast desires, there groweth that carefulness and trouble of mind which is spoken of: for then knowledge is no more *Lumen siccum* [a dry light], whereof Heraclitus the profound said, *Lumen siccum optima anima,* [the dry light is the best soul;] but it becometh *Lumen madidum* or *maceratum,* [a light charged with moisture,] being steeped and infused in the humours of the affections.[5] And as for the third point, it deserveth to be a little stood upon and not to be lightly passed over: for if any man shall think by view and inquiry into these sensible and material things to attain that light whereby he may reveal unto himself the nature or will of God, then indeed is he spoiled by vain philosophy: for the contemplation of God's creatures and works produceth (having regard to the works and creatures themselves) knowledge; but having regard to God, no perfect knowledge, but wonder, which is broken knowledge. And therefore it was most aptly said by one of Plato's school,[6] *That the sense of man carrieth a resemblance with the sun, which (as we see) openeth and revealeth all the terrestrial globe; but then again it obscureth and concealeth the stars and celestial globe: so doth the sense discover natural things, but it darkeneth and shutteth up divine.* And hence it is true that it hath proceeded that divers great learned men have been heretical, whilst they have sought to fly up to the secrets of the Deity by the waxen wings of the senses. And as for the conceit that too much knowledge should incline a man to atheism, and that the ignorance of second causes should make a more devout dependence upon God which is the first cause; first, it is good to ask the question which Job asked of his friends, *Will you lie for God, as one man will do for another, to gratify him?* For certain it is that God worketh nothing in nature but by second causes; and if they would have it otherwise believed, it is mere imposture, as it were in favour towards God; and nothing else but to offer to the author of truth the unclean sacrifice of a lie. But farther, it is an assured truth and a conclusion of experience, that a little or superficial knowledge of philosophy may incline the mind of man to atheism, but a farther proceeding therein doth bring the mind back again to religion; for in the entrance of philosophy, when the second causes, which are next unto the senses, do offer themselves to the mind of man, if it dwell and stay there, it may induce some oblivion of the highest cause; but when a man passeth on farther, and seeth the dependence of causes and the works of Providence; then, according to the allegory of the poets, he will easily believe that the highest link of nature's chain must needs be tied to the foot of Jupiter's chair. To conclude therefore, let no man, upon a weak conceit of sobriety or an ill-applied moderation, think or maintain that a man can search too far or be too well studied in the book of God's word or in the book of God's works; divinity or philosophy; but rather let men endeavour an endless progress or proficience in both; only let men beware that they apply both to charity, and not to swelling; to use, and not to ostentation; and again, that they do not unwisely mingle or confound these learnings together.

And as for the disgraces which learning receiveth from politiques, they be of this nature; that learning doth soften men's minds, and makes them more unapt for the honour and exercise of arms; that it doth mar and pervert men's dispositions for matter of government and policy, in making them too curious and irresolute by variety of reading, or too peremptory or positive by strictness of rules and axioms, or too immoderate and overweening by reason of the greatness of examples, or too incompatible and differing from the times by reason of the dissimilitude of examples; or at least that it doth divert men's travails from action and business, and bringeth them to a love of leisure and privateness; and that it doth bring into states a relaxation of discipline, whilst every man is more ready to argue than to obey and execute. Out of this conceit Cato surnamed the Censor, one of the wisest men indeed that ever lived, when Carneades the philosopher came in embassage to Rome, and that the young men of Rome began to flock about him, being allured with the sweetness and majesty of his eloquence and learning, gave counsel in open senate that they should give him his dispatch with all speed, lest he should infect and inchant the minds and affections of the youth, and at unawares bring in an alteration of the manners and customs of the state. Out of the same conceit or humour did Virgil, turning his pen to the advantage of his country and the disadvantage of his own profession, make a kind of separation between policy and government and between arts and sciences, in the verses so much renowned, attributing and challenging the one to the Romans, and leaving and yielding the other to the Grecians; *Tu regere imperio populos, Romane, memento, Hæ tibi erunt artes,* &c.

[Be thine, O Rome,
With arts of government to rule the nations.]

So likewise we see that Anytus, the accuser of Socrates, laid it as an article of charge and accusation against him that he did with the variety and power of his discourses and disputations withdraw young men from due reverence to the laws and customs of their country; and that he did profess a dangerous and pernicious science, which was to make the worse matter seem the better, and to suppress truth by force of eloquence and speech.

But these and the like imputations have rather a countenance of gravity than any ground of justice: for experience doth warrant that both in persons and in times there hath been a meeting and concurrence in learning and arms, flourishing and excelling in the same men and the same ages. For as for men, there cannot be a better nor the like instance, as of that pair, Alexander the Great and Julius Cæsar the dictator; whereof the one was Aristotle's scholar in philosophy, and the other was Cicero's rival in eloquence; or if any man had rather call for scholars that were great generals than generals that were great scholars, let him take Epaminondas the Theban, or Xenophon the Athenian; whereof the one was the first that abated the power of Sparta, and the other was the first that made way to the overthrow of the monarchy of Persia. And this concurrence is yet more visible in times than in persons, by how much an age is greater object than a man. For both in Ægypt, Assyria, Persia, Græcia, and Rome, the same times that are most renowned for arms are likewise most admired for learning; so that the greatest authors and philosophers and the greatest captains and governors have lived in the same ages. Neither can it otherwise be: for as in man the ripeness of strength of the body and mind cometh much about an age, save that the strength of the body cometh somewhat the more early; so in states, arms and learning, whereof the one correspondeth to the body, the other to the soul of man, have a concurrence or near sequence in times.

And for matter of policy and government, that learning should rather hurt than enable thereunto, is a thing very improbable. We see it is accounted an error to commit a natural body to empiric physicians, which commonly have a few pleasing receits[7] whereupon they are confident and adventurous, but know neither the causes of diseases, nor the complexions[8] of patients, nor peril of accidents, nor the true method of cures. We see it is a like error to rely upon advocates or lawyers which are only men of practice and not grounded in their books, who are many times easily surprised when matter falleth out besides their experience, to the prejudice of the causes they handle. So by like reason it cannot be but a matter of doubtful consequence, if states be managed by empiric statesmen, not well mingled with men grounded in learning. But contrariwise, it is almost without instance contradictory, that ever any government was disastrous that was in the hands of learned governors. For howsover it hath been ordinary with politic men to extenuate and disable[9] learned men by the names of *Pedantes;* yet in the records of time it appeareth in many particulars, that the governments of princes in minority (notwithstanding the infinite disadvantage of that kind of state) have nevertheless excelled the government of princes of mature age, even for that reason which they seek to traduce, which is, that by that occasion the state hath been in the hands of *Pedantes:* for so was the state of Rome for the first five years, which are so much magnified, during the minority of Nero, in the hands of Seneca, a *Pedanti:* so it was again for ten years space or more, during the minority of Gordianus the younger, with great applause and contentation in the hands of Misitheus, a *Pedanti:* so was it before that, in the minority of Alexander Severus, in like happiness, in hands not much unlike, by reason of the rule of the women, who were aided by the teachers and preceptors. Nay let a man look into the government of the bishops of Rome, as by name[10] into the government of Pius Quintus and Sextus Quintus in our times, who were both at their entrance esteemed but as pedantical friars, and he shall find that such popes do greater things, and proceed upon truer principles of estate, than those which have ascended to the papacy from an education and breeding in affairs of estate and courts of princes; for although men bred in learning are perhaps to seek in points of convenience and accommodating for the present, which the Italians call *ragioni di stato*,[11] whereof the same Pius Quintus could not hear spoken with patience, terming them inventions against religion and the moral virtues; yet on the other side, to recompense that, they are perfect in those same plain grounds of religion, justice, honour, and moral virtue; which if they be well and watchfully pursued, there will be seldom use of those other, no more than of physic in a sound or well-dieted body. Neither can the experience of one man's life furnish examples and precedents for the events of one man's life: for as it happeneth sometimes that the grandchild or other descendant resembleth the ancestor more than the son; so many times occurrences of present times may sort better with ancient examples than with those of the later or immediate times: and lastly, the wit of one man can no more countervail learning than one man's means can hold way with a common purse.

And as for those particular seducements or indispositions of the mind for policy and government, which learning is pretended to insinuate; if it be granted that any such thing be, it must be remembered withal, that learning ministereth in every of them greater strength of medicine or remedy, than it offereth cause of indisposition or infirmity. For if by a secret operation it make men perplexed and irresolute, on the other side by plain precept it teacheth them when and upon what ground to resolve; yea, and how to carry things in suspense without prejudice till they resolve. If it make men positive and regular, it teacheth them what things are in their nature demonstrative, and what are conjectural; and as well the use of distinctions and exceptions, as the latitude of principles and rules. If it mislead by disproportion or dissimilitude of examples, it teacheth men the force of circumstances, the errors of comparisons, and all the cautions of application; so that in all these it doth rectify more effectually than it can pervert. And these medicines it conveyeth into men's minds much more forcibly by the quickness and penetration of examples. For let a man look into the errors of Clement the seventh, so lively described by Guicciardine, who served under him, or into the errors of Cicero painted out by his own pencil in his epistles to Atticus, and he will fly apace from being irresolute. Let him look into the errors of Phocion, and he will beware how he be obstinate or inflexible. Let him but read the fable of Ixion, and it will hold him from being vaporous or imaginative. Let him look into the errors of Cato the second, and he will never be one of the Antipodes, to tread opposite to the present world.

And for the conceit[12] that learning should dispose men to leisure and privateness, and make men slothful; it were a strange thing if that which accustometh the mind to a perpetual motion and agitation should induce slothfulness; whereas contrariwise it may be truly affirmed that no kind of men love business for itself but those that are learned; for other persons love it for profit, as an hireling that loves the work for the wages; or for honour, as because it beareth them up in the eyes of men, and refresheth their reputation which otherwise would wear; or because it putteth them in mind of their fortune, and giveth them occasion to pleasure and displeasure; or because it exerciseth some faculty wherein they take pride, and so entertaineth them in good humour and pleasing conceits toward themselves; or because it advanceth any other their ends. So that as it is said of untrue valours that some men's valours are in the eyes of them that look on, so such men's industries are in the eyes of others, or at least in regard of their own designments; only learned men love business as an action according to nature, as agreeable to health of mind as exercise is to health of body, taking pleasure in the action itself, and not in the purchase: so that of all men they are the most indefatigable, if it be towards any business which can hold or detain their mind.

And if any man be laborious in reading and study and yet idle in business and action, it groweth from some weakness of body or softness of spirit, such as Seneca speaketh of; *Quidam tam sunt umbratiles, ut putent in turbido esse quicquid in luce est,* [there are some men so fond of the shade, that they think they are in trouble whenever they are in the light;] and not of learning. Well may it be that such a point of a man's nature may make him give himself to learning, but it is not learning that breedeth any such point in his nature.

And that learning should take up too much time or leisure; I answer, the most active or busy man that hath been or can be hath (no question) many vacant times of leisure, while he expecteth the tides and returns of business, (except he be either tedious and of no dispatch, or lightly and unworthily ambitious to meddle in things that may be better done by others;) and then the question is but how those spaces and times of leisure shall be filled and spent; whether in pleasures or in studies; as was well answered by Demosthenes to his adversary Æschines, that was a man given to pleasure, and told him *that his orations did smell of the lamp: Indeed* (said Demosthenes) *there is a great difference between the things that you and I do by lamp-light.* So as no man need doubt that learning will expulse business; but rather it will keep and defend the possession of the mind against idleness and pleasure, which otherwise at unawares may enter to the prejudice of both.

Again, for that other conceit that learning should undermine the reverence of laws and government, it is assuredly a mere depravation and calumny without all shadow of truth. For to say that a blind custom of obedience should be a surer obligation than duty taught and understood, it is to affirm that a blind man may tread surer by a guide than a seeing man can by a light. And it is without all controversy that learning doth make the minds of men gentle, generous, maniable,[13] and pliant to government; whereas ignorance makes them churlish, thwart, and mutinous: and the evidence of time doth clear this assertion, considering that the most barbarous, rude, and unlearned times have been most subject to tumults, seditions, and changes.

And as to the judgment of Cato the Censor, he was well punished for his blasphemy against learning, in the same kind wherein he offended; for when he was past threescore years old, he was taken with an extreme desire to go to school again and to learn the Greek tongue, to the end to peruse the Greek authors; which doth well demonstrate, that his former censure of the Grecian learning was rather an affected gravity, than according to the inward sense of his own opinion. And as for Virgil's verses, though it pleased him to brave the world in taking to the Romans the art of empire, and leaving to others the arts of subjects; yet so much is manifest, that the Romans never ascended to that height of empire till the time they had ascended to the height of other arts; for in the time of the two first Cæsars, which had the art of government in greatest perfection, there lived the best poet, Virgilius Maro; the best historiographer, Titus Livius; the best antiquary, Marcus Varro; and the best, or second orator, Marcus Cicero, that to the memory of man are known. As for the accusation of Socrates, the time must be remembered when it was prosecuted; which was under the thirty tyrants, the most base, bloody, and envious persons that have governed; which revolution of state was no sooner over, but Socrates, whom they had made a person criminal, was made a person heroical, and his memory accumulate with honours divine and human; and those discourses of his, which were then termed corrupting of manners, were after acknowledged for sovereign medicines of the mind and manners, and so have been received ever since till this day. Let this therefore serve for answer to politiques, which in their humorous[14] severity or in their feigned gravity have presumed to throw imputations upon learning; which redargution[15] nevertheless (save that we know not whether our labours may extend to other ages) were not needful for the present, in regard of the love and reverence towards learning which the example and countenance of two so learned princes, queen Elizabeth and your Majesty, being as Castor and Pollux, *lucida sidera,* stars of excellent light and most benign influence, hath wrought in all men of place and authority in our nation.

Now therefore we come to that third sort of discredit or diminution of credit, that groweth unto learning from learned men themselves, which commonly cleaveth fastest. It is either from their fortune, or from their manners, or from the nature of their studies. For the first, it is not in their power; and the second is accidental; the third only is proper to be handled. But because we are not in hand with true measure, but with popular estimation and conceit, it is not amiss to speak somewhat of the two former. The derogations therefore which grow to learning from the fortune or condition of learned men, are either in respect of scarcity of means, or in respect of privateness of life and meanness of employments.

Concerning want, and that it is the case of learned men usually to begin with little and not to grow rich so fast as other men, by reason they convert not their labours chiefly to lucre and increase; it were good to leave the common place in commendation of poverty to some friar to handle, to whom much was attributed by Machiavel in this point, when he said, *That the kingdom of the clergy had been long before at an end, if the reputation and reverence towards the poverty of friars had not borne out the scandal of the superfluities and excesses of bishops and prelates.* So a man might say that the felicity and delicacy of princes and great persons had long since turned to rudeness and barbarism, if the poverty of learning had not kept up civility and honour of life. But without any such advantages, it is worthy the observation what a reverend and honoured thing poverty of fortune was for some ages in the Roman state, which nevertheless was a state without paradoxes. For we see what Titus Livius saith in his introduction: *Cæterum aut me amor negotii suscepti fallit, aut nulla unquam respublica nec major, nec sanctior nec bonis exem-*

*plis ditior fuit; nec in quam tam seræ avaritia luxuriaque
immigraverint; nec ubi tantus ac tam diu paupertati ac
parsimoniæ honos fuerit:* [that if affection for his subject
did not deceive him, there was never any state in the
world either greater or purer or richer in good examples;
never any into which avarice and luxury made their way
so late; never any in which poverty and frugality were for
so long a time held in so great honour]. We see likewise,
after that the state of Rome was not itself but did degenerate, how that person that took upon him to be counsellor
to Julius Cæsar after his victory, where to begin his restoration of the state, maketh it of all points the most summary
to take away the estimation of wealth: *Verum hæc et
omnia mala pariter cum honore pecuniæ desinent; si neque
magistratus, neque alia vulgo cupienda, venalia, erunt:* [but
these and all other evils (he says) will cease as soon as the
worship of money ceases; which will come to pass when
neither magistracies nor other things that are objects of
desire to the vulgar shall be to be had for money]. To conclude this point, as it was truly said that *rubor est virtutis
color,* [a blush is virtue's colour,] though sometime it come
from vice; so it may be fitly said that *paupertas est virtutis
fortuna,* [poverty is virtue's fortune,] though sometime it
may proceed from misgovernment and accident. Surely
Salomon hath pronounced it, both in censure, *Qui festinat
ad divitias non erit insons,* [he that maketh haste to be rich
shall not be innocent;] and in precept, *Buy the truth, and
sell it not; and so of wisdom and knowledge;* judging that
means were to be spent upon learning, and not learning to
be applied to means. And as for the privateness or obscure-
ness (as it may be in vulgar estimation accounted) of life
of contemplative men; it is a theme so common to extol a
private life, not taxed with sensuality and sloth, in comparison and to the disadvantage of a civil life, for safety, liberty, pleasure, and dignity, or at least freedom from indignity, as no man handleth it but handleth it well; such a
consonancy it hath to men's conceits in the expressing and
to men's consents in the allowing. This only I will add, that

learned men forgotten in states, and not living in the eyes of men, are like the images of Cassius and Brutus in the funeral of Junia; of which not being represented, as many others were, Tacitus saith, *Eo ipso præfulgebant, quod non visebantur;* [they had the preeminence over all—in being left out].

And for meanness of employment, that which is most traduced to contempt is that the government of youth is commonly allotted to them; which age, because it is the age of least authority, it is transferred to the disesteeming of those employments wherein youth is conversant, and which are conversant about youth. But how unjust this traducement is (if you will reduce things from popularity of opinion to measure of reason) may appear in that we see men are more curious what they put into a new vessel than into a vessel seasoned, and what mould they lay about a young plant than about a plant corroborate; so as the weakest terms and times of all things use to have the best applications and helps. And will you hearken to the Hebrew Rabbins? *Your young men shall see visions, and your old men shall dream dreams;* say they youth is the worthier age, for that visions are nearer apparitions of God than dreams. And let it be noted, that howsover the conditions of life of *Pedantes* have been scorned upon theatres, as the ape of tyranny; and that the modern looseness or negligence hath taken no due regard to the choice of school-masters and tutors; yet the ancient wisdom of the best times did always make a just complaint that states were too busy with their laws and too negligent in point of education: which excellent part of ancient discipline hath been in some sort revived of late times by the colleges of the Jesuits; of whom, although in regard of their superstition I may say, *quo meliores, eo deteriores,* [the better the worse;] yet in regard of this, and some other points concerning human learning and moral matters, I may say, as Agesilaus said to his enemy Pharnabazus, *talis quum sis, utinam noster esses,* [they are so good that I wish they were on our side]. And thus much touching the discredits drawn from the fortunes of learned men.

As touching the manners of learned men, it is a thing personal and individual: and no doubt there be amongst them, as in other professions, of all temperatures: but yet so as it is not without truth which is said, that *abeunt studia in mores*, studies have an influence and operation upon the manners of those that are conversant in them.

But upon an attentive and indifferent review, I for my part cannot find any disgrace to learning can proceed from the manners of learned men; not inherent to them as they are learned; except it be a fault (which was the supposed fault of Demosthenes, Cicero, Cato the second, Seneca, and many more) that because the times they read of are commonly better than the times they live in, and the duties taught better than the duties practised, they contend sometimes too far to bring things to perfection, and to reduce the corruption of manners to honesty of precepts or examples of too great height. And yet hereof they have caveats enough in their own walks. For Solon, when he was asked whether he had given his citizens the best laws, answered wisely, *Yea of such as they would receive:* and Plato, finding that his own heart could not agree with the corrupt manners of his country, refused to bear place or office; saying, *That a man's country was to be used as his parents were, that is, with humble persuasions, and not with contestations:* and Cæsar's counsellor put in the same caveat, *Non ad vetera instituta revocans quæ jampridem corruptis moribus ludibrio sunt:* [not to attempt to bring things back to the original institution, now that by reason of the corruption of manners the ancient simplicity and purity had fallen into contempt:] and Cicero noteth this error directly in Cato the second, when he writes to his friend Atticus; *Cato optime sentit, sed nocet interdum reipublicæ; loquitur enim tanquam in republica Platonis, non tanquam in fæce Romuli:* [Cato means excellently well; but he does hurt sometimes to the state; for he talks as if it were Plato's republic that we are living in, and not the dregs of Romulus:] and the same Cicero doth excuse and expound [16] the philosophers for going too far and being too exact in their prescripts, when he saith, *Isti ipsi præceptores virtutis et*

magistri videntur fines officiorum paulo longius quam na-
tura vellet protulisse, ut cum ad ultimum animo contendis-
semus, ibi tamen, ubi oportet, consisteremus: [that they had
set the points of duty somewhat higher than nature would
well bear; meaning belike to allow for shortcomings, and
that our endeavours aiming beyond the mark and falling
short, should light at the right place:] and yet himself might
have said, *Monitus sum minor ipse meis,* [that he fell short
of his own precepts]; for it was his own fault, though not
in so extreme a degree.

Another fault likewise much of this kind hath been incident to learned men; which is, that they have esteemed the
preservation, good, and honour of their countries or masters before their own fortunes or safeties. For so saith
Demosthenes unto the Athenians: *If it please you to note*
it, my counsels unto you are not such whereby I should
grow great amongst you, and you become little amongst
the Grecians: but they be of that nature, as they are some-
times not good for me to give, but are always good for you
to follow. And so Seneca, after he had consecrated that
Quinquennium Neronis[17] to the eternal glory of learned
governors, held on his honest and loyal course of good and
free counsel, after his master grew extremely corrupt in his
government. Neither can this point otherwise be; for learning endueth men's minds with a true sense of the frailty of
their persons, the casualty of their fortunes, and the dignity
of their soul and vocation; so that it is impossible for them
to esteem that any greatness of their own fortune can be a
true or worthy end of their being and ordainment; and
therefore are desirous to give their account to God, and so
likewise to their masters under God (as kings and the
states that they serve), in these words; *Ecce tibi lucrefeci,*
and not *Ecce mihi lucrefeci,* ['Lo, I have gained for thee,'
not 'Lo, I have gained for myself:'] whereas the corrupter sort
of mere politiques, that have not their thoughts established
by learning in the love and apprehension of duty, nor never
look abroad into universality, do refer all things to themselves, and thrust themselves into the centre of the world, as

if all lines should meet in them and their fortunes; never caring in all tempests what becomes of the ship of estates, so they may save themselves in the cockboat of their own fortune; whereas men that feel the weight of duty, and know the limits of self-love, use to make good their places and duties, though with peril. And if they stand in seditious and violent alterations, it is rather the reverence which many times both adverse parts do give to honesty, than any versatile advantage of their own carriage. But for this point of tender sense and fast obligation of duty, which learning doth endue the mind withal, howsoever fortune may tax it and many in the depth of their corrupt principles may despise it, yet it will receive an open allowance, and therefore needs the less disproof or excusation.

Another fault incident commonly to learned men, which may be more probably defended than truly denied, is that they fail sometimes in applying themselves to particular persons; which want of exact application ariseth from two causes; the one, because the largeness of their mind can hardly confine itself to dwell in the exquisite observation or examination of the nature and customs of one person: for it is a speech for a lover and not for a wise man, *Satis magnum alter alteri theatrum sumus*, [each is to other a theatre large enough]. Nevertheless I shall yield, that he that cannot contract the sight of his mind as well as disperse and dilate it, wanteth a great faculty. But there is a second cause, which is no inability but a rejection upon choice and judgment. For the honest and just bounds of observation by one person upon another extend no farther but to understand him sufficiently, whereby not to give him offence, or whereby to be able to give him faithful counsel, or whereby to stand upon reasonable guard and caution in respect of a man's self: but to be speculative into another man, to the end to know how to work him or wind him or govern him, proceedeth from a heart that is double and cloven, and not entire and ingenuous; which as in friendship it is want of integrity, so towards princes or superiors is want of duty. For the custom of the Levant, which is, that subjects do forbear to gaze or fix their eyes upon princes, is in the outward ceremony barbarous; but the moral is good: for men ought not by cunning and bent observations to pierce and penetrate into the hearts of kings, which the Scripture hath declared to be inscrutable.

There is yet another fault (with which I will conclude this part) which is often noted in learned men, that they do many times fail to observe decency and discretion in their behaviour and carriage, and commit errors in small and ordinary points of action; so as the vulgar sort of capacities do make a judgment of them in greater matters by that which they find wanting in them in smaller. But this consequence doth oft deceive men; for which I do refer them over to that which was said by Themistocles, arrogantly and uncivilly being applied to himself out of his own mouth, but being aplied to the general state of this question pertinently and justly; when being invited to touch a lute, he said *he could not fiddle, but he could make a small town a great state.* So no doubt many may be well seen in the passages of government and policy, which are to seek in little and punctual occasions. I refer them also to that which Plato said of his master Socrates, whom he compared to the gallypots of apothecaries, which on the outside had apes and owls and antiques, but contained within sovereign and precious liquors and confections; acknowledging that to an external report he was not without superficial levities and deformities, but was inwardly replenished with excellent virtues and powers. And so much touching the point of manners of learned men.

But in the mean time I have no purpose to give allowance to some conditions and courses base and unworthy, wherein divers professors of learning have wronged themselves and gone too far; such as were those trencher philosophers,[18] which in the later age of the Roman state were usually in the houses of great persons, being little better than solemn parasites; of which kind, Lucian maketh a merry description of the philosopher that the great lady took to ride with her in her coach, and would needs have him carry her little dog, which he doing officiously and yet uncomely, the page scoffed, and said, *That he doubted the philosopher of a Stoic would turn to be a Cynic.*[19] But above all the rest, the gross and palpable flattery whereunto many (not unlearned) have abased and abused their wits and pens, turning (as Du Bartas saith) Hecuba into Helena and Faustina into Lucretia, hath most diminished the price and estimation of learning. Neither is the moral [20] dedications of books and writings, as to patrons, to be commended: for that books (such as are worthy the name of books) ought to have no patrons but truth and reason; and the ancient custom was to dedicate them only to private and equal friends, or to intitle the books with their names; or if to kings and great persons, it was to some such as the argument of the book was fit and proper for. But these and the like courses may deserve rather reprehension than defence.

Not that I can tax or condemn the morigeration[21] or application of learned men to men in fortune. For the answer was good that Diogenes made to one that asked him in mockery, *How it came to pass that philosophers were the followers of rich men, and not rich men of philosophers?* He answered soberly, and yet sharply, *Because the one sort knew what they had need of, and the other did not.* And of the like nature was the answer which Aristippus made, when having a petition to Dionysius and no ear given to him, he fell down at his feet, whereupon Dionysius staid and gave him the hearing and granted it; and afterward some person tender on the behalf of philosophy, reproved Aristippus that he would offer the profession of philosophy such an indignity, as for a private suit to fall at a tyrant's feet: but he answered, *It was not his fault, but it was the fault of Dionysius, that had his ears in his feet.* Neither was it accounted weakness, but discretion, in him that would not dispute his best with Adrianus Cæsar; excusing himself, *That it was reason to yield to him that commanded thirty legions.* These and the like applications and stooping to points of necessity and convenience cannot be disallowed;

for though they may have some outward baseness, yet in a judgment truly made they are to be accounted submissions to the occasion and not to the person.

Now I proceed to those errors and vanities which have intervened amongst the studies themselves of the learned; which is that which is principal and proper to the present argument; wherein my purpose is not to make a justification of the errors, but, by a censure and separation of the errors, to make a justification of that which is good and sound, and to deliver that from the aspersion of the other. For we see that it is the manner of men to scandalize and deprave that which retaineth the state and virtue, by taking advantage upon that which is corrupt and degenerate: as the Heathens in the primitive church used to blemish and taint the Christians with the faults and corruptions of heretics. But nevertheless I have no meaning at this time to make any exact animadversion of the errors and impediments in matters of learning which are more secret and remote from vulgar opinion; but only to speak unto such as do fall under, or near unto, a popular observation.

There be therefore chiefly three vanities in studies, whereby learning hath been most traduced. For those things we do esteem vain, which are either false or frivolous, those which either have no truth or no use: and those persons we esteem vain, which are either credulous or curious; and curiosity is either in matter or words: so that in reason as well as in experience, there fall out to be these three distempers (as I may term them) of learning; the first, fantastical learning; the second, contentious learning; and the last, delicate learning; vain imaginations, vain altercations, and vain affectations; and with the last I will begin. Martin Luther, conducted (no doubt) by an higher Providence, but in discourse of reason finding what a province he had undertaken against the Bishop of Rome and the degenerate traditions of the church, and finding his own solitude, being no ways aided by the opinions of his own time, was enforced to awake all antiquity, and to call former times to his succors to make a party against the

present time; so that the ancient authors, both in divinity
and in humanity, which had long time slept in libraries,
began generally to be read and revolved. This by consequence did draw on a necessity of a more exquisite travail
in the languages original wherein those authors did write,
for the better understanding of those authors and the better advantage of pressing and applying their words. And
thereof grew again a delight in their manner of style and
phrase, and an admiration of that kind of writing; which
was much furthered and precipitated by the enmity and
opposition that the propounders of those (primitive but
seeming new) opinions had against the schoolmen; who
were generally of the contrary part, and whose writings
were altogether in a differing style and form; taking liberty
to coin and frame new terms of art to express their own
sense and to avoid circuit of speech, without regard to the
pureness, pleasantness, and (as I may call it) lawfulness
of the phrase or word. And again, because the great labour
then was with the people, (of whom the Pharisees were
wont to say, *Execrabilis ista turba, quæ non novit legem,*)
[the wretched crowd that has not known the law,] for the
winning and persuading of them, there grew of necessity
in chief price and request eloquence and variety of discourse, as the fittest and forciblest access into the capacity
of the vulgar sort. So that these four causes concurring,
the admiration of ancient authors, the hate of the schoolmen, the exact study of languages, and the efficacy of
preaching, did bring in an affectionate study of eloquence
and copie[22] of speech, which then began to flourish. This
grew speedily to an excess; for men began to hunt more
after words than matter; and more after the choiceness of
the phrase, and the round and clean composition of the
sentence, and the sweet falling of the clauses, and the varying and illustration of their works with tropes and figures,
than after the weight of matter, worth of subject, soundness of argument, life of invention, or depth of judgment.
Then grew the flowing and watery vein of Osorius, the
Portugal bishop, to be in price. Then did Sturmius spend

such infinite and curious pains upon Cicero the orator and
Hermogenes the rhetorician, besides his own books of
periods and imitation and the like. Then did Car of Cambridge, and Ascham, with their lectures and writings almost deify Cicero and Demosthenes, and allure all young
men that were studious unto that delicate and polished kind
of learning. Then did Erasmus take occasion to make the
scoffing echo; *Decem annos consumpsi in legendo Cicer-
one,* [I have spent ten years in reading Cicero:] and the
echo answered in Greek, *one, Asine.*[23] Then grew the learning of the schoolmen to be utterly despised as barbarous.
In sum, the whole inclination and bent of those times was
rather towards copie than weight.

Here therefore [is] the first distemper of learning, when
men study words and not matter: whereof though I have
represented an example of late times, yet it hath been and
will be *secundum majus et minus* [*more or less] in all time.
And how is it possible but this should have an operation to
discredit learning, even with vulgar capacities, when they
see learned men's works like the first letter of a patent or
limned book; which though it hath large flourishes, yet it is
but a letter? It seems to me that Pygmalion's frenzy is a
good emblem or portraiture of this vanity: for words are
but the images of matter; and except they have life of reason and invention, to fall in love with them is all one as to
fall in love with a picture.

But yet notwithstanding it is a thing not hastily to be
condemned, to clothe and adorn the obscurity even of philosophy itself with sensible and plausible elocution. For
hereof we have great examples in Xenophon, Cicero, Seneca, Plutarch, and of Plato also in some degree; and hereof
likewise there is great use; for surely to the severe inquisition of truth, and the deep progress into philosophy, it is
some hinderance; because it is too early satisfactory to the
mind of man, and quencheth the desire of further search,
before we come to a just period; but then if a man be to
have any use of such knowledge in civil occasions, of conference, counsel, persuasion, discourse, or the like; then

shall he find it prepared to his hands in those authors which write in that manner. But the excess of this is so justly contemptible, that as Hercules, when he saw the image of Adonis, Venus' minion, in a temple, said in disdain, *Nil sacri es,* [you are no divinity;] so there is none of Hercules' followers in learning, that is, the more severe and laborious sort of inquirers into truth, but will despise those delicacies and affectations, as indeed capable of no divineness. And thus much of the first disease or distemper of learning.

The second, which followeth, is in nature worse than the former; for as substance of matter is better than beauty of words, so contrariwise vain matter is worse than vain words: wherein it seemeth the reprehension of St. Paul was not only proper for those times, but prophetical for the times following; and not only respective to divinity, but extensive to all knowledge: *Devita profanas vocum novitates, et oppositiones falsi nominis scientiæ:* [shun profane novelties of terms and oppositions of science falsely so called]. For he assigneth two marks and badges of suspected and falsified science; the one, the novelty and strangeness of terms; the other, the strictness of positions, which of necessity doth induce oppositions, and so questions and altercations. Surely, like as many substances in nature which are solid do putrefy and corrupt into worms, so it is the property of good and sound knowledge to putrefy and dissolve into a number of subtile, idle, unwholesome, and (as I may term them) vermiculate questions, which have indeed a kind of quickness and life of spirit, but no soundness of matter or goodness of quality. This kind of degenerate learning did chiefly reign amongst the schoolmen; who having sharp and strong wits, and abundance of leisure, and small variety of reading; but their wits being shut up in the cells of a few authors (chiefly Aristotle their dictator) as their persons were shut up in the cells of monasteries and colleges; and knowing little history, either of nature or time; did out of no great quantity of matter, and infinite agitation of wit, spin out unto us those laborious webs of learning which are extant in their books. For the wit and mind of man, if it work upon matter, which is the contemplation of the creatures of God, worketh according to the stuff, and is limited thereby; but if it work upon itself, as the spider worketh his web, then it is endless, and brings forth indeed cobwebs of learning, admirable for the fineness of thread and work, but of no substance or profit.

This same unprofitable subtility or curiosity is of two sorts; either in the subject itself that they handle, when it is a fruitless speculation or controversy, (whereof there are no small number both in divinity and philosophy,) or in the manner or method of handling of a knowledge; which amongst them was this; upon every particular position or assertion to frame objections, and to those objections, solutions; which solutions were for the most part not confutations, but distinctions: whereas indeed the strength of all sciences is, as the strength of the old man's faggot, in the bond. For the harmony of a science, supporting each part the other, is and ought to be the true and brief confutation and suppression of all the smaller sort of objections; but on the other side, if you take out every axiom, as the sticks of the faggot, one by one, you may quarrel with them and bend them and break them at your pleasure: so that as was said of Seneca, *Verborum minutiis rerum frangit pondera,* [that he broke up the weight and mass of the matter by verbal points and niceties;] so a man may truly say of the schoolmen, *Quæstionum minutiis scientiarum frangunt soliditatem;* [they broke up the solidity and coherency of the sciences by the minuteness and nicety of their questions]. For were it not better for a man in a fair room to set up one great light, or branching candlestick of lights, than to go about with a small watch candle into every corner? And such is their method, that rests not so much upon evidence of truth proved by arguments, authorities, similitudes, examples, as upon particular confutations and solutions of every scruple, cavillation, and objection; breeding for the most part one question as fast it solveth another; even as in the former resemblance, when you carry the light into one corner, you darken the rest: so that the fable and fiction of

Scylla seemeth to be a lively image of this kind of philosophy or knowledge; which was transformed into a comely virgin for the upper parts; but then *Candida succinctam latrantibus inguina monstris,* [there were barking monsters all about her loins:] so the generalities of the schoolmen are for a while good and proportionable; but then when you descend into their distinctions and decisions, instead of a fruitful womb for the use and benefit of man's life, they end in monstrous altercations and barking questions. So as it is not possible but this quality of knowledge must fall under popular contempt, the people being apt to contemn truth upon occasion of controversies and altercations, and to think they are all out of their way which never meet: and when they see such digladiation about subtilities and matter of no use nor moment, they easily fall upon that judgment of Dionysius of Syracusa, *Verba ista sunt senum otiosorum,* [it is the talk of old men that have nothing to do].

Notwithstanding certain it is, that if those schoolmen to their great thirst of truth and unwearied travail of wit had joined variety and universality of reading and contemplation, they had proved excellent lights, to the great advancement of all learning and knowledge. But as they are, they are great undertakers indeed, and fierce with dark keeping; but as in the inquiry of the divine truth their pride inclined to leave the oracle of God's word and to vanish in the mixture of their own inventions, so in the inquisition of nature they ever left the oracle of God's works and adored the deceiving and deformed images which the unequal mirror of their own minds or a few received authors or principles did represent unto them. And thus much for the second disease of learning.

For the third vice or disease of learning, which concerneth deceit or untruth, it is of all the rest the foulest; as that which doth destroy the essential form of knowledge, which is nothing but a representation of truth: for the truth of being and the truth of knowing are one, differing no more than the direct beam and the beam reflected. This vice therefore brancheth itself into two sorts; delight in deceiving, and aptness to be deceived; imposture and credulity; which, although they appear to be of a diverse nature, the one seeming to proceed of cunning, and the other of simplicity, yet certainly they do for the most part concur: for as the verse noteth,

Percontatorem fugito, nam garrulus idem est,[24]

an inquisitive man is a prattler, so upon the like reason a credulous man is a deceiver: as we see it in fame, that he that will easily believe rumours will as easily augment rumours and add somewhat to them of his own; which Tacitus wisely noteth, when he saith, *Fingunt simul creduntque,* [as fast as they believe one tale they make another:] so great an affinity hath fiction and belief.

This facility of credit, and accepting or admitting things weakly authorized or warranted, is of two kinds, according to the subject: for it is either a belief of history (as the lawyers speak, matter of fact), or else of matter of art and opinion. As to the former, we see the experience and inconvenience of this error in ecclesiastical history; which hath too easily received and registered reports and narrations of miracles wrought by martyrs, hermits, or monks of the desert, and other holy men, and their relics, shrines, chapels, and images: which though they had a passage for a time, by the ignorance of the people, the superstitious simplicity of some, and the politic toleration of others, holding them but as divine poesies; yet after a period of time, when the mist began to clear up, they grew to be esteemed but as old wives' fables, impostures of the clergy, illusions of spirits, and badges of antichrist, to the great scandal and detriment of religion.

So in natural history, we see there hath not been that choice and judgment used as ought to have been; as may appear in the writings of Plinius, Cardanus, Albertus, and divers of the Arabians; being fraught with much fabulous matter, a great part not only untried but notoriously untrue, to the great derogation of the credit of natural philosophy with the grave and sober kind of wits. Wherein the wisdom and integrity of Aristotle is worthy to be observed; that having made so diligent and exquisite a history of living creatures, hath mingled it sparingly with any vain or feigned matter; and yet on the other side hath cast all prodigious narrations which he thought worthy the recording into one book; excellently discerning that matter of manifest truth, such whereupon observation and rule was to be built, was not to be mingled or weakened with matter of doubtful credit; and yet again that rarities and reports that seem uncredible are not to be suppressed or denied to the memory of men.

And as for the facility of credit which is yielded to arts and opinions, it is likewise of two kinds; either when too much belief is attributed to the arts themselves, or to certain authors in any art. The sciences themselves which have had better intelligence and confederacy with the imagination of man than with his reason, are three in number; Astrology, Natural Magic, and Alchemy; of which sciences nevertheless the ends or pretences are noble. For astrology pretendeth to discover that correspondence or concatenation which is between the superior globe and the inferior: natural magic pretendeth to call and reduce natural philosophy from variety of speculations to the magnitude of works: and alchemy pretendeth to make separation of all the unlike parts of bodies which in mixtures of nature are incorporate. But the derivations and prosecutions to these ends, both in the theories and in the practices, are full of error and vanity; which the great professors themselves have sought to veil over and conceal by enigmatical writings, and referring themselves to auricular traditions, and such other devices to save the credit of impostures. And yet surely to alchemy this right is due, that it may be compared to the husbandman whereof Æsop makes the fable, that when he died told his sons that he had left unto them gold buried under ground in his vineyard; and they digged over all the ground, and gold they found none, but by reason of their stirring and digging the mould about the roots of their vines, they had a great vintage the year following: so assuredly the search and stir to make gold hath brought to light a great number of good and fruitful inventions and experiments, as well for the disclosing of nature as for the use of man's life.

And as for the overmuch credit that hath been given unto authors in sciences, in making them dictators, that their words should stand, and not counsels to give advice; the damage is infinite that sciences have received thereby, as the principal cause that hath kept them low, at a stay without growth or advancement. For hence it hath comen that in arts mechanical the first deviser comes shortest, and time addeth and perfecteth; but in sciences the first author goeth furthest, and time leeseth and corrupteth. So we see, artillery, sailing, printing, and the like, were grossly managed at the first, and by time accommodated and refined; but contrariwise the philosophies and sciences of Aristotle, Plato, Democritus, Hippocrates, Euclides, Archimedes, of most vigour at the first, and by time degenerate and imbased; whereof the reason is no other, but that in the former many wits and industries have contributed in one; and in the later many wits and industries have been spent about the wit of some one, whom many times they have rather depraved than illustrated. For as water will not ascend higher than the level of the first spring-head from whence it descendeth, so knowledge derived from Aristotle, and exempted from liberty of examination, will not rise again higher than the knowledge of Aristotle. And therefore, although the position be good, *Oportet discentem credere,* [a man who is learning must be content to believe what he is told,] yet it must be coupled with this, *Oportet edoctum judicare,* [when he has learned it he must exercise his judgment and see whether it be worthy of belief;] for disciples do owe unto masters only a temporary belief and a suspension of their own judgment until they be fully instructed, and not an absolute resignation or perpetual captivity: and therefore to conclude this point, I will say no more but, so let great authors have their due, as time which is the author of authors be not deprived of his due, which is further and further to discover truth. Thus have I gone over these three diseases of learning; besides the which, there are some other rather peccant humours than formed diseases, which nevertheless are not so secret and intrinsic but that they fall under a popular observation and traducement, and therefore are not to be passed over.

The first of these is the extreme affecting of two extremities; the one Antiquity, the other Novelty: wherein it seemeth the children of time do take after the nature and malice of the father. For as he devoureth his children, so one of them seeketh to devour and suppress the other; while antiquity envieth there should be new additions, and novelty cannot be content to add but it must deface. Surely the advice of the prophet[25] is the true direction in this matter, *State super vias antiquas, et videte quænam sit via recta et bona, et ambulate in ea:* [stand ye in the old ways, and see which is the good way, and walk therein]. Antiquity deserveth that reverence, that men should make a stand thereupon, and discover what is the best way; but when the discovery is well taken, then to make progression. And to speak truly, *Antiquitas sæculi juventus mundi* [*the antiquity of time is the youth of the world]. These times are the ancient times, when the world is ancient, and not those which we account ancient *ordine retrogrado,* by a computation backward from ourselves.

Another error, induced by the former, is a distrust that any thing should be now to be found out, which the world should have missed and passed over so long time; as if the same objection were to be made to time that Lucian maketh to Jupiter and other the heathen gods, of which he wondereth that they begot so many children in old time and begot none in his time, and asketh whether they were become septuagenary, or whether the law *Pappia,* made against old men's marriages, had restrained them. So it seemeth men doubt lest time is become past children and generation; wherein contrariwise we see commonly the levity and unconstancy of men's judgments, which, till a matter be done, wonder that it can be done; and as soon as it is done, wonder again that it was no sooner done; as we see in the expedition of Alexander into Asia, which at first was prejudged as a vast and impossible enterprise; and yet afterwards it pleaseth Livy to make no more of it than this, *Nil aliud quàm bene ausus vana contemnere:* [it was but taking courage to despise vain apprehensions]. And the same happened to Columbus in the western navigation. But in intellectual matters it is much more common; as may be seen in most of the propositions of Euclid, which till they be demonstrate, they seem strange to our assent; but being demonstrate, our mind accepteth of them by a kind of relation[26] (as the lawyers speak) as if we had known them before.

Another error, that hath also some affinity with the former, is a conceit that of former opinions or sects, after variety and examination, the best hath still prevailed and suppressed the rest; so as if a man should begin the labour of a new search, he were but like to light upon somewhat formerly rejected, and by rejection brought into oblivion: as if the multitude, or the wisest for the multitude's sake, were not ready to give passage rather to that which is popular and superficial than to that which is substantial and profound; for the truth is, that time seemeth to be of the nature of a river or stream, which carrieth down to us that which is light and blown up, and sinketh and drowneth that which is weighty and solid.

Another error, of a diverse nature from all the former, is the over-early and peremptory reduction of knowledge into arts and methods; from which time commonly sciences receive small or no augmentation. But as young men, when they knit and shape perfectly, do seldom grow to a further stature; so knowledge, while it is in aphorisms and observations, it is in growth; but when it once is comprehended in exact methods, it may perchance be further polished and illustrate, and accommodated for use and practice; but it increaseth no more in bulk and substance.

Another error, which doth succeed that which we last

mentioned, is that after the distribution of particular arts and sciences, men have abandoned universality, or *philosophia prima;* which cannot but cease and stop all progression. For no perfect discovery can be made upon a flat or a level: neither is it possible to discover the more remote and deeper parts of any science, if you stand but upon the level of the same science, and ascend not to a higher science.

Another error hath proceeded from too great a reverence, and a kind of adoration of the mind and understanding of man; by means whereof men have withdrawn themselves too much from the contemplation of nature and the observations of experience, and have tumbled up and down in their own reason and conceits. Upon these intellectualists, which are notwithstanding commonly taken for the most sublime and divine philosophers, Heraclitus gave a just censure, saying, *Men sought truth in their own little worlds, and not in the great and common world;* for they disdain to spell and so by degrees to read in the volume of God's works; and contrariwise by continual meditation and agitation of wit do urge and as it were invocate their own spirits to divine and give oracles unto them, whereby they are deservedly deluded.

Another error that hath some connexion with this later is, that men have used to infect their meditations, opinions, and doctrines, with some conceits which they have most admired, or some sciences which they have most applied; and given all things else a tincture according to them, utterly untrue and unproper. So hath Plato intermingled his philosophy with theology, and Aristotle with logic, and the second school of Plato, Proclus and the rest, with the mathematics. For these were the arts which had a kind of primogeniture with them severally. So have the alchemists made a philosophy out of a few experiments of the furnace; and Gilbertus, our countryman, hath made a philosophy out of the observations of a loadstone. So Cicero, when, reciting the several opinions of the nature of the soul, he found a musician that held the soul was but a harmony, saith pleasantly, *Hic ab arte sua non recessit, &c.* [he was constant to his own art]. But of these conceits Aristotle speaketh seriously and wisely, when he saith, *Qui respiciunt ad pauca de facili pronunciant:* [they who take only few points into account find it easy to pronounce judgment].

Another error is an impatience of doubt, and haste to assertion without due and mature suspension of judgment. For the two ways of contemplation are not unlike the two ways of action commonly spoken of by the ancients; the one plain and smooth in the beginning, and in the end impassable; the other rough and troublesome in the entrance, but after a while fair and even. So it is in contemplation; if a man will begin with certainties, he shall end in doubts; but if he will be content to begin with doubts, he shall end in certainties.

Another error is in the manner of the tradition and delivery of knowledge, which is for the most part magistral and peremptory, and not ingenuous and faithful; in a sort as may be soonest believed, and not easiliest examined. It is true that in compendious treatises for practice that form is not to be disallowed. But in the true handling of knowledge, men ought not to fall either on the one side into the vein of Velleius the Epicurean, *Nil tam metuens, quàm ne dubitare aliqua de re videretur,* [who feared nothing so much as the seeming to be in doubt about anything,] nor on the other side into Socrates his ironical doubting of all things; but to propound things sincerely, with more or less asseveration, as they stand in a man's own judgment proved more or less.

Other errors there are in the scope that men propound to themselves, whereunto they bend their endeavours; for whereas the more constant and devote kind of professors of any science ought to propound to themselves to make some additions to their science, they convert their labours to aspire to certain second prizes; as to be a profound interpreter or commenter, to be a sharp champion or defender, to be a methodical compounder or abridger; and so the patrimony of knowledge cometh to be sometimes improved, but seldom augmented.

But the greatest error of all the rest is the mistaking or misplacing of the last or furthest end of knowledge. For men have entered into a desire of learning and knowledge, sometimes upon a natural curiosity and inquisitive appetite; sometimes to entertain their minds with variety and delight; sometimes for ornament and reputation; and sometimes to enable them to victory of wit and contradiction; and most times for lucre and profession; and seldom sincerely to give a true account of their gift of reason, to the benefit and use of men: as if there were sought in knowledge a couch, whereupon to rest a searching and restless spirit; or a terrace, for a wandering and variable mind to walk up and down with a fair prospect; or a tower of state, for a proud mind to raise itself upon; or a fort or commanding ground, for strife and contention; or a shop, for profit or sale; and not a rich storehouse, for the glory of the Creator and the relief of man's estate. But this is that which will indeed dignify and exalt knowledge, if contemplation and action may be more nearly and straitly conjoined and united together than they have been; a conjunction like unto that of the two highest planets, Saturn the planet of rest and contemplation, and Jupiter the planet of civil society and action. Howbeit, I do not mean, when I speak of use and action, that end before-mentioned of the applying of knowledge to lucre and profession: for I am not ignorant how much that diverteth and interrupteth the prosecution and advancement of knowledge; like unto the golden ball thrown before Atalanta, which while she goeth aside and stoopeth to take up, the race is hindered,

Declinat cursus, aurumque volubile tollit.
[*She swerves from the race and picks up the golden ball.]

Neither is my meaning, as was spoken of Socrates, to call philosophy down from heaven to converse upon the earth; that is, to leave natural philosophy aside, and to apply knowledge only to manners and policy. But as both heaven and earth do conspire and contribute to the use and benefit of man, so the end ought to be, from both philosophies to separate and reject vain speculations and whatsoever is empty and void, and to preserve and augment whatsoever is solid and fruitful; that knowledge may not be as a curtesan, for pleasure and vanity only, or as a bond-woman, to acquire and gain to her master's use; but as a spouse, for generation, fruit, and comfort.

Thus have I described and opened, as by a kind of dissection, those peccant humours (the principal of them) which have not only given impediment to the proficience of learning, but have given also occasion to the traducement thereof: wherein if I have been too plain, it must be remembered *Fidelia vulnera amantis, sed dolosa oscula malignantis:* [faithful are the wounds of a friend, but the kisses of an enemy are deceitful]. This I think I have gained, that I ought to be the better believed in that which I shall say pertaining to commendation, because I have proceeded so freely in that which concerneth censure. And yet I have no purpose to enter into a laudative of learning, or to make a hymn to the muses, (though I am of opinion that it is long since their rites were duly celebrated:) but my intent is, without varnish or amplification, justly to weigh the dignity of knowledge in the balance with other things, and to take the true value thereof by testimonies and arguments divine and human.

First therefore, let us seek the dignity of knowledge in the arch-type or first platform, which is in the attributes and acts of God, as far as they are revealed to man and may be observed with sobriety; wherein we may not seek it by the name of learning; for all learning is knowledge acquired, and all knowledge in God is original: and therefore we must look for it by another name, that of wisdom or sapience, as the Scriptures call it.

It is so then, that in the work of the creation we see a double emanation of virtue from God; the one referring more properly to power, the other to wisdom; the one expressed in making the subsistence of the matter, and the other in disposing the beauty of the form. This being supposed, it is to be observed, that for any thing which appeareth in the history of the creation, the confused mass and matter of heaven and earth was made in a moment, and the order and disposition of that chaos or mass was the work of six days; such a note of difference it pleased God to put upon the works of power and the works of wisdom; wherewith concurreth, that in the former it is not set down that God said, *Let there be heaven and earth,* as it is set down of the works following; but actually, that God made heaven and earth: the one carrying the style of a manufacture, and the other of a law, decree, or counsel.

To proceed to that which is next in order, from God to spirits; we find, as far as credit is to be given to the celestial hierarchy of that supposed Dionysius the senator of Athens, the first place or degree is given to the angels of love, which are termed Seraphim; the second to the angels of light, which are termed Cherubim; and the third and so following places to thrones, principalities, and the rest, which are all angels of power and ministry; so as the angels of knowledge and illumination are placed before the angels of office and domination.

To descend from spirits and intellectual forms to sensible and material forms; we read the first form that was created was light, which hath a relation and correspondence in nature and corporal things, to knowledge in spirits and incorporal things.

So in the distribution of days, we see the day wherein God did rest and contemplate his own works, was blessed above all the days wherein he did effect and accomplish them.

After the creation was finished, it is set down unto us that man was placed in the garden to work therein; which work so appointed to him could be no other than work of contemplation; that is, when the end of work is but for exercise and experiment, not for necessity; for there being then no reluctation of the creature, nor sweat of the brow, man's employment must of consequence have been matter of delight in the experiment, and not matter of labour for the use. Again, the first acts which man performed in Paradise consisted of the two summary parts of knowledge; the view of creatures, and the imposition of names. As for the knowledge which induced the fall, it was, as was touched before, not the natural knowledge of creatures, but the moral knowledge of good and evil; wherein the supposition was, that God's commandments or prohibitions were not the originals of good and evil, but that they had other beginnings, which man aspired to know, to the end to make a total defection from God, and to depend wholly upon himself.

To pass on: in the first event or occurrence after the fall of man, we see (as the Scriptures have infinite mysteries, not violating at all the truth of the story or letter,) an image of the two estates, the contemplative state and the active state, figured in the two persons of Abel and Cain, and in the two simplest and most primitive trades of life; that of the shepherd, (who, by reason of his leisure, rest in a place, and living in view of heaven, is a lively image of a contemplative life,) and that of the husbandman: where we see again the favour and election of God went to the shepherd, and not to the tiller of the ground.

So in the age before the flood, the holy records within those few memorials which are there entered and registered have vouchsafed to mention and honour the name of the inventors and authors of music and works in metal. In the age after the flood, the first great judgment of God upon the ambition of man was the confusion of tongues; whereby the open trade and intercourse of learning and knowledge was chiefly imbarred.

To descend to Moses the lawgiver, and God's first pen: he is adorned by the Scriptures with this addition[27] and commendation, that he was *seen in all the learning of the Egyptians;* which nation we know was one of the most ancient schools of the world: for so Plato brings in the Egyptian priest saying unto Solon: *You Grecians are never children; you have no knowledge of antiquity, nor antiquity of knowledge.* Take a view of the ceremonial law of Moses; you shall find, besides the prefiguration of Christ,

the badge or difference of the people of God, the exercise
and impression of obedience, and other divine uses and fruits
thereof, that some of the most learned Rabbins have travelled profitably and profoundly to observe, some of them
a natural, some of them a moral, sense or reduction of
many of the ceremonies and ordinances. As in the law of
the leprosy, where it is said, *If the whiteness have over-
spread the flesh, the patient may pass abroad for clean; but
if there be any whole flesh remaining, he is to be shut up
for unclean;* one of them noteth a principle of nature, that
putrefaction is more contagious before maturity than after:
and another noteth a position of moral philosophy, that
men abandoned to vice do not so much corrupt manners,
as those that are half good and half evil. So in this and very
many other places in that law, there is to be found, besides
the theological sense, much aspersion of philosophy.

So likewise in that excellent book of Job, if it be revolved
with diligence, it will be found pregnant and swelling with
natural philosophy; as for example, cosmography and the
roundness of the world; *Qui extendit aquilonem super
vacuum, et appendit terram super nihilum;* [who stretcheth
out the north upon the empty space, and hangeth the earth
upon nothing;] wherein the pensileness[28] of the earth, the
pole of the north, and the finiteness or convexity of
heaven are manifestly touched. So again matter of astronomy; *Spiritus ejus ornavit cœlos, et obstetricante manu ejus
eductus est Coluber tortuosus:* [by his spirit he hath garnished the heavens; his hand hath formed the crooked
Serpent]. And in another place; *Nunquid conjungere vale-
bis micantes stellas Pleiadas, aut gyrum Arcturi poteris
dissipare?* [canst thou bring together the glittering stars of
the Pleiades, or scatter the array of Arcturus?] where the
fixing of the stars, ever standing at equal distance, is with
great elegancy noted. And in another place, *Qui facit Arc-
turum, et Oriona, et Hyadas, et interiora Austri;* [which
maketh Arcturus, Orion, and Hyades, and the secrets of the
South;] where again he takes knowledge of the depression
of the southern pole, calling it the secrets of the south, be-

cause the southern stars were in that climate unseen. Matter of generation; *Annon sicut lac mulsisti me, et sicut caseum coagulasti me?* &c. [hast thou not drawn me forth like milk, and curdled me like cheese?] Matter of minerals; *Habet argentum venarum suarum principia: et auro locus est in quo conflatur, ferrum de terra tollitur, et lapis solutus calore in æs vertitur:* [surely there is a vein for the silver, and a place for gold where they fine it. Iron is taken out of the earth, and brass is molten out of the stone:] and so forwards in that chapter.

So likewise in the person of Salomon the king, we see the gift or endowment of wisdom and learning, both in Salomon's petition and in God's assent thereunto, preferred before all other terrene and temporal felicity. By virtue of which grant or donative of God, Salomon became enabled not only to write those excellent parables or aphorisms concerning divine and moral philosophy, but also to compile a natural history of all verdure, from the cedar upon the mountain to the moss upon the wall, (which is but a rudiment between putrefaction and an herb,) and also of all things that breathe or move. Nay, the same Salomon the king, although he excelled in the glory of treasure and magnificent buildings, of shipping and navigation, of service and attendance, of fame and renown, and the like, yet he maketh no claim to any of those glories, but only to the glory of inquisition of truth; for so he saith expressly, *The glory of God is to conceal a thing, but the glory of the king is to find it out;* as if, according to the innocent play of children, the Divine Majesty took delight to hide his works, to the end to have them found out; and as if kings could not obtain a greater honour than to be God's playfellows in that game, considering the great commandment of wits and means, whereby nothing needeth to be hidden from them.

Neither did the dispensation of God vary in the times after our Saviour came into the world; for our Saviour himself did first shew his power to subdue ignorance, by his conference with the priests and doctors of the law, before he shewed his power to subdue nature by his miracles. And the coming of the Holy Spirit was chiefly figured and expressed in the similitude and gift of tongues, which are but *vehicula scientiæ*, [carriers of knowledge].

So in the election of those instruments which it pleased God to use for the plantation of the faith, notwithstanding that at the first he did employ persons altogether unlearned otherwise than by inspiration, more evidently to declare his immediate working, and to abase all human wisdom or knowledge; yet nevertheless that counsel of his was no sooner performed, but in the next vicissitude and succession he did send his divine truth into the world waited on with other learnings as with servants or handmaids: for so we see St. Paul, who was only learned amongst the apostles, had his pen most used in the scriptures of the New Testament.

So again we find that many of the ancient bishops and fathers of the Church were excellently read and studied in all the learning of the heathen; insomuch that the edict of the emperor Julianus, (whereby it was interdicted unto Christians to be admitted into schools, lectures, or exercises of learning,) was esteemed and accounted a more pernicious engine and machination against the Christian faith, than were all the sanguinary prosecutions of his predecessors; neither could the emulation and jealousy of Gregory the first of that name, bishop of Rome, ever obtain the opinion of piety or devotion; but contrariwise received the censure of humour,[29] malignity, and pusillanimity, even amongst holy men; in that he designed to obliterate and extinguish the memory of heathen antiquity and authors. But contrariwise it was the Christian Church, which amidst the inundations of the Scythians on the one side from the north-west, and the Saracens from the east, did preserve in the sacred lap and bosom thereof the precious relics even of heathen learning, which otherwise had been extinguished as if no such thing had ever been.

And we see before our eyes, that in the age of ourselves and our fathers, when it pleased God to call the church of

Rome to account for their degenerate manners and ceremonies, and sundry doctrines obnoxious and framed to
uphold the same abuses; at one and the same time it was
ordained by the Divine Providence that there should attend withal a renovation and new spring of all other
knowledges: and on the other side we see the Jesuits, who
partly in themselves and partly by the emulation and
provocation of their example, have much quickened and
strengthened the state of learning,—we see (I say) what
notable service and reparation they have done to the
Roman see.

Wherefore to conclude this part, let it be observed that
there be two principal duties and services, besides ornament and illustration, which philosophy and human learning do perform to faith and religion. The one, because they
are an effectual inducement to the exaltation of the glory
of God: For as the Psalms and other Scriptures do often
invite us to consider and magnify the great and wonderful
works of God, so if we should rest only in the contemplation of the exterior of them as they first offer themselves to
our senses, we should do a like injury unto the majesty of
God as if we should judge or construe of the store of some
excellent jeweller by that only which is set out toward the
street in his shop. The other, because they minister a singular help and preservative against unbelief and error: For
our Saviour saith, *You err, not knowing the Scriptures, nor
the power of God;* laying before us two books or volumes
to study, if we will be secured from error; first the Scriptures, revealing the will of God, and then the creatures
expressing his power; whereof the later is a key unto the
former; not only opening our understanding to conceive
the true sense of the Scriptures, by the general notions of
reason and rules of speech; but chiefly opening our belief,
in drawing us into a due meditation of the omnipotency of
God, which is chiefly signed and engraven upon his works.
Thus much therefore for divine testimony and evidence
concerning the true dignity and value of learning.

As for human proofs, it is so large a field, as in a discourse of this nature and brevity it is fit rather to use choice of those things which we shall produce, than to embrace the variety of them. First therefore, in the degrees of human honour amongst the heathen it was the highest, to obtain to a veneration and adoration as a God. This unto the Christians is as the forbidden fruit. But we speak now separately of human testimony: according to which that which the Grecians call *apotheosis*, and the Latins *relatio inter divos* [*being deified], was the supreme honour which man could attribute unto man; specially when it was given, not by a formal decree or act of state, as it was used among the Roman emperors, but by an inward assent and belief; which honour being so high, had also a degree or middle term; for there were reckoned above human honours, honours heroical and divine; in the attribution and distribution of which honours we see antiquity made this difference: that whereas founders and uniters of states and cities, lawgivers, extirpers of tyrants, fathers of the people, and other eminent persons in civil merit, were honoured but with the titles of worthies or demi-gods; such as were Hercules, Theseus, Minos, Romulus, and the like; on the other side, such as were inventors and authors of new arts, endowments, and commodities towards man's life, were ever consecrated amongst the gods themselves; as was Ceres, Bacchus, Mercurius, Apollo, and others; and justly; for the merit of the former is confined within the circle of an age or a nation; and is like fruitful showers, which though they be profitable and good, yet serve but for that season, and for a latitude of ground where they fall; but the other is indeed like the benefits of heaven, which are permanent and universal. The former again is mixed with strife and perturbation; but the later hath the true character of divine presence, coming in *aura leni* [*like a gentle breeze], without noise or agitation.

Neither is certainly that other merit of learning, in repressing the inconveniencies which grow from man to man, much inferior to the former, of relieving the necessities which arise from nature; which merit was lively set forth by the ancients in that feigned relation of Orpheus theatre; where all beasts and birds assembled, and forgetting their several appetites, some of prey, some of game, some of quarrel, stood all sociably together listening unto the airs and accords of the harp; the sound whereof no sooner ceased, or was drowned by some louder noise, but every beast returned to his own nature: wherein is aptly described the nature and condition of men; who are full of savage and unreclaimed desires, of profit, of lust, of revenge, which as long as they give ear to precepts, to laws, to religion, sweetly touched with eloquence and persuasion of books, of sermons, of harangues, so long is society and peace maintained; but if these instruments be silent, or that sedition and tumult make them not audible, all things dissolve into anarchy and confusion.

But this appeareth more manifestly, when kings themselves, or persons of authority under them, or other governors in commonwealths and popular estates, are endued with learning. For although he might be thought partial to his own profession, that said *Then should people and estates be happy, when either kings were philosophers, or philosophers kings;* yet so much is verified by experience, that under learned princes and governors there have been ever the best times: for howsoever kings may have their imperfections in their passions and customs, yet if they be illuminate by learning, they have those notions of religion, policy, and morality, which do preserve them and refrain them from all ruinous and peremptory errors and excesses; whispering evermore in their ears, when counsellors and servants stand mute and silent. And senators or counsellors likewise which be learned, do proceed upon more safe and substantial principles than counsellors which are only men of experience; the one sort keeping dangers afar off, whereas the other discover them not till they come near hand, and then trust to the agility of their wit to ward or avoid them.

Which felicity of times under learned princes (to keep still the law of brevity, by using the most eminent and selected examples) doth best appear in the age which passed from the death of Domitianus the emperor until the reign of Commodus; comprehending a succession of six princes, all learned or singular favourers and advancers of learning; which age, for temporal respects, was the most happy and flourishing that ever the Roman empire (which then was a model of the world) enjoyed: a matter revealed and prefigured unto Domitian in a dream the night before he was slain; for he thought there was grown behind upon his shoulders a neck and a head of gold, which came accordingly to pass in those golden times which succeeded: of which princes we will make some commemoration; wherein although the matter will be vulgar, and may be thought fitter for a declamation than agreeable to a treatise infolded as this is, yet because it is pertinent to the point in hand, *neque semper arcum tendit Apollo,* [and Apollo does not keep his bow always bent,] and to name them only were too naked and cursory, I will not omit it altogether.

The first was Nerva; the excellent temper of whose government is by a glance in Cornelius Tacitus touched to the life: *Postquam divus Nerva res olim insociabiles miscuisset, imperium et libertatem:* [he united and reconciled two things which used not to go together—government and liberty]. And in token of his learning, the last act of his short reign left to memory was a missive to his adopted son Trajan, proceeding upon some inward discontent at the ingratitude of the times, comprehended in a verse of Homer's;

> Telis, Phœbe, tuis lacrymas ulciscere nostras.
> [O Phœbus, with thy shafts avenge these tears.]

Trajan, who succeeded, was for his person not learned: but if we will hearken to the speech of our Saviour, that saith, *He that receiveth a prophet in the name of a prophet, shall have a prophet's reward,* he deserveth to be placed amongst the most learned princes: for there was not a greater admirer of learning or benefactor of learning; a founder of famous libraries, a perpetual advancer of learned men to office, and a familiar converser with learned professors and preceptors, who were noted to have then most credit in court. On the other side, how much Trajan's virtue and government was admired and renowned, surely no testimony of grave and faithful history doth more lively set forth, than that legend tale of Gregorius Magnus, bishop of Rome, who was noted for the extreme envy he bare towards all heathen excellency: and yet he is reported, out of the love and estimation of Trajan's moral virtues, to have made unto God passionate and fervent prayers for the delivery of his soul out of hell; and to have obtained it, with a caveat that he should make no more such petitions. In this prince's time also the persecutions against the Christians received intermission, upon the certificate of Plinius Secundus, a man of excellent learning and by Trajan advanced.

Adrian, his successor, was the most curious man that lived, and the most universal inquirer; insomuch as it was noted for an error in his mind, that he desired to comprehend all things, and not to reserve himself for the worthiest things; falling into the like humour that was long before noted in Philip of Macedon, who when he would needs over-rule and put down an excellent musician in an argument touching music, was well answered by him again, *God forbid, Sir,* (saith he,) *that your fortune should be so bad, as to know these things better than I.* It pleased God likewise to use the curiosity of this emperor as an inducement to the peace of his church in those days. For having Christ in veneration, not as a God or Saviour, but as a wonder or novelty, and having his picture in his gallery matched with Appollonius (with whom in his vain imagination he thought he had some conformity), yet it served the turn to allay the bitter hatred of those times against the Christian name; so as the church had peace during his time. And for his government civil, although he did not attain to that of Trajan's in glory of arms or perfection of justice, yet in deserving of the weal of the subject he did exceed him. For Trajan erected many famous monuments and buildings; insomuch as Constantine the Great in emulation was wont to call him *Parietaria*, wall flower, because his name was upon so many walls: but his buildings and works were more of glory and triumph than use and necessity. But Adrian spent his whole reign, which was peaceable, in a perambulation or survey of the Roman empire; giving order and making assignation where he went for re-edifying of cities, towns, and forts decayed, and for cutting of rivers and streams, and for making bridges and passages, and for policing of cities and commonalties with new ordinances and constitutions, and granting new franchises and incorporations; so that his whole time was a very restoration of all the lapses and decays of former times.

Antoninus Pius, who succeeded him, was a prince excellently learned; and had the patient and subtile wit of a schoolman; insomuch as in common speech (which leaves no virtue untaxed) he was called *cymini sector*, a carver or divider of cummin seed, which is one of the least seeds; such a patience he had and settled spirit to enter into the least and most exact differences of causes; a fruit no doubt of the exceeding tranquillity and serenity of his mind; which being no ways charged or incumbered either with fears, remorses, or scruples, but having been noted for a man of the purest goodness, without all fiction or affectation, that hath reigned or lived, made his mind continually present and entire. He likewise approached a degree nearer unto Christianity, and became, as Agrippa said unto St. Paul, *half a Christian;* holding their religion and law in good opinion, and not only ceasing persecution, but giving way to the advancement of Christians.

There succeeded him the first *Divi fratres* [*divine brothers], the two adoptive brethren, Lucius Commodus Verus, son to Ælius Verus, who delighted much in the softer kind of learning, and was wont to call the poet Martial his Virgil; and Marcus Aurelius Antoninus; whereof the later, who obscured his colleague and survived him long, was named the Philosopher: who as he excelled all the rest in learning, so he excelled them likewise in perfection of all royal virtues; insomuch as Julianus the emperor, in his book intitled *Cæsares*, being as a pasquil or satire to deride all his predecessors, feigned that they were all invited to a banquet of the gods, and Silenus the jester sat at the nether end of the table and bestowed a scoff on every one as they came in; but when Marcus Philosophus came in, Silenus was gravelled and out of countenance, not knowing where to carp at him; save at the last he gave a glance at his patience towards his wife. And the virtue of this prince, continued with that of his predecessor, made the name of Antoninus so sacred in the world, that though it were extremely dishonoured in Commodus, Caracalla, and Heliogabalus, who all bare the name, yet when Alexander Severus refused the name because he was a stranger to the family, the Senate with one acclamation said, *Quomodo Augustus, sic et Antoninus:* [let the name of Antoninus be as the name of Augustus:] in such renown and veneration was the name of these two princes in those days, that they would have it as a perpetual addition in all the emperors' style. In this emperor's time also the church for the most part was in peace; so as in this sequence of six princes we do see the blessed effects of learning in sovereignty, painted forth in the greatest table of the world.

But for a tablet or picture of smaller volume, (not presuming to speak of your Majesty that liveth,) in my judgment the most excellent is that of queen Elizabeth, your immediate predecessor in this part of Britain; a prince that, if Plutarch were now alive to write lives by parallels, would trouble him, I think, to find for her a parallel amongst women. This lady was endued with learning in her sex singular, and rare even amongst masculine princes; whether we speak of learning of language or of science; modern or ancient; divinity or humanity. And unto the very last year of her life she accustomed to appoint set hours for reading, scarcely any young student in an university more daily or more duly. As for her government, I assure myself I shall not exceed if I do affirm that this part of the island never had forty-five years of better times; and yet not through the calmness of the season, but through the

wisdom of her regiment. For if there be considered of the
one side, the truth of religion established; the constant
peace and security; the good administration of justice; the
temperate use of the prerogative, not slackened, nor much
strained; the flourishing state of learning, sortable[30] to so
excellent a patroness; the convenient estate of wealth and
means, both of crown and subject; the habit of obedience,
and the moderation of discontents; and there be considered
on the other side, the differences of religion, the troubles of
neighbour countries, the ambition of Spain, and opposition
of Rome; and then that she was solitary and of herself:
these things I say considered, as I could not have chosen
an instance so recent and so proper, so I suppose I could
not have chosen one more remarkable or eminent, to the
purpose now in hand; which is concerning the conjunction
of learning in the prince with felicity in the people.

Neither hath learning an influence and operation only
upon civil merit and moral virtue, and the arts or temperature of peace and peaceable government; but likewise it
hath no less power and efficacy in enablement towards
martial and military virtue and prowess; as may be notably
represented in the examples of Alexander the Great and
Cæsar the Dictator, mentioned before, but now in fit place
to be resumed; of whose virtues and acts in war there
needs no note or recital, having been the wonders of time
in that kind; but of their affections towards learning, and
perfections in learning, it is pertinent to say somewhat.

Alexander was bred and taught under Aristotle the great
philosopher, who dedicated divers of his books of philosophy unto him. He was attended with Callisthenes and
divers other learned persons, that followed him in camp,
throughout his journeys and conquests. What price and
estimation he had learning in doth notably appear in these
three particulars: first, in the envy he used to express that
he bare towards Achilles, in this that he had so good a
trumpet of his praises as Homer's verses; secondly, in the
judgment or solution he gave touching that precious cabinet of Darius, which was found among his jewels, whereof

question was made what thing was worthy to be put into it, and he gave his opinion for Homer's works; thirdly, in his letter to Aristotle, after he had set forth his books of nature, wherein he expostulateth with him for publishing the secrets or mysteries of philosophy, and gave him to understand that himself esteemed it more to excel other men in learning and knowledge than in power and empire. And what use he had of learning doth appear, or rather shine, in all his speeches and answers, being full of science and use of science, and that in all variety.

And herein again it may seem a thing scholastical, and somewhat idle, to recite things that every man knoweth; but yet since the argument I handle leadeth me thereunto, I am glad that men shall perceive I am as willing to flatter (if they will so call it) an Alexander or a Cæsar or an Antoninus, that are dead many hundred years since, as any that now liveth: for it is the displaying of the glory of learning in sovereignty that I propound to myself, and not an humour of declaiming in any man's praises. Observe then the speech he used of Diogenes, and see if it tend not to the true state of one of the greatest questions of moral philosophy; whether the enjoying of outward things or the contemning of them be the greatest happiness; for when he saw Diogenes so perfectly contented with so little, he said to those that mocked at his condition, *Were I not Alexander, I would wish to be Diogenes.* But Seneca inverteth it, and saith, *Plus erat quod hic nollet accipere, quàm quod ille posset dare.* There were more things which Diogenes would have refused, than those were which Alexander could have given or enjoyed.

Observe again that speech which was usual with him, *That he felt his mortality chiefly in two things, sleep and lust;* and see if it were not a speech extracted out of the depth of natural philosophy, and liker to have comen out of the mouth of Aristotle or Democritus than from Alexander.

See again that speech of humanity and poesy; when upon the bleeding of his wounds, he called unto him one of his flatterers that was wont to ascribe to him divine honour, and said, *Look, this is very blood; this is not such a liquor as Homer speaketh of, which ran from Venus' hand when it was pierced by Diomedes.*

See likewise his readiness in reprehension of logic, in the speech he used to Cassander upon a complaint that was made against his father Antipater: for when Alexander happed to say, *Do you think these men would have come from so far to complain, except they had just cause of grief?* and Cassander answered, *Yea, that was the matter, because they thought they should not be disproved;* said Alexander laughing, *See the subtilties of Aristotle, to take a matter both ways,* pro et contra, &c.

But note again how well he could use the same art which he reprehended, to serve his own humour, when bearing a secret grudge to Callisthenes because he was against the new ceremony of his adoration, feasting one night where the same Callisthenes was at the table, it was moved by some after supper, for entertainment sake, that Callisthenes who was an eloquent man might speak of some theme or purpose at his own choice; which Callisthenes did; choosing the praise of the Macedonian nation for his discourse, and performing the same with so good manner as the hearers were much ravished; whereupon Alexander, nothing pleased, said, *It was easy to be eloquent upon so good a subject:* but saith he, *Turn your style, and let us hear what you can say against us:* which Callisthenes presently undertook, and did with that sting and life, that Alexander interrupted him, and said, *The goodness of the cause made him eloquent before, and despite made him eloquent then again.*

Consider further, for tropes of rhetoric, that excellent use of a metaphor or translation, wherewith he taxed Antipater, who was an imperious and tyrannous governor: for when one of Antipater's friends commended him to Alexander for his moderation, that he did not degenerate, as his other lieutenants did, into the Persian pride, in use of purple, but kept the ancient habit of Macedon, of black; *True,* (saith Alexander,) *but Antipater is all purple within.*

Or that other, when Parmenio came to him in the plain of Arbella, and shewed him the innumerable multitude of his enemies, specially as they appeared by the infinite number of lights, as it had been a new firmament of stars, and thereupon advised him to assail them by night: whereupon he answered, *That he would not steal the victory.*

For matter of policy, weigh that significant distinction, so much in all ages embraced, that he made between his two friends Hephæstion and Craterus, when he said, *That the one loved Alexander, and the other loved the king;* describing the principal difference of princes' best servants, that some in affection love their person, and others in duty love their crown.

Weigh also that excellent taxation of an error ordinary with counsellors of princes, that they counsel their masters according to the model of their own mind and fortune, and not of their masters; when upon Darius' great offers Parmenio had said, *Surely I would accept these offers, were I as Alexander;* saith Alexander, *So would I, were I as Parmenio.*

Lastly, weigh that quick and acute reply which he made when he gave so large gifts to his friends and servants, and was asked what he did reserve for himself, and he answered, *Hope;* weigh, I say, whether he had not cast up his account aright, because *hope* must be the portion of all that resolve upon great enterprises. For this was Cæsar's portion when he went first into Gaul, his estate being then utterly overthrown with largesses. And this was likewise the portion of that noble prince, howsover transported with ambition, Henry duke of Guise, of whom it was usually said, that he was the greatest usurer in France, because he had turned all his estate into obligations.

To conclude therefore: as certain critics are used to say hyperbolically, *That if all sciences were lost, they might be found in Virgil;* so certainly this may be said truly, there are the prints and footsteps of learning in those few speeches which are reported of this prince: the admiration of whom, when I consider him not as Alexander the Great, but as Aristotle's scholar hath carried me too far.

As for Julius Cæsar, the excellency of his learning needeth not to be argued from his education, or his company,
or his speeches; but in a further degree doth declare itself
in his writings and works; whereof some are extant and
permanent, and some unfortunately perished. For first, we
see there is left unto us that excellent history of his own
wars, which he intitled only a Commentary, wherein all
succeeding times have admired the solid weight of matter,
and the real passages and lively images of actions and persons, expressed in the greatest propriety of words and perspicuity of narration that ever was; which that it was not
the effect of a natural gift, but of learning and precept, is
well witnessed by that work of his intitled *De Analogia*,
being a grammatical philosophy, wherein he did labour to
make this same *vox ad placitum* [*conventional speech] to
become *vox ad licitum* [*correct speech], and to reduce
custom of speech to congruity of speech; and took as it
were the picture of words from the life of reason.

So we receive from him, as a monument both of his
power and learning, the then reformed computation of
the year; well expressing, that he took it to be as great a
glory to himself to observe and know the law of the heavens as to give law to men upon the earth.

So likewise in that book of his *Anti-Cato*, it may easily
appear that he did aspire as well to victory of wit as victory
of war; undertaking therein a conflict against the greatest
champion with the pen that then lived, Cicero the orator.

So again in his book of *Apophthegms* which he collected,
we see that he esteemed it more honour to make himself
but a pair of tables to take the wise and pithy words of
others, than to have every word of his own to be made an
apophthegm or an oracle; as vain princes, by custom of
flattery, pretend to do. And yet if I should enumerate
divers of his speeches, as I did those of Alexander, they are
truly such as Salomon noteth, when he saith, *Verba sapien-
tum tanquam aculei, et tanquam clavi in altum defixi:* [the
words of the wise are as goads, and as nails fixed deep in:]
whereof I will only recite three, not so delectable for elegancy, but admirable for vigour and efficacy.

As first, it is reason he be thought a master of words, that could with one word appease a mutiny in his army; which was thus. The Romans, when their generals did speak to their army, did use the word *Milites* [*soldiers]; but when the magistrates spake to the people, they did use the word *Quirites* [*citizens]. The soldiers were in tumult, and seditiously prayed to be cashiered; not that they so meant, but by expostulation thereof to draw Cæsar to other conditions; wherein he being resolute not to give way, after some silence, he began his speech, *Ego, Quirites* [*I, Citizens]; which did admit them already cashiered; wherewith they were so surprised, crossed, and confused, as they would not suffer him to go on in his speech, but relinquished their demands, and made it their suit to be again called by the name of *Milites*.

The second speech was thus: Cæsar did extremely affect the name of king; and some were set on, as he passed by, in popular acclamation to salute him king; whereupon, finding the cry weak and poor, he put it off thus in a kind of jest, as if they had mistaken his surname; *Non Rex sum sed Cæsar:* [I am not King, but Cæsar:] a speech, that if it be searched, the life and fulness of it can scarce be expressed: for first it was a refusal of the name, but yet not serious: again it did signify an infinite confidence and magnanimity, as if he presumed Cæsar was the greater title; as by his worthiness it is come to pass till this day: but chiefly it was a speech of great allurement towards his own purpose; as if the state did strive with him but for a name, whereof mean families were vested; for Rex was a surname with the Romans, as well as King is with us.

The last speech which I will mention, was used to Metellus; when Cæsar, after war declared, did possess himself of the city of Rome; at which time entering into the inner treasury to take the money there accumulate, Metellus being tribune forbade him: whereto Cæsar said, *That if he did not desist, he would lay him dead in the place;* and presently[31] taking himself up, he added, *Young man, it is harder for me to speak it than to do it. Adolescens, durius est mihi hoc dicere quàm facere.* A speech compounded of the greatest terror and greatest clemency that could proceed out of the mouth of man.

But to return and conclude with him: it is evident himself knew well his own perfection in learning, and took it upon him; as appeared when upon occasion that some spake what a strange resolution it was in Lucius Sylla to resign his dictature, he scoffing at him, to his own advantage, answered, *That Sylla could not skill of letters, and therefore knew not how to dictate.*

And here it were fit to leave this point touching the concurrence of military virtue and learning; (for what example would come with any grace after those two of Alexander and Cæsar?) were it not in regard of the rareness of circumstance that I find in one other particular, as that which did so suddenly pass from extreme scorn to extreme wonder; and it is of Xenophon the philosopher, who went from Socrates' school into Asia, in the expedition of Cyrus the younger against king Artaxerxes. This Xenophon at that time was very young, and never had seen the wars before; neither had any command in the army, but only followed the war as a voluntary, for the love and conversation of Proxenus his friend. He was present when Falinus came in message from the great king to the Grecians, after that Cyrus was slain in the field, and they a handful of men left to themselves in the midst of the king's territories, cut off from their country by many navigable rivers, and many hundred miles. The message imported that they should deliver up their arms, and submit themselves to the king's mercy. To which message before answer was made, divers of the army conferred familiarly with Falinus; and amongst the rest Xenophon happened to say, *Why Falinus, we have now but these two things left, our arms and our virtue; and if we yield up our arms, how shall we make use of our virtue?* Whereto Falinus smiling on him, said, *If I be not deceived, young gentleman, you are an Athenian; and I believe you study philosophy, and it is pretty that you say; but you are much abused if you think your virtue can withstand the king's power.* Here was the scorn; the wonder followed: which was, that this young scholar or philosopher, after all the captains were murdered in parley by treason, conducted those ten thousand foot through the heart of all the king's high countries from Babylon to Græcia in safety, in despite of all the king's forces, to the astonishment of the world, and the encouragement of the Grecians in time succeeding to make invasion upon the kings of Persia; as was after purposed by Jason the Thessalian, attempted by Agesilaus the Spartan, and achieved by Alexander the Macedonian; all upon the ground of the act of that young scholar.

To proceed now from imperial and military virtue to moral and private virtue: first, it is an assured truth which is contained in the verses,

> Scilicet ingenuas didicisse fideliter artes
>> Emolit mores, nec sinit esse feros;

[a true proficiency in liberal learning softens and humanises the manners]. It taketh away the wildness and barbarism and fierceness of men's minds: but indeed the accent had need be upon *fideliter:* [it must be a *true* proficiency:] for a little superficial learning doth rather work a contrary effect. It taketh away all levity, temerity, and insolency, by copious suggestion of all doubts and difficulties, and acquainting the mind to balance reasons on both sides, and to turn back the first offers and conceits of the mind, and to accept of nothing but examined and tried. It taketh away vain admiration of any thing, which is the root of all weakness. For all things are admired, either because they are new, or because they are great. For novelty, no man that wadeth in learning or contemplation throughly, but will find that printed in his heart *Nil novi super terram:* [there is nothing new under the sun]. Neither can any man marvel at the play of puppets, that goeth behind the curtain and adviseth well of the motion. And for magnitude, as Alexander the Great after that he was used to great armies and the great conquests of the spacious provinces

in Asia, when he received letters out of Greece of some
fights and services there, which were commonly for a passage or a fort or some walled town at the most, he said, *It
seemed to him that he was advertised of the battles of the
frogs and the mice, that the old tales went of:* so certainly
if a man meditate much upon the universal frame of nature, the earth with men upon it (the divineness of souls
except) will not seem much other than an ant-hill, whereas
some ants carry corn, and some carry their young, and
some go empty, and all to and fro a little heap of dust. It
taketh away or mitigateth fear of death or adverse fortune;
which is one of the greatest impediments of virtue and
imperfections of manners. For if a man's mind be deeply
seasoned with the consideration of the mortality and corruptible nature of things, he will easily concur with Epictetus, who went forth one day and saw a woman weeping
for her pitcher of earth that was broken, and went forth
the next day and saw a woman weeping for her son that
was dead; and thereupon said, *Heri vidi fragilem frangi,
hodie vidi mortalem mori:* [yesterday I saw a brittle thing
broken, to-day a mortal dead]. And therefore Virgil did
excellently and profoundly couple the knowledge of causes
and the conquest of all fears together, as *concomitantia.*

> Felix qui potuit rerum cognoscere causas,
> Quique metus omnes et inexorabile fatum
> Subjecit pedibus, strepitumque Acherontis avari.
>
> [Happy the man who doth the causes know
> Of all that is: serene he stands, above
> All fears; above the inexorable Fate,
> And that insatiate gulph that roars below.]

It were too long to go over the particular remedies which
learning doth minister to all the diseases of the mind;
sometimes purging the ill humours, sometimes opening the
obstructions, sometimes helping digestion, sometimes increasing appetite, sometimes healing the wounds and
exulcerations thereof, and the like; and therefore I will
conclude with that which hath *rationem totius* [*the es-

sence of the whole matter]; which is, that it disposeth the constitution of the mind not to be fixed or settled in the defects thereof, but still to be capable and susceptible of growth and reformation. For the unlearned man knows not what it is to descend into himself or to call himself to account, nor the pleasure of that *suavissima vita, indies sentire se fieri meliorem,* [to feel himself each day a better man than he was the day before]. The good parts he hath he will learn to shew to the full and use them dexterously, but not much to increase them: the faults he hath he will learn how to hide and colour them, but not much to amend them; like an ill mower, that mows on still and never whets his scythe: whereas with the learned man it fares otherwise, that he doth ever intermix the correction and amendment of his mind with the use and employment thereof. Nay further, in general and in sum, certain it is that *veritas* [*truth] and *bonitas* [*goodness] differ but as the seal and the print; for truth prints goodness, and they be the clouds of error which descend in the storms of passions and perturbations.

From moral virtue let us pass on to matter of power and commandment, and consider whether in right reason there be any comparable with that wherewith knowledge investeth and crowneth man's nature. We see the dignity of the commandment is according to the dignity of the commanded: to have commandment over beasts, as herdsmen have, is a thing contemptible; to have commandment over children, as schoolmasters have, is a matter of small honour; to have commandment over galley-slaves is a disparagement rather than an honour. Neither is the commandment of tyrants much better, over people which have put off the generosity of their minds: and therefore it was ever holden that honours in free monarchies and commonwealths had a sweetness more than in tyrannies; because the commandment extendeth more over the wills of men, and not only over their deeds and services. And therefore when Virgil putteth himself forth to attribute to Augustus Cæsar the best of human honours, he doth it in these words:

victorque volentes
Per populos dat jura, viamque affectat Olympo:
[Moving in conquest onward, at his will
To willing peoples he gives laws, and shapes
Through worthiest deeds on earth his course to Heaven.]

But yet the commandment of knowledge is yet higher than the commandment over the will; for it is a commandment over the reason, belief, and understanding of man, which is the highest part of the mind, and giveth law to the will itself. For there is no power on earth which setteth up a throne or chair of estate in the spirits and souls of men, and in their cogitations, imaginations, opinions, and beliefs, but knowledge and learning. And therefore we see the detestable and extreme pleasure that arch-heretics and false prophets and impostors are transported with, when they once find in themselves that they have a superiority in the faith and conscience of men; so great, that if they have once tasted of it, it is seldom seen that any torture or persecution can make them relinquish or abandon it. But as this is that which the author of the Revelation calleth the depth or profoundness of Satan; so by argument of contraries, the just and lawful sovereignty over men's understanding, by force of truth rightly interpreted, is that which approacheth nearest to the similitude of the divine rule.

As for fortune and advancement, the beneficence of learning is not so confined to give fortune only to states and commonwealths, as it doth not likewise give fortune to particular persons. For it was well noted long ago, that Homer hath given more men their livings than either Sylla or Cæsar or Augustus ever did, notwithstanding their great largesses and donatives and distributions of lands to so many legions. And no doubt it is hard to say whether arms or learning have advanced greater numbers. And in case of sovereignty, we see that if arms or descent have carried away the kingdom, yet learning hath carried the priesthood, which ever hath been in some competition with empire.

Again, for the pleasure and delight of knowledge and learning, it far surpasseth all other in nature: for shall the pleasures of the affections so exceed the senses, as much as the obtaining of desire or victory exceedeth a song or a dinner; and must not of consequence the pleasures of the intellect or understanding exceed the pleasures of the affections? We see in all other pleasures there is satiety, and after they be used, their verdure departeth; which sheweth well they be but deceits of pleasure, and not pleasures; and that it was the novelty which pleased, and not the quality. And therefore we see that voluptuous men turn friars, and ambitious princes turn melancholy. But of knowledge there is no satiety, but satisfaction and appetite are perpetually interchangeable; and therefore appeareth to be good in itself simply, without fallacy or accident. Neither is that pleasure of small efficacy and contentment to the mind of man, which the poet Lucretius describeth elegantly,

Suave mari magno, turbantibus æquora ventis, &c.

It is a view of delight (saith he) *to stand or walk upon the shore side, and to see a ship tossed with tempest upon the sea; or to be in a fortified tower, and to see two battles join upon a plain. But is is a pleasure incomparable, for the mind of man to be settled, landed, and fortified in the certainty of truth; and from thence to descry and behold the errors, perturbations, labours, and wanderings up and down of other men.*

Lastly, leaving the vulgar arguments, that by learning man excelleth man in that wherein man excelleth beasts; that by learning man ascendeth to the heavens and their motions, where in body he cannot come; and the like; let us conclude with the dignity and excellency of knowledge and learning in that whereunto man's nature doth most aspire; which is immortality or continuance; for to this tendeth generation, and raising of houses and families; to this buildings, foundations and monuments; to this tendeth the desire of memory, fame, and celebration; and in effect, the strength of all other human desires. We see then how far the monuments of wit and learning are more durable than the monuments of power or of the hands. For have not the verses of Homer continued twenty-five hundred years or more, without the loss of a syllable or letter; during which time infinite palaces, temples, castles, cities, have been decayed and demolished? It is not possible to have the true pictures or statues of Cyrus, Alexander, Cæsar, no nor of the kings or great personages of much later years; for the originals cannot last, and the copies cannot but leese of the life and truth. But the images of men's wits and knowledges remain in books, exempted from the wrong of time and capable of perpetual renovation. Neither are they fitly to be called images, because they generate still, and cast their seeds in the minds of others, provoking and causing infinite actions and opinions in succeeding ages. So that if the invention of the ship was thought so noble, which carrieth riches and commodities from place to place, and consociateth the most remote regions in participation of their fruits, how much more are letters to be magnified, which as ships pass through the vast seas of time, and make ages so distant to participate of the wisdom, illuminations, and inventions, the one of the other? Nay further, we see some of the philosophers which were least divine and most immersed in the senses and denied generally the immortality of the soul, yet came to this point, that whatsoever motions the spirit of man could act and perform without the organs of the body they thought might remain after death; which were only those of the understanding, and not of the affection; so immortal and incorruptible a thing did knowledge seem unto them to be. But we, that know by divine revelation that not only the understanding but the affections purified, not only the spirit but the body changed, shall be advanced to immortality, do disclaim in[32] these rudiments of the senses. But it must be remembered both in this last point, and so it may likewise be needful in other places, that in probation of the dignity of knowledge or learning I did in the beginning separate divine testimony from human; which method I have pursued, and so handled them both apart.

Nevertheless I do not pretend, and I know it will be impossible for me by any pleading of mine, to reverse the judgment, either of Æsop's cock, that preferred the barley-corn before the gem; or of Midas, that being chosen judge between Apollo president of the Muses, and Pan god of the flocks, judged for plenty; or of Paris, that judged for beauty and love against wisdom and power; or of Agrippina, *occidat matrem, modo imperet,* [let him kill his mother so he be emperor,] that preferred empire with condition never so detestable; or of Ulysses, *qui vetulam prætulit immortalitati,* [that preferred an old woman to an immortality,] being a figure of those which prefer custom and habit before all excellency; or of a number of the like popular judgments. For these things continue as they have been: but so will that also continue whereupon learning hath ever relied, and which faileth not: *Justificata est sapientia a filiis suis:* [wisdom is justified of her children].

THE
SECOND BOOK OF FRANCIS BACON
OF THE
PROFICIENCE
AND
ADVANCEMENT OF LEARNING
DIVINE AND HUMAN

To the King

It might seem to have more convenience, though it come often otherwise to pass, (excellent King,) that those which are fruitful in their generations, and have in themselves the foresight of immortality in their descendants, should likewise be more careful of the good estate of future times; unto which they know they must transmit and commend over their dearest pledges. Queen Elizabeth was a sojourner in the world in respect of her unmarried life; and was a blessing to her own times; and yet so as the impression of her good government, besides her happy memory, is not without some effect which doth survive her. But to your Majesty, whom God hath already blessed with so much royal issue, worthy to continue and represent you for ever, and whose youthful and fruitful bed doth yet promise many the like renovations, it is proper and agreeable to be conversant not only in the transitory parts of good government, but in those acts also which are in their nature permanent and perpetual. Amongst the which (if affection do not transport me) there is not any more worthy than the further endowment of the world with sound and fruitful knowledge: for why should a few received authors stand up like Hercules' Columns,[1] beyond which there should be no sailing or discovering, since we have so bright and benign a star as your Majesty to conduct and prosper us? To return therefore where we left, it remaineth to consider of what kind those acts are, which have been undertaken and performed by kings and others for the increase and advancement of learning: wherein I purpose to speak actively without digressing or dilating.

Let this ground therefore be laid, that all works are overcomen by amplitude of reward, by soundness of direction, and by the conjunction of labours. The first multiplieth endeavour, the second preventeth error, and the third supplieth the frailty of man. But the principal of these is direction: for *claudus in via antevertit cursorem extra viam;* [the cripple that keeps the way gets to the end of the journey sooner than the runner who goes aside;] and Salomon excellently setteth it down, *If the iron be not sharp, it requireth more strength; but wisdom is that which prevaileth;* signifying that the invention or election of the mean is more effectual than any inforcement or accumulation of endeavours. This I am induced to speak, for that (not derogating from the noble intention of any that have been deservers towards the state of learning) I do observe nevertheless that their works and acts are rather matters of magnificence and memory than of progression and proficience, and tend rather to augment the mass of learning in the multitude of learned men than to rectify or raise the sciences themselves.

The works or acts of merit towards learning are conversant about three objects; the places of learning, the books of learning, and the persons of the learned. For as water, whether it be the dew of heaven or the springs of the earth, doth scatter and leese itself in the ground, except it be collected into some receptacle, where it may by union comfort and sustain itself; and for that cause the industry of man hath made and framed spring-heads, conduits, cisterns, and pools, which men have accustomed likewise to beautify and adorn with accomplishments of magnificence and state, as well as of use and necessity; so this excellent liquor of knowledge, whether it descend from divine inspiration or spring from human sense, would soon perish and vanish to oblivion, if it were not preserved in books, traditions, conferences, and places appointed, as universities, colleges, and schools, for the receipt and comforting of the same.

The works which concern the seats and places of learning are four; foundations and buildings, endowments with revenues, endowments with franchises and privileges, institutions and ordinances for government; all tending to quietness and privateness of life, and discharge of cares and troubles; much like the stations which Virgil prescribeth for the hiving of bees:

> Principio sedes apibus statioque petenda,
> Quo neque sit ventis aditus, &c.
> [First for thy bees a quiet station find,
> And lodge them under covert of the wind.]

The works touching books are two: first libraries, which are as the shrines where all the relics of the ancient saints, full of true virtue and that without delusion or imposture, are preserved and reposed; secondly, new editions of authors, with more correct impressions, more faithful translations, more profitable glosses, more diligent annotations, and the like.

The works pertaining to the persons of learned men (besides the advancement and countenancing of them in general) are two: the reward and designation of readers in sciences already extant and invented; and the reward and designation of writers and inquirers concerning any parts of learning not sufficiently laboured and prosecuted.

These are summarily the works and acts, wherein the merits of many excellent princes and other worthy personages have been conversant. As for any particular commemorations, I call to mind what Cicero said, when he gave general thanks; *Difficile non aliquem, ingratum quenquam præterire:* [it were hard to remember all, and yet ungracious to forget any]. Let us rather, according to the Scriptures, look unto that part of the race which is before us than look back to that which is already attained.

First therefore, amongst so many great foundations of colleges in Europe, I find it strange that they are all dedicated to professions, and none left free to arts and sciences at large. For if men judge that learning should be referred to action, they judge well; but in this they fall into the error described in the ancient fable; in which the other parts of the body did suppose the stomach had been idle, because it neither performed the office of motion, as the limbs do, nor of sense, as the head doth; but yet notwithstanding it is the stomach that digesteth and distributeth to all the rest. So if any man think philosophy and universality to be idle studies, he doth not consider that all professions are from thence served and supplied. And this I take to be a great cause that hath hindered the progression of learning, because these fundamental knowledges have been studied but in passage. For if you will have a tree bear more fruit than it hath used to do, it is not any thing you can do to the boughs, but it is the stirring of the earth and putting new mould about the roots that must work it. Neither is it to be forgotten that this dedicating of foundations and dotations to professory learning[2] hath not only had a malign aspect and influence upon the growth of sciences, but hath also been prejudicial to states and governments. For hence it proceedeth that princes find a solitude in regard of able men to serve them in causes of estate, because there is no education collegiate which is free;[3] where such as were so disposed might give themselves to histories, modern languages, books of policy and civil discourse, and other the like enablements unto service of estate.

And because founders of colleges do plant and founders of lectures do water, it followeth well in order to speak of the defect which is in public lectures; namely, in the small-ness and meanness of the salary or reward which in most places is assigned unto them; whether they be lectures of arts, or of professions. For it is necessary to the progression of sci-ences that readers[4] be of the most able and sufficient men; as those which are ordained for generating and propaga-ting of sciences, and not for transitory use. This cannot be, except their condition and endowment be such as may content the ablest man to appropriate his whole labour and continue his whole age in that function and attend-ance; and therefore must have a proportion answerable to that mediocrity or competency of advancement which may be expected from a profession or the practice of a profes-sion. So as, if you will have sciences flourish, you must observe David's military law, which was, *That those which staid with the carriage should have equal part with those which were in the action;* else will the carriages be ill attended: So readers in sciences are indeed the guardians of the stores and provisions of sciences whence men in active courses are furnished, and therefore ought to have equal entertainment with them; otherwise if the fathers in sciences be of the weakest sort or be ill-maintained,

Et patrum invalidi referent jejunia nati:

[the poor keeping of the parents will appear in the poor constitution of the offspring.]

Another defect I note, wherein I shall need some al-chemist to help me, who call upon men to sell their books and to build furnaces; quitting and forsaking Minerva and the Muses as barren virgins, and relying upon Vulcan. But certain it is that unto the deep, fruitful, and operative study of many sciences, specially natural philosophy and physic,[5] books be not only the instrumentals; wherein also the beneficence of men hath not been altogether wanting; for we see spheres, globes, astrolabes, maps, and the like, have been provided as appurtenances to astronomy and cosmography, as well as books: we see likewise that some places instituted for physic have annexed the commodity of gardens for simples of all sorts, and do likewise command the use of dead bodies for anatomies. But these do respect but a few things. In general, there will hardly be any main proficience in the disclosing of nature, except there be some allowance for expenses about experiments; whether they be experiments appertaining to Vulcanus or Dædalus, furnace or engine, or any other kind; and therefore as secretaries and spials of princes and states bring in bills for intelligence,[6] so you must allow the spials and intelligencers of nature to bring in their bills, or else you shall be ill advertised.[7]

And if Alexander made such a liberal assignation to Aristotle of treasure for the allowance of hunters, fowlers, fishers, and the like, that he might compile an History of nature, much better do they deserve it that travail in Arts of nature.[8]

Another defect which I note, is an intermission or neglect in those which are governors in universities of consultation, and in princes or superior persons of visitation; to enter into account and consideration, whether the readings, exercises, and other customs appertaining unto learning, anciently begun and since continued, be well instituted or no; and thereupon to ground an amendment or reformation in that which shall be found inconvenient. For it is one of your Majesty's own most wise and princely maxims, *that in all usages and precedents, the times be considered wherein they first began; which if they were weak or ignorant, it derogateth from the authority of the usage, and leaveth it for suspect.* And therefore in as much as most of the usages and orders of the universities were derived from more obscure times, it is the more requisite they be re-examined. In this kind I will give an instance or two for example sake, of things that are the most obvious and familiar. The one is a matter which though it be ancient and general, yet I hold to be an error; which is, that scholars in universities come too soon and too unripe to logic and rhetoric; arts fitter for graduates than children and novices: for these two, rightly taken, are the gravest of sciences; being the

arts of arts, the one for judgment, the other for ornament;
and they be the rules and directions how to set forth and
dispose matter; and therefore for minds empty and un-
fraught with matter, and which have not gathered that
which Cicero calleth *sylva* and *supellex*, stuff and variety,
to begin with those arts, (as if one should learn to weigh or
to measure or to paint the wind,) doth work but this effect,
that the wisdom of those arts, which is great and universal,
is almost made contemptible, and is degenerate into childish sophistry and ridiculous affectation. And further, the
untimely learning of them hath drawn on by consequence
the superficial and unprofitable teaching and writing of
them, as fitteth indeed to the capacity of children. Another
is a lack I find in the exercises used in the universities,
which do make too great a divorce between invention and
memory; for their speeches are either premeditate *in verbis
conceptis* [*in words already chosen], where nothing is left
to invention, or merely *extemporal*, where little is left to
memory: whereas in life and action there is least use of
either of these, but rather of intermixtures of premeditation
and invention, notes and memory; so as the exercise fitteth
not the practice, nor the image the life; and it is ever a
true rule in exercises, that they be framed as near as may
be to the life of practice; for otherwise they do pervert the
motions and faculties of the mind, and not prepare them.
The truth whereof is not obscure, when scholars come to
the practices of professions, or other actions of civil life;
which when they set into, this want is soon found by themselves, and sooner by others. But this part, touching the
amendment of the institutions and orders of universities, I
will conclude with the clause of Cæsar's letter to Oppius
and Balbus, *Hoc quemadmodum fieri possit, nonnulla mihi
in mentem veniunt, et multa reperiri possunt; de iis rebus
rogo vos ut cogitationem suscipiatis:* [how this may be
done, some things occur to me and more may be thought
of. I would have you take these matters into consideration.]

Another defect which I note, ascendeth a little higher
than the precedent. For as the proficience of learning con-

sisteth much in the orders and institutions of universities in
the same states and kingdoms, so it would be yet more
advanced, if there were more intelligence mutual between
the universities of Europe than now there is. We see there
be many orders and foundations, which though they be
divided under several sovereignties and territories, yet they
take themselves to have a kind of contract, fraternity, and
correspondence one with the other, insomuch as they have
Provincials and Generals.[9] And surely as nature createth
brotherhood in families, and arts mechanical contract
brotherhoods in communalties, and the anointment of God
superinduceth a brotherhood in kings and bishops; so in
like manner there cannot but be a fraternity in learning
and illumination, relating to that paternity which is attributed to God, who is called the Father of illuminations
or lights.

The last defect which I will note is, that there hath not
been, or very rarely been, any public designation of writers
or inquirers concerning such parts of knowledge as may
appear not to have been already sufficiently laboured or
undertaken; unto which point it is an inducement, to enter
into a view and examination what parts of learning have
been prosecuted, and what omitted; for the opinion of
plenty is amongst the causes of want, and the great quantity of books maketh a shew rather of superfluity than lack;
which surcharge nevertheless is not to be remedied by
making no more books, but by making more good books,
which, as the serpent of Moses, might devour the serpents
of the enchanters.

The removing of all the defects formerly enumerate, except the last, and of the active part also of the last, (which
is the designation of writers,) are *opera basilica,* [works for
a king;] towards which the endeavours of a private man
may be but as an image in a crossway, that may point at
the way but cannot go it. But the inducing part of the latter (which is the survey of learning) may be set forward
by private travel. Wherefore I will now attempt to make a
general and faithful perambulation of learning, with an

inquiry what parts thereof lie fresh and waste, and not improved and converted by the industry of man; to the end that such a plot made and recorded to memory may both minister light to any public designation, and also serve to excite voluntary endeavours; wherein nevertheless my purpose is at this time to note only omissions and deficiencies, and not to make any redargution of errors or incomplete prosecutions; for it is one thing to set forth what ground lieth unmanured, and another thing to correct ill husbandry in that which is manured.

In the handling and undertaking of which work I am not ignorant what it is that I do now move and attempt, nor insensible of mine own weakness to sustain my purpose; but my hope is that if my extreme love to learning carry me too far, I may obtain the excuse of affection; for that *it is not granted to man to love and to be wise.* But I know well I can use no other liberty of judgment than I must leave to others; and I for my part shall be indifferently glad either to perform myself or accept from another that duty of humanity, *Nam qui erranti comiter monstrat viam,* &c. [to put the wanderer in the right way]. I do foresee likewise that of those things which I shall enter and register as deficiencies and omissions, many will conceive and censure that some of them are already done and extant; others to be but curiosities, and things of no great use; and others to be of too great difficulty and almost impossibility to be compassed and effected. But for the two first, I refer myself to the particulars. For the last, touching impossibility, I take it those things are to be held possible which may be done by some person, though not by every one; and which may be done by many, though not by any one; and which may be done in succession of ages, though not within the hourglass of one man's life; and which may be done by public designation, though not by private endeavour. But notwithstanding, if any man will take to himself rather that of Salomon, *Dicit piger, Leo est in via,* [the slothful man saith there is a lion in the path,] than that of Vergil, *Possunt quia posse videntur,* [they find it possible because they think it possible,] I shall be content that my labours be esteemed but as the better sort of wishes; for as it asketh some knowledge to demand a question not impertinent, so it requireth some sense to make a wish not absurd.

The parts of human learning have reference to the three parts of Man's Understanding, which is the seat of learning: History to his Memory, Poesy to his Imagination, and Philosophy to his Reason. Divine learning receiveth the same distribution; for the spirit of man is the same, though the revelation of oracle and sense be diverse: so as theology consisteth also of History of the Church; of Parables, which is divine poesy; and of holy Doctrine or precept. For as for that part which seemeth supernumerary, which is Prophecy, it is but divine history; which hath that prerogative over human, as the narration may be before the fact as well as after.

History is Natural, Civil, Ecclesiastical, and Literary; whereof the three first I allow as extant, the fourth I note as deficient. For no man hath propounded to himself the general state of learning to be described and represented from age to age, as many have done the works of nature and the state civil and ecclesiastical; without which the history of the world seemeth to me to be as the statua of Polyphemus with his eye out; that part being wanting which doth most shew the spirit and life of the person. And yet I am not ignorant that in divers particular sciences, as of the juris-consults, the mathematicians, the rhetoricians, the philosophers, there are set down some small memorials of the schools, authors, and books; and so likewise some barren relations touching the invention of arts or usages. But a just story of learning, containing the antiquities and originals of knowledges, and their sects; their inventions, their traditions; their diverse administrations and managings; their flourishings, their oppositions, decays, depressions, oblivions, removes; with the causes and occasions of them, and all other events concerning learning, throughout the ages of the world; I may truly

Historia Literarum

affirm to be wanting. The use and end of which work I do not so much design for curiosity, or satisfaction of those that are the lovers of learning; but chiefly for a more serious and grave purpose, which is this in few words, that it will make learned men wise in the use and administration of learning. For it is not St. Augustine's nor St. Ambrose works that will make so wise a divine, as ecclesiastical history throughly read and observed; and the same reason is of learning.

History of Nature is of three sorts; of nature in course, of nature erring or varying, and of nature altered or wrought; that is, history of Creatures, history of Marvels, and history of Arts. The first of these no doubt is extant, and that in good perfection; the two later are handled so weakly and unprofitably, as I am moved to note them as deficient. For *Historia Naturæ Errantis* I find no sufficient or competent collection of the works of nature which have a digression and deflexion from the ordinary course of generations, productions, and motions; whether they be singularities of place and region, or the strange events of time and chance, or the effects of yet unknown proprieties, or the instances of exception to general kinds. It is true, I find a number of books of fabulous experiments and secrets, and frivolous impostures for pleasure and strangeness. But a substantial and severe collection of the Heteroclites or Irregulars of nature, well examined and described, I find not; specially not with due rejection of fables and popular errors: for as things now are, if an untruth in nature be once on foot, what by reason of the neglect of examination and countenance of antiquity, and what by reason of the use of the opinion in similitudes and ornaments of speech, it is never called down.

The use of this work, honoured with a precedent in Aristotle, is nothing less than to give contentment to the appetite of curious and vain wits, as the manner of Mirabilaries is to do; but for two reasons, both of great weight; the one to correct the partiality of axioms and opinions, which are commonly framed only upon common and familiar examples; the other because from the wonders of nature is the nearest intelligence and passage towards the wonders of art: for it is no more but by following and as it were hounding Nature in her wanderings, to be able to lead her afterwards to the same place again. Neither am I of opinion, in this History of Marvels, that superstitious narrations of sorceries, witchcrafts, dreams, divinations, and the like, where there is an assurance and clear evidence of the fact, be altogether excluded. For it is not yet known in what cases, and how far, effects attributed to superstition do participate of natural causes; and therefore howsoever the practice of such things is to be condemned, yet from the speculation and consideration of them light may be taken, not only for the discerning of the offences, but for the further disclosing of nature. Neither ought a man to make scruple of entering into these things for inquisition of truth, as your Majesty hath shewed in your own example;[10] who with the two clear eyes of religion and natural philosophy have looked deeply and wisely into these shadows, and yet proved yourself to be of the nature of the sun, which passeth through pollutions and itself remains as pure as before. But this I hold fit, that these narrations which have mixture with superstition be sorted by themselves, and not to be mingled with the narrations which are merely and sincerely natural. But as for the narrations touching the prodigies and miracles of religions, they are either not true or not natural; and therefore impertinent for the story of nature.

For History of Nature Wrought or Mechanical, I find
Historia Mechanica some collections made of agriculture, and likewise of manual arts; but commonly with a rejection of experiments familiar and vulgar. For it is esteemed a kind of dishonour unto learning to descend to inquiry or meditation upon matters mechanical, except they be such as may be thought secrets, rarities, and special subtilties; which humour of vain and supercilious arrogancy is justly derided in Plato; where he brings in Hippias, a vaunting sophist, disputing with Socrates, a true and unfeigned inquisitor of truth; where the subject being touching beauty,

Socrates, after his wandering manner of inductions, put
first an example of a fair virgin, and then of a fair horse,
and then of a fair pot well glazed, whereat Hippias was
offended, and said, *More than for courtesy's sake, he did
think much to dispute with any that did allege such base
and sordid instances:* whereunto Socrates answereth, *You
have reason, and it becomes you well, being a man so trim
in your vestiments,* &c. and so goeth on in an irony. But the
truth is, they be not the highest instances that give the se-
curest information; as may be well expressed in the tale so
common of the philosopher, that while he gazed upwards
to the stars fell into the water; for if he had looked down
he might have seen the stars in the water, but looking aloft
he could not see the water in the stars. So it cometh often
to pass that mean and small things discover great better
than great can discover the small; and therefore Aristotle
noteth well, *that the nature of every thing is best seen in
his smallest portions,* and for that cause he inquireth the
nature of a commonwealth, first in a family, and the simple
conjugations of man and wife, parent and child, master and
servant, which are in every cottage: even so likewise the
nature of this great city of the world and the policy thereof
must be first sought in mean concordances and small portions. So we see how that secret of nature, of the turning of
iron touched with the loadstone towards the north, was
found out in needles of iron, not in bars of iron.

But if my judgment be of any weight, the use of History
Mechanical is of all others the most radical and fundamental towards natural philosophy; such natural philosophy as
shall not vanish in the fume of subtile, sublime, or delectable speculation, but such as shall be operative to the endowment and benefit of man's life: for it will not only
minister and suggest for the present many ingenious practices in all trades, by a connexion and transferring of the
observations of one art to the use of another, when the experiences of several mysteries shall fall under the consideration of one man's mind; but further it will give a more
true and real illumination concerning causes and axioms

than is hitherto attained. For like as a man's disposition is never well known till he be crossed, nor Proteus ever changed shapes till he was straitened and held fast; so the passages and variations of nature cannot appear so fully in the liberty of nature, as in the trials and vexations of art.

For Civil History, it is of three kinds; not unfitly to be compared with the three kinds of pictures or images. For of pictures or images, we see some are unfinished, some are perfect, and some are defaced. So of histories we may find three kinds, Memorials, Perfect Histories, and Antiquities; for Memorials are history unfinished, or the first or rough draughts of history, and Antiquities are history defaced, or some remnants of history which have casually escaped the shipwrack of time.

Memorials, or Preparatory History, are of two sorts; whereof the one may be termed Commentaries, and the other Registers. Commentaries are they which set down a continuance of the naked events and actions, without the motives or designs, the counsels, the speeches, the pretexts, the occasions, and other passages of action: for this is the true nature of a Commentary; though Cæsar, in modesty mixed with greatness, did for his pleasure apply the name of a Commentary to the best history of the world. Registers are collections of public acts, as decrees of council, judicial proceedings, declarations and letters of estate, orations, and the like, without a perfect continuance or contexture of the thread of the narration.

Antiquities or Remnants of History are, as was said, *tanquam tabula naufragii,* [like the planks of a shipwreck;] when industrious persons by an exact and scrupulous diligence and observation, out of monuments, names, words, proverbs, traditions, private records and evidences, fragments of stories, passages of books that concern not story, and the like, do save and recover somewhat from the deluge of time.

In these kinds of unperfect histories I do assign no deficience, for they are *tanquam imperfecte mista,* [things imperfectly compounded;] and therefore any deficience in them is but their nature. As for the corruptions and moths of history, which are Epitomes, the use of them deserveth to be banished, as all men of sound judgment have confessed; as those that have fretted and corroded the sound bodies of many excellent histories, and wrought them into base and unprofitable dregs.

History which may be called Just and Perfect History is of three kinds, according to the object which it propoundeth or pretendeth to represent: for it either representeth a Time, or a Person, or an Action. The first we call Chronicles, the second Lives, and the third Narrations or Relations. Of these, although the first be the most complete and absolute kind of history and hath most estimation and glory, yet the second excelleth it in profit and use, and the third in verity and sincerity. For History of Times representeth the magnitude of actions and the public faces and deportments of persons, and passeth over in silence the smaller passages and motions of men and matters. But such being the workmanship of God as he doth hang the greatest weight upon the smallest wires, *maxima e minimis suspendens,* it comes therefore to pass, that such histories do rather set forth the pomp of business than the true and inward resorts thereof. But Lives, if they be well written, propounding to themselves a person to represent in whom actions both greater and smaller, public and private, have a commixture, must of necessity contain a more true, native, and lively representation. So again Narrations and Relations of actions, as the War of Peloponnesus, the Expedition of Cyrus Minor, the Conspiracy of Catiline, cannot but be more purely and exactly true than Histories of Times, because they may choose an argument comprehensible within the notice and instructions of the writer: whereas he that undertaketh the story of a time, especially of any length, cannot but meet with many blanks and spaces which he must be forced to fill up out of his own wit and conjecture.

For the History of Times, (I mean of civil history) the providence of God hath made the distribution: for it hath pleased God to ordain and illustrate two examplar states of the world, for arms, learning, moral virtue, policy, and laws; the state of Græcia, and the state of Rome; the histories whereof occupying the middle part of time, have more ancient to them, histories which may by one common name be termed the Antiquities of the World; and after them, histories which may be likewise called by the name of Modern History.

Now to speak of the deficiencies. As to the Heathen Antiquities of the world, it is in vain to note them for deficient. Deficient they are no doubt, consisting most of fables and fragments; but the deficience cannot be holpen; for antiquity is like fame, *caput inter nubila condit* [*she lifts her head among the clouds], her head is muffled from our sight. For the History of the Exemplar States, it is extant in good perfection. Not but I could wish there were a perfect course of history for Græcia from Theseus to Philopœmen, (what time the affairs of Græcia drowned and extinguished in the affairs of Rome;) and for Rome from Romulus to Justinianus, who may be truly said to be *ultimus Romanorum* [*the last of the Romans]. In which sequences of story the text of Thucydides and Xenophon in the one, and the texts of Livius, Polybius, Sallustius, Cæsar, Appianus, Tacitus, Herodianus in the other, to be kept entire without any diminution at all, and only to be supplied and continued. But this is matter of magnificence, rather to be commended than required: and we speak now of parts of learning supplemental, and not of supererogation.

But for Modern Histories, whereof there are some few very worthy, but the greater part beneath mediocrity, leaving the care of foreign stories to foreign states, because I will not be *curiosus in aliena republica,* [a meddler in other nations' matters,] I cannot fail to represent to your Majesty the unworthiness of the history of England in the main continuance thereof, and the partiality and obliquity of that of Scotland in the latest and largest author that I have seen; supposing that it would be honour for your Majesty and a work very memorable, if this island of Great Britain, as it is now joined in monarchy for the ages to come, so were joined in one history for the times passed; after the manner of the sacred history, which draweth down the story of the Ten Tribes and of the Two Tribes as twins together. And if it shall seem that the greatness of this work may make it less exactly performed, there is an excellent period of a much smaller compass of time, as to the story of England; that is to say, from the Uniting of the Roses to the Uniting of the Kingdoms; a portion of time, wherein to my understanding, there hath been the rarest varieties that in like number of successions of any hereditary monarchy hath been known. For it beginneth with the mixed adeption of a crown, by arms and title; an entry by battle, an establishment by marriage; and therefore times answerable, like waters after a tempest, full of working and swelling, though without extremity of storm; but well passed through by the wisdom of the pilot, being one of the most sufficient kings[11] of all the number. Then followeth the reign of a king, whose actions, howsoever conducted, had much intermixture with the affairs of Europe, balancing and inclining them variably; in whose time also began that great alteration in the state ecclesiastical, an action which seldom cometh upon the stage: then the reign of a minor: then an offer of an usurpation, though it was but as *febris ephemera,* [a diary ague:] then the reign of a queen matched with a foreigner: then of a queen that lived solitary and unmarried, and yet her government so masculine as it had greater impression and operation upon the states abroad than it any ways received from thence: and now last, this most happy and glorious event, that this island of Britain, divided from all the world, should be united in itself; and that oracle of rest given to Æneas, *Antiquam exquirite matrem,* [seek out your ancient mother,] should now be performed and fulfilled upon the nations of England and Scotland, being now reunited in the ancient mother name of Britain, as a full period of all instability and peregrinations: so that as it cometh to pass in massive bodies, that they have certain trepidations and waverings before they fix and settle; so it seemeth that by the providence of God this monarchy, before it was to settle in your Majesty and your generations, (in which I hope it is now established for ever,) it had these prelusive changes and varieties.

For Lives, I do find strange that these times have so little esteemed the virtues of the times, as that the writing of lives should be no more frequent. For although there be not many sovereign princes or absolute commanders, and that states are most collected into monarchies, yet are there many worthy personages that deserve better than dispersed report or barren elogies. For herein the invention of one of the late poets[12] is proper, and doth well enrich the ancient fiction: for he feigneth that at the end of the thread or web of every man's life there was a little medal containing the person's name, and that Time waited upon the shears, and as soon as the thread was cut, caught the medals and carried them to the river of Lethe; and about the bank there were many birds flying up and down, that would get the medals and carry them in their beak a little while, and then let them fall into the river: only there were a few swans, which if they got a name, would carry it to a temple where it was consecrate. And although many men more mortal in their affections than in their bodies, do esteem desire of name and memory but as a vanity and ventosity,

Animi nil magnæ laudis egentes;

[souls that have no care for praise;] which opinion cometh from that root, *non prius laudes contempsimus, quam laudanda facere desivimus;* [men hardly despise praise till they have ceased to deserve it;] yet that will not alter Salomon's judgment, *Memoria justi cum laudibus, at impiorum nomen putrescet;* [the memory of the just is blessed; but the name of the wicked shall rot;] the one flourisheth, the other either consumeth to present oblivion, or turneth to an ill odour. And therefore in that style or addition, which is and hath been long well received and brought in use, *felicis memoriæ, piæ memoriæ, bonæ memoriæ,* [of happy, of pious, of good memory,] we do acknowledge that which Cicero saith, borrowing it from Demosthenes, that *bona fama propria pos-sessio defunctorum;* [good fame is all that a dead man can possess;] which possession I cannot but note that in our times it lieth much waste, and that therein there is a deficience.

For Narrations and Relations of particular actions, there were also to be wished a greater diligence therein; for there is no great action but hath some good pen which attends it. And because it is an ability not common to write a good history, as may well appear by the small number of them; yet if particularity of actions memorable were but tolerably reported as they pass, the compiling of a complete History of Times might be the better expected, when a writer should arise that were fit for it: for the collection of such relations might be as a nursery garden, whereby to plant a fair and stately garden when time should serve.

There is yet another portion of history which Cornelius Tacitus maketh, which is not to be forgotten, specially with that application which he accoupleth it withal, Annals and Journals: appropriating to the former matters of estate, and to the later acts and accidents of a meaner nature. For giving but a touch of certain magnificent buildings, he addeth, *Cum ex dignitate populi Romani repertum sit, res illustres annalibus, talia diurnis urbis actis mandare:* [that it had been thought suitable to the dignity of the Roman people to enter in their *annals* only matters of note and greatness; leaving such things as these to the *journal records* of the city.] So as there is a kind of contemplative heraldry, as well as civil. And as nothing doth derogate from the dignity of a state more than confusion of degrees; so it doth not a little embase the authority of an history, to intermingle matters of triumph or matters of ceremony or matters of novelty with matters of state. But the use of a Journal hath not only been in the history of times, but likewise in the history of persons, and chiefly of actions; for princes in ancient time had, upon point of honour and policy both, journals kept of what passed day by day: for we see the Chronicle which was read before Ahasuerus, when he could not take rest, contained matter of affairs indeed, but such as had passed in his own time, and very lately before: but the Journal of Alexander's house expressed every small particularity, even concerning his person and court; and it is yet an use well received in enterprises memorable, as expeditions of war, navigations, and the like, to keep diaries of that which passeth continually.

I cannot likewise be ignorant of a form of writing which some grave and wise men have used, containing a scattered history of those actions which they have thought worthy of memory, with politic discourse and observation thereupon; not incorporate into the history, but separately, and as the more principal in their intention; which kind of Ruminated History I think more fit to place amongst books of policy,[13] whereof we shall hereafter speak, than amongst books of history; for it is the true office of history to represent the events themselves together with the counsels, and to leave the observations and conclusions thereupon to the liberty and faculty of every man's judgment. But mixtures are things irregular, whereof no man can define.

So also is there another kind of history manifoldly mixed, and that is History of Cosmography: being compounded of natural history, in respect of the regions themselves; of history civil, in respect of the habitations, regiments, and manners of the people; and the mathematics, in respect of the climates and configurations towards the heavens: which part of learning of all others in this latter time hath obtained most proficience. For it may be truly affirmed to the honour of these times, and in a virtuous emulation with antiquity, that this great building of the world had never through-lights made in it, till the age of us and our fathers; for although they had knowledge of the antipodes,

> Nosque ubi primus equis oriens afflavit anhelis,
> Illic sera rubens accendit lumina Vesper:
>
> [And while on us the fresh East breathes from far,
> For them the red West lights her evening star:]

yet that might be by demonstration, and not in fact; and if by travel, it requireth the voyage but of half the globe. But to circle the earth, as the heavenly bodies do, was not done nor enterprised till these later times: and therefore these times may justly bear in their word, not only *plus ultra* [*even further], in precedence of the ancient *non ultra* [*no further], and *imitabile fulmen*[14] in precedence of the ancient *non imitabile fulmen,*

> Demens qui nimbos et non imitable fulmen &c.
> [*Madman, who would mimic the stormcloud and the inimitable thunderbolt]

but likewise *imitabile cœlum* [*imitable heavens]; in respect of the many memorable voyages, after the manner of heaven, about the globe of the earth.

And this proficience in navigation and discoveries may plant also an expectation of the further proficience and augmentation of all sciences; because it may seem they are ordained by God to be coevals, that is, to meet in one age. For so the prophet Daniel speaking of the latter times foretelleth, *Plurimi pertransibunt, et multiplex erit scientia:* [many shall pass to and fro, and knowledge shall be multiplied:] as if the openness and through passage of the world and the increase of knowledge were appointed to be in the same ages; as we see it is already performed in great part; the learning of these later times not much giving place to the former two periods or returns of learning, the one of the Grecians, the other of the Romans.

History Ecclesiastical receiveth the same divisions with History Civil: but further in the propriety thereof may be divided into History of the Church, by a general name; History of Prophecy; and History of Providence. The first describeth the times of the militant church; whether it be fluctuant, as the ark of Noah; or moveable, as the ark in the wilderness; or at rest, as the ark in the temple; that is, the state of the church in persecution, in remove, and in peace. This part I ought in no sort to note as deficient; only I would that the virtue and sincerity of it were according to the mass and quantity. But I am not now in hand with censures, but with omissions.

The second, which is History of Prophecy, consisteth of two relatives, the prophecy and the accomplishment; and therefore the nature of such a work ought to be, that every prophecy of the scripture be sorted with the event fulfilling the same, throughout the ages of the world; both for the better confirmation of faith, and for the better illumination of the church touching those parts of prophecies which are yet unfulfilled; allowing nevertheless that latitude which is agreeable and familar unto divine prophecies; being of the nature of their author, with whom a thousand years are but as one day; and therefore are not fulfilled punctually at once, but have springing and germinant accomplishment throughout many ages, though the height or fulness of them may refer to some one age. This is a work which I find de-
Historia Prophetica ficient, but is to be done with wisdom, sobriety, and reverence, or not at all.

The third, which is History of Providence, containeth that excellent correspondence which is between God's revealed will and his secret will; which though it be so obscure as for the most part it is not legible to the natural man; no, nor many times to those that behold it from the tabernacle; yet at some times it pleaseth God, for our better establishment and the confuting of those which are as without God in the world, to write it in such text and capital letters that, as the prophet saith, *he that runneth by may read it;* that is, mere sensual persons, which hasten by God's judgments and never bend or fix their cogitations upon them, are nevertheless in their passage and race urged to discern it. Such are the notable events and examples of God's judgments, chastisements, deliverances, and blessings. And this is a work which hath passed through the labour of many, and therefore I cannot present as omitted.

There are also other parts of learning which are Appendices to history. For all the exterior proceedings of man consist of words and deeds; whereof history doth properly receive and retain in memory the deeds, and if words, yet but as inducements and passages to deeds; so are there other books and writings, which are appropriate to the custody and receit of words only; which likewise are of three sorts; Orations, Letters, and Brief Speeches or Sayings. Orations are pleadings, speeches of counsel; laudatives, invectives, apologies, reprehensions; orations of formality or ceremony, and the like. Letters are according to all the variety of occasions; advertisements, advices, directions, propositions, petitions, commendatory, expostulatory, satisfactory, of compliment, of pleasure, of discourse, and all other passages of action. And such as are written from wise men are, of all the words of man, in my judgment the best; for they are more natural than orations and public speeches, and more advised than conferences or present speeches. So again letters of affairs from such as manage them or are privy to them are of all others the best instructions for history, and to a diligent reader the best histories in themselves. For Apophthegms, it is a great loss of that book of Cæsar's; for as his history and those few letters of his which we have and those apophthegms which were of his own excel all men's else, so I suppose would his collection of Apophthegms have done; for as for those which are collected by others, either I have no taste in such matters, or else their choice hath not been happy. But upon these three kinds of writings I do not insist, because I have no deficiences to propound concerning them.

Thus much therefore concerning History; which is that part of learning which answereth to one of the cells, domiciles, or offices of the mind of man; which is that of the Memory.

Poesy is a part of learning in measure of words for the most part restrained, but in all other points extremely licensed, and doth truly refer to the Imagination; which, being not tied to the laws of matter, may at pleasure join that which nature hath severed, and sever that which nature hath joined, and so make unlawful matches and divorces of things: *Pictoribus atque poetis,* &c. [Painters and

Poets have always been allowed to take what liberties they would.] It is taken in two senses, in respect of words or matter. In the first sense it is but a character of style, and belongeth to arts of speech, and is not pertinent for the present. In the later, it is (as hath been said) one of the principal portions of learning, and is nothing else but Feigned History, which may be styled as well in prose as in verse.

The use of this Feigned History hath been to give some shadow of satisfaction to the mind of man in those points wherein the nature of things doth deny it; the world being in proportion inferior to the soul; by reason whereof there is agreeable to the spirit of man a more ample greatness, a more exact goodness, and a more absolute variety, than can be found in the nature of things. Therefore, because the acts or events of true history have not that magnitude which satisfieth the mind of man, poesy feigneth acts and events greater and more heroical; because true history propoundeth the successes and issues of actions not so agreeable to the merits of virtue and vice, therefore poesy feigns them more just in retribution, and more according to revealed providence; because true history representeth actions and events more ordinary and less interchanged, therefore poesy endueth them with more rareness, and more unexpected and alternative variations. So as it appeareth that poesy serveth and conferreth to magnanimity, morality, and to delectation. And therefore it was ever thought to have some participation of divineness, because it doth raise and erect the mind, by submitting the shews of things to the desires of the mind; whereas reason doth buckle and bow the mind unto the nature of things. And we see that by these insinuations and congruities with man's nature and pleasure, joined also with the agreement and consort it hath with music, it hath had access and estimation in rude times and barbarous regions, where other learning stood excluded.

The division of poesy which is aptest in the propriety thereof, (besides those divisions which are common unto it with history, as feigned chronicles, feigned lives; and the appendices of history, as feigned epistles, feigned orations, and the rest;) is into Poesy Narrative, Representative, and Allusive. The Narrative is a mere imitation of history, with the excesses before remembered; choosing for subject commonly wars and love, rarely state, and sometimes pleasure or mirth. Representative is as a visible history, and is an image of actions as if they were present, as history is of actions in nature as they are, (that is) past. Allusive or Parabolical is a narration applied only to express some special purpose or conceit. Which later kind of parabolical wisdom was much more in use in the ancient times, as by the fables of Æsop and the brief sentences of the Seven[15] and the use of hieroglyphics may appear. And the cause was, for that it was then of necessity to express any point of reason which was more sharp or subtile than the vulgar in that manner; because men in those times wanted both variety of examples and subtilty of conceit: and as hieroglyphics were before letters, so parables were before arguments: and nevertheless now and at all times they do retain much life and vigour, because reason cannot be so sensible, nor examples so fit.

But there remaineth yet another use of Poesy Parabolical, opposite to that which we last mentioned: for that tendeth to demonstrate and illustrate that which is taught or delivered, and this other to retire and obscure it: that is when the secrets and mysteries of religion, policy, or philosophy are involved in fables or parables. Of this in divine poesy we see the use is authorized. In heathen poesy we see the exposition of fables doth fall out sometimes with great felicity; as in the fable that the giants being overthrown in their war against the gods, the Earth their mother in revenge thereof brought forth Fame:

> Illam Terra parens, irâ irritata deorum,
> Extremam, ut perhibent, Cœo Enceladoque sororem
> Progenuit:

[°Her, as they tell, Mother Earth, when stung by wrath against the gods, bore last sister to Cœus and Enceladus] expounded that when princes and monarchs have suppressed actual and open rebels, then the malignity of people (which is the mother of rebellion) doth bring forth libels and slanders and taxations of the state, which is of the same kind with rebellion, but more feminine. So in the fable that the rest of the gods having conspired to bind Jupiter, Pallas called Briareus with his hundred hands to his aid: expounded that monarchies need not fear any curbing of their absoluteness by mighty subjects, as long as by wisdom they keep the hearts of the people, who will be sure to come in on their side. So in the fable that Achilles was brought up under Chiron the Centaur, who was part a man and part a beast: expounded ingeniously but corruptly by Machiavel, that it belongeth to the education and discipline of princes to know as well how to play the part of the lion in violence and the fox in guile, as of the man in virtue and justice. Nevertheless in many the like encounters, I do rather think that the fable was first, and the exposition devised, than that the moral was first, and thereupon the fable framed. For I find it was an ancient vanity in Chrysippus, that troubled himself with great contention to fasten the assertions of the Stoics upon the fictions of the ancient poets. But yet that all the fables and fictions of the poets were but pleasure and not figure,[16] I interpose no opinion. Surely of those poets which are now extant, even Homer himself, (notwithstanding he was made a kind of Scripture by the later schools of the Grecians,) yet I should without any difficulty pronounce that his fables had no such inwardness in his own meaning; but what they might have upon a more original tradition, is not easy to affirm; for he was not the inventor of many of them.

In this third part of learning, which is poesy, I can report no deficience. For being as a plant that cometh of the lust of the earth, without a formal seed, it hath sprung up and spread abroad more than any other kind. But to ascribe unto it that which is due; for the expressing of affections, passions, corruptions, and customs, we are beholding to poets more than to the philosophers' works; and for wit and eloquence not much less than to orators' harangues. But it is not good to stay too long in the theatre. Let us now pass on to the judicial place or palace of the mind, which we are to approach and view with more reverence and attention.

The knowledge of man is as the waters, some descending from above, and some springing from beneath; the one informed by the light of nature, the other inspired by divine revelation. The light of nature consisteth in the notions of the mind and the reports of the senses; for as for knowledge which man receiveth by teaching, it is cumulative and not original; as in a water that besides his own spring-head is fed with other springs and streams. So then according to these two differing illuminations or originals, knowledge is first of all divided into Divinity and Philosophy.

In Philosophy, the contemplations of man do either penetrate unto God, or are circumferred to Nature, or are reflected or reverted upon Himself. Out of which several inquiries there do arise three knowledges, Divine philosophy, Natural philosophy, and Human philosophy or Humanity. For all things are marked and stamped with this triple character, of the power of God, the difference of nature, and the use of man. But because the distributions and partitions of knowledge are not like several lines that meet in one angle, and so touch but in a point; but are like branches of a tree that meet in a stem, which hath a dimension and quantity of entireness and continuance, before it come to discontinue and break itself into arms and boughs; therefore it is good, before we enter into the former distribution, to erect and constitute one universal science, by the name of *Philosophia Prima,* Primitive or Summary Philosophy, as the main and common way, before we come where the ways part and divide themselves; which science whether I should report as deficient or no, I stand doubtful. For I find a certain rhapsody of Natural Theology, and of divers parts of Logic; and of that part of Natural Philosophy which concerneth the Principles, and of that other part of Natural Philosophy which concerneth the Soul or Spirit; all these strangely commixed and confused; but being examined, it seemeth to me rather a depredation of other sciences, advanced and exalted unto some height of terms, than any thing solid or substantive of itself. Nevertheless I cannot be ignorant of the distinction which is current, that the same things are handled but in several respects; as for example, that logic considereth of many things as they are in notion, and this philosophy as they are in nature; the one in appearance, the other in existence. But I find this difference better made than pursued. For if they had considered Quantity, Similitude, Diversity, and the rest of those Extern Characters of things, as philosophers, and in nature, their inquiries must of force have been of a far other kind than they are. For doth any of them, in handling Quantity, speak of the force of union, how and how far it multiplieth virtue? Doth any give the reason, why some things in nature are so common and in so great mass, and others so rare and in so small quantity? Doth any, in handling Similitude and Diversity, assign the cause why iron should not move to iron, which is more like, but move to the loadstone, which is less like? Why in all diversities of things there should be certain participles in nature, which are almost ambiguous to which kind they should be referred? But there is a mere and deep silence touching the nature and operation of those Common Adjuncts of things, as in nature; and only a resuming and repeating of the force and use of them in speech or argument. Therefore, because in a writing of this nature I avoid all subtility, my meaning touching this original or universal philosophy is thus, in a plain and gross description by negative: *That it be a receptacle for all such profitable observations and axioms as fall not within the compass of any of the special parts of philosophy or sciences, but are more common and of a higher stage.*

Now that there are many of that kind need not be doubted. For example; is not the rule, *Si inæqualibus æqualia addas, omnia erunt inæqualia,* [if equals be added to unequals, the wholes will be unequal,] an axiom as well of justice as of the mathematics? And is there not a true coincidence between commutative and distributive justice, and arithmetical and geometrical proportion? Is not that other rule, *Quæ in eodem tertio conveniunt, et inter se conveniunt,* [things that are equal to the same are equal to each other,] a rule taken from the mathematics, but so potent in logic as all syllogisms are built upon it? Is not the observation, *Omnia mutantur, nil interit,* [all things change, but nothing is lost,] a contemplation in philosophy thus, That the *quantum* of nature is eternal? in natural theology thus, That it requireth the same omnipotence to make somewhat nothing, which at the first made nothing somewhat? according to the scripture, *Didici quod omnia opera quæ fecit Deus perseverent in perpetuum; non possumus eis quicquam addere nec auferre:* [I know that whatsoever God doeth, it shall be for ever; nothing can be put to it, nor anything taken from it]. Is not the ground, which Machiavel wisely and largely discourseth concerning governments, that the way to establish and preserve them is to reduce them *ad principia* [*to a head], a rule in religion and nature as well as in civil administration? Was not the Persian Magic a reduction or correspondence of the principles and architectures of nature to the rules and policy of governments? Is not the precept of a musician, to fall from a discord or harsh accord upon a concord or sweet accord, alike true in affection? Is not the trope of music, to avoid or slide from the close or cadence, common with the trope of rhetoric of deceiving expectation? Is not the delight of the quavering upon a stop[17] in music the same with the playing of light upon the water?

Splendet tremulo sub lumine pontus:
[Beneath the trembling light glitters the sea.]

Are not the organs of the senses of one kind with the organs of reflexion, the eye with a glass, the ear with a cave or strait determined and bounded? Neither are these only similitudes, as men of narrow observation may conceive them to be, but the same footsteps of nature, treading or printing

Philosophia Prima, sive de Fontibus Scientiarum

upon several subjects or matters. This science therefore (as I understand it) I may justly report as deficient; for I see sometimes the profounder sort of wits, in handling some particular argument, will now and then draw a bucket of water out of this well for their present use; but the springhead thereof seemeth to me not to have been visited, being of so excellent use both for the disclosing of nature and the abridgment of art.

This science being therefore first placed as a common parent, like unto Berecynthia, which had so much heavenly issue,

> Omnes cœlicolas, omnes supera alta tenentes:
> [All dwellers in the heaven and upper sky:]

we may return to the former distribution of the three philosophies; Divine, Natural, and Human. And as concerning Divine Philosophy or Natural Theology, it is that knowledge or rudiment of knowledge concerning God which may be obtained by the contemplation of his creatures; which knowledge may be truly termed divine in respect of the object, and natural in respect of the light. The bounds of this knowledge are, that it sufficeth to convince atheism, but not to inform religion: and therefore there was never miracle wrought by God to convert an atheist, because the light of nature might have led him to confess a God: but miracles have been wrought to convert idolaters and the superstitious, because no light of nature extendeth to declare the will and true worship of God. For as all works do shew forth the power and skill of the workman, and not his image; so it is of the works of God; which do shew the omnipotency and wisdom of the maker, but not his image: and therefore therein the heathen opinion differeth from the sacred truth; for they supposed the world to be the image of God, and man to be an extract or compendious image of the world; but the Scriptures never vouchsafe to attribute to the world that honour, as to be the image of God, but only *the work of his hands;* neither do they speak of any other image of God, but man. Wherefore by the contemplation of nature to induce and inforce the acknowledgment of God, and to demonstrate his power, providence, and goodness, is an excellent argument, and hath been excellently handled by divers. But on the other side, out of the contemplation of nature, or ground of human knowledges, to induce any verity or persuasion concerning the points of faith, is in my judgment not safe: *Da fidei quæ fidei sunt:* [give unto Faith that which is Faith's]. For the Heathen themselves conclude as much in that excellent and divine fable of the golden chain: *That men and gods were not able to draw Jupiter down to the earth; but contrariwise, Jupiter was able to draw them up to heaven.* So as we ought not to attempt to draw down or submit the mysteries of God to our reason; but contrariwise to raise and advance our reason to the divine truth. So as in this part of knowledge touching divine philosophy, I am so far from noting any deficience, as I rather note an excess: whereunto I have digressed, because of the extreme prejudice which both religion and philosophy hath received and may receive by being commixed together; as that which undoubtedly will make an heretical religion, and an imaginary and fabulous philosophy.

Otherwise it is of the nature of angels and spirits, which is an appendix of theology both divine and natural, and is neither inscrutable nor interdicted; for although the Scripture saith, *Let no man deceive you in sublime discourse touching the worship of angels, pressing into that he knoweth not,* &c. yet notwithstanding if you observe well that precept, it may appear thereby that there be two things only forbidden, adoration of them, and opinion fantastical of them; either to extol them further than appertaineth to the degree of a creature, or to extol a man's knowledge of them further than he hath ground. But the sober and grounded inquiry which may arise out of the passages of holy Scriptures, or out of the gradations of nature, is not restrained. So of degenerate and revolted spirits, the conversing with them or the employment of them is prohibited, much more any veneration towards them. But the contemplation or science of their nature, their power, their illusions, either by Scripture or reason, is a part of spiritual wisdom. For so the apostle[18] saith, *We are not ignorant of his stratagems*; and it is no more unlawful to inquire the nature of evil spirits than to enquire the force of poisons in nature, or the nature of sin and vice in morality. But this part touching angels and spirits, I cannot note as deficient, for many have occupied themselves in it; I may rather challenge it, in many of the writers thereof, as fabulous and fantastical.

Leaving therefore Divine Philosophy or Natural Theology (not Divinity or Inspired Theology, which we reserve for the last of all, as the haven and sabbath of all man's contemplations), we will now proceed to Natural Philosophy. If then it be true that Democritus said, *That the truth of nature lieth hid in certain deep mines and caves;* and if it be true likewise that the Alchemists do so much inculcate, that Vulcan is a second nature, and imitateth that dexterously and compendiously which nature worketh by ambages[19] and length of time; it were good to divide natural philosophy into the mine and the furnace, and to make two professions or occupations of natural philosophers, some to be pioners and some smiths; some to dig, and some to refine and hammer. And surely I do best allow of a division of that kind, though in more familiar and scholastical terms; namely, that these be the two parts of natural philosophy,—the Inquisition of Causes, and the Production of Effects; Speculative, and Operative; Natural Science, and Natural Prudence. For as in civil matters there is a wisdom of discourse and a wisdom of direction; so is it in natural. And here I will make a request, that for the latter (or at least for a part thereof) I may revive and reintegrate the misapplied and abused name of Natural Magic; which in the true sense is but Natural Wisdom, or Natural Prudence, taken according to the ancient acception, purged from vanity and superstition. Now although it be true, and I know it well, that there is an intercourse between Causes and Effects, so as both these knowledges, Speculative and Operative, have a great connexion between themselves; yet because all true and fruitful Natural Philosophy hath a double scale or ladder, ascendent and descendent; ascending from experiments to the invention of causes, and descending from causes to the invention of new experiments; therefore I judge it most requisite that these two parts be severally considered and handled.

Natural Science or Theory is divided into Physic and Metaphysic: wherein I desire it may be conceived that I use the word Metaphysic in a differing sense from that that is received: and in like manner I doubt not but it will easily appear to men of judgment that in this and other particulars, wheresoever my conception and notion may differ from the ancient, yet I am studious to keep the ancient terms. For hoping well to deliver myself from mistaking by the order and perspicuous expressing of that I do propound, I am otherwise zealous and affectionate to recede as little from antiquity, either in terms or opinions, as may stand with truth and the proficience of knowledge. And herein I cannot a little marvel at the philosopher Aristotle, that did proceed in such a spirit of difference and contradiction towards all antiquity; undertaking not only to frame new words of science at pleasure, but to confound and extinguish all ancient wisdom; insomuch as he never nameth or mentioneth an ancient author or opinion, but to confute and reprove; wherein for glory, and drawing followers and disciples, he took the right course. For certainly there cometh to pass and hath place in human truth, that which was noted and pronounced in the highest truth: *Veni in nomine Patris, nec recipitis me; si quis venerit in nomine suo, eum recipietis;* [I have come in my Father's name, and ye receive me not; if one come in his own name, him ye will receive]. But in this divine aphorism (considering to whom it was applied, namely to Antichrist, the highest deceiver,) we may discern well that *the coming in a man's own name,* without regard of antiquity or paternity, is no good sign of truth; although it be joined with the fortune and success of an *Eum recipietis* [*You will receive Him]. But for this excellent person Aristotle, I will think of him that he learned that humour of his scholar,[20] with whom it seemeth he did emulate, the one to conquer all opinions, as the other to conquer all nations. Wherein nevertheless, it may be, he may at some men's hands that are of a bitter disposition get a like title as his scholar did;

> Felix terrarum prædo, non utile mundo
> Editus exemplum, &c.

[a fortunate robber, who made prize of nations]; so

> Felix doctrinæ prædo,

[a fortunate robber, who made prize of learning]. But to me on the other side that do desire, as much as lieth in my pen, to ground a sociable intercourse between antiquity and proficience, it seemeth best to keep way with antiquity *usque ad aras*, [as far as may be without violating higher obligations;] and therefore to retain the ancient terms, though I sometimes alter the uses and definitions; according to the moderate proceeding in civil government, where although there be some alteration, yet that holdeth which Tacitus wisely noteth, *eadem magistratuum vocabula*, [the name of the magistracies are not changed].

To return therefore to the use and acception of the term Metaphysic, as I do now understand the word: It appeareth by that which hath been already said, that I intend Philosophia Prima, Summary Philosophy, and Metaphysic, which heretofore have been confounded as one, to be two distinct things. For the one I have made as a parent or common ancestor to all knowledge, and the other I have now brought in as a branch or descendent of Natural Science. It appeareth likewise that I have assigned to Summary Philosophy the common principles and axioms which are promiscuous and indifferent to several sciences. I have assigned unto it likewise the inquiry *touching the operation of the relative and adventive characters of essences, as Quantity, Similitude, Diversity, Possibility*, and the rest;

with this distinction and provision; that they be handled as they have efficacy in nature, and not logically. It appeareth likewise that Natural Theology, which heretofore hath been handled confusedly with Metaphysic, I have inclosed and bounded by itself. It is therefore now a question, what is left remaining for Metaphysic; wherein I may without prejudice preserve thus much of the conceit of antiquity, that Physic should contemplate that which is inherent in matter and therefore transitory, and Metaphysic that which is abstracted and fixed. And again that Physic should handle that which supposeth in nature only a being and moving, and Metaphysic should handle that which supposeth further in nature a reason, understanding, and platform. But the difference, perspicuously expressed, is most familiar and sensible. For as we divided Natural Philosophy in general into the Inquiry of Causes and Productions of Effects; so that part which concerneth the Inquiry of Causes we do subdivide, according to the received and sound division of Causes; the one part, which is Physic, enquireth and handleth the Material and Efficient Causes; and the other, which is Metaphysic, handleth the Formal and Final Causes.

Physic (taking it according to the derivation, and not according to our idiom for Medicine,) is situate in a middle term or distance between Natural History and Metaphysic. For Natural History describeth the *variety of things;* Physic, the causes, but *variable or respective causes;* and Metaphysic, the *fixed and constant causes.*

> Limus ut hic durescit, et hæc ut cera liquescit,
> Uno eodemque igni:
>
> [As the same fire which makes the soft clay hard
> Makes hard wax soft:]

Fire is the cause of induration, but respective to clay; fire is the cause of colliquation, but respective to wax; but fire is no constant cause either of induration or colliquation. So then the physical causes are but the efficient and the matter. Physic hath three parts; whereof two respect nature *united* or *collected,* the third contemplateth nature *diffused* or *distributed.* Nature is collected either into one entire *total,* or else into the same *principles* or *seeds.* So as the first doctrine is touching the Contexture or Configuration of things, as *de mundo, de universitate rerum* [*concerning the world, concerning the universality of things]. The second is the doctrine concerning the Principles or Originals of things. The third is the doctrine concerning all Variety and Particularity of things, whether it be of the differing substances, or their differing qualities and natures; whereof there needeth no enumeration, this part being but as a gloss or paraphrase, that attendeth upon the text of Natural History. Of these three I cannot report any as deficient. In what truth or perfection they are handled, I make not now any judgment: but they are parts of knowledge not deserted by the labour of man.

For Metaphysic, we have assigned unto it the inquiry of Formal and Final Causes; which assignation, as to the former of them, may seem to be nugatory and void, because of the received and inveterate opinion that the inquisition of man is not competent to find out *essential forms* or *true differences:* of which opinion we will take this hold; that the invention of Forms is of all other parts of knowledge the worthiest to be sought, if it be possible to be found. As for the possibility, they are ill discoverers that think there is no land when they can see nothing but sea. But it is manifest that Plato in his opinion of Ideas, as one that had a wit of elevation situate as upon a cliff, did descry *that forms were the true object of knowledge;* but lost the real fruit of his opinion, by considering of forms as absolutely abstracted from matter, and not confined and determined by matter; and so turning his opinion upon Theology, wherewith all his natural philosophy is infected. But if any man shall keep a continual watchful and severe eye upon action, operation, and the use of knowledge, he may advise and take notice what are the Forms, the disclosures whereof are fruitful and important to the state of man. For as to the Forms of substances

—Man only except, of whom it is said, *Formavit hominem de limo terræ, et spiravit in faciem ejus spiraculum vitæ,* [He formed man of the dust of the ground, and breathed into his nostrils the breath of life,] and not as of all other creatures, *Producant aquæ, producat terra,* [let the waters bring forth, let the earth bring forth,]—the Forms of Substances I say (as they are now by compounding and transplanting multiplied) are so perplexed, as they are not to be enquired; no more than it were either possible or to purpose to seek in gross *the forms of those sounds which make words,* which by composition and transposition of letters are infinite. But on the other side, to enquire *the form of those sounds or voices which make simple letters* is easily comprehensible, and being known, induceth and manifesteth the forms of all words, which consist and are compounded of them. In the same manner to enquire the Form of a lion, of an oak, of gold, nay of water, of air, is a vain pursuit: but to enquire the Forms of sense, of voluntary motion, of vegetation, of colours, of gravity and levity, of density, of tenuity, of heat, of cold, and all other natures and qualities, which like an alphabet are not many, and of which the essences (upheld by matter) of all creatures do consist; to enquire I say the *true forms* of these, is that part of Metaphysic which we now define of. Not but that Physic doth make inquiry and take consideration of the same natures: but how? Only as to the Material and Efficient Causes of them, and not as to the Forms. For example; if the cause of Whiteness in snow or froth be enquired, and it be rendered thus, *that the subtile intermixture of air and water is the cause,* it is well rendered; but nevertheless, is this the Form of Whiteness? No; but it is the Efficient, which is ever but *vehiculum formæ,* [the Metaphysica, carrier of the Form]. This part of Metaphysic I sive do not find laboured and performed; whereat De Formis et Finibus I marvel not, because I hold it not possible to be Rerum invented by that course of invention which hath been used; in regard that men (which is the root of all error) have made too untimely a departure and too remote a recess from particulars.

But the use of this part of Metaphysic which I report as deficient, is of the rest the most excellent in two respects; the one, because it is the duty and virtue of all knowledge to abridge the infinity of individual experience as much as the conception of truth will permit, and to remedy the complaint of *vita brevis, ars longa,* [life is short and art is long;] which is performed by uniting the notions and conceptions of sciences. For knowledges are as pyramides, whereof history is the basis: so of Natural Philosophy the basis is Natural History; the stage next the basis is Physic; the stage next the vertical point is Metaphysic. As for the vertical point, *Opus quod operatur Deus à principio usque ad finem,* [the work which God worketh from the beginning to the end,] the Summary Law of Nature, we know not whether man's inquiry can attain unto it. But these three be the true *stages* of knowledge; and are to them that are depraved no better than the giants' hills, [Pelion, Ossa, and Olympus, piled upon each other,]

> Ter sunt conati imponere Pelio Ossam,
> Scilicet atque Ossæ frondosum involvere Olympum:

but to those which refer all things to the glory of God, they are as the three acclamations, *Sancte, sancte, sancte;* holy in the description or dilatation of his works, holy in the connexion or concatenation of them, and holy in the union of them in a perpetual and uniform law. And therefore the speculation was excellent in Parmenides and Plato, although but a speculation in them, That all things by scale did ascend to unity. So then always that knowledge is worthiest, which is charged with least multiplicity; which appeareth to be Metaphysic; as that which considereth the Simple Forms or Differences of things, which are few in number, and the degrees and co-ordinations whereof make all this variety. The second respect which valueth and commendeth this part of Metaphysic, is that it doth enfranchise the power of man unto the greatest liberty and possibility of works and effects. For Physic carrieth men in narrow and restrained ways, subject to many accidents of impediments, imitating the ordinary flexuous courses of nature; but *latæ undique sunt sapientibus viæ* [*everywhere hidden are the ways of things]: to sapience (which was anciently defined to be *rerum divinarum et humanarum scientia,* [the knowledge of things human and divine],) there is ever choice of means. For physical causes give light to new invention *in simili materia* [*in like matter]; but whosoever knoweth any *form,* knoweth the utmost possibility of *superinducing that nature upon any variety of matter,* and so is less restrained in operation, either to the basis of the Matter or the condition of the Efficient: which kind of knowledge Salomon likewise, though in a more divine sense, elegantly describeth: *Non arctabuntur gressus tui, et currens non habebis offendiculum;* [thy steps shall not be straitened; thou shalt run and not stumble]. The ways of sapience are not much liable either to particularity or chance.

The second part of Metaphysic is the inquiry of *final* causes, which I am moved to report not as omitted, but as misplaced. And yet if it were but a fault in order, I would not speak of it; for order is matter of illustration, but pertaineth not to the substance of sciences: but this misplacing hath caused a deficience, or at least a great improficience in the sciences themselves. For the handling of final causes mixed with the rest in physical inquiries, hath intercepted the severe and diligent inquiry of all real and physical causes, and given men the occasion to stay upon these satisfactory and specious causes, to the great arrest and prejudice of further discovery. For this I find done not only by Plato, who ever anchoreth upon that shore, but by Aristotle, Galen, and others, which do usually likewise fall upon these flats of *discoursing causes.* For to say that *the hairs of the eye-lids are for a quickset and fence about the sight;* or that *the firmness of the skins and hides of living creatures is to defend them from the extremities of heat or cold;* or that *the bones are for the columns or beams, whereupon the frames of the bodies of living creatures are built;* or that *the leaves of trees are for protecting of the fruit;* or that *the clouds are for watering of the earth;* or that *the solidness of the earth is for the station and mansion of living creatures,* and the like, is well enquired and collected in Metaphysic; but in Physic they are impertinent. Nay, they are indeed but remoras and hinderances to stay and slug the ship from further sailing, and have brought this to pass, that the search of the Physical Causes hath been neglected and passed in silence. And therefore the natural philosophy of Democritus and some others, who did not suppose a mind or reason in the frame of things, but attributed *the form thereof able to maintain itself to infinite essays or proofs of nature,* which they term *fortune,* seemeth to me (as far as I can judge by the recital and fragments which remain unto us) in particularities of physical causes more real and better enquired than that of Aristotle and Plato; whereof both intermingled final causes, the one as a part of theology, and the other as a part of logic, which were the favourite studies respectively of both those persons. Not because those final causes are not true, and worthy to be enquired, being kept within their own province; but because their excursions into the limits of physical causes hath bred a vastness and solitude in that track. For otherwise keeping their precincts and borders, men are extremely deceived if they think there is an enmity or repugnancy at all between them. For the cause rendered, that *the hairs about the eye-lids are for the safeguard of the sight,* doth not impugn the cause rendered, that *pilosity is incident to orifices of moisture; Muscosi fontes,* [the mossy springs,] &c. Nor the cause rendered, that *the firmness of hides is for the armour of the body against extremities of heat or cold,* doth not impugn the cause rendered, that *contraction of pores is incident to the outwardest parts, in regard of their adjacence to foreign or unlike bodies;* and so of the rest: both causes being true and compatible, the one declaring an intention, the other a consequence only. Neither doth this call in question or derogate from divine providence, but highly confirm and exalt it. For as in civil actions he is the greater and deeper politique, that can make other men the instruments of his will and ends and yet never acquaint them with his purpose, so as they shall do it and yet not know what they do, than he that imparteth his meaning to those he employeth; so is the wisdom of God more admirable, when nature intendeth one thing and providence draweth forth another, than if he had communicated to particular creatures and motions the characters and impressions of his providence. And thus much for Metaphysic; the later part whereof I allow as extant, but wish it confined to its proper place.

Nevertheless there remaineth yet another part of Natural Philosophy, which is commonly made a principal part, and holdeth rank with Physic special and Metaphysic; which is Mathematic; but I think it more agreeable to the nature of things and to the light of order to place it as a branch of Metaphysic; for the subject of it being Quantity; not Quantity indefinite, which is but a relative and belongeth to *philosophia prima* (as hath been said,) but Quantity determined or proportionable; it appeareth to be one of the Essential Forms of things; as that that is causative in nature of a number of effects; insomuch as we see in the schools both of Democritus and of Pythagoras, that the one *did ascribe figure to the first seeds of things*, and the other *did suppose numbers to be the principles and originals of things:* and it is true also that of all other forms (as we understand forms) it is the most abstracted and separable from matter, and therefore most proper to Metaphysic; which hath likewise been the cause why it hath been better laboured and enquired than any of the other forms, which are more immersed into matter. For it being the nature of the mind of man (to the extreme prejudice of knowledge) to delight in the spacious liberty of generalities, as in a champion region,[21] and not in the inclosures of particularity; the Mathematics of all other knowledge were the goodliest fields to satisfy that appetite. But for the placing of this science, it is not much material: only we have endeavoured in these our partitions to observe a kind of perspective, that one part may cast light upon another.

The Mathematics are either Pure or Mixed. To the Pure Mathematics are those sciences belonging which handle Quantity Determinate, merely severed from any axioms of natural philosophy; and these are two, Geometry and Arithmetic; the one handling Quantity continued, and the other dissevered. Mixed hath for subject some axioms or parts of natural philosophy, and considereth Quantity determined, as it is auxiliary and incident unto them. For many parts of nature can neither be invented with sufficient subtilty nor demonstrated with sufficient perspicuity nor accommodated unto use with sufficient dexterity, without the aid and intervening of the Mathematics: of which sort are Perspective, Music, Astronomy, Cosmography, Architecture, Enginery, and divers others. In the Mathematics I can report no deficience, except it be that men do not sufficiently understand the excellent use of the Pure Mathematics, in that they do remedy and cure many defects in the wit and faculties intellectual. For if the wit be too dull, they sharpen it; if too wandering, they fix it; if too inherent in the sense, they abstract it. So that as tennis is a game of no use in itself, but of great use in respect it maketh a quick eye and a body ready to put itself into all postures; so in the Mathematics, that use which is collateral and intervenient is no less worthy than that which is principal and intended. And as for the Mixed Mathematics, I may only make this prediction, that there cannot fail to be more kinds of them, as nature grows further disclosed. Thus much of Natural Science, or the part of nature Speculative.

For Natural Prudence, or the part Operative of Natural Philosophy, we will divide it into three parts, Experimental, Philosophical, and Magical; which three parts active have a correspondence and analogy with the three parts Speculative, Natural History, Physic, and Metaphysic. For many operations have been invented, sometimes by a casual incidence and occurrence, sometimes by a purposed experiment; and of those which have been found by an intentional experiment, some have been found out by varying or extending the same experiment, some by transferring and compounding divers experiments the one into the other, which kind of invention an empiric may manage. Again, by the knowledge of physical causes there cannot fail to follow many indications and designations of new particulars, if men in their speculation will keep one eye upon use and practice. But these are but coastings along the shore, *premendo littus iniquum* [*pressing the irregular shore]: for it seemeth to me there can hardly be discovered any radical or fundamental alterations and innovations in nature, either by the fortune and essays of experiments, or by the light and direction of physical causes. If therefore we have reported Metaphysic deficient, it must follow that *Naturalis Magia, sive Physica Operativa Major* we do the like of Natural Magic, which hath relation thereunto. For as for the Natural Magic whereof now there is mention in books, containing certain credulous and superstitious conceits and observations of Sympathies and Antipathies and hidden proprieties, and some frivolous experiments, strange rather by disguisement than in themselves; it is as far differing in truth of nature from such a knowledge as we require, as the story of king Arthur of Britain, or Hugh of Bourdeaux, differs from Cæsar's commentaries in truth of story. For it is manifest that Cæsar did greater things *de vero* than those imaginary heroes were feigned to do. But he did them not in that fabulous manner. Of this kind of learning the fable of Ixion was a figure, who designed to enjoy Juno, the goddess of power; and instead of her had copulation with a cloud, of which mixture were begotten centaurs and chimeras. So whosoever shall entertain high and vaporous imaginations instead of a laborious and sober inquiry of truth, shall beget hopes and beliefs of strange and impossible shapes. And therefore we may note in these sciences which hold so much of imagination and belief, as this degenerate Natural Magic, Alchemy, Astrology, and the like, that in their propositions the description of the means is ever more monstrous than the pretence or end. For it is a thing more probable, that he that knoweth well the natures of Weight, of Colour, of Pliant and Fragile in

respect of the hammer, of Volatile and Fixed in respect of
the fire, and the rest, may superinduce upon some metal
the nature and form of gold by such mechanique as belongeth to the production of the natures afore rehearsed,
than that some grains of the medicine projected [22] should
in a few moments of time turn a sea of quicksilver or other
material into gold. So it is more probable, that he that
knoweth the nature of arefaction,[23] the nature of assimila-
tion of nourishment to the thing nourished, the manner of
increase and clearing of spirits, the manner of the depreda-
tions which spirits make upon the humours and solid parts,
shall by ambages of diets, bathings, anointings, medicines,
motions, and the like, prolong life or restore some degree
of youth or vivacity, than that it can be done with the use
of a few drops or scruples of a liquor or receit. To conclude
therefore, the true Natural Magic, which is that great liberty and latitude of operation which dependeth upon the
knowledge of Forms, I may report deficient, as the relative
thereof is. To which part, if we be serious and incline not
to vanities and plausible discourse, besides the deriving
and deducing the operations themselves from Metaphysic,
there are pertinent two points of much purpose, the one by
way of preparation, the other by way of caution. The first
is, that there be made a *Calendar resembling an inventory*
of the estate of man, containing all the inventions (being
the works or fruits of nature or art) which are
now extant and whereof man is already possessed; out of which doth naturally result a note,
what things are yet held impossible, or not invented; which
calendar will be the more artificial and serviceable, if to
every reputed impossibility you add what thing is extant
which cometh the nearest in degree to that impossibility;
to the end that by these optatives and potentials man's inquiry may be the more awake in deducing direction of
works from the speculation of causes. And secondly, that
those experiments be not only esteemed which have an immediate and present use, but those principally which are of
most universal consequence for invention of other experi-

*Inventarium
Opum huma-
narum*

ments, and those which give most light to the invention of causes; for the invention of the mariner's needle, which giveth the direction, is of no less benefit for navigation than the invention of the sails, which give the motion.

Thus have I passed through Natural Philosophy, and the deficiences thereof; wherein if I have differed from the ancient and received doctrines, and thereby shall move contradiction; for my part, as I affect not to dissent, so I purpose not to contend. If it be truth,

> Non canimus surdis, respondent omnia sylvæ:
> [All as we sing the listening woods reply:]

the voice of nature will consent, whether the voice of man do or no. And as Alexander Borgia was wont to say of the expedition of the French for Naples, that they came with chalk in their hands to mark up their lodgings, and not with weapons to fight; so I like better that entry of truth which cometh peaceably with chalk to mark up those minds[24] which are capable to lodge and harbour it, than that which cometh with pugnacity and contention.

But there remaineth a division of Natural Philosophy according to the *report of the inquiry*, and nothing concerning the matter or subject; and that is Positive and Considerative; when the inquiry reporteth either an Assertion or a Doubt. These doubts or *non liquets* [*reservations] are of two sorts, Particular and Total. For the first, we see a good example thereof in Aristotle's Problems, which deserved to have had a better continuance, but so nevertheless as there is one point whereof warning is to be given and taken. The registering of doubts hath two excellent uses: the one, that it saveth philosophy from errors and falsehoods; when that which is not fully appearing is not collected into assertion, whereby error might draw error, but reserved in doubt: the other, that the entry of doubts are as so many suckers or spunges to draw use of[25] knowledge; insomuch as that which if doubts had not preceded a man should never have advised but passed it over without note, by the suggestion and solicitation of doubts is made to be attended and applied.

But both these commodities do scarcely countervail an inconvenience which will intrude itself, if it be not debarred; which is, that when a doubt is once received men labour rather how to keep it a doubt still than how to solve it, and accordingly bend their wits. Of this we see the familiar example in lawyers and scholars, both which if they have once admitted a doubt, it goeth ever after authorised for a doubt. But that use of wit and knowledge is to be allowed, which laboureth to make doubtful things certain, and not those which labour to make certain things doubtful. There-

Continuatio Problematum in Natura

fore these *calendars of doubts* I commend as excellent things, so that there be this caution used, that when they be throughly sifted and brought to resolution, they be from thenceforth omitted, decarded, and not continued to cherish and encourage men in doubting. To which calendar of doubts or problems, I advise be annexed another calendar, as much or more material, which is *a calendar of popular errors:* I

Catalogus Falsitatum grassantium in historia Naturæ

mean chiefly, in natural history such as pass in speech and conceit, and are nevertheless apparently detected and convicted of untruth; that man's knowledge be not weakened nor imbased by such dross and vanity. As for the *doubts or non liquets general or in total,* I understand those differences of opinions touching the principles of nature and the fundamental points of the same, which have caused the diversity of sects, schools, and philosophies; as that of Empodocles, Pythagoras, Democritus, Parmenides, and the rest. For although Aristotle, as though he had been of the race of the Ottomans, thought he could not reign except the first thing he did he killed all his brethren; yet to those that seek truth and not magistrality, it cannot but seem a matter of great profit to see before them the several opinions touching the foundations of nature; not for any exact truth that can be expected in those theories; for as the same phænomena in astronomy are satisfied by the received astronomy of the diurnal motion and the proper motions of the planets with their eccentrics and epicycles, and like-

wise by the theory of Copernicus who supposed the earth
to move; and the calculations are indifferently agreeable to
both; so the ordinary face and view of experience is many
times satisfied by several theories and philosophies; whereas
to find the real truth requireth another manner of severity and attention. For as Aristotle saith that children at the
first will call every woman mother, but afterward they
come to distinguish according to truth; so experience, if it
be in childhood, will call every philosophy mother, but
when it cometh to ripeness it will discern the true mother.
So as in the mean time it is good to see the several glosses
and opinions upon nature, whereof it may be every one in
some one point hath seen clearer than his fellows. There-
De Antiquis fore I wish some collection to be made painfully
Philosophiis and understandingly *de antiquis philosophiis*
[*out of the ancient philosophers], out of all the possible
light which remaineth to us of them. Which kind of work I
find deficient. But here I must give warning, that it be done
distinctly and severely; the philosophies of every one
throughout by themselves; and not by titles packed and
faggoted up together, as hath been done by Plutarch. For
it is the harmony of a philosophy in itself which giveth it
light and credence; whereas if it be singled and broken, it
will seem more foreign and dissonant. For as when I read
in Tacitus the actions of Nero or Claudius, with circumstances of times, inducements, and occasions, I find them
not so strange; but when I read them in Suetonius Tran-
quillus gathered into titles and bundles, and not in order
of time, they seem more monstrous and incredible; so is it
of any philosophy reported entire, and dismembered by
articles. Neither do I exclude opinions of latter times to be
likewise represented in this calendar of sects of philosophy,
as that of Theophrastus Paracelsus, eloquently reduced into
an harmony by the pen of Severinus the Dane; and that of
Telesius, and his scholar Donius, being as a pastoral philosophy, full of sense but of no great depth; and that of
Fracastorius, who though he pretended not to make any
new philosophy, yet did use the absoluteness of his own

sense upon the old; and that of Gilbertus our countryman, who revived, with some alterations and demonstrations, the opinions of Xenophanes; and any other worthy to be admitted.

Thus have we now dealt with two of the three beams of man's knowledge; that is *Radius Directus,* which is referred to nature, *Radius Refractus,* which is referred to God, and cannot report truly because of the inequality of the medium. There resteth *Radius Reflexus* whereby Man beholdeth and contemplateth himself.

We come therefore now to that knowledge whereunto the ancient oracle directeth us, which is *the knowledge of ourselves;* which deserveth the more accurate handling, by how much it toucheth us more nearly. This knowledge, as it is the end and term of natural philosophy in the intention of man, so notwithstanding it is but a portion of natural philosophy in the continent of nature. And generally let this be a rule, that all partitions of knowledges be accepted rather for lines and veins, than for sections and separations; and that the continuance and entireness of knowledge be preserved. For the contrary hereof hath made particular sciences to become barren, shallow, and erroneous; while they have not been nourished and maintained from the common fountain. So we see Cicero the orator complained of Socrates and his school, that he was the first that separated philosophy and rhetoric; whereupon rhetoric became an empty and verbal art. So we may see that the opinion of Copernicus touching the rotation of the earth, which astronomy itself cannot correct because it is not repugnant to any of the phænomena, yet natural philosophy may correct. So we see also that the science of medicine, if it be destituted and forsaken by natural philosophy, it is not much better than an empirical practice. With this reservation therefore we proceed to Human Philosophy or Humanity, which hath two parts: the one considereth man segregate, or distributively; the other congregate, or in society. So as Human Philosophy is either Simple and

Particular, or Conjugate and Civil. Humanity Particular consisteth of the same parts whereof man consisteth; that is, of knowledges which respect the Body, and of knowledges that respect the Mind. But before we distribute so far, it is good to constitute. For I do take the consideration in general and at large of Human Nature to be fit to be emancipate and made a knowledge by itself; not so much in regard of those delightful and elegant discourses which have been made of the dignity of man, of his miseries, of his state and life, and the like *adjuncts of his common and undivided nature;* but chiefly in regard of the knowledge concerning the *sympathies and concordances between the mind and body,* which, being mixed, cannot be properly assigned to the sciences of either.

This knowledge hath two branches: for as all leagues and amities consist of mutual Intelligence and mutual Offices, so this league of mind and body hath these two parts; *how the one discloseth the other,* and *how the one worketh upon the other;* Discovery, and Impression. The former of these hath begotten two arts, both of Prediction or Prenotion; whereof the one is honoured with the inquiry of Aristotle, and the other of Hippocrates. And although they have of later time been used to be coupled with superstitious and fantastical arts, yet being purged and restored to their true state, they have both of them a solid ground in nature, and a profitable use in life. The first is Physiognomy, which discovereth the disposition of the mind by the lineaments of the body. The second is the Exposition of Natural Dreams, which discovereth the state of the body by the imaginations of the mind. In the former of these I note a deficience. For Aristotle hath very ingeniously and diligently handled the factures of the body, but not the gestures of the body, which are no less comprehensible by art, and of greater use and advantage. For the Lineaments of the body do disclose the disposition and inclination of the mind in general; but the Motions of the countenance and parts do not only so, but do further disclose the present humour and state of the mind and will. For as your Majesty saith most aptly and elegantly, *As the tongue speaketh to the ear, so the gesture speaketh to the eye.* And therefore a number of subtile persons whose eyes do dwell upon the faces and fashions of men, do well know the advantage of this observation, as being most part of their ability; neither can it be denied but that it is a great discovery of dissimulations, and a great direction in business.

The latter branch, touching Impression, hath not been collected into art, but hath been handled dispersedly; and it hath the same relation or antistrophe that the former hath. For the consideration is double: Either *how, and how far the humours and affects*[26] *of the body do alter or work upon the mind;* or again, *how and how far the passions or apprehensions of the mind do alter or work upon the body.* The former of these hath been inquired and considered as a part and appendix of Medicine, but much more as a part of Religion or Superstition. For the physician prescribeth cures of the mind in phrensies and melancholy passions; and pretendeth also to exhibit medicines to exhilarate the mind, to confirm the courage, to clarify the wits, to corroborate the memory, and the like; but the scruples and superstitions of diet and other regiment of the body in the sect of the Pythagoreans, in the heresy of the Manicheans, and in the law of Mahomet, do exceed. So likewise the ordinances in the Ceremonial Law, interdicting the eating of the blood and the fat, distinguishing between beasts clean and unclean for meat, are many and strict. Nay the faith itself being clear and serene from all clouds of Ceremony, yet retaineth the use of fastings, abstinences, and other macerations and humiliations of the body, as things real, and not figurative. The root and life of all which prescripts is, (besides the ceremony,) the consideration of that dependency which the affections of the mind are submitted unto upon the state and disposition of the body. And if any man of weak judgment do conceive that this suffering of the mind from the body doth either question the immortality or derogate from the sovereignty of the soul, he may be taught in easy instances, that the infant in the mother's womb is compatible with the mother and yet separable; and the most absolute monarch is sometimes led by his servants and yet without subjection. As for the reciprocal knowledge, which is the operation of the conceits and passions of the mind upon the body, we see all wise physicians in the prescriptions of their regiments to their patients do ever consider *accidentia animi* [*the nature of the mind], as of great force to further or hinder remedies or recoveries; and more specially it is an inquiry of great depth and worth concerning Imagination, how and how far it altereth the body proper of the imaginant. For although it hath a manifest power to hurt, it followeth not it hath the same degree of power to help; no more than a man can conclude, that because there be pestilent airs, able suddenly to kill a man in health, therefore there should be sovereign airs, able suddenly to cure a man in sickness. But the inquisition of this part is of great use, though it needeth, as Socrates said, *a Delian diver*,[27] being difficult and profound. But unto all this knowledge *de communi vinculo* [*of the common bond], of the concordances between the mind and the body, that part of inquiry is most necessary, which considereth of the *seats* and *domiciles* which the several faculties of the mind do take and occupate in the organs of the body; which knowledge hath been attempted, and is controverted, and deserveth to be much better enquired. For the opinion of Plato, who placed *the understanding in the brain, animosity* (which he did unfitly call *anger,* having a greater mixture with *pride*) *in the heart,* and *concupiscence or sensuality in the liver,* deserveth not to be despised; but much less to be allowed. So then we have constituted (as in our own wish and advice) the inquiry *touching human nature entire,* as a just portion of knowledge to be handled apart.

The knowledge that concerneth man's body is divided as the good of man's body is divided, unto which it referreth. The good of man's body is of four kinds, Health, Beauty, Strength, and Pleasure: so the knowledges are Medicine, or art of Cure; art of Decoration, which is called

Cosmetic; art of Activity, which is called Athletic; and art Voluptuary, which Tacitus truly calleth *eruditus luxus*, [educated luxury]. This subject of man's body is of all other things in nature most susceptible of remedy; but then that remedy is most susceptible of error. For the same subtility of the subject doth cause large possibility and easy failing; and therefore the inquiry ought to be the more exact.

To speak therefore of Medicine, and to resume that we have said, ascending a little higher: The ancient opinion that man was Microcosmus, an abstract or model of the world, hath been fantastically strained by Paracelsus and the alchemists, as if there were to be found in man's body certain correspondences and parallels, which should have respect to all varieties of things, as stars, planets, minerals, which are extant in the great world. But thus much is evidently true, that of all substances which nature hath produced, man's body is the most extremely compounded. For we see herbs and plants are nourished by earth and water; beasts for the most part by herbs and fruits; man by the flesh of beasts, birds, fishes, herbs, grains, fruits, water, and the manifold alterations, dressings, and preparations of these several bodies, before they come to be his food and aliment. Add hereunto that beasts have a more simple order of life, and less change of affections to work upon their bodies; whereas man in his mansion, sleep, exercise, passions, hath infinite variations; and it cannot be denied but that the Body of man of all other things is of the most compounded mass. The Soul on the other side is the simplest of substances, as is well expressed.

> Purumque reliquit
> Æthereum sensum atque auraï simplicis ignem:
> [Pure and unmixed
> The etherial sense is left—mere air and fire.]

So that it is no marvel though the soul so placed enjoy no rest, if that principle be true that *Motus rerum est rapidus extra locum, placidus in loco:* [things move rapidly to their place and calmly in their place]. But to the purpose. This variable composition of man's body hath made it as an instrument easy to distemper; and therefore the poets did well to conjoin Music and Medicine in Apollo: because the office of medicine is but to tune this curious harp of man's body and to reduce it to harmony. So then the subject being so variable hath made the art by consequent more conjectural; and the art being conjectural hath made so much the more place to be left for imposture. For almost all other arts and sciences are judged by acts or master-pieces, as I may term them, and not by the successes and events. The lawyer is judged by the virtue of his pleading, and not by the issue of the cause. The master in the ship is judged by the directing his course aright, and not by the fortune of the voyage. But the physician, and perhaps the politique, hath no particular acts demonstrative of his abil-ity, but is judged most by the event; which is ever but as it is taken: for who can tell, if a patient die or recover, or if a state be preserved or ruined, whether it be art or acci-dent? And therefore many times the impostor is prized, and the man of virtue taxed. Nay, we see [the] weakness and credulity of men is such, as they will often prefer a montabank or witch before a learned physician. And there-fore the poets were clear-sighted in discerning this extreme folly, when they made Æsculapius and Circe brother and sister, both children of the sun, as in the verses,

> Ipse repertorem medicinæ talis et artis
> Fulmine *Phœbigenam* Stygias detrusit ad undas:
> [*Apollo's son* from whom that art did grow
> Jove struck with thunder to the shades below].

And again,

> Dives inaccessos ubi *Solis filia* lucos, &c.
> [Now by the shelves of Circe's coast they run,—
> Circe the rich, the *daughter of the sun*.]

For in all times, in the opinion of the multitude, witches and old women and imposters have had a competition with physicians. And what followeth? Even this, that physicians say to themselves, as Salomon expresseth it upon an higher occasion; *If it befal to me as befalleth to the fools, why should I labour to be more wise?* And therefore I cannot much blame physicians, that they use commonly to intend some other art or practice, which they fancy, more than their profession. For you shall have of them antiquaries, poets, humanists, statesmen, merchants, divines, and in every of these better seen than in their profession; and no doubt upon this ground, that they find that mediocrity and excellency in their art maketh no difference in profit or reputation towards their fortune; for the weakness of patients and sweetness of life and nature of hope maketh men depend upon physicians with all their defects. But nevertheless these things which we have spoken of are courses begotten between a little occasion and a great deal of sloth and default; for if we will excite and awake our observation, we shall see in familiar instances what a predominant faculty the *subtilty of spirit* hath over the *variety of matter or form.* Nothing more variable than faces and countenances; yet men can bear in memory the infinite distinctions of them; nay, a painter with a few shells of colours, and the benefit of his eye and habit of his imagination, can imitate them all that ever have been, are, or may be, if they were brought before him. Nothing more variable than voices; yet men can likewise discern them personally; nay, you shall have a *buffon* or *pantomimus* will express as many as he pleaseth. Nothing more variable than the differing sounds of words; yet men have found the way to reduce them to a few simple letters. So that it is not *the insufficiency or incapacity of man's mind,* but it is *the remote standing or placing thereof,* that breedeth these mazes and incomprehensions: for as the sense afar off is full of mistaking but is exact at hand, so is it of the understanding; the remedy whereof is not to quicken or strengthen the organ, but to go nearer to the object; and therefore there is no doubt but if the physicians will learn and use the true approaches and avenues of nature, they may assume as much as the poet saith:

Et quoniam variant morbi, variabimus artes;
Mille mali species, mille salutis erunt:

[varying their arts according to the variety of diseases,—
for a thousand forms of sickness a thousand methods of
cure]. Which that they should do, the nobleness of their art
doth deserve; well shadowed by the poets, in that they
made Æsculapius to be the son of the Sun, the one being
the fountain of life, the other as the second stream; but infinitely more honoured by the example of our Saviour, who
made the body of man the object of his miracles, as the
soul was the object of his doctrine. For we read not that
ever he vouchsafed to do any miracle about honour, or
money (except that one for giving tribute to Cæsar), but
only about the preserving, sustaining, and healing the body
of man.

Medicine is a science which hath been (as we have said)
more professed than laboured, and yet more laboured than
advanced; the labour having been, in my judgment, rather
in circle than in progression. For I find much iteration, but
small addition. It considereth *causes of diseases*, with the
occasions or impulsions; the *diseases themselves*, with the
accidents; and the *cures*, with the *preservations*. The deficiencies which I think good to note, being a few of many,
and those such as are of a more open and manifest nature,
I will enumerate, and not place.

The first is the discontinuance of the ancient and serious
diligence of Hippocrates, which used to set
down a narrative of the special cases of his patients, and how they proceeded, and how they were judged
by recovery or death. Therefore having an example proper
in the father of the art, I shall not need to allege an example foreign, of the wisdom of the lawyers, who are careful to report new cases and decisions for the direction of
future judgments. This continuance of Medicinal History I
find deficient; which I understand neither to be so infinite
as to extend to every common case, nor so reserved as to
admit none but wonders: for many things are new in the
manner, which are not new in the kind; and if men will

Narrationes medicinales

intend to observe, they shall find much worthy to observe.

In the inquiry which is made by Anatomy I find much

Anatomia comparata deficience: for they inquire of the *parts*, and their *substances, figures,* and *collocations;* but they inquire not of the *diversities of the parts,* the *secrecies of the passages,* and the *seats or nestling of the humours,* nor much of the *footsteps and impressions of diseases:* the reason of which omission I suppose to be, because the first inquiry may be satisfied in the view of one or a few anatomies; but the latter, being comparative and casual, must arise from the view of many. And as to the diversity of parts, there is no doubt but the facture or framing of the inward parts is as full of difference as the outward, and in that is the *cause continent* of many diseases; which not being observed, they quarrel many times with the humours, which are not in fault; the fault being in the very frame and mechanic of the part, which cannot be removed by medicine alterative, but must be accommodate and palliate by diets and medicines familiar. And for the passages and pores, it is true which was anciently noted, that the more subtile of them appear not in anatomies, because they are shut and latent in dead bodies, though they be open and manifest in live: which being supposed, though the inhumanity of *anatomia vivorum* [anatomy of the living subject] was by Celsus justly reproved; yet in regard of the great use of this observation, the inquiry needed not by him so slightly to have been relinquished altogether, or referred to the casual practices of surgery; but might have been well diverted upon the dissection of beasts alive, which notwithstanding the dissimilitude of their parts, may sufficiently satisfy this inquiry. And for the humours, they are commonly passed over in anatomies as purgaments;[28] whereas it is most necessary to observe what cavities, nests, and receptacles the humours do find in the parts, with the differing kind of the humour so lodged and received. And as for the footsteps of diseases, and their devastations of the inward parts, imposthumations, exulcerations, discontinuations, putrefactions, consumptions, contractions, extensions,

convulsions, dislocations, obstructions, repletions, together
with all preternatural substances, as stones, carnosities, ex-
crescences, worms, and the like; they ought to have been
exactly observed by multitude of anatomies and the con-
tribution of men's several experiences, and carefully set
down both historically according to the appearances, and
artificially with a reference to the diseases and symptoms
which resulted from them, in case where the anatomy is of
a defunct patient; whereas now upon opening of bodies
they are passed over slightly and in silence.

In the inquiry of diseases, they do abandon the cures of
Inquisitio　　many, some as in their nature incurable, and
ulterior de　others as past the period of cure; so that Sylla
Morbis in-　and the triumvirs never proscribed so many men
sanabilibus　to die, as they do by their ignorant edicts;
whereof numbers do escape with less difficulty than they
did in the Roman proscriptions. Therefore I will not doubt
to note as a deficience, that they inquire not the perfect
cures of many diseases, or extremities of diseases, but pronouncing them incurable do enact a law of neglect, and
exempt ignorance from discredit.

Nay further, I esteem it the office of a physician not only
De Euthanasia　to restore health, but to mitigate pain and do-
exteriore　　lors; and not only when such mitigation may
conduce to recovery, but when it may serve to make a fair
and easy passage: for it is no small felicity which Augustus
Cæsar was wont to wish to himself, that same *Euthanasia;*
and which was specially noted in the death of Antoninus
Pius, whose death was after the fashion and semblance of
a kindly and pleasant sleep. So it is written of Epicurus,
that after his disease was judged desperate, he drowned
his stomach and senses with a large draught and ingurgita-
tion of wine; whereupon the epigram was made, *Hinc
stygias ebrius hausit aquas;* he was not sober enough to
taste any bitterness of the Stygian water. But the physicians
contrariwise do make a kind of scruple and religion to stay
with the patient after the disease is deplored; whereas, in
my judgment, they ought both to enquire the skill and to

give the attendances for the facilitating and assuaging of the pains and agonies of death.

In the consideration of the Cures of diseases, I find a *Medicinæ Ex-* deficiency in the receipts of propiety respect-*perimentales* ing[29] the particular cures of diseases: for the physicians have frustrated the fruit of tradition and experience by their magistralities, in adding and taking out and changing *quid pro quo* in their receipts, at their pleasures; commanding so over the medicine as the medicine cannot command over the disease. For except it be treacle and mithridatum, and of late *diascordium*,[30] and a few more, they tie themselves to no receipts severely and religiously: for as to the confections of sale which are in the shops, they are for readiness and not for propriety; for they are upon general intentions of purging, opening, comforting, altering, and not much appropriate to particular diseases: and this is the cause why emperics and old women are more happy many times in their cures than learned physicians, because they are more religious in holding their medicines. Therefore here is the deficience which I find, that physicians have not, partly out of their own practice, partly out of the constant probations reported in books, and partly out of the traditions of empirics, set down and delivered over certain *experimental medicines* for the cure of particular diseases, besides their own *conjectural* and *magistral descriptions*. For as they were the men of the best composition in the state of Rome, which either being consuls inclined to the people, or being tribunes inclined to the senate; so in the matter we now handle, they be the best physicians, which being learned incline to the traditions of experience, or being empirics incline to the methods of learning.

In preparation of Medicines, I do find strange, specially considering how mineral medicines have been *Imitatio Na-* extolled, and that they are safer for the outward *turæ in Bal-* *neis et Aquis* than inward parts, that no man hath sought to *Medicinalibus* make an imitation by art of Natural Baths and Medicinable Fountains; which nevertheless are confessed to receive their virtues from minerals: and not so only, but discerned and distinguished from what particular mineral they receive tincture, as sulphur, vitriol, steel, or the like; which nature if it may be reduced to compositions of art, both the variety of them will be increased, and the temper of them will be more commanded.

But lest I grow to be more particular than is agreeable either to my intention or to proportion, I will *Filum Medi-* conclude this part with the note of one defi- *cinale, sive de* cience more, which seemeth to me of greatest *vicibus Medi-* *cinarum* consequence; which is, that the prescripts in use are too compendious to attain their end: for, to my under- standing, it is a vain and flattering opinion to think any medicine can be so sovereign or so happy, as that the receit or use of it can work any great effect upon the body of man. It were a strange speech which spoken, or spoken oft, should reclaim a man from a vice to which he were by na- ture subject. It is order, pursuit, sequence, and interchange of application, which is mighty in nature; which although it require more exact knowledge in prescribing and more precise obedience in observing, yet is recompensed with the magnitude of effects. And although a man would think, by the daily visitations of the physicians, that there were a pursuance in the cure; yet let a man look into their pre- scripts and ministrations, and he shall find them but in- constancies and every day's devices, without any settled providence or project. Not that every scrupulous or super- stitious prescript is effectual, no more than every straight way is the way to heaven; but the *truth of the direction* must precede *severity of observance.*

For Cosmetic, it hath parts civil, and parts effeminate: for cleanness of body was ever esteemed to proceed from a due reverence to God, to society, and to ourselves. As for artificial decoration, it is well worthy of the deficiencies which it hath; being neither fine enough to deceive, nor handsome to use, nor wholesome to please.

For Athletic, I take the subject of it largely; that is to say, for any point of ability whereunto the body of man may be brought, whether it be of *activity* or of *patience;* whereof activity hath two parts, *strength* and *swiftness;* and patience likewise hath two parts, *hardness against wants and extremities,* and *indurance of pain or torment:* whereof we see the practices in tumblers, in savages, and in those that suffer punishment: nay, if there be any other faculty which falls not within any of the former divisions, as in those that dive, that obtain a strange power of containing respiration, and the like, I refer it to this part. Of these things the practices are known, but the philosophy that concerneth them is not much enquired; the rather, I think, because they are supposed to be obtained either by an aptness of nature, which cannot be taught, or only by continual custom, which is soon prescribed; which though it be not true, yet I forbear to note any deficiences; for the Olympian Games are down long since, and the mediocrity of these things is for use; as for the excellency of them, it serveth for the most part but for mercenary ostentation.

For Arts of Pleasure Sensual, the chief deficience in them is of laws to repress them. For as it hath been well observed that the arts which flourish in times while virtue is in growth, are military; and while virtue is in state, are liberal; and while virtue is in declination, are voluptuary; so I doubt that this age of the world is somewhat upon the descent of the wheel. With arts *voluptuary* I couple practices *joculary;* for the deceiving of the senses is one of the pleasures of the senses. As for games of recreation, I hold them to belong to civil life and education. And thus much of that particular Human Philosophy which concerns the Body, which is but the tabernacle of the mind.

For Human Knowledge which concerns the Mind, it hath two parts; the one that enquireth of *the substance or nature of the soul or mind,* the other that enquireth of *the faculties or functions thereof.* Unto the first of these, the considerations of *the original of the soul,* whether it be *native or adventive,* and *how far it is exempted from laws of matter,* and of the *immortality* thereof, and many other points, do appertain: which have been not more laboriously enquired than variously reported; so as the travail therein taken seemeth to have been rather in a maze than in a way. But although I am of opinion that this knowledge may be more really and soundly enquired, even in nature, than it hath been; yet I hold that in the end it must be bounded by religion, or else it will be subject to deceit and delusion; for as the substance of the soul in the creation was not extracted out of the mass of heaven and earth by the benediction of a *producat*,[31] but was immediately inspired from God; so it is not possible that it should be (otherwise than by accident) subject to *the laws of heaven and earth,* which are *the subject of philosophy;* and therefore the true knowledge of the nature and state of the soul, must come by the same inspiration that gave the substance. Unto this part of knowledge touching the soul there be two appendices; which, as they have been handled, have rather vapoured forth fables than kindled truth; Divination and Fascination.

Divination hath been anciently and fitly divided into *artificial* and *natural;* whereof *artificial* is when the mind maketh a prediction by argument, concluding upon signs and tokens; *natural* is when the mind hath a presention by an internal power, without the inducement of a sign. Artificial is of two sorts; either when the argument is coupled with a derivation of causes, which is *rational;* or when it is only grounded upon a coincidence of the effect, which is *experimental:* whereof the later for the most part is superstitious; such as were the heathen observations upon the inspection of sacrifices, the flights of birds, the swarming of bees; and such as was the Chaldean Astrology, and the like. For *artificial divination,* the several kinds thereof are distributed amongst particular knowledges. The Astronomer hath his predictions, as of conjunctions, aspects, eclipses, and the like. The Physician hath his predictions, of death, of recovery, of the accidents and issues of diseases. The Politique hath his predictions; *O urbem venalem, et cito perituram, si emptorem invenerit!* [a city in which all things are for sale and which will fall to the first purchaser,] which stayed not long to be performed, in Sylla first, and after in Cæsar. So as these predictions are now impertinent, and to be referred over. But the divination which springeth from the internal nature of the soul, is that which we now speak of; which hath been made to be of two sorts, *primitive* and by *influxion*. Primitive is grounded upon the supposition that the mind, when it is withdrawn and collected into itself and not diffused into the organs of the body, hath some extent and latitude of prenotion; which therefore appeareth most in sleep, in extasies, and near death; and more rarely in waking apprehensions; and is induced and furthered by those abstinences and observances which make the mind most to consist in itself. By influxion, is grounded upon the conceit that the mind, as a mirror or glass, should take illumination from the foreknowledge of God and spirits; unto which the same regiment doth likewise conduce. For the retiring of the mind within itself is the state which is most susceptible of divine influxions; save that it is accompanied in this case with a fervency and elevation (which the ancients noted by *fury*), and not with a repose and quiet, as it is in the other.

Fascination is the power and act of imagination, intensive upon other bodies than the body of the imaginant: for of that we spake in the proper place: wherein the school of Paracelsus and the disciples of pretended Natural Magic have been so intemperate, as they have exalted the power of the imagination to be much one with the power of miracle-working faith; others that draw nearer to probability, calling to their view the secret passages of things, and especially of the contagion that passeth from body to body, do conceive it should likewise be agreeable to nature that there should be some transmissions and operations from spirit to spirit, without the mediation of the sense; whence the conceits have grown (now almost made civil) of the Mastering Spirit, and the force of confidence, and the like. Incident unto this is the inquiry how to raise and fortify the imagination; for if the imagination fortified have power, then it is material to know how to fortify and exalt it. And herein comes in crookedly and dangerously a palliation of a great part of Ceremonial Magic. For it may be pretended that Ceremonies, Characters, and Charms, do work not by any tacit or sacramental contract with evil spirits, but serve only to strengthen the imagination of him that useth it; as images are said by the Roman church to fix the cogitations and raise the devotions of them that pray before them. But for mine own judgment, if it be admitted that imagination hath power, and that Ceremonies fortify imagination, and that they be used sincerely and intentionally for that purpose; yet I should hold them unlawful, as opposing to that first edict which God gave unto man, *In sudore vultus comedes panem tuum*, [in the sweat of thy brow shalt thou eat bread]. For they propound those noble effects which God hath set forth unto man to be bought at the price of labour, to be attained by a few easy and slothful observances. Deficiences in these knowledges I will report none, other than the general deficience, that it is not known how much of them is verity and how much vanity.

The knowledge which respecteth the Faculties of the Mind of man is of two kinds; the one respecting his Understanding and Reason, and the other his Will, Appetite, and Affection; whereof the former produceth Position or Decree, the later Action or Execution. It is true that the Imagination is an agent or *nuncius* [*messenger] in both provinces, both the judicial and the ministerial. For Sense sendeth over to Imagination before Reason have judged: and Reason sendeth over to Imagination before the Decree can be acted; for Imagination ever precedeth Voluntary Motion: saving that this Janus of Imagination hath differing faces; for the face towards Reason hath the print of Truth, but the face towards Action hath the print of Good; which nevertheless are faces,

Quales decet esse sororum,—

[sister-faces]. Neither is the Imagination simply and only a messenger; but is invested with or at leastwise usurpeth no small authority in itself, besides the duty of the message.

For it was well said by Aristotle, *That the mind hath over the body that commandment, which the lord hath over a bondman; but that reason hath over the imagination that commandment which a magistrate hath over a free citizen;* who may come also to rule in his turn. For we see that in matters of Faith and Religion we raise our Imagination above our Reason; which is the cause why Religion sought ever access to the mind by similitudes, types, parables, visions, dreams. And again in all persuasions that are wrought by eloquence and other impression of like nature, which do paint and disguise the true appearance of things, the chief recommendation unto Reason is from the Imagination. Nevertheless, because I find not any science that doth properly or fitly pertain to the Imagination, I see no cause to alter the former division. For as for Poesy, it is rather a pleasure or play of imagination, than a work or duty thereof. And if it be a work, we speak not now of such parts of learning as the Imagination produceth, but of such sciences as handle and consider of the Imagination; no more than we shall speak now of such knowledges as Reason produceth, (for that extendeth to all philosophy,) but of such knowledges as do handle and inquire of the faculty of Reason: so as Poesy had his true place. As for the power of the Imagination in nature, and the manner of fortifying the same, we have mentioned it in the doctrine *De Anima* [*of the soul], whereunto most fitly it belongeth. And lastly, for Imaginative or Insinuative Reason, which is the subject of Rhetoric, we think it best to refer it to the Arts of Reason. So therefore we content ourselves with the former division, that Human Philosophy which respecteth the faculties of the mind of man hath two parts, Rational and Moral.

The part of Human Philosophy which is rational, is of all knowledges, to the most wits, the least delightful; and seemeth but a net of subtility and spinosity. For as it was truly said, that knowledge is *pabulum animi,* [the food of the mind;] so in the nature of men's appetite to this food, most men are of the taste and stomach of the Israelites in the desert, that would fain have returned *ad ollas carnium,* [to the flesh-pots,] and were weary of manna; which, though it were celestial, yet seemed less nutritive and comfortable. So generally men taste well knowledges that are drenched in flesh and blood, Civil History, Morality, Policy, about the which men's affections, praises, fortunes, do turn and are conversant; but this same *lumen siccum,* [this dry light,] doth parch and offend most men's watery and soft natures. But to speak truly of things as they are in worth, Rational Knowledges are the keys of all other arts; for as Aristotle saith aptly and elegantly, *That the hand is the Instrument of Instruments, and the mind is the Form of Forms:* so these be truly said to be the Art of Arts: neither do they only direct, but likewise confirm and strengthen; even as the habit of shooting doth not only enable to shoot a nearer shoot, but also to draw a stronger bow.

The Arts Intellectual are four in number; divided according to the ends whereunto they are referred: for man's labour is to *invent* that which is *sought* or *propounded;* or to *judge* that which is *invented;* or to *retain* that which is *judged;* or to *deliver over* that which is *retained.* So as the arts must be four; Art of Inquiry or Invention: Art of Examination or Judgment; Art of Custody or Memory; and Art of Elocution or Tradition.

Invention is of two kinds, much differing; the one, of Arts and Sciences; and the other, of Speech and Arguments. The former of these I do report deficient; which seemeth to me to be such a deficience as if in the making of an inventory touching the estate of a defunct it should be set down *that there is no ready money.* For as money will fetch all other commodities, so this knowledge is that which should purchase all the rest. And like as the West-Indies had never been discovered if the use of the mariner's needle had not been first discovered, though the one be vast regions and the other a small motion; so it cannot be found strange if sciences be no further discovered, if the art itself of invention and discovery hath been passed over.

That this part of knowledge is wanting, to my judgment standeth plainly confessed: for first, Logic doth not pretend to invent Sciences or the Axioms of Sciences, but passeth it over with a *cuique in sua arte credendum,* [the knowledge that pertains to each art must be taken on trust from those that profess it]. And Celsus acknowledgeth it gravely, speaking of the empirical and dogmatical sects of physicians, *That medicines and cures were first found out, and then after the reasons and causes were discoursed; and not the causes first found out, and by light from them the medicines and cures discovered.* And Plato in his Theætetus noteth well, *That particulars are infinite, and the higher generalities give no sufficient direction; and that the pith of all sciences, which maketh the arts-man differ from the inexpert, is in the middle propositions, which in every particular knowledge are taken from tradition and experience.* And therefore we see that they which discourse of the inventions and originals of things, refer them rather to chance than to art, and rather to beasts, birds, fishes, serpents, than to men.

> Dictamnum genetrix Cretæa carpit ab Ida,
> Puberibus caulem foliis et flore comantem
> Purpureo: non illa feris incognita capris
> Gramina, cum tergo volucres hæsere sagittæ.

> [A sprig of dittany his mother brought,
> Gathered by Cretan Ide; a stalk it is
> Of woolly leaf, crested with purple flower;
> Which well the wild-goat knows when in his side
> Sticks the winged shaft.]

So that it was no marvel (the manner of antiquity being to consecrate inventors) that the Ægyptians had so few human idols in their temples, but almost all brute:

> Omnigenumque Deum monstra, et latrator Anubis,
> Contra Neptunum et Venerem, contraque Minervam, &c.

> [All kinds and shapes of Gods, a monstrous host,
> The dog Anubis foremost, stood arrayed
> 'Gainst Neptune, Venus, Pallas, &c.]

And if you like better the tradition of the Grecians, and ascribe the first inventions to men, yet you will rather believe that Prometheus first struck the flints, and marvelled at the spark, than that when he first struck the flints he expected the spark; and therefore we see the West-Indian Prometheus[32] had no intelligence with the European, because of the rareness with them of flint, that gave the first occasion. So as it should seem that hitherto men are rather beholden to a wild goat for surgery, or to a nightingale for music, or to the Ibis for some part of physic, or to the pot lid that flew open for artillery, or generally to chance or any thing else, than to Logic, for the invention of arts and sciences. Neither is the form of invention which Virgil describeth much other:

> Ut varias usus meditando extunderet artes
> Paulatim:

[that practice with meditation might by degrees hammer out the arts]. For if you observe the words well, it is no other method than that which brute beasts are capable of, and do put in ure;[33] which is *a perpetual intending or practising some one thing, urged and imposed by an absolute necessity of conservation of being:* for so Cicero saith very truly, *Usus uni rei deditus et naturam et artem sæpe vincit:* [practice applied constantly to one thing will often do more than either nature or art can]. And therefore if it be said of men.

> Labor omnia vincit
> Improbus, et duris urgens in rebus egestas,
>   [Stern labour masters all,
> And want in poverty importunate,]

it is likewise said of beasts, *Quis psittaco docuit suum χαῖρε?* [who taught the parrot to say how d'ye do?] Who taught the raven in a drowth to throw pebbles into an hollow tree where she spied water, that the water might rise so as she might come to it? Who taught the bee to sail through such a vast sea of air, and to find the way from a field in flower a great way off to her hive? Who taught the ant to bite every grain of corn that she burieth in her hill, lest it should take root and grow? Add then the word *extundere* [*to hammer out], which importeth the extreme difficulty, and the word *paulatim* [°little by little], which importeth the extreme slowness, and we are where we were, even amongst the Ægyptians' gods; there being little left to the faculty of Reason, and nothing to the duty of Art, for matter of invention.

Secondly, the induction which the logicians speak of, and which seemeth familiar with Plato, whereby the Principles of sciences may be pretended to be invented, and so the middle propositions by derivation from the principles,— their form of induction, I say, is utterly vicious and incompetent: wherein their error is the fouler, because it is the duty of Art to perfect and exalt Nature; but they contrariwise have wronged, abused, and traduced nature. For he that shall attentively observe how the mind doth gather this excellent dew of knowledge, like unto that which the poet speaketh of, *Aërei mellis cœlestia dona,* [the gift of heaven, aërial honey,] distilling and contriving it out of particulars natural and artificial, as the flowers of the field and garden, shall find that the mind of herself by nature doth manage and act an induction much better than they describe it. For to conclude *upon an enumeration of particulars without instance contradictory* is no conclusion, but a conjecture; for who can assure (in many subjects) upon those particulars which appear of a side, that there are not other on the contrary side which appear not? As if Samuel should have rested upon those sons of Issay which were brought before him, and failed of David, which was in the field. And this form (to say truth) is so gross, as it had not been possible for wits so subtile as have managed these things to have offered it to the world, but that they hasted to their *theories* and *dogmaticals*, and were imperious and scornful toward particulars; which their manner was to use but as *lictores* and *viatores*, for sergeants and whifflers,[34] *ad summovendam turbam* [*for dispersing a crowd], to make

way and make room for their opinions, rather than in their
true use and service. Certainly it is a thing may touch a man
with a religious wonder, to see how the footsteps of seducement are the very same in divine and human truth: for as
in divine truth man cannot endure to become as a child;
so in human, they reputed the attending the Inductions
(whereof we speak) as if it were a second infancy or
childhood.

Thirdly, allow some Principles or Axioms were rightly induced, yet nevertheless certain it is that Middle Propositions cannot be deduced from them in subject of nature by
Syllogism, that is, *by touch and reduction of them to principles in a middle term.* It is true that in sciences popular,
as moralities, laws, and the like, yea and divinity (because
it pleaseth God to apply himself to the capacity of the simplest), that form may have use; and in natural philosophy
likewise, by way of argument or satisfactory reason, *quæ
assensum parit, operis effœta est,* [which procures assent
but can do no work:] but the subtilty of nature and operations will not be enchained in those bonds: for Arguments
consist of Propositions, and Propositions of Words; and
Words are but the current tokens or marks of Popular Notions of things; which notions, if they be grossly and variably collected out of particulars, it is not the laborious
examination either of consequences of arguments or of the
truth of propositions, that can ever correct that error; being
(as the physicians speak) in the first digestion: and therefore it was not without cause, that so many excellent philosophers became Sceptics and Academics, and denied any
certainty of knowledge or comprehension, and held opinion
that the knowledge of man extended only to appearances
and probabilities. It is true that in Socrates it was supposed
to be but a form of irony, *Scientiam dissimulando simulavit,*
[an affectation of knowledge under pretence of ignorance:]
for he used to disable his knowledge, to the end to enhance
his knowledge; like the humour of Tiberius in his beginnings, that would reign, but would not acknowledge so
much; and in the later Academy, which Cicero embraced,

this opinion also of *acatalepsia* (I doubt) was not held sincerely: for that all those which excelled in copie of speech seem to have chosen that sect, as that which was fittest to give glory to their eloquence and variable discourses; being rather like progresses of pleasure than journeys to an end. But assuredly many scattered in both Academies did hold it in subtilty and integrity. But here was their chief error; they charged the deceit upon the Senses; which in my judgment (notwithstanding all their cavillations) are very sufficient to certify and report truth, though not alway immediately, yet by comparison, by help of instrument, and by producing and urging such things as are too subtile for the sense to some effect comprehensible by the sense, and other like assistance. But they ought to have charged the deceit upon *the weakness of the intellectual powers, and upon the manner of collecting and concluding upon the reports of the senses*. This I speak not to disable the mind of man, but to stir it up to seek help: for no man, be he never so cunning or practised, can make a straight line or perfect circle by steadiness of hand, which may be easily done by help of a ruler or compass.

This part of invention, concerning the inven-

Experientia literata, et interpretatio Naturæ

tion of sciences, I purpose (if God give me leave) hereafter to propound; having digested it into two parts; whereof the one I term *Experientia literata*, and the other *Interpretatio Naturæ*: the former being but a degree and rudiment of the latter. But I will not dwell too long, nor speak too great upon a promise.

The invention of speech or argument is not properly an invention: for to invent is to discover that we know not, and not to recover or resummon that which we already know; and the use of this invention is no other but *out of the knowledge whereof our mind is already possessed, to draw forth or call before us that which may be pertinent to the purpose which we take into our consideration*. So as, to speak truly, it is no *Invention*, but a *Remembrance* or *Suggestion*, with an application; which is the cause why the schools do place it after judgment, as subsequent and not precedent. Nevertheless, because we do account it a Chase

as well of deer in an inclosed park as in a forest at large,
and that it hath already obtained the name, let it be called
invention: so as it be perceived and discerned, that the
scope and end of this invention is readiness and present use
of our knowledge, and not addition or amplification thereof.

To procure this ready use of knowledge there are two
courses, Preparation and Suggestion. The former of these
seemeth scarcely a part of Knowledge, consisting rather of
diligence than of any artificial erudition. And herein Aristotle wittily, but hurtfully, doth deride the sophists near
his time, saying, *they did as if one that professed the art of
shoe-making should not teach how to make up a shoe, but
only exhibit in a readiness a number of shoes of all fashions
and sizes.* But yet a man might reply, that if a shoe-maker
should have no shoes in his shop, but only work as he is be-
spoken, he should be weakly customed. But our Saviour,
speaking of Divine Knowledge, saith, *that the kingdom of
heaven is like a good householder, that bringeth forth both
new and old store;* and we see the ancient writers of rhetoric do give it in precept, that pleaders should have the
Places[35] whereof they have most continual use ready handled in all the variety that may be; as that, to speak for the
literal interpretation of the law against equity, and contrary; and to speak for presumptions and inferences against
testimony, and contrary. And Cicero himself, being broken
unto it by great experience, delivereth it plainly, that whatsoever a man shall have occasion to speak of, (if he will
take the pains) he may have it in effect premeditate, and
handled *in thesi* [*in the basic assertions to be made]; so
that when he cometh to a particular, he shall have nothing
to do but to put to names and times and places, and such
other circumstances of individuals. We see likewise the
exact diligence of Demosthenes; who, in regard of the great
force that the entrance and access into causes hath to make
a good impression, had ready framed a number of prefaces
for orations and speeches. All which authorities and precedents may overweigh Aristotle's opinion, that would have
us change a rich wardrobe for a pair of shears.

But the nature of the collection of this provision or preparatory store, though it be common both to logic and rhetoric, yet having made an entry of it here, where it came first to be spoken of, I think fit to refer over the further handling of it to rhetoric.

The other part of Invention, which I term Suggestion, doth assign and direct us to certain *marks* or *places,* which may excite our mind to return and produce such knowledge as it hath formerly collected, to the end we may make use thereof. Neither is this use (truly taken) only to furnish argument to dispute probably with others, but likewise to minister unto our judgment to conclude aright within ourselves. Neither may these Places serve only to apprompt our invention, but also to direct our inquiry. For a faculty of wise interrogating is half a knowledge. For as Plato saith, *Whosoever seeketh, knoweth that which he seeketh for in a general notion; else how shall he know it when he hath found it?* And therefore the larger your Anticipation is, the more direct and compendious is your search. But the same Places which will help us what to produce of that which we know already, will also help us, if a man of experience were before us, what questions to ask; or if we have books and authors to instruct us, what points to search and revolve: so as I cannot report that this part of invention, which is that which the schools call Topics, is deficient.

Nevertheless Topics are of two sorts, *general* and *special.* The general we have spoken to; but the particular hath been touched by some, but rejected generally as inartificial and variable. But leaving the humour which hath reigned too much in the schools, (which is to be vainly subtile in a few things which are within their command, and to reject the rest,) I do receive particular Topics, that is places or directions of invention and inquiry in every particular knowledge, as things of great use; being mixtures of Logic with the matter of sciences; for in these it holdeth, *Ars inveniendi adolescit cum inventis,* [every act of discovery advances the art of discovery;] for as in going of a way we do not only gain that part of the way which is passed, but we gain the better sight of that part of the way which remain-

eth; so every degree of proceeding in a science giveth a
light to that which followeth; which light if we strengthen,
by drawing it forth into questions or places of inquiry, we
Now we pass unto the arts of Judgment, which handle
do greatly advance our pursuit.
the natures of Proofs and Demonstrations; which as to Induction hath a coincidence with Invention; *for in all inductions, whether in good or vicious form, the same action of
the mind which inventeth, judgeth; all one as in the sense;*
but otherwise it is in proof by syllogism; for the proof being
not immediate but by mean, *the invention of the mean* is
one thing, and the *judgment of the consequence* is another;
the one exciting only, the other examining. Therefore for
the real and exact form of judgment we refer ourselves to
that which we have spoken of *Interpretation of Nature.*

For the other judgment by Syllogism, as it is a thing most
agreeable to the mind of man, so it hath been vehemently
and excellently laboured. For the nature of man doth extremely covet to have somewhat in his understanding fixed
and immoveable, and as a rest and support of the mind.
And therefore as Aristotle endeavoureth to prove that in all
motion there is some point quiescent; and as he elegantly
expoundeth the ancient fable of Atlas (that stood fixed and
bare up the heaven from falling) to be meant of the poles
or axle-tree of heaven, whereupon the conversion is accomplished; so assuredly men have a desire to have an Atlas or
axle-tree within to keep them from fluctuation, which is like
to a perpetual peril of falling; therefore men did hasten to
set down some Principles about which the variety of their
disputations might turn.

So then this art of Judgment is but *the reduction of propositions to principles in a middle term:* the Principles to be
agreed by all and exempted from argument; the Middle
Term to be elected at the liberty of every man's invention;
the Reduction to be of two kinds, direct and inverted; the
one when the proposition is reduced to the principle, which
they term a *Probation ostensive;* the other when the contradictory of the proposition is reduced to the contradictory

of the principle, which is that which they call *per incommodum,* or *pressing an absurdity;* the number of middle terms to be as the proposition standeth degrees more or less removed from the principle.

But this art hath two several methods of doctrine; the one by way of direction, the other by way of caution: the former frameth and setteth down a true form of consequence, by the variations and deflexions from which errors and inconsequences may be exactly judged; toward the composition and structure of which form, it is incident to handle the parts thereof, which are propositions, and the parts of propositions, which are simple words; and this is that part of logic which is comprehended in the Analytics.

The second method of doctrine was introduced for expedite use and assurance sake; discovering the more subtile forms of sophisms and illaqueations with their redargutions,[36] which is that which is termed *Elenches.* For although in the more gross sorts of fallacies it happeneth (as Seneca maketh the comparison well) as in juggling feats, which though we know not how they are done, yet we know well it is not as it seemeth to be; yet the more subtile sort of them doth not only put a man besides his answer, but doth many times abuse his judgment.

This part concerning *Elenches* is excellently handled by Aristotle in precept, but more excellently by Plato in example, not only in the persons of the Sophists, but even in Socrates himself; who professing to affirm nothing, but to infirm that which was affirmed by another, hath exactly expressed all the forms of objection, fallace, and redargution. And although we have said that the use of this doctrine is for redargution, yet it is manifest the degenerate and corrupt use is for caption and contradiction; which passeth for a great faculty, and no doubt is of very great advantage: though the difference be good which was made between orators and sophisters, that the one is as the greyhound, which hath his advantage in the race, and the other as the hare, with hath her advantage in the turn, so as it is the advantage of the weaker creature.

But yet further, this doctrine of *Elenches* hath a more

ample latitude and extent than is perceived; namely, unto divers parts of knowledge; whereof some are laboured and other omitted. For first, I conceive (though it may seem at first somewhat strange) that that part which is variably referred sometimes to Logic sometimes to Metaphysic, touching the *common adjuncts of essences*, is but an elenche; for the great sophism of all sophisms being equivocation or ambiguity of words and phrase, specially of such words as are most general and intervene in every inquiry, it seemeth to me that the true and fruitful use (leaving vain subtilties and speculations) of the inquiry of majority, minority, priority, posteriority, identity, diversity, possibility, act, totality, parts, existence, privation, and the like, are but wise cautions against ambiguities of speech. So again the distribution of things into certain tribes, which we call categories or predicaments, are but cautions against the confusion of definitions and divisions.

Secondly, there is a seducement that worketh by the strength of the impression and not by the subtilty of the illaqueation; not so much perplexing the reason as overruling it by power of the imagination. But this part I think more proper to handle when I shall speak of Rhetoric.

But lastly, there is yet a much more important and profound kind of fallacies in the mind of man, which I find not observed or enquired at all, and think good to place here, as that which of all others appertaineth most to rectify judgment: the force whereof is such, as it doth not dazzle or snare the understanding in some particulars, but doth more generally and inwardly infect and corrupt the state thereof. For the mind of man is far from the nature of a clear and equal glass, wherein the beams of things should reflect according to their true incidence; nay, it is rather like an enchanted glass, full of superstition and imposture, if it be not delivered and reduced. For this purpose, let us consider the false appearances that are imposed upon us by the general nature of the mind, beholding them in an example or two; as first, in that instance which is the root of all superstition, namely, *That to the nature of the mind of all men it is consonant for the affirmative or active to affect*[37] *more than the negative or privative:* so that a few times hitting or presence, countervails oft-times failing or absence; as was well answered by Diagoras to him that shewed him in Neptune's temple the great number of pictures of such as had scaped shipwreck and had paid their vows to Neptune, saying, *Advise now, you that think it folly to invocate Neptune in tempest: Yea but* (saith Diagoras) *where are they painted that are drowned?* Let us behold it in another instance, namely, *That the spirit of man, being of an equal and uniform substance, doth usually suppose and feign in nature a greater equality and uniformity than is in truth.* Hence it cometh that the mathematicians cannot satisfy themselves, except they reduce the motions of the celestial bodies to perfect circles, rejecting spiral lines, and labouring to be discharged of eccentrics. Hence it cometh, that whereas there are many things in nature as it were *monodica, sui juris,* [singular, and like nothing but themselves;] yet the cogitations of man do feign unto them relatives, parallels, and conjugates, whereas no such thing is; as they have feigned an element of Fire, to keep square with Earth, Water, and Air, and the like: nay, it is not credible, till it be opened, what a number of fictions and fancies the similitude of human actions and arts, together with the making of man *communis mensura* [*to a common measure], have brought into Natural Philosophy; not much better than the heresy of the Anthropomorphites, bred in the cells of gross and solitary monks, and the opinion of Epicurus, answerable to the same in heathenism, who supposed the gods to be of human shape. And therefore Velleius the Epicurian needed not to have asked, why God should have adorned the heavens with stars, as if he had been an Ædilis, one that should have set forth some magnificent shews or plays. For if that great work-master had been of an human disposition, he would have cast the stars into some pleasant and beautiful works and orders, like the frets[38] in the roofs of houses; whereas one can scarce find a posture in square or triangle or straight line amongst such an infinite number; so differing an harmony there is between the spirit of Man and the spirit of Nature.

Let us consider again the false appearances imposed upon us by every man's own individual nature and custom, in that feigned supposition that Plato maketh of the cave: for certainly if a child were continued in a grot or cave under the earth until maturity of age, and came suddenly abroad, he would have strange and absurd imaginations; so in like manner, although our persons live in the view of heaven, yet our spirits are included in the caves of our own complexions and customs; which minister unto us infinite errors and vain opinions, if they be not recalled to examination. But hereof we have given many examples in one of the errors, or peccant humours, which we ran briefly over in our first book.

And lastly, let us consider the false appearances that are imposed upon us by words, which are framed and applied according to the conceit and capacities of the vulgar sort: and although we think we govern our words, and prescribe it well, *Loquendum ut vulgus, sentiendum ut sapientes,* [a man should speak like the vulgar, and think like the wise;] yet certain it is that words, as a Tartar's bow,[39] do shoot back upon the understanding of the wisest, and mightily entangle and pervert the judgment; so as it is almost necessary in all controversies and disputations to imitate the wisdom of the Mathematicians, in setting down in the very beginning the definitions of our words and terms, that others may know how we accept and understand them, and whether they concur with us or no. For it cometh to pass for want of this, that we are sure to end there where we ought to have begun, which is in questions and differences about words. To conclude therefore, it must be confessed that it is not possible to divorce ourselves from these fallacies and false appearances, because they are inseparable *Elenchi magni,* from our nature and condition of life; so yet *sive de Idolis* nevertheless the caution of them (for all *animi humani,* *nativis et ad-* elenches, as was said, are but cautions) doth *ventitiis* extremely import the true conduct of human judgment. The particular elenches or cautions against these three false appearances I find altogether deficient.

There remaineth one part of judgment of great excellency, which to mine understanding is so slightly touched, as I may report that also deficient; which is the application of the differing kinds of proofs to the differing kinds of subjects; for there being but four kinds of demonstrations, that is, by the immediate consent of the mind or sense; by induction; by sophism; and by congruity, which is that which Aristotle calleth *demonstration in orb or circle,* and not *a notioribus* [*from the known to the unknown]; every of these hath certain subjects in the matter of sciences, in which respectively they have chiefest use; and certain other, from which respectively they ought to be excluded: and the rigour and curiosity in requiring the more severe proofs in some things, and chiefly the facility in contenting ourselves with the more remiss proofs in others, hath been amongst the greatest causes of detriment and hindrance to knowledge. The distributions and assignations of demonstrations, according to the analogy of sciences, I note as deficient.

De Analogia Demonstrationum

The custody or retaining of knowledge is either in Writing or Memory; whereof Writing hath two parts, the nature of the *character,* and the order of the *entry.* For the art of *characters,* or other visible notes of words or things, it hath nearest conjugation with grammar, and therefore I refer it to the due place. For the *disposition* and *collocation* of that knowledge which we preserve in writing, it consisteth in a good digest of common-places; wherein I am not ignorant of the prejudice imputed to the use of commonplace books, as causing a retardation of reading, and some sloth or relaxation of memory. But because it is but a counterfeit thing in knowledges to be forward and pregnant, except a man be deep and full, I hold the entry of commonplaces to be a matter of great use and essence in studying; as that which assureth copie[40] of invention, and contracteth judgment to a strength. But this is true, that of the *methods* of common-places that I have seen, there is none of any sufficient worth; all of them carrying merely the face of a *school,* and not of a *world;* and referring to vulgar matters and pedantical divisions without all life or respect to action.

For the other principal part of the custody of knowledge, which is Memory, I find that faculty in my judgment weakly enquired of. An art there is extant of it; but it seemeth to me that there are better precepts than that art, and better practices of that art than those received. It is certain the art (as it is) may be raised to points of ostentation prodigious: but in use (as it is now managed) it is barren; not burdensome nor dangerous to natural memory, as is imagined, but barren; that is, not dexterous to be applied to the serious use of business and occasions. And therefore I make no more estimation of repeating a great number of names or words upon once hearing, or the pouring forth of a number of verses or rhymes *ex tempore*, or the making of a satirical simile of every thing, or the turning of every thing to a jest, or the falsifying or contradicting of every thing by cavil, or the like, (whereof in the faculties of the mind there is great copie, and such as by device and practice may be exalted to an extreme degree of wonder,) than I do of the tricks of tumblers, funambuloes, baladines;[41] the one being the same in the mind that the other is in the body; matters of strangeness without worthiness.

This art of Memory is but built upon two intentions; the one Prenotion, the other Emblem. Prenotion dischargeth the indefinite seeking of that we would remember, and directeth us to seek in a narrow compass; that is, somewhat that hath congruity with our *place of memory*. Emblem reduceth conceits intellectual to images sensible, which strike the memory more; out of which axioms may be drawn much better practique than that in use; and besides which axioms, there are divers moe touching help of memory, not inferior to them. But I did in the beginning distinguish, not to report those things deficient, which are but only ill managed.

There remaineth the fourth kind of Rational Knowledge, which is transitive, concerning the expressing or transferring our knowledge to others; which I will term by the general name of Tradition or Delivery. Tradition hath three parts; the first concerning the *organ* of tradition; the second concerning the *method* of tradition; and the third concerning the *illustration* of tradition.

For the organ of tradition, it is either Speech or Writing: for Aristotle saith well, *Words are the images of cogitations, and letters are the images of words;* but yet it is not of necessity that cogitations be expressed by the medium of words. For *whatsoever is capable of sufficient differences, and those perceptible by the sense, is in nature competent to express cogitations.* And therefore we see in the commerce of barbarous people that understand not one another's language, and in the practice of divers that are dumb and deaf, that men's minds are expressed in gestures, though not exactly, yet to serve the turn. And we understand further that it is the use of China and the kingdoms of the high Levant to write in Characters Real, which express neither letters nor words in gross, but Things or Notions; insomuch as countries and provinces, which understand not one another's language, can nevertheless read one another's writings, because the characters are accepted more generally than the languages do extend; and therefore they have a vast multitude of characters; as many, I suppose, as radical words.

These Notes of Cogitations are of two sorts; the one when the note hath some similitude or congruity with the notion; the other *ad placitum* [*by general consent], having force only by contract or acceptation. Of the former sort are Hieroglyphics and Gestures. For as to Hieroglyphics, (things of ancient use, and embraced chiefly by the Ægyptians, one of the most ancient nations,) they are but as continued impresses[42] and emblems. And as for Gestures, they are as transitory Hieroglyphics, and are to Hieroglyphics as words spoken are to words written, in that they abide not; but they have evermore, as well as the other, an affinity with the things signified: as Periander, being consulted with how to preserve a tyranny newly usurped, bid the messenger attend and report what he saw him do; and went into his garden and topped all the highest flowers; signifying, that it consisted in the cutting off and keeping low of the nobility and *grandes*. *Ad placitum* are the Characters Real before mentioned, and Words: although some have been willing by curious inquiry, or rather by apt feigning, to have derived imposition of names from reason and intendment; a speculation elegant, and, by reason it searcheth into antiquity, reverent; but sparingly mixed with truth, and of small fruit. This portion of knowledge, touching the Notes of Things and cogitations in general, I find not enquired, but deficient. And although it may seem of no great use, considering that words and writings by letters do far excel all the other ways; yet because this part concerneth as it were the mint of knowledge, (for words are the tokens current and accepted for conceits, as moneys are for values, and that it is fit men be not ignorant that moneys may be of another kind than gold and silver,) I thought good to propound it to better enquiry.

De Notis Rerum

Concerning Speech and Words, the consideration of them hath produced the science of Grammar: for man still striveth to reintegrate himself in those benedictions, from which by his fault he hath been deprived; and as he hath striven against the first general curse by the invention of all other arts, so hath he sought to come forth of the second general curse (which was the confusion of tongues) by the art of Grammar: whereof the use in a mother tongue is small; in a foreign tongue more; but most in such foreign tongues as have ceased to be vulgar tongues, and are turned only to learned tongues. The duty of it is of two natures; the one popular, which is for the speedy and perfect attaining languages, as well for intercourse of speech as for understanding of authors; the other philosophical, examining the power and nature of words as they are the footsteps and prints of reason: which kind of analogy between words and reason is handled *sparsim*, brokenly, though not entirely; and therefore I cannot report it deficient, though I think it very worthy to be reduced into a science by itself.

Unto Grammar also belongeth, as an appendix, the consideration of the Accidents of Words; which are measure, sound, and elevation or accent, and the sweetness and harshness of them; whence hath issued some curious observations in Rhetoric, but chiefly Poesy, as we consider it in respect of the verse and not of the argument: wherein though men in learned tongues do tie themselves to the ancient measures, yet in modern languages it seemeth to me as free to make new measures of verses as of dances; for a dance is a measured pace, as a verse is a measured speech. In these things the sense is better judge than the art;

Cœnæ fercula nostræ
Mallem convivis quam placuisse cocis:

[the dinner is to please the guests that eat it, not the cook that dresses it.] And of the servile expressing antiquity in an unlike and an unfit subject, it is well said, *Quod tempore antiquum videtur, id incongruitate est maxime novum;* [there is nothing more new than an old thing that has ceased to fit].

For Ciphers, they are commonly in letters or alphabets, but may be in words. The kinds of Ciphers (besides the simple ciphers with changes and intermixtures of nulls and non-significants) are many, according to the nature or rule of the infolding; Wheel-ciphers, Key-ciphers, Doubles, &c. But the virtues of them, whereby they are to be preferred, are three; that they be not laborious to write and read; that they be impossible to decipher; and, in some cases, that they be without suspicion. The highest degree whereof is to write *omnia per omnia;*[43] which is undoubtedly possible, with a proportion quintuple at most of the writing infolding to the writing infolded, and no other restraint whatsoever. This art of Ciphering, hath for relative an art of Disciphering; by supposition unprofitable; but, as things are, of great use. For suppose that ciphers were well managed, there be multitudes of them which exclude the discipherer. But in regard of the rawness and unskilfulness of the hands through which they pass, the greatest matters are many times carried in the weakest ciphers.

In the enumeration of these private and retired arts, it may be thought I seek to make a great muster-roll of sciences; naming them for shew and ostentation, and to little other purpose. But let those which are skilful in them judge whether I bring them in only for appearance, or whether in that which I speak of them (though in few marks) there be not some seed of proficience. And this must be remembered, that as there be many of great account in their countries and provinces, which when they come up to the Seat of the Estate are but of mean rank and scarcely regarded; so these arts being here placed with the principal and supreme sciences, seem petty things; yet to such as have chosen them to spend their studies in them, they seem great matters.

For the Method of Tradition, I see it hath moved a controversy in our time. But as in civil business, if there be a meeting and men fall at words there is commonly an end of the matter for that time and no proceeding at all; so in learning, where there is much controversy there is many times little inquiry. For this part of knowledge of Method seemeth to me so weakly enquired as I shall report it deficient.

Method hath been placed, and that not amiss, in Logic, as a part of Judgment: for as the doctrine of Syllogisms comprehendeth the rules of judgment upon that which is invented, so the doctrine of Method containeth the rules of judgment upon that which is to be delivered; for judgment precedeth Delivery, as it followeth Invention. Neither is the method or the nature of the tradition material only to the *use* of knowledge, but likewise to the *progression* of knowledge: for since the labour and life of one man cannot attain to perfection of knowledge, the wisdom of the Tradition is that which inspireth the felicity of continuance and proceeding. And therefore the most real diversity of

method is of method referred to Use, and method referred
to Progression; whereof the one may be termed Magistral,
and the other of Probation.

The later whereof seemeth to be *via deserta et interclusa,*
[a way that is abandoned and stopped up]. For as knowledges are now delivered, there is a kind of contract of error
between the deliverer and the receiver: for he that delivereth knowledge desireth to deliver it in such form as may be
best believed, and not as may be best examined; and he
that receiveth knowledge desireth rather present satisfaction than expectant inquiry; and so rather not to doubt
than not to err: glory making the author not to lay open his
weakness, and sloth making the disciple not to know his
strength.

But knowledge that is delivered as a thread to be spun
on, ought to be delivered and intimated, if it were possible,
in the same method wherein it was invented; and so is it
possible of knowledge induced. But in this same anticipated and prevented knowledge, no man knoweth how he
came to the knowledge which he hath obtained. But yet
nevertheless, *secundum majus et minus* [*more or less], a
man may revisit and descend unto the foundations of his
knowledge and consent; and so transplant it into another
as it grew in his own mind. For it is in knowledges as it is
in plants: if you mean to use the plant, it is no matter for
the roots; but if you mean to remove it to grow, then it is
more assured to rest upon roots than slips. So the delivery
of knowledges (as it is now used) is as of fair bodies of
trees without the roots; good for the carpenter, but not for
the planter; but if you will have sciences grow, it is less
matter for the shaft or body of the tree, so you look well to
the taking up of the roots. Of which kind of
delivery the method of the mathematiques, in
that subject, hath some shadow; but generally I
see it neither put in ure nor put in inquisition,
and therefore note it for deficient.

*De Methodo
sincera, sive
ad filios Sci-
entiarum*

Another diversity of Method there is, which hath some
affinity with the former, used in some cases by the discre-

tion of the ancients, but disgraced since by the impostures of many vain persons, who have made it as a false light for their counterfeit merchandises; and that is, Enigmatical and Disclosed. The pretence whereof is to remove the vulgar capacities from being admitted to the secrets of knowledges, and to reserve them to selected auditors, or wits of such sharpness as can pierce the veil.

Another diversity of Method, whereof the consequence is great, is the delivery of knowledge in Aphorisms, or in Methods; wherein we may observe that it hath been too much taken into custom, out of a few Axioms or observations upon any subject to make a solemn and formal art; filling it with some discourses, and illustrating it with examples, and digesting it into a sensible Method; but the writing in Aphorisms hath many excellent virtues, whereto the writing in Method doth not approach.

For first, it trieth the writer, whether he be superficial or solid: for Aphorisms, except they should be ridiculous, cannot be made but of the pith and heart of sciences; for discourse of illustration is cut off; recitals of examples are cut off; discourse of connexion and order is cut off; descriptions of practice are cut of; so there remaineth nothing to fill the Aphorisms but some good quantity of observation: and therefore no man can suffice, nor in reason will attempt, to write Aphorisms, but he that is sound and grounded. But in Methods,

Tantum series juncturaque pollet,
Tantum de medio sumptis accedit honoris,

[the arrangement and connexion and joining of the parts has so much effect,] as a man shall make a great shew of an art, which if it were disjointed would come to little. Secondly, Methods are more fit to win consent or belief, but less fit to point to action; for they carry a kind of demonstration in orb or circle, one part illuminating another, and therefore satisfy; but particulars, being dispersed, do best agree with dispersed directions. And lastly, Aphorisms, representing a knowledge broken, do invite men to enquire farther; whereas Methods, carrying the shew of a total, do secure men, as if they were at furthest.

Another diversity of Method, which is likewise of great weight, is the handling of knowledge by Assertions and their Proofs, or by Questions and their Determinations; the latter kind whereof, if it be immoderately followed, is as prejudicial to the proceeding of learning, as it is to the proceeding of an army to go about to besiege every little fort or hold. For if the field be kept and the sum of the enterprise pursued, those smaller things will come in of themselves: indeed a man would not leave some important piece enemy at his back. In like manner, the use of confutation in the delivery of sciences ought to be very sparing; and to serve to remove strong preoccupations and prejudgments, and not to minister and excite disputations and doubts.

Another diversity of Methods is *according to the subject or matter which is handled;* for there is a great difference in delivery of the Mathematics, which are the most abstracted of knowledges, and Policy, which is the most immersed: and howsoever contention hath been moved touching an uniformity of method in multiformity of mattter, yet we see how that opinion, besides the weakness of it, hath been of ill desert towards learning, as that which taketh the way to reduce learning to certain empty and barren generalities; being but the very husks and shells of sciences, all the kernel being forced out and expulsed with the torture and press of the method; and therefore as I did allow well of particular Topics for invention, so I do allow likewise of particular Methods of tradition.

Another diversity of judgment in the delivery and teaching of knowledge is *according unto the light and presuppositions of that which is delivered;* for that knowledge which is new and foreign from opinions received, is to be delivered in another form than that that is agreeable and familiar; and therefore Aristotle, when he thinks to tax Democritus, doth in truth commend him, where he saith, *If we shall indeed dispute, and not follow after similitudes,*

&c. For those whose conceits are seated in popular opinions, need only but to prove or dispute; but those whose conceits are beyond popular opinions, have a double labour; the one to make themselves conceived, and the other to prove and demonstrate; so that it is of necessity with them to have recourse to similitudes and translations to express themselves. And therefore in the infancy of learning, and in rude times, when those conceits which are now trivial were then new, the world was full of Parables and Similitudes; for else would men either have passed over without mark or else rejected for paradoxes that which was offered, before they had understood or judged. So in divine learning we see how frequent Parables and Tropes are: for it is a rule, *That whatsoever science is not consonant to presuppositions, must pray in aid of similitudes.*

There be also other diversities of Methods, vulgar and received; as that of Resolution or Analysis, of Constitution or Systasis, of Concealment or Cryptic, &c. which I do allow well of; though I have stood upon those which are *De prudentia* least handled and observed. All which I have *Traditionis* remembered to this purpose, because I would erect and constitute one general inquiry, which seems to me deficient, touching the Wisdom of Tradition.

But unto this part of knowledge concerning Method doth further belong not only the Architecture of the whole frame of a work, but also the several beams and columns thereof; not as to their stuff, but as to their quantity and figure; and therefore Method considereth not only the disposition of the Argument or Subject, but likewise the Propositions; not as to their truth or matter, but as to their limitation and manner. For herein Ramus merited better a great deal in reviving the good rules of Propositions, Καθόλου πρῶτον, κατὰ παντίς, &c.[44] than he did in introducing the canker of Epitomes; and yet (as it is the condition of human things that, according to the ancient fables, *The most precious things have the most pernicious keepers;*) it was so, that the attempt of the one made him fall upon the other. For he had need be well conducted that should design to make Axioms *convertible,* if he make them not withal *circular,* and *non-promovent,* or *incurring into themselves:* but yet the intention was excellent.

The other considerations of Method concerning Propositions are chiefly touching the utmost propositions, which limit the dimensions of sciences; for every knowledge may be fitly said, besides the profundity, (which is the truth and substance of it, that makes it solid,) to have a longitude and a latitude; accounting the latitude towards other sciences, and the longitude towards action; that is, from the greatest generality to the most particular precept: the one giveth rule how far one knowledge ought to intermeddle within the province of another, which is the rule they call Καθαυτὸ;[45] the other giveth rule unto what degree of particularity a knowledge should descend: which latter I find passed over in silence, being in my judgment the more material; for certainly there must be somewhat left to practice; but how much is worthy the inquiry. We see remote and superficial generalities do but offer knowledge to scorn of practical men; and are no more aiding to practice, than an Ortelius' universal map[46] is to direct the way between London and York. The better sort of rules have been not unfitly compared to glasses of steel unpolished, where you may see the images of things, but first they must be filed: so the rules will help, if they be laboured and polished by practice. But how chrystalline they may be made at the first, and how far forth they may be polished aforehand, is the question; the inquiry whereof seemeth to me deficient.

De productione Axiomatum

There hath been also laboured and put in practice a method, which is not a lawful method, but a method of imposture; which is to deliver knowledges in such manner, as men may speedily come to make a shew of learning who have it not: such was the travail of Raymundus Lullius, in making that art which bears his name; not unlike to some books of Typocosmy which have been made since; being nothing but a mass of words of all arts, to give men countenance that those which use the terms might be thought to understand the art; which collections are much like a frip-per's or broker's shop,[47] that hath ends of every thing, but nothing of worth.

Now we descend to that part which concerneth the Illus-tration of Tradition, comprehended in that science which we call Rhetoric, or Art of Eloquence; a science excellent, and excellently well laboured. For although in true value it is inferior to wisdom, as it is said by God to Moses, when he disabled himself for want of this faculty, *Aaron shall be thy speaker, and thou shalt be to him as God;* yet with people it is the more mighty: for so Salomon saith, *Sapiens corde appellabitur prudens, sed dulcis eloquio majora re-periet,* [the wise in heart shall be called prudent, but he that is sweet of speech shall compass greater things;] signifying that profoundness of wisdom will help a man to a name or admiration, but that it is eloquence that prevaileth in an active life. And as to the labouring of it, the emulation of Aristotle with the rhetoricians of his time, and the experi-ence of Cicero, hath made them in their works of Rhetorics exceed themselves. Again, the excellency of examples of eloquence in the orations of Demosthenes and Cicero, added to the perfection of the precepts of eloquence, hath doubled the progression in this art; and therefore the de-ficiences which I shall note will rather be in some collec-tions which may as handmaids attend the art, than in the rules or use of the art itself.

Notwithstanding, to stir the earth a little about the roots of this science, as we have done of the rest: The duty and office of Rhetoric is *to apply Reason to Imagination* for the better moving of the will. For we see Reason is disturbed in the administration thereof by three means; by Illaquea-tion or Sophism, which pertains to Logic; by Imagination or Impression, which pertains to Rhetoric; and by Passion or Affection, which pertains to Morality. And as in negotia-tion with others men are wrought by cunning, by impor-tunity, and by vehemency; so in this negotiation within ourselves men are undermined by Inconsequences, solicited and importuned by Impressions or Observations, and trans-ported by Passions. Neither is the nature of man so unfortunately built, as that those powers and arts should have force to disturb reason, and not to establish and advance it: for the end of Logic is to teach a form of argument to secure reason, and not to entrap it; the end of Morality is to procure the affections to obey reason, and not to invade it; the end of Rhetoric is to fill the imagination to second reason, and not to oppress it: for these abuses of arts come in but *ex obliquo* [*indirectly], for caution.

And therefore it was great injustice in Plato, though springing out of a just hatred of the rhetoricians of his time, to esteem of Rhetoric but as a voluptuary art, resembling it to cookery, that did mar wholesome meats, and help unwholesome by variety of sauces to the pleasure of the taste. For we see that speech is much more conversant in adorning that which is good than in colouring that which is evil; for there is no man but speaketh more honestly than he can do or think: and it was excellently noted by Thucydides in Cleon,[48] that because he used to hold on the bad side in causes of estate, therefore he was ever inveighing against eloquence and good speech; knowing that no man can speak fair of courses sordid and base. And therefore as Plato said elegantly, *That virtue, if she could be seen, would move great love and affection;* so seeing that she cannot be shewed to the Sense by corporal shape, the next degree is to shew her to the Imagination in lively representation: for to shew her to Reason only in subtilty of argument, was a thing ever derided in Chrysippus and many of the Stoics; who thought to thrust virtue upon men by sharp disputations and conclusions, which have no sympathy with the will of man.

Again, if the affections in themselves were pliant and obedient to reason, it were true there should be no great use of persuasions and insinuations to the will, more than of naked proposition and proofs; but in regard of the continual mutinies and seditions of the affections,

> Video meliora, proboque;
> Deteriora sequor:

[whereby they who not only see the better course, but

approve it also, nevertheless follow the worse,] reason
would become captive and servile, if Eloquence of Persuasions did not practise and win the Imagination from the
Affection's part, and contract a confederacy between the
Reason and Imagination against the Affections. For the affections themselves carry ever an appetite to good, as
reason doth; the difference is, that *the affection beholdeth
merely the present; reason beholdeth the future and sum
of time;* and therefore the present filling the imagination
more, reason is commonly vanquished; but after that force
of eloquence and persuasion hath made things future and
remote appear as present, then upon the revolt of the imagination reason prevaileth.

We conclude therefore, that Rhetoric can be no more
charged with the colouring of the worse part, than Logic
with Sophistry, or Morality with Vice. For we know the
doctrines of contraries are the same, though the use be opposite. It appeareth also that Logic differeth from Rhetoric,
not only as the fist from the palm, the one close the other
at large; but much more in this, that Logic handleth reason
exact and in truth, and Rhetoric handleth it as it is planted
in popular opinions and manners. And therefore Aristotle
doth wisely place Rhetoric as between Logic on the one
side and moral or civil knowledge on the other, as partici-
pating of both: for the proofs and demonstrations of Logic
are toward all men indifferent and the same; but the proofs
and persuasions of Rhetoric ought to differ according to
the auditors: ·

Orpheus in sylvis, inter delphinas Arion:

[to be in the woods an Orpheus, among the dolphins an
Arion:] which application, in perfection of idea, ought to
extend so far, that if a man should speak of the same thing
to several persons, he should speak to them all respectively
and several ways: though this *politic part of eloquence in
private speech* it is easy for the greatest orators to want,
whilst by the observing their well-graced forms
of speech they leese the volubility of application: and therefore it shall not be amiss to rec-

*De prudentia
Sermonis
privati*

ommend this to better inquiry; not being curious whether we place it here, or in that part which concerneth policy.

Now therefore will I descend to the deficiences, which (as I said) are but attendances:[49] and first, I do not find the wisdom and diligence of Aristotle well pursued, who began *Colores boni et* to make a collection of *the popular signs and* *mali, simplicis* *colours of good and evil, both simple and com-* *et comparati* *parative,* which are as the Sophisms of Rhetoric (as I touched before). For example:

SOPHISMA [*SOPHISM]

Quod laudatur, bonum: quod vituperatur, malum.
[*What is praised is good; what is blamed, bad.]

REDARGUTIO [*REFUTATION]

Laudet venales qui vult extrudere merces.
Malum est, malum est, inquit emptor: sed cum recesserit, tum gloriabitur.
[*He praises his wares who wants them off his hands.
It's nothing, it's nothing, says the buyer; but after he leaves, he brags.]

The defects in the labour of Aristotle are three: one, that there be but a few of many; another, that their Elenches are not annexed: and the third, that he conceived but a part of the use of them: for their use is not only in probation, but much more in impression. For many forms are equal in signification which are differing in impression; as the difference is great in the piercing of that which is sharp and that which is flat, though the strength of the percussion be the same; for there is no man but will be a little more raised by hearing it said, *Your enemies will be glad of this:*

Hoc Ithacus velit, et magno mercentur Atridæ:
[*This the Ithacan would desire, and the sons of Atreus buy at great ransom.]

than by hearing it said only, *This is evil for you.*
Secondly, I do resume also that which I mentioned

before touching Provision or Preparatory store for the furniture of speech and readiness of invention; which appeareth to be of two sorts; the one in resemblance to a shop of pieces unmade up, the other to a shop of things ready made up; both to be applied to that which is frequent and most in request: the former of these I will call *Antitheta,* and the latter *Formulæ.*

Antitheta are Theses argued *pro et contra;* wherein men

Antitheta
Rerum

may be more large and laborious: but (in such as are able to do it) to avoid prolixity of entry, I wish the seeds of the several arguments to be cast up into some brief and acute sentences; not to be cited, but to be as skeins or bottoms of thread, to be unwinded at large when they come to be used; supplying authorities and examples by reference.

PRO VERBIS LEGIS [*FOR THE WORDS OF THE LAW]

Non est interpretatio, sed divinatio, quæ recedit a literâ.
Cum receditur a literâ, judex transit in legislatorem.
[*Interpretation which departs from the letter is not interpretation but divination.
When the letter is departed from the judge becomes the lawgiver.]

PRO SENTENTIA LEGIS [*FOR THE INTENTION OF THE LAW]

Ex omnibus verbis est eliciendus sensus qui interpretatur singula.
[*The sense by which each word is to be interpreted must be gathered from all the words together.]

Formulæ are but decent and apt passages or conveyances of speech, which may serve indifferently for differing subjects; as of preface, conclusion, digression, transition, excusation, &c. For as in buildings there is great pleasure and use in the well-casting of the stair-cases, entries, doors, windows, and the like; so in speech the conveyances and passages are of special ornament and effect.

A CONCLUSION IN A DELIBERATIVE

So may we redeem the faults passed, and prevent the inconveniences future.

There remain two appendices touching the tradition of
knowledge, the one Critical, the other Pedantical. For all
knowledge is either delivered by teachers, or attained by
men's proper endeavours: and therefore as the principal
part of tradition of knowledge concerneth chiefly writing of
books, so the relative part thereof concerneth reading of
books. Whereunto appertain incidently these considerations. The first is concerning the true correction and edition
of authors; wherein nevertheless rash diligence hath done
great prejudice. For these critics have often presumed that
that which they understand not is false set down: as the
Priest that where he found it written of St. Paul, *Demissus
est per sportam*, [he was let down in a basket,] mended his
book, and made it *Demissus est per portam*, [he was let out
by the gate;] because *sporta* was an hard word, and out of
his reading; and surely their errors, though they be not so
palpable and ridiculous, are yet of the same kind. And
therefore as it hath been wisely noted, the most corrected
copies are commonly the least correct.

The second is concerning the exposition and explication
of authors, which resteth in annotations and commentaries;
wherein it is over usual to blanch the obscure places, and
discourse upon the plain.

The third is concerning the times, which in many cases
give great light to true interpretations.

The fourth is concerning some brief censure and judgment of the authors; that men thereby may make some
election unto themselves what books to read.

And the fifth is concerning the syntax and disposition of
studies; that men may know in what order or pursuit to
read.

For Pedantical knowledge, it containeth that difference
of Tradition which is proper for youth; whereunto appertain divers considerations of great fruit.

As first, the timing and seasoning of knowledge; as with what to initiate them, and from what for a time to refrain them.

Secondly, the consideration where to begin with the easiest and so proceed to the more difficult; and in what courses to press the more difficult and then to turn them to the more easy: for it is one method to practise swimming with bladders, and another to practice dancing with heavy shoes.

A third is the application of learning according unto the propriety of the wits; for there is no defect in the faculties intellectual but seemeth to have a proper cure contained in some studies: as for example, if a child be bird-witted, that is, hath not the faculty of attention, the Mathematics giveth a remedy thereunto; for in them, if the wit be caught away but a moment, one is new to begin. And as sciences have a propriety towards faculties for cure and help, so faculties or powers have a sympathy towards sciences for excellency or speedy profiting; and therefore it is an inquiry of great wisdom, what kinds of wits and natures are most apt and proper for what sciences.

Fourthly, the ordering of exercises is matter of great consequence to hurt or help; for as is well observed by Cicero, men in exercising their faculties, if they be not well advised, do exercise their faults and get ill habits as well as good; so as there is a great judgment to be had in the continuance and intermission of exercises. It were too long to particularise a number of other considerations of this nature, things but of mean appearance, but of singular efficacy. For as the wronging or cherishing of seeds or young plants is that that is most important to their thriving; and as it was noted that the first six kings being in truth as tutors of the state of Rome in the infancy thereof, was the principal cause of the immense greatness of that state which followed: so the culture and manurance of minds in youth hath such a forcible (though unseen) operation, as hardly any length of time or contention of labour can countervail it afterwards. And it is not amiss to observe also how small and mean faculties gotten by education, yet when they fall into great men or great matters, do work great and important effects; whereof we see a notable example in Tacitus of two stage-players, Percennius and Vibulenus, who by their faculty of playing put the Pannonian armies into an extreme tumult and combustion. For there arising a mutiny amongst them upon the death of Augustus Cæsar, Blæsus the lieutenant had committed some of the mutiners; which were suddenly rescued; whereupon Vibulenus got to be heard speak, which he did in this manner:—*These poor innocent wretches, appointed to cruel death, you have restored to behold the light. But who shall restore my brother to me, or life unto my brother? that was sent hither in message from the legions of Germany to treat of the common cause, and he hath murdered him this last night by some of his fencers and ruffians, that he hath about him for his executioners upon soldiers. Answer, Blæsus, what is done with his body? The mortalest enemies do not deny burial. When I have performed my last duties to the corpse with kisses, with tears, command me to be slain besides him; so that these my fellows, for our good meaning and our true hearts to the legions, may have leave to bury us.* With which speech he put the army into an infinite fury and uproar; whereas truth was he had no brother, neither was there any such matter, but he played it merely as if he had been upon the stage.

But to return: we are now come to a period of Rational Knowledges; wherein if I have made the divisions other than those that are received, yet would I not be thought to disallow all those divisions which I do not use. For there is a double necessity imposed upon me of altering the divisions. The one, because it differeth in end and purpose, to sort together those things which are next in nature, and those things which are next in use. For if a secretary of state should sort his papers, it is like in his study or general cabinet he would sort together things of a nature, as treaties, instructions, &c. but in his boxes or particular cabinet he would sort together those that he were like to use together, though of several natures; so in this general cabinet of knowledge it was necessary for me to follow the divisions of the nature of things; whereas if myself had been to handle any particular knowledge, I would have respected the divisions fittest for use. The other, because the bringing in of the deficiences did by consequence alter the partitions of the rest: for let the knowledge extant (for demonstration sake) be fifteen; let the knowledge with the deficiences be twenty; the parts of fifteen are not the parts of twenty; for the parts of fifteen are three and five; the parts of twenty are two, four, five, and ten. So as these things are without contradiction, and could not otherwise be.

We proceed now to that knowledge which considereth of the Appetite and Will of Man; whereof Salomon saith, *Ante omnia, fili, custodi cor tuum; nam inde procedunt actiones vitæ:* [keep thy heart with all diligence, for thereout come the actions of thy life]. In the handling of this science, those which have written seem to me to have done as if a man that professeth to teach to write did only exhibit fair copies of alphabets and letters joined, without giving any precepts or directions for the carriage of the hand and framing of the letters. So have they made good and fair exemplars and copies, carrying the draughts and portraitures of Good, Virtue, Duty, Felicity; propounding them well described as the true objects and scopes of man's will and desires; but how to attain these excellent marks, and how to frame and subdue the will of man to become true and conformable to these pursuits, they pass it over altogether, or slightly and unprofitably. For it is not the disputing *that moral virtues are in the mind of man by habit and not by nature,* or the distinguishing *that generous spirits are won by doctrines and persuasions, and the vulgar sort by reward and punishment,* and the like scattered glances and touches, that can excuse the absence of this part.

The reason of this omission I suppose to be that hidden

rock whereupon both this and many other barks of knowledge have been cast away; which is, that men have despised to be conversant in ordinary and common matters; the judicious direction whereof nevertheless is the wisest doctrine (for life consisteth not in novelties or subtilities); but contrariwise they have compounded sciences chiefly of a certain resplendent or lustrous mass of matter, chosen to give glory either to the subtility of disputations or to the eloquence of discourses. But Seneca giveth an excellent check to eloquence; *Nocet illis eloquentia, quibus non rerum cupiditatem facit, sed sui:* [eloquence does mischief when it draws men's attention away from the matter to fix it on itself]. Doctrines should be such as should make men in love with the lesson, and not with the teacher; being directed to the auditor's benefit, and not to the author's commendation: and therefore those are of the right kind which may be concluded as Demosthenes concludes his counsel, *Quæ si feceritis, non oratorem duntaxat in præsentia laudabitis, sed vosmetipsos etiam non ita multo post statu rerum vestrarum meliore:* [if you follow this advice you will do a grace to yourselves no less than to the speaker,—to him by your vote to-day, to yourselves by the improvement which you will presently find in your affairs].

Neither needed men of so excellent parts to have despaired of a fortune which the poet Virgil promised himself, (and indeed obtained,) who got as much glory of eloquence, wit, and learning in the expressing of the observations of husbandry, as of the heroical acts of Æneas:—

> Nec sum animi dubius, verbis ea vincere magnum
> Quam sit, et angustis his addere rebus honorem.

> [How hard the task alas full well I know
> With charm of words to grace a theme so low.]

And surely if the purpose be in good earnest not to write at leisure that which men may read at leisure, but really to instruct and suborn action and active life, these Georgics of the mind, concerning the husbandry and tillage thereof, are no less worthy than the heroical descriptions of Virtue,

Duty, and Felicity. Wherefore the main and primitive division of moral knowledge seemeth to be into the Exemplar or Platform of Good, and the Regiment or Culture of the Mind; the one describing the nature of good, the other prescribing rules how to subdue, apply, and accommodate the will of man thereunto.

The doctrine touching the Platform or Nature of Good considereth it either Simple or Compared; either the kinds of good, or the degrees of good: in the later whereof those infinite disputations which were touching the supreme degree thereof, which they term felicity, beatitude, or the highest good, the doctrines concerning which were as the heathen divinity, are by the Christian faith discharged. And as Aristotle saith, *That young men may be happy, but not otherwise but by hope;* so we must all acknowledge our minority, and embrace the felicity which is by hope of the future world.

Freed therefore and delivered from this doctrine of the philosophers' heaven, whereby they feigned an higher elevation of man's nature than was, (for we see in what an height of style Seneca writeth, *Vere magnum, habere fragilitatem hominis, securitatem Dei,* [it is true greatness to have in one the frailty of a man and the security of a God,] we may with more sobriety and truth receive the rest of their inquiries and labours. Wherein for the Nature of Good Positive or Simple, they have set it down excellently, in describing the forms of Virtue and Duty, with their situations and postures, in distributing them into their kinds, parts, provinces, actions, and administrations, and the like: nay farther, they have commended them to man's nature and spirit with great quickness of argument and beauty of persuasions; yea, and fortified and intrenched them (as much as discourse can do) against corrupt and popular opinions. Again, for the Degrees and Comparative Nature of Good, they have also excellently handled it in their triplicity of Good, in the comparisons between a contemplative and an active life, in the distinction between virtue with reluctation and virtue secured, in their encounters between honesty and profit, in their balancing of virtue with virtue, and the like; so as this part deserveth to be reported for excellently laboured.

Notwithstanding, if before they had comen to the popular and received notions of virtue and vice, pleasure and pain, and the rest, they had stayed a little longer upon the inquiry concerning the roots of good and evil, and the strings of those roots, they had given, in my opinion, a great light to that which followed; and specially if they had consulted with nature, they had made their doctrines less prolix and more profound; which being by them in part omitted and in part handled with much confusion, we will endeavour to resume and open in a more clear manner.

There is formed in every thing a double nature of good: the one, as every thing is a total or substantive in itself; the other, as it is a part or member of a greater body; whereof the later is in degree the greater and the worthier, because it tendeth to the conservation of a more general form. Therefore we see the iron in particular sympathy moveth to the loadstone; but yet if it exceed a certain quantity, it forsaketh the affection to the loadstone, and like a good patriot moveth to the earth, which is the region and country of massy bodies; so may we go forward, and see that water and massy bodies move to the centre of the earth; but rather than to suffer a divulsion in the continuance of nature, they will move upwards from the centre of the earth, forsaking their duty to the earth in regard of their duty to the world. This double nature of good, and the comparative thereof, is much more engraven upon man, if he degenerate not; unto whom the conservation of duty to the public ought to be much more precious than the conservation of life and being: according to that memorable speech of Pompeius Magnus, when being in commission of purveyance for a famine at Rome, and being dissuaded with great vehemency and instance by his friends about him that he should not hazard himself to sea in an extremity of weather, he said only to them, *Necesse est ut eam, non ut vivam:* [it is needful that I go, not that I live]. But it may be truly affirmed that there was never any philosophy, religion, or other discipline, which did so plainly and highly exalt the good which is communicative, and depress the good which is private and particular, as the Holy Faith; well declaring, that it was the same God that gave the Christian law to men, who gave those laws of nature to inanimate creatures that we spake of before; for we read that the elected saints of God have wished themselves anathematized and razed out of the book of life, in an ecstasy of charity and infinite feeling of communion.

This being set down and strongly planted, doth judge and determine most of the controversies wherein Moral Philosophy is conversant. For first it decideth the question touching the preferment of the contemplative or active life, and decideth it against Aristotle. For all the reasons which he bringeth for the contemplative are private, and respecting the pleasure and dignity of a man's self, (in which respects no question the contemplative life hath the pre-eminence:) not much unlike to that comparison which Pythagoras made for the gracing and magnifying of philosophy and contemplation; who being asked what he was, answered, *That if Hiero were ever at the Olympian games, he knew the manner, that some came to try their fortune for the prizes, and some came as merchants to utter their commodities, and some came to make good cheer and meet their friends, and same came to look on; and that he was one of them that came to look on.* But men must know, that in this theatre of man's life it is reserved only for God and Angels to be lookers on. Neither could the like question ever have been received in the church, notwithstanding their *Pretiosa in oculis Domini mors sanctorum ejus,* [precious in the sight of the Lord is the death of his saints,] by which place they would exalt their civil death and regular professions, but upon this defence, that the monastical life is not simple contemplative, but performeth the duty either of incessant prayers and supplications, which hath been truly esteemed as an office in the church, or else of writing or taking instructions for writing concerning the law of God, as Moses did when he abode so long in the mount. And so we see Henoch the seventh from Adam, who was the first Contemplative and walked with God, yet did also endow the church with prophecy, which St. Jude citeth. But for contemplation which should be finished in itself without casting beams upon society, assuredly divinity knoweth it not.

It decideth also the controversies between Zeno and Socrates and their schools and successions on the one side, who placed felicity in virtue simply or attended; the actions and exercises whereof do chiefly embrace and concern society; and on the other side, the Cyrenaics and Epicureans, who placed it in pleasure, and made virtue (as it is used in some comedies of errors, wherein the mistress and the maid change habits,) to be but as a servant, without which pleasure cannot be served and attended; and the reformed school of the Epicureans, which placed it in serenity of mind and freedom from perturbation; as if they would have deposed Jupiter again, and restored Saturn and the first age, when there was no summer nor winter, spring nor autumn, but all after one air and season; and Herillus, which placed felicity in extinguishment of the disputes of the mind, making no fixed nature of good and evil, esteeming things according to the clearness of the desires, or the reluctation;[50] which opinion was revived in the heresy of the Anabaptists, measuring things according to the motions of the spirit, and the constancy or wavering of belief: all which are manifest to tend to private repose and contentment, and not to point of society.

It censureth also the philosophy of Epictetus, which presupposeth that felicity must be placed in those things which are in our power, lest we be liable to fortune and disturbance: as if it were not a thing much more happy to fail in good and virtuous ends for the public, than to obtain all that we can wish to ourselves in our proper fortune; as Consalvo said to his soldiers, shewing them Naples, and protesting he had rather die one foot forwards than to have his life secured for long by one foot of retreat; whereunto the wisdom of that heavenly leader hath signed, who hath affirmed that *a good conscience is a continual feast:* shewing plainly that the conscience of good intentions, howsoever succeeding, is a more continual joy to nature than all the provision which can be made for security and repose.

It censureth likewise that abuse of philosophy which grew general about the time of Epictetus, in converting it into an occupation or profession; as if the purpose had been, not to resist and extinguish perturbations, but to fly and avoid the causes of them, and to shape a particular kind and course of life to that end; introducing such an health of mind, as was that health of body of which Aristotle speaketh of Herodicus, who did nothing all his life long but intend his health: whereas if men refer themselves to duties of society, as that health of body is best which is ablest to endure all alterations and extremities, so likewise that health of mind is most proper which can go through the greatest temptations and perturbations. So as Diogenes' opinion is to be accepted, who commended not them which abstained, but them which sustained, and could refrain their mind *in præcipitio* [*in full career], and could give unto the mind (as is used in horsemanship) the shortest stop or turn.

Lastly, it censureth the tenderness and want of application in some of the most ancient and reverend philosophers and philosophical men, that did retire too easily from civil business, for avoiding of indignities and perturbations; whereas the resolution of men truly moral ought to be such as the same Consalvo said the honour of a soldier should be, *e telâ crassiore,* [of a stouter web,] and not so fine as that every thing should catch in it and endanger it.

To resume Private or Particular Good, it falleth into the division of Good Active and Passive: for this difference of Good (not unlike to that which amongst the Romans was expressed in the familiar or household terms of Promus and Condus) is formed also in all things; and is best disclosed in the two several appetites in creatures, the one to preserve or continue themselves, and the other to dilate or multiply themselves; whereof the later seemeth to be the worthier. For in nature, the heavens, which are the more worthy, are the agent; and the earth, which is the less worthy, is the patient. In the pleasures of living creatures, that of generation is greater than that of food. In divine doctrine, *Beatius est dare quam accipere:* [it is more blessed to give than to receive]. And in life, there is no man's spirit so soft, but esteemeth the effecting of somewhat that he hath fixed in his desire more than sensuality. Which priority of the Active Good is much upheld by the consideration of our estate to be mortal and exposed to fortune; for if we might have a perpetuity and certainty in our pleasures, the *state* of them would advance their price; but when we see it is but *Magni æstimamus mori tardius,* [we think it a great matter to be a little longer in dying,] and *Ne glorieris de crastino, nescis partum diei,* [boast not thyself of to-morrow, thou knowest not what the day may bring forth,] it maketh us to desire to have somewhat secured and exempted from time; which are only our deeds and works; as it is said *Opera eorum sequuntur eos:* [their works follow them]. The pre-eminence likewise of this Active Good is upheld by the affection which is natural in man towards variety and proceeding; which in the pleasures of the sense (which is the principal part of Passive Good) can have no great latitude: *Cogita quamdiu eadem feceris; cibus, somnus, ludus; per hunc circulum curritur; mori velle non tantum fortis, aut miser, aut prudens, sed etiam fastidiosus potest:* [if you consider, says Seneca, how often you do the same thing over and over; food sleep exercise, and then food sleep exercise again, and so round and round; you will think that there needs neither fortitude nor misery nor wisdom to reconcile a man to death; one might wish to die for mere weariness of being alive]. But in enterprises, pursuits, and purposes of life, there is much variety; whereof men are sensible with pleasure in their inceptions, progressions, recoils, reintegrations, approaches, and attainings to their ends: so as it was well said, *Vita sine proposito languida et vaga est:* [life without an object to pursue is a languid and tiresome thing]. Neither hath this Active Good any identity with the good of society, though in some case it hath an incidence into it: for although it do many times bring forth acts of beneficence, yet it is with a respect private to a man's own power, glory, amplification, continuance; as appeareth plainly when it findeth a contrary subject. For that gigantine state of mind which possesseth the troublers of the world, such as was Lucius Sylla, and infinite other in smaller model, who would have all men happy or unhappy as they were their friends or enemies, and would give form to the world according to their own humours, (which is the true Theomachy,) pretendeth and aspireth to active good, though it recedeth furthest from good of society, which we have determined to be the greater.

To resume Passive Good, it receiveth a subdivision of Conservative and Perfective. For let us take a brief review of that which we have said: we have spoken first of the Good of Society, the intention whereof embraceth the form of Human Nature, whereof we are members and portions, and not our own proper and individual form; we have spoken of Active Good, and supposed it as a part of Private and Particular Good; and rightly; for there is impressed upon all things a triple desire or appetite proceeding from love to themselves; one of preserving and continuing their form; another of advancing and perfecting their form; and a third of multiplying and extending their form upon other things; whereof the multiplying or signature of it upon other things is that which we handled by the name of Active Good. So as there remaineth the conserving of it, and perfecting or raising of it; which later is the highest degree of Passive Good. For to preserve in state is the less, to preserve with advancement is the greater. So in man,

> Igneus est ollis vigor, et cœlestis origo.
> [The living fire that glows those seeds within
> Remembers its celestial origin.]

His approach or assumption to divine or angelical nature is the perfection of his form; the error or false imitation of which good is that which is the tempest of human life; while man, upon the instinct of an advancement formal and essential, is carried to seek an advancement local. For as those which are sick, and find no remedy, do tumble up and down and change place, as if by a remove local they could obtain a remove internal; so is it with men in ambition, when failing of the mean to exalt their nature, they are in a perpetual estuation to exalt their place. So then Passive Good is, as was said, either Conservative or Perfective.

To resume the good of Conservation or Comfort, which consisteth *in the fruition of that which is agreeable to our natures;* it seemeth to be the most pure and natural of pleasures, but yet the softest and the lowest. And this also receiveth a difference, which hath neither been well judged of nor well enquired. For the good of fruition or contentment is placed either in the sincereness of the fruition, or in the quickness and vigour of it; the one superinduced by the equality, the other by vicissitude; the one having less mixture of evil, the other more impression of good. Whether of these is the greater good, is a question controverted; but whether man's nature may not be capable of both, is a question not enquired.

The former question being debated between Socrates and a Sophist, Socrates placing felicity in an equal and constant peace of mind, and the Sophist in much desiring and much enjoying, they fell from argument to ill words: the Sophist saying that Socrates' felicity was the felicity of a block or stone; and Socrates saying that the Sophist's felicity was the felicity of one that had the itch, who did nothing but itch and scratch. And both these opinions do not want their supports. For the opinion of Socrates is much upheld by the general consent even of the Epicures themselves, that virtue beareth a great part in felicity; and if so, certain it is that virtue hath more use in clearing perturbations than in compassing desires. The Sophist's opinion is much favoured by the assertion we last spake of, that good of advancement is greater than good of simple preservation; because every obtaining a desire hath a shew of advancement, as motion though in a circle hath a shew of progression.

But the second question, decided the true way, maketh the former superfluous. For can it be doubted but that there are some who take more pleasure in enjoying pleasures than some other, and yet nevertheless are less troubled with the loss or leaving of them? so as this same *Non uti ut non appetas, non appetere ut non metuas, sunt animi pusilli et diffidentis:* [to abstain from the use of a thing that you may not feel a want of it; to shun the want that you may not fear the loss of it; are the precautions of pusillanimity and cowardice]. And it seemeth to me, that most of the doctrines of the philosophers are more fearful and cautionary than the nature of things requireth. So have they increased the fear of death in offering to cure it. For when they would have a man's whole life to be but a discipline or preparation to die, they must needs make men think that it is a terrible enemy against whom there is no end of preparing. Better saith the poet:

> Qui finem vitæ extremum inter munera ponat
> Naturæ:

[the end of life is to be counted among the boons of nature]. So have they sought to make men's minds too uniform and harmonical, by not breaking them sufficiently to contrary motions: the reason whereof I suppose to be, because they themselves were men dedicated to a private, free, and unapplied course of life. For as we see, upon the lute or like instrument, a *ground*, though it be sweet and have shew of many changes, yet breaketh not the hand to such strange and hard stops and passages as a *set song* or *voluntary;* much after the same manner was the diversity between a philosophical and a civil life. And therefore men are to imitate the wisdom of jewellers; who, if there be a grain or a cloud or an ice which may be ground forth without taking too much of the stone, they help it; but if it should lessen and abate the stone too much, they will not meddle with it: so ought men so to procure serenity as they destroy not magnanimity.

Having therefore deduced the Good of Man which is Private and Particular as far as seemeth fit, we will now return to that good of man which respecteth and beholdeth society, which we may term Duty; because the term of Duty is more proper to a mind well framed and disposed towards others, as the term of Virtue is applied to a mind well formed and composed in itself; though neither can a man understand Virtue without some relation to society, nor Duty without an inward disposition. This part may seem at first to pertain to science civil and politic; but not if it be well observed. For it concerneth the regiment and government of every man over himself, and not over others. And as in architecture the direction of framing the posts, beams, and other parts of building, is not the same with the manner of joining them and erecting the building; and in mechanicals, the direction how to frame an instrument or engine, is not the same with the manner of setting it on work and employing it; and yet nevertheless in expressing of the one you incidently express the aptness towards the other; so the doctrine of conjugation of men in society differeth from that of their conformity thereunto.

This part of Duty is subdivided into two parts; the common duty of every man, as a man or member of a state; the other, the respective or special duty of every man, in his profession, vocation, and place. The first of these is extant and well laboured, as hath been said. The second likewise I may report rather dispersed than deficient; which manner of dispersed writing in this kind of argument I acknowledge to be best. For who can take upon him to write of the proper duty, virtue, challenge, and right of every several vocation, profession and place? For although sometimes a looker on may see more than a gamester, and there be a proverb more arrogant than sound, *That the vale best discovereth the hill;* yet there is small doubt but that men can write best and most really and materially in their own professions; and that the writing of speculative men of active matter for the most part doth seem to men of experience, as Phormio's argument of the wars seemed to Hannibal, to be but dreams and dotage. Only there is one vice which accompanieth them that write in their own professions, that they magnify them in excess. But generally it were to be wished (as that which would make learning indeed solid and fruitful) that active men would or could become writers.

In which kind I cannot but mention, *honoris causa* [*for the sake of honor], your Majesty's excellent book[51] touching the duty of a king: a work richly compounded of divinity, morality, and policy, with great aspersion of all other arts; and being in mine opinion one of the most sound and healthful writings that I have read; not distempered in the heat of invention, nor in the coldness of negligence; not sick of dizziness, as those are who leese themselves in their order; nor of convulsions, as those which cramp in matters impertinent; not savouring of perfumes and paintings, as those do who seek to please the reader more than nature beareth; and chiefly well disposed in the spirits thereof, being agreeable to truth and apt for action; and far removed from that natural infirmity, whereunto I noted those that write in their own professions to be subject, which is, that they exalt it above measure. For your Majesty hath truly described, not a king of Assyria or Persia in their extern glory, but a Moses or a David, pastors of their people. Neither can I ever leese out of my remembrance what I heard your Majesty in the same sacred spirit of government deliver in a great cause of judicature, which was, *That Kings ruled by their laws as God did by the laws of nature, and ought as rarely to put in use their supreme prerogative as God doth his power of working miracles*. And yet notwithstanding, in your book of a free monarchy, you do well give men to understand, that you know the plenitude of the power and right of a King, as well as the circle of his office and duty. Thus have I presumed to allege this excellent writing of your Majesty, as a prime or eminent example of

tractates concerning special and respective duties; wherein
I should have said as much, if it had been written a thousand years since. Neither am I moved with certain courtly
decencies, which esteem it flattery to praise in presence. No,
it is flattery to praise in absence; that is, when either the
virtue is absent, or the occasion is absent; and so the praise
is not natural, but forced, either in truth or in time. But let
Cicero be read in his oration *pro Marcello,* which is nothing
but an excellent table of Cæsar's virtue, and made to his
face; besides the example of many other excellent persons,
wiser a great deal than such observers; and we will never
doubt, upon a full occasion, to give just praises to present
or absent.

But to return: there belongeth further to the handling of
this part touching the duties of professions and vocations, a
Relative or opposite, touching the frauds, cautels, impostures, and vices of every profession; which hath been likewise handled: but how? rather in a satire and cynically, than
seriously and wisely: for men have rather sought by wit to
deride and traduce much of that which is good in professions, than with judgment to discover and sever that which
is corrupt. For, as Salomon saith, He that cometh to seek
after knowledge with a mind to scorn and censure, shall be
sure to find matter for his humour, but no matter for his
instruction: *Quærenti derisori scientiam ipsa se abscondit;
sed studioso fit obviam.* But the managing of this argument
with integrity and truth, which I note as deficient, seemeth
to me to be one of the best fortifications for honesty and
virtue that can be planted. For as the fable goeth of the
Basilisk, that if he see you first you die for it, but if you see
him first he dieth; so is it with deceits and evil arts; which
if they be first espied they leese their life, but if they prevent[52] they endanger. So that we are much beholden to
Machiavel and others, that write what men do and not what
they ought to do. For it is not possible to join serpentine
wisdom with the columbine innocency, except men know
exactly all the conditions of the serpent; his baseness and
going upon his belly, his volubility and lubricity, his envy

and sting, and the rest; that is, all forms and natures of evil.
For without this, virtue lieth open and unfenced. Nay an
honest man can do no good upon those that are wicked to
reclaim them, without the help of the knowledge of evil.
For men of corrupted minds presuppose that honesty groweth out of simplicity of manners, and believing of preachers,
schoolmasters, and men's exterior language: so as, except
you can make them perceive that you know the utmost
reaches of their own corrupt opinions, they despise all morality. *Non recipit stultus verba prudentiæ, nisi ea dixeris
quæ versantur in corde ejus:* [the fool will not listen to the
words of the wise, unless you first tell him what is in his
own heart].

Unto this part touching Respective Duty doth also appertain the duties between husband and wife, parent and
child, master and servant: so likewise the laws of friendship
and gratitude, the civil bond of companies, colleges, and
politic bodies, of neighbourhood, and all other proportion-
ate duties; not as they are parts of government and society,
but as to the framing of the mind of particular persons.

The knowledge concerning good respecting Society doth
handle it also not simply alone, but comparatively; whereunto belongeth the weighing of duties between person and
person, case and case, particular and public: as we see in
the proceeding of Lucius Brutus against his own sons,
which was so much extolled; yet what was said?

Infelix, utcunque ferent ea facta minores:

[unhappy man! whatever judgment posterity shall pass upon
that deed, &c.]. So the case was doubtful, and had opinion
on both sides. Again, we see when M. Brutus and Cassius
invited to a supper certain whose opinions they meant to
feel, whether they were fit to be made their associates, and
cast forth the question touching the killing of a tyrant
being an usurper, they were divided in opinion; some holding that servitude was the extreme of evils, and others that
tyranny was better than a civil war: and a number of the
like cases there are of comparative duty. Amongst which that

of all others is the most frequent, where the question is of a great deal of good to ensue of a small injustice. Which Jason of Thessalia determined against the truth: *Aliqua sunt injuste facienda, ut multa juste fieri possint:* [that there may be justice in many things there must be injustice in some]. But the reply is good, *Authorem præsentis justitiæ habes, sponsorem futuræ non habes:* [the justice that is to be done now is in your power, but where is your security for that which is to be done hereafter?] Men must pursue things which are just in present, and leave the future to the divine Providence. So then we pass on from this general part touching the exemplar and description of good.

Now therefore that we have spoken of this fruit of life, it *De Cultura* remaineth to speak of the husbandry that be- *Animi* longeth thereunto; without which part the former seemeth to be no better than a fair image or statua, which is beautiful to contemplate, but is without life and motion: whereunto Aristotle himself subscribeth in these words: *Necesse est scilicet de virtute dicere, et quid sit, et ex quibus gignatur. Inutile enim fere fuerit virtutem quidem nosse, acquirendæ autem ejus modos et vias ignorare. Non enim de virtute tantum, qua specie sit, quærendum est, sed et quomodo sui copiam faciat: utrumque enim volumus, et rem ipsam nosse, et ejus compotes fieri: hoc autem ex voto non succedet, nisi sciamus et ex quibus et quomodo:* [it is necessary to determine concerning Virtue not only what it is but whence it proceeds. For there would be no use in knowing Virtue without knowing the ways and means of acquiring it. For we have to consider not only what it is, but how it is to be had. For we want both to know virtue and to be virtuous; which we cannot be without knowing both the whence and the how]. In such full words and with such iteration doth he inculcate this part. So saith Cicero in great commendation of Cato the second, that he had applied himself to philosophy *non ita disputandi causa, sed ita vivendi:* [not that he might talk like a philosopher, but that he might live like one]. And although the neglect of our times, wherein few men do hold any consultations touching the reformation of their life, (as Seneca excellently saith, *De partibus vitæ quisque deliberat, de summâ nemo,*) [every man takes thought about the parts of his life, no man about the whole,] may make this part seem superfluous; yet I must conclude with that aphorism of Hippocrates, *Qui gravi morbo correpti dolores non sentiunt, iis mens ægrotat;* [they that are sick and yet feel no pain are sick in their minds;] they need medicine not only to assuage the disease but to awake the sense. And if it be said that the cure of men's minds belongeth to sacred Divinity, it is most true: but yet Moral Philosophy may be preferred [53] unto her as a wise servant and humble handmaid. For as the Psalm saith, *that the eyes of the handmaid look perpetually towards the mistress,* and yet no doubt many things are left to the discretion of the handmaid to discern of the mistress' will; so ought Moral Philosophy to give a constant attention to the doctrines of Divinity, and yet so as it may yield of herself (within due limits) many sound and profitable directions.

This part therefore, because of the excellency thereof, I cannot but find exceeding strange that it is not reduced to written inquiry; the rather because it consisteth of much matter wherein both speech and action is often conversant, and such wherein the common talk of men (which is rare, but yet cometh sometimes to pass) is wiser than their books. It is reasonable therefore that we propound it in the more particularity, both for the worthiness, and because we may acquit ourselves for reporting it deficient; which seemeth almost incredible, and is otherwise conceived and presupposed by those themselves that have written. We will therefore enumerate some heads or points thereof, that it may appear the better what it is, and whether it be extant.

First therefore, in this, as in all things which are practical, we ought to cast up our account, what is in our power and what not; for the one may be dealt with by way of alteration, but the other by way of application only. The husbandman cannot command neither the nature of the earth nor the seasons of the weather; no more can the physician the constitution of the patient nor the variety of accidents. So in the culture and cure of the mind of man, two things are without our command; points of nature, and points of fortune; for to the basis of the one, and the conditions of the other, our work is limited and tied. In these things therefore it is left unto us to proceed by application:

Vincenda est omnis fortuna ferendo:

[all fortune may be overcome by endurance or suffering;] and so likewise,

Vincenda est omnis natura ferendo:

[all nature may be overcome by suffering]. But when that we speak of suffering, we do not speak of a dull and neglected suffering, but of a wise and industrious suffering, which draweth and contriveth use and advantage out of that which seemeth adverse and contrary; which is that property which we call Accommodating or Applying. Now the wisdom of application resteth principally in the exact and distinct knowledge of the precedent state or disposition unto which we do apply: for we cannot fit a garment, except we first take measure of the body.

So then the first article of this knowledge is to set down sound and true distributions and descriptions of the several characters and tempers of men's natures and dispositions, specially having regard to those differences which are most radical in being the fountains and causes of the rest, or most frequent in concurrence or commixture; wherein it is not the handling of a few of them in passage, the better to describe the mediocrities of virtues, that can satisfy this intention; for if it deserve to be considered, *that there are minds which are proportioned to great matters, and others to small,* (which Aristotle handleth or ought to have handled by the name of Magnanimity,) doth it not deserve as well to be considered, *that there are minds proportioned to intend many matters, and others to few?* so that some can divide themselves, others can perchance do exactly well,

but it must be but in few things at once; and so there cometh to be a *narrowness of mind,* as well as a *pusillanimity.*
And again, *that some minds are proportioned to that which
may be dispatched at once, or within a short return of time;
others to that which begins afar off, and is to be won with
length of pursuit;*

Jam tum tenditque fovetque:

[he begins to attend and nurse his project while it is yet
in the cradle;] so that there may be fitly said to be a *lon-
ganimity;* which is commonly also ascribed to God as a
magnanimity. So further deserved it to be considered by
Aristotle, *that there is a disposition in conversation (supposing it in things which do in no sort touch or concern a man's
self) to soothe and please, and a disposition contrary to contradict and cross;* and deserveth it not much better to be
considered, *that there is a disposition, not in conversation
or talk but in matter of more serious nature, (and supposing
it still in things merely indifferent,) to take pleasure in the
good of another, and a disposition contrariwise to take
distaste at the good of another;* which is that property
which we call good-nature or ill-nature, benignity or malignity? And therefore I cannot sufficiently marvel that this
part of knowledge touching the several characters of natures
and dispositions should be omitted both in morality and
policy, considering it is of so great ministery and suppedi-
tation to them both. A man shall find in the traditions of
astrology some pretty and apt divisions of men's natures,
according to the predominances of the planets; *lovers of
quiet, lovers of action, lovers of victory, lovers of honour,
lovers of pleasure, lovers of arts, lovers of change,* and so
forth. A man shall find in the wisest sort of these Relations
which the Italians make touching Conclaves, the natures
of the several Cardinals handsomely and lively painted
forth. A man shall meet with in every day's conference the
denominations of *sensitive, dry, formal, real, humorous,
certain, huomo di prima impressione, huomo di ultima impressione,*[54] and the like: and yet nevertheless this kind of

observations wandereth in words, but is not fixed in inquiry. For the distinctions are found (many of them), but we conclude no precepts upon them; wherein our fault is the greater, because both history, poesy, and daily experience are as goodly fields where these observations grow; whereof we make a few posies to hold in our hands, but no man bringeth them to the confectionary, that receits might be made of them for use of life.

Of much like kind are those impressions of nature, which are imposed upon the mind *by the sex, by the age, by the region, by health and sickness, by beauty and deformity,* and the like, which are inherent and not extern; and again those which are caused by extern fortune; as *sovereignty, nobility, obscure birth, riches, want, magistracy, privateness, prosperity, adversity, constant fortune, variable fortune, rising per saltum, per gradus* [*by bounds, by degrees], and the like. And therefore we see that Plautus maketh it a wonder to see an old man beneficent; *benignitas hujus ut adolescentuli est:* [he is as generous as if he were a young man:] St. Paul concludeth that severity of discipline was to be used to the Cretans, *Increpa eos durè,* [rebuke them sharply,] upon the disposition of their country; *Cretenses semper mendaces, malæ bestiæ, ventres pigri:* [the Cretans are always liars, evil beasts, slow bellies:] Sallust noteth that it is usual with Kings to desire contradictories; *Sed plerumque regiæ voluntates, ut vehementes sunt, sic mobiles, sæpeque ipsæ sibi adversæ:* [royal desires, as they are violent, so are they changeable, and often incompatible with each other:] Tacitus observeth how rarely raising of the fortune mendeth the disposition; *Solus Vespasianus mutatus in melius:* [Vespasian the only one of the emperors that changed for the better:] Pindarus maketh an observation that great and sudden fortune for the most part defeateth men; *Qui magnam felicitatem concoquere non possunt:* [that cannot digest great felicity:] so the Psalm sheweth it is more easy to keep a measure in the enjoying of fortune than in the increase of fortune; *Divitiæ si affluant, nolite cor apponere:* [if riches increase set not your heart

upon them]. These observations and the like I deny not but
are touched a little by Aristotle as in passage in his Rhetorics, and are handled in some scattered discourses; but
they were never incorporate into Moral Philosophy, to
which they do essentially appertain; as the knowledge of
the diversity of grounds and moulds doth to agriculture, and
the knowledge of the diversity of complexions and constitutions doth to the physician; except we mean to follow the
indiscretion of empirics, which minister the same medicines
to all patients.

Another article of this knowledge is the inquiry touching
the affections; for as in medicining of the body it is in order
first to know the divers complexions and constitutions, secondly the diseases, and lastly the cures; so in medicining
of the mind, after knowledge of the divers characters of
men's natures, it followeth in order to know the diseases
and infirmities of the mind, which are no other than the
perturbations and distempers of the affections. For as the
ancient politiques in popular estates were wont to compare
the people to the sea and the orators to the winds, because
as the sea would of itself be calm and quiet if the winds
did not move and trouble it, so the people would be peaceable and tractable if the seditious orators did not set them
in working and agitation; so it may be fitly said, that the
mind in the nature thereof would be temperate and stayed,
if the affections, as winds, did not put it into tumult and
perturbation. And here again I find strange, as before, that
Aristotle should have written divers volumes of Ethics and
never handled the affections, which is the principal subject
thereof; and yet in his Rhetorics, where they are considered
but collaterally and in a second degree (*as they may be
moved by speech*), he findeth place for them, and handleth
them well for the quantity; but where their true place is, he
pretermitteth them. For it is not his disputations about pleasure and pain that can satisfy this inquiry, no more than he
that should generally handle the nature of light can be said
to handle the nature of colours; for pleasure and pain are to
the particular affections as light is to particular colours.

Better travails I suppose had the Stoics taken in this argument, as far as I can gather by that which we have at second hand: but yet it is like it was after their manner, rather in subtilty of definitions (which in a subject of this nature are but curiosities) than in active and ample descriptions and observations. So likewise I find some particular writings of an elegant nature touching some of the affections; as of *anger,* of *comfort upon adverse accidents,* of *tenderness of countenance,* and other. But the poets and writers of histories are the best doctors of this knowledge; where we may find painted forth with great life, how affections are kindled and incited; and how pacified and refrained; and how again contained from act and further degree; how they disclose themselves, how they work, how they vary, how they gather and fortify, how they are inwrapped one within another, and how they do fight and encounter one with another, and other the like particularities: amongst the which this last is of special use in moral and civil matters; how (I say) to set affection against affection, and to master one by another; even as we use to hunt beast with beast and fly bird with bird, which otherwise percase we could not so easily recover: upon which foundation is erected that excellent use of *præmium* [*reward] and *pœna* [*punishment], whereby civil states consist; employing the predominant affections of *fear* and *hope,* for the suppressing and bridling the rest. For as in the government of states it is sometimes necessary to bridle one faction with another, so it is in the government within.

Now come we to those points which are within our own command, and have force and operation upon the mind to affect the will and appetite and to alter manners: wherein they ought to have handled *custom, exercise, habit, education, example, imitation, emulation, company, friends, praise, reproof, exhortation, fame, laws, books, studies:* these as they have determinate use in moralities, from these the mind suffereth, and of these are such receipts and regiments compounded and described, as may seem to recover or preserve the health and good estate of the mind, as far as pertaineth to human medicine: of which number we will visit upon some one or two as an example of the rest, because it were too long to prosecute all; and therefore we do resume Custom and Habit to speak of.

The opinion of Aristotle seemeth to me a negligent opinion, that of those things which consist by nature nothing can be changed by custom; using for example, that if a stone be thrown ten thousand times up, it will not learn to ascend; and that by often seeing or hearing, we do not learn to see or hear the better. For though this principle be true in things wherein nature is *peremptory*, (the reason whereof we cannot now stand to discuss,) yet it is otherwise in things wherein nature admitteth *a latitude*. For he might see that a strait glove will come more easily on with use, and that a wand will by use bend otherwise than it grew, and that by use of the voice we speak louder and stronger, and that by use of enduring heat or cold we endure it the better, and the like: which later sort have a nearer resemblance unto that subject of manners he handleth than those instances which he allegeth. But allowing his conclusion, *that virtues and vices consist in habit*, he ought so much the more to have taught the manner of superinducing that habit: for there be many precepts of the wise ordering the exercises of the mind, as there is of ordering the exercises of the body; whereof we will recite a few.

The first shall be, that we beware we take not at the first either too *high* a strain or too *weak*: for if too high, in a diffident nature you discourage; in a confident nature you breed an opinion of facility, and so a sloth; and in all natures you breed a further expectation than can hold out, and so an insatisfaction on the end: if too weak of the other side, you may not look to perform and overcome any great task.

Another precept is, to practise all things chiefly at two several times, the one when the mind is best disposed, the other when it is worst disposed; that by the one you may gain a great step, by the other you may work out the knots and stonds of the mind, and make the middle times the more easy and pleasant.

Another precept is, that which Aristotle mentioneth by

the way, which is to bear ever towards the contrary extreme of that whereunto we are by nature inclined: like unto the rowing against the stream, or making a wand straight by bending him contrary to his natural crookedness.

Another precept is, that the mind is brought to any thing better, and with more sweetness and happiness, if that whereunto you pretend be not first in the intention, but *tanquam aliud agendo* [*as if while doing something else], because of the natural hatred of the mind against necessity and constraint. Many other axioms there are touching the managing of *Exercise* and *Custom;* which being so conducted, doth prove indeed another nature; but being governed by chance, doth commonly prove but an ape of nature, and bringeth forth that which is lame and counterfeit.

So if we should handle *books* and *studies,* and what influence and operation they have upon manners, are there not divers precepts of great caution and direction appertaining thereunto? Did not one of the fathers in great indignation call Poesy *vinum dæmonum* [*the wine of demons], because it increaseth temptations, perturbations, and vain opinions? Is not the opinion of Aristotle worthy to be regarded, wherein he saith that young men are no fit auditors of moral philosophy, because they are not settled from the boiling heat of their affections, nor attempered with time and experience? And doth it not hereof come, that those excellent books and discourses of the ancient writers (whereby they have persuaded unto virtue most effectually, by representing her in state and majesty, and popular opinions against virtue in their parasites' coats, fit to be scorned and derided,) are of so little effect towards honesty of life, because they are not read and revolved by men in their mature and settled years, but confined almost to boys and beginners? But is it not true also, that much less young men are fit auditors of matters of policy, till they have been throughly seasoned in religion and morality; lest their judgments be corrupted, and made apt to think that there are no true differences of things, but according to utility and fortune; as the verse describes it, *Prosperum et* *felix scelus virtus vocatur;* [a crime that is successful is called a virtue;] and again, *Ille crucem pretium sceleris tulit, hic diadema;* [the same crime is rewarded in one man with a gibbet and in another with a crown;] which the poets do speak satirically, and in indignation on virtue's behalf; but books of policy do speak it seriously and positively; for so it pleaseth Machiavel to say, *that if Cæsar had been overthrown he would have been more odious than ever was Catiline;* as if there had been no difference but in fortune, between a very fury of lust and blood, and the most excellent spirit (his ambition reserved) of the world? Again, is there not a caution likewise to be given of the doctrines of moralities themselves (some kinds of them,) lest they make men too precise, arrogant, incompatible; as Cicero saith of Cato, *In Marco Catone hæc bona quæ videmus divina et egregia, ipsius scitote esse propria; quæ nonnunquam requirimus, ea sunt omnia non a naturâ, sed a magistro:* [his excellencies were his own, his defects came from the school-master]? Many other axioms and advices there are touching those proprieties and effects which studies do infuse and instil into manners. And so likewise is there touching the use of all those other points, of company, fame, laws, and the rest, which we recited in the beginning in the doctrine of morality.

But there is a kind of Culture of the Mind that seemeth yet more accurate and elaborate than the rest, and is built upon this ground; that the minds of all men are at some times in a state more perfect, and at other times in a state more depraved. The purpose therefore of this practice is to fix and cherish the good hours of the mind, and to obliterate and take forth the evil. The fixing of the good hath been practised by two means; vows or constant resolutions; and observances or exercises; which are not to be regarded so much in themselves, as because they keep the mind in continual obedience. The obliteration of the evil hath been practised by two means; some kind of redemption or expiation of that which is past; and an inception or account *de novo* [*beginning anew] for the time to come. But this part seemeth sacred and religious, and justly; for all good Moral Philosophy (as was said) is but an handmaid to religion.

Wherefore we will conclude with that last point which is of all other means the most compendious and summary, and again the most noble and effectual, to the reducing of the mind unto virtue and good estate; which is the electing and propounding unto a man's self good and virtuous ends of his life, such as may be in a reasonable sort within his compass to attain. For if these two things be supposed, that a man set before him honest and good ends, and again that he be resolute, constant, and true unto them, it will follow that he shall mould himself into all virtue at once. And this is indeed like the work of nature; whereas the other course is like the work of the hand. For as when a carver makes an image, he shapes only that part whereupon he worketh; as if he be upon the face, that part which shall be the body is but a rude stone still, till such times as he comes to it; but contrariwise when nature makes a flower or living creature, she formeth rudiments of all the parts at one time; so in obtaining virtue by *habit*, while a man practiseth temperance, he doth not profit much to fortitude, nor the like; but when he dedicateth and applieth himself to *good ends*, look what virtue soever the pursuit and passage towards those ends doth commend unto him, he is invested of a precedent disposition to conform himself thereunto; which state of mind Aristotle doth excellently express himself, that it ought not to be called *virtuous*, but *divine*: his words are these: *Immanitati autem consentaneum est opponere eam, quæ supra humanitatem est, heroicam sive divinam virtutem:* and a little after, *Nam ut feræ neque vitium neque virtus est, sic neque Dei: sed hic quidem status altius quiddam virtute est, ille aliud quiddam a vitio:* [that which answers to the brutal degree of vice is the heroical or divine degree of virtue. . . . For as neither virtue nor vice can be predicated of a brute, so neither can it of a God: the divine condition being something higher than virtue, the brutal something different from vice]. And therefore we may see what celsitude[55] of honour Plinius Secundus attributeth to Trajan in his funeral oration, where he said, *that men needed to make no other prayers to the gods, but that they would continue as good lords to them as Trajan had been;* as if he had not been only an imitation of divine nature, but a pattern of it. But these be heathen and profane passages, having but a shadow of that divine state of mind which religion and the holy faith doth conduct men unto, by imprinting upon their souls Charity, which is excellently called the bond of Perfection, because it comprehendeth and fasteneth all virtues together. And as it is elegantly said by Menander of vain love, which is but a false imitation of divine love, *Amor melior sophista lævo ad humanam vitam,* that love teacheth a man to carry himself better than the sophist or preceptor, which he calleth *left-handed,* because with all his rules and preceptions he cannot form a man so *dexterously,* nor with that facility to prize himself and govern himself, as love can do; so certainly if a man's mind be truly inflamed with charity, it doth work him suddenly into greater perfection than all the doctrine of morality can do, which is but a sophist in comparison of the other. Nay further, as Xenophon observed truly that all other affections, though they raise the mind, yet they do it by distorting and uncomeliness of ecstasies or excesses; but only love doth exalt the mind, and nevertheless at the same instant doth settle and compose it; so in all other excellencies, though they advance nature, yet they are subject to excess; only charity admitteth no excess; for so we see, aspiring to be like God in power, the angels transgressed and fell; *Ascendam, et ero similis Altissimo;* [I will ascend and be like unto the Highest:] by aspiring to be like God in knowledge, man transgressed and fell; *Eritis sicut Dii, scientes bonum et malum;* [ye shall be as Gods, knowing good and evil;] but by aspiring to a similitude of God in goodness or love, neither man nor angel ever transgressed or shall transgress. For unto that imitation we are called: *Diligite inimicos vestros, benefacite eis qui oderunt vos, et orate pro persequentibus et calumniantibus vos, ut sitis filii Patris vestri qui in cœlis, qui solem suum oriri facit super bonos et malos, et pluit super justos et injustos;* [love your enemies, do good to them that hate you, and pray for them which despitefully use you and persecute you; that ye may be the children of your Father which is in Heaven, who maketh his sun to rise on the evil and on the good, and sendeth rain on the just and on the unjust]. So in the first platform of the divine nature itself, the heathen religion speaketh thus, *Optimus Maximus,* [Best and Greatest:] and the sacred Scriptures thus, *Misericordia ejus super omnia opera ejus,* [his mercy is over all his works].

Wherefore I do conclude this part of moral knowledge, concerning the Culture and Regiment of the Mind; wherein if any man, considering the parts thereof which I have enumerated, do judge that my labour is but to collect into an Art or Science that which hath been pretermitted by others as matter of common sense and experience, he judgeth well. But as Philocrates sported with Demosthenes, *You may not marvel (Athenians,) that Demosthenes and I do differ, for he drinketh water, and I drink wine;* and like as we read of an ancient parable of *the two gates of sleep,*

> Sunt geminæ somni portæ: quarum altera fertur
> Cornea, qua veris facilis datur exitus umbris:
> Altera candenti perfecta nitens elephanto,
> Sed falsa ad cœlum mittunt insomnia manes:

> [Two gates there are of sleep; of horn the one,
> By which the true shades pass; of ivory
> Burnished and white the other, but through it
> Into the upper world false dreams are sent:]

so if we put on sobriety and attention, we shall find it a sure maxim in knowledge, that the more pleasant liquor (*of wine*) is the more vaporous, and the braver gate (*of ivory*) sendeth forth the falser dreams.

But we have now concluded *that general part of Human Philosophy, which contemplateth man segregate, and as he consisteth of body and spirit.* Wherein we may further note, that there seemeth to be a relation or conformity between the good of the mind and the good of the body. For as we divided the good of the body into *health, beauty, strength,* and *pleasure;* so the good of the mind inquired in rational and moral knowledges, tendeth to this, to make the mind *sound,* and without perturbation; *beautiful,* and graced with decency; and *strong* and *agile* for all duties of life. These three, as in the body so in the mind, seldom meet, and commonly sever. For it is easy to observe that many have strength of wit and courage, but have neither health from perturbations, nor any beauty or decency in their doings: some again have an elegancy and fineness of carriage, which have neither soundness of honesty, nor substance of sufficiency: and some again have honest and reformed minds, that can neither become themselves nor manage business: and sometimes two of them meet, and rarely all three. As for pleasure, we have likewise determined that the mind ought not to be reduced to stupid, but to retain pleasure; confined rather in the subject of it, than in the strength and vigour of it.

Civil Knowledge is conversant about a subject which of all others is most immersed in matter, and hardliest reduced to axiom. Nevertheless, as Cato the censor said, *That the Romans were like sheep, for that a man might better drive a flock of them, than one of them; for in a flock, if you could get but some few go right, the rest would follow:* so in that respect moral philosophy is more difficile than policy. Again, moral philosophy propoundeth to itself the framing of internal goodness; but civil knowledge requireth only an external goodness; for that as to society sufficeth; and therefore it cometh oft to pass that there be evil times in good governments: for so we find in the holy story, when the kings were good, yet it is added, *Sed adhuc populus non direxerat cor suum ad Dominum Deum patrum suorum;* [but as yet the people had not turned their hearts towards the Lord God of their fathers]. Again, States, as great engines, move slowly, and are not so soon put out of frame: for as in Egypt the seven good years sustained the seven bad, so governments for a time well grounded do bear out errors following: but the resolution of particular persons is more suddenly subverted. These respects do somewhat qualify the extreme difficulty of civil knowledge.

This knowledge hath three parts, according to the three summary actions of society; which are Conversation, Negotiation, and Government. For man seeketh in society comfort, use, and protection: and they be three wisdoms of divers natures, which do often sever; wisdom of the behaviour, wisdom of business, and wisdom of state.

The wisdom of Conversation ought not to be over much affected, but much less despised; for it hath not only an honour in itself, but an influence also into business and government. The poet saith,

Nec vultu destrue verba tuo:

a man may destroy the force of his words with his countenance: so may he of his deeds, saith Cicero; recommending to his brother affability and easy access; *Nil interest habere ostium apertum, vultum clausum;* it is nothing won to admit men with an open door, and to receive them with a shut and reserved countenance. So we see Atticus, before the first interview between Cæsar and Cicero, the war depending, did seriously advise Cicero touching the composing and ordering of his countenance and gesture. And if the government of the countenance be of such effect, much more is that of the speech, and other carriage appertaining to conversation; the true model whereof seemeth to me well expressed by Livy, though not meant for this purpose; *Ne aut arrogans videar, aut obnoxius; quorum alterum est alienæ libertatis obliti, alterum suæ:* the sum of behaviour is to retain a man's own dignity, without intruding upon the liberty of others. On the other side, if behaviour and outward carriage be intended too much, first it may pass into affection,[56] and then *quid deformius quam scenam in vitam transferre,* [what more unseemly than to be always playing a part;] to act a man's life? But although it proceed not to that extreme, yet it consumeth time, and employeth the mind too much. And therefore as we use to advise

young students from company keeping, by saying, *Amici
fures temporis*, [friends are thieves of time;] so certainly the
intending of the discretion of behaviour is a great thief of
meditation. Again, such as are accomplished in that honor
of urbanity please themselves in name, and seldom aspire
to higher virtue; whereas those that have defect in it do
seek comeliness by reputation: for where reputation is, almost every thing becometh; but where that is not, it must
be supplied by *puntos* [*small points] and compliments.
Again, there is no greater impediment of action than an
over-curious observance of decency, and the guide of decency, which is time and season. For as Salomon sayeth,
*Qui respicit ad ventos, non seminat; et qui respicit ad
nubes, non metet;* [he that looketh to the winds doth not
sow, and he that regardeth the clouds shall not reap:] a
man must make his opportunity, as oft as find it. To conclude; Behaviour seemeth to me as a garment of the mind,
and to have the conditions of a garment. For it ought to be
made in fashion; it ought not to be too curious; it ought to
be shaped so as to set forth any good making of the mind,
and hide any deformity; and above all, it ought not to be
too strait or restrained for exercise or motion. But this part
of civil knowledge hath been elegantly handled, and therefore I cannot report it for deficient.

The wisdom touching Negotiation or Business hath not
been hitherto collected into writing, to the great derogation
of learning and the professors of learning. For from this
root springeth chiefly that note or opinion, which by us is
expressed in adage to this effect, that there is no great concurrence between learning and wisdom. For of the three
wisdoms which we have set down to pertain to civil life, for
wisdom of Behaviour, it is by learned men for the most
part despised, as an inferior to virtue and an enemy to
meditation; for wisdom of Government, they acquit themselves well when they are called to it, but that happeneth
to few; but for the wisdom of Business, wherein man's life
is most conversant, there be no books of it, except some few
scattered advertisements, that have no proportion to the

magnitude of this subject. For if books were written of this as the other, I doubt not but learned men with mean experience would far excel men of long experience without learning, and outshoot them in their own bow.

Neither needeth it at all to be doubted that this knowledge should be so variable as it falleth not under precept; for it is much less infinite than science of Government, which we see is laboured and in some part reduced. Of this wisdom it seemeth some of the ancient Romans in the saddest and wisest times were professors; for Cicero reporteth that it was then in use for senators that had name and opinion for general wise men, as Coruncanius, Curius, Lælius, and many others, to walk at certain hours in the Place,[57] and to give audience to those that would use their advice; and that the particular citizens would resort unto them, and consult with them of the marriage of a daughter, or of the employing of a son, or of a purchase or bargain, or of an accusation, and every other occasion incident to man's life; so as there is a wisdom of counsel and advice even in private causes, arising out of an universal insight into the affairs of the world; which is used indeed upon particular cases propounded, but is gathered by general observation of causes of like nature. For so we see in the book which Q. Cicero writeth to his brother *De petitione consulatus* [*Of Seeking the Consulship] (being the only book of business that I know written by the ancients), although it concerned a particular action then on foot, yet the substance thereof consisteth of many wise and politic axioms, which contain not a temporary but a perpetual direction in the case of popular elections. But chiefly we may see in those aphorisms which have place amongst divine writings, composed by Salomon the king, of whom the Scriptures testify that his heart was as the sands of the sea, encompassing the world and all worldly matters; we see, I say, not a few profound and excellent cautions, precepts, positions, extending to much variety of occasions; whereupon we will stay awhile, offering to consideration some number of examples.

Sed et cunctis sermonibus qui dicuntur ne accommodes

*aurem tuam, ne forte audias servum tuum maledicentem
tibi.* [Hearken not unto all words that are spoken, lest thou
hear thy servant curse thee.] Here is concluded the provi-
dent stay of inquiry of that which we would be loth to find:
as it was judged great wisdom in Pompeius Magnus that he
burned Sertorius' papers unperused.

*Vir sapiens si cum stulto contenderit, sive irascatur sive
rideat, non inveniet requiem.* [A wise man if he contend
with a fool, whether he be angry or whether he laugh, shall
find no rest.] Here is described the great disadvantage
which a wise man hath in undertaking a lighter person than
himself; which is such an engagement as whether a man
turn the matter to jest, or turn it to heat, or howsoever he
change copy, he can no ways quit himself well of it.

*Qui delicatè a pueritia nutrit servum suum, postea sentiet
eum contumacem.* [He that delicately bringeth up his servant from a child shall have him become froward at the
length.] Here is signified, that if a man begin too high a
pitch in his favours, it doth commonly end in unkindness
and unthankfulness.

*Vidisti virum velocem in opere suo? Coram regibus stabit,
nec erit inter ignobiles.* [Seest thou a man that is quick in
his business? He shall stand before kings; his place shall
not be among mean men.] Here is observed that, of all virtues for rising to honour, quickness of dispatch is the best;
for superiors many times love not to have those they employ too deep or too sufficient, but ready and diligent.

*Vidi cunctus viventes qui ambulant sub sole, cum adole-
scente secundo qui consurgit pro eo.* [I beheld all the living
which walk under the sun, with the second youth that shall
stand in his place.] Here is expressed that which was noted
by Sylla first, and after him by Tiberius: *Plures adorant
solem orientem quam occidentem vel meridianum,* [there
be more that worship the rising sun than the sun setting or
at mid-day].

*Si spiritus potestatem habentis ascenderit super te, locum
tuum ne dimiseris; quia curatio faciet cessare peccata maxima.* [If the spirit of the ruler rise up against thee, leave not

thy place; for observance will remove great offences.] Here caution is given that upon displeasure, retiring is of all courses the unfittest; for a man leaveth things at worst, and depriveth himself of means to make them better.

Erat civitas parva, et pauci in ea viri: venit contra eam rex magnus, et vadavit eam, intruxitque munitiones per gyrum, et perfecta est obsidio: inventusque est in ea vir pauper et sapiens, et liberavit eam per sapientiam suam; et nullus deinceps recordatus est hominis illius pauperis. [There was a little city and few men within it; and there came a great king against it and besieged it and raised great bulwarks round about it: and there was found in it a poor wise man, and he by his wisdom delivered the city; yet no man remembered that same poor man.] Here the corruption of states is set forth, that esteem not virtue or merit longer than they have use of it.

Mollis responsio frangit iram. [A soft answer defeateth wrath.] Here is noted that silence or rough answer exasperateth; but an answer present and temperate pacifieth.

Iter pigrorum quasi sepes spinarum. [The way of the slothful is as an hedge of thorns.] Here is lively represented how laborious sloth proveth in the end; for when things are deferred till the last instant and nothing prepared beforehand, every step findeth a brier or an impediment, which catcheth or stoppeth.

Melior est finis orationis quam principium. [Better is the end of a speech than the beginning thereof.] Here is taxed the vanity of formal speakers, that study more about prefaces and inducements than upon the conclusions and issues of speech.

Qui cognoscit in judicio faciem, non bene facit; iste et pro buccella panis deseret veritatem. [He that respecteth persons in judgment doth not well; even for a piece of bread will that man depart from the truth.] Here is noted, that a judge were better be a briber than a respecter of persons; for a corrupt judge offendeth not so lightly[58] as a facile.

Vir pauper calumnians pauperes similis est imbri vehementi, in quo paratur fames. [A poor man that beareth witness against the poor is like a sweeping rain which leaveth no food.] Here is expressed the extremity of necessitous extortions, figured in the ancient fable of the full and hungry horse-leech.[59]

Fons turbatus pede, et vena corrupta, est justus cadens coram impio. [A righteous man falling down before the wicked is as a troubled fountain and a corrupt spring.] Here is noted, that one judicial and exemplar iniquity in the face of the world doth trouble the fountains of justice more than many particular injuries passed over by connivance.

Qui subtrahit aliquid a patre et a matre, et dicit hoc non esse peccatum, particeps est homicidii. [Whoso robbeth his father and his mother, and saith it is no transgression, is the companion of a destroyer.] Here is noted, that whereas men in wronging their best friends use to extenuate their fault, as if they might presume or be bold upon them, it doth contrariwise indeed aggravate their fault, and turneth it from injury to impiety.

Noli esse amicus homini iracundo, nec ambulato cum homine furioso. [Make no friendship with an angry man, neither go with a furious man.] Here caution is given, that in the election of our friends we do principally avoid those which are impatient, as those that will espouse us to many factions and quarrels.

Qui conturbat domum suam, possidebit ventum. [He that troubleth his own house shall inherit the wind.] Here is noted, that in domestical separations and breaches men do promise to themselves quieting of their mind and contentment; but still they are deceived of their expectation, and it turneth to wind.

Filius sapiens lætificat patrem: filius vero stultus mœstitia est matri suæ. [A wise son maketh a glad father, but a foolish son is the heaviness of his mother.] Here is distinguished, that fathers have most comfort of the good proof of their sons; but mothers have most discomfort of their ill proof, because women have little discerning of virtue, but of fortune.

Qui celat delictum, quærit amicitiam; sed qui altero sermone repetit, separat fœderatos. [He that covereth a transgression seeketh love, but he that repeateth a matter separateth very friends.] Here caution is given, that reconcilement is better managed by an *amnesty*, and passing over that which is past, than by apologies and excusations.

In omni opere boni erit abundantia; ubi autem verba sunt plurima, ibi frequenter egestas. [In every good work there shall be abundance, but where there are many words there is penury.] Here is noted that words and discourse abound most where there is idleness and want.

Primus in sua causa justus; sed venit altera pars, et inquirit in eum. [He that is first in his own cause seemeth just; but the other party cometh and searcheth him.] Here is observed, that in all causes the first tale possesseth much; in sort that the prejudice thereby wrought will be hardly removed, except some abuse or falsity in the information be detected.

Verba bilinguis quasi simplicia, et ipsa perveniunt ad interiora ventris. [The words of the double-tongued man which seem artless are they that go down to the innermost parts of the belly.] Here is distinguished, that flattery and insinuation which seemeth set and artificial sinketh not far; but that entereth deep which hath shew of nature, liberty, and simplicity.

Qui erudit derisorem, ipse sibi injuriam facit; et qui arguit impium, sibi maculam generat. [He that reproveth a scorner doth himself wrong, and he that rebuketh a wicked man getteth himself a blot.] Here caution is given how we tender reprehension to arrogant and scornful natures, whose manner is to esteem it for contumely, and accordingly to return it.

Da sapienti occasionem, et addetur ei sapientia. [Give opportunity to a wise man, and he will be yet wiser.] Here is distinguished the wisdom brought into habit, and that which is but verbal and swimming only in conceit; for the one upon the occasion presented is quickened and redoubled, the other is amazed and confused.

*Quomodo in equis resplendent vultus prospicientium, sic
corda hominum manifesta sunt prudentibus.* [As the face of
one that looketh upon the water is reflected therein, so the
hearts of men are manifest unto the wise.] Here the mind
of a wise man is compared to a glass, wherein the images of
all diversity of natures and customs are represented; from
which representation proceedeth that application,

Qui sapit, innumeris moribus aptus erit:

[a wise man will know how to apply himself to all sorts of
characters].

Thus have I staid somewhat longer upon these sentences
politic of Salomon than is agreeable to the proportion of an
example; led with a desire to give authority to this part of
knowledge, which I noted as deficient, by so excellent a
precedent; and have also attended them with brief observations, such as to my understanding offer no violence to the
sense, though I know they may be applied to a more divine
use: but it is allowed even in divinity, that some interpretations, yea and some writings, have more of the Eagle than
others. But taking them as instructions for life, they might
have received large discourse, if I would have broken them
and illustrated them by deducements and examples.

Neither was this in use only with the Hebrews; but it is
generally to be found in the wisdom of the more ancient
times, that as men found out any observation that they
thought was good for life, they would gather it and express
it in parable or aphorism or fable. But for fables, they were
vicegerents and supplies where examples failed: now that
the times abound with history, the aim is better when the
mark is alive. And therefore the form of writing which of
all others is fittest for this variable argument of negotiation
and occasions is that which Machiavel chose wisely and
aptly for government; namely, *discourse upon histories or
examples.* For knowledge drawn freshly and in our view
out of particulars, knoweth the way best to particulars
again. And it hath much greater life for practice when the
discourse attendeth upon the example, than when the ex-

ample attendeth upon the discourse. For this is no point of order, as it seemeth at first, but of substance. For when the example is the ground, being set down in an history at large, it is set down with all circumstances, which may sometimes control the discourse thereupon made and sometimes supply it, as a very pattern for action; whereas the examples alleged for the discourse's sake are cited succinctly and without particularity, and carry a servile aspect toward the discourse which they are brought in to make good.

But this difference is not amiss to be remembered, that as history of Times is the best ground for discourse of government, such as Machiavel handleth, so histories of Lives is the most proper for discourse of business, as more conversant in private actions. Nay there is a ground of discourse for this purpose fitter than them both, which is *discourse upon letters*, such as are wise and weighty, as many are of Cicero *ad Atticum* and others. For letters have a great and more particular representation of business than either Chronicles or Lives. Thus have we spoken both of the matter and form of this part of civil knowledge touching Negotiation, which we note to be deficient.

But yet there is another part of this part, which differeth as much from that whereof we have spoken as *sapere* and *sibi sapere*, [*to be wise* and *to be wise for oneself*,] the one moving as it were to the circumference, the other to the centre. For there is a wisdom of counsel, and again there is a wisdom of pressing a man's own fortune; and they do sometimes meet, and often sever. For many are wise in their own ways that are weak for government or counsel; like ants, which is a wise creature for itself, but very hurtful for the garden. This wisdom the Romans did take much knowledge of: *Nam pol sapiens* (saith the comical poet) *fingit fortunam sibi*, [the wise man fashions his fortune for himself;] and it grew to an adage, *Faber quisque fortunæ propriæ*, [every man has tools to make his own fortune with,] and Livy attributeth it to Cato the first, *In hoc viro tanta vis animi et ingenii inerat, ut quocunque loco natus esset, sibi ipse fortunam facturus videretur,* [such was his force of mind and genius that in whatever state he had been born he would have made himself a fortune].

This conceit or position if it be too much declared and professed, hath been thought a thing impolitic and unlucky; as was observed in Timotheus the Athenian; who having done many great services to the estate in his government, and giving an account thereof to the people as the manner was, did conclude every particular with this clause, and in this fortune had no part. And it came so to pass that he never prospered in any thing he took in hand afterward: for this is too high and too arrogant, savouring of that which Ezekiel saith of Pharaoh, *Dicis, Fluvius est meus, et ego feci memet ipsum,* [thou sayest the river is mine, and I made myself;] or of that which another prophet speaketh, that men offer sacrifices to their nets and snares; and that which the poet expresseth,

> Dextra mihi Deus, et telum quod missile libro,
> Nunc adsint!

[my right hand and my spear are the God I trust in]. For these confidences were ever unhallowed, and unblessed. And therefore those that were great politiques indeed ever ascribed their successes to their felicity, and not to their skill or virtue. For so Sylla surnamed himself *Felix,* not *Magnus,* [the Fortunate, not the Great]. So Cæsar said to the master of the ship, *Cæsarem portas et fortunam ejus,* [you carry Cæsar and his fortune].

But yet nevertheless these positions, *Faber quisque fortunæ suæ; Sapiens dominabitur astris; Invia virtuti nulla est via;* [every man should be the maker of his own fortune; the wise man will command his stars; nothing impossible to virtue:] and the like, being taken and used as spurs to industry, and not as stirrups to insolency, rather for resolution than for presumption or outward declaration, have been ever thought sound and good, and are no question imprinted in the greatest minds; who are so sensible of this opinion as they can scarce contain it within. As we see in

Augustus Cæsar, (who was rather diverse from his uncle[60] than inferior in virtue,) how when he died, he desired his friends about him to give him a *Plaudite;* as if he were conscient to himself that he had played his part well upon the stage. This part of knowledge we do report also as deficient: not but that it is practised too much, but it hath not been reduced to writing. And therefore lest it should seem to any that it is not comprehensible by axiom, it is requisite, as we did in the former, that we set down some heads or passages of it.

Faber For-tunæ, sive de Ambitu vitæ

Wherein it may appear at the first a new and unwonted argument to teach men how to raise and make their fortune; a doctrine wherein every man perchance will be ready to yield himself a disciple, till he see the difficulty: for Fortune layeth as heavy impositions as Virtue; and it is as hard and severe a thing to be a true politique, as to be truly moral. But the handling hereof concerneth learning greatly, both in honour and in substance: in honour, because pragmatical men may not go away with an opinion that learning is like a lark, that can mount and sing and please herself, and nothing else; but may know that she holdeth as well of the hawk, that can soar aloft, and can also descend and strike upon the prey: in substance, because it is the perfect law of inquiry of truth, *that nothing be in the globe of matter, which should not be likewise in the globe of crystal, or form;* that is that there be not any thing in being and action, which should not be drawn and collected into contemplation and doctrine. Neither doth learning admire or esteem of this architecture of fortune otherwise than as of an inferior work: for no man's fortune can be an end worthy of his being, and many times the worthiest men do abandon their fortune willingly for better respects: but nevertheless fortune as an organ of virtue and merit deserveth the consideration.

First therefore, the precept which I conceive to be most summary towards the prevailing in fortune, is to obtain that window which Momus did require, who seeing in the frame of man's heart such angles and recesses, found fault

there was not a window to look into them; that is, to procure good informations of particulars touching persons,
their natures, their desires and ends, their customs and
fashions, their helps and advantages, and whereby they
chiefly stand; so again their weaknesses and disadvantages,
and where they lie most open and obnoxious; their friends,
factions, dependances; and again their opposites, enviers,
competitors, their moods and times, *Sola viri molles aditus
et tempora noras* [*You alone have known what way, what
hour the man would yield to soft persuasion]; their principles, rules, and observations, and the like: and this not only
of persons, but of actions; what are on foot from time to
time, and how they are conducted, favoured, opposed; and
how they import, and the like. For the knowledge of present actions is not only material in itself, but without it also
the knowledge of persons is very erroneous: for men change
with the actions; and whiles they are in pursuit they are
one, and when they return to their nature they are another.
These informations of particulars touching persons and actions are as the minor propositions in every active syllogism; for no excellency of observations (which are as the
major propositions) can suffice to ground a conclusion, if
there be error and mistaking in the minors.

That this knowledge is possible, Salomon is our surety;
who saith, *Consilium in corde viri tanquam aqua profunda;
sed vir prudens exhauriet illud,* [counsel in the heart of man
is like deep water; but a man of understanding will draw it
out]. And although the knowledge itself falleth not under
precept, because it is of individuals, yet the instructions for
the obtaining of it may.

We will begin therefore with this precept, according to
the ancient opinion, that the sinews of wisdom are slowness
of belief and distrust; that more trust be given to countenances and deeds than to words; and in words, rather to
sudden passages and surprised words, than to set and purposed words. Neither let that be feared which is said, *fronti
nulla fides,* [no trusting to the face:] which is meant of a
general outward behaviour, and not of the private and sub-

tile motions and labours of the countenance and gesture; which as Q. Cicero elegantly saith, is *animi janua*, the gate of the mind. None more close than Tiberius, and yet Tacitus saith of Gallus, *Etenim vultu offensionem conjectaverat*, [he had seen displeasure in his countenance]. So again, noting the differing character and manner of his commending Germanicus and Drusus in the senate, he saith touching his fashion wherein he carried his speech of Germanicus, thus; *Magis in speciem adornatis verbis, quam ut penitus sentire videretur*, [it was in words too laboured and specious to be taken for what he really felt;] but of Drusus thus; *Paucioribus, sed intentior, et fida oratione*, [he said less, but more earnestly, and in a style of sincerity;] and in another place, speaking of his character of speech when he did any thing that was gracious and popular, he saith that in other things he was *velut eluctantium verborum*, [of a kind of struggling speech;] but then again, *solutius loquebatur quando subveniret*, [he spoke with more freedom when he was speaking in a man's favour]. So that there is no such artificer of dissimulation, nor no such commanded countenance *(vultus jussus)* that can sever from a feigned tale some of these fashions, either a more slight and careless fashion, or more set and formal, or more tedious and wandering, or coming from a man more drily and hardly.

Neither are *deeds* such assured pledges, as that they may be trusted without a judicious consideration of their magnitude and nature: *Fraus sibi in parvis fidem præstruit, ut majore emolumento fallat*, [it is a trick of treachery to win itself credit at the first by fidelity in small things, that being thereupon trusted in greater it may deceive with more advantage;] and the Italian[61] thinketh himself upon the point to be bought and sold, when he is better used than he was wont to be without manifest cause. For small favours, they do but lull men asleep, both as to caution and as to industry, and are as Demosthenes calleth them, *Alimenta socordiæ*, [sops to feed sloth]. So again we see how false the nature of some deeds are, in that particular which Mutianus practised upon Antonius Primus, upon that hollow and unfaithful reconcilement which was made between them;

whereupon Mutianus advanced many of the friends of Antonius: *simul amicis ejus præfecturas et tribunatus largitur,* [making them prefects and tribunes:] wherein under pretence to strengthen him, he did desolate him, and won from him his dependances.

As for *words,* (though they be like waters to physicians, full of flattery and uncertainty,) yet they are not to be despised, specially wth the advantage of passion and affection. For so we see Tiberius upon a stinging and incensing speech of Agrippina came a step forth of his dissimulation, when he said, *You are hurt because you do not reign;* of which Tacitus saith, *Audita hæc raram occulti pectoris vocem elicuere; correptamque Græco versu admonuit, ideo lædi quia non regnaret,* [these words drew from Tiberius the voice, so rarely heard, of his secret heart: he retorted upon her with a Greek verse, that she was hurt, &c.]. And therefore the poet doth elegantly call passions tortures, that urge men to confess their secrets:

> Vino tortus et ira.
> [*Tortured by wine and wrath.]

And experience sheweth, there are few men so true to themselves and so settled, but that, sometimes upon heat, sometimes upon bravery, sometimes upon kindness, sometimes upon trouble of mind and weakness, they open themselves; specially if they be put to it with a counter-dissimulation, according to the proverb of Spain, *Di mentira, y sacaras verdad, Tell a lie and find a truth.*

As for the knowing of men which is at second hand from reports; men's weaknesses and faults are best known from their enemies, their virtues and abilities from their friends, their customs and times from their servants, their conceits and opinions from their familiar friends with whom they discourse most. General fame is light, and the opinions conceived by superiors or equals are deceitful; for to such men are more masked: *Verior fama e domesticis emanat,* [the truer kind of report comes from those who see them at home].

But the soundest disclosing and expounding of men is by

their natures and ends; wherein the weakest sort of men are best interpreted by their natures, and the wisest by their ends. For it was both pleasantly and wisely said (though I think very untruly) by a nuncio of the pope, returning from a certain nation where he served as lieger; whose opinion being asked touching the appointment of one to go in his place, he wished that in any case they did not send one that was too wise; because no very wise man would ever imagine what they in that country were like to do. And certainly it is an error frequent for men to shoot over, and to suppose deeper ends and more compass reaches than are: the Italian proverb being elegant, and for the most part true:

> Di danari, di senno, e di fede,
> Cè nè manco che non credi:

There is commonly less money, less wisdom, and less good faith, than men do account upon.

But Princes upon a far other reason are best interpreted by their natures, and private persons by their ends; for princes being at the top of human desires, they have for the most part no particular ends whereto they aspire, by distance from which a man might take measure and scale of the rest of their actions and desires; which is one of the causes that maketh their hearts more inscrutable. Neither is it sufficient to inform ourselves in men's ends and natures of the variety of them only, but also of the predominancy, what humour reigneth most, and what end is principally sought. For so we see, when Tigellinus saw himself outstripped by Petronius Turpilianus in Nero's humours of pleasures, *metus ejus rimatur*, he wrought upon Nero's fears, whereby he brake the other's neck.

But to all this part of inquiry the most compendious way resteth in three things. The first, to have general acquaintance and inwardness with those which have general acquaintance and look most into the world; and specially according to the diversity of business and the diversity of persons, to have privacy and conversation with some one friend at least which is perfect and well intelligenced in every several kind. The second is to keep a good mediocrity in liberty of speech and secrecy; in most things liberty; secrecy where it importeth; for liberty of speech inviteth and provoketh liberty to be used again, and so bringeth much to a man's knowledge; and secrecy, on the other side, induceth trust and inwardness. The last is the reducing of a man's self to this watchful and serene habit, as to make account and purpose, in every conference and action, as well to observe as to act. For as Epictetus would have a philosopher in every particular action to say to himself, *Et hoc volo, et etiam institutum servare,* [I would do this and keep my course too;] so a politic man in every thing should say to himself, *Et hoc volo, ac etiam aliquid addiscere,* [I would do it and also learn something from it]. I have stayed the longer upon this precept of obtaining good information, because it is a main part by itself, which answereth to all the rest. But, above all things, caution must be taken that men have a good stay and hold of themselves, and that this much knowledge do not draw on much meddling, for nothing is more unfortunate than light and rash intermeddling in many matters; so that this variety of knowledge tendeth in conclusion but only to this, to make a better and freer choice of those actions which may concern us, and to conduct them with the less error and the more dexterity.

The second precept concerning this knowledge is, for men to take good information touching their own person, and well to understand themselves: knowing that, as St. James saith, though men look oft in a glass, yet they do suddenly forget themselves; wherein as the divine glass is the word of God, so the politic glass is the state of the world or times wherein we live; in the which we are to behold ourselves.

For men ought to take an unpartial view of their own abilities and virtues; and again of their wants and impediments; accounting these with the most, and those other with the least; and from this view and examination to frame the considerations following.

First, to consider how the constitution of their nature

sorteth with the general state of the times; which if they find agreeable and fit, then in all things to give themselves more scope and liberty; but if differing and dissonant, then in the whole course of their life to be more close, retired, and reserved: as we see in Tiberius, who was never seen at a play and came not into the senate in twelve of his last years; whereas Augustus Cæsar lived ever in men's eyes, which Tacitus observeth: *Alia Tiberio morum via*, [Tiberius's ways were different].

Secondly, to consider how their nature sorteth with professions and courses of life, and accordingly to make election, if they be free; and, if engaged, to make the departure at the first opportunity: as we see was done by duke Valentine, that was designed by his father to a sacerdotal profession, but quitted it soon after in regard of his parts and inclination; being such nevertheless, as a man cannot tell well whether they were worse for a prince or for a priest.

Thirdly, to consider how they sort with those whom they are like to have competitors and concurrents, and to take that course wherein there is most solitude, and themselves like to be most eminent: as Cæsar Julius did, who at first was an orator or pleader; but when he saw the excellency of Cicero, Hortensius, Catulus, and others, for eloquence, and saw there was no man of reputation for the wars but Pompeius, upon whom the state was forced to rely, he forsook his course begun toward a civil and popular greatness, and transferred his designs to a martial greatness.

Fourthly, in the choice of their friends and dependances, to proceed according to the composition of their own nature; as we may see in Cæsar, all whose friends and followers were men active and effectual, but not solemn or of reputation.

Fifthly, to take special heed how they guide themselves by examples, in thinking they can do as they see others do; whereas perhaps their natures and carriages are far differing; in which error it seemeth Pompey was, of whom Cicero saith, that he was wont often to say, *Sylla potuit, ego non potero?* [Sylla could do it, why not I?] wherein he was much abused, the natures and proceedings of himself and his example being the unlikest in the world; the one being fierce, violent, and pressing the fact; the other solemn, and full of majesty and circumstance, and therefore the less effectual.

But this precept touching the politic knowledge of ourselves hath many other branches whereupon we cannot insist.

Next to the well understanding and discerning of a man's self, there followeth the well opening and revealing a man's self; wherein we see nothing more usual than for the more able man to make the less shew. For there is a great advantage in the well setting forth of a man's virtues, fortunes, merits; and again in the artificial covering of a man's weaknesses, defects, disgraces; staying upon the one, sliding from the other; cherishing the one by circumstances, gracing the other by exposition, and the like: wherein we see what Tacitus saith of Mutianus, who was the greatest politique of his time, *Omnium quæ dixerat feceratque arte quâdam ostentator,* [having a certain art of displaying to advantage all he said and did;] which requireth indeed some art, lest it turn tedious and arrogant; but yet so as ostentation (though it be to the first degree of vanity) seemeth to me rather a vice in manners than in policy: for as it is said, *Audacter calumniare, semper aliquid hæret,* [slander boldly, there is ever some that sticks;] so, except it be in a ridiculous degree of deformity, *Audacter te vendita, semper aliquid hæret,* [put forward your own pretensions boldly—something always sticks]. For it will stick with the more ignorant and inferior sort of men, though men of wisdom and rank do smile at it and despise it; and yet the authority won with many doth countervail the disdain of a few. But if it be carried with decency and government, as with a natural, pleasant, and ingenious[62] fashion; or at times when it is mixed with some peril and unsafety, (as in military persons;) or at times when others are most envied; or with easy and careless passage to it and from it, without dwelling too long or being too serious; or with an equal freedom of taxing a man's self as well as gracing himself; or by occasion of repelling or

putting down others' injury or insolency; it doth greatly add
to reputation: and surely not a few solid natures, that want
this ventosity and cannot sail in the height of the winds,
are not without some prejudice and disadvantage by their
moderation.

But for these flourishes and enhancements of virtue, as
they are not perchance unnecessary, so it is at least necessary that virtue be not disvalued and imbased under the
just price; which is done in three manners: by offering and
obtruding a man's self; wherein men think he is rewarded,
when he is accepted: by doing too much; which will not
give that which is well done leave to settle, and in the end
induceth satiety: and by finding too soon the fruit of a man's
virtue, in commendation, applause, honour, favour; wherein
if a man be pleased with a little, let him hear what is truly
said, *Cave ne insuetus rebus majoribus videaris, si hæc te
res parva sicuti magna delectat,* [if he take so much delight
in a little thing, he will be thought unused to greater things].

But the covering of defects is of no less importance than
the valuing of good parts; which may be done likewise in
three manners; by Caution, by Colour, and by Confidence.
Caution is when men do ingeniously and discreetly avoid
to be put into those things for which they are not proper:
whereas contrariwise bold and unquiet spirits will thrust
themselves into matters without difference, and so publish
and proclaim all their wants. Colour is when men make a
way for themselves to have a construction made of their
faults or wants as proceeding from a better cause, or intended for some other purpose: for of the one it is well said,
Sæpe latet vitium proximitate boni, [a vice will often hide
itself under the shadow of a neighboring virtue;] and
therefore whatsoever want a man hath, he must see that he
pretend the virtue that shadoweth it; as if he be dull, he
must affect gravity; if a coward, mildness; and so the rest:
for the second, a man must frame some probable cause why
he should not do his best, and why he should dissemble his
abilities; and for that purpose must use to dissemble those
abilities which are notorious in him, to give colour that his

true wants are but industries and dissimulations. For Confidence, it is the last but the surest remedy; namely, to depress and seem to despise whatsover a man cannot attain; observing the good principle of the merchants, who endeavour to raise the price of their own commodities, and to beat down the price of others. But there is a confidence that passeth this other; which is, to face out a man's own defects, in seeming to conceive that he is best in those things wherein he is failing; and, to help that again, to seem on the other side that he hath least opinion of himself in those things wherein he is best: like as we shall see it commonly in poets, that if they shew their verses, and you except to any, they will say *that that line cost them more labour than any of the rest;* and presently will seem to disable and suspect rather some other line, which they know well enough to be the best in the number. But above all, in this righting and helping of a man's self in his own carriage, he must take heed he shew not himself dismantled and exposed to scorn and injury, by too much dulceness, goodness, and facility of nature, but shew some sparkles of liberty, spirit, and edge: which kind of fortified carriage, with a ready rescuing of a man's self from scorns, is sometimes of necessity imposed upon men by somewhat in their person of fortune; but it ever succeedeth with good felicity.

Another precept of this knowledge is, by all possible endeavour to frame the mind to be pliant and obedient to occasion; for nothing hindereth men's fortunes so much as this *Idem manebat neque idem decebat,* [continuing the same when the same is no longer fit:] men are where they were, when occasions turn: and therefore to Cato, whom Livy maketh such an architect of fortune, he addeth that he had *versatile ingenium,* [a wit that could turn well]. And thereof it cometh that these grave solemn wits, which must be like themselves and cannot make departures, have more dignity than felicity. But in some it is nature to be somewhat viscous and inwrapped, and not easy to turn. In some it is a conceit that is almost a nature, which is, that men can hardly make themselves believe that they ought to change their course, when they have found good by it in former experience. For Machiavel noteth wisely, how Fabius Maximus would have been temporizing still, according to his old bias, when the nature of the war was altered and required hot pursuit. In some other it is want of point and penetration in their judgment, that they do not discern when things have a period, but come in too late after the occasion; as Demosthenes compareth the people of Athens to country fellows when they play in a fence school, that if they have a blow, then they remove their weapon to that ward,[63] and not before. In some other it is a lothness to leese labours passed, and a conceit that they can bring about occasions to their ply; and yet in the end, when they see no other remedy, then they come to it with disadvantage; as Tarquinius, that gave for the third part of Sibylla's books the treble price, when he might at first have had all three for the simple. But from whatsoever root or cause this restiveness of mind proceedeth, it is a thing most prejudicial; and nothing is more politic than to make the wheels of our mind concentric and voluble with the wheels of fortune.

Another precept of this knowledge, which hath some affinity with that we last spake of, but with difference, is that which is well expressed, *Fatis accede Deisque,* [take the way which the Fates and the Gods offer;] that men do not only turn with the occasions but also run with the occasions, and not strain their credit or strength to over hard or extreme points, but choose in their actions that which is most passable: for this will preserve men from foil, not occupy them too much about one matter, win opinion of moderation, please the most, and make a shew of a perpetual felicity in all they undertake; which cannot but mightily increase reputation.

Another part of this knowledge seemeth to have some repugnancy with the former two, but not as I understand it; and it is that which Demosthenes uttereth in high terms; *Et quemadmodum receptum est, ut exercitum ducat imperator, sic et a cordatis viris res ipsæ ducendæ; ut quæ ipsis videntur, ea gerantur, et non ipsi eventus persequi cogantur;* [as the captain leads the army, so should wise men lead affairs; they should get that done which they think good to be done, and not be forced to follow at the heels of events]. For if we observe, we shall find two differing kinds of sufficiency in managing of business: some can make use of occasions aptly and dexterously, but plot little; some can urge and pursue their own plots well, but cannot accommodate nor take in; either of which is very unperfect without the other.

Another part of this knowledge is the observing a good mediocrity in the declaring or not declaring a man's self: for although depth of secrecy, and making way *qualis est via navis in mari,* [like the way of a ship through the water,] (which the French calleth *sourdes menées,* when men set things in work without opening themselves at all,) be sometimes both prosperous and admirable; yet many times *Dissimulatio errores parit qui dissimulatorem ipsum illaqueant,* [dissimulation breeds mistakes in which the dissembler himself is caught]. And therefore we see the greatest politiques have in a natural and free manner professed their desires, rather than been reserved and disguised in them. For so we see that Lucius Sylla made a kind of profession, *that he wished all men happy or unhappy as they stood his friends or enemies.* So Cæsar, when he went first into Gaul, made no scruple to profess *that he had rather be first in a village than second at Rome.* So again as soon as he had begun the war, we see what Cicero saith of him; *Alter* (meaning of Cæsar) *non recusat, sed quodammodo postulat, ut (ut est) sic appelletur tyrannus,* [he does not refuse, but in a manner demands, to be called what he is—tyrant]. So we may see in a letter of Cicero to Atticus, that Augustus Cæsar in his very entrance into affairs, when he was a dearling of the senate, yet in his harangues to the people would swear *Ita parentis honores consequi liceat,* [as I hope to attain my father's honours;] which was no less than the tyranny, save that, to help it he would stretch forth his hand towards a statua of Cæsar's that was erected in the place: and men laughed and wondered and said Is it possible? or Did you ever hear the like? and yet thought he meant no hurt, he did it so hand-somely and ingenuously. And all these were prosperous: whereas Pompey, who tended to the same end but in a more dark and dissembling manner, as Tacitus saith of him, *Occultior non melior,* [having his intentions better concealed but not better,] wherein Sallust concurreth, *ore probo, animo inverecundo,* [an honest tongue but a shameless mind,] made it his design by infinite secret engines to cast the state into an absolute anarchy and confusion, that the state might cast itself into his arms for necessity and protec-tion, and so the sovereign power be put upon him, and he never seen in it: and when he had brought it (as he thought) to that point, when he was chosen consul alone, as never any was, yet he could make no great matter of it, because men understood him not; but was fain in the end to go the beaten track of getting arms into his hands, by colour of the doubt of Cæsar's designs: so tedious, casual, and un-fortunate are these deep dissimulations; whereof it seemeth Tacitus made this judgment, that they were a cunning of an inferior form in regard of true policy; attributing the one to Augustus, the other to Tiberius, where speaking of Livia he saith, *Et cum artibus mariti simulatione filii bene com-posita,* [that she was of a happy composition, uniting the arts of her husband with the dissimulation of her son;] for surely the continual habit of dissimulation is but a weak and sluggish cunning, and not greatly politic.

Another precept of this Architecture of Fortune is to ac-custom our minds to judge of the proportion or value of things as they conduce and are material to our particular ends; and that to do substantially, and not superficially. For we shall find the logical part (as I may term it) of some men's minds good, but the mathematical part erroneous; that is, they can well judge of consequences, but not of pro-portions and comparison; preferring things of shew and sense before things of substance and effect. So some fall in love with access to princes, others with popular fame and applause, supposing they are things of great purchase; when in many cases they are but matters of envy, peril, and impediment. So some measure things according to the labour and difficulty or assiduity which are spent about them; and think if they be ever moving, that they must needs advance and proceed; as Cæsar saith in a despising manner of Cato the second, when he describeth how laborious and inde-fatigable he was to no great purpose; *Hæc omnia magno studio agebat.* So in most things men are ready to abuse themselves in thinking the greatest means to be best, when it should be the fittest.

As for the true marshalling of men's pursuits towards their fortune as they are more or less material, I hold them to stand thus. First the amendment of their own minds; for the remove of the impediments of the mind will sooner clear the passages of fortune, than the obtaining fortune will remove the impediments of the mind. In the second place I set down wealth and means; which I know most men would have placed first, because of the general use which it beareth towards all variety of occasions. But that opinion I may condemn with like reason as Machiavel doth that other, that moneys were the sinews of the wars; whereas (saith he) the true sinews of the wars are the sin-ews of men's arms, that is, a valiant, populous, and military nation; and he voucheth aptly the authority of Solon, who when Crœsus shewed him his treasury of gold said to him, that if another came that had better iron he would be master of his gold. In like manner it may be truly affirmed that it is not moneys that are the sinews of fortune, but it is the sinews and steel of men's minds, wit, courage, audac-ity, resolution, temper, industry, and the like. In third place I set down reputation, because of the peremptory tides and currents it hath; which if they be not taken in their due time are seldom recovered, it being extreme hard to play an after-game of reputation. And lastly I place honour, which is more easily won by any of the other three, much more by all, than any of them can be pur-chased by honour. To conclude this precept, as there is order and priority in matter, so is there in time, the pre-posterous placing whereof is one of the commonest errors;

while men fly to their ends when they should intend their beginnings, and do not take things in order of time as they come on, but marshal them according to greatness and not according to instance; not observing the good precept, *Quod nunc instat agamus,*

[Despatch we now what stands us now upon].

Another precept of this knowledge is, not to embrace any matters which do occupy too great a quantity of time, but to have that sounding in a man's ears, *Sed fugit interea, fugit irreparabile tempus,* [while he is making ready to do it the time for doing it is gone;] and that is the cause why those which take their course of rising by professions of burden, as lawyers, orators, painful divines, and the like, are not commonly so politic for their own fortune, otherwise than in their ordinary way, because they want time to learn particulars, to wait occasions, and to devise plots.

Another precept of this knowledge is to imitate nature which doth nothing in vain; which surely a man may do, if he do well interlace his business, and bend not his mind too much upon that which he principally intendeth. For a man ought in every particular action so to carry the motions of his mind, and so to have one thing under another, as if he cannot have that he seeketh in the best degree, yet to have it in a second, or so in a third; and if he can have no part of that which he purposed, yet to turn the use of it to somewhat else; and if he cannot make anything of it for the present, yet to make it as a seed of somewhat in time to come; and if he can contrive no effect or substance from it, yet to win some good opinion by it, or the like; so that he should exact an account of himself, of every action to reap somewhat, and not to stand amazed and confused if he fail of that he chiefly meant: for nothing is more impolitic than to mind actions wholly one by one; for he that doth so leeseth infinite occasions which intervene, and are many times more proper and propitious for somewhat that he shall need afterwards, than for that which he urgeth for the present; and therefore men must be perfect in that rule,

Hæc oportet facere, et illa non omittere, [these things ought ye to do, and not to leave the other undone].

Another precept of this knowledge is, not to engage a man's self peremptorily in any thing, though it seem not liable to accident; but ever to have a window to fly out at, or a way to retire; following the wisdom in the ancient fable of the two frogs, which consulted when their plash was dry whither they should go; and the one moved to go down into a pit, because it was not likely the water would dry there; but the other answered, *True, but if it do, how shall we get out again?*

Another precept of this knowledge is that ancient precept of Bias, construed not to any point of perfidiousness but only to caution and moderation, *Et ama tanquam inimicus futurus, et odi tanquam amaturus,* [love your friend as you would love one who may hereafter be your enemy; hate your enemy as one who may hereafter be your friend;] for it utterly betrayeth all utility for men to embark themselves too far in unfortunate friendships, troublesome spleens, and childish and humorous envies or emulations.

But I continue this beyond the measure of an example; led, because I would not have such knowledges which I note as deficient to be thought things imaginative or in the air, or an observation or two much made of; but things of bulk and mass, whereof an end is hardlier made than a beginning. It must be likewise conceived, that in these points which I mention and set down, they are far from complete tractates of them, but only as small pieces for patterns. And lastly, no man I suppose will think that I mean fortunes are not obtained without all this ado; for I know they come tumbling into some men's laps; and a number obtain good fortunes by diligence in a plain way, little intermeddling, and keeping themselves from gross errors.

But as Cicero, when he setteth down an Idea of a perfect Orator, doth not mean that every pleader should be such; and so likewise, when a Prince or a Courtier hath been described by such as have handled those subjects, the mould hath used to be made according to the perfection of the art, and not according to common practice: so I understand it that it ought to be done in the description of a Politic man; I mean politic for his own fortune.

But it must be remembered all this while, that the precepts which we have set down are of that kind which may be counted and called *bonæ artes*, [honest arts]. As for evil arts, if a man would set down for himself that principle of Machiavel, *that a man seek not to attain virtue itself, but the appearance only thereof; because the credit of virtue is a help, but the use of it is cumber;* or that other of his principles, *that he presuppose that men are not fitly to be wrought otherwise but by fear, and therefore that he seek to have every man obnoxious, low, and in strait,* which the Italians call *seminar spine,* to sow thorns; or that other principle contained in the verse which Cicero citeth, *Cadant amici, dummodo inimici intercidant,* [down with friends so enemies go down with them,] as the Triumvirs, which sold every one to other the lives of their friends for the deaths of their enemies; or that other protestation of L. Catilina, to set on fire and trouble states, to the end to fish in droumy[64] waters, and to unwrap their fortunes; *Ego si quid in fortunis meis excitatum sit incendium, id non aqua sed ruina restinguam,* [if my fortunes be set on fire I will put it out not with water but with demolition:] or that other principle of Lysander *that children are to be deceived with comfits, and men with oaths:* and the like evil and corrupt positions, whereof (as in all things) there are more in number than of the good: certainly with these dispensations from the laws of charity and integrity the pressing of a man's fortune may be more hasty and compendious. But it is in life as it is in ways; the shortest way is commonly the foulest, and surely the fairer way is not much about.

But men if they be in their own power and do bear and sustain themselves, and be not carried away with a whirlwind or tempest of ambition, ought in the pursuit of their own fortune to set before their eyes not only that general map of the world, that *all things are vanity and vexation of spirit,* but many other more particular cards and directions:

chiefly that, that Being without well-being is a curse and
the greater being the greater curse, and that all virtue is
most rewarded and all wickedness most punished in itself:
according as the poet saith excellently:

> Quæ vobis, quæ digna, viri, pro laudibus istis
> Præmia posse rear solvi? pulcherrima primum
> Dii *moresque* dabunt vestri:

> [What recompence, O friends, can I hold out
> Worthy such deeds? The best is that ye have, —
> God's blessing and your proper nobleness:]

and so of the contrary. And secondly they ought to look
up to the eternal providence and divine judgment, which
often subverteth the wisdom of evil plots and imaginations,
according to that Scripture, *He hath conceived mischief
and shall bring forth a vain thing*. And although men should
refrain themselves from injury and evil arts, yet this incessant and sabbathless pursuit of a man's fortune leaveth
not tribute which we owe to God of our time; who (we
see) demandeth a tenth of our substance, and a seventh,
which is more strict, of our time: and it is to small purpose
to have an erected face towards heaven, and a perpetual
grovelling spirit upon earth, eating dust as doth the serpent;
Atque affigit humo divinæ particulam auræ, [fixing to earth
the etherial spark divine]. And if any man flatter himself
that he will employ his fortune well though he should obtain it ill, as was said concerning Augustus Cæsar, and after
of Septimius Severus, *that either they should never have
been born or else they should never have died*, they did
so much mischief in the pursuit and ascent of their greatness, and so much good when they were established; yet
these compensations and satisfactions are good to be used,
but never good to be purposed. And lastly, it is not amiss
for men in their race toward their fortune to cool themselves a little with that conceit which is elegantly expressed
by the emperor Charles the fifth in his instructions to the
king his son, *that fortune hath somewhat of the nature of
a woman, that if she be too much wooed she is the farther*

off. But this last is but a remedy for those whose tastes are corrupted: let men rather build upon that foundation which is as a corner-stone of divinity and philosophy, wherein they join close, namely that same *Primum quærite*. For divinity saith, *Primum quærite regnum Dei, et ista omnia adjicientur vobis,* [seek ye first the kingdom of God, and all these things shall be added unto you:] and philosophy saith, *Primum quærite bona animi, cætera aut aderunt aut non oberunt,* [seek ye first the good things of the mind, all other good things will either come or not be wanted]. And although the human foundation hath somewhat of the sand, as we see in M. Brutus when he brake forth into that speech,

> Te colui, Virtus, ut rem; at tu nomen inane es;

[I took thee, Virtue, for a reality, but I find thee an empty name;] yet the divine foundation is upon the rock. But this may serve for a taste of that knowledge which I noted as deficient.

Concerning Government, it is a part of knowledge secret and retired, in both these respects in which things are deemed secret; for some things are secret because they are hard to know, and some because they are not fit to utter. We see all governments are obscure and invisible.

> Totamque infusa per artus
> Mens agitat molem, et magno se corpore miscet.

[In every pore diffused the great mind works,
Stirs all the mass, and thro' the huge frame lives.]

Such is the description of governments. We see the government of God over the world is hidden, insomuch as it seemeth to participate of much irregularity and confusion. The government of the Soul in moving the Body is inward and profound, and the passages thereof hardly to be reduced to demonstration. Again, the wisdom of antiquity (the shadows whereof are in the poets) in the description of torments and pains, next unto the crime of rebellion which was the Giants' offence, doth detest the offence of futility,[65] as in Sisyphus and Tantalus. But this was meant of particulars: nevertheless even unto the general rules and discourses of policy and government there is due a reverent and reserved handling.

But contrariwise in the governors toward the governed all things ought, as far as the frailty of man permitteth, to be manifest and revealed. For so it is expressed in the Scriptures touching the government of God, that this globe, which seemeth to us a dark and shady body, is in the view of God as crystal: *Et in conspectu sedis tanquam mare vitreum simile crystallo*, [and before the Throne there was a sea of glass, like unto crystal]. So unto princes and states, and specially towards wise senates and councils, the natures and dispositions of the people, their conditions and necessities, their factions and combinations, their animosities and discontents, ought to be, in regard of the variety of their intelligences, the wisdom of their observations, and the height of their station where they keep sentinel, in great part clear and transparent. Wherefore, considering that I write to a king that is a master of this science, and is so well assisted, I think it decent to pass over this part in silence, as willing to obtain the certificate which one of the ancient philosophers aspired unto; who being silent, when others contended to make demonstration of their abilities by speech, desired it might be certified for his part, *that there was one that knew how to hold his peace*.

Notwithstanding, for the more public part of government, which is Laws, I think good to note only one deficience; which is, that all those which have written of laws, have written either as philosophers or as lawyers, and none as statesmen. As for the philosophers, they make imaginary laws for imaginary commonwealths; and their discourses are as the stars, which give little light because they are so high. For the lawyers, they write according to the states where they live, what is received law, and not what ought to be law: for the wisdom of a lawmaker is one, and of a lawyer is another. For there are in nature certain fountains of justice, whence all civil laws are derived but as streams; and like as waters do take tinctures and tastes from the soils through which they run, so do civil laws vary according to the regions and governments where they are planted, though they proceed from the same fountains. Again, the wisdom of a lawmaker consisteth not only in a platform of justice, but in the application thereof; taking into consideration by what means laws may be made certain, and what are the causes and remedies of the doubtfulness and incertainty of law; by what means laws may be made apt and easy to be executed, and what are the impediments and remedies in the execution of laws; what influence laws touching private right of *meum* and *tuum* have into the public state, and how they may be made apt and agreeable; how laws are to be penned and delivered, whether in Texts or in Acts; brief or large; with preambles or without; how they are to be pruned and reformed from time to time; and what is the best means to keep them from being too vast in volumes or too full of multiplicity and crossness; how they are to be expounded, when upon causes emergent and judicially discussed, and when upon responses and conferences touching general points or questions; how they are to be pressed, rigorously or tenderly; how they are to be mitigated by equity and good conscience; and whether discretion and strict law are to be mingled in the same courts or kept apart in several courts; again, how the practice, profession, and erudition of law is to be censured and governed; and many other points touching the administration, and (as I may term it) animation of laws. Upon which I insist the less, because I purpose (if God give me leave), having begun a work of this nature in aphorisms, to propound it hereafter noting it in the mean time for deficient.

De prudentia legislatoria, sive de fontibus Juris

And for your Majesty's laws of England, I could say much of their dignity, and somewhat of their defect; but they cannot but excel the civil laws[66] in fitness for the government: for the civil law was *non hos quæsitum munus in usus;* it was not made for the countries which it governeth. Hereof I cease to speak, because I will not intermingle matter of action with matter of general learning.

Thus have I concluded this portion of learning touching Civil Knowledge; and with civil knowledge have concluded Human Philosophy; and with human philosophy, Philosophy in General. And being now at some pause, looking back into that I have passed through, this writing seemeth to me, (*si nunquam fallit imago* [*if the mirror does not lie]) as far as a man can judge of his own work, not much better than that noise or sound which musicians make while they are tuning their instruments; which is nothing pleasant to hear, but yet is a cause why the music is sweeter afterwards. So have I been content to tune the instruments of the muses, that they may play that have better hands. And surely, when I set before me the condition of these times, in which learning hath made her third visitation or circuit, in all the qualities thereof; as the excellency and vivacity of the wits of this age; the noble helps and lights which we have by the travails of ancient writers; the art of printing, which communicateth books to men of all fortunes; the openness of the world by navigation, which hath disclosed multitudes of experiments, and a mass of natural history; the leisure wherewith these times abound, not employing men so generally in civil business, as the states of Græcia did in respect of their popularity,[67] and the state of Rome in respect of the greatness of their monarchy; the present disposition of these times at this instant to peace; the consumption of all that ever can be said in controversies of religion, which have so much diverted men from other sciences; the perfection of your Majesty's learning, which as a phœnix may call whole vollies of wits to follow you; and the inseparable propriety of time, which is ever more and more to disclose truth; I cannot but be raised to this persuasion, that this third period of time will far surpass that of the Græcian and Roman learning: only if men will know their own strength and their own weakness both; and take one from the other light of invention, and not fire of contradiction; and esteem of the inquisition of truth as of an enterprise, and not as of a quality or ornament; and employ wit and magnificence to things of worth and excellency, and not to things vulgar and of popular estimation. As for my labours, if any man shall please himself or others in the reprehension of them, they shall make that ancient and patient request, *Verbera sed audi,* [strike me if you will, only hear me;] let men reprehend them, so they observe and weigh them. For the appeal is (lawful though it may be it shall not be needful) from the first cogitations of men to their second, and from the nearer times to the times further off. Now let us come to that learning, which both the former times were not so blessed as to know, sacred and inspired Divinity, the Sabaoth and port of all men's labours and peregrinations.

The prerogative of God extendeth as well to the reason as to the will of man; so that as we are to obey his law though we find a reluctation in our will, so we are to believe his word though we find a reluctation in our reason. For if we believe only that which is agreeable to our sense, we give consent to the matter and not to the author; which is no more than we would do towards a suspected and discredited witness; but that faith which was accounted to Abraham for righteousness was of such a point as whereat Sarah laughed, who therein was an image of natural reason.

Howbeit (if we will truly consider it) more worthy it is to believe than to know as we now know. For in knowledge man's mind suffereth from sense, but in belief it suffereth from spirit, such one as it holdeth for more authorised than itself, and so suffereth from the worthier agent. Otherwise it is of the state of man glorified; for then faith shall cease, and we shall know as we are known.

Wherefore we conclude that sacred Theology (which in our idiom we call Divinity) is grounded only upon the word and oracle of God, and not upon the light of nature: for it is written, *Cœli enarrant gloriam Dei,* [the Heavens declare the glory of God,] but it is not written, *Cœli enar-*

rant voluntatem Dei, [the Heavens declare the will of God,] but of that it is said, *Ad legem et testimonium: si non fecerint secundum verbum istud,* &c., [to the law and to the testimony: if they do not according to this word, &c.]. This holdeth not only in those points of faith which concern the great mysteries of the Deity, of the Creation, of the Redemption, but likewise those which concern the law moral truly interpreted: *Love your enemies: do good to them that hate you: be like to your heavenly Father, that suffereth his rain to fall upon the just and unjust.* To this it ought to be applauded, *Nec vox Hominem sonat* [*nor is the voice of human tone]: it is a voice beyond the light of nature. So we see the heathen poets, when they fall upon a libertine passion, do still expostulate with laws and moralities, as if they were opposite and malignant to nature: *Et quod natura remittit, invida jura negant,* [what Nature suffers envious laws forbid]. So said Dendamis the Indian unto Alexander's messengers, That he had heard somewhat of Pythagoras and some other of the wise men of Græcia, and that he held them for excellent men: but that they had a fault, which was that they had in too great reverence and veneration a thing they called law and manners. So it must be confessed that a great part of the law moral is of that perfection, whereunto the light of nature cannot aspire. How then is it that man is said to have by the light and law of nature some notions and conceits of virtue and vice, justice and wrong, good and evil? Thus; because the light of nature is used in two several senses; the one, that which springeth from reason, sense, induction, argument, according to the laws of heaven and earth; the other, that which is imprinted upon the spirit of man by an inward instinct, according to the law of conscience, which is a sparkle of the purity of his first estate: in which later sense only he is participant of some light and discerning touching the perfection of the moral law: but how? sufficient to check the vice, but not to inform the duty. So then the doctrine of religion, as well moral as mystical, is not to be attained but by inspiration and revelation from God.

The use notwithstanding of reason in spiritual things, and the latitude thereof, is very great and general: for it is not for nothing that the apostle calleth religion *our reasonable service of God;* insomuch as the very ceremonies and figures of the old law were full of reason and signification, much more than the ceremonies of idolatry and magic, that are full of nonsignificants and surd characters. But most specially the Christian Faith, as in all things so in this, deserveth to be highly magnified; holding and preserving the golden mediocrity in this point between the law of the Heathen and the law of Mahumet, which have embraced the two extremes. For the religion of the Heathen had no constant belief or confession, but left all to the liberty of argument; and the religion of Mahumet on the other side interdicteth argument altogether: the one having the very face of error, and the other of imposture: whereas the Faith doth both admit and reject disputation with difference.

The use of human reason in religion is of two sorts: the former, in the conception and apprehension of the mysteries of God to us revealed; the other, in the inferring and deriving of doctrine and direction thereupon. The former extendeth to the mysteries themselves; but how? by way of illustration, and not by way of argument. The later consisteth indeed of probation and argument. In the former we see God vouchsafeth to descend to our capacity, in the expressing of his mysteries in sort as may be sensible unto us; and doth grift[68] his revelations and holy doctrine upon the notions of our reason, and applieth his inspirations to open our understanding, as the form of the key to the ward of the lock: for the later, there is allowed us an use of reason and argument secondary and respective, although not original and absolute. For after the articles and principles of religion are placed, and exempted from examination of reason, it is then permitted unto us to make derivations and inferences from and according to the analogy of them, for our better direction. In nature this holdeth not; for both the principles are examinable by induction,

though not by a medium or syllogism; and besides, those
principles or first positions have no discordance with that
reason which draweth down and deduceth the inferior
positions. But yet it holdeth not in religion alone, but in
many knowledges both of greater and smaller nature,
namely wherein there are not only *posita* [*fixed and not
subject to argument] but *placita* [*as you please or open
to choice]; for in such there can be no use of absolute reason. We see it familiarly in games of wit, as chess, or the
like; the draughts and first laws of the game are positive,
but how? merely *ad placitum* [*by general consent], and
not examinable by reason; but then how to direct our play
thereupon with best advantage to win the game, is artificial and rational. So in human laws there be many
grounds and maxims which are *placita juris*, positive upon
authority and not upon reason, and therefore not to be dis-
puted: but what is most just, not absolutely, but relatively
and according to those maxims, that affordeth a long field
of disputation. Such therefore is that secondary reason
which hath place in divinity, which is grounded upon the
placets [*assent] of God.

Here therefore I note this deficience, that there hath not
been to my understanding sufficiently enquired
and handled *the true limits and use of reason in
spiritual things*, as a kind of divine dialectic:
which for that it is not done, it seemeth to me
a thing usual, by pretext of true conceiving that which is
revealed, to search and mine into that which is not revealed; and by pretext of enucleating inferences and contradictories, to examine that which is positive; the one sort
falling into the error of Nicodemus, demanding to have
things made more sensible than it pleaseth God to reveal
them; *Quomodo possit homo nasci cum sit senex?* [how
can a man be born when he is old?] the other sort into the
error of the disciples, which were scandalized at a show
of contradiction; *Quid est hoc quod dicit nobis? Modicum,
et non videbitis me; et iterum, modicum, et videbitis me,*

*De usu legi-
timo rationis
humanæ in
divinis*

&c. [what is this that he saith unto us? a little while and ye shall not see me, and again a little while and ye shall see me, &c.]

Upon this I have insisted the more in regard of the great and blessed use thereof; for this point well laboured and defined of would in my judgment be an opiate to stay and bridle not only the vanity of curious speculations, wherewith the schools labour, but the fury of controversies, wherewith the church laboureth. For it cannot but open men's eyes, to see that many controversies do merely pertain to that which is either not revealed or positive; and that many others do grow upon weak and obscure inferences or derivations: which latter sort, if men would revive the blessed style of that great doctor of the Gentiles,[69] would be carried thus, *Ego, non Dominus,* [I, not the Lord,] and again, *Secundum consilium meum,* [according to my counsel;] in opinions and counsels, and not in positions and oppositions. But men are now over-ready to usurp the style *Non ego, sed Dominus,* [not I, but the Lord;] and not so only, but to bind it with the thunder and denunciation of curses and anathemas, to the terror of those which have not sufficiently learned out of Salomon that *the causeless curse shall not come.*

Divinity hath two principal parts; the matter informed or revealed, and the nature of the information or revelation: and with the later we will begin, because it hath most coherence with that which we have now last handled. The nature of the information consisteth of three branches; the limits of the information, the sufficiency of the information, and the acquiring or obtaining the information. Unto the limits of the information belong these considerations; how far forth particular persons continue to be inspired; how far forth the church is inspired; and how far forth reason may be used: the last point whereof I have noted as deficient. Unto the sufficiency of the information belong two considerations; what points of religion are fundamental, and what perfective, being matter of further building and perfection upon one and the same foundation; and again, how the gradations of light according to the dispensation of times are material to the sufficiency of belief.

Here again I may rather give it in advice than note it as

De gradibus unitatis in Civitate Dei

deficient, that the points fundamental, and the points of further perfection only, ought to be with piety and wisdom distinguished: a subject tending to much like end as that I noted before; for as that other were likely to abate the number of controversies, so this is like to abate the heat of many of them. We see Moses when he saw the Israelite and the Ægyptian fight, he did not say, *Why strive you?* but drew his sword and slew the Ægyptian: but when he saw the two Israelites fight, he said, *You are brethren, why strive you?* If the point of doctrine be an Ægyptian, it must be slain by the sword of the Spirit, and not reconciled; but if it be an Israelite, though in the wrong, then, *Why strive you?* We see of the fundamental points, our Saviour penneth the league thus, *He that is not with us, is against us;* but of points not fundamental, thus, *He that is not against us, is with us.* So we see the coat of our Saviour was entire without seam, and so is the doctrine of the Scriptures in itself; but the garment of the Church was of divers colours, and yet not divided. We see the chaff may and ought to be severed from the corn in the ear, but the tares may not be pulled up from the corn in the field: so as it is a thing of great use well to define what and of what latitude those points are, which do make men merely aliens and disincorporate from the Church of God.

For the obtaining of the information, it resteth upon the true and sound interpretation of the Scriptures, which are the fountains of the water of life. The interpretations of the Scriptures are of two sorts; methodical, and solute or at large. For this divine water, which excelleth so much that of Jacob's well,[70] is drawn forth much in the same kind as natural water useth to be out of wells and fountains; either it is first forced up into a cistern, and from thence fetched and derived for use; or else it is drawn and received in buckets and vessels immediately where it springeth. The former sort whereof, though it seem to be the more ready, yet in my judgment is more subject to corrupt. This is that method which hath exhibited unto us the scholastical divinity; whereby divinity hath been reduced into an art, as into a cistern, and the streams of doctrine or positions fetched and derived from thence.

In this men have sought three things, a summary brevity, a compacted strength, and a complete perfection; whereof the two first they fail to find, and the last they ought not to seek. For as to brevity, we see in all summary methods, while men purpose to abridge they give cause to dilate. For the sum or abridgment by contraction becometh obscure, the obscurity requireth exposition, and the exposition is deduced into large commentaries, or into common places and titles, which grow to be more vast than the original writings whence the sum was at first extracted. So we see the volumes of the schoolmen are greater much than the first writings of the fathers, whence the Master of the Sentences[71] made his sum or collection. So in like manner the volumes of the modern doctors of the civil law exceed those of the ancient jurisconsults, of which Tribonian compiled the digest. So as this course of sums and commentaries is that which doth infallibly make the body of sciences more immense in quantity, and more base in substance.

And for strength, it is true that knowledges reduced into exact methods have a shew of strength, in that each part seemeth to support and sustain the other; but this is more satisfactory than substantial; like unto buildings which stand by architecture and compaction,[72] which are more subject to ruin than those which are built more strong in their several parts, though less compacted. But it is plain that the more you recede from your grounds the weaker do you conclude; and as in nature the more you remove yourself from particulars the greater peril of error you do incur, so much more in divinity the more you recede from the Scriptures by inferences and consequences, the more weak and dilute are your positions.

And as for perfection or completeness in divinity, it is not to be sought; which makes this course of artificial divinity the more suspect. For he that will reduce a knowledge into an art, will make it round and uniform: but in divinity many things must be left abrupt and concluded with this: *O altitudo sapientiæ et scientiæ Dei! quam incomprehensibilia sunt judicia ejus, et non investigabiles viæ ejus!* [O the depth of the wisdom and knowledge of God! How incomprehensible are his judgments, and his ways past finding out!] So again the apostle saith, *Ex parte scimus,* [we know in part,] and to have the form of a total where there is but matter for a part, cannot be without supplies by supposition and presumption. And therefore I conclude, that the true use of these Sums and Methods hath place in institutions or introductions preparatory unto knowledge; but in them, or by deducement from them, to handle the main body and substance of a knowledge, is in all sciences prejudicial, and in divinity dangerous.

As to the interpretation of the Scriptures solute and at large, there have been divers kinds introduced and devised; some of them rather curious and unsafe, than sober and warranted. Notwithstanding thus much must be confessed, that the Scriptures, being given by inspiration and not by human reason, do differ from all other books in the author; which by consequence doth draw on some difference to be used by the expositor. For the inditer of them did know four things which no man attains to know; which are, the mysteries of the kingdom of glory; the perfection of the laws of nature; the secrets of the heart of man; and the future succession of all ages. For as to the first, it is said, *He that presseth into the light, shall be oppressed of the glory:* and again, *No man shall see my face and live.* To the second, *When he prepared the heavens I was present, when by law and compass he inclosed the deep.* To the third, *Neither was it needful that any should bear witness to him of Man, for he knew well what was in Man.* And to the last, *From the beginning are known to the Lord all his works.*

From the former two of these have been drawn certain senses and expositions of Scriptures, which had need be contained within the bounds of sobriety; the one anagogical, and the other philosophical. But as to the former, man is not to prevent his time: *Videmus nunc per speculum in ænigmate, tunc autem facie ad faciem:* [now we see through a glass darkly, but then face to face:] wherein nevertheless there seemeth to be a liberty granted, as far forth as the polishing of this glass, or some moderate explication of this ænigma. But to press too far into it, cannot but cause a dissolution and overthrow of the spirit of man. For in the body there are three degrees of that we receive into it; Aliment, Medicine, and Poison; whereof aliment is that which the nature of man can perfectly alter and overcome: medicine is that which is partly converted by nature, and partly converteth nature; and poison is that which worketh wholly upon nature, without that that nature can in any part work upon it. So in the mind whatsoever knowledge reason cannot at all work upon and convert, is a mere intoxication, and endangereth a dissolution of the mind and understanding.

But for the latter, it hath been extremely set on foot of late time by the school of Paracelsus, and some others, that have pretended to find the truth of all natural philosophy in the Scriptures; scandalizing and traducing all other philosophy as heathenish and profane. But there is no such enmity between God's word and his works. Neither do they give honour to the Scriptures, as they suppose, but much imbase them. For to seek heaven and earth in the word of God, whereof it is said, *Heaven and earth shall pass, but my word shall not pass,* is to seek temporary things amongst eternal: and as to seek divinity in philosophy is to seek the living amongst the dead, so to seek philosophy in divinity is to seek the dead amongst the living: neither are the pots or lavers whose place was in the outward part of the temple to be sought in the holiest place of all, where the ark of the testimony was seated. And again, the scope or purpose of the Spirit of God is not to express matters of nature in the Scriptures, otherwise than in passage,[73] and for application to man's capacity and to matters moral or divine. And it is a true rule, *Authoris aliud agentis parva authoritas;* [what a man says incidentally about matters which are not in question has little authority;] for it were a strange conclusion, if a man should use a similitude for ornament or illustration sake, borrowed from nature or history according to vulgar conceit, as of a Basilisk, an Unicorn, a Centaur, a Briareus, an Hydra, or the like, that therefore he must needs be thought to affirm the matter thereof positively to be true. To conclude therefore, these two interpretations, the one by reduction or ænigmatical, the other philosophical or physical, which have been received and pursued in imitation of the rabbins and cabalists, are to be confined with a *Noli altum sapere, sed time,* [be not overwise, but fear.]

But the two later points, known to God and unknown to man, touching *the secrets of the heart, and the successions of time,* doth make a just and sound difference between the manner of the exposition of the Scriptures, and all other books. For it is an excellent observation which hath been made upon the answers of our Saviour Christ to many of the questions which were propounded to him, how that they are impertinent to the state of the question demanded; the reason whereof is, because not being like man, which knows man's thoughts by his words, but knowing man's thoughts immediately, he never answered their words, but their thoughts: much in the like manner it is with the Scriptures, which being written to the thoughts of men, and to the succession of all ages, with a foresight of all heresies, contradictions, differing estates of the church, yea and particularly of the elect, are not to be interpreted only according to the latitude of the proper sense of the place, and respectively towards that present occasion whereupon the words were uttered; or in precise congruity or contexture with the words before or after; or in contemplation of the principal scope of the place; but have in themselves, not only totally or collectively, but distributively in clauses and words, infinite springs and streams of doctrine to water the church in every part; and therefore as the literal sense is as it were the main stream or river; so the moral sense chiefly, and sometimes the allegorical or typical, are they whereof the church hath most use: not that I wish men to be bold in allegories, or indulgent or light in allusions; but that I do much condemn that interpretation of the Scripture which is only after the manner as men use to interpret a profane book.

In this part touching the exposition of the Scriptures, I can report no deficience; but by way of remembrance this I will add: In perusing books of divinity, I find many books of controversies; and many of common places and treatises; a mass of positive divinity, as it is made an art; a number of sermons and lectures, and many prolix commentaries upon the Scriptures, with harmonies and concordances: but that form of writing in divinity, which in my judgment is of all others most rich and precious, is positive divinity collected upon particular texts of Scriptures in brief observations; not dilated into common places, not chasing after controversies, not reduced into method of art; a thing abounding in sermons, which will vanish, but defective in books, which will remain; and a thing wherein this age excelleth. For I am persuaded, and I may speak it with an *Absit invidia verbo,* [meaning no offence,] and no ways in derogation of antiquity, but as in a good emulation between the vine and the olive, that if the choice and best of those observations upon texts of Scriptures which have been made dispersedly in sermons within this your Majesty's island of Britain by the space of these forty years and more (leaving out the largeness of exhortations and applications thereupon) had been set down in a continuance, it had been the best work in divinity which had been written since the apostles' times.

Emanationes Scripturarum in doctrinas positivas

The matter informed by divinity is of two kinds; a matter of belief and truth of opinion, and matter of service and adoration; which is also judged and directed by the former;

the one being as the internal soul of religion, and the other as the external body thereof. And therefore the heathen religion was not only a worship of idols, but the whole religion was an idol in itself; for it had no soul, that is, no certainty of belief or confession; as a man may well think, considering the chief doctors of their church were the poets; and the reason was, because the heathen gods were no jealous gods, but were glad to be admitted into part, as they had reason. Neither did they respect the pureness of heart, so they might have external honour and rites.

But out of these two do result and issue four main branches of divinity; Faith, Manners, Liturgy, and Government. Faith containeth the doctrine of the nature of God, of the attributes of God, and of the works of God. The nature of God consisteth of three persons in unity of Godhead. The attributes of God are either common to the Deity, or respective to the persons. The works of God summary are two, that of the Creation, and that of the Redemption; and both these works, as in total they appertain to the unity of the Godhead, so in their parts they refer to the three persons: that of the Creation, in the mass of the matter to the Father; in the disposition of the form to the Son; and in the continuance and conservation of the being to the Holy Spirit: so that of the Redemption, in the election and counsel to the Father; in the whole act and consummation to the Son; and in the application to the Holy Spirit; for by the Holy Ghost was Christ conceived in flesh, and by the Holy Ghost are the elect regenerate in spirit. This work likewise we consider either effectually in the elect; or privatively in the reprobate; or according to appearance in the visible church.

For Manners, the doctrine thereof is contained in the law, which discloseth sin. The law itself is divided, according to the edition thereof, into the law of Nature, the law Moral, and the law Positive; and according to the style, into Negative and Affirmative, Prohibitions and Commandments. Sin, in the matter and subject thereof, is divided according to the commandments; in the form thereof, it referreth to the three persons in Deity: sins of Infirmity against the Father, whose more special attribute is Power; sins of Ignorance against the Son, whose attribute is Wisdom; and sins of Malice against the Holy Ghost, whose attribute is Grace or Love. In the motions of it, it either moveth to the right hand or to the left; either to blind devotion, or to profane and libertine transgression; either in imposing restraint where God granteth liberty, or in taking liberty where God imposeth restraint. In the degrees and progress of it, it divideth itself into thought, word, or act. And in this part I commend much the deducing of the law of God to cases of conscience; for that I take indeed to be a breaking, and not exhibiting whole, of the bread of life. But that which quickeneth both these doctrines of faith and manners, is the elevation and consent of the heart; whereunto appertain books of exhortation, holy meditation, Christian resolution, and the like.

For the Liturgy or service, it consisteth of the reciprocal acts between God and man; which, on the part of God, are the preaching of the word and the sacraments, which are seals to the covenant, or as the visible word; and on the part of man, invocation of the name of God, and under the law, sacrifices, which were as visible prayers or confessions: but now the adoration being *in spiritu et veritate,* [in spirit and in truth,] there remaineth only *vituli labiorum,* [offerings of the lips;] although the use of holy vows of thankfulness and retribution may be accounted also as sealed petitions.

And for the Government of the church, it consisteth of the patrimony of the church, the franchises of the church, and the offices and jurisdictions of the church, and the laws of the church directing the whole; all which have two considerations, the one in themselves, the other how they stand compatible and agreeable to the civil estate.

This matter of divinity is handled either in form of instruction of truth, or in form of confutation of falsehood. The declinations from religion, besides the privative, which is atheism and the branches thereof, are three; Heresies,

Idolatry, and Witchcraft; Heresies, when we serve the
true God with a false worship; Idolatry, when we worship
false gods, supposing them to be true; and Witchcraft,
when we adore false gods, knowing them to be wicked and
false. For so your Majesty doth excellently well observe,
that Witchcraft is the height of Idolatry. And yet we see
though these be true degrees, Samuel teacheth us that they
are all of a nature, when there is once a receding from the
word of God; for so he saith, *Quasi peccatum ariolandi est
repugnare, et quasi scelus idololatriæ nolle acquiescere;*
[rebellion is as the sin of Witchcraft, and Stubbornness as
the crime of Idolatry].

These things I have passed over so briefly because I can
report no deficience concerning them: for I can find no
space or ground that lieth vacant and unsown in the matter of divinity; so diligent have men been, either in sowing
of good seed or in sowing of tares.

Thus have I made as it were a small Globe of the Intellectual World, as truly and faithfully as I could discover;
with a note and description of those parts which seem to
me not constantly occupate, or not well converted by the
labour of man. In which, if I have in any point receded
from that which is commonly received, it hath been with
a purpose of proceeding *in melius,* and not *in aliud;* a mind
of[74] amendment and proficience, and not of change and
difference. For I could not be true and constant to the
argument I handle, if I were not willing to go beyond
others; but yet not more willing than to have others go
beyond me again: which may the better appear by this,
that I have propounded my opinions naked and unarmed,
not seeking to preoccupate the liberty of men's judgments
by confutations. For in any thing which is well set down,
I am in good hope that if the first reading move an objection, the second reading will make an answer. And in
those things wherein I have erred, I am sure I have not
prejudiced the right by litigious arguments; which certainly
have this contrary effect and operation, that they add

authority to error, and destroy the authority of that which is well invented: for question is an honour and preferment to falsehood, as on the other side it is a repulse to truth. But the errors I claim and challenge to myself as mine own. The good, if any be, is due *tanquam adeps sacrificii,* [as the fat of the sacrifice,] to be incensed to the honour, first of the Divine Majesty, and next of your Majesty, to whom on earth I am most bounden.

[THE CLUE TO THE MAZE—*ca*. 1607]

FILUM LABYRINTHI

SIVE FORMULA INQUISITIONIS

[*THE CLUE TO THE MAZE

OR THE FORMULA OF INQUIRY]

AD FILIOS [*TO HIS SONS]

PARS PRIMA [*PART I]

1. FRANCIS BACON thought in this manner. The knowledge whereof the world is now possessed, especially that of nature, extendeth not to magnitude and certainty of works. The Physician pronounceth many diseases incurable, and faileth oft in the rest. The Alchemists wax old and die in hopes. The Magicians perform nothing that is permanent and profitable. The Mechanics take small light from natural philosophy, and do but spin on their own little threads. Chance sometimes discovereth inventions; but that worketh not in years, but ages. So he saw well, that the inventions known are very unperfect; and that new are not like to be brought to light but in great length of time; and that those which are, came not to light by philosophy.

2. He thought also this state of knowledge was the worse, because men strive (against themselves) to save the credit of ignorance, and to satisfy themselves in this poverty. For the Physician, besides his cauteles[1] of practice, hath this general cautele of art, that he dischargeth the

weakness of his art upon supposed impossibilities: neither can his art be condemned, when itself judgeth. That philosophy also, out of which the knowledge of physic, which now is in use, is hewed, receiveth certain positions and opinions, which (if they be well weighed) induce this persuasion, that no great works are to be expected from art, and the hand of man; as in particular that opinion, *that the heat of the sun and fire differ in kind;* and that other, *that Composition is the work of man, and Mixture is the work of nature,* and the like; all tending to the circumscription of man's power, and to artificial despair; killing in men, not only the comfort of imagination, but the industry of trial; only upon vain glory to have their art thought perfect, and that all is impossible that is not already found. The Alchemist dischargeth his art upon his own errors, either supposing a misunderstanding of the words of his authors, which maketh him listen after auricular traditions; or else a failing in the true proportions and scruples of practice, which maketh him renew infinitely his trials; and finding also that he lighteth upon some mean experiments and conclusions by the way, feedeth upon them, and magnifieth them to the most, and supplieth the rest in hopes. The Magician, when he findeth something (as he conceiveth) above nature effected, thinketh, when a breach is once made in nature, that it is all one to perform great things and small; not seeing that they are but subjects of a certain kind, wherein magic and superstition hath played in all times. The Mechanical person, if he can refine an invention, or put two or three observations or practices together in one, or couple things better with their use, or make the work in less or greater volume, taketh himself for an inventor. So he saw well, that men either persuade themselves of new inventions as of impossibilities; or else think they are already extant, but in secret and in few hands; or that they account of those little industries and additions, as of inventions: all which turneth to the averting of their minds from any just and constant labour to invent further in any quantity.

3. He thought also, when men did set before themselves the variety and perfection of works produced by mechanical arts, they are apt rather to admire the provisions of man, than to apprehend his wants; not considering, that the original inventions and conclusions of nature which are the life of all that variety, are not many nor deeply fetched; and that the rest is but the subtile and ruled motion of the instrument and hand; and that the shop therein is not unlike the library, which in such number of books containeth (for the far greater part) nothing but iterations, varied sometimes in form, but not new in substance. So he saw plainly, that opinion of store was a cause of want; and that both works and doctrines appear many and are few.

4. He thought also, that knowledge is uttered to men, in a form as if every thing were finished; for it is reduced into arts and methods, which in their divisions do seem to include all that may be. And how weakly soever the parts are filled, yet they carry the shew and reason of a total; and thereby the writings of some received authors go for the very art: whereas antiquity used to deliver the knowledge which the mind of man had gathered, in observations, aphorisms, or short and dispersed sentences, or small tractates of some parts that they had diligently meditated and laboured; which did invite men, both to ponder that which was invented, and to add and supply further. But now sciences are delivered to be believed and accepted, and not to be examined and further discovered; and the succession is between master and disciple, and not between inventor and continuer or advancer: and therefore sciences stand at a stay, and have done for many ages, and that which is positive is fixed, and that which is question is kept question, so as the columns of no further proceeding are pitched. And therefore he saw plainly, men had cut themselves off from further invention; and that it is no marvel that that is not obtained, which hath not been attempted but rather shut out and debarred.

5. He thought also, that knowledge is almost generally sought either for delight and satisfaction, or for gain and

profession, or for credit and ornament, and that every of these are as Atalanta's balls, which hinder the race of invention. For men are so far in these courses from seeking to increase the mass of knowledge, as of that mass which is they will take no more than will serve their turn: and if any one amongst so many seeketh knowledge for itself, yet he rather seeketh to know the variety of things, than to discern of the truth and causes of them; and if his inquisition be yet more severe, yet it tendeth rather to judgment than to invention; and rather to discover truth in controversy, than new matter; and if his heart be so large as he propoundeth to himself further discovery or invention, yet it is rather of new discourse and speculation of causes, than of effects and operations: and as for those that have so much in their mouths, action and use and practice and the referring of sciences thereunto, they mean it of application of that which is known, and not of a discovery of that which is unknown. So he saw plainly, that this mark, namely invention of further means to endow the condition and life of man with new powers or works, was almost never yet set up and resolved in man's intention and inquiry.

6. He thought also, that, amongst other knowledges, natural philosophy hath been the least followed and laboured. For since the Christian faith, the greatest number of wits have been employed, and the greatest helps and rewards have been converted upon divinity. And before time likewise, the greatest part of the studies of philosophers was consumed in moral philosophy, which was as the heathen divinity. And in both times a great part of the best wits betook themselves to law, pleadings, and causes of estate; specially in the time of the greatness of the Romans, who by reason of their large empire needed the service of all their able men for civil business. And the time amongst the Grecians in which natural philosophy seemed most to flourish, was but a short space; and that also rather abused in differing sects and conflicts of opinions, than profitably spent: since which time, natural philosophy was never any profession, nor never possessed any whole man, except per-

chance some monk in a cloister, or some gentleman in the country, and that very rarely; but became a science of passage, to season a little young and unripe wits, and to serve for an introduction to other arts, specially physic and the practical mathematics. So as he saw plainly, that natural philosophy hath been intended by few persons, and in them hath occupied the least part of their time, and that in the weakest of their age and judgment.

7. He thought also, how great opposition and prejudice natural philosophy had received by superstition, and the immoderate and blind zeal of religion; for he found that some of the Grecians which first gave the reason of thunder, had been condemned of impiety; and that the cosmographers which first discovered and described the roundness of the earth, and the consequence thereof touching the *Antipodes,* were not much otherwise censured by the ancient fathers of the Christian Church; and that the case is now much worse, in regard of the boldness of the schoolmen and their dependances in the monasteries, who having made divinity into an art, have almost incorporated the contentious philosophy of Aristotle into the body of Christian religion. And generally he perceived in men of devout simplicity, this opinion, that the secrets of nature were the secrets of God and part of that glory whereinto the mind of man if it seek to press shall be oppressed; and that the desire in men to attain to so great and hidden knowledge, hath a resemblance with that temptation which caused the original fall: and on the other side in men of a devout policy, he noted an inclination to have the people depend upon God the more, when they are less acquainted with second causes; and to have no stirring in philosophy, lest it may lead to an innovation in divinity, or else should discover matter of further contradiction to divinity. But in this part resorting to the authority of the Scriptures, and holy examples, and to reason, he rested not satisfied alone, but much confirmed. For first he considered that the knowledge of nature, by the light whereof man discerned of every living creature, and imposed names according to their

propriety, was not the occasion of the fall; but the moral knowledge of good and evil, affected to the end to depend no more upon God's commandments, but for man to direct himself; neither could he find in any Scripture, that the inquiry and science of man in any thing, under the mysteries of the Deity, is determined and restrained, but contrariwise allowed and provoked; for concerning all other knowledge the Scripture pronounceth, *That it is the glory of God to conceal, but it is the glory of man (or of the king, for the king is but the excellency of man) to invent;* and again, *The spirit of man is as the lamp of God, wherewith he searcheth every secret;* and again most effectually, *That God hath made all things beautiful and decent, according to the return of their seasons; also that he hath set the world in man's heart, and yet man cannot find out the work which God worketh from the beginning to the end;* shewing that the heart of man is a continent of that concave or capacity, wherein the content of the world (that is, all forms of the creatures and whatsoever is not God) may be placed or received; and complaining that through the variety of things and vicissitudes of times (which are but impediments and not impuissances) man cannot accomplish his invention. In precedent also he set before his eyes, that in those few memorials before the flood, the Scripture honoureth the name of the inventors of music and works in metal; that Moses had this addition of praise, that he was seen in all the learning of the Egyptians; that Solomon, in his grant of wisdom from God, had contained as a branch thereof, that knowledge whereby he wrote a natural history of all verdor, from the cedar to the moss, and of all that breatheth; that the book of Job, and many places of the prophets, have great aspersion of natural philosophy; that the Church in the bosom and lap therof, in the greatest injuries of times, ever preserved (as holy relics) the books of philosophy and all heathen learning; and that when Gregory the bishop of Rome became adverse and unjust to the memory of heathen antiquity, it was censured for pusillanimity in him, and the honour thereof soon after restored, and his own memory almost persecuted by his successor Sabinian; and lastly in our times and the ages of our fathers, when Luther and the divines of the Protestant Church on the one side, and the Jesuits on the other, have enterprised to reform, the one the doctrine, the other the discipline and manners of the Church of Rome, he saw well how both of them have awaked to their great honour and succour all human learning. And for reason, there cannot be a greater and more evident than this; that all knowledge and specially that of natural philosophy tendeth highly to the magnifying of the glory of God in his power, providence and benefits; appearing and engraven in his works, which without this knowledge are beheld but as through a veil; for if the heavens in the body of them do declare the glory of God to the eye, much more do they in the rule and decrees of them declare it to the understanding. And another reason not inferior to this is, that the same natural philosophy principally amongst all other human knowledge doth give an excellent defence against both extremes of religion, superstition and infidelity; for both it freeth the mind from a number of weak fancies and imaginations, and it raiseth the mind to acknowledge that to God all things are possible: for to that purpose speaketh our Saviour in that first canon against heresies delivered upon the case of the resurrection, *You err, not knowing the Scriptures, nor the power of God;* teaching that there are but two fountains of heresy, not knowing the will of God revealed in the Scriptures, and not knowing the power of God revealed or at least made most sensible in his creatures. So as he saw well, that natural philosophy was of excellent use to the exaltation of the Divine Majesty; and that which is admirable, that being a remedy of superstition, it is nevertheless an help to faith. He saw likewise that the former opinions to the prejudice thereof had no true ground; but must spring either out of mere ignorance, or out of an excess of devotion, to have divinity all in all, whereas it should be only above all (both which states of mind may be best pardoned); or else out of worse causes,

namely out of envy, which is proud weakness and deserveth to be despised; or out of some mixture of imposture, to tell a lie for God's cause; or out of an impious dif-
fidence, as if men should fear to discover some things in
nature which might subvert faith. But still he saw well,
howsoever these opinions are in right reason reproved, yet
they leave not to be most effectual hindrances to natural
philosophy and invention.

8. He thought also, that there wanted not great contrariety to the further discovery of sciences, in regard of
the orders and customs of universities, and also in regard
of common opinion. For in universities and colleges men's
studies are almost confined to certain authors, from which
if any dissenteth or propoundeth matter of redargution,[2] it
is enough to make him thought a person turbulent; whereas
if it be well advised, there is a great difference to be made between matters contemplative and active. For in government
change is suspected, though to the better; but it is natural
to arts to be in perpetual agitation and growth; neither is
the danger alike of new light, and of new motion or remove. And for vulgar and received opinions, nothing is
more usual nor more usually complained of, than that it is
imposed for arrogancy and presumption for men to authorise themselves against antiquity and authors, towards
whom envy is ceased, and reverence by time amortised; it
not being considered what Aristotle himself did (upon
whom the philosophy that now is chiefly dependeth); who
came with a professed contradiction to all the world, and
did put all his opinions upon his own authority and argument, and never so much as nameth an author but to confute and reprove him; and yet his success well fulfilled the
observation of Him that said, *If a man come in his own
name, him will you receive.* Men think likewise, that if they
should give themselves to the liberty of invention and travail of inquiry, that they shall light again upon some conceits and contemplations which have been formerly offered
to the world, and have been put down by better, which
have prevailed and brought them to oblivion; not seeing

that howsoever the property and breeding of knowledges is in great and excellent wits, yet the estimation and price of them is in the multitude, or in the inclinations of princes and great persons meanly learned. So as those knowledges are like to be received and honoured, which have their foundation in the subtility or finest trial of common sense, or such as fill the imagination; and not such knowledge as is digged out of the hard mine of history and experience, and falleth out to be in some points as adverse to common sense or popular reason, as religion, or more. Which kind of knowledge, except it be delivered with strange advantages of eloquence and power, may be likely to appear and disclose a little to the world and straight to vanish and shut again. So that time seemeth to be of the nature of a river or flood, that bringeth down to us that which is light and blown up, and sinketh and drowneth that which is solid and grave. So he saw well, that both in the state of religion, and in the administration of learning, and in common opinion, there were many and continual stops and traverses to the course of invention.

9. He thought also, that the invention of works and further possibility was prejudiced in a more special manner than that of speculative truth; for besides the impediments common to both, it hath by itself been notably hurt and discredited by the vain promises and pretences of Alchemy, Magic, Astrology, and such other arts, which (as they now pass) hold much more of imagination and belief than of sense and demonstration. But to use the poets' language, men ought to have remembered that although Ixion of a cloud in the likeness of Juno begat Centaurs and Chimæras, yet Jupiter also of the true Juno begat Vulcan and Hebe. Neither is it just to deny credit to the greatness of the acts of Alexander, because the like or more strange have been feigned of an Amadis or an Arthur, or other fabulous worthies. But though this in true reason should be, and that men ought not to make a confusion of unbelief; yet he saw well it could not otherwise be in event, but that experience of untruth had made access to truth more difficult, and

that the ignominy of vanity had abated all greatness of mind.

10. He thought also, there was found in the mind of man an affection naturally bred, and fortified and furthered by discourse and doctrine, which did pervert the true proceeding towards active and operative knowledge. This was a false estimation, that it should be as a diminution to the mind of man to be much conversant in experiences and particulars subject to sense and bound in matter, and which are laborious to search, ignoble to meditate, harsh to deliver, illiberal to practise, infinite as is supposed in number, and no ways accommodate to the glory of arts. This opinion or state of mind received much credit and strength by the school of Plato, who thinking that particulars rather revived the notions or excited the faculties of the mind, than merely informed; and having mingled his philosophy with superstition, which never favoureth the sense; extolleth too much the understanding of man in the inward light thereof. And again Aristotle's school, which giveth the due to the sense in assertion, denieth it in practice much more than that of Plato. For we see the schoolmen, Aristotle's succession, which were utterly ignorant of history, rested only upon agitation of wit; whereas Plato giveth good example of inquiry by induction and view of particulars; though in such a wandering manner as is of no force or fruit. So that he saw well, that the supposition of the sufficiency of man's mind hath lost the means thereof.

FROM

[THE WISDOM OF THE ANCIENTS—1609]

DE SAPIENTIA VETERUM

PREFACE

THE most ancient times (except what is preserved of them in the scriptures) are buried in oblivion and silence: to that silence succeeded the fables of the poets: to those fables the written records which have come down to us. Thus between the hidden depths of antiquity and the days of tradition and evidence that followed there is drawn a veil, as it were, of fables, which come in and occupy the middle region that separates what has perished from what survives.

Now I suppose most people will think I am but entertaining myself with a toy, and using much the same kind of licence in expounding the poets' fables which the poets themselves did in inventing them; and it is true that if I had a mind to vary and relieve my severer studies with some such exercise of pleasure for my own or my reader's recreation, I might very fairly indulge in it. But that is not my meaning. Not but that I know very well what pliant stuff fable is made of, how freely it will follow any way you please to draw it, and how easily with a little dexterity and discourse of wit meanings which it was never meant to bear may be plausibly put upon it. Neither have I forgotten that there has been old abuse of the thing in practice; that many, wishing only to gain the sanction and reverence of antiquity for doctrines and inventions of their own, have tried to twist the fables of the poets into that sense; and that this is neither a modern vanity nor a rare one, but old of standing and frequent in use; that Chrysippus long ago, interpreting the oldest poets after the manner of an interpreter of dreams, made them out to be Stoics; and that the Alchemists more absurdly still have discovered in the pleasant and sportive fictions of the transformation of bodies, allusion to experiments of the furnace. All this I have duly examined and weighed; as well as all the levity and looseness with which people indulge their fancy in the matter of allegories; yet for all this I cannot change my mind. For in the first place to let the follies and licence of a few detract from the honour of parables in general is not to be allowed; being indeed a boldness savouring of profanity; seeing that religion delights in such veils and shadows, and to take them away would be almost to interdict all communion between divinity and humanity. But passing that and speaking of human wisdom only, I do certainly for my own part (I freely and candidly confess) incline to this opinion,—that beneath no small number of the fables of the ancient poets there lay from the very beginning a mystery and an allegory. It may be that my reverence for the primitive time carries me too far, but the truth is that in some of these fables, as well in the very frame and texture of the story as in the propriety of the names by which the persons that figure in it are distinguished, I find a conformity and connexion with the thing signified, so close and so evident that one cannot help believing such a signification to have been designed and meditated from the first, and purposely shadowed out. For who is there so impenetrable and that can so shut his eyes to a plain thing, but when he is told that after the *Giants* were put down, *Fame* sprang up as their posthumous sister, he will at once see that it is meant of those murmurs of parties and seditious rumours which always circulate for a time after the suppression of a rebellion? Or again who can hear that the *Giant Typhon* cut off and carried away *Jupiter's* sinews, and that *Mercury* stole them from Typhon and gave them back to Jupiter; without at once perceiving that it relates to successful rebellions, by which kings have their sinews both of money and authority cut off; yet not so but that by fair words and wise edicts the minds of the subjects may be presently reconciled, and as it were stolen back, and so kings recover their strength? Or who can hear that in that memorable expedition of the gods against the giants the braying of *Silenus's ass* had a principal stroke in putting the giants to flight, and not be sure that the incident was invented in allusion to the vast attempts of rebels, dissipated as they commonly are by empty rumours and vain terrors? Then again there is a conformity and significancy in the very names, which must be clear to everybody. Metis, Jupiter's wife, plainly means counsel; Typhon, swelling; Pan, the universe; Nemesis, revenge; and the like. And what if we find here and there a bit of real history underneath, or some things added only for ornament, or times confounded, or part of one fable transferred to another and a new allegory introduced? Such things could not but occur in stories invented (as these were) by men who both lived in different ages and had different ends, some being more modern, some more ancient, some having in their thoughts natural philosophy, others civil affairs; and therefore they need not trouble us.

But there is yet another sign, and one of no small value, that these fables contain a hidden and involved meaning; which is, that some of them are so absurd and stupid upon the face of the narrative taken by itself, that they may be said to give notice from afar and cry out that there is a parable below. For a fable that is probable may be thought to have been composed merely for pleasure, in imitation of history. But when a story is told which could never have entered any man's head either to conceive or relate on its own account, we must presume that it had some further reach. What a fiction (for instance) is that of Jupiter and Metis! Jupiter took Metis to wife: as soon as he saw that she was with child, he ate her up; whereupon he grew to be with child himself; and so brought forth out of his head Pallas in armour! Surely I think no man had ever a dream so monstrous and extravagant, and out of all natural ways of thinking.

But the consideration which has most weight with me is this, that few of these fables were invented, as I take it, by those who recited and made them famous,—Homer, Hesiod, and the rest. For had they been certainly the production of that age and of those authors by whose report they have come down to us, I should not have thought of looking for anything great or lofty from such a source. But it will appear upon an attentive examination that they are delivered not as new inventions then first published, but as stories already received and believed. And since they are told in different ways by writers nearly contemporaneous, it is easy to see that what all the versions have in common came from ancient tradition, while the parts in which they vary are the additions introduced by the several writers for embellishment—a circumstance which gives them in my eyes a much higher value: for so they must be regarded as neither being the inventions nor belonging to the age of the poets themselves, but as sacred relics and light airs breathing out of better times, that were caught from the traditions of more ancient nations and so received into the flutes and trumpets of the Greeks.

Nevertheless, if any one be determined to believe that the allegorical meaning of the fable was in no case original and genuine, but that always the fable was first and the allegory put in after, I will not press that point; but allowing him to enjoy that gravity of judgment (of the dull and leaden order though it be) which he affects, I will attack him, if indeed he be worth the pains, in another manner upon a fresh ground. Parables have been used in two ways, and (which is strange) for contrary purposes. For they serve to disguise and veil the meaning, and they serve also to clear and throw light upon it. To avoid dispute then, let us give up the former of these uses. Let us suppose that these fables were things without any definite purpose, made only for pleasure. Still there remains the latter use. No force of wit can deprive us of that. Nor is there any man of ordinary learning that will object to the reception of it as a thing grave and sober, and free from all vanity; of prime use to the sciences, and sometimes indispensable: I mean the employment of parables as a method of teaching, whereby inventions that are new and abstruse and remote from vulgar opinions may find an easier passage to the understanding. On this account it was that in the old times, when the inventions and conclusions of human reason (even those that are now trite and vulgar) were as yet new and strange, the world was full of all kinds of fables, and enigmas, and parables, and similitudes: and these were used not as a device for shadowing and concealing the meaning, but as a method of making it understood; the understandings of men being then rude and impatient of all subtleties that did not address themselves to the sense,—indeed scarcely capable of them. For as hieroglyphics came before letters, so parables came before arguments. And even now if any one wish to let new light on any subject into men's minds, and that without offence or harshness, he must still go the same way and call in the aid of similitudes.

Upon the whole I conclude with this: the wisdom of the primitive ages was either great or lucky; great, if they knew what they were doing and invented the figure to shadow the meaning; lucky, if without meaning or intending it they fell upon matter which gives occasion to such worthy contemplations. My own pains, if there be any help in them, I shall think well bestowed either way: I shall be throwing light either upon antiquity or upon nature itself.

That the thing has been attempted by others I am of

course aware, but if I may speak what I think freely without mincing it, I must say that the pains which have been hitherto taken that way, though great and laborious, have gone near to deprive the inquiry of all its beauty and worth; while men of no experience in affairs, nor any learning beyond a few commonplaces, have applied the sense of the parables to some generalities and vulgar observations, without attaining their true force, their genuine propriety, or their deeper reach. Here, on the other hand, it will be found (if I mistake not) that though the subjects be old, yet the matter is new; while leaving behind us the open and level parts we bend our way towards the nobler heights that rise beyond.

2

TYPHON

OR THE REBEL

THE poets tell us that Juno being angry that Jupiter had brought forth Pallas by himself without her help, implored of all the gods and goddesses that she also might bring forth something without the help of Jupiter: to which when wearied with her violence and importunity they had assented, she smote the earth, which quaking and opening gave birth to Typhon, a huge and hideous monster. He was given to a serpent by way of foster-father to be nursed. As soon as he was grown up he made war upon Jupiter, whom in the conflict he took prisoner; and bearing him on his shoulders to a remote and obscure region, cut out the sinews of his hands and feet, and carrying them away, left him there helpless and mutilated. Then came Mercury, and having stolen the sinews from Typhon gave them back to Jupiter, who finding his strength restored attacked the monster again. And first he struck him with a thunderbolt, which made a wound the blood whereof engendered serpents; then, as he fell back and fled, threw upon him the mountain Ætna and crushed him beneath the weight.

The fable has been composed in allusion to the variable fortune of kings and the rebellions that occur from time to time in monarchies. For kings and their kingdoms are properly, like Jupiter and Juno, man and wife. But it sometimes happens that the king, depraved by the long habit of ruling, turns tyrant and takes all into his own hands; and not caring for the consent of his nobles and senate, brings forth as it were by himself; that is to say, administers the government by his own arbitrary and absolute authority. Whereat the people aggrieved endeavour on their part to set up some head of their own. This generally begins with the secret solicitation of nobles and great persons, whose connivency being obtained, an attempt is then made to stir the people. Thence comes a kind of swelling in the State, which is signified by the infancy of Typhon. And this condition of affairs is fostered and nourished by the innate depravity and malignant disposition of the common people, which is to kings like a serpent full of malice and mischief; till the disaffection spreading and gathering strength breaks out at last into open rebellion; which because of the infinite calamities it inflicts both on kings and peoples is represented under the dreadful image of Typhon, with a hundred heads, denoting divided powers; flaming mouths, for devastations by fire; belts of snakes, for the pestilences which prevail, especially in sieges; iron hands, for slaughters; eagle's talons, for rapine; feathery body, for perpetual rumours, reports, trepidations, and the like. And sometimes these rebellions grow so mighty that the king is forced, as if carried off on the shoulders of the rebels, to abandon the seat and principal cities of his kingdom, and to contract his forces, and betake himself to some remote and obscure province; his sinews both of money and majesty being cut off. And yet if he bears his fortune wisely, he presently by the skill and industry of Mercury recovers those sinews again; that is to say, by affability and wise edicts and gracious speeches he reconciles the minds of his subjects, and awakens in them an alacrity to grant him supplies, and so recovers the vigour of his authority. Nevertheless, having learned prudence and caution, he is commonly unwilling to set all upon the toss of fortune, and therefore avoids a pitched battle, but tries first by some memorable exploit to destroy the reputation of the rebels: in which if he succeed, the rebels feeling themselves shaken and losing their confidence, resort first to broken and empty threats, like serpent's hisses, and then finding their case desperate take to flight. And then is the time, when they are beginning to fall to pieces, for the king with the entire forces and mass of his kingdom, as with the mountain Ætna, to pursue and overwhelm them.

11

ORPHEUS

OR PHILOSOPHY

THE story of Orpheus, which though so well known has not yet been in all points perfectly well interpreted, seems meant for a representation of universal Philosophy. For Orpheus himself,—a man admirable and truly divine, who being master of all harmony subdued and drew all things after him by sweet and gentle measures,—may pass by an easy metaphor for philosophy personified. For as the works of wisdom surpass in dignity and power the works of strength, so the labours of Orpheus surpass the labours of Hercules.

Orpheus, moved by affection for his wife who had been snatched from him by an untimely death, resolved to go down to Hell and beg her back again of the Infernal Powers; trusting to his lyre. Nor was he disappointed. For so soothed and charmed were the infernal powers by the sweetness of his singing and playing, that they gave him leave to take her away with him; but upon one condition; she was to follow behind him, and he was not to look back until they had reached the confines of light. From this however in the impatience of love and anxiety he could not refrain. Before he had quite reached the point of safety, he looked back; and so the covenant was broken, and she sud-

denly fell away from him and was hurried back into Hell.
From that time Orpheus betook himself to solitary places,
a melancholy man and averse from the sight of women;
where by the same sweetness of his song and lyre he drew
to him all kinds of wild beasts, in such manner that putting
off their several natures, forgetting all their quarrels and
ferocity, no longer driven by the stings and furies of lust,
no longer caring to satisfy their hunger or to hunt their
prey, they all stood about him gently and sociably, as in a
theatre, listening only to the concords of his lyre. Nor was
that all: for so great was the power of his music that it
moved the woods and the very stones to shift themselves
and take their stations decently and orderly about him. And
all this went on for some time with happy success and great
admiration; till at last certain Thracian women, under the
stimulation and excitement of Bacchus, came where he was;
and first they blew such a hoarse and hideous blast upon
a horn that the sound of his music could no longer be heard
for the din: whereupon, the charm being broken that had
been the bond of that order and good fellowship, confusion
began again; the beasts returned each to his several nature
and preyed one upon the other as before; the stones and
woods stayed no longer in their places: while Orpheus himself was torn to pieces by the women in their fury, and his
limbs scattered about the fields: at whose death, Helicon
(river sacred to the Muses) in grief and indignation buried his
waters under the earth, to reappear elsewhere.

The meaning of the fable appears to be this. The singing
of Orpheus is of two kinds; one to propitiate the infernal
powers, the other to draw the wild beasts and the woods.
The former may be best understood as referring to natural
philosophy; the latter to philosophy moral and civil. For
natural philosophy proposes to itself, as its noblest work
of all, nothing less than the restitution and renovation of
things corruptible, and (what is indeed the same thing in
a lower degree) the conservation of bodies in the state in
which they are, and the retardation of dissolution and putrefaction. Now certainly if this can be effected at all, it can-

not be otherwise than by due and exquisite attempering and adjustment of parts in nature, as by the harmony and perfect modulation of a lyre. And yet being a thing of all others the most difficult, it commonly fails of effect; and fails (it may be) from no cause more than from curious and premature meddling and impatience. Then Philosophy finding that her great work is too much for her, in sorrowful mood, as well becomes her, turns to human affairs; and applying her powers of persuasion and eloquence to insinuate into men's minds the love of virtue and equity and peace, teaches the peoples to assemble and unite and take upon them the yoke of laws and submit to authority, and forget their ungoverned appetites, in listening and conforming to precepts and discipline; whereupon soon follows the building of houses, the founding of cities, the planting of fields and gardens with trees; insomuch that the stones and the woods are not unfitly said to leave their places and come about her. And this application of Philosophy to civil affairs is properly represented, and according to the true order of things, as subsequent to the diligent trial and final frustration of the experiment of restoring the dead body to life. For true it is that the clearer recognition of the inevitable necessity of death sets men upon seeking immortality by merit and renown. Also it is wisely added in the story, that Orpheus was averse from women and from marriage; for the sweets of marriage and the dearness of children commonly draw men away from performing great and lofty services to the commonwealth; being content to be perpetuated in their race and stock, and not in their deeds.

But howsoever the works of wisdom are among human things the most excellent, yet they too have their periods and closes. For so it is that after kingdoms and commonwealths have flourished for a time, there arise perturbations and seditions and wars; amid the uproars of which, first the laws are put to silence, and then men return to the depraved conditions of their nature, and desolation is seen in the fields and cities. And if such troubles last, it is not long before letters also and philosophy are so torn in pieces that no traces of them can be found but a few fragments, scattered here and there like planks from a shipwreck; and then a season of barbarism sets in, the waters of Helicon being sunk under the ground, until, according to the appointed vicissitude of things, they break out and issue forth again, perhaps among other nations, and not in the places where they were before.

17

CUPID

OR THE ATOM

THE accounts given by the poets of Cupid, or Love, are not properly applicable to the same person; yet the discrepancy is such that one may see where the confusion is and where the similitude, and reject the one and receive the other.

They say then that Love was the most ancient of all the gods; the most ancient therefore of all things whatever, except Chaos, which is said to have been coeval with him; and Chaos is never distinguished by the ancients with divine honour or the name of a god. This Love is introduced without any parent at all; only, that some say he was an egg of Night. And himself out of Chaos begot all things, the gods included. The attributes which are assigned to him are in number four: he is always an infant; he is blind; he is naked; he is an archer. There was also another Love, the youngest of all the gods, son of Venus, to whom the attributes of the elder are transferred, and whom in a way they suit.

The fable relates to the cradle and infancy of nature, and pierces deep. This Love I understand to be the appetite or instinct of primal matter; or to speak more plainly, *the natural motion of the atom;* which is indeed the original and unique force that constitutes and fashions all things out of matter. Now this is entirely without parent; that is, without cause. For the cause is as it were parent of the effect; and of this virtue there can be no cause in nature (God always excepted): there being nothing before it, therefore no efficient; nor anything more original in nature, therefore neither kind nor form. Whatever it be therefore, it is a thing positive and inexplicable. And even if it were possible to know the method and process of it, yet to know it by way of cause is not possible; it being, next to God, the cause of causes—itself without cause. That the method even of its operation should ever be brought within the range and comprehension of human inquiry, is hardly perhaps to be hoped; with good reason therefore it is represented as an egg hatched by night. Such certainly is the judgment of the sacred philosopher, when he says, *He hath made all things beautiful according to their seasons; also he hath submitted the world to man's inquiry, yet so that man cannot find out the work which God worketh from the beginning to the end.* For the summary law of nature, that impulse of desire impressed by God upon the primary particles of matter which makes them come together, and which by repetition and multiplication produces all the variety of nature, is a thing which mortal thought may glance at, but can hardly take in.

Now the philosophy of the Greeks, which in investigating the material principles of things is careful and acute, in inquiring the principles of motion, wherein lies all vigour of operation, is negligent and languid; and on the point now in question seems to be altogether blind and babbling; for that opinion of the Peripatetics which refers the original impulse of matter to privation, is little more than words—a name for the thing rather than a description of it. And those who refer it to God, though they are quite right in that, yet they ascend by a leap and not by steps. For beyond all doubt there is a single and summary law in which nature centres and which is subject and subordinate to God; the same in fact which in the text just quoted is meant by the words, *The work which God worketh from the beginning to the end.* Democritus considered the matter more deeply; and having first given the atom some dimension and shape, attributed to it a single desire or primary motion simply and absolutely, and a second by comparison. For he thought that all things move by their proper nature towards the centre of the world; but that that which has more matter, moving thither faster, strikes aside that which has less, and forces it to go the other way. This however was but a narrow theory, and framed with reference to too few particulars: for it does not appear that either the motion of the heavenly bodies in circle, or the phenomena of contraction and expansion, can be reduced to this principle, or reconciled with it. As for Epicurus's opinion of the declination and fortuitous agitation of the atom, it is a relapse to trifling and ignorance. So it is but too plain that the parentage of this Cupid is wrapped in night.

Let us now consider his attributes. He is described with great elegance as a little child, and a child for ever; for things compounded are larger and are affected by age; whereas the primary seeds of things, or atoms, are minute and remain in perpetual infancy.

Most truly also is he represented as naked: for all compounds (to one that considers them rightly) are masked and clothed; and there is nothing properly naked, except the primary particles of things.

The blindness likewise of Cupid has an allegorical meaning full of wisdom. For it seems that this Cupid, whatever he be, has very little providence; but directs his course, like a blind man groping, by whatever he finds nearest; which makes the supreme divine Providence all the more to be admired, as that which contrives out of subjects peculiarly empty and destitute of providence, and as it were blind, to educe by a fatal and necessary law all the order and beauty of the universe.

His last attribute is archery: meaning that this virtue is such as acts at a distance: for all operation at a distance is like shooting an arrow. Now whoever maintains the theory of the atom and the vacuum (even though he suppose the vacuum not to be collected by itself but intermingled through space), necessarily implies the action of the virtue of the atom at a distance: for without this no motion could be originated, by reason of the vacuum interposed; but all things would remain fixed and immovable.

As for that younger Cupid, it is with reason that he is reported to be the youngest of the gods; since until the species were constituted he could have no operation. In the description of him the allegory changes its aim and passes to morals. And yet there remains a certain conformity between him and the elder Cupid. For Venus excites the general appetite of conjunction and procreation; Cupid, her son, applies the appetite to an individual object. From Venus therefore comes the general disposition, from Cupid the more exact sympathy. Now the general disposition depends upon causes near at hand, the particular sympathy upon principles more deep and fatal, and as if derived from that ancient Cupid, who is the source of all exquisite sympathy.

25

ATALANTA

OR PROFIT

ATALANTA, who was remarkable for swiftness, was matched to run a race with Hippomenes. The conditions were that if Hippomenes won he was to marry Atalanta, if he lost he was to be put to death; and there seemed to be no doubt about the issue, since the matchless excellence of Atalanta in running had been signalised by the death of many competitors. Hippomenes therefore resorted to an artifice. He provided himself with three golden apples, and carried them with him. The race began. Atalanta ran ahead. He seeing himself left behind bethought him of his stratagem, and rolled forward one of the golden apples, so that she might see it,—not straight forwards, but a little on one side, that it might not only delay her but also draw her out of the course. She, with a woman's eagerness, attracted by the beauty of the apple, left the course, ran after it, and stooped to take it up. Hippomenes in the meantime made good way along the course and got before her. She however by force of her natural swiftness made good the loss of time and was again foremost; when Hippomenes a second and a third time interrupted her in the same way, and so at last by craft not speed won the race.

The story carries in it an excellent allegory, relating to the contest of Art with Nature. For Art, which is meant by Atalanta, is in itself, if nothing stand in the way, far swifter than Nature and, as one may say, the better runner, and comes sooner to the goal. For this may be seen in almost everything; you see that fruit grows slowly from the kernel, swiftly from the graft; you see clay harden slowly into stones, fast into baked bricks: so also in morals, oblivion and comfort of grief comes by nature in length of time; but philosophy (which may be regarded as the art of living) does it without waiting so long, but forestalls and anticipates the day. But then this prerogative and vigour of art is retarded, to the infinite loss of mankind, by those golden apples. For there is not one of the sciences or arts which follows the true and legitimate course constantly forth till it reach its end; but it perpetually happens that arts stop in their undertakings half way, and forsake the course, and turn aside like Atalanta after profit and commodity,—

Leaving the course the rolling gold to seize.

And therefore it is no wonder if Art cannot outstrip Nature, and according to the agreement and condition of the contest put her to death or destroy her; but on the contrary Art remains subject to Nature, as the wife is subject to the husband.

28

SPHINX

OR SCIENCE

SPHINX, says the story, was a monster combining many shapes in one. She had the face and voice of a virgin, the wings of a bird, the claws of a griffin. She dwelt on the ridge of a mountain near Thebes and infested the roads, lying in ambush for travellers, whom she would suddenly attack and lay hold of; and when she had mastered them, she propounded to them certain dark and perplexed riddles, which she was thought to have obtained from the Muses. And if the wretched captives could not at once solve and interpret the same, as they stood hesitating and confused she cruelly tore them to pieces. Time bringing no abatement of the calamity, the Thebans offered to any man who should expound the Sphinx's riddles (for this was the only way to subdue her) the sovereignty of Thebes as his reward. The greatness of the prize induced Œdipus, a man of wisdom and penetration, but lame from wounds in his feet, to accept the condition and make the trial: who presenting himself full of confidence and alacrity before the Sphinx, and being asked what kind of animal it was which was born four-footed, afterwards became two-footed, then three-footed, and at last four-footed again, answered readily that it was man; who at his birth and during his infancy sprawls on all four, hardly attempting to creep; in a little while walks upright on two feet; in later years leans on a walking-stick and so goes as it were on three; and at last in extreme age and decrepitude, his sinews all failing, sinks into a quadruped again, and keeps his bed. This was the right answer and gave him the victory; whereupon he slew the Sphinx; whose body was put on the back of an ass and carried about in triumph; while himself was made according to compact King of Thebes.

The fable is an elegant and a wise one, invented apparently in allusion to Science; especially in its application to practical life. Science, being the wonder of the ignorant and unskilful, may be not absurdly called a monster. In figure and aspect it is represented as many-shaped, in allusion to the immense variety of matter with which it deals. It is said to have the face and voice of a woman, in respect of its beauty and facility of utterance. Wings are added because the sciences and the discoveries of science spread and fly abroad in an instant; the communication of knowledge being like that of one candle with another, which lights up at once. Claws, sharp and hooked, are ascribed to it with great elegance, because the axioms and arguments of science penetrate and hold fast the mind, so that it has no means of evasion or escape; a point which the sacred philosopher also noted: *The words of the wise are as goads, and as nails driven deep in.* Again, all knowledge may be regarded as having its station on the heights of mountains; for it is deservedly esteemed a thing sublime and lofty, which looks down upon ignorance as from an eminence, and has moreover a spacious prospect on every side, such as we find on hill-tops. It is described as infesting the roads, because at every turn in the journey or pilgrimage of human life, matter and occasion for study assails and encounters us. Again Sphinx proposes to men a variety of hard questions and riddles which she received from the Muses. In these, while they remain with the Muses, there is probably no cruelty; for so long as the object of meditation and inquiry is merely to know, the understanding is not oppressed or straitened by it, but is free to wander and expatiate, and finds in the very uncertainty of conclusion and variety of choice a certain pleasure and delight; but when they pass from the Muses to Sphinx, that is from contemplation to practice, whereby there is necessity for present action, choice, and decision, then they begin to be painful and cruel; and unless they be solved and disposed of, they strangely torment and worry the mind, pulling it first this way and then that, and fairly tearing it to pieces. Moreover the riddles of the Sphinx have always a twofold condition attached to them; distraction and laceration of mind, if you fail to solve them; if you succeed, a kingdom. For he who understands his subject is master of his end; and every workman is king over his work.

Now of the Sphinx's riddles there are in all two kinds; one concerning the nature of things, another concerning the nature of man; and in like manner there are two kinds of kingdom offered as the reward of solving them; one over nature, and the other over man. For the command over things natural,—over bodies, medicines, mechanical powers, and infinite other of the kind—is the one proper and ultimate end of true natural philosophy; however the philosophy of the School,[1] content with what it finds, and swelling with talk, may neglect or spurn the search after realities and works. But the riddle proposed to Œdipus, by the solution of which he became King of Thebes, related to the nature of man; for whoever has a thorough insight into the nature of man may shape his fortune almost as he will, and is born for empire; as was well declared concerning the arts of the Romans,—

> Be thine the art,
> O Rome, with government to rule the nations,
> And to know whom to spare and whom to abate,
> And settle the condition of the world.

And therefore it fell out happily that Augustus Cæsar, whether on purpose or by chance, used a Sphinx for his seal. For he certainly excelled in the art of politics if ever man did; and succeeded in the course of his life in solving most happily a great many new riddles concerning the nature of man, which if he had not dexterously and readily answered he would many times have been in imminent danger of destruction. The fable adds very prettily that when the Sphinx was subdued, her body was laid on the back of an ass: for there is nothing so subtle and abstruse, but when it is once thoroughly understood and published to the world, even a dull wit can carry it. Nor is that other point to be passed over, that the Sphinx was subdued by a lame man with club feet; for men generally proceed too fast and in too great a hurry to the solution of the Sphinx's riddles; whence it follows that the Sphinx has the better of them, and instead of obtaining the sovereignty by works and effects, they only distract and worry their minds with disputations.

THE GREAT INSTAURATION

INSTAURATIO MAGNA 1620

PROEMIUM

FRANCIS OF VERULAM

REASONED THUS WITH HIMSELF

AND JUDGED IT TO BE FOR THE INTEREST
OF THE PRESENT AND FUTURE GENERATIONS
THAT THEY SHOULD BE MADE ACQUAINTED
WITH HIS THOUGHTS

BEING convinced that the human intellect makes its own difficulties, not using the true helps which are at man's disposal soberly and judiciously; whence follows manifold ignorance of things, and by reason of that ignorance mischiefs innumerable; he thought all trial should be made, whether that commerce between the mind of man and the nature of things, which is more precious than anything on earth, or at least than anything that is of the earth, might by any means be restored to its perfect and original condition, or if that may not be, yet reduced to a better condition than that in which it now is. Now that the errors which have hitherto prevailed, and which will prevail for ever, should (if the mind be left to go its own way), either by the natural force of the understanding or by help of the aids and instruments of Logic, one by one correct themselves, was a thing not to be hoped for: because the primary notions of things which the mind readily and passively imbibes, stores up, and accumulates (and it is from them that all the rest flow) are false, confused, and overhastily abstracted from the facts; nor are the secondary and subsequent notions less arbitrary and inconstant; whence it follows that the entire fabric of human reason which we employ in the inquisition of nature, is badly put together and built up, and like some magnificent structure without any foundation. For while men are occupied in admiring and applauding the false powers of the mind, they pass by and throw away those true powers, which, if it be supplied with the proper aids and can itself be content to wait upon nature instead of vainly affecting to overrule her, are within its reach. There was but one course left, therefore,—to try the whole thing anew upon a better plan, and to commence a total reconstruction of sciences, arts, and all human knowledge, raised upon the proper foundations. And this, though in the project and undertaking it may seem a thing infinite and beyond the powers of man, yet when it comes to be dealt with it will be found sound and sober, more so than what has been done hitherto. For of this there is some issue; whereas in what is now done in the matter of science there is only a whirling round about, and perpetual agitation, ending where it began. And although he was well aware how solitary an enterprise it is, and how hard a thing to win faith and credit for, nevertheless he was resolved not to abandon either it or himself; nor to be deterred from trying and entering upon that one path, which is alone open to the human mind. For better it is to make a beginning of that which may lead to something, than to engage in a perpetual struggle and pursuit in courses which have no exit. And certainly the two ways of contemplation are much like those two ways of action, so much celebrated, in this—that the one, arduous and difficult in the beginning, leads out at last into the open country; while the other, seeming at first sight easy and free from obstruction, leads to pathless and precipitous places.

Moreover, because he knew not how long it might be before these things would occur to any one else, judging especially from this, that he has found no man hitherto who has applied his mind to the like, he resolved to publish at once so much as he has been able to complete. The cause of which haste was not ambition for himself, but solicitude for the work; that in case of his death there might remain some outline and project of that which he had conceived, and some evidence likewise of his honest mind and inclination towards the benefit of the human race. Certain it is that all other ambition whatsoever seemed poor in his eyes compared with the work which he had in hand; seeing that the matter at issue is either nothing, or a thing so great that it may well be content with its own merit, without seeking other recompence.

EPISTLE DEDICATORY

TO OUR MOST GRACIOUS AND MIGHTY
PRINCE AND LORD

JAMES

BY THE GRACE OF GOD
OF GREAT BRITAIN, FRANCE, AND
IRELAND KING
DEFENDER OF THE FAITH, ETC.

MOST GRACIOUS AND MIGHTY KING

Your Majesty may perhaps accuse me of larceny, having stolen from your affairs so much time as was required for this work. I know not what to say for myself. For of time there can be no restitution, unless it be that what has been abstracted from your business may perhaps go to the memory of your name and the honour of your age; if these things are indeed worth anything. Certainly they are quite new; totally new in their very kind: and yet they are copied from a very ancient model; even the world itself and the nature of things and of the mind. And to say truth, I am wont for my own part to regard this work as a child of time rather than of wit; the only wonder being that the first notion of the thing, and such great suspicions concerning matters long established, should have come into any man's mind. All the rest follows readily enough. And no doubt there is something of accident (as we call it) and luck as well in what men think as in what they do or say. But for this accident which I speak of, I wish that if there be any good in what I have to offer, it may be ascribed to the infinite mercy and goodness of God, and to the felicity of your Majesty's times; to which as I have been an honest and affectionate servant in my life, so

426

after my death I may yet perhaps, through the kindling of this new light in the darkness of philosophy, be the means of making this age famous to posterity; and surely to the times of the wisest and most learned of kings belongs of right the regeneration and restoration of the sciences. Lastly, I have a request to make—a request no way unworthy of your Majesty, and which especially concerns the work in hand; namely, that you who resemble Solomon in so many things—in the gravity of your judgments, in the peacefulness of your reign, in the largeness of your heart, in the noble variety of the books which you have composed— would further follow his example in taking order for the collecting and perfecting of a Natural and Experimental History, true and severe (unincumbered with literature and book-learning), such as philosophy may be built upon,—such, in fact, as I shall in its proper place describe: that so at length, after the lapse of so many ages, philosophy and the sciences may no longer float in air, but rest on the solid foundation of experience of every kind, and the same well examined and weighed. I have provided the machine, but the stuff must be gathered from the facts of nature. May God Almighty long preserve your Majesty!

Your Majesty's

Most bounden and devoted

Servant,

FRANCIS VERULAM,

CHANCELLOR

PREFACE

That the state of knowledge is not prosperous nor greatly advancing; and that a way must be opened for the human understanding entirely different from any hitherto known, and other helps provided, in order that the mind may exercise over the nature of things the authority which properly belongs to it.

IT seems to me that men do not rightly understand either their store or their strength, but overrate the one and underrate the other. Hence it follows, that either from an extravagant estimate of the value of the arts which they possess, they seek no further; or else from too mean an estimate of their own powers, they spend their strength in small matters and never put it fairly to the trial in those which go to the main. These are as the pillars of fate set in the path of knowledge; for men have neither desire nor hope to encourage them to penetrate further. And since opinion of store is one of the chief causes of want, and satisfaction with the present induces neglect of provision for the future, it becomes a thing not only useful, but absolutely necessary, that the excess of honour and admiration with which our existing stock of inventions is regarded be in the very entrance and threshold of the work, and that frankly and without circumlocution, stripped off, and men be duly warned not to exaggerate or make too much of them. For let a man look carefully into all that variety of books with which the arts and sciences abound, he will find everywhere endless repetitions of the same thing, varying in the method of treatment, but not new in substance, insomuch that the whole stock, numerous as it appears at first view, proves on examination to be but scanty. And for its value and utility it must be plainly avowed that that wisdom which we have derived principally from the Greeks is but like the boyhood of knowledge, and has the characteristic property of boys: it can talk, but it cannot generate; for it is fruitful of controversies but barren of works. So that the state of learning as it now is appears to be represented to the life in the old fable of Scylla, who had the head and face of a virgin, but her womb was hung round with barking monsters, from which she could not be delivered. For in like manner the sciences to which we are accustomed have certain general positions which are specious and flattering; but as soon as they come to particulars, which are as the parts of generation, when they should produce fruit and works, then arise contentions and barking disputations, which are the end of the matter and all the issue they can yield. Observe also, that if sciences of this kind had any life in them, that could never have come to pass which has been the case now for many ages—that they stand almost at a stay, without receiving any augmentations worthy of the human race; insomuch that many times not only what was asserted once is asserted still, but what was a question once is a question still, and instead of being resolved by discussion is only fixed and fed; and all the tradition and succession of schools is still a succession of masters and scholars, not of inventors and those who bring to further perfection the things invented. In the mechanical arts we do not find it so; they, on the contrary, as having in them some breath of life, are continually growing and becoming more perfect. As originally invented they are commonly rude, clumsy, and shapeless; afterwards they acquire new powers and more commodious arrangements and constructions; in so far that men shall sooner leave the study and pursuit of them and turn to something else, than they arrive at the ultimate perfection of which they are capable. Philosophy and the intellectual sciences, on the contrary, stand like statues, worshipped and celebrated, but not moved or advanced. Nay, they sometimes flourish most in the hands of the first author, and afterwards degenerate. For when men have once made over their judgments to others' keeping, and (like those senators whom they called *Pedarii*[1]) have agreed to support some one person's opinion, from that time they make no enlargement of the sciences themselves, but fall to the servile office of embellishing certain individual authors and increasing their retinue. And let it not be said that the sciences have been growing gradually till they have at last reached their full stature, and so (their course being completed) have settled in the works of a few writers; and that there being now no room for the invention of better, all that remains is to embellish and cultivate those things which have been invented already. Would it were so! But the truth is that this appropriating of the sciences has its origin in nothing better than the confidence of a few persons and the sloth and indolence of the rest. For after the sciences had been in several parts perhaps cultivated and handled diligently, there has risen up some man of bold disposition, and famous for methods and short ways which people like, who has in appearance reduced them to an art, while he has in fact only spoiled all that the others had done. And yet this is what posterity like, because it makes the work short and easy, and saves further inquiry, of which they are weary and impatient. And if any one take this general acquiescence and consent for an argument of weight, as being the judgment of Time, let me tell him that the reasoning on which he relies is most fallacious and weak. For, first, we are far from knowing all that in the matter of sciences and arts has in various ages and places been brought to light and published; much less, all that has been by private persons secretly attempted and stirred; so neither the births nor the miscarriages of Time are entered in our records. Nor, secondly, is the consent itself and the time it has continued a consideration of much worth. For however various are the forms of civil polities, there is but one form of polity in the sciences; and that always has been and always will be popular. Now the doctrines which find most favour with the populace are those which are either contentious and pugnacious, or specious and empty; such, I say, as either entangle assent or tickle it. And therefore no doubt the greatest wits in each successive age have been forced out of their own course; men of capacity and intellect above the vulgar having been fain, for reputation's sake, to bow to the judgment of the time and the multitude; and thus if any contemplations of a higher order took light anywhere, they were presently blown out by the winds of vulgar opinions. So that Time is like a river, which has brought down to us things light and puffed up, while those which are weighty and solid have sunk. Nay, those very authors who have usurped a kind of dictatorship in the sciences and taken upon them to lay down the law with such confidence, yet when from time to time they come to themselves again, they fall to complaints of the subtlety of nature, the hiding-places of truth, the obscurity of things, the entanglement of causes, the weakness of the human mind; wherein nevertheless they show themselves never the more modest, seeing that they will rather lay the blame upon the common condition of men and nature than upon themselves. And then whatever any art fails to attain, they ever set it down upon the authority of that art itself as impossible of attainment; and how can art be found guilty when it is judge in its own cause? So it is but a device for exempting ignorance from ignominy. Now for those things which are delivered and received, this is their condition: barren of works, full of questions; in point of enlargement slow and languid; carrying a show of perfection in the whole, but in the parts ill filled up; in selection popular, and unsatisfactory even to those who propound them; and therefore fenced round and set forth with sundry artifices. And if there be any who have determined to make trial for themselves, and put their own strength to the work of advancing the boundaries of the sciences, yet have they not ventured to cast themselves completely loose from received opinions or to seek their knowledge at the fountain; but they think they have done some great thing if they do but add and introduce into the existing sum of science something of their own; prudently considering with themselves that by making the addition they can assert their liberty, while they retain the credit of modesty by assenting to the rest. But these mediocrities and middle ways so much praised, in deferring to opinions and customs, turn to the great detriment of the sciences. For it is hardly possible at once to admire an author and to go beyond him; knowledge being as water, which will not rise above the level from which it fell. Men of this kind, therefore, amend some things, but advance little; and improve the condition of knowledge, but do not extend its range. Some, indeed, there have been who have gone more boldly to work, and taking it all for an open matter and giving their genius full play, have made a passage for themselves and their own opinions by pulling down and demolishing former ones; and yet all their stir has but little advanced the matter; since their aim has been not to extend philosophy and the arts in substance and value, but only to change doctrines and transfer the kingdom of opinions to themselves; whereby little has indeed been gained, for though the error be the opposite of the other, the causes of erring are the same in both. And if there have been any who, not binding themselves either to other men's opinions or to their own, but loving liberty, have desired to engage others along with themselves in search, these, though honest in intention, have been weak in endeavour. For they have been content to follow probable reasons, and are carried round in a whirl of arguments, and in the promiscuous liberty of search have relaxed the severity of inquiry. There is none who has dwelt upon experience and the facts of nature as long as is necessary. Some there are indeed who have committed themselves to the waves of experience, and almost turned mechanics; yet these again have in their very experiments pursued a kind of wandering inquiry, without any regular system of operations. And besides they have mostly proposed to themselves certain petty tasks, taking it for a great matter to work out some single discovery;—a course of proceeding at once poor in aim and unskilful in design. For no man can rightly and successfully investigate the nature of anything in the thing itself; let him vary his experiments as laboriously as he will, he never comes to a resting-place, but still finds something to seek beyond. And there is another thing to be remembered; namely, that all industry in experimenting has begun with proposing to itself certain definite works to be accomplished, and has pursued them with premature and unseasonable eagerness; it has sought, I say, experiments of Fruit, not experiments of Light; not imitating the divine procedure, which in its first day's work created light only and assigned to it one entire day; on which day it produced no material work, but proceeded to that on the days following. As for those who have given the first place to Logic, supposing that the surest helps to the sciences were to be found in that, they have indeed most truly and excellently perceived that the human intellect left to its own course is not to be trusted; but then the remedy is altogether too weak for the disease; nor is it without evil in itself. For the Logic which is received, though it be very properly applied to civil business and to those arts which rest in discourse and opinion, is not nearly subtle enough to deal with nature; and in offering at what it cannot master, has done more to establish and perpetuate error than to open the way to truth.

Upon the whole therefore, it seems that men have not been happy hitherto either in the trust which they have placed in others or in their own industry with regard to the sciences; especially as neither the demonstrations nor the experiments as yet known are much to be relied upon. But the universe to the eye of the human understanding is framed like a labyrinth; presenting as it does on every side so many ambiguities of way, such deceitful resemblances of objects and signs, natures so irregular in their lines, and so knotted and entangled. And then the way is still to be made by the uncertain light of the sense, sometimes shining out, sometimes clouded over, through the woods of experience and particulars; while those who offer themselves for guides are (as was said) themselves also puzzled, and increase the number of errors and wanderers. In circumstances so difficult neither the natural force of man's judgment nor even any accidental felicity offers any chance of success. No excellence of wit, no repetition of chance experiments, can overcome such difficulties as these. Our steps must be guided by a clue, and the whole way from the very first perception of the senses must be laid out upon a sure plan. Not that I would be understood to mean that nothing whatever has been done in so many ages by so great labours. We have no reason to be ashamed of the discoveries which have been made, and no doubt the ancients proved themselves in everything that turns on wit and abstract meditation, wonderful men. But as in former ages when men sailed only by observation of the stars, they could indeed coast along the shores of the old continent or cross a few small and mediterranean seas; but before the ocean could be traversed and the new world discovered, the use of the mariner's needle, as a more faithful and certain guide, had to be found out; in like manner the discoveries which have been hitherto made in the arts and sciences are such as might be made by practice, meditation, observation, argumentation,—for they lay near to the senses, and immediately beneath common notions; but before we can reach the remoter and more hidden parts of nature, it is necessary that a more perfect use and application of the human mind and intellect be introduced.

For my own part at least, in obedience to the everlasting love of truth, I have committed myself to the uncertainties and difficulties and solitudes of the ways, and relying on the divine assistance have upheld my mind both against the shocks and embattled ranks of opinion, and against my own private and inward hesitations and scruples, and against the fogs and clouds of nature, and the phantoms flitting about on every side; in the hope of providing at last for the present and future generations guidance more faithful and secure. Wherein if I have made any progress, the way has been opened to me by no other means than the true and legitimate humiliation of the human spirit. For all those who before me have applied themselves to the invention of arts have but cast a glance or two upon facts and examples and experience, and straightway proceeded, as if invention were nothing more than an exercise of thought, to invoke their own spirits to give them oracles. I, on the contrary, dwelling purely and constantly among the facts of nature, withdraw my intellect from them no further than may suffice to let the images and rays of natural objects meet in a point, as they do in the sense of vision; whence it follows that the strength and excellency of the wit has but little to do in the matter. And the same humility which I use in inventing I employ likewise in teaching. For I do not endeavour either by triumphs of confutation, or pleadings of antiquity, or assumption of authority, or even by the veil of obscurity, to invest these inventions of mine with any majesty; which might easily be done by one who sought to give lustre to his own name rather than light to other men's minds. I have not sought (I say) nor do I seek either to force or ensnare men's judgments, but I lead them to things themselves and the concordances of things, that they may see for themselves what they have, what they can dispute, what they can add and contribute to the common stock. And for myself, if in anything I have been either too credulous or too little awake and attentive, or if I have fallen off by the way and left the inquiry incomplete, nevertheless I so present these things naked and open, that my errors can be marked and set aside before the mass of knowledge be further infected by them; and it will be easy also for others to continue and carry on my labours. And by these means I suppose that I have established for ever a true and lawful marriage between the empirical and the rational faculty, the unkind and ill-starred divorce and separation of which has thrown into confusion all the affairs of the human family.

Wherefore, seeing that these things do not depend upon myself, at the outset of the work I most humbly and fervently pray to God the Father, God the Son, and God the

Holy Ghost, that remembering the sorrows of mankind and the pilgrimage of this our life wherein we wear out days few and evil, they will vouchsafe through my hands to endow the human family with new mercies. This likewise I humbly pray, that things human may not interfere with things divine, and that from the opening of the ways of sense and the increase of natural light there may arise in our minds no incredulity or darkness with regard to the divine mysteries; but rather that the understanding being thereby purified and purged of fancies and vanity, and yet not the less subject and entirely submissive to the divine oracles, may give to faith that which is faith's. Lastly, that knowledge being now discharged of that venom which the serpent infused into it, and which makes the mind of man to swell, we may not be wise above measure and sobriety, but cultivate truth in charity.

And now having said my prayers I turn to men; to whom I have certain salutary admonitions to offer and certain fair requests to make. My first admonition (which was also my prayer) is that men confine the sense within the limits of duty in respect of things divine: for the sense is like the sun, which reveals the face of earth, but seals and shuts up the face of heaven. My next, that in flying from this evil they fall not into the opposite error, which they will surely do if they think that the inquisition of nature is in any part interdicted or forbidden. For it was not that pure and uncorrupted natural knowledge whereby Adam gave names to the creatures according to their propriety, which gave occasion to the fall. It was the ambitious and proud desire of moral knowledge to judge of good and evil, to the end that man may revolt from God and give laws to himself, which was the form and manner of the temptation. Whereas of the sciences which regard nature, the divine philosopher declares that "it is the glory of God to conceal a thing, but it is the glory of the King to find a thing out." Even as though the divine nature took pleasure in the innocent and kindly sport of children playing at hide and seek, and vouchsafed of his kindness and goodness to admit the human spirit for his playfellow at that game. Lastly, I would address one general admonition to all; that they consider what are the true ends of knowledge, and that they seek it not either for pleasure of the mind, or for contention, or for superiority to others, or for profit, or fame, or power, or any of these inferior things; but for the benefit and use of life; and that they perfect and govern it in charity. For it was from lust of power that the angels fell, from lust of knowledge that man fell; but of charity there can be no excess, neither did angel or man ever come in danger by it.

The requests I have to make are these. Of myself I say nothing; but in behalf of the business which is in hand I entreat men to believe that it is not an opinion to be held, but a work to be done; and to be well assured that I am labouring to lay the foundation, not of any sect or doctrine, but of human utility and power. Next, I ask them to deal fairly by their own interests, and laying aside all emulations and prejudices in favour of this or that opinion, to join in consultation for the common good; and being now freed and guarded by the securities and helps which I offer from the errors and impediments of the way, to come forward themselves and take part in that which remains to be done. Moreover, to be of good hope, nor to imagine that this Instauration of mine is a thing infinite and beyond the power of man, when it is in fact the true end and termination of infinite error; and seeing also that it is by no means forgetful of the conditions of mortality and humanity, (for it does not suppose that the work can be altogether completed within one generation, but provides for its being taken up by another); and finally that it seeks for the sciences not arrogantly in the little cells of human wit, but with reverence in the greater world. But it is the empty things that are vast: things solid are most contracted and lie in little room. And now I have only one favour more to ask (else injustice to me may perhaps imperil the business itself)—that men will consider well how far, upon that which I must needs assert (if I am to be consistent with myself), they are entitled to judge and decide upon these doctrines of mine; inasmuch as all that premature human reasoning which anticipates inquiry, and is abstracted from the facts rashly and sooner than is fit, is by me rejected (so far as the inquisition of nature is concerned), as a thing uncertain, confused, and ill built up; and I cannot be fairly asked to abide by the decision of a tribunal which is itself on its trial.

THE PLAN OF THE WORK

THE WORK IS IN SIX PARTS:

1. *The Divisions of the Sciences*

2. *The New Organon; or Directions concerning the Interpretation of Nature*

3. *The Phenomena of the Universe; or a Natural and Experimental History for the foundation of Philosophy*

4. *The Ladder of the Intellect*

5. *The Forerunners; or Anticipations of the New Philosophy*

6. *The New Philosophy; or Active Science*

THE ARGUMENTS OF THE SEVERAL PARTS

IT being part of my design to set everything forth, as far as may be, plainly and perspicuously (for nakedness of the mind is still, as nakedness of the body once was, the companion of innocence and simplicity), let me first explain the order and plan of the work. I distribute it into six parts.

The first part [2] exhibits a summary or general description of the knowledge which the human race at present possesses. For I thought it good to make some pause upon that which is received; that thereby the old may be more easily made perfect and the new more easily approached. And I hold the improvement of that which we have to be as much an object as the acquisition of more. Besides which it will make me the better listened to; for "He that is ignorant (says the proverb) receives not the words of knowledge, unless thou first tell him that which is in his own heart."

439

We will therefore make a coasting voyage along the shores of the arts and sciences received; not without importing into them some useful things by the way.

In laying out the divisions of the sciences however, I take into account not only things already invented and known, but likewise things omitted which ought to be there. For there are found in the intellectual as in the terrestial globe waste regions as well as cultivated ones. It is no wonder therefore if I am sometimes obliged to depart from the ordinary divisions. For in adding to the total you necessarily alter the parts and sections; and the received divisions of the sciences are fitted only to the received sum of them as it stands now.

With regard to those things which I shall mark as omitted, I intend not merely to set down a simple title or a concise argument of that which is wanted. For as often as I have occasion to report anything as deficient, the nature of which is at all obscure, so that men may not perhaps easily understand what I mean or what the work is which I have in my head, I shall always (provided it be a matter of any worth) take care to subjoin either directions for the execution of such work, or else a portion of the work itself executed by myself as a sample of the whole: thus giving assistance in every case either by work or by counsel. For if it were for the sake of my own reputation only and other men's interests were not concerned in it, I would not have any man think that in such cases merely some light and vague notion has crossed my mind, and that the things which I desire and offer at are no better than wishes; when they are in fact things which men may certainly command if they will, and of which I have formed in my own mind a clear and detailed conception. For I do not propose merely to survey these regions in my mind, like an augur taking auspices, but to enter them like a general who means to take possession.—So much for the first part of the work.

Having thus coasted past the ancient arts, the next point is to equip the intellect for passing beyond. To the second part therefore belongs the doctrine concerning the better and more perfect use of human reason in the inquisition of things, and the true helps of the understanding: that thereby (as far as the condition of mortality and humanity allows) the intellect may be raised and exalted, and made capable of overcoming the difficulties and obscurities of nature. The art which I introduce with this view (which I call *Interpretation of Nature*) is a kind of logic; though the difference between it and the ordinary logic is great; indeed immense. For the ordinary logic professes to contrive and prepare helps and guards for the understanding, as mine does; and in this one point they agree. But mine differs from it in three points especially; viz. in the end aimed at; in the order of demonstration; and in the starting point of the inquiry.

For the end which this science of mine proposes is the invention not of arguments but of arts; not of things in accordance with principles, but of principles themselves; not of probable reasons, but of designations and directions for works. And as the intention is different, so accordingly is the effect; the effect of the one being to overcome an opponent in argument, of the other to command nature in action.

In accordance with this end is also the nature and order of the demonstrations. For in the ordinary logic almost all the work is spent about the syllogism. Of induction the logicians seem hardly to have taken any serious thought, but they pass it by with a slight notice, and hasten on to the formulæ of disputation. I on the contrary reject demonstration by syllogism, as acting too confusedly, and letting nature slip out of its hands. For although no one can doubt that things which agree in a middle term agree with one another (which is a proposition of mathematical certainty), yet it leaves an opening for deception; which is this. The syllogism consists of propositions; propositions of words; and words are the tokens and signs of notions. Now if the very notions of the mind (which are as the soul of words and the basis of the whole structure) be improperly and overhastily abstracted from facts, vague, not sufficiently definite, faulty in short in many ways, the whole edifice tumbles. I therefore reject the syllogism; and that not only as regards principles (for to principles the logicians themselves do not apply it) but also as regards middle propositions; which, though obtainable no doubt by the syllogism, are, when so obtained, barren of works, remote from practice, and altogether unavailable for the active department of the sciences. Although therefore I leave to the syllogism and these famous and boasted modes of demonstration their jurisdiction over popular arts and such as are matter of opinion (in which department I leave all as it is), yet in dealing with the nature of things I use induction throughout, and that in the minor propositions as well as the major. For I consider induction to be that form of demonstration which upholds the sense, and closes with[3] nature, and comes to the very brink of operation, if it does not actually deal with it.

Hence it follows that the order of demonstration is likewise inverted. For hitherto the proceeding has been to fly at once from the sense and particulars up to the most general propositions, as certain fixed poles for the argument to turn upon, and from these to derive the rest by middle terms: a short way, no doubt, but precipitate; and one which will never lead to nature, though it offers an easy and ready way to disputation. Now my plan is to proceed regularly and gradually from one axiom to another, so that the most general are not reached till the last: but then when you do come to them you find them to be not empty notions, but well defined, and such as nature would really recognise as her first principles, and such as lie at the heart and marrow of things.

But the greatest change I introduce is in the form itself of induction and the judgment made thereby. For the induction of which the logicians speak, which proceeds by simple enumeration, is a puerile thing; concludes at hazard; is always liable to be upset by a contradictory instance; takes into account only what is known and ordinary; and leads to no result.

Now what the sciences stand in need of is a form of

induction which shall analyse experience and take it to pieces, and by a due process of exclusion and rejection lead to an inevitable conclusion. And if that ordinary mode of judgment practised by the logicians was so laborious, and found exercise for such great wits, how much more labour must we be prepared to bestow upon this other, which is extracted not merely out of the depths of the mind, but out of the very bowels of nature.

Nor is this all. For I also sink the foundations of the sciences deeper and firmer; and I begin the inquiry nearer the source than men have done heretofore; submitting to examination those things which the common logic takes on trust. For first, the logicians borrow the principles of each science from the science itself; secondly, they hold in reverence the first notions of the mind; and lastly, they receive as conclusive the immediate informations of the sense, when well disposed. Now upon the first point, I hold that true logic ought to enter the several provinces of science armed with a higher authority than belongs to the principles of those sciences themselves, and ought to call those putative principles to account until they are fully established. Then with regard to the first notions of the intellect; there is not one of the impressions taken by the intellect when left to go its own way, but I hold it for suspected, and no way established, until it has submitted to a new trial and a fresh judgment has been thereupon pronounced. And lastly, the information of the sense itself I sift and examine in many ways. For certain it is that the senses deceive; but then at the same time they supply the means of discovering their own errors; only the errors are here, the means of discovery are to seek.

The sense fails in two ways. Sometimes it gives no information, sometimes it gives false information. For first, there are very many things which escape the sense, even when best disposed and no way obstructed; by reason either of the subtlety of the whole body, or the minuteness of the parts, or distance of place, or slowness or else swiftness of motion, or familiarity of the object, or other causes. And again when the sense does apprehend a thing its apprehension is not much to be relied upon. For the testimony and information of the sense has reference always to man, not to the universe; and it is a great error to assert that the sense is the measure of things.

To meet these difficulties, I have sought on all sides diligently and faithfully to provide helps for the sense—substitutes to supply its failures, rectifications to correct its errors; and this I endeavour to accomplish not so much by instruments as by experiments. For the subtlety of experiments is far greater than that of the sense itself, even when assisted by exquisite instruments; such experiments, I mean, as are skilfully and artificially devised for the express purpose of determining the point in question. To the immediate and proper perception of the sense therefore I do not give much weight; but I contrive that the office of the sense shall be only to judge of the experiment, and that the experiment itself shall judge of the thing. And thus I conceive that I perform the office of a true priest of the sense (from which all knowledge in nature must be sought, unless men mean to go mad) and a not unskilful interpreter of its oracles; and that while others only profess to uphold and cultivate the sense, I do so in fact. Such then are the provisions I make for finding the genuine light of nature and kindling and bringing it to bear. And they would be sufficient of themselves, if the human intellect were even, and like a fair sheet of paper with no writing on it. But since the minds of men are strangely possessed and beset, so that there is no true and even surface left to reflect the genuine rays of things, it is necessary to seek a remedy for this also.

Now the idols, or phantoms, by which the mind is occupied are either adventitious or innate. The adventitious come into the mind from without; namely, either from the doctrines and sects of philosophers, or from perverse rules of demonstration. But the innate are inherent in the very nature of the intellect, which is far more prone to error than the sense is. For let men please themselves as they will in admiring and almost adoring the human mind, this is certain: that as an uneven mirror distorts the rays of objects according to its own figure and section, so the mind, when it receives impressions of objects through the sense, cannot be trusted to report them truly, but in forming its notions mixes up its own nature with the nature of things.

And as the first two kinds of idols are hard to eradicate, so idols of this last kind cannot be eradicated at all. All that can be done is to point them out, so that this insidious action of the mind may be marked and reproved (else as fast as old errors are destroyed new ones will spring up out of the ill complexion of the mind itself, and so we shall have but a change of errors, and not a clearance); and to lay it down once for all as a fixed and established maxim, that the intellect is not qualified to judge except by means of induction, and induction in its legitimate form. This doctrine then of the expurgation of the intellect to qualify it for dealing with truth, is comprised in three refutations: the refutation of the Philosophies; the refutation of the Demonstrations; and the refutation of the Natural Human Reason. The explanation of which things, and of the true relation between the nature of things and the nature of the mind, is as the strewing and decoration of the bridal chamber of the Mind and the Universe, the Divine Goodness assisting; out of which marriage let us hope (and be this the prayer of the bridal song) there may spring helps to man, and a line and race of inventions that may in some degree subdue and overcome the necessities and miseries of humanity. This is the second part of the work.

But I design not only to indicate and mark out the ways, but also to enter them. And therefore the third part of the work embraces the Phenomena of the Universe; that is to say, experience of every kind, and such a natural history as may serve for a foundation to build philosophy upon. For a good method of demonstration or form of interpreting nature may keep the mind from going astray or stumbling, but it is not any excellence of method that can supply it with the material of knowledge. Those however who aspire not to guess and divine, but to discover and know; who propose not to devise mimic and fabulous worlds of their own, but to examine and dissect the nature of this very world itself; must go to facts themselves for everything. Nor can the place of this labour and search and worldwide perambulation be supplied by any genius or meditation or argumentation; no, not if all men's wits could meet in one. This therefore we must have, or the business must be for ever abandoned. But up to this day such has been the condition of men in this matter, that it is no wonder if nature will not give herself into their hands.

For first, the information of the sense itself, sometimes failing, sometimes false; observation, careless, irregular, and led by chance; tradition, vain and fed on rumour; practice, slavishly bent upon its work; experiment, blind, stupid, vague, and prematurely broken off; lastly, natural history trivial and poor;—all these have contributed to supply the understanding with very bad materials for philosophy and the sciences.

Then an attempt is made to mend the matter by a preposterous subtlety and winnowing of argument. But this comes too late, the case being already past remedy; and is far from setting the business right or sifting away the errors. The only hope therefore of any greater increase or progress lies in a reconstruction of the sciences.

Of this reconstruction the foundation must be laid in natural history, and that of a new kind and gathered on a new principle. For it is in vain that you polish the mirror if there are no images to be reflected; and it is as necessary that the intellect should be supplied with fit matter to work upon, as with safeguards to guide its working. But my history differs from that in use (as my logic does) in many things,—in end and office, in mass and composition, in subtlety, in selection also and setting forth, with a view to the operations which are to follow.

For first, the object of the natural history which I propose is not so much to delight with variety of matter or to help with present use of experiments, as to give light to the discovery of causes and supply a suckling philosophy with its first food. For though it be true that I am principally in pursuit of works and the active department of the sciences, yet I wait for harvest-time, and do not attempt to mow the moss or to reap the green corn. For I well know that axioms once rightly discovered will carry whole troops of works along with them, and produce them, not here and there one, but in clusters. And that unseasonable and puerile hurry to snatch by way of earnest at the first works which come within reach, I utterly condemn and reject, as an Atalanta's apple that hinders the race. Such then is the office of this natural history of mine.

Next, with regard to the mass and composition of it: I mean it to be a history not only of nature free and at large (when she is left to her own course and does her work her own way),—such as that of the heavenly bodies, meteors, earth and sea, minerals, plants, animals,—but much more of nature under constraint and vexed; that is to say, when by art and the hand of man she is forced out of her natural state, and squeezed and moulded. Therefore I set down at length all experiments of the mechanical arts, of the operative part of the liberal arts, of the many crafts which have not yet grown into arts properly so called, so far as I have been able to examine them and as they conduce to the end in view. Nay (to say the plain truth) I do in fact (low and vulgar as men may think it) count more upon this part both for helps and safeguards than upon the other; seeing that the nature of things betrays itself more readily under the vexations of art than in its natural freedom.

Nor do I confine the history to Bodies; but I have thought it my duty besides to make a separate history of such Virtues as may be considered cardinal in nature. I mean those original passions or desires of matter which constitute the primary elements of nature; such as Dense and Rare, Hot and Cold, Solid and Fluid, Heavy and Light, and several others.

Then again, to speak of subtlety: I seek out and get together a kind of experiments much subtler and simpler than those which occur accidentally. For I drag into light many things which no one who was not proceeding by a regular and certain way to the discovery of causes would have thought of inquiring after; being indeed in themselves of no great use; which shows that they were not sought for on their own account; but having just the same relation to things and works which the letters of the alphabet have to speech and words—which, though in themselves useless, are the elements of which all discourse is made up.

Further, in the selection of the relations and experiments I conceive I have been a more cautious purveyor than those who have hitherto dealt with natural history. For I admit nothing but on the faith of eyes, or at least of careful and severe examination; so that nothing is exaggerated for wonder's sake, but what I state is sound and without mixture of fables or vanity. All received or current falsehoods also (which by strange negligence have been allowed for many ages to prevail and become established) I proscribe and brand by name; that the sciences may be no more troubled with them. For it has been well observed that the fables and superstitions and follies which nurses instil into children do serious injury to their minds; and the same consideration makes me anxious, having the management of the childhood as it were of philosophy in its course of natural history, not to let it accustom itself in the beginning to any vanity. Moreover, whenever I come to a new experiment of any subtlety (though it be in my own opinion certain and approved), I nevertheless subjoin a clear account of the manner in which I made it; that men knowing exactly how each point was made out, may see whether there be any error connected with it, and may arouse themselves to devise proofs more trustworthy and exquisite, if such can be found; and finally, I interpose everywhere admonitions and scruples and cautions, with a religious care to eject, repress, and as it were exorcise every kind of phantasm.

Lastly, knowing how much the sight of man's mind is distracted by experience and history, and how hard it is at the first (especially for minds either tender or preoccupied) to become familiar with nature, I not unfrequently subjoin observations of my own, being as the first offers, inclinations, and as it were glances of history towards philosophy; both by way of an assurance to men that they will not be kept for ever tossing on the waves of experience, and also that when the time comes for the intellect to begin its work, it may find everything the more ready. By such a natural history then as I have described, I conceive that a safe and convenient approach may be made to nature, and matter supplied of good quality and well prepared for the understanding to work upon.

And now that we have surrounded the intellect with faithful helps and guards, and got together with most careful selection a regular army of divine works, it may seem that we have no more to do but to proceed to philosophy itself. And yet in a matter so difficult and doubtful there are still some things which it seems necessary to premise, partly for convenience of explanation, partly for present use.

Of these the first is to set forth examples of inquiry and invention according to my method, exhibited by anticipation in some particular subjects; choosing such subjects as are at once the most noble in themselves among those under inquiry, and most different one from another; that there may be an example in every kind. I do not speak of those examples which are joined to the several precepts and rules by way of illustration (for of these I have given plenty in the second part of the work); but I mean actual types and models, by which the entire process of the mind and the whole fabric and order of invention from the beginning to the end, in certain subjects, and those various and remarkable, should be set as it were before the eyes. For I remember that in the mathematics it is easy to follow the demonstration when you have a machine beside you; whereas without that help all appears involved and more subtle than it really is. To examples of this kind,—being in fact nothing more than an application of the second part in detail and at large,—the fourth part of the work is devoted.

The fifth part is for temporary use only, pending the completion of the rest; like interest payable from time to time until the principal be forthcoming. For I do not make so blindly for the end of my journey, as to neglect anything useful that may turn up by the way. And therefore I include in this fifth part such things as I have myself discovered, proved, or added,—not however according to the true rules and methods of interpretation, but by the ordinary use of the understanding in inquiring and discovering. For besides that I hope my speculations may in virtue of my continual conversancy with nature have a value beyond the pretensions of my wit, they will serve in the meantime for wayside inns, in which the mind may rest and refresh itself on its journey to more certain conclusions. Nevertheless I wish it to be understood in the meantime that they are conclusions by which (as not being discovered and proved by the true form of interpretation) I do not at all mean to bind myself. Nor need any one be alarmed at such suspension of judgment, in one who maintains not simply that nothing can be known, but only that nothing can be known except in a certain course and way; and yet establishes provisionally certain degrees of assurance, for use and relief until the mind shall arrive at a knowledge of causes in which it can rest. For even those schools of philosophy which held the absolute impossibility of knowing anything were not inferior to those which took upon them to pronounce. But then they did not provide helps for the sense and understanding, as I have done, but simply took away all their authority: which is quite a different thing— almost the reverse.

The sixth part of my work (to which the rest is subservient and ministrant) discloses and sets forth that philosophy which by the legitimate, chaste, and severe course of inquiry which I have explained and provided is at length developed and established. The completion however of this last part is a thing both above my strength and beyond my hopes. I have made a beginning of the work— a beginning, as I hope, not unimportant:—the fortune of the human race will give the issue;—such an issue, it may be, as in the present condition of things and men's minds cannot easily be conceived or imagined. For the matter in hand is no mere felicity of speculation, but the real business and fortunes of the human race, and all power of operation. For man is but the servant and interpreter of nature: what he does and what he knows is only what he has observed of nature's order in fact or in thought; beyond this he knows nothing and can do nothing. For the chain of causes cannot by any force be loosed or broken, nor can nature be commanded except by being obeyed. And so those twin objects, human Knowledge and human Power, do really meet in one; and it is from ignorance of causes that operation fails.

And all depends on keeping the eye steadily fixed upon the facts of nature and so receiving their images simply as they are. For God forbid that we should give out a dream of our own imagination for a pattern of the world; rather may he graciously grant to us to write an apocalypse or true vision of the footsteps of the Creator imprinted on his creatures.

Therefore do thou, O Father, who gavest the visible light as the first fruits of creation, and didst breathe into the face of man the intellectual light as the crown and consummation thereof, guard and protect this work, which coming from thy goodness returneth to thy glory. Thou when thou turnedst to look upon the works which thy hands had made, sawest that all was very good, and didst rest from thy labours. But man, when he turned to look upon the work which his hands had made, saw that all was vanity and vexation of spirit, and could find no rest therein. Wherefore if we labour in thy works with the sweat of our brows thou wilt make us partakers of thy vision and thy sabbath. Humbly we pray that this mind may be steadfast in us, and that through these our hands, and the hands of others to whom thou shalt give the same spirit, thou wilt vouchsafe to endow the human family with new mercies.

THE
FIRST PART OF THE INSTAURATION
WHICH COMPRISES THE
DIVISIONS OF THE SCIENCES
IS WANTING
But some account of them will be found in
the Second Book of the
"PROFICIENCE AND ADVANCEMENT OF
LEARNING
DIVINE AND HUMAN"

NEXT COMES
THE
SECOND PART OF THE INSTAURATION
WHICH EXHIBITS
THE ART ITSELF OF INTERPRETING
NATURE
AND OF THE TRUER EXERCISE
OF THE INTELLECT
Not however in the form of a regular Treatise,
but only a Summary digested
into Aphorisms

THE

SECOND PART OF THE WORK

WHICH IS CALLED

THE NEW ORGANON

OR

TRUE DIRECTIONS

CONCERNING

THE INTERPRETATION OF NATURE

[NOVUM ORGANUM]

PREFACE

Those who have taken upon them to lay down the law of nature as a thing already searched out and understood, whether they have spoken in simple assurance or professional affectation, have therein done philosophy and the sciences great injury. For as they have been successful in inducing belief, so they have been effective in quenching and stopping inquiry; and have done more harm by spoiling and putting an end to other men's efforts than good by their own. Those on the other hand who have taken a contrary course, and asserted that absolutely nothing can be known,—whether it were from hatred of the ancient sophists, or from uncertainty and fluctuation of mind, or even from a kind of fulness of learning, that they fell upon this opinion,—have certainly advanced reasons for it that are not to be despised; but yet they have neither started from true principles nor rested in the just conclusion, zeal and affectation having carried them much too far. The more ancient of the Greeks (whose writings are lost) took up with better judgment a position between these two extremes,—between the presumption of pronouncing on everything, and the despair of comprehending anything; and though frequently and bitterly complaining of the difficulty of inquiry and the obscurity of things, and like impatient horses champing the bit, they did not the less follow up their object and engage with Nature; thinking (it seems) that this very question,—viz. whether or no anything can be known,—was to be settled not by arguing, but by trying. And yet they too, trusting entirely to the force of their understanding, applied no rule, but made everything turn upon hard thinking and perpetual working and exercise of the mind.

Now my method, though hard to practise, is easy to explain; and it is this. I propose to establish progressive stages of certainty. The evidence of the sense, helped and guarded by a certain process of correction, I retain. But the mental operation which follows the act of sense I for the most part reject; and instead of it I open and lay out a new and certain path for the mind to proceed in, starting directly from the simple sensuous perception. The necessity of this was felt no doubt by those who attributed so much importance to Logic; showing thereby that they were in search of helps for the understanding, and had no confidence in the native and spontaneous process of the mind. But this remedy comes too late to do any good, when the mind is already, through the daily intercourse and conversation of life, occupied with unsound doctrines and beset on all sides by vain imaginations. And therefore that art of Logic, coming (as I said) too late to the rescue, and no way able to set matters right again, has had the effect of fixing errors rather than disclosing truth. There remains but one course for the recovery of a sound and healthy condition,—namely, that the entire work of the understanding be commenced afresh, and the mind itself be from the very outset not left to take its own course, but guided at every step; and the business be done as if by machinery. Certainly if in things mechanical men had set to work with their naked hands, without help or force of instruments, just as in things intellectual they have set to work with little else than the naked forces of the understanding, very small would the matters have been which, even with their best efforts applied in conjunction, they could have attempted or accomplished. Now (to pause awhile upon this example and look in it as in a glass) let us suppose that some vast obelisk were (for the decoration of a triumph or some such magnificence) to be removed from its place, and that men should set to work upon it with their naked hands; would not any sober spectator think them mad? And if they should then send for more people, thinking that in that way they might manage it, would he not think them all the madder? And if they then proceeded to make a selection, putting away the weaker hands, and using only the strong and vigorous, would he not think them madder than ever? And if lastly, not content with this, they resolved to call in aid the art of athletics, and required all their men to come with hands, arms, and sinews well anointed and medicated according to the rules of art, would he not cry out that they were only taking pains to show a kind of method and discretion in their madness? Yet just so it is that men proceed in matters intellectual,—with just the same kind of mad effort and useless combination of forces,—when they hope great things either from the number and co-operation or from the excellency and acuteness of individual wits; yea, and when they endeavour by Logic (which may be considered as a kind of athletic art) to strengthen the sinews of the understanding; and yet with all this study and endeavour it is apparent to any true judgment that they are but applying the naked intellect all the time; whereas in every great work to be done by the hand of man it is manifestly impossible, without instruments and machinery, either for the strength of each to be exerted or the strength of all to be united.

Upon these premises two things occur to me of which, that they may not be overlooked, I would have men reminded. First it falls out fortunately as I think for the allaying of contradictions and heart-burnings, that the honour and reverence due to the ancients remains untouched and undiminished; while I may carry out my designs and at the same time reap the fruit of my modesty. For if I profess that I, going the same road as the ancients, have something better to produce, there must needs have been some comparison or rivalry between us (not to be avoided by any art of words) in respect of excellency or ability of wit; and though in this there would be nothing unlawful or new (for if there be anything misapprehended by them, or falsely laid down, why may not I, using a liberty common to all, take exception to it?) yet the contest, however just and allowable, would have been an unequal one perhaps, in respect of the measure of my own powers. As it is however,—my object being to open a new way for the understanding, a way by them untried and unknown,—the case is altered; party zeal and emulation are at an end; and I appear merely as a guide to point out the road; an office of small authority, and depending more upon a kind of luck than upon any ability or excellency. And thus much relates to the persons only. The other point of which I would have men reminded relates to the matter itself.

Be it remembered then that I am far from wishing to interfere with the philosophy which now flourishes, or with any other philosophy more correct and complete than this which has been or may hereafter be propounded. For I do not object to the use of this received philosophy, or others like it, for supplying matter for disputations or ornaments for discourse,—for the professor's lecture and for the business of life. Nay more, I declare openly that for these uses the philosophy which I bring forward will not be much available. It does not lie in the way. It cannot be caught up in passage. It does not flatter the understanding by conformity with preconceived notions. Nor will it come down to the apprehension of the vulgar except by its utility and effects.

Let there be therefore (and may it be for the benefit of both) two streams and two dispensations of knowledge;

and in like manner two tribes or kindreds of students in philosophy—tribes not hostile or alien to each other, but bound together by mutual services;—let there in short be one method for the cultivation, another for the invention, of knowledge.

And for those who prefer the former, either from hurry or from considerations of business or for want of mental power to take in and embrace the other (which must needs be most men's case), I wish that they may succeed to their desire in what they are about, and obtain what they are pursuing. But if any man there be who, not content to rest in and use the knowledge which has already been discovered, aspires to penetrate further; to overcome, not an adversary in argument, but nature in action; to seek, not pretty and probable conjectures but certain and demonstrable knowledge;—I invite all such to join themselves, as true sons of knowledge, with me, that passing by the outer courts of nature, which numbers have trodden, we may find a way at length into her inner chambers. And to make my meaning clearer and to familiarise the thing by giving it a name, I have chosen to call one of these methods or ways *Anticipation of the Mind*, the other *Interpretation of Nature*.

Moreover I have one request to make. I have on my own part made it my care and study that the things which I shall propound should not only be true, but should also be presented to men's minds, how strangely soever preoccupied and obstructed, in a manner not harsh or unpleasant. It is but reasonable however (especially in so great a restoration of learning and knowledge) that I should claim of men one favour in return; which is this; If any one would form an opinion or judgment either out of his own observation, or out of the crowd of authorities, or out of the forms of demonstration (which have now acquired a sanction like that of judicial laws), concerning these speculations of mine, let him not hope that he can do it in passage or by the by; but let him examine the thing thoroughly; let him make some little trial for himself of the way which I describe and lay out; let him familiarise his thoughts with that subtlety of nature to which experience bears witness; let him correct by seasonable patience and due delay the depraved and deep-rooted habits of his mind; and when all this is done and he has begun to be his own master, let him (if he will) use his own judgment.

[BOOK I]

APHORISMS

CONCERNING

THE INTERPRETATION OF NATURE

AND

THE KINGDOM OF MAN

Aphorism

I

Man, being the servant and interpreter of Nature, can do and understand so much and so much only as he has observed in fact or in thought of the course of nature: beyond this he neither knows anything nor can do anything.

II

Neither the naked hand nor the understanding left to itself can effect much. It is by instruments and helps that the work is done, which are as much wanted for the understanding as for the hand. And as the instruments of the hand either give motion or guide it, so the instruments of the mind supply either suggestions for the understanding or cautions.

461

III

Human knowledge and human power meet in one; for where the cause is not known the effect cannot be produced. Nature to be commanded must be obeyed; and that which in contemplation is as the cause is in operation as the rule.

IV

Towards the effecting of works, all that man can do is to put together or put asunder natural bodies. The rest is done by nature working within.

V

The study of nature with a view to works is engaged in by the mechanic, the mathematician, the physician, the alchemist, and the magician; but by all (as things now are) with slight endeavour and scanty success.

VI

It would be an unsound fancy and self-contradictory to expect that things which have never yet been done can be done except by means which have never yet been tried.

VII

The productions of the mind and hand seem very numerous in books and manufactures. But all this variety lies in an exquisite subtlety and derivations from a few things already known; not in the number of axioms.

VIII

Moreover the works already known are due to chance and experiment rather than to sciences; for the sciences we now possess are merely systems for the nice ordering and setting forth of things already invented; not methods of invention or directions for new works.

IX

The cause and root of nearly all evils in the sciences is this—that while we falsely admire and extol the powers of the human mind we neglect to seek for its true helps.

X

The subtlety of nature is greater many times over than the subtlety of the senses and understanding; so that all those specious meditations, speculations, and glosses in which men indulge are quite from the purpose,* only there is no one by to observe it.

XI

As the sciences which we now have do not help us in finding out new works, so neither does the logic which we now have help us in finding out new sciences.

XII

The logic now in use serves rather to fix and give stability to the errors which have their foundation in commonly received notions than to help the search after truth. So it does more harm than good.

XIII

The syllogism is not applied to the first principles of sciences, and is applied in vain to intermediate axioms; being no match for the subtlety of nature. It commands assent therefore to the proposition, but does not take hold of the thing.

* Literally, "are a thing insane." The meaning appears to be, that these speculations, being founded upon such an inadequate conception of the case, must necessarily be so wide of the truth that they would seem like mere madness if we could only compare them with it: like the aim of a man blindfolded to bystanders looking on.—J.S.

XIV

The syllogism consists of propositions, propositions consist of words, words are symbols of notions. Therefore if the notions themselves (which is the root of the matter) are confused and over-hastily abstracted from the facts, there can be no firmness in the superstructure. Our only hope therefore lies in a true induction.

XV

There is no soundness in our notions whether logical or physical. Substance, Quality, Action, Passion, Essence itself, are not sound notions: much less are Heavy, Light, Dense, Rare, Moist, Dry, Generation, Corruption, Attraction, Repulsion, Element, Matter, Form, and the like; but all are fantastical and ill defined.

XVI

Our notions of less general species, as Man, Dog, Dove, and of the immediate perceptions of the sense, as Hot, Cold, Black, White, do not materially mislead us; yet even these are sometimes confused by the flux and alteration of matter and the mixing of one thing with another. All the others which men have hitherto adopted are but wanderings, not being abstracted and formed from things by proper methods.

XVII

Nor is there less of wilfulness and wandering in the construction of axioms than in the formations of notions; not excepting even those very principles which are obtained by common induction; but much more in the axioms and lower propositions educed by the syllogism.

XVIII

The discoveries which have hitherto been made in the sciences are such as lie close to vulgar notions, scarcely beneath the surface. In order to penetrate into the inner and further recesses of nature, it is necessary that both notions and axioms be derived from things by a more sure and guarded way; and that a method of intellectual operation be introduced altogether better and more certain.

XIX

There are and can be only two ways of searching into and discovering truth. The one flies from the senses and particulars to the most general axioms, and from these principles, the truth of which it takes for settled and immoveable, proceeds to judgment and to the discovery of middle axioms. And this way is now in fashion. The other derives axioms from the senses and particulars, rising by a gradual and unbroken ascent, so that it arrives at the most general axioms last of all. This is the true way, but as yet untried.

XX

The understanding left to itself takes the same course (namely, the former) which it takes in accordance with logical order. For the mind longs to spring up to positions of higher generality, that it may find rest there; and so after a little while wearies of experiment. But this evil is increased by logic, because of the order and solemnity of its disputations.

XXI

The understanding left to itself, in a sober, patient, and grave mind, especially if it be not hindered by received doctrines, tries a little that other way, which is the right one, but with little progress; since the understanding, unless directed and assisted, is a thing unequal, and quite unfit to contend with the obscurity of things.

XXII

Both ways set out from the senses and particulars, and rest in the highest generalities; but the difference between them is infinite. For the one just glances at experiment and particulars in passing, the other dwells duly and orderly among them. The one, again, begins at once by establishing certain abstract and useless generalities, the other rises by gradual steps to that which is prior and better known in the order of nature.

XXIII

There is a great difference between the Idols of the human mind and the Ideas of the divine. That is to say, between certain empty dogmas, and the true signatures and marks set upon the works of creation as they are found in nature.

XXIV

It cannot be that axioms established by argumentation should avail for the discovery of new works; since the subtlety of nature is greater many times over than the subtlety of argument. But axioms duly and orderly formed from particulars easily discover the way to new particulars, and thus render sciences active.

XXV

The axioms now in use, having been suggested by a scanty and manipular experience and a few particulars of most general occurrence, are made for the most part just large enough to fit and take these in: and therefore it is no wonder if they do not lead to new particulars. And if some opposite instance, not observed or not known before, chance to come in the way, the axiom is rescued and preserved by some frivolous distinction; whereas the truer course would be to correct the axiom itself.

XXVI

The conclusions of human reason as ordinarily applied in matter of nature, I call for the sake of distinction *Anticipations of Nature* (as a thing rash or premature). That reason which is elicited from facts by a just and methodical process, I call *Interpretation of Nature*.

XXVII

Anticipations are a ground sufficiently firm for consent; for even if men went mad all after the same fashion, they might agree one with another well enough.

XXVIII

For the winning of assent, indeed, anticipations are far more powerful than interpretations; because being collected from a few instances, and those for the most part of familiar occurrence, they straightway touch the understanding and fill the imagination; whereas interpretations on the other hand, being gathered here and there from very various and widely dispersed facts, cannot suddenly strike the understanding; and therefore they must needs, in respect of the opinions of the time, seem harsh and out of tune; much as the mysteries of faith do.

XXIX

In sciences founded on opinions and dogmas, the use of anticipations and logic is good; for in them the object is to command assent to the proposition, not to master the thing.

XXX

Though all the wits of all the ages should meet together and combine and transmit their labours, yet will no great progress ever be made in science by means of anticipations; because radical errors in the first concoction of the mind are not to be cured by the excellence of functions and remedies subsequent.

XXXI

It is idle to expect any great advancement in science from the superinducing and engrafting of new things upon old. We must begin anew from the very foundations, unless we would revolve for ever in a circle with mean and contemptible progress.

XXXII

The honour of the ancient authors, and indeed of all, remains untouched; since the comparison I challenge is not of wits or faculties, but of ways and methods, and the part I take upon myself is not that of a judge, but of a guide.

XXXIII

This must be plainly avowed: no judgment can be rightly formed either of my method or of the discoveries to which it leads, by means of anticipations (that is to say, of the reasoning which is now in use); since I cannot be called on to abide by the sentence of a tribunal which is itself on its trial.

XXXIV

Even to deliver and explain what I bring forward is no easy matter; for things in themselves new will yet be apprehended with reference to what is old.

XXXV

It was said by Borgia of the expedition of the French into Italy, that they came with chalk in their hands to mark out their lodgings, not with arms to force their way in. I in like manner would have my doctrine enter quietly into the minds that are fit and capable of receiving it; for confutations cannot be employed, when the difference is upon first principles and very notions and even upon forms of demonstration.

XXXVI

One method of delivery alone remains to us; which is simply this: we must lead men to the particulars themselves, and their series and order; while men on their side must force themselves for awhile to lay their notions by and begin to familiarise themselves with facts.

XXXVII

The doctrine of those who have denied that certainty could be attained at all, has some agreement with my way of proceeding at the first setting out; but they end in being infinitely separated and opposed. For the holders of that doctrine assert simply that nothing can be known; I also assert that not much can be known in nature by the way which is now in use. But then they go on to destroy the authority of the senses and understanding; whereas I proceed to devise and supply helps for the same.

XXXVIII

The idols and false notions which are now in possession of the human understanding, and have taken deep root therein, not only so beset men's minds that truth can hardly find entrance, but even after entrance obtained, they will again in the very instauration of the sciences meet and trouble us, unless men being forewarned of the danger fortify themselves as far as may be against their assaults.

XXXIX

There are four classes of Idols which beset men's minds. To these for distinction's sake I have assigned names,—calling the first class *Idols of the Tribe;* the second, *Idols of the Cave;* the third, *Idols of the Market-place;* the fourth, *Idols of the Theatre.*

XL

The formation of ideas and axioms by true induction is no doubt the proper remedy to be applied for the keeping off and clearing away of idols. To point them out, however, is of great use; for the doctrine of Idols is to the Interpretation of Nature what the doctrine of the refutation of Sophisms is to common Logic.

XLI

The Idols of the Tribe have their foundation in human
nature itself, and in the tribe or race of men. For it is a
false assertion that the sense of man is the measure of
things. On the contrary, all perceptions as well of the sense
as of the mind are according to the measure of the individual and not according to the measure of the universe. And
the human understanding is like a false mirror, which, receiving rays irregularly, distorts and discolours the nature
of things by mingling its own nature with it.

XLII

The Idols of the Cave are the idols of the individual man.
For every one (besides the errors common to human nature
in general) has a cave or den of his own, which refracts
and discolours the light of nature; owing either to his own
proper and peculiar nature; or to his education and conversation with others; or to the reading of books, and the
authority of those whom he esteems and admires; or to the
differences of impressions, accordingly as they take place in
a mind preoccupied and predisposed or in a mind indifferent and settled; or the like. So that the spirit of man (according as it is meted out to different individuals) is in fact
a thing variable and full of perturbation, and governed as it
were by chance. Whence it was well observed by Heraclitus that men look for sciences in their own lesser worlds,
and not in the greater or common world.

XLIII

There are also Idols formed by the intercourse and association of men with each other, which I call Idols of the Market-place, on account of the commerce and consort of men
there. For it is by discourse that men associate; and words
are imposed according to the apprehension of the vulgar.
And therefore the ill and unfit choice of words wonderfully
obstructs the understanding. Nor do the definitions or explanations wherewith in some things learned men are wont

to guard and defend themselves, by any means set the matter right. But words plainly force and overrule the understanding, and throw all into confusion, and lead men away into numberless empty controversies and idle fancies.

XLIV

Lastly, there are Idols which have immigrated into men's minds from the various dogmas of philosophies, and also from wrong laws of demonstration. These I call Idols of the Theatre; because in my judgment all the received systems are but so many stage-plays, representing worlds of their own creation after an unreal and scenic fashion. Nor is it only of the systems now in vogue, or only of the ancient sects and philosophies, that I speak; for many more plays of the same kind may yet be composed and in like artificial manner set forth; seeing that errors the most widely different have nevertheless causes for the most part alike. Neither again do I mean this only of entire systems, but also of many principles and axioms in science, which by tradition, credulity, and negligence have come to be received.

But of these several kinds of Idols I must speak more largely and exactly, that the understanding may be duly cautioned.

XLV

The human understanding is of its own nature prone to suppose the existence of more order and regularity in the world than it finds. And though there be many things in nature which are singular and unmatched, yet it devises for them parallels and conjugates and relatives which do not exist. Hence the fiction that all celestial bodies move in perfect circles; spirals and dragons being (except in name) utterly rejected. Hence too the element of Fire with its orb[1] is brought in, to make up the square with the other three which the sense perceives. Hence also the ratio of density[2] of the so-called elements is arbitrarily fixed at ten to one. And so on of other dreams. And these fancies affect not dogmas only, but simple notions also.

XLVI

The human understanding when it has once adopted an opinion (either as being the received opinion or as being agreeable to itself) draws all things else to support and agree with it. And though there be a greater number and weight of instances to be found on the other side, yet these it either neglects and despises, or else by some distinction sets aside and rejects; in order that by this great and pernicious predetermination the authority of its former conclusions may remain inviolate. And therefore it was a good answer that was made by one who when they showed him hanging in a temple a picture of those who had paid their vows as having escaped shipwreck, and would have him say whether he did not now acknowledge the power of the gods,—"Aye," asked he again, "but where are they painted that were drowned after their vows?" And such is the way of all superstition, whether in astrology, dreams, omens, divine judgments, or the like; wherein men, having a delight in such vanities, mark the events where they are fulfilled, but where they fail, though this happen much oftener, neglect and pass them by. But with far more subtlety does this mischief insinuate itself into philosophy and the sciences; in which the first conclusion colours and brings into conformity with itself all that come after, though far sounder and better. Besides, independently of that delight and vanity which I have described, it is the peculiar and perpetual error of the human intellect to be more moved and excited by affirmatives than by negatives; whereas it ought properly to hold itself indifferently[3] disposed towards both alike. Indeed in the establishment of any true axiom, the negative instance is the more forcible of the two.

XLVII

The human understanding is moved by those things most which strike and enter the mind simultaneously and suddenly, and so fill the imagination; and then it feigns and supposes all other things to be somehow, though it cannot see how, similar to those few things by which it is surrounded. But for that going to and fro to remote and heterogeneous instances, by which axioms are tried as in the fire, the intellect is altogether slow and unfit, unless it be forced thereto by severe laws and overruling authority.

XLVIII

The human understanding is unquiet; it cannot stop or rest, and still presses onward, but in vain. Therefore it is that we cannot conceive of any end or limit to the world; but always as of necessity it occurs to us that there is something beyond. Neither again can it be conceived how eternity has flowed down to the present day; for that distinction which is commonly received of infinity in time past and in time to come can by no means hold; for it would thence follow that one infinity is greater than another, and that infinity is wasting away and tending to become finite. The like subtlety arises touching the infinite divisibility of lines, from the same inability of thought to stop. But this inability interferes more mischievously in the discovery of causes: for although the most general principles in nature ought to be held merely positive, as they are discovered, and cannot with truth be referred to a cause; nevertheless the human understanding being unable to rest still seeks something prior in the order of nature. And then it is that in struggling towards that which is further off it falls back upon that which is more nigh at hand; namely, on final causes: which have relation clearly to the nature of man rather than to the nature of the universe; and from this source have strangely defiled philosophy. But he is no less an unskilled and shallow philosopher who seeks causes of that which is most general, than he who in things subordinate and subaltern omits to do so.

XLIX

The human understanding is no dry light, but receives an infusion from the will and affections; whence proceed sciences which may be called "sciences as one would." For what a man had rather were true he more readily believes. Therefore he rejects difficult things from impatience of research; sober things, because they narrow hope; the deeper things of nature, from superstition; the light of experience, from arrogance and pride, lest his mind should seem to be occupied with things mean and transitory; things not commonly believed, out of deference to the opinion of the vulgar. Numberless in short are the ways, and sometimes imperceptible, in which the affections colour and infect the understanding.

L

But by far the greatest hindrance and aberration of the human understanding proceeds from the dulness, incompetency, and deceptions of the senses; in that things which strike the sense outweigh things which do not immediately strike it, though they be more important. Hence it is that speculation commonly ceases where sight ceases; insomuch that of things invisible there is little or no observation. Hence all the working of the spirits inclosed in tangible bodies lies hid and unobserved of men. So also all the more subtle changes of form in the parts of coarser substances (which they commonly call alteration, though it is in truth local motion through exceedingly small spaces) is in like manner unobserved. And yet unless these two things just mentioned be searched out and brought to light, nothing great can be achieved in nature, as far as the production of works is concerned. So again the essential nature of our common air, and of all bodies less dense than air (which are very many), is almost unknown. For the sense by itself is a thing infirm and erring; neither can instruments for enlarging or sharpening the senses do much; but all the truer kind of interpretation of nature is effected by instances and experiments fit and apposite; wherein the sense decides touching the experiment only, and the experiment touching the point in nature and the thing itself.

LI

The human understanding is of its own nature prone to abstractions and gives a substance and reality to things which are fleeting. But to resolve nature into abstractions is less to our purpose than to dissect her into parts; as did the school of Democritus, which went further into nature than the rest. Matter rather than forms should be the object of our attention, its configurations and changes of configuration, and simple action, and law of action or motion; for forms are figments of the human mind, unless you will call those laws of action forms.

LII

Such then are the idols which I call *Idols of the Tribe;* and which take their rise either from the homogeneity of the substance of the human spirit, or from its preoccupation, or from its narrowness, or from its restless motion, or from an infusion of the affections, or from the incompetency of the senses, or from the mode of impression.

LIII

The *Idols of the Cave* take their rise in the peculiar constitution, mental or bodily, of each individual; and also in education, habit, and accident. Of this kind there is a great number and variety; but I will instance those the pointing out of which contains the most important caution, and which have most effect in disturbing the clearness of the understanding.

LIV

Men become attached to certain particular sciences and speculations, either because they fancy themselves the authors and inventors thereof, or because they have bestowed the greatest pains upon them and become most habituated to them. But men of this kind, if they betake themselves to philosophy and contemplations of a general character, distort and colour them in obedience to their former fancies; a thing especially to be noticed in Aristotle, who made his natural philosophy a mere bond-servant to his logic, thereby rendering it contentious and well nigh useless. The race of chemists again out of a few experiments of the furnace have built up a fantastic philosophy, framed with reference to a few things; and Gilbert also, after he had employed himself most laboriously in the study and observation of the loadstone, proceeded at once to construct an entire system in accordance with his favourite subject.

LV

There is one principal and as it were radical distinction between different minds, in respect of philosophy and the sciences; which is this: that some minds are stronger and apter to mark the differences of things, others to mark their resemblances. The steady and acute mind can fix its contemplations and dwell and fasten on the subtlest distinctions: the lofty and discursive mind recognises and puts together the finest and most general resemblances. Both kinds however easily err in excess, by catching the one at gradations the other at shadows.

LVI

There are found some minds given to an extreme admiration of antiquity, others to an extreme love and appetite for novelty; but few so duly tempered that they can hold the mean, neither carping at what has been well laid down by the ancients, nor despising what is well introduced by the moderns. This however turns to the great injury of the sciences and philosophy; since these affectations of antiquity and novelty are the humours of partisans rather than judgments; and truth is to be sought for not in the felicity of any age, which is an unstable thing, but in the light of nature and experience, which is eternal. These factions therefore must be abjured, and care must be taken that the intellect be not hurried by them into assent.

LVII

Contemplations of nature and of bodies in their simple form break up and distract the understanding, while contemplations of nature and bodies in their composition and configuration overpower and dissolve the understanding: a distinction well seen in the school of Leucippus and Democritus as compared with the other philosophies. For that school is so busied with the particles that it hardly attends to the structure; while the others are so lost in admiration of the structure that they do not penetrate to the simplicity of nature. These kinds of contemplation should therefore be alternated and taken by turns; that so the understanding may be rendered at once penetrating and comprehensive, and the inconveniences above mentioned, with the idols which proceed from them, may be avoided.

LVIII

Let such then be our provision and contemplative prudence for keeping off and dislodging the *Idols of the Cave*, which grow for the most part either out of the predominance of a favourite subject, or out of an excessive tendency to compare or to distinguish, or out of partiality for particular ages, or out of the largeness or minuteness of the objects contemplated. And generally let every student of nature take this as a rule,—that whatever his mind seizes and dwells upon with peculiar satisfaction is to be held in suspicion, and that so much the more care is to be taken in dealing with such questions to keep the understanding even and clear.

LIX

But the *Idols of the Market-place* are the most troublesome of all: idols which have crept into the understanding through the alliances of words and names. For men believe that their reason governs words; but it is also true that words react on the understanding; and this it is that has rendered philosophy and the sciences sophistical and inactive. Now words, being commonly framed and applied according to the capacity of the vulgar, follow those lines of division which are most obvious to the vulgar understanding. And whenever an understanding of greater acuteness or a more diligent observation would alter those lines to suit the true divisions of nature, words stand in the way and resist the change. Whence it comes to pass that the high and formal discussions of learned men end oftentimes in disputes about words and names; with which (according to the use and wisdom of the mathematicians) it would be more prudent to begin, and so by means of definitions reduce them to order. Yet even definitions cannot cure this evil in dealing with natural and material things; since the definitions themselves consist of words, and those words beget others: so that it is necessary to recur to individual instances, and those in due series and order; as I shall say presently when I come to the method and scheme for the formation of notions and axioms.

LX

The idols imposed by words on the understanding are of two kinds. They are either names of things which do not exist (for as there are things left unnamed through lack of observation, so likewise are there names which result from fantastic suppositions and to which nothing in reality corresponds), or they are names of things which exist, but yet confused and ill-defined, and hastily and irregularly derived from realities. Of the former kind are Fortune, the Prime Mover, Planetary Orbits, Element of Fire, and like fictions which owe their origin to false and idle theories. And this class of idols is more easily expelled, because to get rid of them it is only necessary that all theories should be steadily rejected and dismissed as obsolete.

But the other class, which springs out of a faulty and unskilful abstraction, is intricate and deeply rooted. Let us take for example such a word as *humid;* and see how far the several things which the word is used to signify agree with each other; and we shall find the word *humid* to be nothing else than a mark loosely and confusedly applied to denote a variety of actions which will not bear to be reduced to any constant meaning. For it both signifies that which easily spreads itself round any other body; and that which in itself is indeterminate and cannot solidise; and that which readily yields in every direction; and that which easily divides and scatters itself; and that which easily unites and collects itself; and that which readily flows and is put in motion; and that which readily clings to another body and wets it; and that which is easily reduced to a liquid, or being solid easily melts. Accordingly when you come to apply the word,—if you take it in one sense, flame is humid; if in another, air is not humid; if in another, fine dust is humid; if in another, glass is humid. So that it is easy to see that the notion is taken by abstraction only from water and common and ordinary liquids, without any due verification.

There are however in words certain degrees of distortion and error. One of the least faulty kinds is that of names of substances, especially of lowest species and well-deduced (for the notion of *chalk* and of *mud* is good, of *earth* bad); a more faulty kind is that of actions, as *to generate, to corrupt, to alter;* the most faulty is of qualities (except such as are the immediate objects of the sense) as *heavy, light, rare, dense,* and the like. Yet in all these cases some notions are of necessity a little better than others, in proportion to the greater variety of subjects that fall within the range of the human sense.

LXI

But the *Idols of the Theatre* are not innate, nor do they steal into the understanding secretly, but are plainly impressed and received into the mind from the play-books of philosophical systems and the perverted rules of demonstration. To attempt refutations in this case would be merely inconsistent with what I have already said: for since we agree neither upon principles nor upon demonstrations there is no place for argument. And this is so far well, in-

asmuch as it leaves the honour of the ancients untouched.
For they are no wise disparaged—the question between
them and me being only as to the way. For as the saying
is, the lame man who keeps the right road outstrips the runner who takes a wrong one. Nay it is obvious that when a
man runs the wrong way, the more active and swift he is
the further he will go astray.

But the course I propose for the discovery of sciences is
such as leaves but little to the acuteness and strength of
wits, but places all wits and understandings nearly on a
level. For as in the drawing of a straight line or a perfect
circle, much depends on the steadiness and practice of the
hand, if it be done by aim of hand only, but if with the aid
of rule or compass, little or nothing; so is it exactly with my
plan. But though particular confutations would be of no
avail, yet touching the sects and general divisions of such
systems I must say something; something also touching the
external signs which show that they are unsound; and finally
something touching the causes of such great infelicity and
of such lasting and general agreement in error; that so the
access to truth may be made less difficult, and the human
understanding may the more willingly submit to its purga-
tion and dismiss its idols.

LXII

Idols of the Theatre, or of Systems, are many, and there
can be and perhaps will be yet many more. For were it not
that now for many ages men's minds have been busied with
religion and theology; and were it not that civil governments, especially monarchies, have been averse to such
novelties, even in matters speculative; so that men labour
therein to the peril and harming of their fortunes,—not only
unrewarded, but exposed also to contempt and envy; doubtless there would have arisen many other philosophical sects
like to those which in great variety flourished once among
the Greeks. For as on the phenomena of the heavens many
hypotheses may be constructed, so likewise (and more also)
many various dogmas may be set up and established on the

phenomena of philosophy. And in the plays of this philosophical theatre you may observe the same thing which is
found in the theatre of the poets, that stories invented for
the stage are more compact and elegant, and more as one
would wish them to be, than true stories out of history.

In general however there is taken for the material of philosophy either a great deal out of a few things, or a very
little out of many things; so that on both sides philosophy is
based on too narrow a foundation of experiment and natural
history, and decides on the authority of too few cases. For
the Rational School of philosophers snatches from experience a variety of common instances, neither duly ascertained
nor diligently examined and weighed, and leaves all the rest
to meditation and agitation of wit.

There is also another class of philosophers, who having
bestowed much diligent and careful labour on a few experiments, have thence made bold to educe and construct systems; wresting all other facts in a strange fashion to conformity therewith.

And there is yet a third class, consisting of those who out
of faith and veneration mix their philosophy with theology
and traditions; among whom the vanity of some has gone
so far aside as to seek the origin of sciences among spirits
and genii. So that this parent stock of errors—this false philosophy—is of three kinds; the Sophistical, the Empirical,
and the Superstitious.

LXIII

The most conspicuous example of the first class was Aristotle, who corrupted natural philosophy by his logic: fash-
ioning the world out of categories; assigning to the human
soul, the noblest of substances, a genus from words of the
second intention;[4] doing the business of density and rarity
(which is to make bodies of greater or less dimensions, that
is, occupy greater or less spaces), by the frigid distinction
of act and power; asserting that single bodies have each a
single and proper motion, and that if they participate in any
other, then this results from an external cause; and impos-

ing countless other arbitrary restrictions on the nature of things; being always more solicitous to provide an answer to the question and affirm something positive in words, than about the inner truth of things; a failing best shown when his philosophy is compared with other systems of note among the Greeks. For the Homœomera of Anaxagoras; the Atoms of Leucippus and Democritus; the Heaven and Earth of Parmenides; the Strife and Friendship of Empedocles; Heraclitus's doctrine how bodies are resolved into the in-different nature of fire, and remoulded into solids; have all of them some taste of the natural philosopher,—some savour of the nature of things, and experience, and bodies; whereas in the physics of Aristotle you hear hardly anything but tue words of logic; which in his metaphysics also, under a more imposing name, and more forsooth as a realist than a nomi-nalist, he has handled over again. Nor let any weight be given to the fact, that in his books on animals and his prob-lems, and other of his treatises, there is frequent dealing with experiments. For he had come to his conclusion be-fore; he did not consult experience, as he should have done, in order to the framing of his decisions and axioms; but having first determined the question according to his will, he then resorts to experience, and bending her into con-formity with his placets[5] leads her about like a captive in a procession; so that even on this count he is more guilty than his modern followers, the schoolmen, who have abandoned experience altogether.

LXIV

But the Empirical school of philosophy gives birth to dog-mas more deformed and monstrous than the Sophistical or Rational school. For it has its foundations not in the light of common notions, (which though it be a faint and super-ficial light, is yet in a manner universal, and has reference to many things,) but in the narrowness and darkness of a few experiments. To those therefore who are daily busied with these experiments, and have infected their imagination with them, such a philosophy seems probable and all but

certain; to all men else incredible and vain. Of this there is
a notable instance in the alchemists and their dogmas;
though it is hardly to be found elsewhere in these times,
except perhaps in the philosophy of Gilbert.[6] Nevertheless
with regard to philosophies of this kind there is one caution
not to be omitted; for I foresee that if ever men are roused
by my admonitions to betake themselves seriously to experiment and bid farewell to sophistical doctrines, then indeed through the premature hurry of the understanding to
leap or fly to universals and principles of things, great danger may be apprehended from philosophies of this kind;
against which evil we ought even now to prepare.

LXV

But the corruption of philosophy by superstition and an
admixture of theology is far more widely spread, and does
the greatest harm, whether to entire systems or to their
parts. For the human understanding is obnoxious[7] to the
influence of the imagination no less than to the influence of
common notions. For the contentious and sophistical kind
of philosophy ensnares the understanding; but this kind, being fanciful and tumid and half poetical, misleads it more by
flattery. For there is in man an ambition of the understanding, no less than of the will, especially in high and lofty
spirits.

Of this kind we have among the Greeks a striking example in Pythagoras, though he united with it a coarser
and more cumbrous superstition; another in Plato and his
school, more dangerous and subtle. It shows itself likewise
in parts of other philosophies, in the introduction of abstract forms and final causes and first causes, with the omission in most cases of causes intermediate, and the like.
Upon this point the greatest caution should be used. For
nothing is so mischievous as the apotheosis of error; and
it is a very plague of the understanding for vanity to become the object of veneration. Yet in this vanity some of
the moderns have with extreme levity indulged so far as to
attempt to found a system of natural philosophy on the first

chapter of Genesis, on the book of Job, and other parts of the sacred writings; seeking for the dead among the living: which also makes the inhibition and repression of it the more important, because from this unwholesome mixture of things human and divine there arises not only a fantastic philosophy but also an heretical religion. Very meet it is therefore that we be sober-minded, and give to faith that only which is faith's.

LXVI

So much then for the mischievous authorities of systems, which are founded either on common notions, or on a few experiments, or on superstition. It remains to speak of the faulty subject-matter of contemplations, especially in natural philosophy. Now the human understanding is infected by the sight of what takes place in the mechanical arts, in which the alteration of bodies proceeds chiefly by composition or separation, and so imagines that something similar goes on in the universal nature of things. From this source has flowed the fiction of elements, and of their concourse for the formation of natural bodies. Again, when man contemplates nature working freely, he meets with different species of things, of animals, of plants, of minerals; whence he readily passes into the opinion that there are in nature certain primary forms which nature intends to educe, and that the remaining variety proceeds from hindrances and aberrations of nature in the fulfilment of her work, or from the collision of different species and the transplanting of one into another. To the first of these speculations we owe our primary qualities of the elements; to the other our occult properties and specific virtues; and both of them belong to those empty *compendia* of thought wherein the mind rests, and whereby it is diverted from more solid pursuits. It is to better purpose that the physicians bestow their labour on the secondary qualities of matter, and the operations of attraction, repulsion, attenuation, conspissation,[8] dilatation, astriction, dissipation, maturation, and the like; and were it not that by those two compendia which I have mentioned (elementary qualities, to wit, and specific virtues) they corrupted their correct observations in these other matters,—either reducing them to first qualities and their subtle and incommensurable mixtures, or not following them out with greater and more diligent observation to third and fourth qualities, but breaking off the scrutiny prematurely,—they had made much greater progress. Nor are powers of this kind (I do not say the same, but similar) to be sought for only in the medicines of the human body, but also in the changes of all other bodies.

But it is a far greater evil that they make the quiescent principles, *wherefrom*, and not the moving principles, *whereby*, things are produced, the object of their contemplation and inquiry. For the former tend to discourse, the latter to works. Nor is there any value in those vulgar distinctions of motion which are observed in the received system of natural philosophy, as generation, corruption, augmentation, diminution, alteration, and local motion. What they mean no doubt is this:—If a body, in other respects not changed, be moved from its place, this is *local motion;* if without change of place or essence, it be changed in quality, this is *alteration;* if by reason of the change the mass and quantity of the body do not remain the same, this is *augmentation* or *diminution;* if they be changed to such a degree that they change their very essence and substance and turn to something else, this is *generation* and *corruption.* But all this is merely popular, and does not at all go deep into nature; for these are only measures and limits, not kinds of motion. What they intimate is *how far,* not *by what means,* or *from what source.* For they do not suggest anything with regard either to the desires of bodies or to the development of their parts: it is only when that motion presents the thing grossly and palpably to the sense as different from what it was, that they begin to mark the division. Even when they wish to suggest something with regard to the causes of motion, and to establish a division with reference to them, they introduce with the greatest negligence a distinction between motion natural and violent; a distinction which is itself drawn entirely from a vulgar notion, since all violent motion is also in fact natural; the external efficient simply setting nature working otherwise than it was before. But if, leaving all this, any one shall observe (for instance) that there is in bodies a desire of mutual contact, so as not to suffer the unity of nature to be quite separated or broken and a vacuum thus made; or if any one say that there is in bodies a desire of resuming their natural dimensions or tension, so that if compressed within or extended beyond them, they immediately strive to recover themselves, and fall back to their old volume and extent; or if any one say that there is in bodies a desire of congregating towards masses of kindred nature,—of dense bodies, for instance, towards the globe of the earth, of thin and rare bodies towards the compass of the sky; all these and the like are truly physical kinds of motion;—but those others are entirely logical and scholastic, as is abundantly manifest from this comparison.

Nor again is it a less evil, that in their philosophies and contemplations their labour is spent in investigating and handling the first principles of things and the highest generalities of nature; whereas utility and the means of working result entirely from things intermediate. Hence it is that men cease not from abstracting nature till they come to potential and uninformed matter, nor on the other hand from dissecting nature till they reach the atom; things which, even if true, can do but little for the welfare of mankind.

LXVII

A caution must also be given to the understanding against the intemperance which systems of philosophy manifest in giving or withholding assent; because intemperance of this kind seems to establish Idols and in some sort to perpetuate them, leaving no way open to reach and dislodge them.

This excess is of two kinds: the first being manifest in those who are ready in deciding, and render sciences dogmatic and magisterial; the other in those who deny that we can know anything, and so introduce a wandering kind of inquiry that leads to nothing; of which kinds the former subdues, the latter weakens the understanding. For the philosophy of Aristotle, after having by hostile confutations destroyed all the rest (as the Ottomans serve their brothers), has laid down the law on all points; which done, he proceeds himself to raise new questions of his own suggestion, and dispose of them likewise; so that nothing may remain that is not certain and decided: a practice which holds and is in use among his successors.

The school of Plato, on the other hand, introduced *Acatalepsia*,[9] at first in jest and irony, and in disdain of the older sophists, Protagoras, Hippias, and the rest, who were of nothing else so much ashamed as of seeming to doubt about anything. But the New Academy made a dogma of it, and held it as a tenet. And though their's is a fairer seeming way than arbitrary decisions; since they say that they by no means destroy all investigation, like Pyrrho and his Refrainers, but allow of some things to be followed as probable, though of none to be maintained as true; yet still when the human mind has once despaired of finding truth, its interest in all things grows fainter; and the result is that men turn aside to pleasant disputations and discourses and roam as it were from object to object, rather than keep on a course of severe inquisition. But, as I said at the beginning and am ever urging, the human senses and understanding, weak as they are, are not to be deprived of their authority, but to be supplied with helps.

LXVIII

So much concerning the several classes of Idols, and their equipage: all of which must be renounced and put away with a fixed and solemn determination, and the understanding thoroughly freed and cleansed; the entrance into the kingdom of man, founded on the sciences, being not much other than the entrance into the kingdom of heaven, whereinto none may enter except as a little child.

LXIX

But vicious demonstrations are as the strongholds and
defences of Idols; and those we have in logic do little else
than make the world the bond-slave of human thought, and
human thought the bond-slave of words. Demonstrations
truly are in effect the philosophies themselves and the
sciences. For such as *they* are, well or ill established, such
are the systems of philosophy and the contemplations which
follow. Now in the whole of the process which leads from
the sense and objects to axioms and conclusions, the demonstrations which we use are deceptive and incompetent. This
process consists of four parts, and has as many faults. In
the first place, the impressions of the sense itself are faulty;
for the sense both fails us and deceives us. But its shortcomings are to be supplied, and its deceptions to be corrected. Secondly, notions are ill drawn from the impressions
of the senses, and are indefinite and confused, whereas they
should be definite and distinctly bounded. Thirdly, the induction is amiss which infers the principles of sciences by
simple enumeration, and does not, as it ought, employ exclusions and solutions (or separations) of nature. Lastly,
that method of discovery and proof according to which the
most general principles are first established, and then intermediate axioms are tried and proved by them, is the parent
of error and the curse of all science. Of these things however, which now I do but touch upon, I will speak more
largely, when, having performed these expiations and purgings of the mind, I come to set forth the true way for the
interpretation of nature.

LXX

But the best demonstration by far is experience, if it go
not beyond the actual experiment. For if it be transferred to
other cases which are deemed similar, unless such transfer
be made by a just and orderly process, it is a fallacious
thing. But the manner of making experiments which men
now use is blind and stupid. And therefore, wandering and

straying as they do with no settled course, and taking counsel only from things as they fall out, they fetch a wide circuit and meet with many matters, but make little progress; and sometimes are full of hope, sometimes are distracted; and always find that there is something beyond to be sought. For it generally happens that men make their trials carelessly, and as it were in play; slightly varying experiments already known, and, if the thing does not answer, growing weary and abandoning the attempt. And even if they apply themselves to experiments more seriously and earnestly and laboriously, still they spend their labour in working out some one experiment, as Gilbert with the magnet, and the chemists with gold; a course of proceeding not less unskilful in the design than small in the attempt. For no one successfully investigates the nature of a thing in the thing itself; the inquiry must be enlarged, so as to become more general.

And even when they seek to educe some science or theory from their experiments, they nevertheless almost always turn aside with overhasty and unseasonable eagerness to practice; not only for the sake of the uses and fruits of the practice, but from impatience to obtain in the shape of some new work an assurance for themselves that it is worth their while to go on; and also to show themselves off to the world, and so raise the credit of the business in which they are engaged. Thus, like Atalanta, they go aside to pick up the golden apple, but meanwhile they interrupt their course, and let the victory escape them. But in the true course of experience, and in carrying it on to the effecting of new works, the divine wisdom and order must be our pattern. Now God on the first day of creation created light only, giving to that work an entire day, in which no material substance was created. So must we likewise from experience of every kind first endeavour to discover true causes and axioms; and seek for experiments of Light, not for experiments of Fruit. For axioms rightly discovered and established supply practice with its instruments, not one by one, but in clusters, and draw after them trains and troops of works. Of the paths however of experience, which no less than the paths of judgment are impeded and beset, I will speak hereafter; here I have only mentioned ordinary experimental research as a bad kind of demonstration. But now the order of the matter in hand leads me to add something both as to those *signs* which I lately mentioned,—(signs that the systems of philosophy and contemplation in use are in a bad condition)—and also as to the *causes* of what seems at first so strange and incredible. For a knowledge of the signs prepares assent; an explanation of the causes removes the marvel: which two things will do much to render the extirpation of Idols from the understanding more easy and gentle.

LXXI

The sciences which we possess come for the most part from the Greeks. For what has been added by Roman, Arabic, or later writers is not much nor of much importance; and whatever it is, it is built on the foundation of Greek discoveries. Now the wisdom of the Greeks was professorial and much given to disputations; a kind of wisdom most adverse to the inquisition of truth. Thus that name of Sophists, which by those who would be thought philosophers was in contempt cast back upon and so transferred to the ancient rhetoricians, Gorgias, Protagoras, Hippias, Polus, does indeed suit the entire class, Plato, Aristotle, Zeno, Epicurus, Theophrastus, and their successors Chrysippus, Carnades, and the rest. There was this difference only, that the former class was wandering and mercenary, going about from town to town, putting up their wisdom to sale, and taking a price for it; while the latter was more pompous and dignified, as composed of men who had fixed abodes, and who opened schools and taught their philosophy without reward. Still both sorts, though in other respects unequal, were professorial; both turned the matter into disputations, and set up and battled for philosophical sects and heresies; so that their doctrines were for the most part (as Dionysius not unaptly rallied Plato) "the talk of idle old men to ignorant youths." But the elder of the Greek philosophers, Empedocles, Anaxagoras, Leucippus, Democritus, Parmenides, Heraclitus, Xenophanes, Philolaus, and the rest (I omit Pythagoras as a mystic), did not, so far as we know, open schools; but more silently and severely and simply,— that is, with less affectation and parade,—betook themselves to the inquisition of truth. And therefore they were in my judgment more successful; only that their works were in the course of time obscured by those slighter persons who had more which suits and pleases the capacity and tastes of the vulgar: time, like a river, bringing down to us things which are light and puffed up, but letting weighty matters sink. Still even they were not altogether free from the failing of their nation; but leaned too much to the ambition and vanity of founding a sect and catching popular applause. But the inquisition of truth must be despaired of when it turns aside to trifles of this kind. Nor should we omit that judgment, or rather divination, which was given concerning the Greeks by the Ægyptian priest,—that "they were always boys, without antiquity of knowledge or knowledge of antiquity." Assuredly they have that which is characteristic of boys; they are prompt to prattle, but cannot generate; for their wisdom abounds in words but is barren of works. And therefore the signs which are taken from the origin and birth-place of the received philosophy are not good.

LXXII

Nor does the character of the time and age yield much better signs than the character of the country and nation. For at that period there was but a narrow and meagre knowledge either of time or place; which is the worst thing that can be, especially for those who rest all on experience. For they had no history, worthy to be called history, that went back a thousand years; but only fables and rumours of antiquity. And of the regions and districts of the world they knew but a small portion; giving indiscriminately the name of Scythians to all in the North, of Celts to all in the

West; knowing nothing of Africa beyond the hither side of Æthiopia, of Asia beyond the Ganges; much less were they acquainted with the provinces of the New World, even by hearsay or any well-founded rumour; nay, a multitude of climates and zones, wherein innumerable nations breathe and live, were pronounced by them to be uninhabitable; and the travels of Democritus, Plato, and Pythagoras, which were rather suburban excursions than distant journeys, were talked of as something great. In our times on the other hand both many parts of the New World and the limits on every side of the Old World are known, and our stock of experience has increased to an infinite amount. Wherefore if (like astrologers) we draw signs from the season of their nativity or birth, nothing great can be predicted of those systems of philosophy.

LXXIII

Of all signs there is none more certain or more noble than that taken from fruits. For fruits and works are as it were sponsors and sureties for the truth of philosophies. Now, from all these systems of the Greeks, and their ramifications through particular sciences, there can hardly after the lapse of so many years be adduced a single experiment which tends to relieve and benefit the condition of man, and which can with truth be referred to the speculations and theories of philosophy. And Celsus ingenuously and wisely owns as much, when he tells us that the experimental part of medicine was first discovered, and that afterwards men philosophised about it, and hunted for and assigned causes; and not by an inverse process that philosophy and the knowledge of causes led to the discovery and development of the experimental part. And therefore it was not strange that among the Ægyptians, who rewarded inventors with divine honours and sacred rites, there were more images of brutes than of men; inasmuch as brutes by their natural instinct have produced many discoveries, whereas men by discussion and the conclusions of reason have given birth to few or none.

Some little has indeed been produced by the industry of chemists; but it has been produced accidentally and in passing, or else by a kind of variation of experiments, such as mechanics use; and not by any art or theory; for the theory which they have devised rather confuses the experiments than aids them. They too who have busied themselves with natural magic, as they call it, have but few discoveries to show, and those trifling and imposture-like. Wherefore, as in religion we are warned to show our faith by works, so in philosophy by the same rule the system should be judged of by its fruits, and pronounced frivolous if it be barren; more especially if, in place of fruits of grape and olive, it bear thorns and briars of dispute and contention.

LXXIV

Signs also are to be drawn from the increase and progress of systems and sciences. For what is founded on nature grows and increases; while what is founded on opinion varies but increases not. If therefore those doctrines had not plainly been like a plant torn up from its roots, but had remained attached to the womb of nature and continued to draw nourishment from her, that could never have come to pass which we have seen now for twice a thousand years; namely, that the sciences stand where they did and remain almost in the same condition; receiving no noticeable increase, but on the contrary, thriving most under their first founder, and then declining. Whereas in the mechanical arts, which are founded on nature and the light of experience, we see the contrary happen, for these (as long as they are popular) are continually thriving and growing, as having in them a breath of life; at first rude, then convenient, afterwards adorned, and at all times advancing.

LXXV

There is still another sign remaining (if sign it can be called, when it is rather testimony, nay, of all testimony the most valid); I mean the confession of the very author-

ities whom men now follow. For even they who lay down
the law on all things so confidently, do still in their more
sober moods fall to complaints of the subtlety of nature,
the obscurity of things, and the weakness of the human
mind. Now if this were all they did, some perhaps of a
timid disposition might be deterred from further search,
while others of a more ardent and hopeful spirit might be
whetted and incited to go on farther. But not content to
speak for themselves, whatever is beyond their own or
their master's knowledge or reach they set down as beyond
the bounds of possibility, and pronounce, as if on the
authority of their art, that it cannot be known or done; thus
most presumptuously and invidiously turning the weakness
of their own discoveries into a calumny on nature herself,
and the despair of the rest of the world. Hence the school
of the New Academy, which held *Acatalepsia* as a tenet
and doomed men to perpetual darkness. Hence the opinion
that Forms or true differences of things (which are in fact
laws of pure act) are past finding out and beyond the
reach of man. Hence too those opinions in the department
of action and operation; as that the heat of the sun and of
fire are quite different in kind,—lest men should imagine
that by the operations of fire anything like the works of
nature can be educed and formed. Hence the notion that
composition only is the work of man, and mixture of none
but nature,—lest men should expect from art some power
of generating or transforming natural bodies. By this sign,
therefore, men will easily take warning not to mix up their
fortunes and labours with dogmas not only despaired of
but dedicated to despair.

LXXVI

Neither is this other sign to be omitted;—that formerly
there existed among philosophers such great disagreement,
and such diversities in the schools themselves; a fact which
sufficiently shows that the road from the senses to the
understanding was not skilfully laid out, when the same
groundwork of philosophy (the nature of things to wit)

was torn and split up into such vague and multifarious errors. And although in these times disagreements and diversities of opinion on first principles and entire systems are for the most part extinguished, still on parts of philosophy there remain innumerable questions and disputes, so that it plainly appears that neither in the systems themselves nor in the modes of demonstration is there anything certain or sound.

LXXVII

And as for the general opinion that in the philosophy of Aristotle at any rate there is great agreement; since after its publication the systems of older philosophers died away, while in the times which followed nothing better was found; so that it seems to have been so well laid and established as to have drawn both ages in its train; I answer in the first place, that the common notion of the falling off of the old systems upon the publication of Aristotle's works is a false one; for long afterwards, down even to the times of Cicero and subsequent ages, the works of the old philosophers still remained. But in the times which followed, when on the inundation of barbarians into the Roman empire human learning had suffered shipwreck, then the systems of Aristotle and Plato, like planks of lighter and less solid material, floated on the waves of time, and were preserved. Upon the point of consent also men are deceived, if the matter be looked into more keenly. For true consent is that which consists in the coincidence of free judgments, after due examination. But far the greater number of those who have assented to the philosophy of Aristotle have addicted themselves thereto from prejudgment and upon the authority of others; so that it is a following and going along together, rather than consent. But even if it had been a real and widespread consent, still so little ought consent to be deemed a sure and solid confirmation, that it is in fact a strong presumption the other way. For the worst of all auguries is from consent in matters intellectual (divinity excepted, and politics were there is right

of vote). For nothing pleases the many unless it strikes
the imagination, or binds the understanding with the bands
of common notions, as I have already said. We may very
well transfer therefore from moral to intellectual matters,
the saying of Phocion, that if the multitude assent and ap-
plaud men ought immediately to examine themselves as to
what blunder or fault they may have committed. This sign
therefore is one of the most unfavourable. And so much for
this point; namely, that the signs of truth and soundness in
the received systems and sciences are not good; whether
they be drawn from their origin, or from their fruits, or
from their progress, or from the confessions of their founders, or from general consent.

LXXVIII

I now come to the *causes* of these errors, and of so long a
continuance in them through so many ages; which are very
many and very potent;—that all wonder how these considerations which I bring forward should have escaped men's
notice till now, may cease; and the only wonder be, how
now at last they should have entered into any man's head
and become the subject of his thoughts; which truly I myself esteem as the result of some happy accident, rather
than of any excellence of faculty in me; a birth of Time
rather than a birth of Wit. Now, in the first place, those so
many ages, if you weigh the case truly, shrink into a very
small compass. For out of the five and twenty centuries
over which the memory and learning of men extends, you
can hardly pick out six that were fertile in sciences or favourable to their development. In times no less than in
regions there are wastes and deserts. For only three revolutions and periods of learning can properly be reckoned;
one among the Greeks, the second among the Romans, and
the last among us, that is to say, the nations of Western
Europe; and to each of these hardly two centuries can
justly be assigned. The intervening ages of the world, in
respect of any rich or flourishing growth of the sciences,
were unprosperous. For neither the Arabians nor the

Schoolmen need be mentioned; who in the intermediate
times rather crushed the sciences with a multitude of
treatises, than increased their weight. And therefore the
first cause of so meagre a progress in the sciences is duly
and orderly referred to the narrow limits of the time that
has been favourable to them.

LXXIX

In the second place there presents itself a cause of great
weight in all ways; namely, that during those very ages in
which the wits and learning of men have flourished most,
or indeed flourished at all, the least part of their diligence
was given to natural philosophy. Yet this very philosophy
it is that ought to be esteemed the great mother of the
sciences. For all arts and all sciences, if torn from this root,
though they may be polished and shaped and made fit for
use, yet they will hardly grow. Now it is well known that
after the Christian religion was received and grew strong,
by far the greater number of the best wits applied themselves to theology; that to this both the highest rewards
were offered, and helps of all kinds most abundantly supplied; and that this devotion to theology chiefly occupied
that third portion or epoch of time among us Europeans of
the West; and the more so because about the same time
both literature began to flourish and religious controversies
to spring up. In the age before, on the other hand, during
the continuance of the second period among the Romans,
the meditations and labours of philosophers were principally employed and consumed on moral philosophy, which
to the Heathen was as theology to us. Moreover in those
times the greatest wits applied themselves very generally
to public affairs; the magnitude of the Roman empire requiring the services of a great number of persons. Again,
the age in which natural philosophy was seen to flourish
most among the Greeks, was but a brief particle of time;
for in early ages the Seven Wise Men, as they were called,
(all except Thales) applied themselves to morals and politics; and in later times, when Socrates had drawn down

philosophy from heaven to earth, moral philosophy became more fashionable than ever, and diverted the minds of men from the philosophy of nature.

Nay, the very period itself in which inquiries concerning nature flourished, was by controversies and the ambitious display of new opinions corrupted and made useless. Seeing therefore that during those three periods natural philosophy was in a great degree either neglected or hindered, it is no wonder if men made but small advance in that to which they were not attending.

LXXX

To this it may be added that natural philosophy, even among those who have attended to it, has scarcely ever possessed, especially in these later times, a disengaged and whole man (unless it were some monk studying in his cell, or some gentleman in his country-house), but that it has been made merely a passage and bridge to something else. And so this great mother of the sciences has with strange indignity been degraded to the offices of a servant; having to attend on the business of medicine or mathematics, and likewise to wash and imbue youthful and unripe wits with a sort of first dye, in order that they may be the fitter to receive another afterwards. Meanwhile let no man look for much progress in the sciences—especially in the practical part of them—unless natural philosophy be carried on and applied to particular sciences, and particular sciences be carried back again to natural philosophy. For want of this, astronomy, optics, music, a number of mechanical arts, medicine itself,—nay, what one might more wonder at, moral and political philosophy, and the logical sciences,—altogether lack profoundness, and merely glide along the surface and variety of things; because after these particular sciences have been once distributed and established, they are no more nourished by natural philosophy; which might have drawn out of the true contemplation of motions, rays, sounds, texture and configuration of bodies, affections, and intellectual perceptions, the means of imparting to them fresh strength and growth. And therefore it is nothing strange if the sciences grow not, seeing they are parted from their roots.

LXXXI

Again there is another great and powerful cause why the sciences have made but little progress; which is this. It is not possible to run a course aright when the goal itself has not been rightly placed. Now the true and lawful goal of the sciences is none other than this: that human life be endowed with new discoveries and powers. But of this the great majority have no feeling, but are merely hireling and professorial; except when it occasionally happens that some workman of acuter wit and covetous of honour applies himself to a new invention; which he mostly does at the expense of his fortunes. But in general, so far are men from proposing to themselves to augment the mass of arts and sciences, that from the mass already at hand they neither take nor look for anything more than what they may turn to use in their lectures, or to gain, or to reputation, or to some similar advantage. And if any one out of all the multitude court science with honest affection and for her own sake, yet even with him the object will be found to be rather the variety of contemplations and doctrines than the severe and rigid search after truth. And if by chance there be one who seeks after truth in earnest, yet even he will propose to himself such a kind of truth as shall yield satisfaction to the mind and understanding in rendering causes for things long since discovered, and not the truth which shall lead to new assurance of works and new light of axioms. If then the end of the sciences has not as yet been well placed, it is not strange that men have erred as to the means.

LXXXII

And as men have misplaced the end and goal of the sciences; so again, even if they had placed it right, yet they have chosen a way to it which is altogether erroneous and impassable. And an astonishing thing it is to one who rightly considers the matter, that no mortal should have seriously applied himself to the opening and laying out of a road for the human understanding direct from the sense, by a course of experiment orderly conducted and well built up; but that all has been left either to the mist of tradition, or the whirl and eddy of argument, or the fluctuations and mazes of chance and of vague and ill-digested experience. Now let any man soberly and diligently consider what the way is by which men have been accustomed to proceed in the investigation and discovery of things; and in the first place he will no doubt remark a method of discovery very simple and inartificial; which is the most ordinary method, and is no more than this. When a man addresses himself to discover something, he first seeks out and sets before him all that has been said about it by others; then he begins to meditate for himself; and so by much agitation and working of the wit solicits and as it were evokes his own spirit to give him oracles: which method has no foundation at all, but rests only upon opinions and is carried about with them.

Another may perhaps call in logic to discover it for him; but that has no relation to the matter except in name. For logical invention does not discover principles and chief axioms, of which arts are composed, but only such things as appear to be consistent with them. For if you grow more curious and importunate and busy, and question her of probations and invention of principles or primary axioms, her answer is well known: she refers you to the faith you are bound to give to the principles of each separate art.

There remains simple experience; which, if taken as it comes, is called accident; if sought for, experiment. But this kind of experience is no better than a broom without its band, as the saying is;—a mere groping, as of men in the dark, that feel all round them for the chance of finding their way; when they had much better wait for daylight. or light a candle, and then go. But the true method of experience on the contrary first lights the candle, and then by means of the candle shows the way; commencing as it does with experience duly ordered and digested, not bungling or erratic, and from it educing axioms, and from established axioms again new experiments; even as it was not without order and method that the divine word operated on the created mass. Let men therefore cease to wonder that the course of science is not yet wholly run, seeing that they have gone altogether astray; either leaving and abandoning experience entirely, or losing their way in it and wandering round and round as in a labyrinth; whereas a method rightly ordered leads by an unbroken route through the woods of experience to the open ground of axioms.

LXXXIII

This evil however has been strangely increased by an opinion or conceit, which though of long standing is vain and hurtful; namely, that the dignity of the human mind is impaired by long and close intercourse with experiments and particulars, subject to sense and bound in matter; especially as they are laborious to search, ignoble to meditate, harsh to deliver, illiberal to practise, infinite in number, and minute in subtlety. So that it has come at length to this, that the true way is not merely deserted, but shut out and stopped up; experience being, I do not say abandoned or badly managed, but rejected with disdain.

LXXXIV

Again, men have been kept back as by a kind of enchantment from progress in the sciences by reverence for antiquity, by the authority of men accounted great in philosophy, and then by general consent. Of the last I have spoken above.

As for antiquity, the opinion touching it which men entertain is quite a negligent one, and scarcely consonant with the word itself. For the old age of the world is to be accounted the true antiquity; and this is the attribute of our own times, not of that earlier age of the world in which the ancients lived; and which, though in respect of us it was the elder, yet in respect of the world it was the younger. And truly as we look for greater knowledge of human things and a riper judgment in the old man than in the young, because of his experience and of the number and variety of the things which he has seen and heard and thought of; so in like manner from our age, if it but knew its own strength and chose to essay and exert it, much more might fairly be expected than from the ancient times, inasmuch as it is a more advanced age of the world, and stored and stocked with infinite experiments and observations.

Nor must it go for nothing that by the distant voyages and travels which have become frequent in our times, many things in nature have been laid open and discovered which may let in new light upon philosophy. And surely it would be disgraceful if, while the regions of the material globe,—that is, of the earth, of the sea, and of the stars,— have been in our times laid widely open and revealed, the intellectual globe should remain shut up within the narrow limits of old discoveries.

And with regard to authority, it shows a feeble mind to grant so much to authors and yet deny time his rights, who is the author of authors, nay rather of all authority. For rightly is truth called the daughter of time, not of authority. It is no wonder therefore if those enchantments of antiquity and authority and consent have so bound up men's powers that they have been made impotent (like persons bewitched) to accompany with the nature of things. .

LXXXV

Nor is it only the admiration of antiquity, authority, and consent, that has forced the industry of man to rest satisfied with the discoveries already made; but also an admiration for the works themselves of which the human race has long been in possession. For when a man looks at the variety and the beauty of the provision which the mechanical arts have brought together for men's use, he will certainly be more inclined to admire the wealth of man than to feel his wants: not considering that the original observations and operations of nature (which are the life and moving principle of all that variety) are not many nor deeply fetched, and that the rest is but patience, and the subtle and ruled motion of the hand and instruments;—as the making of clocks (for instance) is certainly a subtle and exact work: their wheels seem to imitate the celestial orbs, and their alternating and orderly motion, the pulse of animals: and yet all this depends on one or two axioms of nature.

Again, if you observe the refinement of the liberal arts, or even that which relates to the mechanical preparation of natural substances; and take notice of such things as the discovery in astronomy of the motions of the heavens, of harmony in music, of the letters of the alphabet (to this day not in use among the Chinese) in grammar: or again in things mechanical, the discovery of the works of Bacchus and Ceres—that is, of the arts of preparing wine and beer, and of making bread; the discovery once more of the delicacies of the table, of distillations and the like; and if you likewise bear in mind the long periods which it has taken to bring these things to their present degree of perfection (for they are all ancient except distillation), and again (as has been said of clocks) how little they owe to observations and axioms of nature, and how easily and obviously and as it were by casual suggestion they may have been discovered; you will easily cease from wondering, and on the contrary will pity the condition of mankind, seeing that in a course of so many ages there has been so great a dearth and barrenness of arts and inventions. And yet these very discoveries which we have just mentioned, are older than philosophy and intellectual arts. So that, if the truth must be spoken, when the rational and dogmatical sciences began, the discovery of useful works came to an end.

And again, if a man turn from the workshop to the li brary, and wonder at the immense variety of books he sees there, let him but examine and diligently inspect their matter and contents, and his wonder will assuredly be turned the other way; for after observing their endless repetitions, and how men are ever saying and doing what has been said and done before, he will pass from admiration of the variety to astonishment at the poverty and scantiness of the subjects which till now have occupied and possessed the minds of men.

And if again he descend to the consideration of those arts which are deemed curious rather than safe, and look more closely into the works of the Alchemists or the Magicians, he will be in doubt perhaps whether he ought rather to laugh over them or to weep. For the Alchemist nurses eternal hope, and when the thing fails, lays the blame upon some error of his own; fearing either that he has not sufficiently understood the words of his art or of his authors (whereupon he turns to tradition and auricular whispers), or else that in his manipulations he has made some slip of a scruple in weight or a moment in time (whereupon he repeats his trials to infinity); and when meanwhile among the chances of experiment he lights upon some conclusions either in aspect new or for utility not contemptible, he takes these for earnest of what is to come, and feeds his mind upon them, and magnifies them to the most, and supplies the rest in hope. Not but that Alchemists have made a good many discoveries, and presented men with useful inventions. But their case may be well compared to the fable of the old man, who bequeathed to his sons gold buried in a vineyard, pretending not to know the exact spot; whereupon the sons applied themselves diligently to the digging of the vineyard, and though no gold was found there, yet the vintage by that digging was made more plentiful.

Again the students of natural magic, who explain everything by Sympathies and Antipathies, have in their idle and most slothful conjectures ascribed to substances wonderful virtues and operations; and if ever they have produced works, they have been such as aim rather at admiration and novelty than at utility and fruit.

In superstitious magic on the other hand (if of this also we must speak), it is especially to be observed that they are but subjects of a certain and definite kind wherein the curious and superstitious arts, in all nations and ages, and religions also, have worked or played. These therefore we may pass. Meanwhile it is nowise strange if opinion of plenty has been the cause of want.

LXXXVI

Further, this admiration of men for knowledges and arts,— an admiration in itself weak enough, and well-nigh childish, —has been increased by the craft and artifices of those who have handled and transmitted sciences. For they set them forth with such ambition and parade, and bring them into the view of the world so fashioned and masked, as if they were complete in all parts and finished. For if you look at the method of them and the divisions, they seem to embrace and comprise everything which can belong to the subject. And although these divisions are ill filled out and are but as empty cases, still to the common mind they present the form and plan of a perfect science. But the first and most ancient seekers after truth were wont, with better faith and better fortune too, to throw the knowledge which they gathered from the contemplation of things, and which they meant to store up for use, into aphorisms; that is, into short and scattered sentences, not linked together by an artificial method; and did not pretend or profess to embrace the entire art. But as the matter now is, it is nothing strange if men do not seek to advance in things delivered to them as long since perfect and complete.

LXXXVII

Moreover the ancient systems have received no slight accession of reputation and credit from the vanity and levity of those who have propounded new ones; especially in the active and practical department of natural philosophy. For there have not been wanting talkers and dreamers who, partly from credulity, partly in imposture, have loaded man-

kind with promises, offering and announcing the prolongation of life, the retardation of age, the alleviation of pain,
the repairing of natural defects, the deceiving of the senses;
arts of binding and inciting the affections, of illuminating
and exalting the intellectual faculties, of transmuting substances, of strengthening and multiplying motions at will, of
making impressions and alterations in the air, of bringing
down and procuring celestial influences; arts of divining
things future, and bringing things distant near, and revealing things secret; and many more. But with regard to these
lavish promisers, this judgment would not be far amiss; that
there is as much difference in philosophy between their vanities and true arts, as there is in history between the exploits
of Julius Cæsar or Alexander the Great, and the exploits of
Amadis of Gaul or Arthur of Britain. For it is true that those
illustrious generals really did greater things than these
shadowy heroes are even feigned to have done; but they
did them by means and ways of action not fabulous or
monstrous. Yet surely it is not fair that the credit of true
history should be lessened because it has sometimes been
injured and wronged by fables. Meanwhile it is not to be
wondered at, if a great prejudice is raised against new propositions, especially when works are also mentioned, because
of those impostors who have attempted the like; since their
excess of vanity, and the disgust it has bred, have their
effect still in the destruction of all greatness of mind in
enterprises of this kind.

LXXXVIII

Far more however has knowledge suffered from littleness
of spirit and the smallness and slightness of the tasks which
human industry has proposed to itself. And what is worst of
all, this very littleness of spirit comes with a certain air of
arrogance and superiority.

For in the first place there is found in all arts one general
device, which has now become familiar,—that the author
lays the weakness of his art to the charge of nature: whatever his art cannot attain he sets down on the authority of

the same art to be in nature impossible. And truly no art can be condemned if it be judge itself. Moreover the philosophy which is now in vogue embraces and cherishes certain tenets, the purpose of which (if it be diligently examined) is to persuade men that nothing difficult, nothing by which nature may be commanded and subdued, can be expected from art or human labour; as with respect to the doctrine that the heat of the sun and of fire differ in kind, and to that other concerning mixture, has been already observed. Which things, if they be noted accurately, tend wholly to the unfair circumscription of human power, and to a deliberate and factitious despair; which not only disturbs the auguries of hope, but also cuts the sinews and spur of industry, and throws away the chances of experience itself; and all for the sake of having their art thought perfect, and for the miserable vain glory of making it believed that whatever has not yet been discovered and comprehended can never be discovered or comprehended hereafter.

And even if a man apply himself fairly to facts, and endeavour to find out something new, yet he will confine his aim and intention to the investigation and working out of some one discovery and no more; such as the nature of the magnet, the ebb and flow of the sea, the system of the heavens, and things of this kind, which seem to be in some measure secret, and have hitherto been handled without much success. Whereas it is most unskilful to investigate the nature of anything in the thing itself; seeing that the same nature which appears in some things to be latent and hidden is in others manifest and palpable; wherefore in the former it produces wonder, in the latter excites no attention; as we find it in the nature of consistency, which in wood or stone is not observed, but is passed over under the appellation of solidity, without further inquiry as to why separation or solution of continuity is avoided; while in the case of bubbles, which form themselves into certain pellicles, curiously shaped into hemispheres, so that the solution of continuity is avoided for a moment, it is thought a subtle matter. In fact what in some things is accounted a secret has in others a manifest and well known nature, which will never be recognised as long as the experiments and thoughts of men are engaged on the former only.

But generally speaking, in mechanics old discoveries pass for new, if a man does but refine or embellish them, or unite several in one, or couple them better with their use, or make the work in greater or less volume than it was before, or the like.

Thus then it is no wonder if noble inventions and worthy of mankind have not been brought to light, when men have been contented and delighted with such trifling and puerile tasks, and have even fancied that in them they have been endeavouring after, if not accomplishing, some great matter.

LXXXIX

Neither is it to be forgotten that in every age Natural Philosophy has had a troublesome adversary and hard to deal with; namely, superstition, and the blind and immoderate zeal of religion. For we see among the Greeks that those who first proposed to men's then uninitiated ears the natural causes for thunder and for storms, where thereupon found guilty of impiety. Nor was much more forbearance shown by some of the ancient fathers of the Christian church to those who on most convincing grounds (such as no one in his senses would now think of contradicting) maintained that the earth was round, and of consequence asserted the existence of the antipodes.

Moreover, as things now are, to discourse of nature is made harder and more perilous by the summaries and systems of the schoolmen; who having reduced theology into regular order as well as they were able, and fashioned it into the shape of an art, ended in incorporating the contentious and thorny philosophy of Aristotle, more than was fit, with the body of religion.

To the same result, though in a different way, tend the speculations of those who have taken upon them to deduce the truth of the Christian religion from the principles of

philosophers, and to confirm it by their authority; pomp-
ously solemnising this union of the sense and faith as a lawful marriage, and entertaining men's minds with a pleasing
variety of matter, but all the while disparaging things divine by mingling them with things human. Now in such
mixtures of theology with philosophy only the received doctrines of philosophy are included; while new ones, albeit
changes for the better, are all but expelled and exterminated.

Lastly, you will find that by the simpleness of certain
divines, access to any philosophy, however pure, is well
nigh closed. Some are weakly afraid lest a deeper search
into nature should transgress the permitted limits of sober-
mindedness; wrongfully wresting and transferring what is
said in holy writ against those who pry into sacred mysteries, to the hidden things of nature, which are barred by
no prohibition. Others with more subtlety surmise and reflect that if second causes are unknown everything can more
readily be referred to the divine hand and rod; a point in
which they think religion greatly concerned; which is in
fact nothing else but to seek to gratify God with a lie.
Others fear from past example that movements and changes
in philosophy will end in assaults on religion. And others
again appear apprehensive that in the investigation of nature something may be found to subvert or at least shake
the authority of religion, especially with the unlearned. But
these two last fears seem to me to savour utterly of carnal
wisdom; as if men in the recesses and secret thoughts of
their hearts doubted and distrusted the strength of religion
and the empire of faith over the sense, and therefore feared
that the investigation of truth in nature might be dangerous to them. But if the matter be truly considered, natural
philosophy is after the word of God at once the surest medicine against superstition, and the most approved nourishment for faith, and therefore she is rightly given to religion
as her most faithful handmaid, since the one displays the
will of God, the other his power. For he did not err who
said "Ye err in that ye know not the Scriptures and the
power of God," thus coupling and blending in an indis-

soluble bond information concerning his will and meditation concerning his power. Meanwhile it is not surprising
if the growth of Natural Philosophy is checked, when religion, the thing which has most power over men's minds, has
by the simpleness and incautious zeal of certain persons
been drawn to take part against her.

XC

Again, in the customs and institutions of schools, academies, colleges, and similar bodies destined for the abode of
learned men and the cultivation of learning, everything is
found adverse to the progress of science. For the lectures
and exercises there are so ordered, that to think or specu-
late on anything out of the common way can hardly occur
to any man. And if one or two have the boldness to use any
liberty of judgment, they must undertake the task all by
themselves; they can have no advantage from the company
of others. And if they can endure this also, they will find
their industry and largeness of mind no slight hindrance to
their fortune. For the studies of men in these places are
confined and as it were imprisoned in the writings of certain
authors, from whom if any man dissent he is straightway
arraigned as a turbulent person and an innovator. But surely
there is a great distinction between matters of state and the
arts; for the danger from new motion and from new light
is not the same. In matters of state a change even for the
better is distrusted, because it unsettles what is established;
these things resting on authority, consent, fame and opinion,
not on demonstration. But arts and sciences should be like
mines, where the noise of new works and further advances
is heard on every side. But though the matter be so according to right reason, it is not so acted on in practice; and the
points above mentioned in the administration and government of learning put a severe restraint upon the advancement of the sciences.

XCI

Nay, even if that jealousy were to cease, still it is enough to check the growth of science, that efforts and labours in this field go unrewarded. For it does not rest with the same persons to cultivate sciences and to reward them. The growth of them comes from great wits; the prizes and rewards of them are in the hands of the people, or of great persons, who are but in very few cases even moderately learned. Moreover this kind of progress is not only unrewarded with prizes and substantial benefits; it has not even the advantage of popular applause. For it is a greater matter than the generality of men can take in, and is apt to be overwhelmed and extinguished by the gales of popular opinions. And it is nothing strange if a thing not held in honour does not prosper.

XCII

But by far the greatest obstacle to the progress of science and to the undertaking of new tasks and provinces therein, is found in this—that men despair and think things impossible. For wise and serious men are wont in these matters to be altogether distrustful; considering with themselves the obscurity of nature, the shortness of life, the deceitfulness of the senses, the weakness of the judgment, the difficulty of experiment and the like; and so supposing that in the revolution of time and of the ages of the world the sciences have their ebbs and flows; that at one season they grow and flourish, at another wither and decay, yet in such sort that when they have reached a certain point and condition they can advance no further. If therefore any one believes or promises more, they think this comes of an ungoverned and unripened mind, and that such attempts have prosperous beginnings, become difficult as they go on, and end in confusion. Now since these are thoughts which naturally present themselves to grave men and of great judgment, we must take good heed that we be not led away by our love for a most fair and excellent object to relax or diminish the

severity of our judgment; we must observe diligently what
encouragement dawns upon us and from what quarter;
and, putting aside the lighter breezes of hope, we must
thoroughly sift and examine those which promise greater
steadiness and constancy. Nay, and we must take state-
prudence too into our counsels, whose rule is to distrust,
and to take the less favourable view of human affairs. I am
now therefore to speak touching Hope; especially as I am
not a dealer in promises, and wish neither to force nor to
ensnare men's judgments, but to lead them by the hand
with their good will. And though the strongest means of in-
spiring hope will be to bring men to particulars; especially
to particulars digested and arranged in my Tables of Discovery (the subject partly of the second, but much more of
the fourth part of my Instauration), since this is not merely
the promise of the thing but the thing itself; nevertheless
that everything may be done with gentleness, I will proceed
with my plan of preparing men's minds; of which preparation to give hope is no unimportant part. For without it the
rest tends rather to make men sad (by giving them a worse
and a meaner opinion of things as they are than they now
have, and making them more fully to feel and know the
unhappiness of their own condition) than to induce any
alacrity or to whet their industry in making trial. And therefore it is fit that I publish and set forth those conjectures of
mine which make hope in this matter reasonable; just as
Columbus did, before that wonderful voyage of his across
the Atlantic, when he gave the reasons for his conviction
that new lands and continents might be discovered besides
those which were known before; which reasons, though rejected at first, were afterwards made good by experience,
and were the causes and beginnings of great events.

XCIII

The beginning is from God: for the business which is in
hand, having the character of good so strongly impressed
upon it, appears manifestly to proceed from God, who is
the author of good, and the Father of Lights. Now in di-

vine operations even the smallest beginnings lead of a certainty to their end. And as it was said of spiritual things, "The kingdom of God cometh not with observation," so is it in all the greater works of Divine Providence; everything glides on smoothly and noiselessly, and the work is fairly going on before men are aware that it has begun. Nor should the prophecy of Daniel be forgotten, touching the last ages of the world:—"Many shall go to and fro, and knowledge shall be increased;" clearly intimating that the thorough passage of the world (which now by so many distant voyages seems to be accomplished, or in course of accomplishment), and the advancement of the sciences, are destined by fate, that is, by Divine Providence, to meet in the same age.

XCIV

Next comes a consideration of the greatest importance as an argument of hope; I mean that drawn from the errors of past time, and of the ways hitherto trodden. For most excellent was the censure once passed upon a government that had been unwisely administered. "That which is the worst thing in reference to the past, ought to be regarded as best for the future. For if you had done all that your duty demanded, and yet your affairs were no better, you would not have even a hope left you that further improvement is possible. But now, when your misfortunes are owing, not to the force of circumstances, but to your own errors, you may hope that by dismissing or correcting these errors, a great change may be made for the better." In like manner, if during so long a course of years men had kept the true road for discovering and cultivating sciences, and had yet been unable to make further progress therein, bold doubtless and rash would be the opinion that further progress is possible. But if the road itself has been mistaken, and men's labour spent on unfit objects, it follows that the difficulty has its rise not in things themselves, which are not in our power, but in the human understanding, and the use and application thereof, which admits of remedy and medicine.

It will be of great use therefore to set forth what these errors are; for as many impediments as there have been in times past from this cause, so many arguments are there of hope for the time to come. And although they have been partly touched before, I think fit here also, in plain and simple words, to represent them.

XCV

Those who have handled sciences have been either men of experiment or men of dogmas. The men of experiment are like the ant; they only collect and use: the reasoners resemble spiders, who make cobwebs out of their own substance. But the bee takes a middle course; it gathers its material from the flowers of the garden and of the field, but transforms and digests it by a power of its own. Not unlike this is the true business of philosophy; for it neither relies solely or chiefly on the powers of the mind, nor does it take the matter which it gathers from natural history and mechanical experiments and lay it up in the memory whole, as it finds it; but lays it up in the understanding altered and digested. Therefore from a closer and purer league between these two faculties, the experimental and the rational, (such as has never yet been made) much may be hoped.

XCVI

We have as yet no natural philosophy that is pure; all is tainted and corrupted; in Aristotle's school by logic; in Plato's by natural theology; in the second school of Platonists, such as Proclus and others, by mathematics, which ought only to give definiteness to natural philosophy, not to generate or give it birth. From a natural philosophy pure and unmixed, better things are to be expected.

XCVII

No one has yet been found so firm of mind and purpose as resolutely to compel himself to sweep away all theories and common notions, and to apply the understanding, thus made fair and even, to a fresh examination of particulars.

Thus it happens that human knowledge, as we have it, is a mere medley and ill-digested mass, made up of much credulity and much accident, and also of the childish notions which we at first imbibed.

Now if any one of ripe age, unimpaired senses, and well-purged mind, apply himself anew to experience and particulars, better hopes may be entertained of that man. In which point I promise to myself a like fortune to that of Alexander the Great; and let no man tax me with vanity till we have heard the end; for the thing which I mean tends to the putting off of all vanity. For of Alexander and his deeds Æschines spake thus: "Assuredly we do not live the life of mortal men; but to this end were we born, that in after ages wonders might be told of us;" as if what Alexander had done seemed to him miraculous. But in the next age Titus Livius took a better and a deeper view of the matter, saying in effect, that Alexander "had done no more than take courage to despise vain apprehensions." And a like judgment I suppose may be passed on myself in future ages: that I did no great things, but simply made less account of things that were accounted great. In the meanwhile, as I have already said, there is no hope except in a new birth of science; that is, in raising it regularly up from experience and building it afresh; which no one (I think) will say has yet been done or thought of.

XCVIII

Now for grounds of experience—since to experience we must come—we have as yet had either none or very weak ones; no search has been made to collect a store of particular observations sufficient either in number, or in kind, or in certainty, to inform the understanding, or in any way adequate. On the contrary, men of learning, but easy withal and idle, have taken for the construction or for the confirmation of their philosophy certain rumours and vague fames or airs of experience, and allowed to these the weight of lawful evidence. And just as if some kingdom or state were to direct its counsels and affairs, not by letters and reports from ambassadors and trustworthy messengers, but by the gossip of the streets; such exactly is the system of management introduced into philosophy with relation to experience. Nothing duly investigated, nothing verified, nothing counted, weighed, or measured, is to be found in natural history: and what in observation is loose and vague, is in information deceptive and treacherous. And if any one thinks that this is a strange thing to say, and something like an unjust complaint, seeing that Aristotle, himself so great a man, and supported by the wealth of so great a king, has composed so accurate a history of animals; and that others with greater diligence, though less pretence, have made many additions; while others, again, have compiled copious histories and descriptions of metals, plants, and fossils; it seems that he does not rightly apprehend what it is that we are now about. For a natural history which is composed for its own sake is not like one that is collected to supply the understanding with information for the building up of philosophy. They differ in many ways, but especially in this; that the former contains the variety of natural species only, and not experiments of the mechanical arts. For even as in the business of life a man's disposition and the secret workings of his mind and affections are better discovered when he is in trouble than at other times; so likewise the secrets of nature reveal themselves more readily under the vexations of art than when they go their own way. Good hopes may therefore be conceived of natural philosophy, when natural history, which is the basis and foundation of it, has been drawn up on a better plan; but not till then.

XCIX

Again, even in the great plenty of mechanical experiments, there is yet a great scarcity of those which are of most use for the information of the understanding. For the mechanic, not troubling himself with the investigation of truth, confines his attention to those things which bear upon his particular work, and will not either raise his mind or stretch out his hand for anything else. But then only will there be good ground of hope for the further advance of knowledge, when there shall be received and gathered together into natural history a variety of experiments, which are of no use in themselves, but simply serve to discover causes and axioms; which I call *"Experimenta lucifera,"* experiments of *light,* to distinguish them from those which I call *"fructifera,"* experiments of *fruit.*

Now experiments of this kind have one admirable property and condition; they never miss or fail. For since they are applied, not for the purpose of producing any particular effect, but only of discovering the natural cause of some effect, they answer the end equally well whichever way they turn out; for they settle the question.

C

But not only is a greater abundance of experiments to be sought for and procured, and that too of a different kind from those hitherto tried; an entirely different method, order, and process for carrying on and advancing experience must also be introduced. For experience, when it wanders in its own track, is, as I have already remarked, mere groping in the dark, and confounds men rather than instructs them. But when it shall proceed in accordance with a fixed law, in regular order, and without interruption, then may better things be hoped of knowledge.

CI

But even after such a store of natural history and experience as is required for the work of the understanding, or of philosophy, shall be ready at hand, still the understanding is by no means competent to deal with it off hand and by memory alone; no more than if a man should hope by force of memory to retain and make himself master of the computation of an ephemeris. And yet hitherto more has been done in matter of invention by thinking than by writing; and experience has not yet learned her letters. Now no course of invention can be satisfactory unless it be carried on in writing. But when this is brought into use, and experience has been taught to read and write, better things may be hoped.

CII

Moreover, since there is so great a number and army of particulars, and that army so scattered and dispersed as to distract and confound the understanding, little is to be hoped for from the skirmishings and slight attacks and desultory movements of the intellect, unless all the particulars which pertain to the subject of inquiry shall, by means of Tables of Discovery, apt, well arranged, and as it were animate, be drawn up and marshalled; and the mind be set to work upon the helps duly prepared and digested which these tables supply.

CIII

But after this store of particulars has been set out duly and in order before our eyes, we are not to pass at once to the investigation and discovery of new particulars or works; or at any rate if we do so we must not stop there. For although I do not deny that when all the experiments of all the arts shall have been collected and digested, and brought within one man's knowledge and judgment, the mere transferring of the experiments of one art to others may lead, by means of that experience which I term *literate*,[10] to the discovery of many new things of service to the life and state of man, yet it is no great matter that can be hoped from that; but from the new light of axioms, which having been educed from those particulars by a certain method and rule, shall in their turn point out the way again to new particulars, greater things may be looked for. For our road does not lie on a level, but ascends and descends; first ascending to axioms, then descending to works.

CIV

The understanding must not however be allowed to jump and fly from particulars to remote axioms and of almost the highest generality (such as the first principles, as they are

called, of arts and things), and taking stand upon them as
truths that cannot be shaken, proceed to prove and frame
the middle axioms by reference to them; which has been
the practice hitherto; the understanding being not only carried that way by a natural impulse, but also by the use of
syllogistic demonstration trained and inured to it. But then,
and then only, may we hope well of the sciences, when in
a just scale of ascent, and by successive steps not interrupted or broken, we rise from particulars to lesser axioms;
and then to middle axioms, one above the other; and last
of all to the most general. For the lowest axioms differ but
slightly from bare experience, while the highest and most
general (which we now have) are notional and abstract
and without solidity. But the middle are the true and solid
and living axioms, on which depend the affairs and fortunes of men; and above them again, last of all those which
are indeed the most general; such I mean as are not abstract, but of which those intermediate axioms are really
limitations.

The understanding must not therefore be supplied with
wings, but rather hung with weights, to keep it from leap-
ing and flying. Now this has never yet been done; when it
is done, we may entertain better hopes of the sciences.

CV

In establishing axioms, another form of induction must
be devised than has hitherto been employed; and it must be
used for proving and discovering not first principles (as
they are called) only, but also the lesser axioms, and the
middle, and indeed all. For the induction which proceeds
by simple enumeration is childish; its conclusions are pre-
carious, and exposed to peril from a contradictory instance;
and it generally decides on too small a number of facts, and
on those only which are at hand. But the induction which
is to be available for the discovery and demonstration of
sciences and arts, must analyse nature by proper rejections
and exclusions; and then, after a sufficient number of negatives, come to a conclusion on the affirmative instances:

which has not yet been done or even attempted, save only by Plato, who does indeed employ this form of induction to a certain extent for the purpose of discussing definitions and ideas. But in order to furnish this induction or demonstration well and duly for its work, very many things are to be provided which no mortal has yet thought of; insomuch that greater labour will have to be spent in it than has hitherto been spent on the syllogism. And this induction must be used not only to discover axioms, but also in the formation of notions. And it is in this induction that our chief hope lies.

CVI

But in establishing axioms by this kind of induction, we must also examine and try whether the axiom so established be framed to the measure of those particulars only from which it is derived, or whether it be larger and wider. And if it be larger and wider, we must observe whether by indicating to us new particulars it confirm that wideness and largeness as by a collateral security; that we may not either stick fast in things already known, or loosely grasp at shadows and abstract forms; not at things solid and realised in matter. And when this process shall have come into use, then at last shall we see the dawn of a solid hope.

CVII

And here also should be remembered what was said above concerning the extending of the range of natural philosophy to take in the particular sciences, and the referring or bringing back of the particular sciences to natural philosophy; that the branches of knowledge may not be severed and cut off from the stem. For without this the hope of progress will not be so good.

CVIII

So much then for the removing of despair and the raising of hope through the dismissal or rectification of the errors of past time. We must now see what else there is to ground hope upon. And this consideration occurs at once—that if many useful discoveries have been made by accident or upon occasion, when men were not seeking for them but were busy about other things; no one can doubt but that when they apply themselves to seek and make this their business, and that too by method and in order and not by desultory impulses, they will discover far more. For although it may happen once or twice that a man shall stumble on a thing by accident which, when taking great pains to search for it, he could not find; yet upon the whole it unquestionably falls out the other way. And therefore far better things, and more of them, and at shorter intervals, are to be expected from man's reason and industry and direction and fixed application, than from accident and animal instinct and the like, in which inventions have hitherto had their origin.

CIX

Another argument of hope may be drawn from this,— that some of the inventions already known are such as before they were discovered it could hardly have entered any man's head to think of; they would have been simply set aside as impossible. For in conjecturing what may be men set before them the example of what has been, and divine of the new with an imagination preoccupied and coloured by the old; which way of forming opinions is very fallacious; for streams that are drawn from the springheads of nature do not always run in the old channels.

If, for instance, before the invention of ordnance, a man had described the thing by its effects, and said that there was a new invention, by means of which the strongest towers and walls could be shaken and thrown down at a great distance; men would doubtless have begun to think over all the ways of multiplying the force of catapults and mechanical engines by weights and wheels and such machinery for ramming and projecting; but the notion of a fiery blast suddenly and violently expanding and exploding would hardly have entered into any man's imagination or fancy; being a

thing to which nothing immediately analogous had been
seen, except perhaps in an earthquake or in lightning, which
as *magnalia* or marvels of nature, and by man not imitable,
would have been immediately rejected.

In the same way, if before the discovery of silk, any one
had said that there was a kind of thread discovered for the
purposes of dress and furniture, which far surpassed the
thread of linen or of wool in fineness and at the same time
in strength, and also in beauty and softness; men would
have begun immediately to think of some silky kind of vege-
table, or of the finer hair of some animal, or of the feathers
and down of birds; but of a web woven by a tiny worm, and
that in such abundance, and renewing itself yearly, they
would assuredly never have thought. Nay, if any one had
said anything about a worm, he would no doubt have been
laughed at as dreaming of a new kind of cobwebs.

So again, if before the discovery of the magnet, any one
had said that a certain instrument had been invented by
means of which the quarters and points of the heavens could
be taken and distinguished with exactness; men would have
been carried by their imagination to a variety of conjectures concerning the more exquisite construction of astro-
nomical instruments; but that anything could be discovered
agreeing so well in its movements with the heavenly bodies,
and yet not a heavenly body itself, but simply a substance
of metal or stone, would have been judged altogether incredible. Yet these things and others like them lay for so
many ages of the world concealed from men, nor was it by
philosophy or the rational arts that they were found out at
last, but by accident and occasion; being indeed, as I said,
altogether different in kind and as remote as possible from
anything that was known before; so that no preconceived
notion could possibly have led to the discovery of them.

There is therefore much ground for hoping that there are
still laid up in the womb of nature many secrets of excellent
use, having no affinity or parallelism with any thing that is
now known, but lying entirely out of the beat of the imagination, which have not yet been found out. They too no

doubt will some time or other, in the course and revolution of many ages, come to light of themselves, just as the others did; only by the method of which we are now treating they can be speedily and suddenly and simultaneously presented and anticipated.

CX

But we have also discoveries to show of another kind, which prove that noble inventions may be lying at our very feet, and yet mankind may step over without seeing them. For however the discovery of gunpowder, of silk, of the magnet, of sugar, of paper, or the like, may seem to depend on certain properties of things themselves and nature, there is at any rate nothing in the art of printing which is not plain and obvious. Nevertheless for want of observing that although it is more difficult to arrange types of letters than to write letters by the motion of the hand, there is yet this difference between the two, that types once arranged serve for innumerable impressions, but letters written with the hand for a single copy only; or perhaps again for want of observing that ink can be so thickened as to colour without running (particularly when the letters face upwards and the impression is made from above)—for want, I say, of observing these things, men went for so many ages without this most beautiful discovery, which is of so much service in the propagation of knowledge.

But such is the infelicity and unhappy disposition of the human mind in this course of invention, that it first distrusts and then despises itself: first will not believe that any such thing can be found out; and when it is found out, cannot understand how the world should have missed it so long. And this very thing may be justly taken as an argument of hope; namely, that there is a great mass of inventions still remaining, which not only by means of operations that are yet to be discovered, but also through the transferring, comparing, and applying of those already known, by the help of that Learned Experience of which I spoke, may be deduced and brought to light.

CXI

There is another ground of hope that must not be omitted. Let men but think over their infinite expenditure of understanding, time, and means on matters and pursuits of far less use and value; whereof if but a small part were directed to sound and solid studies, there is no difficulty that might not be overcome. This I thought good to add, because I plainly confess that a collection of history natural and experimental, such as I conceive it and as it ought to be, is a great, I may say a royal work, and of much labour and expense.

CXII

Meantime, let no man be alarmed at the multitude of particulars, but let this rather encourage him to hope. For the particular phenomena of art and nature are but a handful to the inventions of the wit, when disjoined and separated from the evidence of things. Moreover this road has an issue in the open ground and not far off; the other has no issue at all, but endless entanglement. For men hitherto have made but short stay with experience, but passing her lightly by, have wasted an infinity of time on meditations and glosses of the wit. But if some one were by that could answer our questions and tell us in each case what the fact in nature is, the discovery of all causes and sciences would be but the work of a few years.

CXIII

Moreover I think that men may take some hope from my own example. And this I say not by way of boasting, but because it is useful to say it. If there be any that despond, let them look at me, that being of all men of my time the most busied in affairs of state, and a man of health not very strong (whereby much time is lost), and in this course altogether a pioneer, following in no man's track, nor sharing these counsels with any one, have nevertheless by resolutely entering on the true road, and submitting my mind to

Things, advanced these matters, as I suppose, some little way. And then let them consider what may be expected (after the way has been thus indicated) from men abounding in leisure, and from association of labours, and from successions of ages: the rather because it is not a way over which only one man can pass at a time (as is the case with that of reasoning), but one in which the labours and industries of men (especially as regards the collecting of experience) may with the best effect be first distributed and then combined. For then only will men begin to know their strength, when instead of great numbers doing all the same things, one shall take charge of one thing and another of another.

CXIV

Lastly, even if the breath of hope which blows on us from that New Continent were fainter than it is and harder to perceive; yet the trial (if we would not bear a spirit altogether abject) must by all means be made. For there is no comparison between that which we may lose by not trying and by not succeeding; since by not trying we throw away the chance of an immense good; by not succeeding we only incur the loss of a little human labour. But as it is, it appears to me from what has been said, and also from what has been left unsaid, that there is hope enough and to spare, not only to make a bold man try, but also to make a sober-minded and wise man believe.

CXV

Concerning the grounds then for putting away despair, which has been one of the most powerful causes of delay and hindrance to the progress of knowledge, I have now spoken. And this also concludes what I had to say touching the *signs* and *causes* of the errors, sluggishness, and ignorance which have prevailed; especially since the more subtle causes, which do not fall under popular judgment and observation, must be referred to what has been said on the Idols of the human mind.

And here likewise should close that part of my Instauration, which is devoted to pulling down: which part is performed by three refutations; first, by the refutation of the *natural human reason,* left to itself; secondly, by the refutation of the *demonstrations;* and thirdly, by the refutation of the *theories,* or the received systems of philosophy and doctrine. And the refutation of these has been such, as alone it could be: that is to say, by signs and the evidence of causes; since no other kind of confutation was open to me, differing as I do from others both on first principles and on rules of demonstration.

It is time therefore to proceed to the art itself and rule of interpreting nature; still however there remains something to be premised. For whereas in this first book of aphorisms I proposed to prepare men's minds as well for understanding as for receiving what is to follow; now that I have purged and swept and levelled the floor of the mind, it remains that I place the mind in a good position and as it were in a favourable aspect towards what I have to lay before it. For in a new matter, it is not only the strong preoccupation of some old opinion that tends to create a prejudice, but also a false preconception or prefiguration of the new thing which is presented. I will endeavour therefore to impart sound and true opinions as to the things I propose, although they are to serve only for the time, and by way of interest (so to speak), till the thing itself, which is the principal, be fully known.

CXVI

First, then, I must request men not to suppose that after the fashion of ancient Greeks, and of certain moderns, as Telesius, Patricius, Severinus, I wish to found a new sect in philosophy. For this is not what I am about; nor do I think that it matters much to the fortunes of men what abstract notions one may entertain concerning nature and the principles of things; and no doubt many old theories of this kind can be revived and many new ones introduced; just as many theories of the heavens may be supposed, which agree well enough with the phenomena and yet differ with each other.

But for my part I do not trouble myself with any such speculative and withal unprofitable matters. My purpose, on the contrary, is to try whether I cannot in very fact lay more firmly the foundations, and extend more widely the limits, of the power and greatness of man. And although on some special subjects and in an incomplete form I am in possession of results which I take to be far more true and more certain and withal more fruitful than those now received, (and these I have collected into the fifth part of my Instauration,) yet I have no entire or universal theory to propound. For it does not seem that the time is come for such an attempt. Neither can I hope to live to complete the sixth part of the Instauration (which is destined for the philosophy discovered by the legitimate interpretation of nature), but hold it enough if in the intermediate business I bear myself soberly and profitably, sowing in the meantime for future ages the seeds of a purer truth, and performing my part towards the commencement of the great undertaking.

CXVII

And as I do not seek to found a school, so neither do I hold out offers or promises of particular works. It may be thought indeed, that I who make such frequent mention of works and refer everything to that end, should produce some myself by way of earnest. But my course and method, as I have often clearly stated and would wish to state again, is this,—not to extract works from works or experiments from experiments (as an empiric), but from works and experiments to extract causes and axioms, and again from those causes and axioms new works and experiments, as a legitimate interpreter of nature. And although in my tables of discovery (which compose the fourth part of the Instauration), and also in the examples of particulars (which I have adduced in the second part), and moreover in my observations on the history (which I have drawn out in the third part), any reader of even moderate sagacity and intelligence will everywhere observe indications and outlines of many noble works; still I candidly confess that the natural history which I now have, whether collected from books or from my own investigations, is neither sufficiently copious nor verified with sufficient accuracy to serve the purposes of legitimate interpretation.

Accordingly, if there be any one more apt and better prepared for mechanical pursuits, and sagacious in hunting out works by the mere dealing with experiment, let him by all means use his industry to gather from my history and tables many things by the way, and apply them to the production of works, which may serve as interest until the principal be forthcoming. But for myself, aiming as I do at greater things, I condemn all unseasonable and premature tarrying over such things as these; being (as I often say) like Atalanta's balls. For I do not run off like a child after golden apples, but stake all on the victory of art over nature in the race; nor do I make haste to mow down the moss or the corn in blade, but wait for the harvest in its due season.

CXVIII

There will be found no doubt, when my history and tables of discovery are read, some things in the experiments themselves that are not quite certain, or perhaps that are quite false; which may make a man think that the foundations and principles upon which my discoveries rest are false and doubtful. But this is of no consequence; for such things must needs happen at first. It is only like the occurrence in a written or printed page of a letter or two mistaken or misplaced; which does not much hinder the reader, because such errors are easily corrected by the sense. So likewise may there occur in my natural history many experiments which are mistaken and falsely set down, and yet they will presently by the discovery of causes and axioms be easily expunged and rejected. It is nevertheless true that if the mistakes in natural history and experiments are important, frequent, and continual, they cannot possibly be corrected or amended by any felicity of wit or art. And therefore, if in my natural history, which has been collected and tested with so much diligence, severity, and I may say religious care, there still lurk at intervals certain falsities or errors in the particulars,—what is to be said of common natural history, which in comparison with mine is so negligent and inexact? and what of the philosophy and sciences built on such a sand (or rather quicksand)? Let no man therefore trouble himself for this.

CXIX

There will be met with also in my history and experiments many things which are trivial and commonly known; many which are mean and low; many, lastly, which are too subtle and merely speculative, and that seem to be of no use; which kind of things may possibly avert and alienate men's interest.

And first for those things which seem common; let men bear in mind that hitherto they have been accustomed to do no more than refer and adapt the causes of things which rarely happen to such as happen frequently; while of those which happen frequently they never ask the cause, but take them as they are for granted. And therefore they do not investigate the causes of weight, of the rotation of heavenly bodies, of heat, cold, light, hardness, softness, rarity, density, liquidity, solidity, animation, inanimation, similarity, dissimilarity, organisation, and the like; but admitting these as self-evident and obvious, they dispute and decide on other things of less frequent and familiar occurrence.

But I, who am well aware that no judgment can be passed on uncommon or remarkable things, much less anything new brought to light, unless the causes of common things, and the causes of those causes, be first duly examined and found out, am of necessity compelled to admit the commonest things into my history. Nay, in my judgment philosophy has been hindered by nothing more than this,—that things of familiar and frequent occurrence do not arrest and detain the thoughts of men, but are received in passing without any inquiry into their causes; insomuch that information concerning things which are not known is not oftener wanted than attention concerning things which are.

<h3 style="text-align:center">CXX</h3>

And for things that are mean or even filthy,—things which (as Pliny says) must be introduced with an apology,—such things, no less than the most splendid and costly, must be admitted into natural history. Nor is natural history polluted thereby; for the sun enters the sewer no less than the palace, yet takes no pollution. And for myself, I am not raising a capitol or pyramid to the pride of man, but laying a foundation in the human understanding for a holy temple after the model of the world. That model therefore I follow. For whatever deserves to exist deserves also to be known, for knowledge is the image of existence; and things mean and splendid exist alike. Moreover as from certain putrid substances—musk, for instance, and civet—the sweetest odours are sometimes generated, so too from mean and sordid instances there sometimes emanates excellent light and information. But enough and more than enough of this; such fastidiousness being merely childish and effeminate.

<h3 style="text-align:center">CXXI</h3>

But there is another objection which must be more carefully looked to: namely, that there are many things in this History which to common apprehension, or indeed to any understanding accustomed to the present system, will seem to be curiously and unprofitably subtle. Upon this point therefore above all I must say again what I have said already,—that at first and for a time I am seeking for experiments of light, not for experiments of fruit; following therein, as I have often said, the example of the divine creation; which on the first day produced light only, and assigned to it alone one entire day, nor mixed up with it on that day any material work.

To suppose therefore that things like these are of no use is the same as to suppose that light is of no use, because it is not a thing solid or material. And the truth is that the knowledge of simple natures well examined and defined is as light; it gives entrance to all the secrets of nature's workshop, and virtually includes and draws after it whole bands and troops of works, and opens to us the sources of the noblest axioms; and yet in itself it is of no great use. So also the letters of the alphabet in themselves and apart have no use or meaning, yet they are the subject-matter for the composition and apparatus of all discourse. So again the seeds of things are of much latent virtue, and yet of no use except in their development. And the scattered rays of light itself, until they are made to converge, can impart none of their benefit.

But if objection be taken to speculative subtleties, what is to be said of the schoolmen, who have indulged in subtleties to such excess? in subtleties too that were spent on words, or at any rate on popular notions (which is much the same thing), not on facts or nature; and such as were useless not only in their origin but also in their consequences; and not like those I speak of, useless indeed for the present, but promising infinite utility hereafter. But let men be assured of this, that all subtlety of disputation and discourse, if not applied till after axioms are discovered, is out of season and preposterous; and that the true and proper or at any rate the chief time for subtlety is in weighing experience and in founding axioms thereon; for that other subtlety, though it grasps and snatches at nature, yet can never take hold of her. Certainly what is said of opportunity or fortune is most true of nature; she has a lock in front, but is bald behind.

Lastly, concerning the disdain to receive into natural history things either common, or mean, or over-subtle and in their original condition useless, the answer of the poor woman to the haughty prince, who had rejected her petition as an unworthy thing and beneath his dignity, may be taken for an oracle,—"Then leave off being king." For most certain it is that he who will not attend to things like these, as being too paltry and minute, can neither win the kingdom of nature nor govern it.

CXXII

It may be thought also a strange and a harsh thing that we should at once and with one blow set aside all sciences and all authors; and that too without calling in any of the ancients to our aid and support, but relying on our own strength.

And I know that if I had chosen to deal less sincerely, I might easily have found authority for my suggestions by referring them either to the old times before the Greeks (when natural science was perhaps more flourishing, though it made less noise, not having yet having passed into the pipes and trumpets of the Greeks), or even, in part at least, to some of the Greeks themselves; and so gained for them both support and honour; as men of no family devise for themselves by the good help of genealogies the nobility of a descent from some ancient stock. But for my part, relying on the evidence and truth of things, I reject all forms of fiction and imposture; nor do I think that it matters any more to the business in hand, whether the discoveries that shall now be made were long ago known to the ancients, and have their settings and their risings according to the vicissitude of things and course of ages, than it matters to mankind whether the new world be that island of Atlantis with which the ancients were acquainted, or now discovered for the first time. For new discoveries must be sought from the light of nature, not fetched back out of the darkness of antiquity.

And as for the universality of the censure, certainly if the matter be truly considered, such a censure is not only more probable but more modest too, than a partial one would be. For if the errors had not been rooted in primary notions, there must have been some true discoveries to correct the false. But the errors being fundamental, and not so much of false judgment as of inattention and oversight, it is no wonder that men have not obtained what they have not tried for, nor reached a mark which they never set up, nor finished a course which they never entered on or kept.

And as for the presumption implied in it; certainly if a man undertakes by steadiness of hand and power of eye to describe a straighter line or more perfect circle than any one else, he challenges a comparison of abilities; but if he only says that he with the help of a rule or a pair of compasses can draw a straighter line or a more perfect circle than any one else can by eye and hand alone, he makes no great boast. And this remark, be it observed, applies not merely to this first and inceptive attempt of mine, but to all that shall take the work in hand hereafter. For my way of discovering sciences goes far to level men's wits, and leaves but little to individual excellence; because it performs everything by the surest rules and demonstrations. And therefore I attribute my part in all this, as I have often said, rather to good luck than to ability, and account it a birth of time rather than of wit. For certainly chance has something to do with men's thoughts, as well as with their works and deeds.

CXXIII

I may say then of myself that which one said in jest (since it marks the distinction so truly), "It cannot be that we should think alike, when one drinks water and the other drinks wine." Now other men, as well in ancient as in modern times, have in the matter of sciences drunk a crude liquor like water, either flowing spontaneously from the understanding, or drawn up by logic, as by wheels from a well. Whereas I pledge mankind in a liquor strained from countless grapes, from grapes ripe and fully seasoned, collected in clusters, and gathered, and then squeezed in the press, and finally purified and clarified in the vat. And therefore it is no wonder if they and I do not think alike.

CXXIV

Again, it will be thought, no doubt, that the goal and mark of knowledge which I myself set up (the very point which I object to in others) is not the true or the best; for that the contemplation of truth is a thing worthier and loftier than all utility and magnitude of works; and that this long and anxious dwelling with experience and matter and the fluctuations of individual things, drags down the mind to earth, or rather sinks it to a very Tartarus of turmoil and confusion; removing and withdrawing it from the serene tranquillity of abstract wisdom, a condition far more heavenly. Now to this I readily assent; and indeed this which they point at as so much to be preferred, is the very thing of all others which I am about. For I am building in the human understanding a true model of the world, such as it is in fact, not such as a man's own reason would have it to be; a thing which cannot be done without a very diligent dissection and anatomy of the world. But I say that those foolish and apish images of worlds which the fancies of men have created in philosophical systems, must be utterly scattered to the winds. Be it known then how vast a difference there is (as I said above) between the Idols of the human mind and the Ideas of the divine. The former are nothing more than arbitrary abstractions; the latter are the creator's own stamp upon creation, impressed and defined in matter by true and exquisite lines. Truth therefore and utility are here the very same things: and works themselves are of greater value as pledges of truth than as contributing to the comforts of life.

CXXV

It may be thought again that I am but doing what has been done before; that the ancients themselves took the same course which I am now taking; and that it is likely therefore that I too, after all this stir and striving, shall come at last to some one of those systems which prevailed in ancient times. For the ancients too, it will be said, provided at the outset of their speculations a great store and abundance of examples and particulars, digested the same into notebooks under heads and titles, from them completed their systems and arts, and afterwards, when they understood the matter, published them to the world,—adding a few examples here and there for proof and illustration; but thought it superfluous and inconvenient to publish their notes and minutes and digests of particulars; and therefore did as builders do,—after the house was built they removed the scaffolding and ladders out of sight. And so no doubt they did. But this objection (or scruple rather) will be easily answered by any one who has not quite forgotten what I have said above. For the form of inquiry and discovery that was in use among the ancients is by themselves professed, and appears on the very face of their writings. And that form was simply this. From a few examples and particulars (with the addition of common notions and perhaps of some portion of the received opinions which have been most popular) they flew at once to the most general conclusions, or first principles of science: taking the truth of these as fixed and immoveable, they proceeded by means of intermediate propositions to educe and prove from them the inferior conclusions; and out of these they framed the art. After that, if any new particulars and examples repugnant to their dogmas were mooted and adduced, either they subtly moulded them into their system by distinctions or explanations of their rules, or else coarsely got rid of them by exceptions; while to such particulars as were not repugnant they laboured to assign causes in conformity with those their principles. But this was not the natural history and experience that was wanted; far from it; and besides, that flying off to the highest generalities ruined all.

CXXVI

It will also be thought that by forbidding men to pronounce and to set down principles as established until they have duly arrived through the intermediate steps at the highest generalities, I maintain a sort of suspension of the judgment, and bring it to what the Greeks call *Acatalepsia*, —a denial of the capacity of the mind to comprehend truth. But in reality that which I meditate and propound is not *Acatalepsia*, but *Eucatalepsia;* not denial of the capacity to understand, but provision for understanding truly; for I do not take away authority from the senses, but supply them with helps: I do not slight the understanding, but govern it. And better surely it is that we should know all we need to know, and yet think our knowledge imperfect, than that we should think our knowledge perfect, and yet not know anything we need to know.

It may also be asked (in the way of doubt rather than objection) whether I speak of natural philosophy only, or whether I mean that the other sciences, logic, ethics, and politics, should be carried on by this method. Now I certainly mean what I have said to be understood of them all; and as the common logic, which governs by the syllogism, extends not only to natural but to all sciences; so does mine also, which proceeds by induction, embrace everything. For I form a history and tables of discovery for anger, fear, shame, and the like; for matters political; and again for the mental operations of memory, composition and division, judgment and the rest; not less than for heat and cold, or light, or vegetation, or the like. But nevertheless since my method of interpretation, after the history has been prepared and duly arranged, regards not the working and discourse of the mind only (as the common logic does) but the nature of things also, I supply the mind with such rules and guidance that it may in every case apply itself aptly to the nature of things. And therefore I deliver many and diverse precepts in the doctrine of Interpretation, which in some measure modify the method of invention according to the quality and condition of the subject of the inquiry.

On one point not even a doubt ought to be entertained; namely, whether I desire to pull down and destroy the philosophy and arts and sciences which are at present in use. So far from that, I am most glad to see them used, cultivated, and honoured. There is no reason why the arts which are now in fashion should not continue to supply matter for disputation and ornaments for discourse, to be employed for the convenience of professors and men of business; to be in short like current coin, which passes among men by consent. Nay I frankly declare that what I am introducing will be but little fitted for such purposes as these, since it cannot be brought down to common apprehension, save by effects and works only. But how sincere I am in my professions of affection and good will towards the received sciences, my published writings, especially the books on the Advancement of Learning, sufficiently show; and therefore I will not attempt to prove it further by words. Meanwhile I give constant and distinct warning that by the methods now in use neither can any great progress be made in the doctrines and contemplative part of sciences, nor can they be carried out to any magnitude of works.

CXXIX

It remains for me to say a few words touching the excellency of the end in view. Had they been uttered earlier, they might have seemed like idle wishes; but now that hopes have been raised and unfair prejudices removed, they may perhaps have greater weight. Also if I had finished all myself, and had no occasion to call in others to help and take part in the work, I should even now have abstained from such language, lest it might be taken as a proclamation of my own deserts. But since I want to quicken the industry and rouse and kindle the zeal of others, it is fitting that I put men in mind of some things.

In the first place then, the introduction of famous discoveries appears to hold by far the first place among human actions; and this was the judgment of the former ages. For to the authors of inventions they awarded divine honours; while to those who did good service in the state (such as founders of cities and empires, legislators, saviours of their country from long endured evils, quellers of tyrannies, and the like) they decreed no higher honours than heroic. And certainly if a man rightly compare the two, he will find that this judgment of antiquity was just. For the benefits of discoveries may extend to the whole race of man, civil benefits only to particular places; the latter last not beyond a few ages, the former through all time. Moreover the reformation of a state in civil matters is seldom brought in without violence and confusion; but discoveries carry blessings with them, and confer benefits without causing harm or sorrow to any.

Again, discoveries are as it were new creations, and imitations of God's works; as well sang the poet:—[11]

> "To man's frail race great Athens long ago
> First gave the seed whence waving harvests grow,
> And *re-created* all our life below."

And it appears worthy of remark in Solomon, that though mighty in empire and in gold; in the magnificence of his works, his court, his household, and his fleet; in the lustre of his name and the worship of mankind; yet he took none of these to glory in, but pronounced that "The glory of God is to conceal a thing; the glory of the king to search it out."

Again, let a man only consider what a difference there is between the life of men in the most civilised province of Europe, and in the wildest and most barbarous districts of New India;[12] he will feel it be great enough to justify the saying that "man is a god to man," not only in regard of aid and benefit, but also by a comparison of condition. And this difference comes not from soil, not from climate, not from race, but from the arts.

Again, it is well to observe the force and virtue and consequences of discoveries; and these are to be seen nowhere more conspicuously than in those three which were unknown to the ancients, and of which the origin, though recent, is obscure and inglorious; namely, printing, gunpowder, and the magnet. For these three have changed the whole face and state of things throughout the world; the first in literature, the second in warfare, the third in navigation; whence have followed innumerable changes; insomuch that no empire, no sect, no star seems to have exerted greater power and influence in human affairs than these mechanical discoveries.

Further, it will not be amiss to distinguish the three kinds and as it were grades of ambition in mankind. The first is of those who desire to extend their own power in their native country; which kind is vulgar and degenerate. The second is of those who labour to extend the power of their country and its dominion among men. This certainly has more dignity, though not less covetousness. But if a man endeavour to establish and extend the power and dominion of the human race itself over the universe, his ambition (if ambition it can be called) is without doubt both a more wholesome thing and a more noble than the other two. Now the empire of man over things depends wholly on the arts and sciences. For we cannot command nature except by obeying her.

Again, if men have thought so much of some one particular discovery as to regard him as more than man who has been able by some benefit to make the whole human race his debtor, how much higher a thing to discover that by means of which all things else shall be discovered with ease! And yet (to speak the whole truth), as the uses of light are infinite, in enabling us to walk, to ply our arts, to read, to recognise one another; and nevertheless the very beholding of the light is itself a more excellent and a fairer thing than all the uses of it;—so assuredly the very contemplation of things, as they are, without superstition or imposture, error or confusion, is in itself more worthy than all the fruit of inventions.

Lastly, if the debasement of arts and sciences to purposes of wickedness, luxury, and the like, be made a ground of objection, let no one be moved thereby. For the same may be said of all earthly goods; of wit, courage, strength, beauty, wealth, light itself, and the rest. Only let the human race recover that right over nature which belongs to it by divine bequest, and let power be given it; the exercise thereof will be governed by sound reason and true religion.

CXXX

And now it is time for me to propound the art itself of interpreting nature; in which, although I conceive that I have given true and most useful precepts, yet I do not say either that it is absolutely necessary (as if nothing could be done without it) or that it is perfect. For I am of opinion that if men had ready at hand a just history of nature and experience, and laboured diligently thereon; and if they could bind themselves to two rules,—the first, to lay aside received opinions and notions; and the second, to refrain the mind for a time from the highest generalisations, and those next to them,—they would be able by the native and genuine force of the mind, without any other art, to fall into my form of interpretation. For interpretation is the true and natural work of the mind when freed from impediments. It is true however that by my precepts everything will be in more readiness, and much more sure.

Nor again do I mean to say that no improvement can be made upon these. On the contrary, I that regard the mind not only in its own faculties, but in its connection with things, must needs hold that the art of discovery may advance as discoveries advance.

A PRAYER

OR

PSALM

(1621)

Most gracious Lord God, my merciful Father, from my
youth up, my Creator, my Redeemer, my Comforter. Thou
(O Lord) soundest and searchest the depths and secrets of
all hearts; thou knowledgest the upright of heart, thou
judgest the hypocrite, thou ponderest men's thought and
doings as in a balance, thou measurest their intentions as
with a line, vanity and crooked ways cannot be hid from
thee.

Remember (O Lord) how thy servant walked before
thee: remember what I have first sought, and what hath
been principal in mine intentions. I have loved thy assem-
blies, I have mourned for the divisions of thy Church, I
have delighted in the brightness of thy sanctuary. This
vine which thy right hand hath planted in this nation, I
have ever prayed unto thee that it might have the first
and the latter rain; and that it might stretch her branches
to the seas and to the floods. The state and bread of the
poor and oppressed have been precious in mine eyes: I

541

have hated all cruelty and hardness of heart: I have (though in a despised weed) procured the good of all men. If any have been mine enemies, I thought not of them; neither hath the sun almost set upon my displeasure; but I have been as a dove, free from superfluity of maliciousness. Thy creatures have been my books, but thy Scriptures much more. I have sought thee in the courts, fields, and gardens, but I have found thee in thy temples.

Thousand have been my sins, and ten thousand my transgressions; but thy sanctifications have remained with me, and my heart, through thy grace, hath been an unquenched coal upon thy altar. O Lord, my strength, I have since my youth met with thee in all my ways, by thy fatherly compassions, by thy comfortable chastisements, and by thy most visible providence. As thy favours have increased upon me, so have thy corrections; so as thou hast been alway near me, O Lord; and ever as my wordly blessings were exalted, so secret darts from thee have pierced me; and when I ascended before men, I have descended in humiliation before thee.

And now when I thought most of peace and honour, thy hand is heavy upon me, and hath humbled me, according to thy former loving-kindness, keeping me still in thy fatherly school, not as a bastard, but as a child. Just are thy judgments upon me for my sins, which are more in number than the sands of the sea, but have no proportion to thy mercies; for what are the sands of the sea, to the sea, earth, heavens? and all these are nothing to thy mercies.

Besides my innumerable sins, I confess before thee, that I am debtor to thee for the gracious talent of thy gifts and graces, which I have neither put into a napkin, nor put it (as I ought) to exchanges, where it might have been made best profit; but misspent it in things for which I was least fit; so as I may truly say, my soul hath been a stranger in the course of my pilgrimage. Be merciful unto me (O Lord) for my Saviour's sake, and receive me into thy bosom, or guide me in thy ways.

NEW ATLANTIS
A WORK UNFINISHED

WRITTEN BY

THE RIGHT HONOURABLE

FRANCIS LORD VERULAM,

VISCOUNT ST. ALBAN

[1624]

TO THE READER

THIS fable my Lord devised, to the end that he might exhibit therin a model or description of a college instituted for the interpreting of nature and the producing of great and marvellous works for the benefit of men, under the name of Salomon's House, or the College of the Six Days' Works. And even so far his Lordship hath proceeded, as to finish that part. Certainly the model is more vast and high than can possibly be imitated in all things; notwithstanding most things therein are within men's power to effect. His Lordship thought also in this present fable to have composed a frame of Laws, or of the best state or mould of a commonwealth; but foreseeing it would be a long work, his desire of collecting the Natural History diverted him, which he preferred many degrees before it.

This work of the *New Atlantis* (as much as concerneth the English edition) his Lordship designed for this place; in regard it hath so near affinity (in one part of it) with the preceding Natural History.

W. RAWLEY[1]

NEW ATLANTIS

We sailed from Peru, (where we had continued by the space of one whole year,) for China and Japan, by the South Sea; taking with us victuals for twelve months; and had good winds from the east, though soft and weak, for five months' space and more. But then the wind came about, and settled in the west for many days, so as we could make little or no way, and were sometimes in purpose to turn back. But then again there arose strong and great winds from the south, with a point east; which carried us up (for all that we could do) towards the north: by which time our victuals failed us, though we had made good spare of them. So that finding ourselves in the midst of the greatest wilderness of waters in the world, without victual, we gave ourselves for lost men, and prepared for death. Yet we did lift up our hearts and voices to God above, who *showeth his wonders in the deep;* beseeching him of his mercy, that as in the beginning he discovered [2] the face of the deep, and brought forth dry land, so he would now discover land to us, that we might not perish. And it came to pass that the next day about evening, we saw within a kenning[3] before us, towards the north, as it were thick clouds, which did put us in some hope of land; knowing how that part of the South Sea was utterly unknown; and might have islands or continents, that hitherto were not come to light. Wherefore we bent our course thither, where we saw the appearance of land, all that night; and in the dawning of the next day, we might plainly discern that it was a land; flat to our sight, and full of boscage;[4] which made it shew the more dark. And after an hour and a half's sailing, we entered into a good haven, being the port of a fair city; not great indeed, but well built, and that gave a pleasant view from the sea: and we thinking every minute long till we were on land, came close to the shore, and offered to land. But straightways we saw divers of the people, with bastons[5] in their hands, as it were forbidding us to land; yet without any cries or fierceness, but only as warning us off by signs that they made. Whereupon being not a little discomforted, we were advising with ourselves what we should do. During which time there made forth to us a small boat, with about eight persons in it; whereof one of them had in his hand a tipstaff of a yellow cane, tipped at both ends with blue, who came aboard our ship, without any show of distrust at all. And when he saw one of our number present himself somewhat afore the rest, he drew forth a little scroll of parchment, (somewhat yellower than our parchment, and shining like the leaves of writing tables, but otherwise soft and flexible,) and delivered it to our foremost man. In which scroll were written in ancient Hebrew, and in ancient Greek, and in good Latin of the School,[6] and in Spanish, these words; "Land ye not, none of you; and provide to be gone from this coast within sixteen days, except you have further time given you. Meanwhile, if you want fresh water, or victual, or help for your sick, or that your ship needeth repair, write down your wants, and you shall have that which belongeth to mercy." This scroll was signed with a stamp of cherubins' wings, not spread but hanging downwards, and by them a cross. This being delivered, the officer returned, and left only a servant with us to receive our answer. Consulting hereupon amongst ourselves, we were much perplexed. The denial of landing and hasty warning us away troubled us much; on the other side, to find that the people had languages and were so full of humanity, did comfort us not a little. And above all, the sign of the cross to that instrument was to us a great rejoicing, and as it were a certain presage of good. Our answer was in the Spanish tongue; "That for our ship, it was well; for we had rather met with calms and contrary winds than any tempests. For our sick, they were many, and in very ill case; so that if they were not permitted to land, they ran danger of their lives." Our other wants we set down in particular; adding, "that we had some little store of merchandise, which if it pleased them to deal for, it might supply our wants without being chargeable unto them." We offered some reward in pistolets[7] unto the servant, and a piece of crimson velvet to be presented to the officer; but the servant took them not, nor would scarce look upon them; and so left us, and went back in another little boat which was sent for him.

About three hours after we had dispatched our answer, there came towards us a person (as it seemed) of place. He had on him a gown with wide sleeves, of a kind of water chamolet,[8] of an excellent azure colour, far more glossy than ours; his under apparel was green; and so was his hat, being in the form of a turban, daintily made, and not so huge as the Turkish turbans; and the locks of his hair came down below the brims of it. A reverend man was he to behold. He came in a boat, gilt in some part of it, with four persons more only in that boat; and was followed by another boat, wherein were some twenty. When he was come within a flight-shot[9] of our ship, signs were made to us that we should send forth some to meet him upon the water; which we presently did in our ship-boat, sending the principal man amongst us save one, and four of our number with him. When we were come within six yards of their boat, they called to us to stay, and not to approach farther; which we did. And thereupon the man whom I before described stood up, and with a loud voice in Spanish, asked, "Are ye Christians?" We answered, "We were;" fearing the less, because of the cross we had seen in the subscription. At which answer the said person lifted up his right hand towards heaven, and drew it softly to his mouth, (which is the gesture they use when they thank God,) and then said: "If ye will swear (all of you) by the merits of the Saviour that ye are no pirates, nor have shed blood lawfully nor unlawfully within forty days past, you may have licence to come on land." We said, "We were all ready to take that oath." Whereupon one of those that were with him, being (as it seemed) a notary, made an entry of this act. Which done, another of the attendants of the great person, which was with him in the same boat, after his lord had spoken a little to him, said aloud; "My lord would have you know, that it is not of pride or greatness that he cometh not aboard your ship; but for that in your answer you declare that you have many sick amongst you, he was warned by the Conservator of Health of the city that he should keep a distance." We bowed ourselves towards him, and answered, "We were his humble servants; and accounted for great honour and singular humanity towards us that which was already done; but hoped well that the nature of the sickness of our men was not infectious." So he returned; and a while after came the notary to us aboard our ship; holding in his hand a fruit of that country, like an orange, but of colour between orange-tawney and scarlet, which cast a most excellent odour. He used it (as it seemeth) for a preservative against infection. He gave us our oath; "By the name of Jesus and his merits:" and after told us that the next day by six of the clock in the morning we should be sent to, and brought to the Strangers' House, (so he called it,) where we should be accommodated of things both for our whole and for our sick. So he left us; and when we offered him some pistolets, he smiling said, "He must not be twice paid for one labour": meaning (as

I take it) that he had salary sufficient of the state for his service. For (as I after learned) they call an officer that taketh rewards, *twice paid.*

The next morning early, there came to us the same officer that came to us at first with his cane, and told us, "He came to conduct us to the Strangers' House; and that he had prevented [10] the hour, because we might have the whole day before us for our business. "For," said he, "if you will follow my advice, there shall first go with me some few of you, and see the place, and how it may be made convenient for you; and then you may send for your sick, and the rest of your number which ye will bring on land." We thanked him, and said, "That this care which he took of desolate strangers God would reward." And so six of us went on land with him: and when we were on land, he went before us, and turned to us, and said, "He was but our servant, and our guide." He led us through three fair streets; and all the way we went there were gathered some people on both sides standing in a row; but in so civil a fashion, as if it had been not to wonder at us but to welcome us; and divers of them, as we passed by them, put their arms a little abroad; which is their gesture when they bid any welcome. The Strangers' House is a fair and spacious house, built of brick, of somewhat a bluer colour than our brick; and with handsome windows, some of glass, some of a kind of cambric oiled. He brought us first into a fair parlour above stairs, and then asked us, "What number of persons we were? And how many sick?" We answered "We were in all (sick and whole) one and fifty persons, whereof our sick were seventeen." He desired us to have patience a little, and to stay till he came back to us; which was about an hour after; and then he led us to see the chambers which were provided for us, being in number nineteen: they having cast it (as it seemeth) that four of those chambers, which were better than the rest, might receive four of the principal men of our company, and lodge them alone by themselves; and the other fifteen chambers were to lodge us two and two together. The chambers were handsome and cheerful chambers, and furnished civilly. The he led us to a long gallery, like a dorture,[11] where he showed us all along the one side (for the other side was but wall and window) seventeen cells, very neat ones, having partitions of cedar wood. Which gallery and cells, being in all forty, (many more than we needed,) were instituted as an infirmary for sick persons. And he told us withal, that as any of our sick waxed well, he might be removed from his cell to a chamber; for which purpose there were set forth ten spare chambers, besides the number we spake of before. This done, he brought us back to the parlour, and lifting up his cane a little, (as they do when they give any charge or command,) said to us, "Ye are to know that the custom of the land requireth, that after this day and to-morrow, (which we give you for removing of your people from your ship,) you are to keep within doors for three days. But let it not trouble you, nor do not think yourselves restrained, but rather left to your rest and ease. You shall want nothing, and there are six of our people appointed to attend you, for any business you may have abroad." We gave him thanks with all affection and respect, and said, "God surely is manifested in this land." We offered him also twenty pistolets; but he smiled, and only said; "What? twice paid!" And so he left us. Soon after our dinner was served in; which was right good viands, both for bread and meat: better than any collegiate diet that I have known in Europe. We had also drink of three sorts, all wholesome and good; wine of the grape; a drink of grain, such as is with us our ale, but more clear; and a kind of cider made of a fruit of that country; a wonderful pleasing and refreshing drink. Besides, there were brought in to us great store of those scarlet oranges for our sick; which (they said) were an assured remedy for sickness taken at sea. There was given us also a box of small grey or whitish pills, which they wished our sick should take, one of the pills every night before sleep; which (they said) would hasten their recovery. The next day, after that our trouble of carriage and removing of our men and goods out of our ship was somewhat settled and quiet, I thought good to call our company together; and when they were assembled said unto them; "My dear friends, let us know ourselves, and how it standeth with us. We are men cast on land, as Jonas was out of the whale's belly, when we were as buried in the deep: and now we are on land, we are but between death and life; for we are beyond both the old world and the new; and whether ever we shall see Europe, God only knoweth. It is a kind of miracle hath brought us hither: and it must be little less that shall bring us hence. Therefore in regard of our deliverance past, and our danger present and to come, let us look up to God, and every man reform his own ways. Besides we are come here amongst a Christian people, full of piety and humanity: let us not bring that confusion of face upon ourselves, as to show our vices or unworthiness before them. Yet there is more. For they have by commandment (though in form of courtesy) cloistered us within these walls for three days: who knoweth whether it be not to take some taste of our manners and conditions? and if they find them bad, to banish us straightways; if good, to give us further time. For these men that they have given us for attendance may withal have an eye upon us. Therefore for God's love, and as we love the weal of our souls and bodies, let us so behave ourselves as we may be at peace with God, and may find grace in the eyes of this people." Our company with one voice thanked me for my good admonition, and promised me to live soberly and civilly, and without giving any the least occasion of offence. So we spent our three days joyfully and without care, in expectation what would be done with us when they were expired. During which time, we had every hour joy of the amendment of our sick; who thought themselves cast into some divine pool of healing, they mended so kindly and so fast.

The morrow after our three days were past, there came to us a new man that we had not seen before, clothed in blue as the former was, save that his turban was white, with a small red cross on the top. He had also a tippet of fine linen. At his coming in, he did bend to us a little, and put his arms abroad. We of our parts saluted him in a very lowly and submissive manner; as looking that from him we should receive sentence of life or death. He desired to speak with some few of us: whereupon six of us only stayed and the rest avoided[12] the room. He said, "I am by office governor of this House of Strangers, and by vocation I am a Christian priest; and therefore am come to you to offer you my service, both as strangers and chiefly as Christians. Some things I may tell you, which I think you will not be unwilling to hear. The state hath given you licence to stay on land for the space of six weeks: and let it not trouble you if your occasions ask further time, for the law in this point is not precise; and I do not doubt but myself shall be able to obtain for you such further time as may be convenient. Ye shall also understand, that the Strangers' House is at this time rich, and much aforehand; for it hath laid up revenue these thirty-seven years; for so long it is since any stranger arrived in this part: and therefore take ye no care; the state will defray you all the time you stay; neither shall you stay one day the less for that. As for any merchandise ye have brought, ye shall be well used, and have your return either in merchandise or in gold and silver: for to us it is all one. And if you have any other request to make, hide it not. For ye shall find we will not make your countenance to fall by the answer ye shall receive. Only this I must tell you, that none of you must go above a *karan*" (that is with them a mile and an half) "from the walls of the city, without especial leave." We answered, after we had looked awhile one upon another admiring this gracious and parent-like usage; "That we could not tell what to say: for we wanted words to express our thanks; and his noble free offers left us nothing to ask. It seemed to us that we had before us a picture of our salvation in heaven; for we that were awhile since in the jaws of death, were now brought into a place where we found nothing but consolations. For the commandment laid upon us, we would not fail to obey it, though it was impossible but our hearts should be inflamed to tread further upon this happy and holy ground." We added; "That our tongues should first cleave to the roofs of our mouths, ere we should forget either his reverend person or this whole nation in our prayers." We also most humbly besought him to accept of us as his true servants, by as just a right as ever men on earth were bounden; laying and presenting both our persons and all we had at his feet. He said; "He was a priest, and looked for a priest's reward: which was our brotherly love and the good of our souls and bodies." So he went from us, not without tears of tenderness in his eyes; and left us also confused with joy and kindness, saying amongst ourselves, "That we were come into a land of angels, which did appear to us daily and prevent us with comforts, which we thought not of, much less expected."

The next day, about ten of the clock, the governor came to us again, and after salutations said familiarly, "That he was come to visit us": and called for a chair, and sat him down: and we, being some ten of us, (the rest were of the meaner sort, or else gone abroad,) sat down with him. And when we were set, he began thus: "We of this island of Bensalem," (for so they call it in their language,) "have this; that by means of our solitary situation, and of the laws of secrecy which we have for our travellers, and our rare admission of strangers, we know well most part of the habitable world, and are ourselves unknown. Therefore because he that knoweth least is fittest to ask questions, it is more reason, for the entertainment of the time, that ye ask me questions, than that I ask you." We answered; "That we humbly thanked him that he would give us leave so to do: and that we conceived by the taste we had already, that there was no worldly thing on earth more worthy to be known than the state of that happy land. But above all," (we said,) "since that we were met from the several ends of the world, and hoped assuredly that we should meet one day in the kingdom of heaven, (for that we were both parts Christians,) we desired to know (in respect that land was so remote, and so divided by vast and unknown seas, from the land where our Saviour walked on earth,) who was the apostle of that nation, and how it was converted to the faith?" It appeared in his face that he took great contentment in this our question: he said, "Ye knit my heart to you, by asking this question in the first place; for it sheweth that you *first seek the kingdom of heaven;* and I shall gladly and briefly satisfy your demand.

"About twenty years after the ascension of our Saviour, it came to pass that there was seen by the people of Renfusa, (a city upon the eastern coast of our island,) within night, (the night was cloudy and calm,) as it might be some mile into the sea, a great pillar of light; not sharp, but in form of a column or cylinder, rising from the sea a great way up towards heaven: and on the top of it was seen a large cross of light, more bright and resplendent than the body of the pillar. Upon which so strange a spectacle, the people of the city gathered apace together upon the sands, to wonder; and so after put themselves into a number of small boats, to go nearer to this marvellous sight. But when the boats were come within about sixty yards of the pillar, they found themselves all bound, and could go no further; yet so as they might move to go about, but might not approach nearer: so as the boats stood all as in a theatre, beholding this light as an heavenly sign. It so fell out, that there was in one of the boats one of the wise men of the society of Salomon's House; which house or college (my good brethren) is the very eye of this kingdom; who having awhile attentively and devoutly viewed and contemplated this pillar and cross, fell down upon his face; and then raised himself upon his knees, and lifting up his hands to heaven, made his prayers in this manner:

"'Lord God of heaven and earth, thou hast vouchsafed of thy grace to those of our order, to know thy works of creation, and the secrets of them; and to discern (as far as appertaineth to the generations of men) between divine miracles, works of nature, works of art, and impostures and illusions of all sorts. I do here acknowledge and testify before this people, that the thing which we now see before our eyes is thy Finger and a true Miracle; and forasmuch as we learn in our books that thou never workest miracles but to a divine and excellent end, (for the laws of nature are thine own laws, and thou exceedest them not but upon great cause,) we most humbly beseech thee to prosper this great sign, and to give us the interpretation and use of it in mercy; which thou dost in some part secretly promise by sending it unto us.'

"When he had made his prayer, he presently found the boat he was in moveable and unbound; whereas all the rest remained still fast; and taking that for an assurance of leave to approach, he caused the boat to be softly and with silence rowed towards the pillar. But ere he came near it, the pillar and cross of light brake up, and cast itself abroad, as it were, into a firmament of many stars; which also vanished soon after, and there was nothing left to be seen but a small ark or chest of cedar, dry, and not wet at all with water, though it swam. And in the fore-end of it, which was towards him, grew a small green branch of palm; and when the wise man had taken it with all reverence into his boat, it opened of itself, and there were found in it a Book and a Letter; both written in fine parchment, and wrapped in sindons[13] of linen. The Book contained all the canonical books of the Old and New Testament, according as you have them, (for we know well what the Churches with you receive); and the Apocalypse itself, and some other books of the New Testament which were not at that time written, were nevertheless in the Book. And for the Letter, it was in these words:

" 'I Bartholomew, a servant of the Highest, and Apostle of Jesus Christ, was warned by an angel that appeared to me in a vision of glory, that I should commit this ark to the floods of the sea. Therefore I do testify and declare unto that people where God shall ordain this ark to come to land, that in the same day is come unto them salvation and peace and good-will, from the Father, and from the Lord Jesus.'

"There was also in both these writings, as well the Book as the Letter, wrought a great miracle, conform to that of the Apostles in the original Gift of Tongues. For there being at that time in this land Hebrews, Persians, and Indians, besides the natives, every one read upon the Book and Letter, as if they had been written in his own language. And thus was this land saved from infidelity (as the remain of the old world was from water) by an ark, through the apostolical and miraculous evangelism of St. Bartholomew." And here he paused, and a messenger came, and called him from us. So this was all that passed in that conference.

The next day, the same governor came again to us immediately after dinner and excused himself, saying, "That the day before he was called from us somewhat abruptly, but now he would make us amends, and spend time with us, if we held his company and conference agreeable." We answered, "That we held it so agreeable and pleasing to us, as we forgot both dangers past and fears to come, for the time we heard him speak; and that we thought an hour spent with him, was worth years of our former life." He bowed himself a little to us, and after we were set again, he said; "Well, the questions are on your part." One of our number said, after a little pause; "That there was a matter we were no less desirous to know, than fearful to ask, lest we might presume too far. But encouraged by his rare humanity towards us, (that could scarce think ourselves strangers, being his vowed and professed servants,) we would take the hardiness to propound it: humbly beseeching him, if he thought it not fit to be answered, that he would pardon it, though he rejected it." We said; "We well observed those his words, which he formerly spake, that this happy island where we now stood was known to few, and yet knew most of the nations of the world; which we found to be true, considering they had the languages of Europe, and knew much of our state and business; and yet we in Europe (notwithstanding all the remote discoveries and navigations of this last age,) never heard any of the least inkling or glimpse of this island. This we found wonderful strange; for that all nations have inter-knowledge one of another either by voyage into foreign parts, or by strangers that come to them: and though the traveller into a foreign country doth commonly know more by the eye, than he that stayeth at home can by relation of the traveller; yet both ways suffice to make a mutual knowledge, in some degree, on both parts. But for this island, we never heard tell of any ship of theirs that had been seen to arrive upon any shore of Europe; no, nor of either the East or West Indies; nor yet of any ship of any other part of the world that had made return from them. And yet the marvel rested not in this. For the situation of it (as his lordship said) in the secret conclave of such a vast sea might cause it. But then that they should have knowledge of the languages, books, affairs, of those that lie such a distance from them, it was a thing we could not tell what to make of; for that it seemed to us a condition and propriety of divine powers and beings, to be hidden and unseen to others, and yet to have others open and as in a light to them." At this speech the governor gave a gracious smile, and said; "That we did well to ask pardon for this question we now asked; for that it imported as if we thought this land a land of magicians, that sent forth spirits of the air into all parts, to bring them news and intelligence of other countries." It was answered by us all, in all possible humbleness, but yet with a countenance taking knowledge that we knew that he spake it but merrily, "That we were apt enough to think there was somewhat supernatural in this island; but yet rather as angelical than magical. But to let his lordship know truly what it was that made us tender and doubtful to ask this question, it was not any such conceit,[14] but because we remembered he had given a touch in his former speech, that this land had laws of secrecy touching strangers." To this he said; "You remember it aright; and therefore in that I shall say to you I must reserve some particulars, which it is not lawful for me to reveal; but there will be enough left to give you satisfaction.

"You shall understand (that which perhaps you will scarce think credible) that about three thousand years ago, or somewhat more, the navigation of the world, (specially for remote voyages,) was greater than at this day. Do not think with yourselves that I know not how much it is increased with you within these six-score years: I know it well: and yet I say greater then than now; whether it was, that the example of the ark, that saved the remnant of men from the universal deluge, gave men confidence to adventure upon the waters; or what it was; but such is the truth. The Phœnicians, and especially the Tyrians, had great fleets. So had the Carthaginians, their colony, which is yet further west. Toward the east, the shipping of Egypt and of Palestina was likewise great. China also, and the great Atlantis (that you call America), which have now but junks and canoes, abounded then in tall ships. This island (as appeareth by faithful registers of those times) had then fifteen hundred strong ships, of great content. Of all this there is with you sparing memory, or none; but we have large knowledge thereof.

"At that time, this land was known and frequented by the ships and vessels of all the nations before named. And (as it cometh to pass) they had many times men of other countries, that were no sailors, that came with them; as Persians, Chaldeans, Arabians; so as almost all nations of might and fame resorted hither; of whom we have some stirps[15] and little tribes with us at this day. And for our own ships, they went sundry voyages, as well to your Straits,[16] which you call the Pillars of Hercules, as to other parts in the Atlantic and Mediterrane Seas; as to Paquin[17] (which is the same with Cambaline) and Quinzy,[18] upon the Oriental Seas, as far as to the borders of the East Tartary.

"At the same time, and an age after, or more, the inhabitants of the great Atlantis did flourish. For though the narration and description which is made by a great man[19] with you, that the descendants of Neptune planted there; and of the magnificent temple, palace, city, and hill; and the manifold streams of goodly navigable rivers, (which, as so many chains, environed the same site and temple); and the several degrees of ascent whereby men did climb up to the same, as if it had been a *scala cœli* [*ladder to heaven]; be all poetical and fabulous: yet so much is true, that the said country of Atlantis, as well that of Peru, then called Coya, as that of Mexico, then named Tyrambel, were mighty and proud kingdoms in arms, shipping, and riches: so mighty, as at one time, (or at least within the space of ten years) they both made two great expeditions; they of Tyrambel through the Atlantic to the Mediterrane Sea; and they of Coya through the South Sea upon this our island. And for the former of these, which was into Europe, the same author amongst you (as it seemeth) had some relation from the Egyptian priest whom he citeth. For assuredly such a thing there was. But whether it were the ancient Athenians that had the glory of the repulse and resistance of those forces, I can say nothing: but certain it is, there never came back either ship or man from that voyage. Neither had the other voyage of those of Coya upon us had better fortune, if they had not met with enemies of greater clemency. For the king of this island (by name Altabin) a wise man and a great warrior, knowing well both his own strength and that of his enemies, handled the matter so, as he cut off their land-forces from their ships; and entoiled both their navy and their camp with a greater power than theirs, both by sea and land; and compelled them to render themselves without striking stroke: and after they were at his mercy, contenting himself only with their oath that they should no more bear arms against him, dismissed them all in safety. But the Divine Revenge overtook not long after those proud enterprises. For within less than the space of one hundred years, the great Atlantis was utterly lost and destroyed: not by a great earthquake, as your man saith, (for that whole tract is little subject to earthquakes,) but by a particular deluge or inundation; those countries having, at this day, far greater rivers and far higher mountains to pour down waters, than any part of the old world. But it is true that the same inundation was not deep; not past forty foot, in most places, from the ground: so that although it destroyed man and beast generally, yet some few wild inhabitants of the wood escaped. Birds also were saved by flying to the high trees and woods. For as for men, although they had buildings in many places higher than the depth of the water, yet that inundation, though it were shallow, had a long continuance; whereby they of the vale that were not drowned, perished for want of food and other things necessary. So as marvel you not at the thin population of America, nor at the rudeness and ignorance of the people; for you must account your inhabitants of America as a young people; younger a thousand years, at the least, than the rest of the world; for that there was so much time between the universal flood and their particular inundation. For the poor remnant of human seed which remained in their mountains peopled the country again slowly, by little and little; and being simple and savage people, (not like Noah and his sons, which was the chief family of the earth,) they were not able to leave letters, arts, and civility to their posterity; and having likewise in their mountainous habitations been used (in respect of the extreme cold of those regions) to clothe themselves with the skins of tigers, bears, and great hairy goats, that they have in those parts; when after they came down into the valley, and found the intolerable heats which are there, and knew no means of lighter apparel, they were forced to begin the custom of going naked, which continueth at this day. Only they take great pride and delight in the feathers of birds, and this also they took from those their ancestors of the mountains, who were invited unto it by the infinite flights of birds that came up to the high grounds, while the waters stood below. So you see, by this main accident of time, we lost our traffic with the Americans, with whom of all others, in regard they lay nearest to us, we had most commerce. As for the other parts of the world, it is most manifest that in the ages following (whether it were in respect of wars, or by a natural revolution of time,) navigation did every where greatly decay; and specially far voyages (the rather by the use of galleys, and such vessels as could hardly brook the ocean,) were altogether left and omitted. So then, that part of intercourse which could be from other nations to sail to us, you see how it hath long since ceased; except it were by some rare accident, as this of yours. But now of the cessation of that other part of intercourse, which might be by our sailing to other nations, I must yield you some other cause. For I cannot say (if I shall say truly,) but our shipping, for number, strength, mariners, pilots, and all things that appertain to navigation, is as great as ever: and therefore why we should sit at home, I shall now give you an account by itself: and it will draw nearer to give you satisfaction to your principal question.

"There reigned in this island, about nineteen hundred years ago, a King, whose memory of all others we most adore; not superstitiously, but as a divine instrument, though a mortal man; his name was Solamona: and we esteem him as the lawgiver of our nation. This king had a *large heart*, inscrutable for good; and was wholly bent to make his kingdom and people happy. He therefore, taking into consideration how sufficient and substantive this land was to maintain itself without any aid at all of the foreigner; being five thousand six hundred miles in circuit, and of rare fertility of soil in the greatest part thereof; and finding also the shipping of this country might be plentifully set on work, both by fishing and by transportations from port to port, and likewise by sailing unto some small islands that are not far from us, and are under the crown and laws of this state; and recalling into his memory the happy and flourishing estate wherein this land then was, so as it might be a thousand ways altered to the worse, but scarce any one way to the better; thought nothing wanted to his noble and heroical intentions, but only (as far as human foresight might reach) to give perpetuity to that which was in his time so happily established. Therefore amongst his other fundamental laws of this kingdom, he did ordain the interdicts and prohibitions which we have touching entrance of strangers; which at that time (though it was after the calamity of America) was frequent; doubting novelties, and commixture of manners. It is true, the like law against the admission of strangers without licence is an ancient law in the kingdom of China, and yet continued in use. But there it is a poor thing; and hath made them a curious, ignorant, fearful, foolish nation. But our lawgiver made his law of another temper. For first, he hath preserved all points of humanity, in taking order and making provision for the relief of strangers distressed; whereof you have tasted." At which speech (as reason was) we all rose up, and bowed ourselves. He went on. "That king also, still desiring to join humanity and policy together; and thinking it against humanity to detain strangers here against their wills, and against policy that they should return and discover their knowledge of this estate, he took this course: he did ordain that of the strangers that should be permitted to land, as many (at all times) might depart as would; but as many as would stay should have very good conditions and means to live from the state. Wherein he saw so far, that now in so many ages since the prohibition, we have memory not of one ship that ever returned; and but of thirteen persons only, at several times, that chose to return in our bottoms. What those few that returned may have reported abroad I know not. But you must think, whatsover they have said could be taken where they came but for a dream. Now for our travelling from hence into parts abroad, our Lawgiver thought fit altogether to restrain it. So is it not in China. For the Chineses sail where they will or can; which sheweth that their law of keeping out strangers is a law of pusillanimity and fear. But this restraint of ours hath one only exception, which is admirable; preserving the good which cometh by communicating with strangers, and avoiding the hurt; and I will now open it to you. And here I shall seem a little to digress, but you will by and by find it pertinent. Ye shall understand (my dear friends) that amongst the excellent acts of that king, one above all hath the pre-eminence. It was the erection and institution of an Order or Society which we call *Salomon's House;* the noblest foundation (as we think) that ever was upon the earth; and the lanthorn of this kingdom. It is dedicated to the study of the Works and Creatures of God. Some think it beareth the founder's name a little corrupted, as if it should be Solamona's House. But the records write it as it is spoken. So as I take it to be denominate of the King of the Hebrews, which is famous with you, and no stranger to us. For we have some parts of his works which with you are lost; namely, that Natural History which he wrote, of all plants, from the *cedar of Libanus* to the *moss that groweth out of the wall,* and of all *things that have life and motion.* This maketh me think that our king, finding himself to symbolize in many things with that king of the Hebrews (which lived many years before him), honoured him with the title of this foundation. And I am the rather induced to be of this opinion, for that I find in ancient records this Order or Society is sometimes called Salomon's House, and sometimes the College of the Six Days Works; whereby I am satisfied that our excellent king had learned from the Hebrews that God had created the world and all that therein is within six days; and therefore he instituting that House for the finding out of the true nature of all things, (whereby God might have the more glory in the workmanship of them, and men the more fruit in the use of them,) did give it also that second name. But now to come to our present purpose. When the king had forbidden to all his people navigation into any part that was not under his crown, he made nevertheless this ordinance; That every twelve years there should be set forth out of this kingdom two ships, appointed to several voyages; That in either of these ships there should be a mission of three of the Fellows or Brethren of Salomon's House; whose errand was only to give us knowledge of the affairs and state of those countries to which they were designed, and especially of the sciences, arts, manufactures, and inventions of all the world; and withal to bring unto us books, instruments, and patterns in every kind; That the ships, after they had landed the brethren, should return; and that the brethren should stay abroad till the new mission. These ships are not otherwise fraught, than with store of victuals, and good quantity of treasure to remain with the brethren, for the buying of such things and rewarding of such persons as they should think fit. Now for me to tell you how the vulgar sort of mariners are contained from being discovered at land; and how they that must be put on shore for any time, colour themselves under the names of other nations; and to what places these voyages have been designed; and what places of *rendez-vous* are appointed for the new missions; and the like circumstances of the practique; I may not do it: neither is it much to your desire. But thus you see we maintain a trade, not for gold, silver, or jewels; nor for silks; nor for spices; nor any other commodity of matter; but only for God's first creature, which was *Light*: to have *light* (I say) of the growth of all parts of the world." And when he had said this, he was silent; and so were we all. For indeed we were all astonished to hear so strange things so probably told. And he, perceiving that we were willing to say somewhat but had it not ready, in great courtesy took us off, and descended to ask us questions of our voyage and fortunes; and in the end concluded, that we might do well to think with ourselves what time of stay we would demand of the state; and bade us not to scant ourselves; for he would procure such time as we desired. Whereupon we all rose up, and presented ourselves to kiss the skirt of his tippet; but he would not suffer us; and so took his leave. But when it came once amongst our people that the state used to offer conditions to strangers that would stay, we had work enough to get any of our men to look to our ship, and to keep them from going presently to the governor to crave conditions. But with much ado we refrained them, till we might agree what course to take.

We took ourselves now for free men, seeing there was no danger of our utter perdition; and lived most joyfully, going abroad and seeing what was to be seen in the city and places adjacent within our tedder;[20] and obtaining acquaintance with many of the city, not of the meanest quality; at whose hands we found such humanity, and such a freedom and desire to take strangers as it were into their bosom, as was enough to make us forget all that was dear to us in our own countries: and continually we met with many things right worthy of observation and relation; as indeed, if there be a mirror in the world worthy to hold men's eyes, it is that country. One day there were two of our company bidden to a Feast of the Family, as they call it. A most natural, pious, and reverend custom it is, showing that nation to be compounded of all goodness. This is the manner of it. It is granted to any man that shall live to see thirty persons descended of his body alive together, and all above three years old, to make this feast; which is done at the cost of the state. The Father of the Family, whom they call the *Tirsan*, two days before the feast, taketh to him three of such friends as he liketh to choose; and is assisted also by the governor of the city or place where the feast is celebrated; and all the persons of the family, of both sexes, are summoned to attend him. These two days the Tirsan sitteth in consultation concerning the good estate of the family. There, if there be any discord or suits between any of the family, they are compounded and appeased. There, if any of the family be distressed or decayed, order is taken for their relief and competent means to live. There, if any be subject to vice, or take ill courses, they are reproved and censured. So likewise direction is given touching marriages, and the courses of life which any of them should take, with divers other the like orders and advices. The governor assisteth, to the end to put in execution by his public authority the decrees and orders of the Tirsan, if they should be disobeyed; though that seldom needeth; such reverence and obedience they give to the order of nature. The Tirsan doth also then ever choose one man from amongst his sons, to live in house with him: who is called ever after the Son of the Vine. The reason will hereafter appear. On the feastday, the Father or Tirsan cometh forth after divine service into a large room where the feast is celebrated; which room hath an half-pace[21] at the upper end. Against the wall, in

the middle of the half-pace is a chair placed for him, with a
table and carpet before it. Over the chair is a state,[22] made
round or oval, and it is of ivy; an ivy somewhat whiter than
ours, like the leaf of a silver asp,[23] but more shining; for it
is green all winter. And the state is curiously wrought with
silver and silk of divers colours, broiding or binding in the
ivy; and is ever of the work of some of the daughters
of the family; and veiled over at the top with a fine net of
silk and silver. But the substance of it is true ivy; whereof,
after it is taken down, the friends of the family are desirous
to have some leaf or sprig to keep. The Tirsan cometh forth
with all his generation or lineage, the males before him,
and the females following him; and if there be a mother
from whose body the whole lineage is descended, there is a
traverse[24] placed in a loft above on the right hand of the
chair, with a privy door, and a carved window of glass,
leaded with gold and blue; where she sitteth, but is not
seen. When the Tirsan is come forth, he sitteth down in the
chair; and all the lineage place themselves against the wall,
both at his back and upon the return[25] of the half-pace, in
order of their years without difference of sex; and stand
upon their feet. When he is set; the room being always full
of company, but well kept and without disorder; after some
pause there cometh in from the lower end of the room a
Taratan (which is as much as an herald) and on either side
of him two young lads; whereof one carrieth a scroll of
their shining yellow parchment; and the other a cluster of
grapes of gold, with a long foot or stalk. The herald and
children are clothed with mantles of sea-water green sattin;
but the herald's mantle is streamed with gold, and hath a
train. Then the herald with three curtesies, or rather inclinations, cometh up as far as the half-pace; and there first
taketh into his hand the scroll. This scroll is the King's
Charter, containing gift of revenew, and many privileges,
exemptions, and points of honour, granted to the Father of
the Family; and is ever styled and directed, *To such an one
our well-beloved friend and creditor:* which is a title proper
only to this case. For they say the king is debtor to no man,

but for propagation of his subjects. The seal set to the king's charter is the king's image, imbossed or moulded in gold; and though such charters be expedited of course, and as of right, yet they are varied by discretion, according to the number and dignity of the family. This charter the herald readeth aloud; and while it is read, the father or Tirsan standeth up, supported by two of his sons, such as he chooseth. Then the herald mounteth the half-pace, and delivereth the charter into his hand: and with that there is an acclamation by all that are present in their language, which is thus much: *Happy are the people of Bensalem.* Then the herald taketh into his hand from the other child the cluster of grapes, which is of gold, both the stalk and the grapes. But the grapes are daintily enamelled; and if the males of the family be the greater number, the grapes are enamelled purple, with a little sun set on the top; if the females, then they are enamelled into a greenish yellow, with a crescent on the top. The grapes are in number as many as there are descendants of the family. This golden cluster the herald delivereth also to the Tirsan; who presently delivereth it over to that son that he had formerly chosen to be in house with him: who beareth it before his father as an ensign of honour when he goeth in public, ever after; and is thereupon called the Son of the Vine. After this ceremony ended, the father or Tirsan retireth; and after some time cometh forth again to dinner, where he sitteth alone under the state, as before; and none of his descendants sit with him, of what degree or dignity soever, except he hap to be of Salomon's House. He is served only by his own children, such as are male; who perform unto him all service of the table upon the knee; and the women only stand about him, leaning against the wall. The room below the half-pace hath tables on the sides for the guests that are bidden; who are served with great and comely order; and towards the end of dinner (which in the greatest feasts with them lasteth never above an hour and an half) there is an hymn sung, varied according to the invention of him that composeth it, (for they have excellent poesy,) but the subject of it is (always) the praises of Adam and Noah and Abraham; whereof the former two peopled the world, and the last was the Father of the Faithful: concluding ever with a thanksgiving for the nativity of our Saviour, in whose birth the births of all are only blessed. Dinner being done, the Tirsan retireth again; and having withdrawn himself alone into a place where he maketh some private prayers, he cometh forth the third time, to give the blessing; with all his descendants, who stand about him as at the first. Then he calleth them forth by one and by one, by name, as he pleaseth, though seldom the order of age be inverted. The person that is called (the table being before removed) kneeleth down before the chair, and the father layeth his hand upon his head, or her head, and giveth the blessing in these words: *Son of Bensalem, (or Daughter of Bensalem,) thy father saith it; the man by whom thou hast breath and life speaketh the word; The blessing of the everlasting Father, the Prince of Peace, and the Holy Dove be upon thee, and make the days of thy pilgrimage good and many.* This he saith to every of them; and that done, if there be any of his sons of eminent merit and virtue, (so they be not above two,) he calleth for them again; and saith, laying his arm over their shoulders, they standing; *Sons, it is well ye are born, give God the praise, and persevere to the end.* And withal delivereth to either of them a jewel, made in the figure of an ear of wheat, which they ever after wear in the front of their turban or hat. This done, they fall to music and dances, and other recreations, after their manner, for the rest of the day. This is the full order of that feast.

By that time six or seven days were spent, I was fallen into strait acquaintance with a merchant of that city, whose name was Joabin. He was a Jew, and circumcised: for they have some few stirps of Jews yet remaining among them, whom they leave to their own religion. Which they may the better do, because they are of a far differing disposition from the Jews in other parts. For whereas they hate the name of Christ, and have a secret inbred rancour against the people amongst whom they live: these (contrariwise) give unto our Saviour many high attributes, and love the nation of Bensalem extremely. Surely this man of whom I speak would ever acknowledge that Christ was born of a Virgin, and that he was more than a man; and he would tell how God made him ruler of the Seraphims which guard his throne; and they call him also the *Milken Way,* and the *Eliah* of the *Messiah;* and many other high names; which though they be inferior to his divine Majesty, yet they are far from the language of other Jews. And for the country of Bensalem, this man would make no end of commending it: being desirous, by tradition among the Jews there, to have it believed that the people thereof were of the generations of Abraham, by another son, whom they call Nachoran; and that Moses by a secret cabala ordained the laws of Bensalem which they now use; and that when the Messiah should come, and sit in his throne at Hierusalem, the king of Bensalem should sit at his feet, whereas other kings should keep a great distance. But yet setting aside these Jewish dreams, the man was a wise man, and learned, and of great policy, and excellently seen in the laws and customs of that nation. Amongst other discourses, one day I told him I was much affected with the relation I had from some of the company, of their custom in holding the Feast of the Family; for that (methought) I had never heard of a solemnity wherein nature did so much preside. And because propagation of families proceedeth from the nuptial copulation, I desired to know of him what laws and customs they had concerning marriage; and whether they kept marriage well; and whether they were tied to one wife? For that where population is so much affected, and such as with them it seemed to be, there is commonly permission of plurality of wives. To this he said, "You have reason for to commend that excellent institution of the Feast of the Family. And indeed we have experience, that those families that are partakers of the blessing of that feast do flourish and prosper ever after in an extraordinary manner. But hear me now, and I will tell you what I know. You shall understand that there is not under the heavens so chaste a nation as this of Bensalem; nor so free from all pollution or foulness. It is the virgin of the world. I remember I have read in one of your European books, of an holy hermit amongst you that desired to see the Spirit of Fornication; and there appeared to him a little foul ugly Æthiop. But if he had desired to see the Spirit of Chastity of Bensalem, it would have appeared to him in the likeness of a fair beautiful Cherubin. For there is nothing amongst mortal men more fair and admirable, than the chaste minds of this people. Know therefore, that with them there are no stews, no dissolute houses, no courtesans, nor any thing of that kind. Nay they wonder (with detestation) at you in Europe, which permit such things. They say ye have put marriage out of office: for marriage is ordained a remedy for unlawful concupiscence; and natural concupiscence seemeth as a spur to marriage. But when men have at hand a remedy more agreeable to their corrupt will, marriage is almost expulsed. And therefore there are with you seen infinite men that marry not, but chuse rather a libertine and impure single life, than to be yoked in marriage; and many that do marry, marry late, when the prime and strength of their years is past. And when they do marry, what is marriage to them but a very bargain; wherein is sought alliance, or portion, or reputation, with some desire (almost indifferent) of issue; and not the faithful nuptial union of man and wife, that was first instituted. Neither is it possible that those that have cast away so basely so much of their strength, should greatly esteem children, (being of the same matter,) as chaste men do. So likewise during marriage, is the case much amended, as it ought to be if those things were tolerated only for necessity? No, but they remain still as a very affront to marriage. The haunting of those dissolute places, or resort to courtesans, are no more punished in married men than in bachelors. And the depraved custom of change, and the delight in meretricious embracements, (where sin is turned into art,) maketh marriage a dull thing, and a kind of imposition or tax. They hear you defend these things, as done to avoid greater evils; as advoutries,[26] deflouring of virgins,

unnatural lust, and the like. But they say this is a preposterous wisdom; and they call it *Lot's offer*, who to save his
guests from abusing, offered his daughters: nay they say
farther that there is little gained in this; for that the same
vices and appetites do still remain and abound; unlawful
lust being like a furnace, that if you stop the flames altogether, it will quench; but if you give it any vent, it will
rage. As for masculine love, they have no touch of it; and
yet there are not so faithful and inviolate friendships in the
world again as are there; and to speak generally, (as I said
before,) I have not read of any such chastity in any people
as theirs. And their usual saying is, *That whosoever is un-
chaste cannot reverence himself;* and they say, *That the
reverence of a man's self is, next religion, the chiefest bridle
of all vices.*" And when he had said this, the good Jew
paused a little; whereupon I, far more willing to hear him
speak on than to speak myself, yet thinking it decent that
upon his pause of speech I should not be altogether silent,
said only this; "That I would say to him, as the widow of
Sarepta said to Elias; that he was come to bring to memory
our sins; and that I confess the righteousness of Bensalem
was greater than the righteousness of Europe." At which
speech he bowed his head, and went on in this manner:
"They have also many wise and excellent laws touching
marriage. They allow no polygamy. They have ordained
that none do intermarry or contract, until a month be
passed from their first interview. Marriage without consent
of parents they do not make void, but they mulct it in the
inheritors: for the children of such marriages are not admitted to inherit above a third part of their parents' inheritance. I have read in a book of one of your men,[27] of a Feigned
Commonwealth, where the married couple are permitted,
before they contract, to see one another naked. This they
dislike; for they think it a scorn to give a refusal after so
familiar knowledge: but because of many hidden defects in
men and women's bodies, they have a more civil way; for
they have near every town a couple of pools, (which they
call *Adam and Eve's pools*,) where it is permitted to one of

the friends of the man, and another of the friends of the woman, to see them severally[28] bathe naked."

And as we were thus in conference, there came one that seemed to be a messenger, in a rich huke,[29] that spake with the Jew: whereupon he turned to me and said; "You will pardon me, for I am commanded away in haste." The next morning he came to me again, joyful as it seemed, and said, "There is word come to the governor of the city, that one of the Fathers of Salomon's House will be here this day seven-night: we have seen none of them this dozen years. His coming is in state; but the cause of his coming is secret. I will provide you and your fellows of a good standing to see his entry." I thanked him, and told him, "I was most glad of the news." The day being come, he made his entry. He was a man of middle stature and age, comely of person, and had an aspect as if he pitied men. He was clothed in a robe of fine black cloth, with wide sleeves and a cape. His under garment was of excellent white linen down to the foot, girt with a girdle of the same; and a sindon or tippet of the same about his neck. He had gloves that were curious, and set with stone; and shoes of peach-coloured velvet. His neck was bare to the shoulders. His hat was like a helmet, or Spanish Montera; and his locks curled below it decently: they were of colour brown. His beard was cut round, and of the same colour with his hair, somewhat lighter. He was carried in a rich chariot without wheels, litter-wise; with two horses at either end, richly trapped in blue velvet embroidered; and two footmen on each side in the like attire. The chariot was all of cedar, gilt, and adorned with crystal; save that the fore-end had pannels of sapphires, set in borders of gold, and the hinder-end the like of emeralds of the Peru colour. There was also a sun of gold, radiant, upon the top, in the midst; and on the top before, a small cherub of gold, with wings displayed. The chariot was covered with cloth of gold tissued upon blue. He had before him fifty attendants, young men all, in white sattin loose coats to the mid-leg; and stockings of white silk; and shoes of blue velvet; and hats of blue velvet; with fine plumes of divers colours, set round like hat-bands. Next before the chariot went two men, bare-headed, in linen garments down to the foot, girt, and shoes of blue velvet; who carried the one a crosier, the other a pastoral staff like a sheep-hook; neither of them of metal, but the crosier of balm-wood, the pastoral staff of cedar. Horsemen he had none, neither before nor behind his chariot: as it seemeth, to avoid all tumult and trouble. Behind his chariot went all the officers and principals of the Companies of the City. He sat alone, upon cushions of a kind of excellent plush, blue; and under his foot curious carpets of silk of divers colours, like the Persian, but far finer. He held up his bare hand as he went, as blessing the people, but in silence. The street was wonderfully well kept: so that there was never any army had their men stand in better battle-array, than the people stood. The windows likewise were not crowded, but every one stood in them as if they had been placed. When the shew was past, the Jew said to me; "I shall not be able to attend you as I would, in regard of some charge the city hath laid upon me, for the entertaining of this great person." Three days after, the Jew came to me again, and said; "Ye are happy men; for the Father of Salomon's House taketh knowledge of your being here, and commanded me to tell you that he will admit all your company to his presence, and have private conference with one of you that ye shall choose: and for this hath appointed the next day after to-morrow. And because he meaneth to give you his blessing he hath appointed it in the forenoon." We came at our day and hour, and I was chosen by my fellows for the private access. We found him in a fair chamber, richly hanged, and carpeted under foot, without any degrees[30] to the state. He was set upon a low throne richly adorned, and a rich cloth of state over his head, of blue satin embroidered. He was alone, save that he had two pages of honour, on either hand one, finely attired in white. His under-garments were the like that we saw him wear in the chariot; but instead of his gown, he had on him a mantle with a cape, of the same fine black, fastened about him. When we came in, as we were taught, we bowed low at our first entrance; and when we were come near his chair, he stood up, holding forth his hand ungloved, and in posture of blessing; and we every one of us stooped down, and kissed the hem of his tippet. That done, the rest departed, and I remained. Then he warned the pages forth of the room, and caused me to sit down beside him, and spake to me thus in the Spanish tongue:

"God bless thee, my son; I will give thee the greatest jewel I have. For I will impart unto thee, for the love of God and men, a relation of the true state of Salomon's House. Son, to make you know the true state of Salomon's House, I will keep this order. First, I will set forth unto you the end of our foundation. Secondly, the preparations and instruments we have for our works. Thirdly, the several employments and functions whereto our fellows are assigned. And fourthly, the ordinances and rites which we observe.

"The End of our Foundation is the knowledge of Causes, and secret motions of things; and the enlarging of the bounds of Human Empire, to the effecting of all things possible.

"The Preparations and Instruments are these. We have large and deep caves of several depths: the deepest are sunk six hundred fathom; and some of them are digged and made under great hills and mountains: so that if you reckon together the depth of the hill and the depth of the cave, they are (some of them) above three miles deep. For we find that the depth of a hill, and the depth of a cave from the flat, is the same thing; both remote alike from the sun and heaven's beams, and from the open air. These caves we call the Lower Region. And we use them for all coagulations, indurations,[31] refrigerations, and conservations of bodies. We use them likewise for the imitation of natural mines; and the producing also of new artificial metals, by compositions and materials which we use, and lay there for many years. We use them also sometimes, (which may seem strange,) for curing of some diseases, and for prolongation of life in some hermits that choose to live there, well accommodated of all things necessary; and indeed live very long; by whom also we learn many things.

"We have burials in several earths, where we put divers cements, as the Chineses do their porcellain. But we have them in greater variety, and some of them more fine. We have also great variety of composts, and soils, for the making of the earth fruitful.

"We have high towers; the highest about half a mile in height; and some of them likewise set upon high mountains; so that the vantage of the hill with the tower is in the highest of them three miles at least. And these places we call the Upper Region: accounting the air between the high places and the low, as a Middle Region. We use these towers, according to their several heights and situations, for insolation,[32] refrigeration, conservation; and for the view of divers meteors; as winds, rain, snow, hail; and some of the fiery meteors also. And upon them, in some places, are dwellings of hermits, whom we visit sometimes, and instruct what to observe.

"We have great lakes both salt and fresh, whereof we have use for the fish and fowl. We use them also for burials of some natural bodies: for we find a difference in things buried in earth or in air below the earth, and things buried in water. We have also pools, of which some do strain fresh water out of salt; and others by art do turn fresh water into salt. We have also some rocks in the midst of the sea, and some bays upon the shore, for some works wherein is required the air and vapour of the sea. We have likewise violent streams and cataracts, which serve us for many motions: and likewise engines for multiplying and enforcing[33] of winds, to set also on going divers motions.

"We have also a number of artificial wells and fountains, made in imitation of the natural sources and baths; as tincted upon[34] vitriol, sulphur, steel, brass, lead, nitre, and other minerals. And again we have little wells for infusions of many things, where the waters take the virtue quicker and better than in vessels or basons. And amongst them we have a water which we call Water of Paradise, being, by that we do to it, made very sovereign for health, and prolongation of life.

"We have also great and spacious houses, where we imitate and demonstrate meteors; as snow, hail, rain, some artificial rains of bodies and not of water, thunders, lightnings; also generations of bodies in air; as frogs, flies, and divers others.

"We have also certain chambers, which we call Chambers of Health, where we qualify the air as we think good and proper for the cure of divers diseases, and preservation of health.

"We have also fair and large baths, of several mixtures, for the cure of diseases, and the restoring of man's body from arefaction:[35] and others for the confirming of it in strength of sinews, vital parts, and the very juice and substance of the body.

"We have also large and various orchards and gardens, wherein we do not so much respect beauty, as variety of ground and soil, proper for divers trees and herbs: and some very spacious, where trees and berries are set whereof we make divers kinds of drinks, besides the vineyards. In these we practise likewise all conclusions of grafting and inoculating, as well of wild-trees as fruit-trees, which produceth many effects. And we make (by art) in the same orchards and gardens, trees and flowers to come earlier or later than their seasons; and to come up and bear more speedily than by their natural course they do. We make them also by art greater much than their nature; and their fruit greater and sweeter and of differing taste, smell, colour, and figure, from their nature. And many of them we so order, as they become of medicinal use.

"We have also means to make divers plants rise by mixtures of earths without seeds; and likewise to make divers new plants, differing from the vulgar; and to make one tree or plant turn into another.

"We have also parks and inclosures of all sorts of beasts and birds, which we use not only for view or rareness, but likewise for dissections and trials; that thereby we may take light what may be wrought upon the body of man. Wherein we find many strange effects; as continuing life in them, though divers parts, which you account vital, be perished and taken forth; resuscitating of some that seem dead in appearance; and the like. We try also all poisons and other medicines upon them, as well of chirurgery as physic. By art likewise, we make them greater or taller than their kind is; and contrariwise dwarf them, and stay their growth: we make them more fruitful and bearing than their kind is; and contrariwise barren and not generative. Also we make them differ in colour, shape, activity, many ways. We find means to make commixtures and copulations of different kinds; which have produced many new kinds, and them not barren, as the general opinion is. We make a number of kinds of serpents, worms, flies, fishes, of putrefaction; whereof some are advanced (in effect) to be perfect creatures, like beasts or birds; and have sexes, and do propagate. Neither do we this by chance, but we know beforehand of what matter and commixture what kind of those creatures will arise.

"We have also particular pools, where we make trials upon fishes, as we have said before of beasts and birds.

"We have also places for breed and generation of those kinds of worms and flies which are of special use; such as are with you your silk-worms and bees.

"I will not hold you long with recounting of our brew-houses, bake-houses, and kitchens, where are made divers drinks, breads, and meats, rare and of special effects. Wines we have of grapes; and drinks of other juice of fruits, of grains, and of roots: and of mixtures with honey, sugar, manna, and fruits dried and decocted. Also of the tears or woundings of trees, and of the pulp of canes. And these drinks are of several ages, some to the age or last of forty years. We have drinks also brewed with several herbs, and roots, and spices; yea with several fleshes, and white meats; whereof some of the drinks are such, as they are in effect meat and drink both: so that divers, especially in age, do desire to live with them, with little or no meat or bread. And above all, we strive to have drinks of extreme thin parts, to insinuate into the body, and yet without all biting, sharpness, or fretting; insomuch as some of them put upon the back of your hand will, with a little stay, pass through to the palm, and yet taste mild to the mouth. We have also waters which we ripen in that fashion, as they become nourishing; so that they are indeed excellent drink; and many will use no other. Breads we have of several grains, roots, and kernels: yea and some of flesh and fish dried; with divers kinds of leavenings and seasonings: so that some do extremely move appetites; some do nourish so, as divers do live of them, without any other meat; who live very long. So for meats, we have some of them so beaten and made tender and mortified, yet without all corrupting, as a weak heat of the stomach will turn them into good chylus, as well as a strong heat would meat otherwise prepared. We have some meats also and breads and drinks, which taken by men enable them to fast long after; and some other, that used make the very flesh of men's bodies sensibly more hard and tough, and their strength far greater than otherwise it would be.

"We have dispensatories, or shops of medicines. Wherein you may easily think, if we have such variety of plants and living creatures more than you have in Europe, (for we know what you have,) the simples, drugs, and ingredients of medicines, must likewise be in so much the greater variety. We have them likewise of divers ages, and long fermentations. And for their preparations, we have not only all manner of exquisite distillations and separations, and especially by gentle heats and percolations through divers strainers, yea and substances; but also exact forms of composition, whereby they incorporate almost, as they were natural simples.

"We have also divers mechanical arts, which you have not; and stuffs made by them; as papers, linen, silks, tissues; dainty works of feathers of wonderful lustre; excellent dyes, and many others; and shops likewise, as well for such as are not brought into vulgar use amongst us as for those that are. For you must know that of the things before recited, many of them are grown into use throughout the kingdom; but yet if they did flow from our invention, we have of them also for patterns and principals.

"We have also furnaces of great diversities, and that keep great diversity of heats; fierce and quick; strong and constant; soft and mild; blown, quiet; dry, moist; and the like. But above all, we have heats in imitation of the sun's and heavenly bodies' heats, that pass divers inequalities and (as it were) orbs, progresses, and returns, whereby we produce admirable effects. Besides, we have heats of dungs, and of bellies and maws of living creatures, and of their bloods and bodies; and of hays and herbs laid up moist; of lime unquenched; and such like. Instruments also which generate heat only by motion. And farther, places for strong insolations; and again, places under the earth, which by nature or art yield heat. These divers heats we use, as the nature of the operation which we intend requireth.

"We have also perspective-houses, where we make demonstrations of all lights and radiations; and of all colours; and out of things uncoloured and transparent, we can represent unto you all several colours; not in rain-bows, as it is in gems and prisms, but of themselves single. We represent also all multiplications of light, which we carry to great distance, and make so sharp as to discern small points and lines; also all colorations of light: all delusions and deceits of the sight in figures, magnitudes, motions, colours: all demonstrations of shadows. We find also divers means, yet unknown to you, of producing of light originally from divers bodies. We procure means of seeing objects afar off; as in the heaven and remote places; and represent things near as afar off, and things afar off as near; making feigned distances. We have also helps for the sight, far above spectacles and glasses in use. We have also glasses and means to see small and minute bodies perfectly and distinctly; as the shapes and colours of small flies and worms, grains and flaws in gems, which cannot otherwise be seen; observations in urine and blood, not otherwise to be seen. We make artificial rain-bows, halos, and circles about light. We represent also all manner of reflexions, refractions and multiplications of visual beams of objects.

"We have also precious stones of all kinds, many of them of great beauty, and to you unknown; crystals likewise; and glasses of divers kinds; and amongst them some of metals vitrificated, and other materials besides those of which you make glass. Also a number of fossils, and imperfect minerals, which you have not. Likewise loadstones of prodigious virtue; and other rare stones, both natural and artificial.

"We have also sound-houses, where we practise and demonstrate all sounds, and their generation. We have harmonies which you have not, of quarter-sounds, and lesser slides of sounds. Divers instruments of music likewise to you unknown, some sweeter than any you have; together with bells and rings that are dainty and sweet. We represent small sounds as great and deep; likewise great sounds extenuate and sharp; we make divers tremblings and warblings of sounds, which in their original are entire. We represent and imitate all articulate sounds and letters, and the voices and notes of beasts and birds. We have certain helps which set to the ear do further the hearing greatly. We have also divers strange and artificial echoes, reflecting the voice many times, and as it were tossing it: and some that give back the voice louder than it came; some shriller, and some deeper; yea, some rendering the voice differing in the letters or articulate sound from that they receive. We have also means to convey sounds in trunks and pipes, in strange lines and distances.

"We have also perfume-houses; wherewith we join also practices of taste. We multiply smells, which may seem strange. We imitate smells, making all smells to breathe out of other mixtures than those that give them. We make divers imitations of taste likewise, so that they will deceive any man's taste. And in this house we contain also a confiture house; where we make all sweet-meats, dry and moist, and divers pleasant wines, milks, broths, and sallets, far in greater variety than you have.

"We have also engine-houses, where are prepared engines and instruments for all sorts of motions. There we imitate and practise to make swifter motions than any you have, either out of your muskets or any engine that you have; and to make them and multiply them more easily, and with small force, by wheels and other means: and to make them stronger, and more violent than yours are; exceeding your greatest cannons and basilisks.[36] We represent also ordnance and instruments of war, and engines of all kinds: and likewise new mixtures and compositions of gun-powder, wildfires burning in water, and unquenchable. Also fireworks of all variety both for pleasure and use. We imitate also flights of birds; we have some degrees of flying in the air; we have ships and boats for going under water, and brooking of seas; also swimming-girdles and supporters. We have divers curious clocks, and other like motions of return,[37] and some perpetual motions. We imitate also motions of living creatures, by images of men, beasts, birds, fishes, and serpents. We have also a great number of other various motions, strange for equality, fineness, and subtilty.

"We have also a mathematical house, where are represented all instruments, as well of geometry as astronomy, exquisitely made.

"We have also houses of deceits of the senses; where we represent all manner of feats of juggling, false apparitions, impostures, and illusions; and their fallacies. And surely you will easily believe that we that have so many things truly natural which induce admiration, could in a world of particulars deceive the senses, if we would disguise those things and labour to make them seem more miraculous. But we do hate all impostures and lies: insomuch as we have severely forbidden it to all our fellows, under pain of ignominy and fines, that they do not shew any natural work or thing, adorned or swelling; but only pure as it is, and without all affectation of strangeness.

"These are (my son) the riches of Salomon's House.

"For the several employments and offices of our fellows; we have twelve that sail into foreign countries, under the names of other nations, (for our own we conceal;) who bring us the books, and abstracts, and patterns of experiments of all other parts. These we call Merchants of Light.

"We have three that collect the experiments which are in all books. These we call Depredators.

"We have three that collect the experiments of all mechanical arts; and also of liberal sciences; and also of practices which are not brought into arts. These we call Mystery-men.

"We have three that try new experiments, such as themselves think good. These we call Pioners or Miners.

"We have three that draw the experiments of the former four into titles and tables, to give the better light for the drawing of observations and axioms out of them. These we call Compilers.

"We have three that bend themselves, looking into the experiments of their fellows, and cast about how to draw out of them things of use and practice for man's life, and knowledge as well for works as for plain demonstration of causes, means of natural divinations, and the easy and clear discovery of the virtues and parts of bodies. These we call Dowry-men or Benefactors.

"Then after divers meetings and consults of our whole number, to consider of the former labours and collections, we have three that take care, out of them, to direct new experiments, of a higher light, more penetrating into nature than the former. These we call Lamps.

"We have three others that do execute the experiments so directed, and report them. These we call Inoculators.

"Lastly, we have three that raise the former discoveries by experiments into greater observations, axioms, and aphorisms. These we call Interpreters of Nature.

"We have also, as you must think, novices and apprentices, that the succession of the former employed men do not fail; besides a great number of servants and attendants, men and women. And this we do also: we have consultations, which of the inventions and experiences which we have discovered shall be published, and which not: and take all an oath of secrecy, for the concealing of those which we think fit to keep secret: though some of those we do reveal sometimes to the state, and some not.

"For our ordinances and rites: we have two very long and fair galleries: in one of these we place patterns and samples of all manner of the more rare and excellent inventions: in the other we place the statua's of all principal inventors. There we have the statua of your Columbus, that discovered the West Indies: also the inventor of ships: your monk that was the inventor of ordnance and of gunpowder: the inventor of music: the inventor of letters: the inventor of printing: the inventor of observations of astronomy: the inventor of works in metal: the inventor of glass: the inventor of silk of the worm: the inventor of wine: the inventor of corn and bread: the inventor of sugars: and all these by more certain tradition than you have. Then have we divers inventors of our own, of excellent works; which since you have not seen, it were too long to make descriptions of them; and besides, in the right understanding of those descriptions you might easily err. For upon every invention of value, we erect a statua to the inventor, and give him a liberal and honourable reward. These statua's are some of brass; some of marble and touch-stone; some of cedar and other special woods gilt and adorned: some of iron; some of silver; some of gold.

"We have certain hymns and services, which we say daily of laud and thanks to God for his marvellous works: and forms of prayers, imploring his aid and blessing for the illumination of our labours, and the turning of them into good and holy uses.

"Lastly, we have circuits or visits of divers principal cities of the kingdom; where, as it cometh to pass, we do publish such new profitable inventions as we think good. And we do also declare natural divinations of diseases, plagues, swarms of hurtful creatures, scarcity, tempests, earthquakes, great inundations, comets, temperature of the year, and divers other things; and we give counsel thereupon what the people shall do for the prevention and remedy of them."

And when he had said this, he stood up; and I, as I had been taught, kneeled down; and he laid his right hand upon my head, and said; "God bless thee, my son, and God bless this relation which I have made. I give thee leave to publish it for the good of other nations; for we here are in God's bosom, a land unknown." And so he left me; having assigned a value of about two thousand ducats,[38] for a bounty to me and my fellows. For they give great largesses where they come upon all occasions.

[THE REST WAS NOT PERFECTED.]

NOTES

ESSAYS

1. Of Truth

1. "affecting." Desiring. The verb "to affect," which Bacon frequently uses, virtually never carries its modern sense of pretending.
2. "the sects of philosophers." Pyrrho and the ancient Sceptics who held that assured knowledge is unattainable.
3. "certain discoursing wits." Renaissance sceptics like Cornelius Heinrich Agrippa who wrote *Of the Vanity and Uncertainty of the Sciences* (1527), Franciscus Sanchez who wrote *That Nothing May Be Known* (1576), and the essayist Michel Montaigne.
4. "One of the later school of the Grecians." The satirist Lucian.
5. "One of the Fathers." Either St. Jerome or more probably St. Augustine in his *Confessions*.
6. "The poet." The Epicurean poet Lucretius, author of *De rerum natura* (*Of the Nature of Things*).

2. OF DEATH

1. "And by him that spake only as a philosopher." The Roman essayist Lucius Annaeus Seneca, who spoke only as a philosopher in the sense that he was not a Christian.
2. "Better saith he." The Roman satirist Juvenal.
3. "*Nunc dimittis.*" "Now thou lettest thy servant depart," Luke 2. 29.

3. OF UNITY IN RELIGION

1. "The Doctor of the Gentiles." St. Paul.
2. "a master of scoffing." François Rabelais.
3. "cross." Contrasting.
4. "one of the fathers." St. Augustine.
5. "The massacre . . . the powder treason." The St. Bartholomew's Day massacre of the Huguenots (1572) and the Gunpowder Plot to destroy King James I and Parliament (1605).
6. "Mercury rod." The caduceus or staff by which Hermes summoned souls from or sent them to Hades.
7. "the apostle." St. James.
8. "a wise father." Probably St. Cyprian.

8. OF MARRIAGE AND SINGLE LIFE

1. "he was reputed." The philosopher Thales who was included among the Seven Wise Men of the ancient world.

9. OF ENVY

1. "the *lot.*" The spell.

10. OF LOVE

1. "he that preferred Helena." The judgment of the shepherd Paris, who tragically preferred Venus's gift of the most beautiful woman (Helen of Troy) to the gifts of Juno (power) or of Pallas Athene (wisdom).

11. OF GREAT PLACE

1. "sufficiency." Ability.

12. OF BOLDNESS

1. "Popular states." Democracies.

13. OF GOODNESS AND GOODNESS OF NATURE

1. "to the bough." To the gallows as suicides. The misanthrope Timon of Athens warned his fellow citizens of his intention to fell a fig tree of his that had been much used by those committing suicide and urged those of like mind to hurry before the tree was cut down.
2. "knee timber." Timber with a natural angular bend.
3. "the noble tree." The frankincense whose bark was slit to obtain aromatic resin.

14. OF NOBILITY

1. "stirps." Families.

15. OF SEDITIONS AND TROUBLES

1. "when things grow to equality." When distinction lessens between the ruler and those who are ruled.
2. *"primum mobile."* According to the old astronomy, the great circle that carried all the planets from east to west about the earth every twenty-four hours, producing the succession of day and night.
3. "the orbs are out of frame." The stars and planets have left their orbits.
4. "the best mines above ground." The manufactures, trade, and shipping that made the Netherlands prosperous.

16. OF ATHEISM

1. "the Legend." *The Golden Legend* of Jacobus de Voragine, a popular thirteenth-century collection of saints' lives and miracles.
2. "that school." The ancient Greek school of atomic philosophers who held that the physical universe was created by the chance collocation of atoms. According to this philosophy, the gods had nothing to do with either creating or governing the universe.

3. "four mutable elements, and one immutable fifth essence." According to the traditional Aristotelian physics in Bacon's day, everything material beneath the orbit of the moon was formed of the four elements (earth, water, air, and fire) and was in an unceasing state of flux, whereas the region above the moon was made up of a mysterious but stable fifth element called the quintessence.

17. OF SUPERSTITION

1. "to save." To account for. The same sense is again employed below in the phrase "to save the practice of the church."

18. OF TRAVEL

1. "card." Map.
2. "prick in." Plant or embroider.

19. OF EMPIRE

1. "Alexander the Great," etc. According to legend, Alexander wept because there were no more worlds he could conquer; Diocletian handed over rule of the Roman Empire to others after years of uninterrupted success; and the Holy Roman Emperor Charles V spent the last years of his life (1550 to 1558) in a monastery.
2. "*vena porta.*" The large vein conveying blood to the liver.

20. OF COUNSEL

1. "Salomon's son." Rehoboam, whose reign was catastrophic.
2. "*cabinet* counsels." Secret, unofficial councils.
3. "to grind with a hand-mill." To do things for himself.
4. "Morton and Fox." John Morton, Archbishop of Canterbury, and Richard Fox, Bishop of Winchester, the king's ablest advisers.
5. "the fable." Of Metis and Jupiter told above.
6. "indifferent." Impartial. Bacon always uses the word in this sense.
7. "take the wind of him." Learn his intentions and wishes.
8. "*placebo.*" Literally, "I shall please you." Agreement and flattery.

21. OF DELAYS

1. "Sibylla's offer." The Sibyl offered to sell nine books to the Roman king Tarquin. He refused to buy, whereupon she destroyed three books. The Sibyl repeated the offer, the king again refused, and the Sibyl destroyed three more. Tarquin then capitulated and bought the remaining three books at the price of the original nine. These Sibylline books, containing religious information and political policies, were among the cherished national treasures of Rome.

22. OF CUNNING

1. "to wait upon him . . . with your eye." To keep your eyes on him.
2. "as Narcissus did." Messalina, dissolute wife of the emperor Claudius, went through a marriage ceremony with another man. The freedman Narcissus persuaded two women to break the news to the emperor and then have him summon Narcissus to furnish the details.
3. "be apposed of." Be posed with.

23. OF WISDOM FOR A MAN'S SELF

1. "set a bias upon their bowl." Make a bowling ball curve— i.e., self-interest may deflect a servant from loyalty to his master.

24. OF INNOVATIONS

1. "of course." In due course.
2. "pairs." Impairs.

25. OF DISPATCH

1. "passages." Transitions.
2. "to the person." To the speaker himself.
3. "too material." Too blunt.
4. "more pregnant of direction." A more fertile suggestion as to how to proceed.

26. Of Seeming Wise

1. "the Apostle." St. Paul.
2. "to bear it." To succeed.
3. "blanch." Avoid.
4. "inward beggar." Actually a beggar no matter what his outward show.

27. Of Friendship

1. "him that spake it." Aristotle, *Politics*, i. 1.
2. "Epimenides the Candian," etc. Epimenides of Crete, a philosopher-poet (Sixth Century B.C.), is said to have slept fifty-seven years in a cave; Numa, the legendary second king of Rome, retired to a cave from time to time to receive counsel from the nymph Egeria; Empedocles, a Greek philosopher (Fifth Century B.C.), allegedly threw himself into the crater of Mt. Etna; and Apollonius was an ascetic magician of the First Century A.D.
3. "affections." The emotions in general.
4. *"cloth of Arras."* Pictorial tapestry.
5. "The four and twenty letters." The alphabet, "i" and "j" and "u" and "v" being regarded as single letters.

28. Of Expense

1. "of even hand." Income and expenditure properly related.
2. "to certainties." Budgeted expenses and assured income.
3. "Interest." Paying out interest.

29. Of the True Greatness of Kingdoms and Estates.

1. "staddles." Young trees left after underbrush is cleared.
2. "Nebuchadnezzar's tree of monarchy." Nebuchadnezzar dreamed of a large tree cut down to a stump, a vision interpreted to mean the temporary loss of his empire.
3. *"jus commercii,"* etc. The rights of trading, marrying, inheriting property, voting, and holding public office.
4. "the Pragmatical Sanction." A Spanish royal decree of 1622 granting certain privileges to married persons and to couples with six or more children.

5. "prest." Prompt.
6. "a veteran army." A standing army.
7. "abridgment." Epitome.
8. "set up their rest." Staked everything.

31. OF SUSPICION

1. "to account upon such suspicions as true." To provide remedies as though the suspicions were true.
2. "*Sospetto licentia fede.*" Suspicion licenses faith—i.e., frees men (so they think) from their usual moral obligations.

32. OF DISCOURSE

1 "of touch." Touching.
2. "a flout or dry blow." A broadly satiric contradiction or an ironic, mocking understatement.
3. "without a good speech of interlocution." Without the ability to converse well.

33. OF PLANTATIONS

1. "certify over to their country." Send home bad reports.
2. "artichokes of Hierusalem." Sunflowers.
3. "Virginia." Complaints were made that the Virginia colony put too much effort into growing tobacco for quick profit and too little into diversified crops that would make the colony self-sustaining.
4. "bay-salt." Salt produced by evaporating sea water in the sun.
5. "Soap-ashes." Ashes used in making soap.

34. OF RICHES

1. "value unsound men." Extend credit to those whose credit is worthless.
2. "the first sugar man in the Canaries." The first man to raise sugar cane in the Canary Islands.
3. "glorious." Ostentatious.

35. OF PROPHECIES

1. "the King's style." James I was king of Great Britain, having combined the crowns of Scotland and of England.

2. "Octogesimus octavus," etc. " '88 is the wonderful year." Regiomontanus was the Latin patronymic of Johannes Mueller, a fifteenth-century German astronomer and astrologer.
3. "collect." Infer.

36. OF AMBITION

1. "choler." According to the conventional physiology of Bacon's time, choler was one of the four humors (bodily liquids), specifically yellow bile.
2. "adust." Burned.
3. "seeled." Having the eyelids sewn shut, a term of falconry.
4. "obnoxious." Liable.
5. "bravery." Display.

37. OF MASQUES AND TRIUMPHS

1. "Masques and Triumphs." Masques were courtly entertainments that featured dancing, pantomime, and song, whereas triumphs were public entertainments that usually consisted of processions and pageants.
2. "broken music." Music played by a string ensemble.
3. "by catches." A round for three or more unaccompanied voices written as a single melody with one singer after another 'catching up' his part in turn.
4. "into figure." Ending the dance with an elaborate pattern such as forming a diamond, a chain, or a set of letters.
5. "oes, or spangs." Sequins and spangles.
6. "anti-masques." A grotesque or comic interlude designed as contrast to the masque proper.
7. "turquets." Little Turks.
8. "justs, and tourneys, and barriers." Jousts were single combats between two horsemen armed with spears; tourneys were similar group combats; and barriers were group combats with swords.

38. OF NATURE IN MEN

1. "converse in those things they do not affect." Deal with those things they do not desire.

39. Of Custom and Education

1. "friar Clement," etc. Assassins of various Renaissance kings.
2. "of the first blood." Murdering for the first time.
3. "votary resolution." Resolution confirmed by a vow.
4. "the sect of their wise men." The Gymnosophists or ascetic philosophers of India.
5. "queching." Flinching.
6. "a with." A limber twig.

40. Of Fortune

1. *"desemboltura." Desenvoltura*, a relaxed grace such as one finds in a gifted natural athlete.
2. "stonds." Impediments.
3. "in respect of." When compared with.

41. Of Usury

1. Title. Usury was the practice of charging interest on loans, not necessarily at an exorbitant rate. Charging any interest was in disrepute and was made illegal for a time in sixteenth-century England.
2. "tithe." A tenth part, ten percent being the legalized rate of interest in England when Bacon was writing.
3. "orange-tawney bonnets." Medieval law had required Jews to wear some distinguishing feature of dress, and yellow headgear was often specified.
4. "Some others," etc. The meaning here is obscure, but the sense may be as follows: Some men have created dubious but ingenious schemes for legalizing pawnshops, for reporting each person's income and expenses, and other such proposals.
5. *"vena porta."* See note on Essay 19.
6. "five in the hundred." Five percent.
7. "the price of land." Bacon's proposal means in effect that real estate loans should be legalized at six percent as against a five percent legal rate for other loans.
8. "to colour other men's monies." To lend other men's money for them.

42. OF YOUTH AND AGE

1. "Cosmus," etc. Cosimo de' Medici who started to rule Florence in 1537 at the age of seventeen; Gaston, Count de Foix, born 1331, was a distinguished commander at the age of fourteen.
2. "care not to innovate." Plunge recklessly into innovations.
3. "Hermogenes." A Greek rhetorician of the Second Century A.D. who lost his memory at twenty-five.

43. OF BEAUTY

1. "almost." Generally.
2. "favour." Features.
3. "motion." Both general bearing and expression of countenance.
4. "by pardon." By making allowances.

44. OF DEFORMITY

1. "obnoxious and officious." Dutiful and ready to serve.
2. "Agesilaus," etc. Agesilaus was a lame king of Sparta, Zanger was a deformed son of Solyman the Magnificent, the fabulist Aesop was supposedly a hunchback, Pedro de la Gasca (conqueror of Pizarro in Peru) had overly long legs, and Socrates had a proverbially ugly face.

45. OF BUILDING

1. "seat." Site.
2. "knap." Knoll.
3. "Momus." The god of fault-finding.
4. "lurcheth." Snatches.
5. "returns." Sides extending back from the front of a building.
6. "open newel." Open stairwell of a curving staircase.
7. "chambers of presence." Formal reception rooms.
8. "inbowed." Bay.
9. "antecamera, and recamera." Anteroom and retiring room.
10. "avoidances." Outlets.
11. "tarrasses." Terraces.

46. Of Gardens

1. "pine-apple-trees." Pines.
2. "flags." Iris.
3. "stoved." Hot-housed.
4. "warm set." Planted where it will get as much sun as possible.
5. "mezereon-tree." A dwarf bay tree.
6. "chamaïris." Iris.
7. "ribes." Currants.
8. "rasps." Raspberries.
9. "genitings, quadlins." Early apples.
10. "melocotones." A variety of peach.
11. "wardens." A variety of pear.
12. "bullaces." Wild plum.
13. "bent." Bent-grass.
14. "for letting your prospect upon." Because of blocking your view of.
15. "deceive." Rob of nourishment.

47. Of Negociating

1. "practice." Good management.

48. Of Followers and Friends

1. "ill intelligence." Misunderstanding based on misinformation.
2. "glorious." Vainglorious.
3. "all is of favour." Everything depends on winning the master's favor.
4. "to be of the last impression." To act on most recent impressions.

49. Of Suitors

1. "to make an information." The phrase is ambiguous. It may mean to gain information about or to deliver information against someone.
2. "In suits of favour . . . for his discovery." The sentence is confused, but the general meaning is that in requests for

favor, the first petitioner should cautiously be given a slight advantage because he has taken the trouble to bring a situation to someone's attention.

3. "rise in his suit." Begin by making modest requests.

50. OF STUDIES

1. "proyning." Pruning.
2. "flashy." Insipid.
3. "reins." Kidneys.
4. "to beat over." To treat fully.

51. OF FACTION

1. "indifferent." Impartial.
2. "lightly goeth away with it." Ordinarily and easily gains by it.
3. "the League of France." The League of the Holy Trinity which flourished during the 1570's and 1580's to support Catholic vs. Protestant interests in France. Henry III was by times conciliatory toward it and even on occasion headed it, but ultimately had to fight it.
4. *"primum mobile."* See note on Essay 15.

52. OF CEREMONIES

1. "real." Of sterling worth.
2. "queen Isabella." Of Castile, patroness of Columbus.
3. "point device." Precise.

53. OF PRAISE

1. "catch-poles." Contemptuous term for constables.

54. OF VAIN-GLORY

1. "glorious." Vainglorious.
2. "bravery." Ostentation.
3. *"cross lies."* Lies told to each of two parties in a dispute.
4. "virtue was never . . . at the second hand." The sense is obscure, but the passage may mean that virtue has largely to be its own reward because human nature is slow to praise genuine but unassertive virtue.
5. "cessions." Yielding to others.

55. OF HONOUR AND REPUTATION

1. "broken upon another." In contrast to those who have tried something and failed.
2. "*Siete partidas.*" The basic code of Spanish law.
3. "M. Regulus, and the two Decii." Marcus Regulus, a Roman general taken prisoner by Carthage, was sent home to negotiate a peace. He urged the Romans to continue the war, then returned to Carthage to meet his death by torture. The two Decii, father and son, were Romans who charged the enemy to meet certain death.

56. OF JUDICATURE

1. "chop." Chop logic, i.e., to answer back by bandying words and petty arguments.
2. "foot-pace . . . and purprise." Dais and environs.
3. "catching and polling." Arresting and seizing.
4. "may trench to point of estate." May approach some affair of state.

57. OF ANGER

1. "*upon that it falls.*" On that upon which it falls.
2. "Consalvo." Fernandez Gonsalvo, the Great Captain of Cordova, a famous sixteenth-century mercenary soldier.
3. "*communia maledicta.*" General abuse as contrasted with personal abuse, "extreme bitterness of words aculeate and proper."

58. OF VICISSITUDE OF THINGS

1. "Elias." The Old Testament prophet Elijah.
2. "the succession of Sabinian." Sabinian (Seventh Century) suceeded St. Gregory as Pope.
3. "Plato's great year." The period, alluded to in Plato's *Timaeus,* during which the stars and planets returned to the position they had been in at Creation. The span of this period was variously estimated at from 12,000 to 365,000 years.
4. "arietations." Uses of the battering ram.

5. "philology." Speculative philosophical writing as in Plato's *Timaeus* and *Critias*.

DE INTERPRETATIONE NATURAE

1. "Generals." Generalizations.

OF THE PROFICIENCE AND ADVANCEMENT OF LEARNING

BOOK I

1. "the Law." The Mosaic code of the Hebrews.
2. "The wisest king." Solomon.
3. "the apostle." St. Paul.
4. "coarctation." Restriction.
5. "the affections." The emotions in general.
6. "one of Plato's school." Philo Judaeus, a Jewish scholar of Alexandria (First Century A.D.).
7. "receits." Recipes.
8. "complexions." Temperaments and constitutions.
9. "extenuate and disable." Depreciate and disparage.
10. "by name." For example.
11. "to seek . . . *ragioni di stato.*" Deficient in finding expedients and in temporizing, which the Italians call 'reasons of state.'
12. "conceit." Conception, with the further implication of fanciful idea.
13. "Maniable." Manageable.
14. "humorous." Abnormal.
15. "redargution." Refutation.
16. "excuse and expound." Apologizes for them and shows why they did it.
17. "*Quinquennium Neronis.*" The first five years of Nero's reign, during which his tutor Seneca was his chief adviser, were years of remarkably good government as compared to the later years of his reign.
18. "trencher philosophers." Those who used their conversational skill to obtain dinner invitations.
19. "*Cynic.*" The word itself means 'doglike,' as well as being the name of a philosophic school.

20. "moral." Customary.
21. "morigeration." Compliance.
22. "copie." Copiousness, rhetorical facility.
23. "*one, Asine.*" The Greek word *one* means ass.
24. This is translated in the next clause in the text.
25. "the prophet." Jeremiah.
26. "relation." Demonstration.
27. "addition." Honor.
28. "pensileness." Hanging position.
29. "humour." Caprice.
30. "sortable." Fitting.
31. "presently." Instantly.
32. "disclaim in." Renounce.

BOOK II

1. "Hercules' Columns." The Straits of Gibraltar.
2. "dotations to professory learning." Endowments for professional training.
3. "free." Liberal as opposed to professional.
4. "readers." Instructors.
5. "physic." Medicine.
6. "intelligence." Reports furnished.
7. "advertised." Advised.
8. "Arts of nature." Working upon and altering nature by art.
9. "Provincials and Generals." Local and general officers.
10. "your own example." James I had written a treatise on demonology and witchcraft.
11. "one of the most sufficient kings." Henry VII, the first of the Tudors, who was succeeded in turn by Henry VIII (in whose reign the Reformation occurred), the boy king Edward VI, the unwilling usurper Lady Jane Grey (nine days a queen), Mary I (who married Philip of Spain), Elizabeth I, and James VI of Scotland, who became James I of England as well.
12. "one of the late poets." Ariosto in his *Orlando Furioso* (1516), Books 34 and 35.
13. "policy." The art of government.

14. "imitabile fulmen." Imitable thunderbolt., i.e., gunpowder.
15. "the brief sentences of the Seven." The maxims ascribed to the Seven Wise Men of the ancient world: Solon, Thales, Pittacus, Bias, Chilon, Cleobulus, and Periander.
16. "figure." Serious meaning expressed in figurative language.
17. "quavering upon a stop." Producing a vibrato or a trill.
18. "the apostle." St. Paul.
19. "ambages." Roundabout ways.
20. "his scholar." Alexander the Great.
21. "champion region." Region of open fields.
22. "medicine projected." The hoped-for chemical.
23. "arefaction." Drying up.
24. "with chalk to mark up those minds." Bacon alludes to the custom of the royal progress or tour when an official (the harbinger) was sent ahead to designate the quarters in which the monarch and his retinue would be housed.
25. "draw use of." Increase.
26. "affects." Temperament.
27. *"a Delian diver."* One who can go deep.
28. "purgaments." Excretions.
29. "receipts of propriety respecting." Proper prescriptions for.
30. *"diascordium."* A preparation of antimony.
31. *"producat."* The command, "Let it come forth."
32. "the West-Indian Prometheus." The Indian who first produced fire by rubbing pieces of wood together.
33. "in ure." Into use.
34. *"lictores* and *viatores,* for sergeants and whifflers." The Latin and English terms are roughly synonymous and mean the officers attending a judge, the first to clear the way and the second to summon the accused before him.
35. "Places." Commonplaces or topics.
36. "illaqueations with their redargutions." Entangling arguments with their refutations.
37. *"to affect."* To require.
38. "frets." Figured roof ornaments.
39. "as a Tartar's bow." The Tartars were supposed to be able to shoot backward as well as they could forward.
40. "copie." Facility.

41. "funabuloes, baladines." Rope dancers, ballet dancers.
42. "impresses." Pictures.
43. "*omnia per omnia.*" A cipher conveying any words under cover of any other words, provided that the latter contain not less than five times as many letters.
44. "Καθόλου," etc. That they should be true generally, primarily, and essentially. Ramus was a sixteenth-century French logician who tried to revolutionize logic by a system of dichotomies ("the canker of Epitomes") by which problems of logical analysis could be much simplified.
45. "Καθαυτό." The rule that propositions should be true *essentially.*
46. "Ortelius' universal map." The world map of Ortelius, the great Renaissance cartographer.
47. "fripper's or broker's." Secondhand clothing or pawnbroker's.
48. "in Cleon." In criticism of Cleon.
49. "attendances." Rough notes.
50. "reluctation." Resistance to them.
51. Bacon alludes to the *Basilikon Doron* (1599) by James I.
52. "prevent." Come first before they are anticipated.
53. "preferred." Recommended.
54. "*Huomo di prima impressione,*" etc. A man who bases his opinions on first impressions . . . or on last impressions.
55. "celsitude." Height.
56. "affection." Affectation.
57. "the Place." The Forum.
58. "lightly." Readily.
59. "Fable of the full and hungry horse-leech." This fable has not been identified.
60. "his uncle." Julius Caesar.
61. "the Italian." Bacon alludes to an Italian proverb, 'whoever caresses me more than ordinarily either has deceived or wants to deceive me.'
62. "ingenious." Ingenuous.
63. "ward." Defensive position.
64. "droumy." Troubled.
65. "futility." Idle curiosity.

66. "civil laws." So-called Roman law based upon a code, as opposed to English or common law, which is based upon precedents.
67. "popularity." Democratic system.
68. "grift." Engraft.
69. "doctor of the Gentiles." St. Paul.
70. "Jacob's well." A well at which Jesus drank, contrasting its waters with his own teachings.
71. "the Master of the Sentences." Peter the Lombard, Bishop of Paris whose *Sententiae* (Twelfth Century) in four books was a summary of accepted theological doctrine.
72. "by architecture and compaction." Bacon is thinking of narrow, high houses built in crowded urban conditions as opposed to rambling castles built in open country.
73. "in passage." In passing.
74. "a mind of." Mindful of.

THE CLUE TO THE MAZE

1. "cauteles." Reservations or exceptions made as a precaution.
2. "redargution." Refutation.

THE WISDOM OF THE ANCIENTS

1. "of the School." Of the speculative medieval Scholastics.

THE GREAT INSTAURATION

1. "*Pedarii*." Senators of no eminence who vote as their leaders tell them to.
2. "the first part." Bacon regarded *The Advancement of Learning* as an unfinished draft of part one of the great instauration. The remaining parts of the instauration, aside from *The New Organon*, which itself was not wholly perfected, were left only in samples or wholly unwritten.
3. "closes with." Comes to grips with.

NOVUM ORGANUM

1. "Fire with its orb." According to the old astronomy, the four elements—earth, water, air, and fire—lay in spheres having

a common center at the middle of the earth, the sphere of fire (in its purest form) supposedly existing just beneath the orbit of the moon.

2. "the ratio of density." According to this fanciful table of weights, air was presumed to be ten times heavier than fire, water ten times heavier than air, and earth ten times the weight of an equal volume of water.

3. "indifferently." Impartially.

4. "words of the second intention." The meaning is not clear. Perhaps the meaning is that Aristotle, in his treatise *De Anima* (*Of the Soul*) described the soul in terms which Bacon felt to be more appropriate to physical objects instead of ascribing it to the first cause, God.

5. "placets." 'If-you-please's.'

6. "Gilbert." William Gilbert, Bacon's English contemporary, whose treatise *De Magnete* (1600) is a landmark in the history of science. But Bacon felt that Gilbert drew broader and more dogmatic conclusions about the nature of the physical universe than his evidence warranted.

7. "obnoxious." Susceptible.

8. "conspissation." Condensation.

9. *"Acatalepsia."* The habit of reserving judgment.

10. *"literate."* Spelling it out.

11. "the poet." The Roman poet Lucretius.

12. "New India." The West Indies.

NEW ATLANTIS

1. "W. Rawley." William Rawley, Bacon's chaplain and first biographer, who published the *New Atlantis* in 1627, the year following Bacon's death.

2. "discovered." Opened.

3. "within a kenning." Within sight.

4. "boscage." Woods.

5. "bastons." Staves.

6. "Latin of the School." Classical as opposed to medieval Latin.

7. "pistolets." Gold coins.

8. "water chamolet." Camlet, a rich Angora fabric marked with wavy lines.

9. "a flight-shot." The distance an arrow could be shot, between two and three hundred yards.

10. "prevented." Come before.

11. "dorture." Dormitory.

12. "avoided." Left.

13. "sindons." Cloth in which liturgical documents are wrapped.

14. "conceit." Fanciful idea.

15. "stirps." Families.

16. "your Straits." The Straits of Gibraltar.

17. "Paquin." Pekin.

18. "Quinzy." Hangchow.

19. "a great man." Plato in *Critias* and *Timaeus*.

20. "tedder." Tether, namely the limit of a mile and a half imposed on the visitors earlier.

21. "half-pace." Dais.

22. "state." Canopy.

23. "asp." Aspen.

24. "traverse." Curtain.

25. "return." Sides.

26. "advoutries." Adulteries.

27. "one of your men." Sir Thomas More, author of *Utopia* (1516).

28. "severally." Separately.

29. "huke." A hooded, furred cape.

30. "without any degrees," etc. Without any steps leading up to the canopied throne.

31. "indurations." Hardening processes.

32. "insolation." Exposure to the sun.

33. "enforcing." Reinforcing.

34. "tincted upon." Tinctured with.

35. "arefaction." Drying up.

36. "basilisks." A variety of cannon.

37. "return." Oscillation.

38 "ducats." Gold coin worth about $2.25.

MODERN LIBRARY GIANTS

A series of full-sized library editions of books that formerly were available only in cumbersome and expensive sets.
THE MODERN LIBRARY GIANTS REPRESENT A
SELECTION OF THE WORLD'S GREATEST BOOKS

These volumes contain from 600 to 1,400 pages each

G39. THE BASIC WRITINGS OF SIGMUND FREUD.
G40. THE COMPLETE TALES AND POEMS OF EDGAR ALLAN POE.
G41. FARRELL, JAMES T. Studs Lonigan.
G42. THE POEMS AND PLAYS OF TENNYSON.
G43. DEWEY, JOHN. Intelligence in the Modern World: John Dewey's Philosophy.
G44. DOS PASSOS, JOHN. U. S. A.
G45. STOIC AND EPICUREAN PHILOSOPHERS
G46. A NEW ANTHOLOGY OF MODERN POETRY.
G47. THE ENGLISH PHILOSOPHERS FROM BACON TO MILL.
G48. THE METROPOLITAN OPERA GUIDE.
G49. TWAIN, MARK. Tom Sawyer and Huckleberry Finn.
G50. WHITMAN, WALT. Leaves of Grass.
G51. THE BEST-KNOWN NOVELS OF GEORGE ELIOT.
G52. JOYCE, JAMES. Ulysses.
G53. SUE, EUGENE. The Wandering Jew.
G54. AN ANTHOLOGY OF FAMOUS BRITISH STORIES.
G55. O'NEILL, EUGENE. Nine Plays by
G56. THE WISDOM OF CATHOLICISM.
G57. MELVILLE. Selected Writings of Herman Melville.
G58. THE COMPLETE NOVELS OF JANE AUSTEN.
G59. THE WISDOM OF CHINA AND INDIA.
G60. DOSTOYEVSKY, FYODOR. The Idiot.
G61. SPAETH, SIGMUND. A Guide to Great Orchestral Music.
G62. THE POEMS, PROSE AND PLAYS OF PUSHKIN.
G63. SIXTEEN FAMOUS BRITISH PLAYS.
G64. MELVILLE, HERMAN. Moby Dick.
G65. THE COMPLETE WORKS OF RABELAIS.
G66. THREE FAMOUS MURDER NOVELS
   Before the Fact, Francis Iles.
   Trent's Last Case, E. C. Bentley.
   The House of the Arrow, A. E. W. Mason.
G67. ANTHOLOGY OF FAMOUS ENGLISH AND AMERICAN POETRY.
G68. THE SELECTED WORK OF TOM PAINE.
G69. ONE HUNDRED AND ONE YEARS' ENTERTAINMENT.
G70. THE COMPLETE POETRY OF JOHN DONNE AND WILLIAM BLAKE.
G71. SIXTEEN FAMOUS EUROPEAN PLAYS.
G72. GREAT TALES OF TERROR AND THE SUPERNATURAL.
G73. A SUB-TREASURY OF AMERICAN HUMOR.
G74. ST. AUGUSTINE. The City of God.
G75. SELECTED WRITINGS OF ROBERT LOUIS STEVENSON.
G76. GRIMM AND ANDERSEN, TALES OF
G77. AN ANTHOLOGY OF FAMOUS AMERICAN STORIES.
G78. HOLMES, OLIVER WENDELL. The Mind and Faith of Justice Holmes.
G79. THE WISDOM OF ISRAEL.
G80. DREISER, THEODORE. An American Tragedy.